A Cultural History of Computer Graphics

A Cultural History of Computer Graphics presents a fundamentally new approach to analyzing digital images aesthetically through the example of 3D computer graphics (CG). While numerous methods for creating digital imagery have long existed, the advent of AI-generated content is causing a rise in debates and conflict. It is becoming increasingly difficult to aesthetically differentiate digital photographs, CG and AI images, and yet, because these types of images carry different cultural or even political implications, it is becoming increasingly important to do so. In response to the need of new methods to culturally decode digital imagery, this book starts from the production process and describes computer graphics as an independent method of expression, containing a specific ideological concept of realism. Through this study, it becomes clear that a particular understanding of the world is inscribed in computer graphics software and, consequently, the image creation process. As the image surface does not reveal much about these cultural artifacts, it becomes necessary to focus on the historical development of this imaging practice and analyze it production-aesthetically. In its own unique way, this is true for every digital imaging method. Each embodies its own sense of the world that is only accessible through their production aesthetics. This book will be of great interest to researchers of computer graphics, 3D image generation and the cultural history of computer-generated imagery.

"Computer graphics is a constantly evolving field, presenting new technical opportunities and challenges that demand attention. As such, it is rare to step back and reflect on how intentionality, philosophical perspectives, applied practice and visual culture influence its development, or to consider its broader cultural impact. However, this perspective is essential for recognizing emerging trends, fostering creativity and innovation, agency and collaboration, as well as allowing for more informed and ethically conscious decisions moving forward. As the field of computer graphics undergoes a significant transformation with the rise of machine learning and AI technologies, it is an opportune moment to reflect on how past contributors and practitioners have influenced technological development. Dr. Scheler is uniquely positioned to cast light on the dynamics of agency and cooperation in computer-based art and design, and offers a perspective rooted in the research goals and philosophies of those who pioneered the field. This insight should inspire originality and invite a deeper cultural reflection in future researchers in the fields of technology and cultural history alike."
—**Vita Berezina-Blackburn,** *The Ohio State University*

"The current excitement surrounding images generated by generative AI that look like photographs obscures the fact that there is an older and, for some time to come, arguably more important tradition: photorealistic computer graphics. Research in this field began as early as the 1960s. Scheler traces this development and, more importantly, embeds it in a cultural history of realism. This outstanding study makes a very important contribution to our understanding of today's digital visual culture and, at the same time, allows us to read the traditions that have shaped it. Ultimately, it also succeeds in providing a successful classification of AI-generated images."
—**Jens Schröter,** *Professor of Media Studies, University of Bonn*

A Cultural History of Computer Graphics

Carolin Scheler

CRC Press
Taylor & Francis Group
Boca Raton London New York

CRC Press is an imprint of the
Taylor & Francis Group, an **informa** business

This book was originally published in 2023 in the German language with Transcript Independent Academic Publishing, Bielefeld, under the title *Computergrafik – Zur Geschichte und Produktionsästhetik synthetischer Bilder.*

This work was funded by the German Research Foundation (DFG) as part of the Research Training Group 2477 "Aesthetic Practice" (project number: 394082147) and submitted as a dissertation at the University of Hildesheim. The defense took place on November 10, 2022, in Hildesheim. The supervisors were Prof Dr Thomas Lange (University of Hildesheim) and Prof Dr Friedrich Weltzien (Hanover University of Applied Sciences and Arts).

Designed cover image: Carolin Scheler

First edition published 2026
by CRC Press
2385 NW Executive Center Drive, Suite 320, Boca Raton FL 33431

and by CRC Press
4 Park Square, Milton Park, Abingdon, Oxon, OX14 4RN

CRC Press is an imprint of Taylor & Francis Group, LLC

ISBN: 9781041094005 (hbk)
ISBN: 9781041088158 (pbk)
ISBN: 9781003649861 (ebk)

DOI: 10.1201/9781003649861

Typeset in Minion
by KnowledgeWorks Global Ltd.

Contents

Preface

With this English edition my book is finally "coming home." For several reasons I had originally decided to write my thesis in German, but I always had it in the back of my mind to perhaps publish this title in English language one day – simply because I have written about a topic that is deeply connected with US culture and because all the archival material I worked with is also written in English language. Aside from this, my research adds to a discourse that has so far mostly taken place in the English-speaking research community.

That said, I do see some "German traits" in my thesis that are also quite authentic. Even though the book has been translated, I have stuck to my original, rather descriptive style of writing, which is also informed by my phenomenological approach. It leads to a language that neither praises all too much nor judges heavily. It might to an English-speaking reader sound a bit dry and impersonal from time to time. This should not be misunderstood for a lack of appreciation for the issues and people that I wrote about. It is rather the contrary – I have only written about this topic and dove into all the archival material, because I was deeply interested in the developments and thoughts of all the pioneers. My research was always led by a deep curiosity and respect for the material and all those individuals I "encountered" along the way.

In large parts this edition is a direct translation of the German book, only minor changes, that could deepen my findings in a few details, have been made in two chapters – the one on Charles A. Csuri and the one on Gordon W. Romney. In both cases this was initiated through a very inspiring thought exchange during the process of clearing the copyrights of their images – once with Csuri's daughter Caroline Csuri and once with Gordon W. Romney himself. Significant changes to the narrative I pursue here were, however, not made.

A noteworthy change that this edition went through is, however, my decision to add a whole chapter to the book. It discusses at least briefly the newer developments that took place in the field of generative AI and connects them to the narrative I pursue throughout the book. Since starting my research, the topic of generative AI became increasingly relevant – especially in the course of the last few years. This is why I seized the opportunity to comment on this development in light of my findings on earlier forms of computer graphics. The chapter therefore adds a dimension to this book that I had originally not anticipated. Hopefully it is apt to demonstrate how the fundamentally new approach I decided to develop to aesthetically analyze digital imagery can also be suitable to examine newer methods of synthetic imaging.

It should further be mentioned here that except for this last chapter DeepL Pro was used to produce a draft translation of the German edition. Nevertheless, I did revise the entire text throughout. Whenever a source was not published in an English translation, I carefully reworked the AI translation of the German sources, so they would reflect what was originally written as accurately as possible.

To comprehend my book in all its dimensions, I believe it is best to read it in chronological order from beginning to end – I do set up a narrative that will be understood more thoroughly this way. It is, however, also possible to jump directly to sections that spark interest to the reader. If something is unclear, cross-references will lead to other places in the book that discuss aspects in more detail. Finally, my hope is that this book initiates conversations, because, most importantly, I understand it as a contribution to an ongoing discussion that encourages continuous exploration of new thoughts and versatile perspectives.

Acknowledgments

I would like to take this opportunity to thank all the people who have supported this project in many different ways over the past years. Special thanks go to my two supervisors, Prof Dr Friedrich Weltzien and Prof Dr Thomas Lange. Since my master's degree at Hanover University of Applied Sciences and Arts, my second supervisor Friedrich Weltzien has accompanied me every step of the way from my practical design background into the world of cultural theory. I particularly remember his encouragement to recognize a valuable approach for research in my practical questions. His careful guidance smoothed the entire path and shaped the project. In a personally and professionally valuable addition, I was fortunate to win Thomas Lange as my first reviewer of my doctoral project at the University of Hildesheim. His precise feedback and his supervision as part of the DFG Research Training Group "Aesthetic Practice" made a significant contribution to bringing the project to a successful conclusion. In addition to the very valuable financial support, I would like to thank Prof Dr Andreas Hetzel as spokesperson at the time and Dr Sonja Dinter as coordinator. Both of them played a decisive role in shaping and promoting my position as a researcher within the Research Training Group.

In an academic context, I would also like to thank the members of the doctoral colloquium at the Department of Design and Media at Hanover University of Applied Sciences and Arts. I particularly want to acknowledge Prof Dr Martin Scholz, who also supported my master's degree and my teaching activities, as well as my colleagues Katrin Brümmer, Annerose Keßler, Dr Katharina Krämer, Dr Alexandra Panzert, Dr Saskia Plankert, Sylvia Thys and Antonia Ulrich. Additionally, I would like to thank all my students for their challenging questions and their inspiring thoughts. Our discussions have left valuable traces that can in one way or another be directly found in this study as well.

My project's method was further supported substantially by Prof Dr Annette Geiger (University of the Arts Bremen). My heartfelt thanks go to her. I am also tremendously grateful to Vita Berezina-Blackburn and Prof Maria Palazzi at Ohio State University, who have played an important role in shaping my thoughts. My time at ACCAD (Advanced Computing Center for the Arts and Design) was of fundamental importance for my research. I also deeply appreciate Vita Berezina-Blackburn's support in facilitating an exchange with Kyoung Swearingen, a long-time Pixar employee, which was very enriching for my research. I would like to thank Kyoung Swearingen for her willingness to enter into dialogue with me. The same applies to Dominik Pott, who as a 3D artist provided valuable insights into his work.

For this English edition of my book, I additionally had the chance to speak with Caroline Csuri, daughter of Charles A. Csuri who founded the ACCAD. I am deeply grateful for our inspiring exchange of ideas and for her generous permission to reproduce so many of her father's works in this edition. In this regard I am also thankful to James F. Blinn – not only for granting me permission to print his images, but also for his invaluable support in connecting me with Edwin Catmull, Henri Gouraud, Martin Newell and Gordon W. Romney, who kindly gave me their permissions to reproduce their images as well. Moreover, my email exchange with Gordon W. Romney has turned into a very insightful conversation. The permissions granted by all the other individuals and institutions are also much appreciated. I would further like to thank Alan Warburton and his thoughts on the final chapter of this book. The chapter was partly born out of a very inspiring conversation with him.

I am also especially grateful to my editor Elliott Morsia at Taylor & Francis and my production editor Jennifer Stair at CRC Press. Their proactive and helpful support as well as their clear and attentive communication style always made it seem like every challenge in the process of publishing this volume can be overcome. I am deeply grateful to their interest in this project and the support along the way.

Finally, I would like to express my heartfelt thanks to my friends and family. In various ways I was supported by Anja Egbers, Dr Matthias Bock, Dr Hendrik Hachmann, Sarah Haggard, Xianyu Bonnie Hao, Kathrin Jobczyk, Almut Schmitt, Theo Schreiber, Lisa Schulten, Shagana Shanmuganathan and Dr Petrissa Zell. Conversations with all of them continuously influence much of my thinking. In addition to their friendship, Petrissa Zell and Hendrik Hachmann were also valuable resources for technical consultations in the field of computer science. Especially their input on my last chapter on artificial intelligence has sharpened my thoughts tremendously.

The loving support of my parents Dorothea Seyfarth-Scheler and Thomas Scheler forms an essential foundation for this work. They fostered an artistic and creative environment in which curious exchange and thought experiments were not only possible, but strongly encouraged. In this sense, both my parents and my siblings Dr Corinna Scheler and David Scheler have significantly influenced this study through their free spirit, their sincere interest in my research and countless intensive discussions.

Last but not least, my wife Dr Kerstin Prietzel supported me with tireless commitment. I am particularly indebted to her, as she has accompanied and supported this project on many different levels. Her moral support as well as countless moments of advice and feedback at various stages of its development are essential pillars on which this project stands. I hope that one day I will be able to return the favor for this extraordinary form of support, not only from her but also from all the other people mentioned here.

About the Author

Carolin Scheler is a researcher in the fields of digital visual culture, media archaeology and animation studies, currently planning a postdoctoral research project. Her educational background is in the practical field of 3D animation and cultural theory, which she studied at the University of Applied Sciences and Arts Hanover, Germany, and The Ohio State University, United States. From 2015 to 2018 she worked as a research assistant at the University of Applied Sciences and Arts Hanover in the Department of Media, Information and Design. During the same period, she was also a research assistant at the Institute of Fine Arts and Art History at the University of Hildesheim, where she later earned her doctorate in the Department of Cultural Studies and Aesthetic Communication in 2022. As part of the Research Training Group "Aesthetic Practice," her scholarly work was funded by the German Research Foundation in the years from 2019 to 2022. Since 2022, Carolin Scheler has been a lecturer in cultural theory at the University of the Arts Bremen in the Department of Art and Design. She has also been working as a lecturer at the University of Applied Sciences and Arts Hanover in the Department of Media, Information and Design since 2018. At these universities, she teaches in the field of digital media studies, animation theory, art theory, humor theory and academic writing as well as supervising BAs and MAs.

I

Introduction

> Technological systems index their makers' theories of action, modeling both users and machines by framing their interaction.[1]
>
> *DANIEL CARDOSO LLACH (2015)*

This study describes an aesthetic of digital three-dimensional (3D) computer graphics – an aesthetic that can be applied to any type of image created using commercial 3D graphics software. This objective also establishes a fundamental assumption of this study, as the following elaborations are based on the hypothesis that 3D computer graphics share a common aesthetic and thus also a common context of meaning that applies equally to all images of this kind. The term "context of meaning" is used here in the sense of Hans Blumenberg and will be examined more closely in the next chapter. Although this premise suggests that the study has an image-theoretical focus, this categorization is only partially adequate. In the following, questions of pictoriality and image generation are central, but – according to another basic assumption of the study – digital 3D graphics cannot be fully grasped purely in terms of image aesthetics.[2]

The reason for this is that the graphics – even if they originate from the same software environment – can take on an infinite number of different appearances. As Figures I.1–I.4 illustrate, the fact that 3D computer graphics are an original and independent imaging technique is difficult and sometimes impossible to recognize through reception alone. The four examples demonstrate that 3D images can have not only a photorealistic but, for instance, also a flat cartoon aesthetic. This initial observation makes it difficult to describe the actual object of research at the beginning of the study, as the images relevant to this investigation would have to be described at a time when they cannot yet be described satisfactorily. However, being able to do this, that is, to capture the specifics of computer-generated images, is a key objective of the study. All four of the images mentioned were created using the same image-generation process. Each of the images is a synthetic computer-generated 3D graphic. They all share a similar production process due to the fact that they originate from a common software environment (see also Section 2.1). With this reference to the production process, the subject of this study now becomes clearer. Although it is ultimately about images, due to the inconsistent appearance of these images, the focus is rather on their production. Numerous other examples could be shown, as the range of what can be produced synthetically using 3D graphics software is not yet exhausted with these four images. However, these four graphics are sufficient to illustrate the purpose of this study: The aim is to find out what unites them, how they can be understood as an independent means of expression[3] – similar to what is perhaps possible for painting or photography. However, if a common aesthetic cannot be proven in terms of visual aesthetics and if similarities in terms of reception aesthetics are not readily recognizable, the intention of this study is to grasp the aesthetics of 3D graphics in terms of production aesthetics.

DOI: 10.1201/9781003649861-1

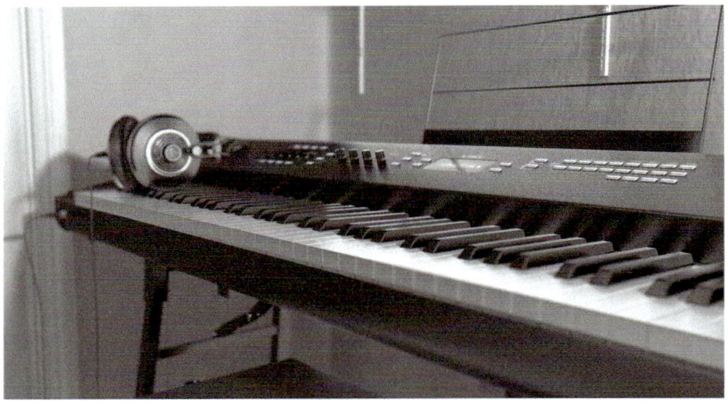

FIGURE I.1 Image by the author, *study*, 2011, 3D computer graphic. (© Carolin Scheler. Autodesk screen shots reprinted courtesy of Autodesk, Inc.)

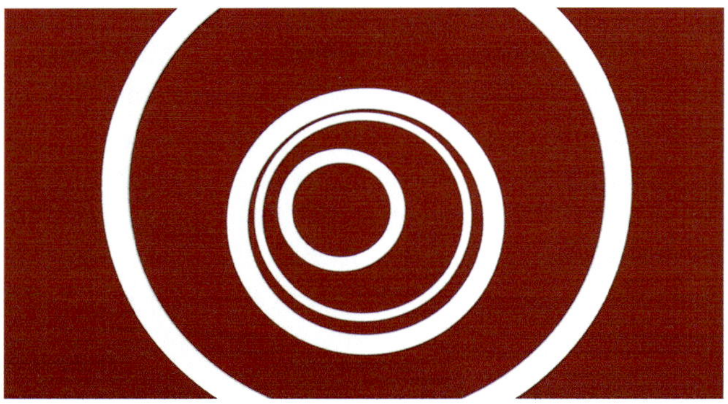

FIGURE I.2 Image by the author, still from *For as Long as it Lasts*, 2014, 3D computer graphic. (© Carolin Scheler. Autodesk screen shots reprinted courtesy of Autodesk, Inc.)

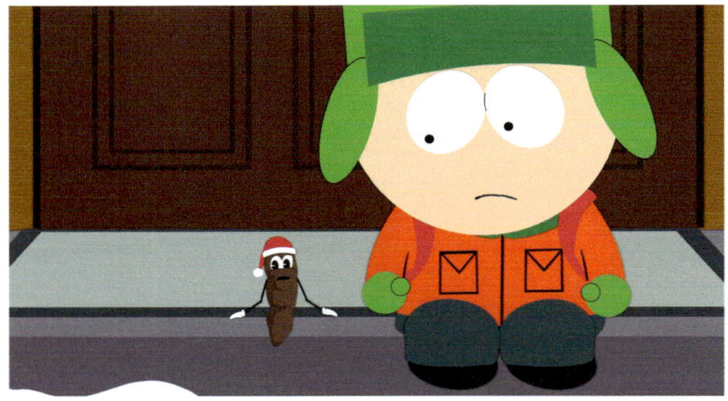

FIGURE I.3 Trey Parker, director, still from *South Park – The Problem with a Poo*, 2018, 3D computer graphic. (© Comedy Central. Photo 12 / Alamy Stock Photo.)

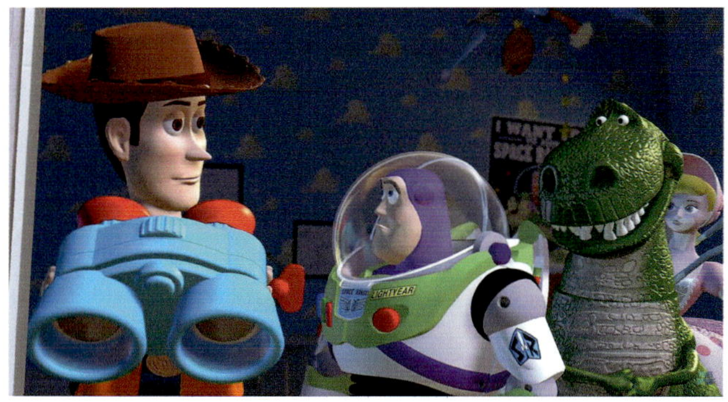

FIGURE I.4 John Lasseter, director, still from *Toy Story*, 1995, 3D computer graphic. (© 1995 Disney/Pixar.)

The aim of this production-aesthetic perspective is to find out what motivation lies behind the creation of these types of images by focusing on the production process, assuming that describable commonalities can be better recognized there than in the different pictorial forms of 3D computer graphics. So when it comes to finding out what motivates people to create images with computers, it becomes clear that my focus is not primarily directed toward the computer or the technology, but rather the people who work with computers for specific reasons. These include, on the one hand, those who have created the possibility of generating computer graphics in the first place and, on the other hand, those who make use of these possibilities. The production-aesthetic perspective of this study is therefore concerned with the practice of generating images on the computer and the question of whether this practice can be captured by common aesthetic parameters.

For the purposes of this study, the term 3D computer graphics must be narrowed down in one respect: The focus here is on those graphics that are used in the broadest sense in popular culture or in artistic-experimental contexts. On the other hand, representations that are created for architecture or industrial design, for example, are not the focus. Although they can also be described as 3D graphics, as they visualize a virtual 3D space like the images discussed in this study, they come from a different software landscape – despite having common historical roots (this is explained more precisely in Section 1.3).

What characterizes the software for popular culture and artistic-experimental fields of application and distinguishes it from the programs used in architecture and industrial design is the above-mentioned diversity of possible visual worlds that can be created with it. In addition to its use in building construction, software for the disciplines of architecture and industrial design is often used to create photorealistic images to visualize concepts for buildings and products that have not yet been realized. While this would also be possible with the software for popular culture, it is not exclusively focused on photorealistic imagery. As illustrated by the examples, these kinds of graphics programs can be used to imitate the aesthetics of many different imaging processes. In addition to creating individual, standalone images, the computer graphics process can also be used to generate image elements that can later be seamlessly combined with image elements from other digital processes, for example when it comes to integrating fantasy creatures or effects into a real-life feature film. As these examples and the sample images show, the software is often used for moving images, but this type of application is of secondary importance in the context of this study. The focus is solely on aspects of the production of imagery.

In addition to the terms 3D computer graphics and 3D graphics, I will also use the terms computer graphics, 3D image or synthetic image. The latter term is a reference to the phrase "l'image de synthèse," which is frequently used in French-language discourse. In this discourse it is occasionally employed in contrast to the term "l'image numérique"[4] to indicate that it is not simply digital images that are meant, but specifically those graphics that are artificially generated on the computer. Although, in contrast to the terms "3D computer graphics" and "3D graphics," the terms "computer graphics" and "synthetic image" lack the reference "3D," in the context of this study, with all these terms, I refer to an imaging process that depicts a virtual 3D space. The technological environment in which these images are created will be explained in more detail in Section 2.1, but it should already be pointed out here that when the terms "computer graphics" and "synthetic image" are used in the context of this study, they do not refer to two-dimensional (2D) computer graphics that can be generated using illustration programs. Images of this type or other 2D digital products such as digital photographs are not the subject of this study, nor are images that create a three-dimensional impression of films on a screen at the movie theater with the aid of glasses. The increasingly relevant graphics that can now be generated using artificial neural networks will briefly be addressed in a short outlook at the end of this study. It is here where I will present how the findings of this study can easily be transferred to the realm of AI imagery.

NOTES

1. Daniel Cardoso Llach, *Builders of the Vision. Software and the Imagination of Design* (New York: Routledge, 2015), 46.
2. The concept of imagery used in this study is based on an understanding of pictoriality as described, for example by Annette Geiger and Bianca Holtschke in their volume *Piktogrammatik*. Although the authors refer conceptually to the pictogram, Geiger and Holtschke understand it as a broader concept that can also be applied to the computer graphics discussed in this study: "With the help of the term 'pictogrammatics,' a theoretical framework can be established that sharpens the view of the systematics of signs and examines how entire sets of rules and reference systems are composed from individual sign elements (shapes, lines, arrows, contours, structures, colors, etc.). Shapes and colors are used in pictorial representations to make knowledge and thinking, but also perception and feeling, visually tangible. The resulting pictograms would not be legible if they did not refer to an inventory of signs; all communication ultimately presupposes the framework of a grammar. Although picture grammar is based on the idea of depicting perceived reality, this certainly does not mean that reality itself can be depicted. Rather, the real is interpreted and signified. The pictorial signs are to be understood as empowerment, even self-empowerment, the drawing shows that one has recognized and understood something, that one knows how to convey the corresponding knowledge through an abstracting representation. Precisely because the creative freedom is greater than one might think, a grammar of images is required. Its rules have to be created specifically and do not arise by themselves." Annette Geiger, Bianca Holtschke, "Einleitung. Grafisches Gestalten als Weltwissen und Bilderordnung," in *Piktogrammatik. Grafisches Gestalten als Weltwissen und Bilderordnung*, ed. Annette Geiger and Bianca Holtschke (Bielefeld: transcript, 2021), 11–12. In this sense, I set out to develop a grammar of 3D computer graphics.
3. The term "medium" is deliberately not used here, as this study does not intend to develop a media theory. Rather, it is assumed that a media-theoretical examination of 3D computer graphics can only take place in connection with the knowledge gained here about its production process. Nevertheless, in the course of the study, significant intersections to questions of media theory emerge at certain points, as will, for example, become clear in Section 1.1.
4. See e.g. Edmond Couchot, Norbert Hillaire, *L'art numérique. Comment la technologie vient au monde de l'art* (Paris: Flammarion, 2003), 22–23.

CHAPTER 1

Methodology and Structure of the Study

1.1 METHODOLOGY – OVERCOMING LEAPS

> [T]he problem of technology essentially has to do with the manner in which man is *responsible* for history; this was in fact true long before it could be perceived and become vivid that technology actually determines man's existence, and indeed, decides his possibilities.[1]
>
> *HANS BLUMENBERG (1963)*

Why might it be useful to explore the practice of image-making with the computer against the backdrop of a unifying aesthetic for 3D computer graphics? One possible starting point for an answer to this question lies in the observation that with the various digital imaging processes that I have mentioned so far – such as digital photography, artificial neural networks and 3D graphics – there are now several means that can be used to create images that give the impression of having been recorded photographically. At the same time, however, based on the guiding hypothesis for my investigation, I am assuming that each of these processes has its very own production-aesthetic context of meaning. What I mean by this can be illustrated by a further image example. The three portraits in Figures 1.1–1.3 are a digital photograph, a 3D computer graphic and an image created by an artificial neural network. Although from a visual-aesthetic as well as a reception-aesthetic angle the pictures clearly depict three different people, the portraits do not differ in any way from a purely technical point of view. Their "material" is completely identical in each case – all the examples are ordinary JPG files. As US media theorist Peter Lunenfeld notes, "[r]emember that the '*photorealistic*' graphic and the digital photograph are compositionally indistinguishable from each other, as they are at base simply representations of binary pairs: yes/no, 0/1, on/off."[2] The images or the image files themselves therefore do not reveal that the people whose faces are shown in the computer graphic and in the artificial image do not exist. The portraits can be placed next to each other on a completely equal footing, but, following Nelson Goodman, an aesthetic difference only starts to exist at the moment when the respective origin of the images is known.[3] However, since, as the examples presented here demonstrate, an investigation of the visual aesthetics or reception aesthetics can no longer easily grasp the respective aesthetic dimension of the three imaging processes, it is necessary – at least if the aim is to understand their respective independent aesthetics – to take the production of the images into account. Although there are potentially also digital images whose origin is communicated in terms of image aesthetics, the examples show that in the digital environment, a production-aesthetic perspective that traces the origin of the images is becoming increasingly important in determining their aesthetics.

Incidentally, this is an observation that can also apply to the field of text or music production. While knowing the context in which an online post was created is important in text production, especially with

DOI: 10.1201/9781003649861-2

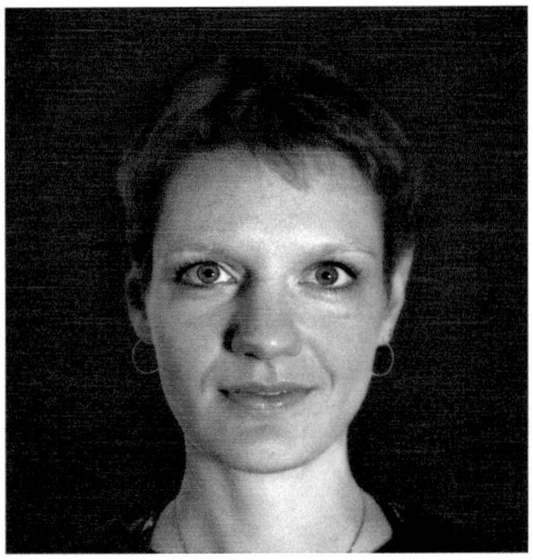

FIGURE 1.1 Image by the author, *Portrait*, 2022, digital photography. (© Carolin Scheler.)

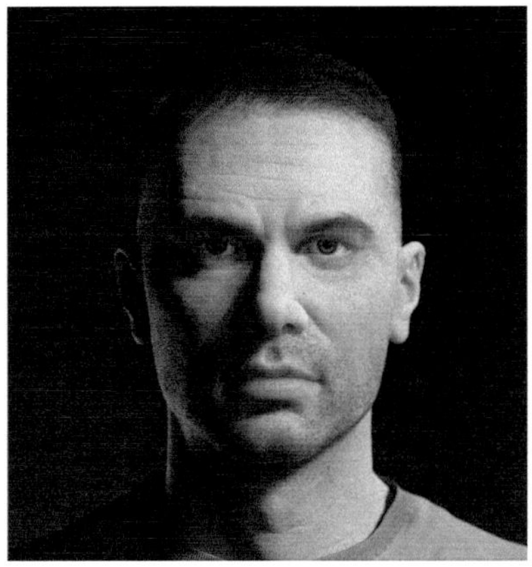

FIGURE 1.2 Paweł Somogyi, *Steve* (fictional person), 2022, 3D computer graphic. (© Paweł Somogyi.)

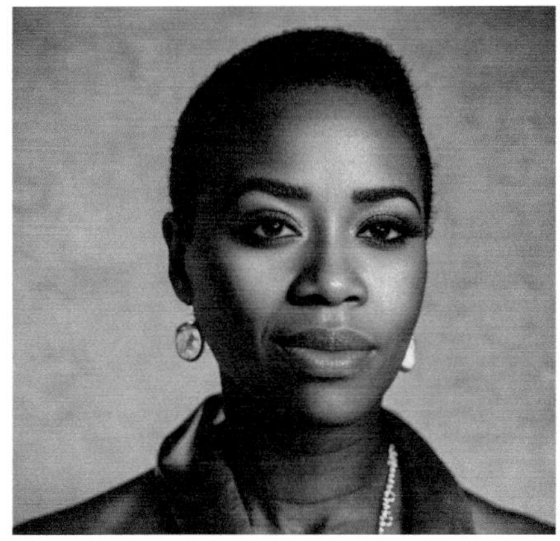

FIGURE 1.3 neural.love, *portrait of a middle aged black woman looking into the camera*, 2023, AI generated image. (© CC0.)

regard to the phenomenon of "fake news," the situation in music is similar to that in image production: Here too, human hearing can no longer easily distinguish between analogously recorded and subsequently digitized sounds, which also applies to synthetic music that was created from the outset using digital samples or with the help of an artificial neural network. The aim of using the production-aesthetic perspective to understand the respective products against the backdrop of their individual aesthetic dimension can therefore also have a political dimension – especially in the area of text production. At the same time, the question of the manipulability of people through digital media is not the guiding principle of my study.

With the aim to differentiate between the digital processes and to consider them each in their own aesthetics, I therefore do not directly enter into the debate on the manipulability of digital images that took place primarily in the 1980s, 1990s and 2000s, although some of these positions are discussed below. Rather, aspects of this debate are taken up indirectly. I see an intellectual affinity, for example, with an argumentative line pursued by the cultural scientist Birgit Schneider. In her paper *Wissenschaftsbilder zwischen digitaler Transformation und Manipulation Einige Anmerkungen zur Diskussion des "digitalen Bildes"*[4] (Scientific Images between Digital Transformation and Manipulation. Some Notes on the Discussion of the "Digital Image"), Schneider presents an alternative way of analyzing digital images. Her aim is to draw attention to so-called scientific images, which – such as climate models – are concerned with visualizing data. In order to show that such types of images cannot be captured by prominent narrative strands of the debate on digital imagery, she first traces the central positions of this discussion and then makes a proposal to expand this debate to include a new perspective. In addition to a brief mention of Marshall McLuhan, her summary of the most influential positions to date begins with Max Bense, who in the 1950s and 1960s was concerned with early forms of computer graphics still on paper.[5] With Jean Baudrillard, Schneider then jumps to the 1970s, a period in which digital images could now be output on displays. In this context, she emphasizes that to some extent Baudrillard's contribution to the debate still shapes the way we deal with digital images today and that his thinking continues in a similar form in positions such as those of Vilém Flusser or Paul Virilio:

> Since then, philosophy and visual studies, art history, information and media theory as well as semiotics have contributed very different aspects to the question of the status of digital images, whereby the hypotheses have only rarely been tested on the basis of empirical material. The point of intersection here was, on the one hand, the invoked crisis of representation, which was assessed either as loss or liberation. In this early phase […], the visual worlds on the

> basis of which this early debate was conducted either implicitly or explicitly hardly touched on the fields of scientific imagery that was changing due to digital technologies, but were primarily borrowed from popular cultural areas of application, such as animated films, computer games, image manipulation and cyberspace applications, which could be negotiated under the concepts of virtuality and simulation.[6]

Although in my discussion I explicitly focus on the object of research criticized by Schneider when I am dealing primarily with those computer graphics that belong to a popular cultural spectrum in the broadest sense, I am nevertheless taking up her proposal for an alternative perspective on digital images, because it can also be made fruitful in the context of this study. Her main point of criticism is that in the debate on digital imagery, reference is still very rarely, and in many cases not at all, made to the numerical dimension of images or to the dimension that Frieder Nake, a pioneer of computer art, describes as the "sub-surface" (German: Unterfläche) of the image, in contrast to the surface of the image.[7] However, this dimension becomes particularly relevant with regard to the investigation of scientific images, because here the algorithmic sub-surface of the images is an essential component. The visualization of a data set in these images is never mimetic and at the same time, it is not an illusion. Instead, the visual surface of the scientific images is always an attempt to reproduce the sub-surface as objectively as possible. In order to make it comprehensible "to which 'reality' the images refer behind their coding,"[8] Schneider therefore proposes, with reference to Bruno Latour, to trace the chains of reference between the image surface and its underlying algorithmic nature when examining scientific images.[9]

Although Schneider deals with a different object of investigation, in I do tie in with her approach of no longer conducting the debate on digital imagery solely in relation to the surface of the images, but also taking into account their production process. Although Schneider herself does not use the term production aesthetics, her following statement can be understood as a methodological starting point for my discussion:

> The surface alone does not have to show its processing, because even if it is not an a priori property of digital images to conceal their construction and manipulations, it is nevertheless a mistake to believe that one can necessarily see the conditions of an image's production from the formal conditions; the image surfaces do not have to bear the traces of their construction within themselves, and it is usually no longer possible to trace on the image surface which visualization effects, programs and decisions led to a particular image.[10]

So if the potentially identical appearance of the three different imaging processes of digital photography, 3D graphics and artificial intelligence (AI) forms the starting point in this chapter, it is not to address questions about the manipulability of images or image techniques but rather to ask how and why it has come about that there are now three processes that can produce photographic or photorealistic images. This angle makes it possible to no longer automatically suspect manipulative intentions behind the images, but instead to first take them seriously in their aesthetics. Studying the people who originally developed the ability to create photorealistic computer graphics can then also help us to better understand the digitalized world and to approach digital images that conceal their own nature not with doubt,[11] but with confidence. And according to my main hypothesis, this task can in the diverse digital image landscape only be fulfilled from the perspective of practice.

So what methodological foundation can this study be placed on? My aim to describe here a unifying aesthetic for 3D graphics, which appear so diverse, can be backed up by technology-philosophical positions. The phenomenological approach of the philosopher Hans Blumenberg is drawn upon for this purpose. The fact that a phenomenological mode of thought can be suitable for the approach of focusing on the practice and more or less disregarding the sensually perceptible facade of the images may seem contradictory at this point. After all, the aim here is to react to the 3D computer graphics analytically rather than sensually. Blumenberg's examination of Edmund Husserl's phenomenology can show how this contradiction can be resolved.

In his 1963 essay *Phenomenological Aspects on Life-World and Technization*, Blumenberg explores questions about the technization of the human being against the backdrop of Husserl's phenomenology.[12] Blumenberg's starting point is the debate on the separation between nature and technology that has been established since antiquity, i.e. the traditional confrontation of the two concepts "natura naturans" and "natura naturata." He reminds us that since the modern era at the latest, technology has also been seen as an instrument of human self-empowerment. Technology seemed to dominate nature more and more and thus increasingly provoke what Blumenberg phrases "calls to order"[13] one of them being, for instance, Husserl's well-known demand at the beginning of the 20th century: "[T]o the things themselves!"[14]

Blumenberg's concern is to understand how this plea can be understood in relation to technology. He asks "what in the case of technology was 'the thing itself.'"[15] He rejects the idea of a primordial state in which humans may once have found themselves and from which they suddenly decided to live in a *technicized* way instead of *naturally* from one day to the next. Instead, he suggests that the technization of mankind should not be seen as a radical change, but as a development whose beginning cannot be determined and which has always taken place in a process. However, the assumption that humans are technicized by nature is also too simplistic for him. Neither the idea of an antithesis between nature and technology nor the idea that man has always been mechanized could provide a possible answer to the question of "the thing itself" in relation to technology. According to Blumenberg, in order to avoid having to approach the technization of human beings from either a negative or a positive stance, it is appropriate to use a mode of thought that makes it possible to approach the technization *without bias*. He therefore chooses the method that was developed with precisely this claim of impartiality: Husserl's phenomenology.[16]

Some of Husserl's concepts play a particularly central role in Blumenberg's analysis, such as "intentionality," the "life-world," the "universe of obviousnesses" and the "phenomenological reduction." I want to briefly explain them below in order to be able to build on them in the further course of this chapter: Husserl chooses the concept of intentionality – as Blumenberg explains – for his concern to face the "things themselves" in an unbiased, merely descriptive way. Husserl uses the term "intentionality" to describe the process of consciously directing our perceptual apparatus toward our environment in order to approach things purposefully.[17] Blumenberg, however, points out the great challenge of surrendering to intentionality in everyday life: "Mundane and practical life may [...] out of necessity content itself with fragments of intuitions, with indications and intimations, with formulae and signs [...]."[18] Although Blumenberg – unlike Husserl – rejects the idea of a non-technicized primordial state, he agrees with the necessity proclaimed by Husserl to get *behind* this layer of signs again. Husserl calls this immediate dimension, freed from all intermediate levels, the "life-world." This is a "universe of what is pre-given as obvious,"[19] which, however, according to Blumenberg's explanation, corresponds to an unattainable state of a beginning without history. Nevertheless, the goal of phenomenological reduction is ultimately to at least approach this state. Blumenberg explains this process as follows:

> The life-world was discovered by constantly refining the main methodological instrument of phenomenology, the so-called phenomenological reduction. With this *reduction*, every assertion was to be suspended that could not be traced back to the immediate givenness of consciousness – above all, the "general thesis" of the transcendent existence of a world independent of consciousness.[20]

According to this statement phenomenological reduction assumes an even higher position than the supposedly neutral natural sciences, i.e. the theorization of phenomena. Here too, access to the "thing itself" can only be achieved with the help of phenomenological reduction, but as long as theory does not follow this principle, it merely takes place within a constructed frame of reference that is detached from the life-world. The same applies to an even greater extent to the technization. According to Blumenberg Husserl regarded it as the materialized realization of previous theoretical considerations – that is, as a continuation of theory.[21] Blumenberg uses Husserl's idea of an extreme distance between the life-world and technology as a starting point for his own argumentation. Here he also establishes the concept of the context of meaning, which is central to my study.

Blumenberg uses the example of an electric doorbell to illustrate the distance between the life-world and technology. Whereas earlier models required a cord to be pulled or a switch to be turned in order to mechanically produce a ringing sound, with the electric version the sound is no longer directly produced but only triggered. There is no longer any connection or, as Blumenberg calls it, any *context of meaning* between the action performed and the sound:

> The desired effect is kept ready for our use, available for us, as it were, within the design of the apparatus; indeed, it carefully hides its conditionality and the complexity of its realization from us in order to suggest itself to us as something effortlessly available. For the sake of this suggestion of the always-ready, the technical world, regardless of all its functional requirements, is a sphere of casings, disguises, nonspecific façades, and blinds.[22]

Blumenberg goes on to explain that this is also the reason why we sometimes hit the light switch instead of the doorbell in the hallway of an apartment block. He therefore states,

> The self-presentation of the technical object [...] seems to do everything in its power not to let questions arise in the first place – and not just questions concerning the secrets of its design and its functional principle, but above all, questions concerning its right to exist.[23]

So, technology, like the theory that preceded it, is in its existence not only detached from the life-world, technical achievements also inadvertently join the life-world, the "universe of obviousnesses," they no longer trigger any questions – we take these developments as they are, although their context of meaning is no longer communicated.[24]

Blumenberg's example of the electric doorbell can be directly applied to the images I presented above. They, too, leave the impression of an "always-ready" façade whose "right to exist" is often not questioned. Especially in the everyday flood of images, we seem to be taking them completely for granted. In this context, Blumenberg refers to the paradox described by Husserl that, although technical achievements claim to *reveal* something on the one hand, they always contribute to *concealing* something on the other. This paradox applies greatly to these images. Blumenberg interprets Husserl's choice to speak only of *concealing* instead of, for example, destroying, quite positively: "[I]t is a gentle image for the lost context of meaning when Husserl says that science 'hovers as if in empty space above the life-world.' The position of phenomenological analysis cannot be pushed until it reaches its antithesis."[25]

But even if Husserl's phenomenology does not represent an opposing position to technology, the question remains what "the thing itself" could be in relation to technology. How can we deal with the problem of *revelation* and *concealment*? For Husserl, historical consciousness is of immense importance at this point. As a human it is important to take responsibility for the fragmented perception caused by our technization. Blumenberg explains that man "wants to move ahead, so to speak, 'in leaps.' He omits history."[26] According to Blumenberg, with his phenomenology, Husserl "wants to restore history – history in an absolute sense. Its basic demand is to 'repeat the entire history … of the subjective activities.'"[27]

At this point, Blumenberg recognizes a contradiction inherent in Husserl's phenomenology, which Blumenberg, however, ultimately uses as a constructive approach. Husserl's plea to turn to "the things themselves" was intended to serve as a kind of therapy for the theorized and increasingly technicized world that had gone astray, in order to return to the "life-world." However, the phenomenological reduction that he developed in order to do justice to this claim was nothing more than a *method*, a theorized process. Husserl's idea that the reduction is directed toward infinity is decisive for Blumenberg's realization, because implicitly such a never-ending process means that it takes place in consecutive and applicable steps. It is therefore a cognitive process that could take place in a very similar way in the natural sciences.[28] Each individual step represents an *intermediate realization* that can subsequently be built upon. In this respect, Husserl's approach itself would be detached from the life-world. Not even his phenomenology can therefore fulfill the principle of unbiased observation, which is why Blumenberg comes to the conclusion that "at the lowest elemental level of its achievements, the human intellect is always already engaged in formalization."[29]

However, instead of speaking of a theory's "*loss* of meaning"[30] as Husserl does, Blumenberg suggests that the formalization underlying human thought should be understood as a voluntary "*renunciation* of meaning."[31] In this context, he refers, for example, to Euclid's geometry: In some cases, Euclid deliberately renounced the final resolution of a problem in order to create a space in this renunciation that allows insights even before the argumentation has been finalized. Blumenberg thus concludes that "perhaps there would still be no geometry today,"[32] if Euclid had always waited for the final proof of a theoretical problem. Phenomenological reduction cannot be brought to a close either, and yet it produces insights.

Husserl was aware of this contradiction, which is why he was able to grant sciences such as mathematics their right to exist. However, it was important to Husserl that the original meaning of a theory, from which it was developed, was always known. Blumenberg ultimately interprets Husserl as him seeing the main task of his phenomenology "[to] vicariously [...] administer the treasure of the structures of meaning that technization has skipped."[33] Unlike mathematics, Husserl saw phenomenology as capable of fulfilling this task and taking responsibility for the restoration of meaning. In order to pursue this sense of responsibility and, with regard to technization, to make our way back to the "universe of obviousnesses," it is necessary to consciously decide to no longer take anything for granted, which is why Blumenberg puts it more succinctly: "To call into question even the last and most hidden self-evidences could almost be stated as the program of phenomenology."[34] But, as Blumenberg points out, there is once again a deep contradiction in the phenomenological approach. For if nothing in our perception can be taken for granted, suddenly everything that appears to us is only *one* possibility of many. In other words, it is pure contingency. But it is precisely contingency that makes us as humans inventive. If we see everything as a possibility, it stands to reason that we will begin to push the limits of this scope of possibility to see how far we can go. Contingency *encourages* our technization. Yes, phenomenology *encourages* technization; it is itself one of its motors.[35] For this reason, phenomenology – and this is Blumenberg's final conclusion – can only be understood in the sense of a dialectical suspension: "We may thus regard the idealized 'life-world' in Husserl's thinking as the correlate to and corrective for the increase in contingency unnoticed in technization."[36]

But how can this realization be applied in practice? Where would Husserl's method lead in relation to the questions posed in my own study? Blumenberg points out that phenomenology's claim to take nothing for granted, especially in relation to technization, has given rise to a very topical and radical method.[37] While phenomenological reduction can certainly allow the *renunciation* of meaning and trust that insights will emerge even *before* the questions posed have been answered, this renunciation of meaning is never successful in relation to our technization. In terms of contingency, Blumenberg understands technology as "ultimately designed to enhance a finite given capacity, that of human existence."[38] If the phenomenological reduction is focused on a technical achievement, it always exposes this enhancement and thus also the motives for it.

According to Blumenberg, Husserl himself was not even aware of the topicality of his own method in relation to our technization. The leaps caused by technologies would be particularly visible, for example, when they are used in regions of the world in which they were not developed, in which technization had no historical motivation at all. According to Blumenberg, in order to get closer to the "things themselves" in relation to technization and to understand their context of meaning, it is necessary to ask *why* we humans push our own existential capacities to such an extent.[39]

This conceptual background explains the actual focus of my study. Instead of concentrating on the surface of the images, my aim is to shed light on the background of the images, to determine how and why 3D graphics are created in a certain way. My aim is therefore to inquire into the *meaning* of these images and the motivation behind their creation. In order to make Blumenberg's model practicable as a method, the previously announced production-aesthetic approach is suitable for my investigation.

In this sense, my study also ties in with creativity theorist Friedrich Weltzien's paper *Produktionsästhetik als Methode* (Production Aesthetics as a Method). In it, Weltzien explains the advantages of focusing on the production of a work:

> By focusing on the creative process itself in addition to formal analysis or reception-aesthetic approaches, historical contextualization, biographies or intention research,

> dimensions of meaning are opened up that would be much more difficult or even impossible to grasp and describe by other means.[40]

Another particular characteristic that Weltzien mentions in relation to this definition of a production-aesthetic research method is that it can often unite aspects that are rarely focused on together in other research approaches.[41] The extent to which this also comes into play in my study is discussed again at the end of this section.

The aim should therefore be to understand and describe (as in "restore") the creative process that led to the 3D graphics we have today in a step-by-step manner and – acknowledging the fundamental phenomenological requirement – to approach this with the greatest possible impartiality. Which decisions were made by which people at what time and for what reason? However, if the aim is to relate this question not only to a single image and its production, but to the computer graphics imaging process as a whole, then this decision has consequences for the scope of this study.

The focus then shifts from those who use the software to those who have developed it. This shift in focus is based on the assumption that it is precisely in the tension-filled field *between* the development and use of software that the leaps Blumenberg talks about can be identified. Overcoming these leaps means understanding the context of meaning of 3D graphics and of the practice of creating them, because the software has been developed for certain reasons that those who use it may not even be aware of. Nevertheless, the practice of creating 3D graphics is always characterized by certain aesthetic parameters that were once the basis for the development of the software. Individual work steps are so self-evident (or *obvious* in Husserl's terms) that their cultural background is often no longer recognized. Thus, when 3D graphics software is used around the world today to produce synthetic images, the production-aesthetic aspects of other, previous programmers and developers are constantly passed on.

The history of software development for 3D computer graphics therefore concerns not only all 3D computer graphics equally but also the practice with which images of this kind are created. Although each individual graphic within the software has emerged from an independent production-aesthetic process, the practice is always influenced by the software and thus also by production-aesthetic features that are anchored in it. These features constitute the underlying context of meaning of 3D computer graphics. Before an individual graphic can be analyzed in order to perhaps also describe it in terms of visual aesthetics, it is necessary to know the historical context underlying the imaging technique itself. Blumenberg's examination of Husserl shows *why* it is necessary to work in this way when the creative process takes place in a highly technical environment. This is the only way to overcome the leaps in order to try and return "to the things themselves" and to help make a possible context of meaning recognizable. The history of software development therefore contains the *common* context of meaning of all 3D graphics and thus also the knowledge that is needed to make 3D computer graphics aesthetically comprehensible.

The production-aesthetic method, as it is to be understood here against the background of Blumenberg, adds a historical dimension to the study, which ultimately makes software *development* the actual object of investigation. The shift in the starting point, which now no longer focuses on the 3D graphics themselves, but rather on the history of the software required to create these graphics, makes it possible to understand my production-aesthetic study not only as an image-theoretical or praxeological study, but rather as a media-archeological examination that is able to unite all of these perspectives. The concept of media archeology is based on Erkki Huhtamo's and Jussi Parikka's definition:

> Media Archaeology rummages textual, visual, and auditory archives as well as collections of artifacts, emphasizing both the discursive and the material manifestations of culture. Its explorations move fluidly between disciplines, although it does not have a permanent home within any of them. Such "nomadicism," rather than being a hindrance, may in fact match its goals and working methods, allowing it to roam across the landscape of the humanities and social sciences and occasionally to leap into the arts.[42]

In many respects, Huhtamo and Parikka's description of how to work with media-archeological approaches applies to my study's methodology. My main focus is on archival materials that can be used to trace the individual decisions that led to the development of graphics software. However, in order to be able to analyze these decisions more comprehensively in terms of cultural history, the study will examine the field of art at the end of the production-aesthetic examination of computer technology developments in order to apply the art historical findings to the results on graphics software. Huhtamo and Parikka's definition of the media-archeological approach legitimizes this step, which will be explained in more detail in the following section on the study's structure. There, the archival documents analyzed will also be presented in more detail. Additionally, in the next section I will demonstrate that I adopt another approach that is characteristic of media archeology, because if my aim is to tell a cultural history of 3D computer graphics, then approaches that are not (or hardly) embedded in today's commercially available software should also be taken into account. As Huhtamo and Parikka aptly point out, even the "[d]ead ends, losers, and inventions that never made it into a material product [...] have important stories to tell."[43]

1.2 STRUCTURE OF THE STUDY

The study consists of five parts. The first contains sections on my research method and the current state of research, as well as a brief technical and historical introduction to computer graphics. Parts II and III, respectively, present historical developments at the *Massachusetts Institute of Technology* (MIT) and the *University of Utah* – two research institutions that played a key role in the emergence of 3D graphics software. Part IV discusses art-historical image concepts that emerged in the United States, which are then applied to developments in computer technology. In Part V, the findings from the previous chapters are synthesized, placed in a wider cultural-historical context of American Studies and interpreted against this backdrop. The study ends with a brief conclusion, although I do offer in a last chapter a short outlook in which I transfer the findings of my study to the newer generative AI tools.

In the first part, i.e. in the next section, I present the current state of research, which my study builds on, followed by a brief technical insight into the software environment in which the 3D graphics whose history I am analyzing in this study are created. Being able to understand the practice at least to some extent seems necessary in order to be able to better comprehend both the way in which I am undertaking the historiography here and the findings that I produce with my study. Before moving on to the second part of the study, I provide an initial, brief outline of historical events in order to establish an overview of key figures and milestones in computer technology from the outset, which I then examine in greater depth step by step.

In Parts II and III, I mainly direct my attention to historical individuals whose research – at least from a production-aesthetical perspective – still shapes the imaging process of computer graphics today. To gain a deeper understanding of the contingency of the developments, I here also draw direct comparisons to artists and developers whose ideas ultimately did not influence the software used today to the same extent. The brief overview of events at the beginning of the book allows readers to quickly familiarize themselves with the individuals presented in more depth later on. My main focus in this study is on the historical development of the software, which took place in its main stages within the United States in the 1960s and 1970s. The research material for Parts II and III consists essentially of primary sources from the fields of engineering and computer science. Particularly revealing in this context are master's theses, dissertations and conference papers which produced new findings and developments in the field of human-machine interaction and computer graphics display options.

While in Part II, I focus on developments at the *Lincoln Laboratory* of the MIT in Boston, Massachusetts, in Part III, I deal with developments at the *Computer Science Department* at the *University of Utah*.

Based on the findings of the previous chapters, Part IV of the study is devoted to the phenomenon of "American Realism" – understood here not as a historical category, but rather an aesthetic one and as such as a collection of different figurative artistic movements in the United States. This angle helps to identify concepts of imaging typical to the United States, considering the basic computer graphics algorithms were mainly developed there. The decision to deal with "realist" painterly traditions in the United States is justified by the fact that a specific concept of "realism" can be identified as a major point of reference for the developers of computer graphics algorithms. It is therefore assumed that by looking at a historical epoch of art, insights can be gained into today's digital imaging process. As an aesthetic paradigm, the historical development of "American Realism" has the potential to create topicality, which this study exploits.[44]

In order to specifically describe and comprehend – in the sense of Blumenberg – the "context of meaning" of 3D computer graphics in Part V, all the findings from the previous chapters are synthesized into a larger cultural-historical concept. I here pursue indications that have crystallized while researching the production-aesthetical relations between the art-historical insights and the computer-graphical approaches. The synthesis of the two fields takes place with reference to *The Machine in the Garden: Technology and the Pastoral Ideal in America* by the US cultural historian and American Studies researcher Leo Marx published in 1964.[45] His examination of the technological progress in the United States and its effects on the cultural developments there is used in conclusion to address the question of what the emergence of graphics software means for the practice of making images on the computer. Therefore, the study finally leads back to the practitioner's perspective and the question of how to deal with this legacy that is inscribed into the software, even if only briefly. After a short summary in Chapter 12, Chapter 13 presents how the historical developments and cultural values related to computer graphics are production-aesthetically, but also visually perpetuated within the newer environment of artificial neural networks.

1.3 CURRENT STATE OF RESEARCH

> Spanning scientific, academic, and popular discourses, this dominant image of technology in design [...] is so engrained that it has become a lens through which we come to see design practices socially, historically, and conceptually in technological terms. Furthermore, by organizing views about architecture, product design, engineering, and urbanism our technological imagination of design fundamentally structures the intellectual work of designers across fields [...].[46]
>
> *DANIEL CARDOSO LLACH (2015)*

The task of describing a state of research for this study could generally be approached from two perspectives: On the one hand, it is possible to present studies in which software has also been investigated from a phenomenological or even production-aesthetic angle, but this perspective threatens to move the graphic software under investigation out of focus, as this research approach has not yet been used for this purpose. Nevertheless, the 1987 monograph *Electric Language: A Philosophical Study of Word Processing* by the philosopher Michael Heim, which addresses the topic of computer-aided word processing from a phenomenological perspective, at least demonstrates the advantages of such an approach. It is presented first in the following. However, as the graphics software and the images it generates are central to this study a further starting point for presenting the state of research can, on the other hand, also be found in the fundamental concern of this study, which is to look behind the façade of the images. This concern is also addressed by media historian and theorist Jacob Gaboury in his 2021 study *Image Objects: An Archaeology of Computer Graphics.* He is, like me, interested in investigating computer graphics by acknowledging that they encompass more than just their visible surface. While he follows a similar goal with this angle, in terms of methodology, he is not working phenomenologically. Also he is neither or hardly concerned with the image aesthetics, nor with the production aesthetics of synthetic imaging. Rather, he predominantly works in a documentary manner.[47] The consequences of exploring a similar object of research using these different approaches will become clear later in this section. Gaboury's study is presented in detail in second place. To conclude the state of research, I will present the 2015 study *Builders of the Vision: Software and the Imagination of Design* by the architect Daniel Cardoso Llach which pursues a very similar concern to my study. Despite a different professional outset – he focuses primarily on architecture and computer-aided design (CAD) – he also looks at the development of software from the perspective of design practice. Cardoso Llach's approach can therefore be regarded as a direct starting point for my own study. His book is particularly apt to illustrate the desideratum that I have addressed in my research: While he covers one path of a fork in the road – the one related to architecture, I cover the other – the one related to computer graphics.

So how can software development be understood phenomenologically? In his 1987 study *Electric Language: A Philosophical Study of Word Processing*, Heim deals with the phenomenon of computer-aided word processing. Although he does not consider graphics software in his study, the mindset with which he approaches his research can, at least to some extent, be considered groundbreaking for the following explanations, because with his desire to work phenomenologically, he expresses the claim, similar to Blumenberg, to initially examine his subject neither from a negative nor from an affirmative perspective. Before a judgment can be made or one can join either side, the changes brought about by a new technology must first be understood.[48] His way to express himself reflects the point in time at which Heim undertook his investigation because, as he himself puts it, he was working on the subject at a time when software phenomena such as computerized word processing were still a source of amazement. He even recognizes a potential in this amazement, because once the technology has become a habit, it becomes invisible, making it less obvious as an object of investigation.[49] The moment of amazement has long since passed in the field of 3D graphics, as it is often no longer even recognizable for what it is. In terms of thought, Heim is also related to Blumenberg here, as Heim also anticipates that the technologized life-world will one day be taken for granted. Although the age in which Heim published his study has passed and people no longer marvel at computerized text or image processing, Heim's mindset serves as a model for my study. My stance on the developments that have led to 3D graphics software is, as described in the methods section, therefore neither euphoric nor negative. Rather, I approach the historical steps – similar to Heim – in a dialectical manner. He explains what he means by this in his 1999 essay *The Cyberspace Dialectic*, in which he first describes how most debates on the then emerging digitality were characterized either by a deep rejection or a euphoric approval. Instead of joining one of the two sides, he proposes a dialectic approach to the phenomenon: "We might learn to balance the idealist's enthusiasm for computerized life with the need to ground ourselves more deeply in the felt earth that the realist affirms to be our primary reality."[50]

While Heim describes the electronic text editing process itself on the computer in phenomenological terms and places it in a wider cultural-historical context,[51] I devote my focus solely to the steps that took place before the software available today even existed. Heim ultimately comes to the realization that electronic text processing changes our thinking and writing processes, although he always remains true to his careful gauging mindset when making this observation.[52] In the end, however, his approach differs from the one I adopt in my own study, because to me it is no longer a question of describing a potential break with previous practices, but rather of discovering continuities.[53]

With this fundamental concern, I follow an agenda that is in its basic mindset related to the concept of "remediation," because as Jay D. Bolter and Richard Grusin note in their 1999 study *Remediation: Understanding New Media*, "[n]o medium today, and certainly no single media event, seems to do its cultural work in isolation from other media, any more than it works in isolation from other social and economic forces."[54] Although my primary aim is not to find out which old media have found their way into a new one,[55] but rather to identify an overarching concept of imagery, my study is based on the fundamental assumption that certain worldviews survive in software, which also characterized image-making before the age of the computer. With this proximity to Bolter and Grusin, the concern of my approach differs completely from that of the film and media scholar Jacob Gaboury, who in his study *Image Objects: An Archaeology of Computer Graphics* mentioned at the beginning of this section, emphasizes, "[r]efusing popular narratives of convergence and remediation, I argue that computer graphics is a unique medium distinct from those earlier visual forms it seeks to simulate."[56] A key reason why Gaboury rejects the conceptual approach of remediation for his scrutinization of computer graphics is that he does not regard them solely as a pictorial phenomenon. As the title of his study announces, he develops the concept of *image objects* in the context of his investigation, with which he wants to indicate that he views computer graphics rather as a phenomenon that can assume several states at the same time. Gaboury argues that every smartphone, car or even most buildings are also computer-graphic shapes. Many of these everyday objects exist not only as a file on a computer but also as a visualization and as an object in our environment.[57] Gaboury thus ascribes an omnipresent and very central role to computer-graphic developments:

> In fact, computer graphics are as old as the modern computer itself, and their development marks a fundamental transformation not only in the way we make images, but in the way we mediate our world through the computer, and in turn come to reimagine the world as computational. We live in a world that has been structured by the visual regime of computer graphics.[58]

Although, unlike Gaboury, I exclusively address the pictorial nature of 3D computer graphics and although I do not take into account the points of intersection in which computer graphics intervene in our environment in the form of physical objects, his observation shows how relevant the examination of the field of 3D computer graphics is.

In his study, Gaboury derives the concept of the object on two interlinked levels. The first relates to the reciprocal connection that in the history of computer graphics, everyday objects were often measured at the beginning in order to test the process of virtual modeling, and that, conversely, almost all everyday objects in our immediate environment today come from this very virtual environment. So while the virtual environment is populated by objects that once had their origins in our everyday lives, our environment is now populated by objects whose origins can be identified in the virtual environment.[59] The second level, from which Gaboury derives the concept of the object, refers to the software environment itself and the object-oriented programming paradigm on which every computer is based today. The object-oriented programming paradigm is particularly central in my own study (see, for example, Section 3.2 in this study). In the long term, it has prevailed over the original and older procedural programming paradigm, which, in contrast to the new approach that enabled interactive operation of the computer, functions in a process-based and linear manner. The change that took place in the 1970s from one paradigm to the other had far-reaching consequences. This development is also central for Gaboury:

> *Image Objects* tells a second story about the emergence of a new object form, and along with it the transformation of computation as a technical and cultural practice. Prior to the 1960s, computers were machines built for the procedural calculation of numerical data. They functioned hierarchically, with large mainframes designed for solving predetermined problems or processing data according to predetermined procedures. [...] The development of computer graphics [...] marks a reorientation of computer science toward the object world such that it could be made subject to computational forms of simulation, transforming the computer from a *tool* for procedural calculation into a *medium* structured by a distinct ontological claim.[60]

Gaboury refers to the media artist and theorist Casey Alt when he says that the object-oriented programming paradigm has turned the computer into a medium. Central to Alt and his position is the computer scientist Alan Kay, who first coined the term "object-oriented" in the 1970s when developing his programming language *Smalltalk* and who is also credited with designing the first prototype of a laptop with the "Dynabook."[61] As Gaboury then explains, the reciprocal cycle of "real" and "virtual" objects was only made possible by the paradigm shift from a procedural to an object-oriented programming approach indicated in his quote.[62] In contrast to Gaboury, who focuses mainly on the object-oriented paradigm,[63] the two programming approaches and their effects on creative processes are assessed in detail within my book, particularly in Section 3.2 and Chapter 4. However, similarities to Gaboury emerge in my study with regard to the observation that the newer object-oriented approach brought about significant changes that are still relevant today. Yet while Gaboury takes these innovations as an opportunity to ascribe to *image objects* an independent mediality that is not orientated toward previous media, my book comes to the opposite conclusion: Only through the object-oriented programming paradigm it became possible to carry – or *remediate* – concepts and worldviews into the software and thus into our everyday interactions. Although Gaboury links the "medial autonomy" of *image objects* to the object-oriented programming paradigm and at the same time relies on Alt's hypothesis that Kay medialized the computer with it, Alt himself points out the extent to which the object-oriented paradigm leads to practices and ideologies entering today's software environment. As Alt emphasizes, the new programming paradigm was deliberately conceptualized by Kay in order to create credible simulations. Kay's original idea was that anyone could create programs according to their own creative ideas, and he himself regrets that his system did not develop in this open direction: "In the end, the greatest irony of object orientation may be that no one was more disturbed by its voracious, all-consuming logic than Alan Kay himself, who, only a few years after creating Smalltalk, actively lobbied for its destruction."[64] Gaboury's argument that the object-oriented structure of *image objects* leads to a new mediality that does not tie in with any previous concept can be refuted not only by Alt but also by the inventor of the concept himself. The way in which the dynamic described here by Alt has developed is shown in the context of my study in a comprehensive production-aesthetic investigation. In order to deepen Alt's findings on the object-oriented approach, I place a special focus as well on procedural processes, as these were *also* used to generate computer graphics. The production-aesthetic comparison of both programming approaches and the way in which they are used for synthetic image generation is one of the main concerns of my study. However, Alan Kay is placed in the background here; instead, previous developments are shown which he later built upon with his ideas in the 1970s.

As can now be seen, Gaboury also chooses a historical perspective for his investigation in order to characterize 3D graphics as an *image object.* With his historical reappraisal of the emergence of graphics software and hardware, he presents an extremely up-to-date and comprehensive history of computer graphics.[65] The archival materials he works with show a considerable overlap with those that are also examined in the historiography undertaken in my book. As Gaboury only published his research shortly before my research was completed, it becomes clear that Gaboury and I have dealt with the subject of our research in overlapping time periods and independently of each other as well as for the first time in such a comprehensive manner. On the one hand, this parallelism shows how relevant the subject of the research is, and on the other hand, the results of the studies show how differently research materials can be interpreted and read if the fundamental research objective and the method differ in each case. The following remarks can show why Gaboury's research approach comes to the conclusion that no remediation has taken place, although it can already be anticipated that the production-aesthetic method can certainly be used to uncover the extent to which other imaging media and associated image concepts have found their way into the graphics software.

For both Gaboury and me, the developments that took place at the *University of Utah* in the 1960s and 1970s are particularly central, with Gaboury's view even reaching into the 1980s. A main focus of both his and my own study is on the research project *Graphical Man/Machine Communications* carried out in Utah as well as on the dissertations and research papers prepared during the course of this project. It is interesting that Gaboury's and my own book, which were produced independently of each other and in parallel, trace an extremely consistent historical development overall, despite the different interpretations they make. Gaboury also traces the origins of today's graphics software at its core back not only to developments in the United States in general, but specifically to the project at the *University of Utah.* He summarizes the influence of the research carried out there as follows:

> In the period from roughly 1965 to 1980, the faculty and graduates of the Utah program were responsible for no less than inventing the very concepts that make modern computer graphics possible, and many of the school's graduates went on to become industry leaders in the field of computing in the second half of the twentieth century. The founders of Pixar, Adobe, Silicon Graphics, Netscape, Atari, and WordPerfect were all students at Utah during this period, and dozens of key researchers at Xerox PARC, NASA's Jet Propulsion Laboratory, the New York Institute of Technology, and Industrial Light & Magic all began their careers in Salt Lake City. The University of Utah was the epicenter of graphical development for the first fifteen years of the discipline, and its archives and papers form the foundation of this book.[66]

Gaboury's handling of the research material, to which he refers again here and which, as mentioned, also forms the basis of my study to a great extent, is in large parts more comprehensive than mine. His historiography attempts to precisely encompass all developments and technical conditions in a broad sense. In direct comparison to my approach, Gaboury covers a much larger radius of investigation, but at the same time, due to his claim to present an all-encompassing history he occasionally loses sight of details, which in turn are given special attention in my study.[67] While the production-aesthetical approach of my book by no means leads to an all-encompassing history of computer graphics, my discussion is often more precise in detail than Gaboury's. However, many of the developments I describe could be located in a larger context with Gaboury.

The different approach to the historical material is ultimately due to the respective research perspectives each study chooses. While Gaboury's starting point are technical conditions, my starting point are the people who worked with the technology or developed it. In Gaboury's own words, the effects of this fundamental decision to turn away from human-centered narratives can be explained, because having technology be the central focus in his investigation is the main reason why he comes to conclusions that are contrary to those of my research:

> I ask not simply how computer graphics developed over the second half of the twentieth century, or who helped shape the discipline through research and innovation, but rather what historical technologies structured and limited the field as it evolved, and how those technologies continue to determine the ways we engage with computational images today.[68]

While I tie in with the last aspect of this statement and ask how the technology developed at that time still has an impact today, I do not, for instance, like Gaboury does, assume that the work of the developers was structured by the technological conditions at the time, but rather that the researchers developed their technology according to specific ideas and pushed it forward until their goal was achieved – a process that has not yet been completed, as paradoxically even Gaboury himself notes[69] by referring to a "quest for realism"[70] that is still motivating computer graphical research today. He also speaks of an overarching vision that was necessary for the development of computer graphics.[71] However, since Gaboury starts with technology, there is no discussion of the deeper cultural motives that could lie behind its development. In a footnote, in which he adds a comment on his methodology, it becomes clear that he does acknowledge the risks that his decision to refrain from a human-centered focus[72] may entail:

> This focus on objects rather than the culture of the people that produced them runs the risk of erasing the agency of human subjects and the deeply political context in which these objects were produced, used, and circulated. As media historian Laine Nooney suggests, "Media archaeology so often ignores: human specificity, the way enactments of power fall upon certain types of bodies more than others." My hope is that this book creates a space for precisely this work by attending to the material conditions for the emergence of early computer graphics while opening a space for research that expands on the historical articulation of computer graphics within cultures and communities of practice.[73]

Ultimately, I understand Gaboury and his historiography as part of the paradigm examined in my book: It is striking that Gaboury – because of his focus on technology rather than the humans behind it – does not distance himself from the events in his account of technological developments. Rather, he considers the developments to be self-evident and even necessary. This impression can be exemplified by a technical explanation that Gaboury gives of the phenomenon of the so-called "hidden surface problem," which also becomes relevant at certain points later on in my discussion. This problem refers to the calculation of virtual models as opaque, i.e. non-transparent objects, a process that represented a major challenge at the beginning of computer graphics endeavors. Today, this function is taken for granted when using 3D graphics software, as will be explained in the following section:

> The hidden surface problem is significant not only because it is such a crucial challenge for the nascent field of computer graphics but because it also forms the basis of a much larger set of concerns for computational visualization. Without an understanding of the opacity of an object, the shape of its surfaces,

> and their relation to one another, it is impossible to accurately model their interaction with a given environment. Shading, lighting, shadow, collision, and any number of additional effects are dependent on a suitable means of identifying and describing the structure of an object, and a hidden surface algorithm is the first step in calculating a reasonably efficient means to do so since it produces data for each significant point of an object that may be compared against surrounding points and processed through additional visualization algorithms.[74]

The phenomena of "shading," light and shadow addressed here by Gaboury are not questioned by him as such, and in contrast to my approach, this intention does not represent the concern of his investigation. One aspect that further reinforces the impression that Gaboury does not step out of the paradigm I examine in this study is the fact that he does not refer in his monograph to parallel developments, such as ones that have taken place in France, for instance. Particularly noteworthy here is the software *Anyflo* by the computer artist Michel Bret, which he has been developing since 1985 and which is always available in a current version as a free download on his website.[75] In his essay *Tools for Artists*, published in 1991, he explains why he designed his own software:

> Artists seldom have the choice other than to put up with softwares which they did not develop or to build their own tools. The first choice, being by far the most frequent one, has left most of them hopeless. The second one really affects a small amount of creative people. [...]
>
> In order to give the creators immediate access to the synthesis standard methods, without rewriting everything and without being dependent of aesthetic choices made or not, I have designed the ANYFLO software which is an interactive open system built around an interpreter.[76]

Bret provides an example of the aesthetic decisions he is referring to here in his 1994 essay *L'artiste et l'ordinateur* (The Artist and the Computer). Here he notes that the generally available programs for creating synthetic images only allow us to work in a virtual space that is constructed in central perspective in order to create objects with smooth and flawless surfaces.[77] The aspects of shading, light and shadow, which all contribute to the aesthetics of these objects described by Bret, are therefore not a necessity in synthetic image creation. In her 2001 study *Le Réalisme dans l'image informatique* (Realism in Computer Graphics), art historian Ondine Bréaud even describes the flawless 3D graphics as a link "entre la science et le kitsch!"[78] In contrast to Bréaud, I do not initially judge the aesthetic ideas against the background of which today's commercial 3D graphics programs were created, but what the French discourse on the synthetic images can show is that it is also possible to leave the paradigm and look at synthetic image creation "from the outside." A more detailed examination of Bret's computer-technological developments does not take place within the framework of my study. As explained above, the focus is on the one hand on those approaches that have found their way into today's software, and on the other hand on parallel approaches that also originated in the United States but do not or hardly persist in today's programs. Although a comparative analysis of Bret's software, for example, would presumably be very informative, in this study the decision was made in favor of those developments that have a greater geographical or, in some cases, conceptual proximity and thus also better comparability with the approaches that have survived in commercial software to this day. A more precise explanation of this decision is provided again at the beginning of the respective relevant chapters. See in particular Chapter 4.

With regard to the notes made by Bret and Bréaud to 3D software and the visual aesthetics of 3D graphics, the question now arises as to whether it is possible to completely detach the examination of these images and their creation from the usual discourses on mimetic image design, as Gaboury suggests: "Popular discourses of realism and fidelity dominate our analysis of digital image technologies, but are derived from uncritical appropriation of those formal qualities that have historically defined prior modes of image making."[79] The accusation that Gaboury expresses here does not hold up against the background of Bret's observations, for example, as he not only critically but, as a computer artist, also professionally engages with the imagery firmly anchored in commercial software.

In principle, Gaboury's desire not to focus exclusively on the pictorial level of computer graphics is in some sense a standpoint that corresponds to the concern of my book as I also think it is necessary to look at more than just the surface of the image. However, I consider 3D technology first and foremost as an imaging method. The reason for this lies – again – in my production-aesthetic angle, because this reveals, as Bret's comments also demonstrate, that aspects such as visual "realism" and central perspective did not become part of 3D computer graphics by chance, but emerged from an intended motive of the developers. Gaboury's criticism of approaches that examine computer graphics in regard to techniques such as perspective projection, as well as his reference to the fact that an examination of central perspective construction did not take place in the development of computer graphics,[80] therefore does not hold against the background of a production-aesthetical investigation. An examination of the work processes and decisions can show the extent to which the perspective construction for the creation of computer graphics was integrated into the software processes with elaborate and very conscious gauging.

The production-aesthetic approach I choose here thus corresponds to Gaboury's desire to analyze the images not only on the basis of their surface, but it fulfills this requirement without losing sight of the fact that 3D graphics often remain figurative and perspectively constructed images and that not every open program file is destined to become an everyday object. Both approaches, Gaboury's and mine, can be viewed as alternatives or even supplements to each other. Each study can gain something from the other. Gaboury's study gives the scope of my book more weight. Although he does not consider this aspect, with his study it becomes evident that the worldviews and concepts of imagery that are anchored in the software characterize not only every 3D graphic created with it but also numerous objects in our direct physical everyday environment.

The last study to be presented in the context of this state of research is from 2015 and, as mentioned at the beginning, is called *Builders of the Vision: Software and the Imagination of Design*. As an architect, the author of the monograph, Daniel Cardoso Llach, turns to the ideas with which the software for CAD regularly used in his discipline today, was developed, because "seeing software systems as infrastructures situates them as cultural artifacts within economic, institutional, and political frames, and as embodiments of their makers' worldviews, ambitions, and desires."[81] He therefore picks quite a different approach to Gaboury and, in turn, one quite similar to my own. He is, like me, interested in the worldviews that shape his actions as an architect when he works with the software. I take up the term "cultural artifact," used by Cardoso Llach, for my own study.

Cardoso Llach seeks the answers to his questions in the historical development of architectural software and thus provides one of the few studies that not only *describe* technological developments and contexts but also ask *why* they were developed in a certain way. His concern is therefore directly related to mine. Parallels can also be shown in terms of methodology, because his study primarily adopts a production-aesthetical approach to investigation, although he does not use the term itself. A major methodological difference to my book, however, lies in the fact that Cardoso Llach places the CAD software and its development in a very comprehensive historical context, which initially starts with Leon Battista Alberti in the Renaissance, but is supplemented selectively by insights from ancient Greece and ancient Rome.[82] Based on this historical framework, he identifies a specific understanding that emerged in relation to the field of architecture during the Renaissance at the latest. This understanding is closely linked to the idea that the intellectual design work stands above the material, i.e. above the manual labor of actually constructing the buildings. Cardoso Llach uses the phrase "mind over matter"[83] for this cultural development and describes the separation between intellectual and practical work as an "Albertian split."[84] Regarding the 3D computer graphics, which Cardoso Llach does not focus on in his book, a retrospective into the Renaissance is a familiar pattern of investigation, since the synthetic images – as Gaboury has also noted – are often also linked to cultural artifacts from the Renaissance, in this case especially to the central perspective construction.[85] Although for my research approach I deliberately chose not to trace the course of this phenomenon all the way back to the Renaissance and instead rather focus on the development of visual culture in the

United States as a cultural-historical framework for investigation, the principle of "mind over matter" can also be rediscovered in this narrower framework (see also endnote 34 in Chapter 11).

The most pronounced connection to Cardoso Llach's book lies in the specific object of investigation, because the more recent historical events in terms of software development that he researched – compared to the Renaissance – are also located in the United States. Cardoso Llach's study even intersects with the same historical figures who play a central role in my book. Particularly noteworthy here is the engineer Steven A. Coons, who was actively promoting CAD research at MIT in the 1950s and 1960s. Coons is a key figure both for Cardoso Llach's and my book.[86] The reason for this overlap is that, from a purely historical point of view, the early efforts in computer graphics were closely related to developments in the field of CAD. However, since Cardoso Llach examines Coons from the perspective of architecture and I explore Coons with regard to a concept of imagery, the results of my research can be seen as a supplement to Cardoso Llach's research (see in particular Section 5.1).

A unifying field of investigation, on which both Cardoso Llach's findings on today's architectural software and those of my book on today's graphics software are based, lies in Coons' considerations on how to work creatively with the computer. This facet of Coons is interesting because he has dealt extensively with how and whether creative processes can be automated by the computer, which is why numerous hints can be found in his documents about how he thought about creativity and design. According to Cardoso Llach, Coons and his colleagues at MIT were therefore not simply engineers trying to master technical problems, but "ambitious design theorists and philosophers reconfiguring the concept of design in computational terms."[87] Cardoso Llach even describes Coons as *the* design theorist of the 20th century,[88] because

> [w]hile Coons's important contributions to computational geometry have been recognized, his key role as a design technologist and theorist has so far been overlooked. [...] [T]he fields of architecture and design have yet to recognize and understand how these early theories of computational design, developed outside the field of architecture, came to shape the technological landscapes architects and designers continue to inhabit today.[89]

The results of my book can not only confirm this finding of Cardoso Llach's but also expand it, because what he observes in relation to Coons could only occur thanks to the paradigm shift from procedural to object-oriented programming described above – a development that Cardoso Llach does not focus on in-depth. My book sharpens the findings of both Gaboury and Cardoso Llach by examining the role Coons plays within this programming paradigm. Coons has recognized and reflected on how difficult it is to bring together theory of creativity with computer-technological considerations. Cardoso Llach also hints at this connection but concentrates primarily on the design aspects and puts the computer-technological framework somewhat more in the background.

Coons is not only a key figure in historical developments[90] but also the fork in the road mentioned above. Cardoso Llach himself notes that Coons was not only central to further developments in the field of architecture, but that he also had an influence on his student Ivan E. Sutherland.[91] In 1963, Sutherland developed the graphics program *Sketchpad*, which plays a central role in my discussion and is also regarded as the starting point for Alan Kay's programming language *Smalltalk*.[92] Kay and Sutherland met at the *University of Utah* as part of the research project *Graphical Man/Machine Communications*, in which Sutherland later participated as a colleague of Dave Evans. Sutherland passed on the knowledge he had learned at MIT not only to Kay but also to Edwin Catmull, who later became a founding member of *Pixar Animation Studios*.[93] Both Sutherland and Coons were members of the thesis committee for Catmull's dissertation.[94] The popular cultural landscape of 3D graphics and their software focused on in my study can thus be traced back to Coons; nonetheless, this divergence has not yet been explored in depth, particularly concerning the image concepts prevalent in the software. While Cardoso Llach thus comprehensively describes Coons' influence on today's architectural software, I aim to analyze the role Coons played in regard to the image concept on which the software used today for 3D graphics is based. It can be assumed that Coons is relevant not only for the field of CAD but also for the landscape of popular culture. Coons' influence on this critical fork in the road also becomes clear, for example, in Rebecca Ann Perry's study *Rigging the World: 3D Modeling and the Seduction of the Real*, in which she traces the history of virtual modeling.[95] Perry herself adopts a practical perspective, as she also works in the industry as a so-called 3D artist alongside her historical research work (the term "3D artist" is explained further in the following chapter). In her study, she also points to a close connection between Sutherland and Coons. However, since her focus is on the field of virtual models, she does not deal comprehensively with the imagery and the aesthetics of 3D computer graphics. A more targeted examination of her findings will take place at a later point in my discussion.[96]

While Cardoso Llach thus comprehensively presents Coons' influence on today's architectural software, and Perry to the field of modeling, my book aims to examine the role of Coons with regard to the image concepts inherent in today's 3D graphics software. Since Cardoso Llach does not go further than to merely mention Coons' influence on computer graphics, the events in Utah are of no relevance to him in this regard.[97] Instead, he decided to do an empirical examination of how his historical findings, and especially Coons' influence, survive in today's work contexts in the field of architecture. The conceptual basis of Cardoso Llach's investigation is his fundamental assumption that "[w]hat the machine offers is not absolute freedom, but the freedom to create exactly what is afforded by the system's multiple geometric, material, and computational constraints – that is, an infinitely small subset of objects."[98] In order to explore how the software often does not liberate work, but often even restricts it, Cardoso Llach spent 11 months in Abu Dhabi, where he accompanied construction projects as an architect and researcher. As he points out, his intention with this part of his study is not to fully analyze the extent to which his observations apply to projects worldwide in which the software is used. Rather, according to Cardoso Llach, the specific results of his empirical research in Abu Dhabi provide an exemplary insight into the cultural and historical process of standardization in the construction industry through the use of standardized software.[99] This dynamic is particularly evident in Abu Dhabi:

> Software infrastructures are part of larger political landscapes. The official representations of Abu Dhabi, as seen in advertisements, newspapers, and public exhibitions, seek to fashion the emirate's capital as a global metropolis and as a hub of business and culture. This projected modernity is figured, as anthropologist Ahmed Kanna has pointed out, as a white European upper-class utopia.[100]

Cardoso Llach illustrates this dynamic described by Kanna with the fact that construction projects are being initiated or have already been realized in Abu Dhabi under the supervision of world-famous architects, for example, to build branches of the *Guggenheim Museum*, the *Louvre* or *New York University*.[101] For construction projects of this kind, not only standardized software is generally used but also a working infrastructure designed by the software developers, in which the 3D model of a future building represents the central point of reference for everyone who is involved in the project.[102] Cardoso Llach's research ultimately shows that when working with local construction companies, these standardized work processes do not always proceed as they were designed but are often even undermined and not taken seriously.[103]

Overall, these insights into the discipline of architecture and the standardized technological processes used in regions such as the United Arab Emirates are almost an exemplary illustration of Hans Blumenberg's references to the consequences that can occur when technologies are used in regions where they did not originate. In a way, Cardoso Llach also fulfills Blumenberg's wish to close the gaps in the history of technology in order to overcome the leaps that we as humans make with it. Cardoso Llach's research approach also demonstrates that this can only succeed if the human forms the starting point of the investigation. Both he and I find it problematic to view technology as an autonomous entity acting independently from people, because in this perspective those who were involved in the design of technology and the consequences associated with the influence of these people would remain hidden.[104] Just as Cardoso Llach reveals it for the field of architecture, I aim to examine the history of 3D graphics software to uncover "how [...] software is not merely an instrument of design but also a versatile metaphor – and a crucial infrastructure – reconfiguring conceptions of design, work, authorship, and what it means to be human."[105] The technologies we humans develop and with which we interact on a daily basis are therefore only *one* possible way of navigating the technological world. One of my main concerns is therefore to understand the ubiquitous and often even invisible use of 3D graphics and the practice of creating them as a "space of *possibility*."[106]

NOTES

1. Hans Blumenberg, "Phenomenological Aspects on Life-World and Technization (1963)," in *History, Metaphors, Fables: A Hans Blumenberg Reader*, trans. and ed. Hannes Bajohr, Florian Fuchs and Joe Paul Kroll (Ithaca: Cornell University Press, 2022), 372, emphasis in original.
2. Peter Lunenfeld, *Snap to Grid: A User's Guide to Digital Arts, Media, and Cultures* (Cambridge: MIT Press, 2000), 189.
3. See Nelson Goodman, *Languages of Art: An Approach to a Theory of Symbols* (Indianapolis: The Bobbs-Merrill Company, Inc., 1976), 103–7.
4. See Birgit Schneider, "Wissenschaftsbilder zwischen digitaler Transformation und Manipulation. Einige Anmerkungen zur Diskussion des 'digitalen Bildes,'" in *Logik des Bildlichen*, ed. Martina Heßler and Dieter Mersch (Bielefeld: transcript, 2015), 188–200.
5. See Schneider, "Wissenschaftsbilder," 188.
6. Schneider refers here to Jean Baudrillard, *Agonie des Realen* (Berlin: Merve, 1978), and Vilém Flusser, *Into the Universe of Technical Images*, trans. Nancy Ann Roth (Minneapolis: University of Minnesota Press, 2011). In relation to Virilio, Schneider also mentions the concepts of derealization and dematerialization. See for example Paul Virilio, *War and Cinema: The Logistics of Perception*, trans. Patrick Camiller (London, New York: Verso, 1989). Under the heading *Images under general suspicion or "the precarious image"* Schneider presents numerous other central positions on the question of the manipulability of digital images, including those of the media theorist Jens Schröter and the architect William J. Mitchell (not to be confused with the art historian William J. T. Mitchell). See Schneider, "Wissenschaftsbilder," 190–92. See also William J. Mitchell, *The Reconfigured Eye. Visual Truth in the Post-Photographic Era* (Cambridge: MIT Press, 2001), and see Jens Schröter, "Das Ende der Welt. Analoge vs. digitale Bilder – mehr und weniger 'Realität'?", in *Analog/Digital – Opposition oder Kontinuum? Zur Theorie und Geschichte einer Unterscheidung*, ed. Jens Schröter and Alexander Böhnke (Bielefeld: transcript, 2004). In a further section, Schneider deals with Claus Pias' proposal to analyze digital images under the pretext that they do not exist. As Schneider explains, Pias means that "[a]t the level of the human recipient [...] the images are analog." Schneider, "Wissenschaftsbilder," 193. See also Claus Pias, "Das digitale Bild gibt es nicht. Über das (Nicht-)Wissen der Bilder und die informatische Illusion," *zeitenblicke* 2, no 1 (2003), https://mediarep.org/handle/doc/4845.
7. See Schneider, "Wissenschaftsbilder," 194, 196, and see Frieder Nake, "Das doppelte Bild," in *BAND 3,2 Digitale Form*, ed. Katja Müller-Helle and Claudia Blümle (Berlin: De Gruyter, 2006), 47. In this context, Schneider refers to an intellectual affinity between Nake's and Lev Manovich's positions. In the latter's relevant monograph *Language of New Media*, Manovich distinguishes between a "cultural layer" and a "computer layer." Lev Manovich, *The Language of New Media* (Cambridge: MIT Press, 2001), 46.
8. Schneider, "Wissenschaftsbilder," 198.
9. See Schneider, "Wissenschaftsbilder," 198. Schneider refers to Bruno Latour *Pandora's Hope. Essays on the Reality of Science Studies* (Cambridge: Harvard University Press, 2000).
10. Schneider, "Wissenschaftsbilder," 197.
11. Peter Lunenfeld describes photographs that were taken digitally rather than analogously as *dubitative* images. The "dubitative" is defined by him as "inclined or given to doubt." He uses the term to describe the digital age, which he also calls the "age of the dubitative." Lunenfeld, *Snap to Grid*, 167, 171.
12. See Blumenberg, "Life-World and Technization."
13. Blumenberg, "Life-World and Technization," 360.
14. See Blumenberg, "Life-World and Technization," 360.
15. Blumenberg, "Life-World and Technization," 361.
16. See Blumenberg, "Life-World and Technization," 367.
17. See Blumenberg, "Life-World and Technization," 368. Blumenberg also notes that Husserl adopted the term "intentionality" from Franz Brentano.
18. Blumenberg, "Life-World and Technization," 368–69.
19. Blumenberg quotes Edmund Husserl, *The Crisis of European Sciences and Transcendental Phenomenology: An Introduction to Phenomenological Philosophy*, trans. David Carr (Evanston: Northwestern University Press, 1970), 180.
20. Blumenberg, "Life-World and Technization," 376, emphasis in original.
21. See Blumenberg, "Life-World and Technization," 378–83.
22. Blumenberg, "Life-World and Technization," 385.
23. Blumenberg, "Life-World and Technization," 386.
24. See Blumenberg, "Life-World and Technization," 386–87.
25. Blumenberg, "Life-World and Technization," 383. Blumenberg quotes Edmund Husserl, *Die Krisis der europäischen Wissenschaften und die transzendentale Phänomenologie: Eine Einleitung in die phänomenologische Philosophie*, ed. Walter Biemel (The Hague: Nijhoff, 1976), 448.
26. Blumenberg, "Life-World and Technization," 384.

27. Blumenberg, "Life-World and Technization," 387. Blumenberg quotes Edmund Husserl, *Experience and Judgment: Investigations in a Genealogy of Logic*, ed. Ludwig Landgrebe, trans. Spencer Churchill and Karl Ameriks (Evanston: Northwestern University Press, 1973), 49.
28. See Blumenberg, "Life-World and Technization," 387–92.
29. Blumenberg, "Life-World and Technization," 392.
30. Blumenberg, "Life-World and Technization," 391, emphasis in original.
31. Blumenberg, "Life-World and Technization," 391, emphasis in original.
32. Blumenberg, "Life-World and Technization," 392.
33. Blumenberg, "Life-World and Technization," 393.
34. Blumenberg, "Life-World and Technization," 396.
35. See Blumenberg, "Life-World and Technization," 395–96.
36. Blumenberg, "Life-World and Technization," 397–98.
37. See Blumenberg, "Life-World and Technization," 398–99.
38. Blumenberg, "Life-World and Technization," 399.
39. See Blumenberg, "Life-World and Technization," 398–99.
40. Friedrich Weltzien, "Produktionsästhetik als Methode," in *Praxis. Ausüben. Begreifen*, ed. Michael Corsten (Weilerswist: Velbrück, 2021), 221. With the phenomenon of digital products, Weltzien identifies an area of investigation that he sees as particularly suitable for a production-aesthetic approach, since disinformation, for example, can often only be deciphered by looking at the production process. See Friedrich Weltzien, "Produktionsästhetik als Methode," 231–32.
41. See Friedrich Weltzien, "Produktionsästhetik als Methode," 232–33.
42. Erkki Huhtamo and Jussi Parikka, "Introduction: An Archaeology of Media Archaeology," in *Media Archaeology. Approaches, Applications, and Implications*, ed. Erkki Huhtamo and Jussi Parikka (Berkeley, Los Angeles: University of California Press, 2011), 3. Huhtamo and Parikka trace the origins of media archeology back to various individuals, including Michel Foucault's "archaeology of knowledge." His approach was subsequently taken up by both Anglo-American and German-language research, albeit in two different ways. While the Anglo-American tradition initially focused on socio-cultural aspects, the German-language approach primarily made the technical conditions of media the starting point of the investigation. In this context, Huhtamo and Parikka emphasize in particular Friedrich Kittler and his publications *Aufschreibesysteme* and *Grammophon Film Typewriter*. See Huhtamo and Parikka, "Introduction," 8–9. My study ties in with Huhtamo and Parikka, as the authors express a very open and flexible understanding of media archeology. They state, "[a]lthough this term [media archaeology] does not designate an academic discipline [...], it has appeared in an increasing number of studies, and university courses and lectures have also been given under this heading. [...] [T]here is no general agreement about either the principles or the terminology of media archaeology. Yet the term has inspired historically tuned research and is beginning to encourage scholars to define their principles and to reflect on their theoretical and philosophical implications." Huhtamo and Parikka, "Introduction," 2.
43. Huhtamo and Parikka, "Introduction," 3.
44. See also the concept of history as developed in the anthology *What's the Use? Constellations of Art, History, and Knowledge*: Here, history is understood "as a constantly changing creation of the present" since "periods appear also not to be fixed, but reveal their malleable quality because they are the subject of working minds, determined to put forward an understanding of the present through reflecting on the past appearing in the present." Nick Aikens, Thomas Lange et al., eds., *What's the Use? Constellations of Art, History, and Knowledge. A Critical Reader* (Amsterdam: Valiz, 2016), 11. Drawing on Walter Benjamin's concept of constellations, Lange describes the fluid interweaving of historical epochs with the present: "Constellations show the expanded and interwoven matrix of layers of time revealing multiple connections to later, or previous, past and present times." Thomas Lange, "Constellating History – Introduction," in *What's the Use? Constellations of Art, History, and Knowledge. A Critical Reader*, ed. Nick Aikens, Thomas Lange et al. (Amsterdam: Valiz, 2016), 16.
45. See Leo Marx, *The Machine in the Garden. Technology and the Pastoral Ideal in America* (Oxford: Oxford University Press USA, 2000). Following the publication of his study, Marx was subjected to various accusations, which will be briefly addressed here. As the Americanists Eric Erbacher, Nicole Maruo-Schröder and Florian Sedlmeier explain in the introduction to their anthology *Rereading the Machine in the Garden*, Marx was above all accused of perpetuating the narrative of American exceptionalism with his study, thereby simultaneously expressing the idea of a uniform and thus one-sided historiography for the United States. This is why Erbacher, Maruo-Schröder and Sedlmeier place Marx in a tradition of Americanist studies that has since been superseded by the so-called New Americanists. In contrast to the previous tradition, this new Americanist theory takes up positions from the fields of cultural studies, gender studies and post-structuralist approaches. As the editors of the volume also note, Marx responded to the accusations

leveled against him not only in a number of essays but also in the new edition of his monograph, which I also refer to in my study. See Eric Erbacher, Nicole Maruo-Schröder and Florian Sedlmeier, "Introduction: Rereading *The Machine in the Garden*," in *Rereading the Machine in the Garden. Nature and Technology in American Culture*, ed. Eric Erbacher, Nicole Maruo-Schröder and Florian Sedlmeier (Frankfurt am Main: Campus, 2014), 1–2. Marx himself describes how his study is accused of adopting an elitist, white and male perspective and thus ignoring the differences in US society. The newer research approaches in his discipline, he describes in an appreciative manner, are geared toward also taking into account the differences in society, i.e. factors such as social class formation, ethnic origin or gender-related developments. He therefore explains that he could no longer write some of the very unifying sentences in his study on the behavior of "Americans" in the same way today and also lists other aspects that he would take up today in his thinking. At the same time, he defends his study by pointing out that he is not describing a uniform society with a universalizing attitude, but that he is certainly pointing to divisions caused by the technology that emerged in US history and which was not equally supported by everyone. He even emphasizes that he underestimated the topicality of the conflict, which he locates at its core in the 19th century. Shortly after the publication of his study in 1964, the student protests began, which directly continued the conflict described by Marx. See Marx, *Machine in the Garden*, 381–84. My study is orientated toward the stance also taken by Erbacher, Maruo-Schröder and Sedlmeier in their reappraisal of Marx's study, for here they describe the image of the machine invading the garden as still being formative for numerous artistic, cinematic and literary works. Although the image may not be all-encompassing for US history, they nevertheless want to honor "its significance in artistic productions from a U.S. context" with their volume. Erbacher, Maruo-Schröder, Sedlmeier, "Introduction," 9.

46. Daniel Cardoso Llach, *Builders of the Vision: Software and the Imagination of Design* (New York: Routledge, 2015), xii.
47. As the title of his study suggests, Gaboury himself also describes his approach as media archeological. See Jacob Gaboury, *Image Objects. An Archaeology of Computer Graphics* (Cambridge: MIT Press, 2021), 5.
48. See Michael Heim, *Electric Language. A Philosophical Study of Word Processing* (New Haven: Yale University Press, 1987), 4.
49. See Michael Heim, *Electric Language*, 6–7.
50. Michael Heim, "The Cyberspace Dialectic," in *Digital Dialectic: New Essays on New Media*, ed. Peter Lunenfeld (Cambridge: MIT Press, 1999), 41.
51. Before Heim turns to electronic text processing in his study, he traces how the interplay of thought, writing and language has shaped and changed up to the present day, starting from Greek antiquity. He initially builds on the arguments of Eric Havelock and Walter J. Ong, but also to critically reflect on and eventually renew their respective positions in relation to the phenomenon of electronic text processing. See Heim, *Electric Language*, 21–69.
52. See Heim, *Electric Language*, 192–224.
53. Despite his cautious gauging stance, Heim remains true to the style of the debates held at the time. As he points out, these were often divided into supportive and negative positions. This is often accompanied by the idea that the innovations brought about by digitality were so radical that they even caused a break with previous media. Edmont Couchot, for example, a French pioneer of digital art, works with the concept of rupture. In his joint study with Norbert Hillaire, *L'art numérique. Comment la technologie vient au monde de l'art*, he expresses the view that digital forms of expression, especially pictorial ones, radically break with all previous techniques: "Le numérique est [...] en rupture avec les techniques figuratives traditionelles, mais il est aussi capable de se réapproprier les techniques non numériques qu'il simule de très près et de composer avec elles [...]." Edmond Couchot, Norbert Hillaire, *L'art numérique. Comment la technologie vient au monde de l'art* (Paris: Flammarion, 2003), 28. Couchot and Hillaire regret that the possibility of always imitating other processes with the computer would not reveal the extent to which it represented a new and independent means of expression. At the same time, they also describe a continuity that takes place with the computer, as it continues the traditional tension between science and art. Similar to cubism, for example, digital art translates abstract models of reality into a sensually perceptible level through the algorithm on which it is based. See Couchot and Hillaire, *L'art numérique,* 30–33. With their view that the computer simulates previous means of expression on the one hand, but can, on the other, also create new modes of expression that are unique to it, they take a similar position – much earlier, incidentally – to Lev Manovich in his 2013 study *Software Takes Command*. In it, he defines the computer as a meta-medium that takes up and reproduces all previous techniques in the form of simulations, but also allows new, as yet unknown techniques to emerge from it. See Lev Manovich, *Software Takes Command* (New York: Bloomsbury Academic, 2013), e.g. 112.
54. Bolter and Grusin assume that the only thing new about new media is *how* they carry out remediation. Jay D. Bolter, Richard Grusin, *Remediation: Understanding New Media* (Cambridge: MIT Press, 1999), 15. The concept or rather the mindset of remediation can also be found in Jens Schröter, *3D: History, Theory and Aesthetics*

of the Transplane Image (New York: Bloomsbury Academic, 2009). In his monograph, Schröter develops the concept and history of the technological transplane image, by which he includes all forms of representation that appear spatially when viewed, such as stereoscopies, holograms or virtual realities using head-mounted displays. The last example in particular gives rise to some points of contact with Schröter in my study. In his study, he comprehensively criticizes Jonathan Crary's position that the mode of viewing changed fundamentally at the beginning of the 19th century with the shift from geometric to physiological optics and made processes such as stereoscopy possible in the first place. While Crary even speaks of a rupture, Schröter suggests that the development of the technological transplane image should not be understood in a linear fashion, but rather "as layers or as a palimpsest of simultaneous and different forms of optical knowledge [...]. The optical/visual media – and thus also the transplanar images – emerge from these different forms of optical knowledge [...]." Schröter, *3D*, 12. See also Schröter, *3D*, 4–12, and see Jonathan Crary, *Techniques of the Observer. On Vision and Modernity in the Nineteenth Century* (Cambridge: MIT Press, 1992), 1–24.

55. The idea that every new medium contains an old medium goes back to Marshall McLuhan. See Marshall McLuhan, *Understanding Media: The Extensions of Man* (London: Routledge & Kegan Paul Ltd, 1968), 8.
56. Gaboury, *Image Objects*, 4.
57. See Gaboury, *Image Objects*, 7.
58. Gaboury, *Image Objects*, 3.
59. See Gaboury, *Image Objects*, 8–9.
60. Gaboury, *Image Object*, 6–7, emphasis in original.
61. See Casey Alt, "Objects of Our Affection. How Object Orientation Made Computers a Medium," in *Media Archaeology. Approaches, Applications, and Implications*, ed. Erkki Huhtamo and Jussi Parikka (Berkeley, Los Angeles: University of California Press, 2011), 284–85. See also Gaboury, *Image Objects*, 17, 141, 209. Alt convincingly places the object-oriented approach in the context of systems theory and cybernetics. From the perspective of production aesthetics, however, no explicit and direct references to the fields can be recognized, which is why these are not addressed in my study. See Alt, "Objects of Our Affection," 280–81.
62. See Gaboury, *Image Objects*, 7.
63. Gaboury provides a brief explanation of the procedural programming paradigm in comparison to the object-oriented approach and also illustrates both systems with a schematic diagram. See Gaboury, *Image Objects*, 127–29.
64. Alt, "Objects of Our Affection," 299. Manovich, who also links the definition of the computer as a metamedium to Alan Kay's developments, argues in a similar fashion as Gaboury. The concept of remediation is also not sufficient for Manovich to determine the modes of expression of the computer. Manovich bases his arguments on Alan Kay's statements, but without taking into account the fact that he later differentiated himself from the momentum that his own achievements have created in the further course of software development. Manovich also ignores Casey Alt's findings and instead assumes that Kay's visions had been fulfilled without restriction. See Manovich, *Software Takes* Command, e.g. 162.
65. A monograph published at exactly the same time as Gaboury's also deals with historical developments in the field of computer graphics, but with the aim of tracing the history of the pixel. The author of this work, Alvy Ray Smith, was involved in the founding of *Pixar Animation Studios* together with Edwin Catmull. As a result, Smith plays a central role in the history of computer graphics, which is why he is considered part of the object of investigation in this study and is mentioned in this function in several chapters. Findings from his monograph that are relevant to my study are taken up at appropriate points. He endeavors to be comprehensive in his historical explanations. Nevertheless, he often deals with historical facts about the pixel from a mathematical perspective. In his presentation of the more recent history of the pixel, he focuses on examples from the field of popular culture computer graphics and computer animation instead of looking at the fields of film or gaming. However, his explanations of the technical properties of the pixel can in principle be applied to all these areas. He makes a general distinction between pixels that are captured, such as in digital photography, and pixels that are created synthetically ("*take* and *make*"). He justifies his decision to focus primarily on the latter by the fact that he himself was involved in this development. See Alvy R. Smith, *A Biography of the Pixel* (Cambridge: MIT Press, 2021), 6–7.
66. Gaboury, *Image Objects*, 6. It is striking that Gaboury considers the developments at the *University of Utah* to be neglected by previous research. His assessment can only be explained by the fact that he does not mention other studies that have also dealt extensively with research at the *University of Utah*, such as the historical and practice-oriented study *Rigging the World: 3D Modeling and the Seduction of the Real* by Rebecca Perry and the older historical account *The Algorithmic Image* by Robert Rivlin. See Rebecca A. Perry, "Rigging the World: 3D Modeling and the Seduction of the Real" (PhD diss., Massachusetts Institute of Technology, 2014), MIT Libraries, DSpace@MIT (900615015), and see Robert Rivlin, *The Algorithmic Image: Graphic Visions of the Computer Age* (Redmond: Microsoft Press, 1986). Tom Sito, cited by Gaboury himself, also provides extensive

explanations of the technical achievements made at the *University of Utah* in his historiography of computer animation. See Tom Sito, *Moving Innovation: A History of Computer Animation* (Cambridge: MIT Press, 2013).

67. This observation can be exemplified by a statement Gaboury makes about the computer graphics pioneer William A. Fetter. While Gaboury refers to Fetter as an example of the rethinking that initiated the shift from the procedural to the object-oriented programming paradigm, a production-aesthetic examination of Fetter's approach reveals that the computer graphics Gaboury refers to were created by Fetter using the procedural programming paradigm. See Gaboury, *Image Objects*, 12–17, and Section 4.2 in this study.
68. Gaboury, *Image Objects*, 4–5.
69. See Gaboury, *Image Objects*, 28.
70. Gaboury, *Image Objects*, 27. Gaboury considers Ivan E. Sutherland's paper *The Ultimate Display*, in which he illustratively expresses the vision of a completely immersive reproduction of our physical reality, as particularly influential for the pursuit of realism. Gaboury does not undertake an in-depth examination of a possible concept of realism. See Ivan E. Sutherland, "The Ultimate Display," in *Information Processing 1965. Proceedings of IFIP Congress. Part 2*, ed. Wayne A. Kalenich (Washington: Spartan, 1965). Sutherland plays a central role in my study, but his concepts in *The Ultimate Display* are only of secondary relevance here.
71. See Gaboury, *Image Objects*, 32–33.
72. See Gaboury, *Image Objects*, 5–6.
73. Gaboury, *Image Objects*, 204. Gaboury quotes Laine Nooney, "A Pedestal, a Table, a Love Letter: Archaeologies of Gender in Videogame History," *Game Studies* 13, no. 2 (2013). http://gamestudies.org/1302/articles/nooney. In Chapter 12, the conclusion of my study, I briefly discuss again why the study takes a human-centered perspective as its starting point instead of, for example, post-humanist approaches.
74. Gaboury, *Image Objects*, 46.
75. See "Anyflo philosophy," Anyflo philosophy, Michel Bret, accessed December 5, 2021, https://anyflo.com/distribution/distribution_eng/env/philosophie.htm.
76. Michel Bret, "Tools for Artists," in *Computer Animation '91*, ed. Nadia Magnenat Thalmann and Daniel Thalmann (Tokyo: Springer Japan, 1991), 187–88. Being aware that the machine is always involved in creative decisions when working artistically with the computer, the computer artist Anne-Sarah Le Meur examines in her study *Création artistique en image de synthèse. Expression de la corporéité* the process of artistic creation on the computer, both on the basis of creative works by others and her own artistic practice. Bret's software Anyflo plays a central role in her research as well as in her artistic work. See Anne-Sarah Le Meur, "Création artistique en image de synthèse: Expression de la corporéité" (PhD diss., Université de Paris VIII, 1999), 11, 95, 360–61.
77. See Michel Bret, "L'artiste et l'ordinateur," in *Les images numériques: Créations françaises*, ed. Daisy Hochart (Condé-sur-Noireau: Ed. Corlet-Télérama, CinémAction TV 10, 1994), 68.
78. Ondine Bréaud, *Le Réalisme dans l'image informatique: Étude des années 1980 et 1990* (Paris: Harmattan, 2001), 114. In her study, Bréaud examines the realism of synthetic images on the level of visual aesthetics. Central to her study is the relationship between the commercial realist images of the 1980s and 1990s and computer art from the same period. She rejects the idea of a break with previous means of expression, which is why she initially pursues the aim of finding out to what extent the computer-generated images stand in a certain tradition of previous image production. She contextualizes the realism of commercial images by drawing comparisons with the advertising industry. In her opinion, it was a time when nothing old or dirty was allowed to be shown – even the Gulf War was depicted cleanly and bloodlessly in the media and cosmetic surgery was also experiencing a boom at the time. The synthetic images were just as distracting from the truth as advertising photography. She also makes references to US photorealistic painting, but to Bréaud their images also merely fulfilled the demands of the zeitgeist. Bréaud therefore does not ask *why* all these pictures are aesthetically very similar. She does not inquire into a deeper cultural context of the computer images. Instead, she comes to the conclusion that, on the one hand, the realism of the images was only strived for in order to present the technological possibilities, which – she assumes – on the other hand leads to the images remaining in a self-referential cycle by only referring to their technology. For Bréaud, the solution to this problem lies in using the computer to strive for an image aesthetic that resists the hyperreality and transparency of the medium. See Bréaud, *Réalisme dans l'image informatique*, 16, 143–46, 155–57.
79. Gaboury, *Image Objects*, 11.
80. See Gaboury, *Image Objects*, 23, 35.
81. Cardoso Llach, *Builders of the Vision*, 4.
82. See Cardoso Llach, *Builders of the Vision*, 15, 18.
83. Cardoso Llach, *Builders of the Vision*, 1.
84. Cardoso Llach, *Builders of the Vision*, 1.
85. See e.g. Bolter and Grusin, *Remediation*, 26. However, Bolter and Grusin also point out that the perspective projection in computer graphics is mathematically perfect, whereas it did not fulfill this requirement in the Renaissance. Manovich also refers the realism of synthetic images to the aspect of mimesis and the grapes painted by the ancient Greek artist Zeuxis. See

Lev Manovich, "Synthetic Realism: The Mythology of Computer Graphics," *Afterimage* 20, no. 2 (1992): 14, https://doi.org/10.1525/aft.1992.20.2.12.

86. See Cardoso Llach, *Builders of the Vision*, xvi.
87. Cardoso Llach, *Builders of the Vision*, xvi.
88. See Cardoso Llach, *Builders of the Vision*, 56.
89. Cardoso Llach, *Builders of the Vision*, 54.
90. Gaboury also addresses the influence of Coons but only refers to the so-called "Coons Surface Patch," a mathematical calculation model for the computer-aided representation of curved surfaces. See Gaboury, *Image Objects*, 94–95.
91. See Cardoso Llach, *Builders of the Vision*, 71.
92. See Casey Alt, "The Materialities of Maya: Making Sense of Object-Orientation," *Configurations* 10, no. 3 (2002): 409–10, https://doi.org/10.1353/con.2004.0002.
93. See, for example, Cardoso Llach, *Builders of the Vision*, 71–72.
94. See Edwin Catmull, "A Subdivision Algorithm for Computer Display of Curved Surfaces" (PhD diss., University of Utah, 1974), J. Willard Marriott Library (712681), [i].
95. See Perry, "Rigging the World."
96. Alvy Ray Smith also gives Coons a central role in his biography of the pixel and in this context also refers to the common roots of CAD and computer graphics. However, Smith assumes that Coons was not interested in images, but primarily in producing objects and components. See Smith, *Pixel*, 263. Smith does not mention that Coons co-authored a comprehensive graphics manual with his colleague John T. Rule. It is examined in detail in my study with regard to Coons' image concepts. See John T. Rule and Steven A. Coons, *Graphics* (New York: McGraw-Hill, 1961). See also Section 5.1 in this study.
97. See Cardoso Llach, *Builders of the Vision*, 73–84.
98. Cardoso Llach, *Builders of the Vision*, xii.
99. See Cardoso Llach, *Builders of the Vision*, 8–9.
100. Cardoso Llach, *Builders of the Vision*, 108. Cardoso Llach refers here to Ahmed Kanna, *Dubai: The City as Corporation* (Minneapolis: University of Minnesota Press, 2011). According to Cardoso Llach, Kanna's descriptions of the influence of Western traditions on urban planning in Dubai could also be applied to his own experiences and observations that he was able to make in Abu Dhabi. See Cardoso Llach, *Builders of the Vision*, 111–12.
101. See Cardoso Llach, *Builders of the Vision*, 116–17.
102. The infrastructure that Cardoso Llach is talking about here is referred to in architecture as Building Information Modeling, or BIM for short. Cardoso Llach explains how BIM was conceived and how it is related to CAD software as follows: "Expressing an economic imperative to reduce the distance between design and manufacturing to increase industrial production, the renewed CAD discourse reimagined design and building practices entirely around a digital model placed at the center of a multidisciplinary array of actors. This ambition of centralized control underpins the technology project known in industry today as Building Information Modeling (BIM) – essentially an effort towards standardized models containing all aspects of a building's design in a three-dimensional description. By standardizing design descriptions, the BIM project indexes an infrastructural impulse to colonize and re-organize a vastly complex landscape of design and building practices and actors." Cardoso Llach, *Builders of the Vision*, 86.
103. See Cardoso Llach, *Builders of the Vision*, 121–34.
104. See Cardoso Llach, *Builders of the Vision*, 2.
105. Cardoso Llach, *Builders of the Vision*, 1–2.
106. Cardoso Llach, *Builders of the Vision*, xvii, emphasis in original. Cardoso Llach's phrasing is reminiscent of Annette Geiger's monograph *Andersmöglichsein. Zur Ästhetik des Designs* (The Possibility of Being Different: On an Aesthetic of Design). In it, Geiger describes a design aesthetic that defines the field of design as a *space of possibility*: "All design begins with the realization that we have the choice to design our things and media, our communications and relationships, our technologies, economies and ecologies differently – otherwise there would be no need for designers to think about the good choice of forms. Design therefore presupposes the recognition of creative freedom; there is no inevitability that could lead to a single correct form." Annette Geiger, *Andersmöglichsein. Zur Ästhetik des Designs* (Bielefeld: transcript, 2018), 15. My study, which does not deal with the design of technology, but with the design of computerized processes, therefore responds to Geiger's chapter entitled *Mensch und Technik: Wer gestaltet wen?* (Man and Technology: Who Designs Whom?). See Geiger, *Andersmöglichsein*, 103–26.

CHAPTER 2

Introductory Overview

2.1 STARTING FROM SCRATCH – THE PRACTICE OF SYNTHETIC IMAGE GENERATION

> If you want to learn Maya, it might seem overwhelming at first. That's okay, just remember to take it step by step.[1]
>
> *AUTODESK MAYA® (2022)*

To tie in with the terminology mentioned at the end of the last chapter, this section deals with the question of what *possibilities* the three-dimensional (3D) graphics software available today can offer for the practice of creating 3D images. The software landscape, the historical development of which will be explored in the following parts, will now be presented from a practical perspective. This is important, because first, the questions from which this study has developed stem directly from an angle of a practitioner. Second, the significance of the findings from the following parts for the practice of creating 3D graphics becomes much clearer when the reader knows how 3D computer graphics can be generated in graphics software in the first place. The focus here is on the software landscape that is used in commercial contexts, for example in popular culture or for artistic-experimental purposes. There are numerous different programs from different companies, each of which has established itself in specific areas of application.[2]

The first feature that characterizes this software landscape is the sense of community among those who work with it. Being able to use this software also means being part of a global community, which often exchanges information on usage methods, new processes and application advice in special forums on the Internet. Perry encountered this sense of community in her research when conducting numerous interviews on the practice of virtual modeling:

> Though they [the interviewees] are geographically widely dispersed, and may work either alone or in groups nearly the size of small cities, almost without exception they described themselves as belonging to a close, tight-knit community, where "everyone knows everyone." They felt this to be true even though the community numbers many thousands of people working in studios in many different cities and countries. [...] In addition, distances and cultures are bridged and the sense of community is reinforced through interaction with common software packages and concepts, through sharing data, tools and circulating objects, through personal connections with others and through the development of a shared aesthetic.[3]

So what characterizes the software landscape that this community works with? In addition to his own practical experience of working with the software, explanations are also provided by 3D artist Dominik Pott, who has been working in the commercial feature film industry for around ten years in the field of computer-aided special effects for both computer-animated films and live-action films. This section is largely based on an interview I conducted with Pott.[4] The term 3D artist generally describes a person who works in any way with the software described here. It

DOI: 10.1201/9781003649861-3

does not yet indicate the exact field of work, because as can be seen from Pott's specialization in the area of effects and Perry's focus on modeling, different disciplines can be identified for the creation of 3D graphics, each of which requires a slightly different level of expertise. As a rule, however, those who work specifically in one of the areas also have an idea of the fields of activity of the others, as all disciplines are closely interlinked. They intertwine in the production process in a complex manner. As this study is primarily concerned with the phenomenon of computer-generated imagery, the software features used in the areas of animation and simulation of effects will only be touched on in the background here. The focus is on those features within the software that serve to generate an image – regardless of whether the image is later to exist as a still image or is used in an animated sequence or in a film.

This initial insight into the various disciplines illustrates that 3D graphics programs are extremely complex software systems that – comparable to the individual technical crews in a theater or on a film set – combine numerous different disciplines in a single computer application. It is therefore usually possible to customize the user interface of such a program for your own discipline and only display those functions that are relevant to your own area of work. This basic structure applies equally to all 3D graphics programs of this type. The main individual disciplines that are anchored in the software will now be listed, to better comprehend, within the historical analysis of my study, how these different areas came about and why they play a role in the software today.

The fields of discipline involved in the process of creating a computer-generated image can essentially be limited to the areas of modeling, shading, texturing, rendering and compositing. With the topic of virtual lighting, there is another field that is central to the creation of 3D graphics. As will be shown in the further course of this study, this statement also applies with regard to the history of the creation of synthetic images.[5] However, as the aim of this section is merely to provide a basic insight into the practice of synthetic image generation using 3D graphics software, the highly technical sub-area of light is not addressed here in its own right, but rather in direct connection with the related disciplines of shading and rendering. As will become clear in the course of this section and the entire study, both areas are directly related to virtual light sources and would not be feasible without them. While the areas of modeling, shading and texturing take place within the software itself and will be given special attention here, the rendering process is often carried out by an independent and also interchangeable software plugin within the 3D application. Standalone rendering programs are also used. Compositing takes place in a completely independent software environment but is closely linked to the work steps previously carried out within the 3D graphics program. Some elements from the area of compositing – insofar as they are directly relevant to this study – will therefore also be presented.

In addition to the usual menus and context menus for all sub-disciplines, the interface of 3D graphics software essentially consists of a viewport, which is a view through a virtual camera lens. When the program is opened, a so-called grid can usually be seen here – a square area lying in perspective in virtual space, which can be understood as a coordination system and indicates the mathematical zero point in virtual 3D space. It is primarily used for orientation in this virtual space and also provides a basis for proportions, as it is divided into units of measurement. You can work interactively in the displayed view of this camera, the so-called perspective view (Figure 2.1). The viewport is particularly essential for modeling – the first step in the creation of 3D graphics – because virtual objects and figures can be created directly in the camera's field of view as so-called 3D models.[6] The camera also offers additional viewing perspectives for this purpose, so that a model can also be viewed and edited directly from above, from the front or from the side, for example. These so-called views with the names "top," "side" and "front" have no perspective distortion, unlike the "perspective view" (Figure 2.2).

In principle, virtual models can be created in two different ways in the 3D graphics programs described here. On the one hand, there is a method with which objects can be modeled with maximum precision on the basis of mathematical functions. On the other hand, there is a polygon-based method that can be used to achieve technically less precise but much more flexible results. While precise models are required in industrial design, for example, in order to be able to produce components accurately, polygon-based models are predominantly used in the field of popular

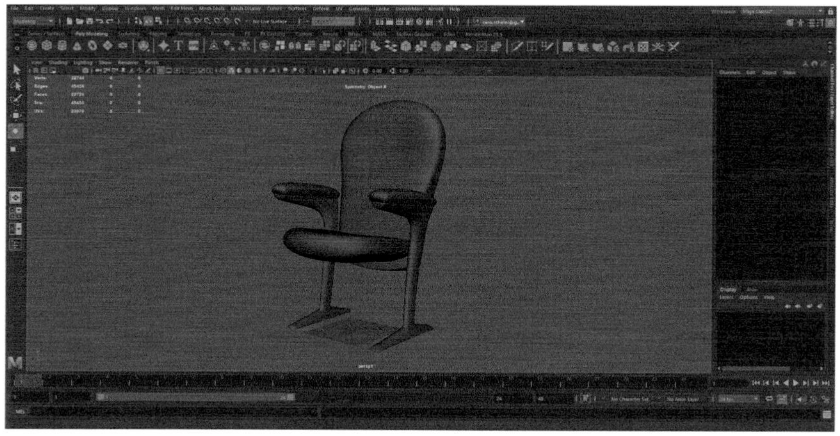

FIGURE 2.1 Screenshot by the author, *"perspective view" in Autodesk Maya*, 2021. (Autodesk screen shots reprinted courtesy of Autodesk, Inc.)

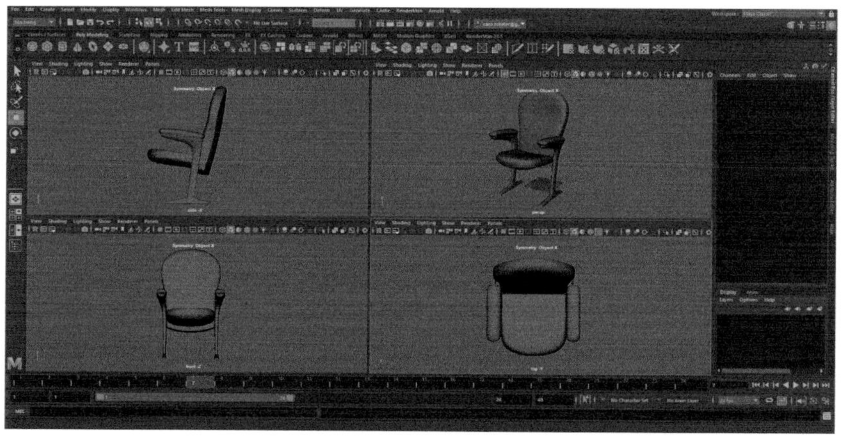

FIGURE 2.2 Screenshot by the author, *"perspective, side, front and top view" in Autodesk Maya*, 2021. (Autodesk screen shots reprinted courtesy of Autodesk, Inc.)

culture. The following descriptions therefore only refer to this approach. Polygon models consist of faces, edges and so-called vertices (plural for vertex). Using an ordinary globe as an example, a polygon model can be described particularly well, as the faces, edges and vertices would roughly correspond to the appearance of the lines of longitude and latitude on the globe. The quadrilaterals created by the intersecting lines on the globe would in this example be the polygons. They therefore form ring-shaped paths, which also applies in principle to more complex models, even if the paths in those might not always be as uniform and straightforward as on a sphere (Figure 2.3). Within the program it is then possible to decide whether the models should be displayed as "wireframe" or as "solid" (Figures 2.4 and 2.5). The wireframe mode shows the model as a transparent grid, which can easily be visually misleading, especially with complex models, as in this display mode it is not clear which lines of the grid are in the foreground, and which are in the background. For the modeling process, it can be helpful to also keep an eye on the vertices on the back of a model, but to gain a better overall view, there is the mode of displaying models as "solids." They are then displayed with a simple basic shading, so that only those surfaces that are in the foreground can be seen. Every 3D graphics program provides basic geometric volumes, so-called primitives, to get you started with the polygon-based modeling process, which can be modified to become more complex models. The most common basic shapes are limited to a cube, a sphere, a torus, a cone and a cylinder, although a few other

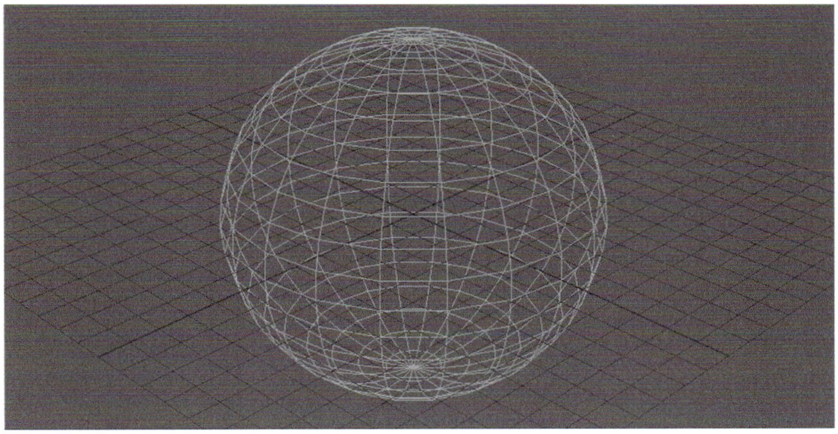

FIGURE 2.3 Screenshot by the author, *Wireframe-view of a sphere in Autodesk Maya*, 2021. (Autodesk screen shots reprinted courtesy of Autodesk, Inc.)

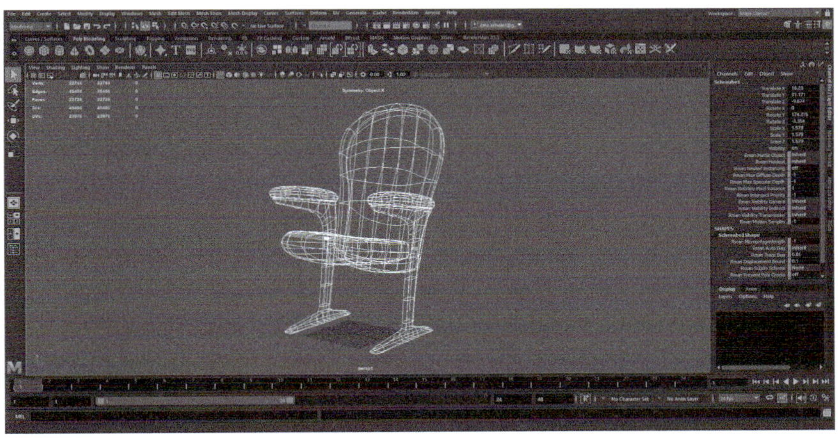

FIGURE 2.4 Screenshot by the author, *Wireframe-view of a cinema chair in Autodesk Maya* (3D model by the author), 2021. (Autodesk screen shots reprinted courtesy of Autodesk, Inc.)

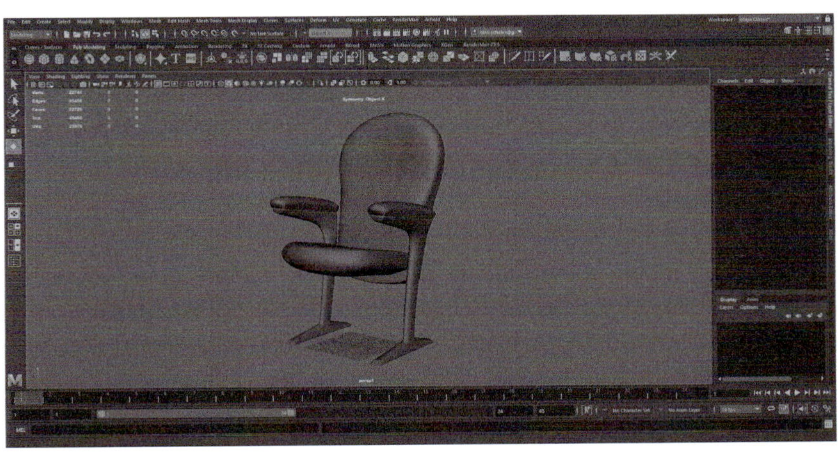

FIGURE 2.5 Screenshot by the author, *Solid of a cinema chair in Autodesk Maya* (3D Model by the author), 2021. (Autodesk screen shots reprinted courtesy of Autodesk, Inc.)

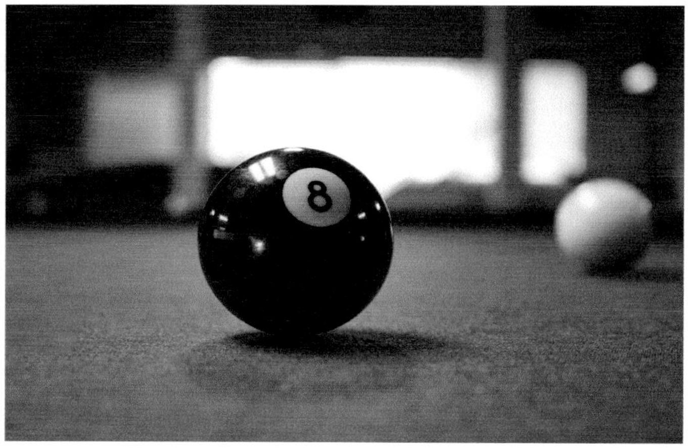

FIGURE 2.6 Pixabay, *Billard ball*, 2019, digital photography.

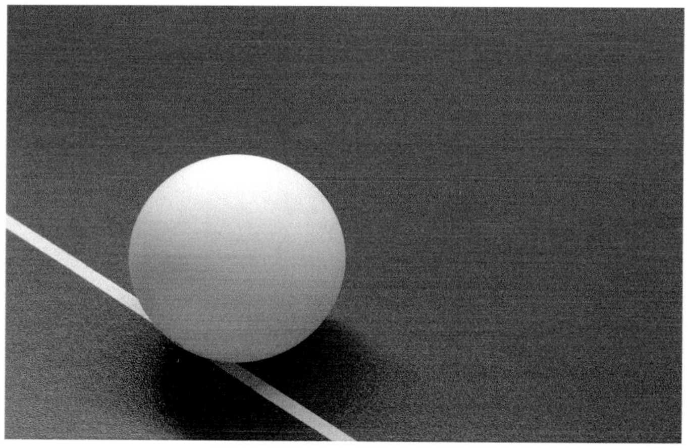

FIGURE 2.7 Pixabay, *Table tennis ball*, 2019, digital photography.

models, such as a tube or a pyramid, are also available depending on the program. How the modeling process actually works will not be discussed here, but it should be noted that similar tools exist in all programs to design the desired object starting from the basic shape.[7]

The next step toward the finished image is to determine and recreate the materiality of the object. For this purpose, the area of shading exists. It is decisive for the appearance of the objects in the image and is also closely interlinked with the area of texturing. There are numerous different so-called shaders and each of these shaders basically contains settings, for example in the form of sliders, behind which mathematical calculations are hidden. These settings can be used to regulate how the artificial light in the virtual space should react to the surface of the material, i.e. whether – as with the smooth surface of a billiard ball – the light is focused in a small, sharply defined white dot or whether it is scattered over a diffuse area on the material surface, as happens with a table tennis ball, for example (Figures 2.6 and 2.7). With the help of so-called bump maps, a shader can also process height and depth information, for example if one wishes for a sphere to have the appearance of a basketball. If a bump map is used, shading is simulated during the image calculation so that – in simplified terms – the impression is created that the ball has a relief on the surface, such as the nubs on a basketball. This feature makes it possible to avoid having to model such fine structures individually. Instead, they can be added later in the shading. The idea of creating such an effect on a purely visual level, rather than in the geometry of the object, was developed by James F. Blinn in the 1970s,[8]

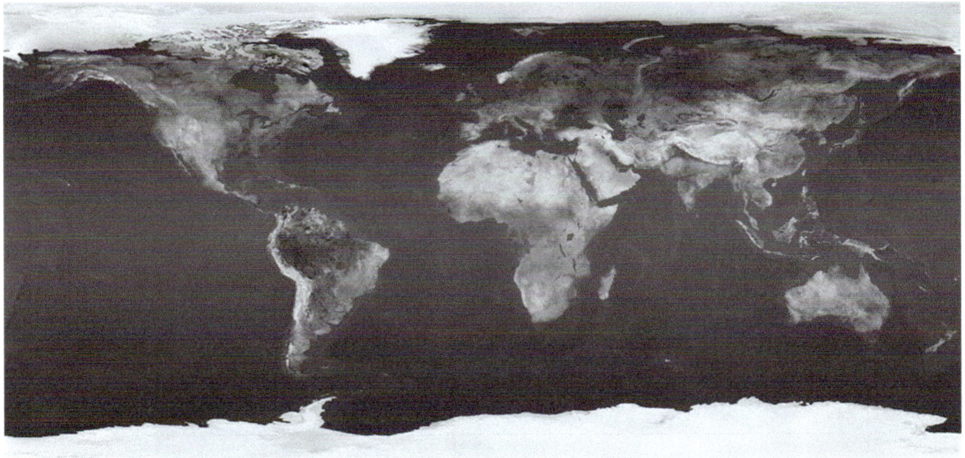

FIGURE 2.8 James Hastings-Trew, *earth texture map*, undated, photomontage. (Copyright © James Hastings-Trew/ public domain.)

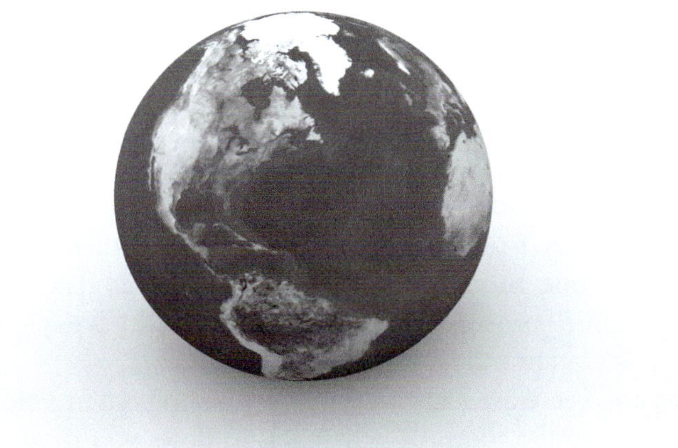

FIGURE 2.9 Image by the author, Sphere textured with the *earth texture map* in previous figure, 2022, 3D computer graphic.

who will become relevant again within the historiography of this study. Bump maps can be used in any 3D application and are a standard feature.[9]

In addition to the surface structure, the color of an object can also be determined with a shader. Although it is possible to color an entire virtual object or just individual polygons with a specific color, the coloring is rarely created in this way. So-called textures are usually used instead. They can be explained again using the example of the globe. Instead of coloring polygons individually in a blue hue to indicate the world's oceans, for example all details of the world map are displayed in a flat image that can then be "wrapped" around the globe, so to speak. Photographs or photomontages can also be used for this purpose (Figures 2.8 and 2.9). Historically, Edwin Catmull is another author who can be specifically identified for this particular feature.[10] His idea of adding textures to objects predates Blinn's bump maps by several years.

Overall, it can be said that shading is a particularly central area of 3D computer graphics. Generally, 3D computer programs contain extensive libraries with preset shaders, so that it is possible to quickly create the effect of gold, glass or concrete, for example. With the help of sliders, further settings can then be made to the shader so that your own ideas can be realized to a certain extent. These shader libraries are also the place within the software where most references to

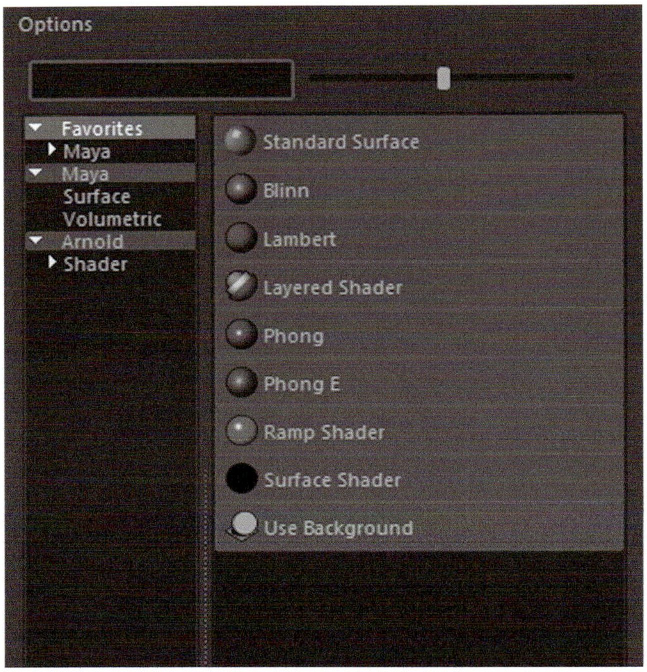

FIGURE 2.10 Screenshot by the author, *Detail of the Hypershade Editor in Autodesk Maya*, 2022. (Autodesk screen shots reprinted courtesy of Autodesk, Inc.)

the authors behind them can be found (Figure 2.10). While Catmull does not appear by name within the software, a shader with the name Blinn exists, for example, because the algorithm processed in the shader is based on a light calculation model that was originally developed by Blinn. There are also shaders with the names Phong and Gouraud, both of which also refer to their authors Bui Tuong Phong and Henri Gouraud. Although these shaders were developed in the 1970s in the United States and newer shading methods have long since been available,[11] they are – even if rarely – still in use today. The German software manufacturer Maxon, for example, uses a Gouraud shader as standard in the 3D graphics software *Cinema 4D* to display models as "solids." The shader is explained on the program manufacturer's help pages online. It is "[t]he highest quality display mode for viewports. All objects are shaded with smoothing and light sources are taken into account."[12] The detail that the Gouraud shader is integrated into the *Cinema 4D* program as a default setting can be viewed as an example of one of the leaps described by Blumenberg, as the shader was not – like the software – developed in Europe. The fact that Gouraud had specific ideas when developing his shader does not play a role in practice, at least not at first glance, as this study can show. This observation also applies to the Phong shader. It was also implemented in *Cinema 4D* and its functionality is explained on the help pages as follows:

> Phong is a function built into Cinema 4D that allows you to give an object made up of triangles and squares a round, smooth surface (Phong shading) during image calculation. For example, a sphere that is made up of a hundred faces and normally appears faceted can hardly be distinguished from the perfect sphere when Phong is switched on.[13]

The problem behind the faceted appearance of the sphere commented on here will be explained in detail in Sections 7.1.2 and 7.1.3, but these examples can already illustrate that many of the people involved in the development of 3D graphics at the time are still shaping the software landscape today. For this reason, these people form the starting point of my analysis I pursue in this study. In the next section, I will therefore first provide a brief historical overview of them, before going into detail about their respective contributions to the development of

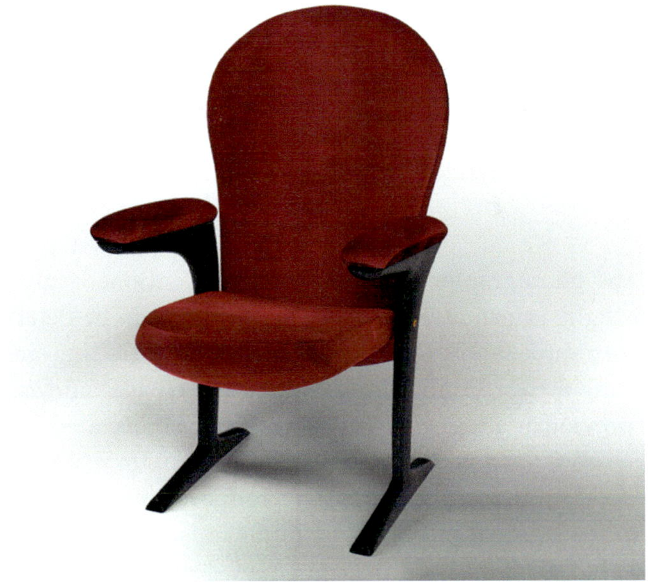

FIGURE 2.11 Image by the author, *Cinema chair*, 2013, 3D computer graphic. (© Carolin Scheler. Autodesk screen shots reprinted courtesy of Autodesk, Inc.)

3D computer graphics in Parts II and III. First, however, I am now presenting the final steps required to create a finished 3D graphic.

After shading has been used to define how the virtually generated light reacts to the textured surfaces for all objects, rendering is the step that creates a fixed 3D graphic from an open file, which – to put it simply – can then be saved on the computer as a JPG, for example (Figure 2.11). Rendering is therefore first and foremost the translation of a virtual 3D scene into a two-dimensional (2D) surface and as such this process is one of the most complex and computationally intensive processing steps. The task of a so-called render engine is to process all the settings previously defined in the 3D program in a particularly effective and at the same time aesthetically pleasing way. The aspect of aesthetic appeal – and this is a central point in the context of my discussion – should not be a fixed criterion for computer-aided image generation, and yet certain ideas prevail for this work step, which are generally strived for in the generation of 3D computer graphics. Here, for the first time, it becomes clear what my question regarding a common context of meaning of 3D graphics is aimed at. Before I systematically and production-aesthetically examine the work steps presented here within the following parts of my study, it can be anticipated at this point already that an aesthetically successful result is often associated with photorealistic qualities. In the best-case scenario, a render engine is therefore designed to be able to generate images from the 3D scene that – if you put your mind to it – no longer differ from a photograph. The "Physically Based Rendering," which has been established in the industry more than ten years ago,[14] is also based on this principle. In their handbook *Physically Based Rendering: From Theory to Implementation*, the authors Matt Pharr, Wenzel Jakob and Greg Humphreys present their rendering system *pbrt* and its areas of application:

> `pbrt` and the contents of this book focus exclusively on *photorealistic rendering*, which can be defined variously as the task of generating images that are indistinguishable from those that a camera would capture in a photograph or as the task of generating images that evoke the same response from a human observer as looking at the actual scene. There are many reasons to focus on photorealism. Photorealistic images are crucial for the movie special-effects industry because computer-generated imagery must often be mixed seamlessly with footage of the real world. In entertainment applications where

> all of the imagery is synthetic, photorealism is an effective tool for making the observer forget that he or she is looking at an environment that does not actually exist. Finally, photorealism gives a reasonably well-defined metric for evaluating the quality of the rendering system's output.[15]

In order to do justice to the photographic style, a render engine processes the light information from the virtual environment, for example, and calculates light refractions and reflections for those objects to which these properties were previously assigned using a shader.[16]

The render engine can also store the depth information of the virtual space in the finished image files in the form of metadata, so that areas of the image can be blurred to simulate a depth of field as if focusing a scene with a camera lens. This happens either during the rendering process itself or later during compositing. In addition, the rendering process also includes steps that are not directly related to the aesthetics of the image, but rather to the technical conditions that arise when images are displayed on screens. For example, a render engine must translate a continuous 3D scene into a screen-compliant raster with a specific resolution. This process usually results in an artifact known as aliasing, which is noticeable as a staircase effect on diagonal or curved edges and contours in the image. The render engine is therefore equipped with "anti-aliasing," a highly computationally intensive algorithm that can counteract this effect. In addition, the size of the image files to be output can also be specified in the rendering process, so that they can either be turned into high-resolution video recordings or prepared for printing, for example. The area of rendering is so comprehensive that there is also independent software for this step in the work process, which can either be integrated as a plugin in a 3D application or communicate with the graphics software as an independent program. One of the leading render engines in the commercial feature film industry is the *RenderMan* software,[17] which also goes back to the computer scientist Edwin Catmull.[18] Today, the now widespread approach of "physically based rendering" is also implemented in *RenderMan*.[19]

The last area – compositing – is used to post-process the images calculated by the render engine. This step is carried out separately in independent software systems that are designed for this task. As this is strictly speaking a 2D graphics application due to the processing of image files, this area is already outside the scope of this study. Nevertheless, it should be mentioned briefly, as numerous visual elements that are characteristic of 3D computer graphics are often only added in this step. These include, for example, the already-mentioned subsequently generated depth of field, which can be determined using metadata in the image, color grading and adjustment of light reflections as well as shadows. "Errors," such as film grain, can also be integrated into the images in this final processing step, for example if the 3D graphics are to be introduced into a real film environment and adapted to the noise of the film footage.

The decision to finalize 3D graphics as part of compositing is based on the fact that it takes both less time and computing power if, for example, a depth of field is subsequently inserted into a 2D environment. If it were output directly by the render engine – which would also be possible – the entire 3D scene would have to be converted into a 2D image again if a change was requested. These types of post-processing therefore ensure that an image does not have to be re-rendered from the 3D environment if, for example, changes are required. Instead, it can be edited in the compositing program until the desired image aesthetic is achieved.

To summarize, there is one final aspect that affects all of these different work steps, because generally, every software system mentioned here is part of an agile and reciprocal process. This means that the software is never finished in the true sense of the word but is fundamentally based on a feedback loop between application and development. In the third edition of their monograph, Pharr, Jakob and Humphreys also refer in their acknowledgments to feedback from the community, for example in the form of so-called bug reports, i.e. weak points in the system that often only become visible in the application and can later be stabilized through such feedback loops.[20] As a starting point for my study, however, it is important to note that every new software development and improvement in the field of 3D graphics continues to operate within a more or less fixed framework that is not questioned as such. Therefore, the hypothesis for the following investigation is that all improvements are always developed against the backdrop of an overarching aesthetic goal, to which even the cycle of feedback and improvement is subordinate. The vast majority of innovations merely consist of making the systems simpler and more efficient. Fundamental changes with regard to the aesthetic possibilities, on the other hand, are not part of the dynamic described here and are at best offered in open-source systems (see endnote 2).[21] The individual sub-disciplines described in this section, which are reflected in the software today, have developed on the basis of this overarching idea. At the beginning of the history of computer graphics, the individual fields were not yet differentiated from each other in the same way; they only gradually crystallized into individual areas with this clarity. At the end of this section, the following question therefore arises: Which visual conception marked the beginning of the development of 3D computer graphics? Why does the creative process of producing 3D graphics take place in the way described here?

2.2 THE PRACTICE OF 3D COMPUTER GRAPHICS FROM A HISTORICAL PERSPECTIVE – A BRIEF OVERVIEW

> Almost every influential person in the modern computer-graphics community either passed through the University of Utah or came into contact with it in some way [...].[22]
>
> *ROBERT RIVLIN (1986)*

The historical investigation of the software environment from which 3D graphics emerge is directly linked to the practical perspective presented in the previous section. This means that the historiography I undertake in this study is developed directly along a path of knowledge that only opens up when one works practically with the software. This path of knowledge is now briefly presented in order to outline the essential steps of my historiography for the purpose of orientation. Part II of the study begins with a comprehensive review of the events outlined in this section.

As described in the previous section, material properties can be assigned to a virtual object within a computer program for 3D graphics using the central function of shading. The special characteristic of this program feature is that – in contrast to other settings – direct references to the authors are made in the shader libraries of various programs via the names of individual shaders available for selection. I mentioned the three computer scientists Henri Gouraud, Bui Tuong Phong and James F. Blinn in this context. Although the shading algorithms were developed by the three computer scientists back in the 1970s, the question of their origins is, from the perspective of the production process, therefore extremely topical. In addition, based on the shaders, it is possible to consider whether other program functions with a neutral name can also be traced back to specific people who once approached the development of these operating functions with certain ideas. In order to find an entry point into the investigation of these ideas, it is therefore possible to first follow the names of Gouraud, Phong and Blinn and thus jump directly into the 1970s. All three researchers developed the three shaders in succession and with reference to the previous ones as part of their dissertations: Gouraud in 1971, Phong in 1973 and Blinn in 1978.[23] The leap from today's practice, which leads 40–50 years into the past without any intermediate steps, is quite surprising, as software is usually renewed within a few years and a new program version is generally presented every year. So how can it be that, despite the rapid technological development that is common in this industry, there are not only fragments, but even central operating components that are now around 40 or 50 years old? Once again, I follow the hypothesis that a concept must have emerged at that time as to how computer-aided three-dimensional representations could be produced and what standards or principles they should follow, especially visually. The fundamental views on this are still relevant today. This assumption allows and even requires taking a direct leap into the past in order to trace the understanding of these computer graphics that were then a fairly novel phenomenon. With what goal and against what background were technologies such as the three shaders developed? And can other computer graphics achievements from that time be filtered out that are still relevant today and thus still convey the values that characterized the development process back then? These are the central questions that will be explored in the second and third parts of the study.

The practical path of knowledge can be continued via the three shaders and their authors. Gouraud's and Phong's dissertations took place as part of the same research project; Blinn refers to both of his predecessors a few years later, especially to Phong, as Blinn's work is directly based on Phong's approach.[24] The frame in which Gouraud and Phong developed their shaders is the *Graphical Man/Machine Communications* research project I already mentioned above in the current state of research, which was carried out from 1966 to 1973 under the direction of physicist and computer scientist Dave Evans at the *Computer Science Department* of the *University of Utah* and which is also the focus of Gaboury's investigation.[25] Evans was involved in the founding of this department in 1965, which has since been renamed *Kahlert School of Computing.*[26] Until the completion of the research project, he was also the chairman of the new department and, in this capacity, brought Ivan E. Sutherland into the project as a further leading researcher in 1968.[27] At the same time, the two colleagues founded the company *Evans & Sutherland*, which is still active today under different management and which used to specialize primarily in the creation of computer graphics flight simulations.[28] According to its own website, it is "the world's first computer graphics company."[29] Given his previous research focus, integrating Sutherland into the project was an obvious choice. After all, with the development of the *Sketchpad* program at MIT in 1963 he had already pursued a similar goal to that later pursued by Evans at the *University of Utah*. The written report that summarizes Sutherland's dissertation project and describes the *Sketchpad* program is called *Sketchpad: A Man-Machine Graphical Communication System.*[30] The aim of his program was to facilitate communication between humans and computers with the help of graphical commands. Sutherland thus fundamentally rethought the programming process, which is why *Sketchpad* is often referred to as one of the first object-oriented programs, even though the term itself was not introduced until the 1970s by Alan Kay.[31] As *Sketchpad* plays a central role not only in general with regard to the development of computer technology but also in relation to the history of computer-generated images, Chapter 3 provides a thorough examination of the program and Sutherland's ideas. The chapter on Sutherland thus also forms the introduction to the historiography I pursue in my study.

Although Sutherland only became involved in Evans' research project in Utah two years after it was established and thus five years after Sutherland worked on *Sketchpad*, he played an influential role in his colleague's project in another capacity from the very beginning. After completing his dissertation at MIT, Sutherland was head of the *Information Processing Techniques Office* (IPTO) from 1963 to 1965, a department of the *Advanced Research Projects Agency* (ARPA), now known as the *Defense Advanced Research Projects Agency* (DARPA).[32] This is a research agency set up by the US military in 1958 to fund research projects of potential military relevance with substantial sums of money. The organization was founded as a direct response to the Soviet Union's success in 1957 as the first nation to put a satellite, called *Sputnik I*, into the Earth's orbit.[33] NASA describes the impact this event had on the United States as follows: "While the Sputnik launch was a single event, it marked the start of the space age and the U.S.–U.S.S.R space race."[34] DARPA's historical documentation also addresses the shock that the Soviet Union's lead triggered in the United States:

> "Now, somehow, in some way, the sky seemed almost alien," then-Senate Majority Leader Lyndon B. Johnson recalled feeling on that night, adding that he remembered "the profound shock of realizing that it might be possible for another nation to achieve technological superiority over this great country of ours." Ever since its establishment on February 7, 1958, ARPA – which later added the D for defense at the front of its name – has been striving to keep that technological superiority in the hands of the United States.[35]

In his position as head of the IPTO, it was ultimately Sutherland's task to continue to ensure this goal of "technological superiority" and to select projects in the field of computer technology that he considered to fulfill the relevant criteria and prove worthy of funding. In this role, he was therefore directly responsible for enabling Dave Evans to carry out the *Graphical Man/Machine Communications* research project at the *Computer Science Department* of the *University of Utah.*[36] Furthermore, as Sutherland himself reported in an interview, he had a great deal of freedom in terms of project selection:

> There really was not very much fuss in ARPA. In fact, to get something done, what I had to do was convince myself and convince my boss. [...] [M]y understanding of the mechanism was that if I could convince the ARPA director that something was sensible to do, it got done. [...] I do not think that I did anything that was so outrageous that it would be brought into question. But there was really very little required. There were justifications required.[37]

From a production-aesthetic perspective, two aspects emerge here that appear to be groundbreaking for the development of computer-graphic images. Not only does Ivan E. Sutherland play a central role on several levels, but the historical context that led to the founding of ARPA also provides a significant production-aesthetic detail that, at least in the background, advanced the development of 3D computer graphics. For although Evans' research project was only launched nine years after the Soviet Sputnik success, the spirit of research that accompanied the work at the *University of Utah* becomes clear here: A technological defeat to another nation should, if possible, not be repeated, and as can be seen from Gouraud, Phong and Blinn's shading algorithms, the essential components that still have a considerable influence on the way computer graphics software works today were developed within the *Graphical Man/Machine Communications* research project and in subsequent studies at the same location. A detailed description of these developments take place in Part III.

However, before looking at Evans' and Sutherland's work in Utah, the first step is to present Sutherland's preliminary intellectual work, as the practical rethinking of the programming process that he brought about forms a foundation on which all further steps in this study are based. Central to this is the technical report that he wrote as part of his doctoral thesis to describe the development and functionality of the *Sketchpad* program. In addition to the technical and mathematical explanations, the report provides crucial information about Sutherland's motivation. In terms of production aesthetics, it is thus possible to deduce from the report the ideas with which he later influenced Evans' research project in addition to his purely technical achievements. To get a deeper understanding of these ideological aspects, I also include Sutherland's research context at MIT in my historical investigation, as I assume that his intentions were influenced by this environment. The focus here is on Steven Anson Coons, who was an Associate Professor of Engineering Graphics at MIT in the Department of Mechanical Engineering in the 1960s and, in this capacity, a member of Sutherland's thesis committee.[38] Robert W. Mann, an MIT colleague of Coons, reports that he was the only one of Sutherland's supervisors who had a background as a draftsman.[39] Coons also worked intensively on the question of how human creativity could be reconciled with machine intelligence. According to Mann, Sutherland actively approached Coons to recruit him as a member of the thesis committee,[40] which is why the findings produced by Sutherland can be understood much more profoundly if Coons is also taken into account in the historiography.

In order to better comprehend the new programming approaches and their impact on the production process, it is useful to focus on other parallel developments that are not directly related to the *University of Utah* and MIT. The research of Charles A. Csuri and William A. Fetter, also pioneers in the field of computer graphics, is particularly suitable for this purpose. Csuri was an artist who began exploring the computer as a means of expression in the 1950s. Like Coons before his work at MIT, Fetter worked as a draftsman in the field of aircraft construction, although Fetter saw himself primarily as a communication designer.[41] At about the same time that Sutherland and Coons began exploring new methods of human-computer interaction, both Csuri and Fetter were working with established methods of procedural programming. Their work was based on completely independent ideas, both in terms of visual language and the role of the computer in their creative work. They form a contrast not only to each other but also to the developments at MIT and at the *University of Utah*.

The developments at MIT are presented as follows in the second part of this book: First, Sutherland's *Sketchpad* program is drawn upon to illustrate the rethinking that took place in the programming process in the 1960s. This is followed by Chapter 4, in which first Csuri's and then Fetter's production processes are analyzed and contrasted with Sutherland's approach. Chapter 5 finally introduces Coons. This chapter forms the transition to Part III of the study, which deals with research at the *University of Utah*. Edwin Catmull, one of the founders of the animation studio Pixar, forms the end point of my historical investigation, as he is the first person to express Coons' and Sutherland's graphic and ideological values to their full extent not only on a production-aesthetic level but also on a visual aesthetic level. An overview of all the people mentioned in the historiography can be found in an organizational chart on the last page of this book.

NOTES

1. "Learning Maya." Help, Autodesk Maya, accessed January 1, 2021. https://help.autodesk.com/view/MAYAUL/2022/ENU/?guid=GUID-4191EE54-4500-4FFC-BF29-BA6C1EAD9F58.
2. The types of software listed below are examples, although this is not an exhaustive list of all available programs. *Autodesk Maya* is established in the feature film industry, although *Autodesk* also markets *3ds Max*® software, which is primarily used in the gaming sector. See Casey Alt, "The Materialities of Maya: Making Sense of Object-Orientation," *Configurations* 10, no. 3 (2002): 395–96. Maxon's *Cinema 4D* is a product developed in Germany, and *Blender* is a non-commercial open-source platform originating in the Netherlands. While *Cinema 4D* is considered to be particularly intuitive to use, as emphasized by media artist Mark Gmehling, for example, *Blender* is valued for being open-source software that can be extensively expanded to include new aesthetic options. See Carolin Scheler, "Ein Atelier im virtuellen Raum. 3D als Ausdrucksmedium" (Master's thesis, Hanover University of Applied Sciences and Arts, 2015), 102; see "History," Blender, accessed December 8, 2021, https://www.blender.org/about/history/; see Blender, "Japanese anime studio Khara moving to Blender," *User Stories*, August 15, 2019, https://www.blender.org/user-stories/japanese-anime-studio-khara-moving-to-blender/?utm_source=www-homepage.
3. See Rebecca A. Perry, "Rigging the World: 3D Modeling and the Seduction of the Real" (PhD diss., Massachusetts Institute of Technology, 2014), MIT Libraries, DSpace@MIT (900615015), 28–29.
4. See Dominik Pott, interview by the author, August 16, 2020, transcript, Research Online/Data, https://doi.org/10.25625/Z27EP6.
5. Pott, who I asked to describe a typical process to create a 3D image, also mentions the concept phase, in which a story and an aesthetic for a project are initially defined in the form of sketches, collages or painted images as part of pre-production. This step usually takes place before the software is used, or it is carried out in other computer programs, which is why this phase is excluded here. See Pott, interview, 30–31.
6. Pott also mentions the viewport as a central component of the user interface of a 3D graphics program, including the remark that models can be created and textured there. This second function is also discussed in this section. He also mentions an area in which individual parameters can be set for each individual 3D object, as well as an editor in which the elements in the viewport as well as the associated textures and other properties can be displayed in a structure tree. Each setting made is part of a hierarchy chain that can also be viewed and edited there. The functions described by Pott go beyond the basic presentation of the software and are therefore only listed here as a side note. See Pott, interview, 28–29.
7. One of these overarching functions, which is used very frequently in the modeling process, is the ability to extrude surfaces, which means that the model is given a kind of outgrowth at this point based on a polygon. The tool is therefore suitable for adding details to an object and making it more complex overall.
8. See James F. Blinn, "Computer Display of Curved Surfaces" (PhD diss., University of Utah, 1978), J. Willard Marriott Library (105596).
9. In addition to the bump map feature, all of the 3D applications analyzed here also have a process that uses displacement maps to change the geometry of the object through the shading settings. What this means in concrete terms can also be explained using the example of the basketball: With bump mapping, the silhouette of the ball remains smooth, which is why bump maps are particularly suitable when the outline of an object cannot be seen. This effect can be avoided with a displacement map, as it creates actual bumps on the surface of an object that are recognizable in the silhouette. The nubs of the basketball would also be raised at the edge of the ball. The advantage of a displacement map is that not every nub has to be modeled individually, but that all nubs can be created simultaneously in a single processing step with the shading. The disadvantage of this method is that it is considerably more computationally intensive than the bump map. Raised irregularities on the surface affect the incidence of light and shadows, which requires considerably more calculations than with the bump map, which ignores this effect in the silhouette. For an explanation of the difference between bump and displacement maps, see also Matt Pharr, Wenzel Jakob and Greg Humphreys, *Physically Based Rendering: From Theory to Implementation* (Cambridge: Morgan Kaufmann, 2017), 592.

10. See Edwin Catmull, "A Subdivision Algorithm for Computer Display of Curved Surfaces" (PhD diss., University of Utah, 1974), J. Willard Marriott Library (712681).
11. Pott refers, for example, to the so-called Principled Shader, which is discussed in detail in Section 10.2. See Pott, interview, 20, 22–23.
12. "Shading," Maxon, accessed December 9, 2021. https://help.maxon.net/c4d/s26/en-us/Default.htm#html/DBASEDRAW-BASEDRAW_GROUP_VIEW.html.
13. "Phong," Maxon, accessed March 25, 2021. https://help.maxon.net/c4d/r23/de-de/Default.htm#html/TPHONG.html?Highlight=Phong. Pott notes that older shaders, such as the Phong calculation model, are hardly relevant in practice today. At the same time, the examples cited in connection with *Cinema 4D* nevertheless show that the first developed shaders are still used, even if these are special use cases. Additionally, it becomes clear in the course of my study that newer shading methods are at least conceptually linked to the earlier ones. See Pott, interview, 21.
14. See Pharr, Jakob and Humphreys, *Physically Based Rendering*, 1.
15. Pharr, Jakob and Humphreys, *Physically Based Rendering*, xx, all emphases in original.
16. The beginnings of physically based rendering can be traced back to the 1980s. See Pharr, Jakob and Humphreys, *Physically Based Rendering*, 48. The development is based on the intention to simplify the areas of shading and rendering. The aim was to create a comprehensive virtual physical environment in which all objects and their surfaces react uniformly to external circumstances such as light, something that was not yet possible with Phong and Blinn's shaders, for example. Pharr, Jakob and Humphreys describe how the work of shading and rendering was organized before this approach was developed: "Earlier, when reflection models that didn't necessarily conserve energy were used, an object might be placed in a single lighting environment while its surface reflection parameters were adjusted. The object might look great in that environment, but it would often appear completely wrong when moved to another lighting environment because surfaces were actually reflecting too little or too much energy: surface properties had been set to unreasonable values." Pharr, Jakob and Humphreys, *Physically Based Rendering*, 52.
17. In an article written for *Wired* magazine, Peter Rubin describes *RenderMan* as "perhaps the most transformative software Hollywood has ever seen." Peter Rubin, "Happy 30th Birthday to the Engine That Powered the CGI Revolution," *Wired*, December 17, 2018, https://www.wired.com/story/renderman-30th-anniversary/.
18. See Jacob Gaboury, *Image Objects. An Archaeology of Computer Graphics* (Cambridge: MIT Press, 2021), 145.
19. See Pharr, Jakob and Humphreys, *Physically Based Rendering*, 51.
20. See Pharr, Jakob and Humphreys, *Physically Based Rendering*, xxvi. Pott is also directly involved in the feedback loops described here in his day-to-day work. In addition to his focus on effects, he describes himself as a pipeline programmer, which is a field of work in which the aim is to optimize the work processes of the individual sub-disciplines. This often involves automating processes, such as the automatic creation and naming of files. In this way, someone who is working on an animation scene can concentrate solely on this task without having to consider how and where to save their open file. See Pott, interview, 3–4.
21. Nevertheless, Manovich also notes that open-source software is often built according to the same principles as its commercial counterpart. See Lev Manovich, *Software Takes Command* (New York: Bloomsbury Academic, 2013), 37–38.
22. Robert Rivlin, *The Algorithmic Image: Graphic Visions of the Computer Age* (Redmond: Microsoft Press, 1986), 27.
23. See Henri Gouraud, "Computer Display of Curved Surfaces" (PhD diss., University of Utah, 1971), ProQuest (7127878); see Bui T. Phong, "Illumination for Computer-Generated Images" (PhD diss., University of Utah, 1973), J. Willard Marriott Library (1602050); see Blinn, "Computer Display of Curved Surfaces."
24. See Blinn, "Computer Display of Curved Surfaces," vii.
25. The time period can be determined on the basis of research reports, which Evans produced every six months to present the status of the project. The project was divided into two research periods, which is why the reports were not produced at the same pace throughout. See David C. Evans, "Graphical Man/Machine Communications: November 1966" (research report, University of Utah, 1966), J. Willard Marriott Library (703452); see David C. Evans, "Graphical Man/Machine Communications: May 1967" (research report, University of Utah, 1967), J. Willard Marriott Library (704511); see David C. Evans, "Graphical Man/Machine Communications: February 1968" (research report, University of Utah, 1968), J. Willard Marriott Library (707101); see David C. Evans, "Graphical Man/Machine communications: November 1968" (research report, University of Utah, 1968), J. Willard Marriott Library (703204); see David C. Evans, "Graphical Man/Machine Communications: May 1969" (research report, University of Utah, 1969), J. Willard Marriott Library (702679); see David C. Evans, "Graphical Man/Machine Communications: November 1969" (research report, University of Utah, 1969), J. Willard Marriott Library (706332); see David C. Evans, "Graphical Man/Machine Communications: May 1971" (research report, University of Utah, 1971),

J. Willard Marriott Library (703517); see David C. Evans, "Graphical Man/Machine Communications: June 1971" (research report, University of Utah, 1971), J. Willard Marriott Library (702407); see David C. Evans, "Graphical Man/Machine Communications: December 1971" (research report, University of Utah, 1971), J. Willard Marriott Library (702292); see David C. Evans, "Graphical Man/Machine Communications: June 1972" (research report, University of Utah, 1972), J. Willard Marriott Library (702817); see David C. Evans, "Graphical Man/Machine Communications: December 1972" (research report, University of Utah, 1972), J. Willard Marriott Library (706529).

26. See "History," University of Utah, accessed June 19, 2025, https://www.cs.utah.edu/resources/history/.
27. In the reports written by Evans every six months, Sutherland's name appears for the first time in the November 1968 report. See Evans, "Graphical Man/Machine communications: November 1968," 7. Sutherland is not listed as a "senior investigator" in the "Computer Graphics Techniques" section until November 1969. Evans, "Graphical Man/Machine Communications: November 1969," 1.
28. See Gaboury, *Image Objects*, 147, 245.
29. "A Cosm Company: About – Evans & Sutherland," Evans & Sutherland, accessed on December 9, 2021, https://www.es.com/about/. Gaboury chooses a more cautious wording and emphasizes that the company was "one of the first commercial computer graphics firms in the United States [...]." Gaboury, *Image Objects*, 18.
30. See Ivan E. Sutherland, "Sketchpad. A Man-Machine Graphical Communication System" (PhD diss., Massachusetts Institute of Technology, 1963), MIT Libraries, DSpace@MIT (15036306).
31. See Casey Alt, "Objects of Our Affection. How Object Orientation Made Computers a Medium," in *Media Archaeology. Approaches, Applications, and Implications*, ed. Erkki Huhtamo and Jussi Parikka (Berkeley, Los Angeles: University of California Press, 2011), 282. See also Section 1.3, the current state of research in my study.
32. See Ivan E. Sutherland, oral history interview by William Aspray, May 1, 1989, transcript, University Digital Conservancy, Charles Babbage Institute, University of Minnesota, https://conservancy.umn.edu/handle/11299/107642, 2.
33. See "The Sputnik Surprise," DARPA, accessed on December 10, 2021, https://www.darpa.mil/about-us/timeline/creation-of-darpa.
34. "Sputnik and the Dawn of the Space Age," NASA, accessed on December 10, 2021, https://history.nasa.gov/sputnik.html.
35. "The Sputnik Surprise."
36. See Sutherland, interview by Aspray, 15–17.
37. Sutherland, interview by Aspray, 11. It is clear from the interview that Evans had also already received funding from ARPA for an earlier project initiated by Sutherland's predecessor J. C. R. Licklider. Evans and other researchers who had received funding from Licklider acted as role models for Sutherland: "I felt that those were the kind of senior people in the field, and they had a pretty clear idea as to what good things to do were." Sutherland, interview by Aspray, 8.
38. See, e.g., Sutherland, interview by Aspray, 5.
39. The thesis committee was chaired by electrical engineer Claude E. Shannon. See Robert W. Mann, "Computer-Aided Design – 1959 through 1965 – in the Design and Graphics Division of MIT's Mechanical Engineering Department," in *Fundamental Developments of Computer-Aided Geometric Modeling*, ed. Les A. Piegl (London: Academic Press, 1993), 385. Reference to Shannon is made again in the following chapters. See in particular Section 3.1.
40. Sutherland also describes this event in his report: "I made contact with the Computer Aided Design Group at MIT which was composed partly of the people of the MIT Electronic Systems Laboratory [...] who developed APT [Automatically Programmed Tool] and partly of people in the Mechanical Engineering Department who brought a knowledge of the problems faced by designers to the project. [...] I was able to visit many separate laboratories for discussion and ideas without becoming so attached to any one that I was forced into its way of thinking. In particular, members of the Mechanical Engineering Department, notably Professor Steven A. Coons, who agreed to serve on my thesis committee, suggested mechanical design problems and applications." Sutherland, "Sketchpad" (1963a), 25–26.
41. Coons worked as a mathematician and designer for *Chance-Vought Aircraft* from 1940 to 1947. In the 1930s he had also taken up work as an illustrator in the publishing industry, which he continued to do during his employment at MIT. See Mann, "Computer-Aided Design," 382. Fetter worked for the *Boeing Company* and produced computer graphics primarily for military aircraft. At the same time, he saw his computer-graphic communication methods as transferable to other areas, such as the design of motorways, architecture, shipbuilding, industrial design and urban planning. See the chapters 'Typical Applications' and 'Other Applications' in William A. Fetter, *Computer Graphics in Communication. Written for the Course Content Development Study in Engineering Graphics, supported by the National Science Foundation* (New York: McGraw-Hill, 1965).

II

The Computer as a Creative Partner

The Early Developments of Computer Graphics at the
Massachusetts Institute of Technology

Ivan E. Sutherland's *Sketchpad* and the Birth of the "Universal" Computer Drawing

> The Sketchpad system makes it possible for a man and a computer to converse rapidly through the medium of line drawings. Heretofore, most interaction between men and computers has been slowed down by the need to reduce all communication to written statements that can be typed; in the past, we have been writing letters to rather than conferring with our computers.[1]
>
> –*IVAN E. SUTHERLAND (1963)*

As part of his dissertation project from 1961[2] to 1963, Sutherland investigated the interaction between humans and computers. His research consisted of two components: First, the practical concern of developing a computer program, which he called *Sketchpad* and whose main task was to facilitate communication between the computer and humans, and second, a written documentation of his approach in the form of a technical report, which describes the evolution of the program and explains the key findings of the research. Sutherland's report, entitled *Sketchpad: A Man-Machine Graphical Communication System* forms the basis of this chapter. I am referring to an edition of the report published in the UK at the Computer Laboratory of the *University of Cambridge* that has been edited and contextualized with a foreword by Alan Blackwell and Kerry Rodden in 2003. The conclusions that can be drawn from Sutherland's research can be considerably deepened by Blackwell and Rodden's contextualization. Sutherland himself supported the new publication of his report – on the one hand ideally, on the other hand also quite practically by proofreading the texts scanned from the original.[3] In the previous chapter, I noted that he sparked a rethinking in the programming process with *Sketchpad*. Blackwell and Rodden confirm the special role that not only the program but also the associated report played:

> Ivan Sutherland's Sketchpad is one of the most influential computer programs ever written by an individual, as recognized in his citation for the Turing award in 1988. The Sketchpad program itself had limited distribution – executable versions were limited to a customized machine at the MIT Lincoln Laboratory – so its influence has been via the ideas that it introduced rather than in its execution. Sutherland's dissertation describing Sketchpad was a critical channel by which those ideas were propagated, along with a movie of the program in use, and a widely-cited conference publication [...]. [W]e believe it [the report] deserves wider readership – hence the electronic archival publication.[4]

DOI: 10.1201/9781003649861-5

Blackwell and Rodden's comment demonstrates that particularly the conceptual innovations brought about by *Sketchpad* can be identified based on the report. I argue that Sutherland's intellectual and practical conception of *Sketchpad* took place against the backdrop of a certain understanding of images and the world as well as a certain idea of creativity, which still characterizes today's production process of synthetic images in a decisive way. The aim of this chapter is therefore to use Sutherland's documentation and the foreword by Blackwell and Rodden to determine the extent to which this assumption can be confirmed and thus to gain insights into the way in which *Sketchpad* influences the production process of today's 3D computer graphics.

Sutherland's central idea was to enable potential users of the computer to communicate with the machine by means of graphical input without the need to have any special computer skills,[5] although it should be noted here that the computer Sutherland was working on in no way resembles today's devices (Figures 3.1 and 3.2). The machine will be presented in more detail in the further course of the chapter, but what can be said now is that at the time, communicative access to computers was usually reserved exclusively for people who were familiar with the use of programming language commands. Even a light pen developed a few years earlier, which could be used to make entries on a CRT screen, did nothing to change the fact that specialized knowledge remained a prerequisite for operating the computer. Sutherland utilized the new light pen for his project. Without it, his idea of a graphical input option on the computer, which was also suitable for non-experts, would not have been realizable. In the report he explains how his project built on a field of research that was still in its infancy: "I had been surprised that so little practical work had been done in application of computers to line drawing, especially since display systems and light pens were relatively common when my work began."[6]

He learned about the possibility of drawing on a display from his colleague Herschel H. Loomis, who did "some preliminary drawing work"[7] and shared this experience with Sutherland. Loomis' research intention was to develop a program that could be used as a "'sketch pad' for the drawing of logical block diagrams."[8] Although he uses the same terminology as Sutherland, Loomis does not mention any other possible applications or visual-aesthetic references apart from the possibility of drawing block diagrams. Sutherland developed much more extensive visions for his drawing program. With *Sketchpad*, he not only considerably expanded Loomis' drawing intentions but also developed a fundamentally new approach, especially with regard to the use of the computer.[9] What did Sutherland mean by what he called "line drawings"? An answer to this question can be deduced from the areas of application he presents at the beginning of his report. He lists a

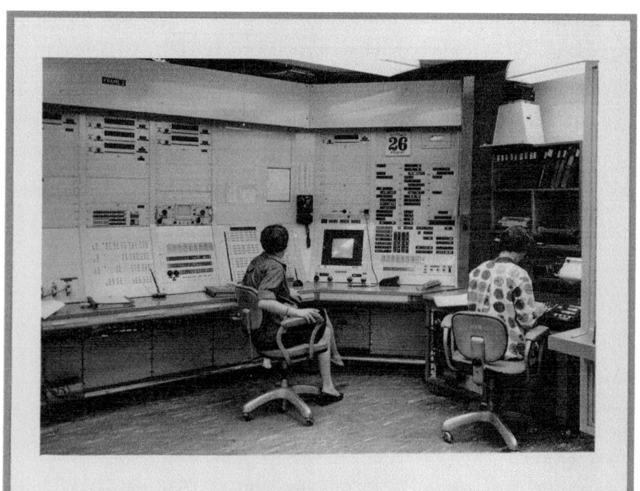

FIGURE 3.1 MIT Museum, *TX-2 Computer*, undated, photography. (Courtesy MIT Museum.)

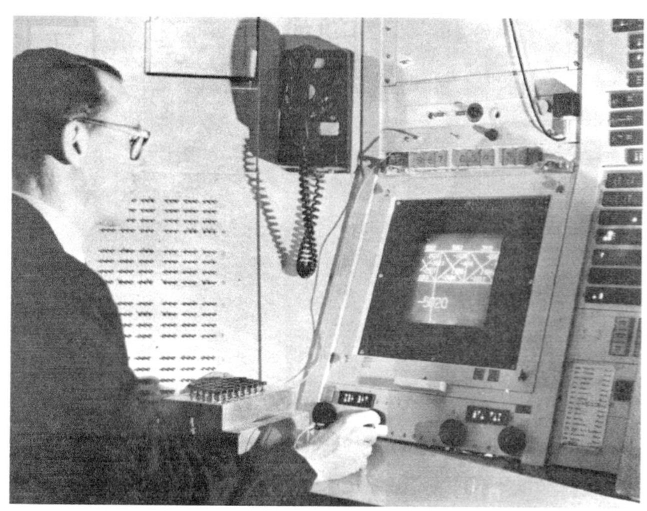

FIGURE 3.2 Ivan E. Sutherland, *TX-2 operating area – Sketchpad in use*, 1963, photography.

total of four: The use is (1) for small changes to existing drawings, (2) for gaining a scientific or technical understanding of graphically representable operations, (3) as a topological input device, for example, for the simulation of circuits and (4) for producing highly repetitive drawings.[10] According to this list, the areas of application of *Sketchpad* are primarily aimed at solving technical questions and problems. In his introduction, Sutherland emphasizes that at the beginning of his research, technical drawings had never been produced on a screen in the way that he had made possible with *Sketchpad*: "[C]onsequently no one knew what it would be like."[11] This statement by Sutherland can be further clarified on the basis of Blackwell's and Rodden's analysis, as it is difficult to understand the challenges Sutherland faced given the ubiquitous use of computers today:

> As with many early publications of computer science, this dissertation is also interesting for the way in which it explores important concepts that are now considered familiar, but which at the time demanded continual small discoveries by every researcher. [...] The struggles of developing custom hardware while also exploring far-reaching abstractions are also far removed from current research experiences.[12]

In their foreword, Blackwell and Rodden highlight several chapters from Sutherland's report. One of these, Chapter 9 "Examples and Conclusions," is also of particular importance to my discussion, as it is here that Sutherland discusses further possible uses of his program in the form of an outlook – aside from the four technical applications of *Sketchpad*. His subsection "Artistic Drawings"[13] is particularly central to my research. Without defining what could constitute the artistic demands of a drawing, Sutherland devotes himself here to the free and creative use of his program and thus provides particularly central insights into his worldview and his understanding of images. I will scrutinize this outlook of Sutherland's in the last of the following four thematic blocks: In the first step, I will highlight his technical equipment and, in a second step, the change that took place in the programming process as a result of *Sketchpad*. In the third step I will examine how these changes have influenced creative processes on the computer, not only back then but also today. In the fourth and final step, I will analyze the free use of *Sketchpad*.

3.1 MULTI-PURPOSE COMPUTERS AND LIGHT PENS – SUTHERLAND'S HARDWARE EQUIPMENT

Although Sutherland was not the first to come up with the idea of drawing on a screen with a pen, he was the first to systematically acknowledge that graphic input on a computer can be used as a control element to communicate with the machine. The insights he gained from the development of *Sketchpad* at that time made a fundamental contribution to the way computers are used today. In their foreword, Blackwell and Rodden also emphasize the change that Sutherland's intention alone brought about in the way computers are used:

> After 40 years, ideas introduced in Sketchpad still influence how every computer user thinks about computing. It made fundamental contributions in the area of human-computer interaction, being one of the first graphical user interfaces. It exploited the light-pen, predecessor of the mouse, allowing the user to point at and interact with objects displayed on the screen. This anticipated many of the interaction conventions of direct manipulation, including clicking a button to select a visible object, and dragging to modify it.[14]

Although this statement by Blackwell and Rodden clearly illustrates the points of reference to the use of computers today, and although I do not intend to downplay the influence of *Sketchpad* on today's computers, I nevertheless assume that Sutherland did not start from scratch with his invention but built on existing work structures beyond Loomis that fostered his ideas. One indicator for this hypothesis is the interdisciplinary nature of his program. Even in the acknowledgments of his report, it is clear from which fields of discipline Sutherland was influenced during the work on his project. He had studied electrical engineering,[15] which is why it is obvious that he first emphasizes his doctoral supervisor, the mathematician and electrical engineer Claude E. Shannon. He also mentions Marvin Minsky, who developed the first simulation of a neural network in 1951.[16] Additionally, he thanks

Steven Anson Coons and Douglas T. Ross, both members of a research group based at MIT at the time, which focused on the field of computer-aided design (CAD). Finally, he mentions Wesley A. Clark who was instrumental in designing the TX-2 computer in 1957,[17] on which Sutherland was later able to develop *Sketchpad*. The field of computer science did not yet exist at that time.[18] Coons played a particularly central role, especially with regard to the understanding of images that still underlies computer graphics today. A separate chapter will therefore be devoted to him in the further course of my study. I will now take a look at Clark and the TX-2 computer, because the way it was designed already anticipated an application like *Sketchpad*.

Before Sutherland realized *Sketchpad* on the TX-2 computer, he used its predecessor, the TX-0, in 1960, which was also equipped with a screen and a light pen. Even then, he had the idea of making it possible to produce line drawings on the computer in the future.[19] He finally approached Clark with his idea in order to agree with him on the potential use of the TX-2 for his project: "I owe a great deal to Mr. Clark's initial enthusiasm and, though I didn't know it at the time, to the many design features he had incorporated into TX-2 seemingly with just such a project in mind."[20] With his statement on the design features of the computer, Sutherland refers to a technical report written by Clark on the development of the computer in 1957.[21] A key feature of both models, the TX-0 and the TX-2, which Clark mentions right at the beginning of his report, is the ability of the computers to process operations in real time. In addition to the CRT screen, with which the TX-2 was also equipped, particular emphasis was placed on increased performance with the TX-2. However, in a subsection entitled "Design Objectives," Clark notes the following:

> In describing design objectives, it should be pointed out that speed of operation was *not* the primary consideration to which all other attributes were sacrificed. [...] The principal objective was rather that of achieving a balance among the factors of speed, reliability, simplicity, flexibility, and general virtue.[22]

In a discussion that took place in connection with Clark's contribution and was also printed in the report, Clark goes on to explain what use he had in mind for his computer: "What motivated the computer was an obvious desire to make something better. [...] This machine is to be used in simulating physical systems."[23] Clark's fairly abstract description of the use of the TX-2 becomes somewhat more concrete in the presentation that followed his at the same conference in 1957. In it, the authors John M. Frankovich and H. Phillip Peterson describe the TX-2 as a "general purpose computer."[24] The term provides an insight into the then-developing idea of using computers not only for special fields but also for general types of application. At that time, the claim of a universality of the devices was envisioned for the first time. In the summary of the report by Frankovich and Peterson, this claim is taken up again, but here they open up a view of a problem that is still debated today and which Sutherland was also confronted with in his development of *Sketchpad*: "However, this versatility and efficiency is not accompanied by a disastrous loss in simplicity. The system organization is such that details can be easily ignored by the naive programmer, without the details having even subtly obtrusive effects."[25] The juxtaposition of the versatile use on the one hand and the concern about a possible loss of complexity on the other is central to this statement. The authors assert that the TX-2 does not lead to an oversimplification of processes despite its versatility, but that a "naive" user can operate it more easily. According to the authors' definition, however, this user must still be understood as someone who knows how to program, as it is clear from their descriptions of the TX-2's operation that the inputs are made via written commands.[26] Ultimately, with *Sketchpad* Sutherland changed the requirements for operating the computer and made it possible to enter graphic elements without being able to program. He describes the way in which the operation was set up for inexperienced users: "The user group experience showed that relatively new users with no programming knowledge could produce simple drawings with the system if a skilled user (myself) prepared the building blocks necessary."[27] Similar to Frankovich and Peterson, Sutherland here opens up a comparison between experienced and "naive" users. However, the problem that emerges with Frankovich and Peterson is further intensified with Sutherland. The separation that Sutherland describes so explicitly here is reminiscent of a statement by media philosopher Vilém Flusser, which he made around 30 years later in 1991 in his essay *Digital Apparition*. Without referring to Sutherland, Flusser speaks here of a "division of society into a few programmers who think numerically and many programmed people who think literally."[28] Blackwell and Rodden also address the juxtaposition of these two groups in their preface. They illustrate the extent to which the challenge that Sutherland faced with his claim is still relevant today. According to them, Sutherland was still trying to use graphical input options to make communication with the computer easier and therefore more generalized, while at the same time hoping to *maintain* the complexity that can be achieved with the input of written commands. However, the current design of user interfaces shows that Sutherland's aspiration could not prevail in the long term:

> In contrast, direct manipulation interfaces have since succeeded by reducing the levels of abstraction exposed to the user. Ongoing research in end-user programming continues to struggle with the question of how to reduce the cognitive challenges of abstract manipulation. Nevertheless, Sutherland's attempt to remove the division between users and programmers was not the only system that, in failing to do so, provided the imaginative leap to a new programming paradigm.[29]

Blackwell and Rodden refer here to the *Simula* programming language, which followed a similar approach to *Sketchpad* and can also be categorized as part of the object-oriented programming paradigm.[30] While *Simula* was the first official and widely used object-oriented programming language, the object-oriented approach was already anticipated conceptually with *Sketchpad* a few years earlier, as noted at the beginning of this chapter. Blackwell and Rodden's reference to the then-new programming paradigm is therefore central to the rest of this chapter and to my study as a whole.

3.2 DEVELOPERS AND USERS – A NEW FIELD OF TENSION

Until Sutherland's *Sketchpad*, the usual approach was to describe a process on the computer from start to finish, which means that the goal needed to be known at the start of a process and was aimed for from the outset.[31] *Sketchpad*, on the other hand, was designed in such a way that the process could begin openly, and once a result had been produced, it could be changed subsequently. With Sutherland's *Sketchpad*, a change from the procedural to the so-called object-oriented programming paradigm took place for the first time. Although Sutherland himself did not yet use the term object-oriented programming, he developed his own terms for the program features he designed, which make the paradigm shift recognizable. The individual operations are presented and defined in a glossary at the end of his report. Many of these operating elements are still in use today, such as copying or deleting an element. The object-oriented programming process can be illustrated particularly well with Sutherland's so-called instances. Sutherland himself ascribes them a particularly central role within *Sketchpad*, as they are "[t]he most powerful tool [...] for creating large complex drawings quickly and easily."[32] Sutherland explains the term as follows:

> A fixed geometry subpicture represented very compactly in storage by reference to a *master* and indication by four numbers of the size, rotation, and location of the subpicture. Internal structure of an instance is visible and may contain other instances, but since it is identical in appearance to the *master* it cannot be changed without changing the *master*. Except for size, rotation, and location, all instances of one *master* look the same.[33]

This abstract definition can be illustrated, for example, using a schematic representation of an electrical circuit. If the circuit is to contain several light bulbs, it is sufficient to first draw one light bulb as a *master* image. Then, instances of this image can be created to represent the other light bulbs. Each instance can have its own position in the image, but its appearance is always identical to the master image. If you wish to make a change to all light bulbs, it is sufficient to change only the master image. All instances in the circuit adapt at the same time. And if one of the light bulbs is to be used for something else, one of the instances can be converted into a copy, making it an independent object that can be changed without affecting the appearance of the previously connected instances. The instance would be removed from the hierarchical structure and saved as a copy parallel to the master drawing of the light bulb as a separate structure.[34] This distinction between instance and copy developed by Sutherland has been preserved to this day. Both the software and the hardware are different today, but comparable functions can be found in everyday computer use.[35]

These two *Sketchpad* functions, and particularly the parallel processes and hierarchies shown, illustrate what characterizes the new paradigm: A procedural programming process would, in contrast, have had to be restarted if a change had been requested to a finished circuit drawing. Sutherland recognized that the ability to make subsequent changes opens up the work process. The consequence of this new way of working on the computer that is particularly relevant to my analysis is the possibility of no longer having to know the work goal at the start of the activity. It was only during his work on *Sketchpad* that Sutherland realized that this new openness in the work process expanded the field of application for his program beyond what he had previously anticipated:

> The organization of the elements of the drawing into types has facilitated the generalization of the programs which comprise the Sketchpad system. The effort toward generality came relatively late in the research effort because I did not at first appreciate the power that a general approach could bring. Considerable reprogramming was done, however, to include as much generality as possible.[36]

Sutherland's use of the term "generality" is reminiscent of the preliminary work of his colleagues, who designed the TX-2, on which Sutherland programmed *Sketchpad*, as a "general purpose computer." However, the fact that *Sketchpad* made it possible for the first time to work with the computer without being able to program gave the term "generality" a new level of meaning. *Sketchpad* could not only be used as a *general* drawing program, but it also opened up the *general* possibility for everyone to work with it for the first time. With this opening, which refers not only to the work process itself but also to the circle of users, Sutherland provides a central basis for the question I pursue in my study about the production process and the assumption that computer graphics share a common context of meaning: As long as not every person has the ability to program, the possibility of a *general* use of the computer can only be attained by *predefining* work processes on the computer. Sutherland therefore had to create a framework, or more precisely: a *limitation*, in order to enable greater freedom in the application of his program. In addition, his work encouraged the division between programmers and users, i.e. between experts and laymen. The shift to the object-oriented programming paradigm therefore means that half of the production process for digital products remains hidden. While the procedural programming process contains the entire production process of a finished image, because the fields of development and application still basically coincide here, the object-oriented programming paradigm divides the production process into two phases for the first time: One that concerns the developer and one that concerns the user. However, the first phase can only be surmised as a trace[37] in the form of available operations. The second phase, the application of the operations, is the visible part of the creative process. Designing a synthetic image, for instance, only begins here on the surface of the user interface. For all digital products that are not created as part of a procedural programming process, it is therefore true that their production process is divided into two phases and that they share a common context of meaning in the first, hidden phase, regardless of which production steps take place in the second phase. Sutherland's contribution to the common context of meaning of synthetic images therefore becomes evident on this basic level. However, to understand the creation of synthetic images in terms of production aesthetics, it is not only necessary to know that there are available operations behind which a programming process is concealed but also to ask how the selection of these operations came about. What was the intention to develop certain program features and not others? What are the motives behind the intention? Based on the selection of program features that Sutherland developed for *Sketchpad*, his worldview and a particular understanding of images can be discerned. To illustrate this, in the last two sections I will present some of these features and their artistic application.

3.3 COPY AND PASTE – INTERACTION AND EFFICIENCY IN *SKETCHPAD*

Blackwell and Rodden's observation that Sutherland was unable to overcome the boundary between user and programmer (see also in Section 3.1) can be further emphasized based on the findings from the previous section. Sutherland was the first to bring about with such clarity the two phases in the production process and, along with it, an even stronger separation between the developer and user. Although, according to Blackwell and Rodden, Sutherland's own aim was not to reduce the complexity of communication with the computer, he was forced to define certain operations that he found useful when working with *Sketchpad*, as his program was also intended to be suitable for non-experts. Since he was convinced of the general applicability of his program, which would, for instance, differ from specialist requirements such as in the field of engineering drawing, the program features he developed are an expression of his conviction that he would be able to implement this general usage requirement. In his report, it becomes clear that he does not question whether general functions are possible at all but rather presupposes them:

> In the process of making the Sketchpad system operate, a few very general functions were developed which make no reference at all to the specific types of entities on which they operate. These general functions give the Sketchpad system the ability to operate on a wide range of problems. The motivation for making the functions as general as possible came from the desire to get as much result as possible from the programming effort involved. For example, the general function for expanding instances makes it possible for Sketchpad to handle *any* fixed geometry subpicture. The rewards that come from implementing general functions are so great that the author has become reluctant to write any programs for specific jobs.[38]

How is it that Sutherland so naturally assumed the possibility of a general benefit of his program? His phrasing "as general as possible"[39] expresses implicitly that he must have been aware of the extent to which every general function is nevertheless accompanied by a restriction or at least a definition, but here it becomes clear once again that to him such a definition does not contradict his idea of generality.

Sutherland's mindset becomes even more evident when considering his so-called constraints. These are commands in programming language that define the relationship between several elements in the form of conditions.[40] Sutherland's own definition of the term confirms that the use of constraints is a consciously applied restriction: "A specific storage representation of a relationship between *variables* which limits the freedom of the *variables*, i.e., reduces the number of degrees of freedom of the system."[41] Sutherland has programmed a series of such constraints so that they can be called up and applied at any time when creating a drawing in *Sketchpad*. Alongside the features of copies and instances, to him, the constraints form an essential part of *Sketchpad*, as they "[relate] the parts of a drawing in any computable way."[42] Sutherland uses an example to explain the constraints he has developed for *Sketchpad*:

> When we asked that the vertices of the hexagon lie on the circle we were making use of a basic relationship between picture parts that is built into the system. Basic relationships (atomic constraints) to make lines vertical, horizontal, parallel, or perpendicular; to make points lie on lines or circles; to make symbols appear upright, vertically above one another or be of equal size; and to relate symbols to other drawing parts such as points and lines have been included in the system. It is so easy to program new constraint types that the set of atomic constraints was expanded from five to the seventeen listed in Appendix A in a period of about two days; specialized constraint types may be added as needed.[43]

In order to program the constraints, Sutherland therefore tried to anticipate many different conditions that could arise during the drawing process, such as how lines in the image relate to each other, i.e. whether they should, for example, appear parallel or at right angles to each other. At the same time, he explains in the introduction to his report that the original decision to create a drawing feature on the computer was not to recreate the conventional tools required to produce design drawings, but primarily to find out what

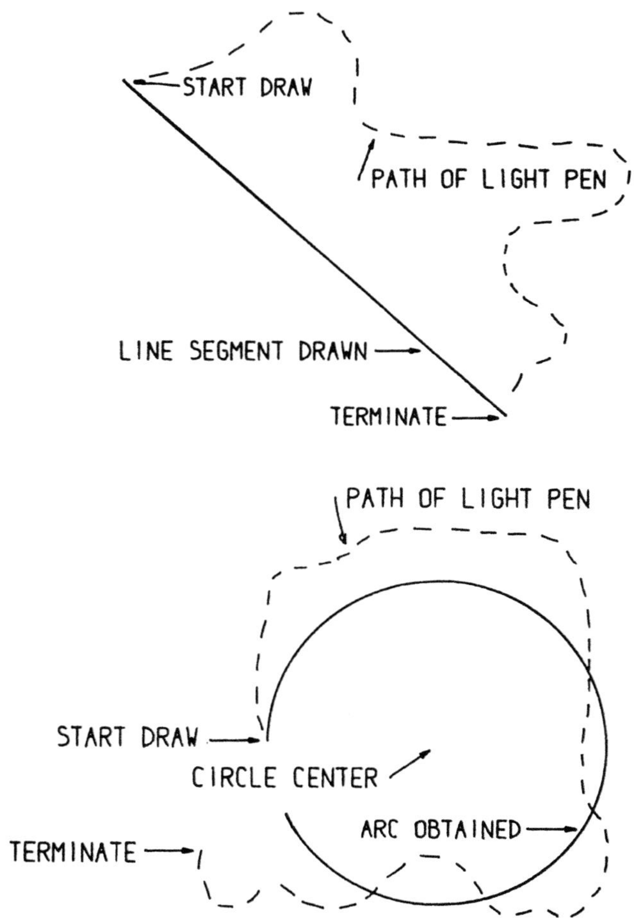

FIGURE 3.3 Ivan E. Sutherland, *Line and circle drawing*, 1963, Sketchpad drawing.

purposes such a system might later be suitable for. Therefore, the drawing process in *Sketchpad* is not directly comparable with drawing on paper, as also Figure 3.3 illustrates:

> [I]t was implicit in the research nature of the work that simple new facilities should be discovered which, when implemented, should be useful in a wide range of applications, preferably including some unforseen [*sic*] ones. It has turned out that the properties of a computer drawing are entirely different from a paper drawing not only because of the accuracy, ease of drawing, and speed of erasing provided by the computer, but also primarily because of the ability to move drawing parts around on a computer drawing without the need to erase them. Had a working system not been developed, our thinking would have been too strongly influenced by a lifetime of drawing on paper to discover many of the useful services that the computer can provide.[44]

Sutherland's description points to a reciprocity between old and new production processes that has characterized the development of *Sketchpad*. On the one hand, the very differences that Sutherland lists in contrast to the conventional drawing process demonstrate that they still serve as the starting point for programming new tools, because a deviation can only be conceived from an existing phenomenon. On the other hand, however, it becomes apparent here to what extent Sutherland articulates clear ideas for the use of the computer that give the drawing process a completely new character of its own, even though these ideas refer back to the traditional process. That this new way of working with the computer, initiated by Sutherland, has survived to this day can be demonstrated by the fact that the program features that Sutherland developed are reminiscent of the everyday use of computer programs today. Even common word processing programs offer simple layout options in which objects can be duplicated, moved, rotated, deleted or aligned in a certain relationship to one another using comparable functions to those Sutherland had developed.[45] My examination of Sutherland's *Sketchpad* thus demonstrates that each of these functions, which are still available today and seem so natural, was defined and developed at a specific point in time with a specific motivation. And although Sutherland's exemplary description shows that he endeavored to achieve with the extensibility of the constraints the greatest possible freedom in their use, an inexperienced user of any program remains dependent on previously defined features. The restrictions associated with these features, which – as mentioned – paradoxically facilitate and thus democratize general access to the devices, are reflected in the term 'constraints' in a very literal sense.

But against which backdrop did Sutherland develop his constraints? If he wanted to use *Sketchpad* to break away from conventional drawing on paper – as described above – and he himself emphasized that "the Sketchpad drawing itself is entirely different from the trail of carbon left on a piece of paper,"[46] how did he decide which functions would become part of *Sketchpad* and which would not? Since – as he states – it would not have been a challenge for him to develop further operation modes, he nevertheless prioritized certain production steps with those that his program version had ready at the end of his research. As I described previously, according to Sutherland, *Sketchpad* was particularly suitable for drawings that serve to solve technical questions and problems. Despite his references to the differences between the drawing tools used on the computer and on paper, his report provides evidence in the sense of the reciprocity I mentioned above that a certain idea of a conventional drawing process served him as a point of orientation in *Sketchpad*, not in terms of craftsmanship, but at least conceptually:

> Construction of a drawing with Sketchpad is *itself* a model of the design process. The locations of the points and lines of the drawing model the variables of a design, and the goemetric [*sic*] constraints applied to the points and lines of the drawing model the design constraints which limit the values of design variables. The ability of Sketchpad to satisfy the geometric constraints applied to the parts of a drawing models the ability of a good designer to satisfy all the design conditions imposed by the limitations of his materials, cost, etc. In fact, since designers in many fields produce nothing themselves but a drawing of a part, design conditions may well be thought of as applying to the drawing of a part rather than to the part itself. If such design conditions were added to Sketchpad's vocabulary of constraints the computer could assist a user not only in arriving at a nice looking drawing, but also in arriving at a sound design.[47]

Sutherland's view that the drawing process within *Sketchpad* is itself a model of a design process explicitly underlines my assumption that the design of this first graphical computer application was conceived against the backdrop of existing work processes – an observation that does not change the fact that new workflows and processes in the operation of the computer can later also emerge. This reciprocity inherent in the development process of *Sketchpad* illustrates a phenomenon that can also be observed elsewhere in the context of software development. The phenomenon is taken up again and discussed in detail, for example, in the chapter on Steven Coons in Section 5.2.

Sutherland's consideration of conventional design processes provides insights into his understanding of creative processes, which also provides clues to his conception of images. If one recalls the fields of application that Sutherland primarily envisioned for the use of *Sketchpad*, it becomes clear that he was initially primarily concerned with drawings in technical contexts. His concept of "universality" could therefore be limited exclusively to the range of technical drawings which actually do follow a specific and perhaps universal set of rules, as they must be unambiguously legible when used in the production of components. Nevertheless, Sutherland's report gives reason to assume that his idea of a universal field of application for *Sketchpad* includes drawings outside of technical professions. In the abstract alone, he announces: "[Sketchpad] has been seen to draw electrical, mechanical, scientific, mathematical, and animated drawings; it is a general purpose system."[48] Although it is clear that Sutherland did not refer to general design principles but to specific ones that were probably only customary in his work environment, his report shows that he attributed universal validity to this highly specialist and therefore one-sided approach. This mindset could be explained by the fact that Sutherland presumably had the conception of a universally valid pictoriality. In other words, he may have been convinced that the images traditionally used in his environment represent the entire spectrum of all possible pictorial worlds:

> The usual picture for human consumption displays only lines, circles, text, digits, and instances. However certain very useful abstractions are represented in the ring structure storage which give the drawing the properties desired by the user. [...] To make it possible for a user to manipulate these abstractions, each abstraction must be able to be seen on the display if desired. [...] The light pen demonstrative language [...] is sufficient for making all changes to objects or abstractions which can be displayed. To make Sketchpad's light pen language universal, *all* objects and abstractions represented in Sketchpad's ring structure can be displayed.[49]

It is not clear what type of image Sutherland is describing here with the phrase "usual picture." However, his reference to the representation of instances initially suggests that he is referring exclusively to images created in *Sketchpad*. But while for him this usual picture typically consists of lines and circles as well as text elements, numbers and instances, he offers – with the possible modifications of these components – an approach with which any conceivable change could be made to an image, provided the alterations could be viewed on the display. This characteristic of his program leads him to classify the operating options he has developed within *Sketchpad* as universal. Therefore it can be assumed that with his phrase "usual picture" he actually wants to express that universally valid images not only exist but also that they can be created using equally universally valid design principles. Given this context, it is understandable why he does not regard the discrepancy between experts and laypeople as problematic. For if, according to his conception, his program reproduces universally valid parameters, the available program features are not, strictly speaking, restrictions, or if they are, then only those that apply equally to all forms of imagery, regardless of whether a computer is even involved in the creation or not. Sutherland clearly had no fear of overlooking anything or of influencing potential users in a one-sided way.

This mindset can be illustrated particularly impressively in his final subsection, in which he presents his "Artistic Drawings."[50] Here it becomes evident to what extent the program features he developed fulfill – at least from his perspective – his idea of a universal application possibility. At the same time, these examples show that the supposed universality reflects a very specific idea of pictoriality that is confined to a narrow framework. In order to condense and sharpen the results presented so far, Sutherland's "Artistic Drawings" will now be discussed in the last section of this chapter.

3.4 *SKETCHPAD* AND ART – OPEN WORK PROCESSES ON THE COMPUTER

Sutherland explores the artistic application of *Sketchpad* in a separate subsection, which he calls "Artistic Drawings." This is embedded in the final chapter, "Examples and Conclusions,"[51] in which Sutherland presents prospects for the further use of *Sketchpad*. As I have already pointed out above, Sutherland linked the openness of *Sketchpad* to the program's universal applicability. It could therefore be argued, to put it bluntly, that Sutherland's idea of the "universality" of his program not only includes free and artistic drawings but is actually dependent on them. Accordingly, only a completely free use of *Sketchpad* can be the justification for him to refer to the program as a "general purpose system."[52] If *Sketchpad* had been designed exclusively for the production of technical drawings that are always subject to strict rules, neither this designation nor the announcement of a universal application would have been valid. At the same time, however, it can be questioned whether *Sketchpad* could really allow for a completely free use. In this final section on Sutherland, I therefore propose that his very idea of being able to develop a universal design tool with pre-programmed application modules expresses, again, not only a particular worldview, but also a certain conception of images. This conception becomes particularly apparent in the examples that Sutherland presents to demonstrate the free use of his program. His idea of artistic work, which he expresses in his subsection "Artistic Drawings," is not to be evaluated here; I rather focus on the insights that can be derived from his examples with regard to the aim of my study, which is to describe 3D computer graphics in terms of production aesthetics.

In an earlier section of his report, Sutherland expresses the vision of an infinitely expandable program and thus indirectly an inexhaustible source of free, creative work. He calls the section "The as yet undreamt of things that will be displayed."[53] This phrasing suggests that Sutherland seems almost proud to have found a way to think of programming a computer so openly that no goal needs to be defined beforehand. The explanation that follows remains vague with regard to the artistic application of his program, but it picks up on the eagerness of the title:

> At the present time the need for dotted lines and circles, including center lines, dark lines, etc. and the need for a ratio type unitless scalar for representing angles and proportions is clear. Conic sections would be useful. What other kinds of things may become useful for special purposes is as yet unknown. Sketchpad attempts to be big enough to incorporate anything easily.[54]

In the summary of his report – even before he turns to the "Artistic Drawings" – he expresses this vision more clearly. He begins his conclusion with the aspect of efficiency. For example, he emphasizes that the production of complex technical drawings can be completed much more quickly using *Sketchpad*, in contrast to the manual approach. For example, a drawing of 900 hexagons took around half an hour, "including the time taken to figure out how to do it."[55] According to a prognosis from the drafting department with which Sutherland consulted, it would have taken two days to complete manually (Figure 3.4).[56] In addition to numerous other examples of the use of *Sketchpad* in the area of technical drawings or for engineering calculations, which primarily serve to optimize existing processes,[57] Sutherland turns to a feature of his program that he considers "[b]y far the most interesting application of Sketchpad."[58] This production-aesthetic detail is also informative for my research interest. These are so-called linkages, i.e. gears and mechanisms in which different elements of a component – and in Sutherland's case a drawing – can be linked and set in motion. An example that is not mentioned by Sutherland but which can be used to illustrate what is meant by this in engineering is the scissor mechanism used in lifting platforms.[59] Sutherland emphasizes that a manipulation option

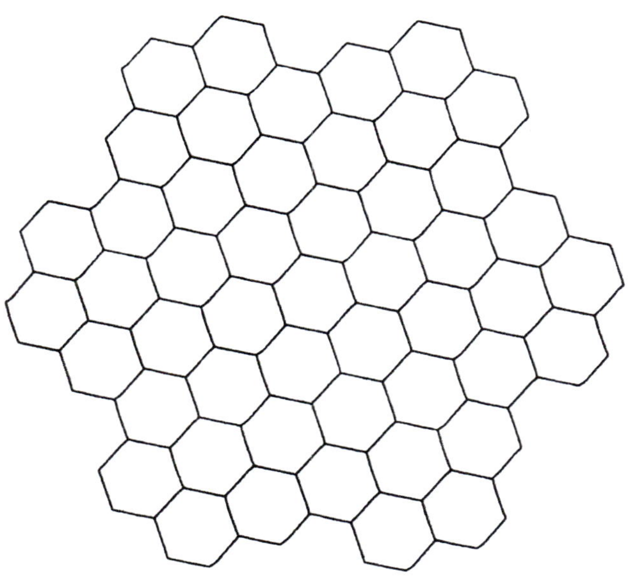

FIGURE 3.4 Ivan E. Sutherland, *Hexagonal pattern*, 1963, Sketchpad drawing.

in the form of moving computer graphics has never existed before,[60] and so it is precisely this function that for him holds the greatest potential for the free, creative use of *Sketchpad*, as he explains in the subsection "Artistic Drawings":

> Sketchpad need not be applied only to engineering drawings. The ability to put motion into the drawings suggests that it would be exciting to try making cartoons. The capability of Sketchpad to store previously drawn information on magnetic tape means that every cartoon component ever drawn is available for future use. If the almost identical but slightly different frames that are required for making a motion picture cartoon could be produced semi-automatically, the entire Sketchpad system could justify itself economically in yet another way.[61]

Although Sutherland's prediction was not realized to any great extent within *Sketchpad*, it is clear that with his idea of animating computer graphic elements, he anticipated a later, commercially very promising use of computer graphics. Blackwell and Rodden also emphasize: "Now, of course, we are used to seeing entire feature films created from computer graphics."[62] Against this background, it seems reasonable that about ten years later, Sutherland himself became a member of Edwin Catmull's thesis committee, who, as described in the introduction, conducted research as a doctoral student in Utah and later realized the vision of animated computer graphics with the *Pixar Animation Studios* in commercially very successful pioneering work. While the aspect of animation is not my focus, it is all the more important for my further investigation that a visual-aesthetic bridge can be built from Sutherland to Catmull. This connection is evident in the fact that Catmull first made a concept of images visible in his Pixar films that can already be recognized in Sutherland's work. The visual approaches that he pursued in his free use of *Sketchpad*, and that can be linked to Catmull, I will now analyze in the final part of this section. However, I will explore the connection between Sutherland and Catmull more comprehensively at a later point, after I have also brought Coons' conception of imagery into focus. Nevertheless, it can already be stated here that before a specific understanding of images emerged with Catmull in a wide-ranging way, also on a visual or rather *visible* level, the mere concept of what an image could or should be was gradually inscribed in the genealogy of computer graphics software development in the form of ready-to-use program features, as for example established by Sutherland. Therefore, the central question remains: On which conception of images did Sutherland base his program features? An answer to this question is necessary to understand the starting point of the developments that have reached – at least from the perspective I adopt with this study – an end point with Catmull.

To illustrate the openness of *Sketchpad* and its potential for animation, Sutherland uses a drawing of a stylized face of a girl created with the light pen.[63] Simple contours made up of geometric elements such as lines and circles are used to depict key features of the face and the surrounding hair (Figure 3.5). Sutherland describes how he could make the girl blink by creating detailed drawings of one of the two eyes in an open, half-open and closed state and displaying them in quick succession. He calls this process "cartooning by substitution"[64] which, as he explains, represents one of two ways of animating with the help of *Sketchpad*. Sutherland is satisfied with the effect of this method: "Doing this on the computer display has amused many visitors."[65] With the second animation method, which utilizes the 'linkages' explained above, the girl's hair could also be made to swing. According to Sutherland, this approach is "the more usual form of cartooning seen in movies,"[66] although he does not explain why he holds this view. He also does not provide any examples, but it is possible to discern two different levels of meaning in his use of the term "cartooning." On the one hand, as the quote above indicates, he uses it synonymously with the term cartoon animation; on the other hand, he uses it to describe the process of sketching, as his second example shows. In it, he again presents the drawing of a female face, and he emphasizes:

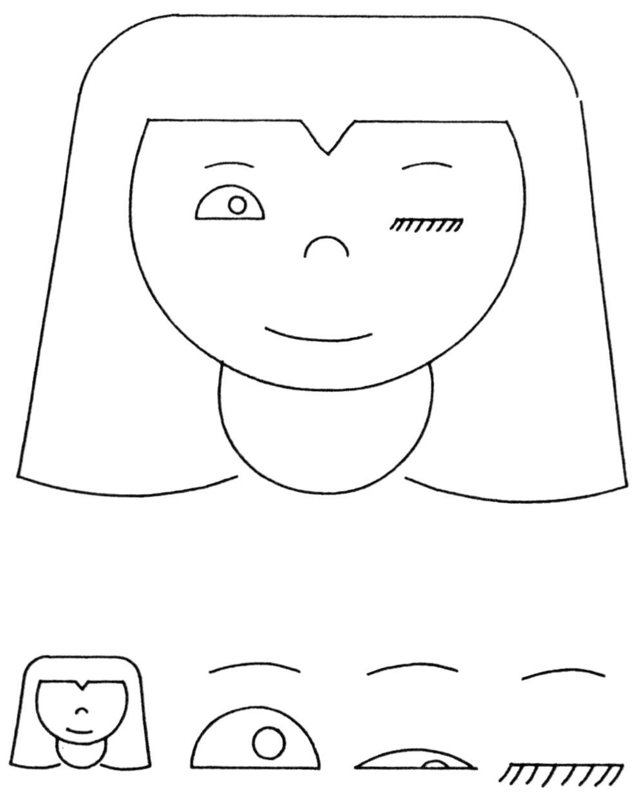

FIGURE 3.5 Ivan E. Sutherland, *Winking girl and components*, 1963, Sketchpad drawing.

> Aside from its economics as a teaching or amusement device, cartooning can bring the insights which are the prime value of Sketchpad drawings. The girl seen in Figure 9.9 was traced from a photograph into the Sketchpad system. The photograph was read into the computer by a facsimile machine used in another project and shown in outline on the computer display. This outline was then traced with wax pencil on the display face. Later, with Sketchpad in the computer, the outline was made into a Sketchpad drawing by tracing the wax line with the light pen.[67]

Here, Sutherland announces a key insight for him, and, as he points out later in his chapter, it relates not only to the described drawing process but above all to the post-processing of the image – it was, in this manner, possible for the first time because of *Sketchpad*. Sutherland illustrates his experiments with further pictures. While one illustration shows the "original" line drawing, another one shows an edited version of the face. In it the mouth and eyes were first removed to create a face without any facial features (Figure 3.6). Subsequently, everything but one eye was removed from a saved version of the original drawing, and, in a second process,

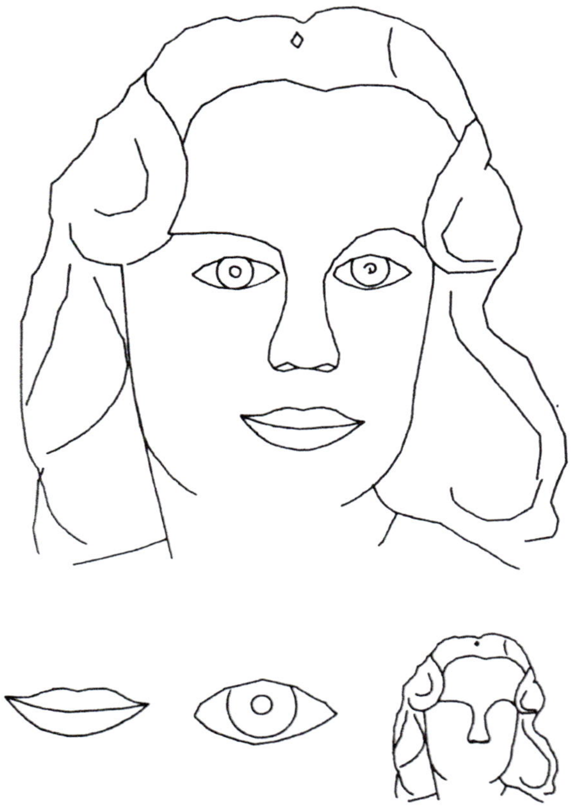

FIGURE 3.6 Ivan E. Sutherland, *Girl traced from photograph*, 1963, Sketchpad drawing.

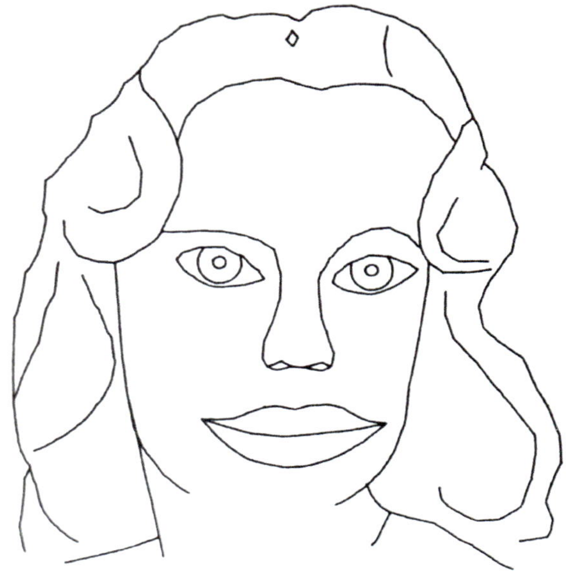

FIGURE 3.7 Ivan E. Sutherland, *Girl with features changed*, 1963, Sketchpad drawing.

everything but the mouth, so that three individual components of the face could now be saved separately: The "empty" face, one eye and the mouth. Sutherland then rearranged the individual facial features, first duplicating the single eye and then reinserting the new pair of eyes together with the mouth in a slightly enlarged form in their original position (Figure 3.7). In his descriptions of this free and creative approach to *Sketchpad*, it becomes clear not only that he understood these work steps as an artistic process but also, above all, that Sutherland saw the program as part of this process. This creates the impression that Sutherland regarded his program as an equal and independent partner from whom he could learn something and with whom he could pursue a creative task in collaborative cooperation:

> In refitting the features to the blank face, we discovered that, although the original girl was a sweet looking miss, an entirely different character appears if her mouth is made larger [...]. Using a computer to partially automate an artistic process has brought me, a non-artist, some understanding of the effect of certain features on the appearance of a face. It is the understanding that can be gained from computer drawings that is more valuable than mere production of a drawing for shop use.[68]

Sutherland's reflections on how *Sketchpad* can be used beyond purely technical issues provide insights on two levels: First, it becomes clear that he understood artistic processes as open processes, in which the definition of a goal is not the main focus; second, he confirms here my assumption that it is precisely these artistic approaches that enable him to speak of a "general purpose system." In his opinion, it is primarily the artistic activities that can exploit the potential of his program.

Although it is true that *Sketchpad* has for the first time facilitated such great openness in working with the computer that artistic, or at least free, creative processes can also benefit from it, the exemplary drawings show how strongly the creative process was dictated by the functions within *Sketchpad*. In the previous section, I considered whether Sutherland's statement about the "usual picture for human consumption,"[69] which, according to him, consists solely of lines, circles, text, numbers and instances, refers exclusively to designs in technical contexts. In connection with the operating functions of *Sketchpad*, which he considered to be universal, I concluded that Sutherland actually did have the idea of universal design principles or a universal pictoriality that goes beyond technical concerns. This conclusion can be confirmed based on the two drawings that he defined as "artistic drawings." However, I do not want to argue here that he deliberately based his development of the drawing tools within *Sketchpad* on a specific concept of image or art. Yet, the image examples make it evident that he considered the tools, that he developed for technical purposes, suitable as well for artistic and, consequently, general use. It could therefore be argued that Sutherland viewed images in general, including artistic images, as technical drawings and accordingly as drawings that are not only very precise but also predictable. Within this defined framework, Sutherland has thus developed operating functions that can be used in a variety of ways, even by non-experts, and that can also be used experimentally – as he demonstrates – but which, in accordance with the assumption I made at the beginning of this part, always reproduce his idea of pictoriality and consequently a certain way of working.

In two respects, it can now be shown to what extent this visual language anchored in *Sketchpad* cannot – as Sutherland claimed – be considered universal: First, this can be illustrated by referring to the research context in which Sutherland's work took place. As I mentioned earlier, I want to bring Steven A. Coons into focus for this purpose. Coons was a member of Sutherland's thesis committee and the only one of the members Sutherland mentions, for example, in his acknowledgments, who had a background as a draftsman and experience in the field of CAD. On the one hand, Coons can therefore be used to definitively derive Sutherland's visual language paradigm; on the other hand, Coons can also be used to illustrate how this understanding of images was able to find its way into the operation of the computer. Second, the insights into Sutherland's concept of images can be sharpened if the path of the historiography I pursue here is supplemented by some exemplary parallel developments in the field of computer graphics. These developments can be seen as parallel simply because, unlike Sutherland, they did not pursue the goal of exploring communication between humans and computers but instead took image generation itself as their starting point. As Sutherland's new approach was not yet widespread, these alternative approaches followed the procedural programming paradigm. In terms of production aesthetics, they therefore form a contrast to Sutherland's work method. Before focusing on Coons, these parallel developments will first be described.

NOTES

1. Ivan E. Sutherland, "Sketchpad: A Man-Machine Graphical Communication System" (technical report, ed. Alan Blackwell and Kerry Rodden, University of Cambridge, 2003), Computer Laboratory (UCAM-CL-TR-574), 17.
2. See Ivan E. Sutherland, "Sketchpad. A Man-Machine Graphical Communication System" (PhD diss., Massachusetts Institute of Technology, 1963), MIT Libraries, DSpace@MIT (15036306), 24.
3. The text of the original version was not changed: "We also chose not to correct any errors we found in the original document, in order to provide the textual equivalent of a facsimile edition. These include a few spelling errors (to Ivan's embarrassment), and also the rather idiosyncratic fact that the original dissertation had two pages 106." Alan Blackwell and Kerry Rodden, "Preface," in "Sketchpad: A Man-Machine Graphical Communication System" (technical report by Ivan E. Sutherland, ed. Alan Blackwell and Kerry Rodden, University of Cambridge, 2003), Computer Laboratory (UCAM-CL-TR-574), 5.
4. Blackwell and Rodden, "Preface," 3. The conference paper referred to here bears the same name as the report and summarizes the results presented in detail therein in an abridged form. The page numbers given by Blackwell and Rodden in their bibliography differ from the information given in the conference catalog. See Ivan E. Sutherland, "Sketchpad," in *Proceedings of the Spring Joint Computer Conference – AFIPS '63*, ed. E. Calvin Johnson (New York: ACM Press, 1963). There is no bibliographical reference to the film mentioned by the authors here. It can be assumed that they are referring to a 1964 television program produced by MIT, which shows not only the use of *Sketchpad* but also the *Sketchpad III* version of the program developed by the later Master's student Timothy Johnson, which also enabled perspective drawings

for the first time. Both Johnson's contribution and the film are discussed again in Chapters 5 and 7. See John Fitch, *MIT Science Reporter*, "Computer Sketchpad," directed by Russell Morash (Boston: National Educational Television, 1964).

5. See Sutherland, "Sketchpad" (2003), 35.
6. Sutherland, "Sketchpad" (2003), 32.
7. Sutherland, "Sketchpad" (2003), 31. See Herschel H. Loomis, "Graphical Manipulation Techniques Using the Lincoln TX-2 Computer" (technical report, Massachusetts Institute of Technology, 1960). MIT Libraries, Distinctive Collections.
8. Loomis, "Graphical Manipulation Techniques," 1.
9. In accordance with the procedural programming paradigm, Loomis lists so-called "Program Flow Diagrams" in his document, in which the procedural structure of his approach becomes visible. See Loomis, "Graphical Manipulation Techniques," 16–18.
10. See Sutherland, "Sketchpad" (2003), 28–29.
11. Sutherland, "Sketchpad" (2003), 28.
12. Blackwell and Rodden, "Preface," 4.
13. Sutherland, "Sketchpad" (2003), 107.
14. Blackwell and Rodden, "Preface," 3.
15. He completed his bachelor's degree at the *Carnegie Institute of Technology* (now *Carnegie Mellon University*) and his master's degree at the *California Institute of Technology*. See, e.g., Ivan E. Sutherland, "An Interview with Ivan Sutherland," interview by Karen A. Frenkel, *Communications of the ACM* 32, no. 6 (1989): 711, https://doi.org/10.1145/63526.63531
16. Sutherland got to know the mathematician and electrical engineer Claude E. Shannon together with his brother Bert in his youth, long before he later conducted research at MIT. Shannon had a great influence on Sutherland through this early encounter, as Sutherland himself describes. See Sutherland, interview by Frenkel, 712; see "Marvin Minsky," MIT, Marvin Minsky, accessed December 11, 2021. https://web.media.mit.edu/~minsky/
17. See Wesley A. Clark, "The Lincoln TX-2 Computer Development," in *Western Joint Computer Conference – IRE-AIEE-ACM '57*, ed. Morton M. Astrahan (New York: ACM Press, 1957).
18. While Sutherland was still working on the completion of *Sketchpad* at MIT, a new department was formed there in 1963, which was initially known as *Project MAC* (Multiple Access Computing or Machine-Aided Cognition) and only later adopted the term computer science. In an interview conducted in 1989, Sutherland refers to the fact that he was able to show *Sketchpad* to some of those involved in the founding of *Project MAC*, but that he himself was not involved. At the same time, it is clear from the interview that *Project MAC* was also supported by ARPA, albeit before Sutherland's own employment there. See Sutherland, interview by Aspray, 4, 8. Today, the department is called *Computer Science & Artificial Intelligence Lab* (CSAIL). Similar to the research project in Utah, the beginnings of these research fields were also supported at MIT with military funds: "CSAIL has its roots in two MIT computing powerhouses: The Laboratory for Computer Science (LCS) and the Artificial Intelligence Laboratory (AI Lab). [...] LCS was founded in 1963 as Project MAC (Multiple Access Computing or Machine-Aided Cognition), a project sponsored by the Department of Defense to develop a computer system accessible to a large number of people." "Mission & History," MIT, CSAIL, accessed on December 11, 2021, https://www.csail.mit.edu/about/mission-history.
19. See Sutherland, "Sketchpad" (2003), 31.
20. Sutherland, "Sketchpad" (2003), 31.
21. The naming of the two generations of the computer is derived from technical features that characterize the two devices, which is why there is no TX-1 model: "After some thought about the various possible minimal machines, a design was completed in which the word length would be 18 bits – a graceful half of the projected final form. We began to refer to this computer as the TX-0 and to the projected machine as the TX-2." Clark, "The Lincoln TX-2," 144.
22. Clark, "The Lincoln TX-2," 144, emphasis in original.
23. Clark, "The Lincoln TX-2," 145.
24. John M. Frankovich and H. Phillip Peterson, "A Functional Description of the Lincoln TX-2 Computer," in *Western Joint Computer Conference – IRE-AIEE-ACM '57*, ed. M. M. Astrahan (New York: ACM Press, 1957), 150.
25. Frankovich and Peterson, "A Functional Description of TX-2," 154.
26. See Frankovich and Peterson, "A Functional Description of TX-2," 146.
27. Sutherland, "Sketchpad" (2003), 35.
28. Vilém Flusser, "Digitaler Schein," in *Digitaler Schein: Ästhetik der elektronischen Medien*, ed. Florian Rötzer (Frankfurt am Main: Suhrkamp, 1991), 151. In the English translation of Flusser's essay, the part in which the quote can be found has been omitted. See Vilém Flusser, "Digital Apparition," in *Electronic Culture: Technology and Visual Representation*, ed. Timothy Druckrey (New York: Aperture, 1996).
29. Blackwell and Rodden, "Preface," 3–4.
30. *Simula* is a programming language developed by two Norwegian computer scientists, Ole-Johan Dahl and Kristen Nygaard, in the 1960s. Casey Alt describes how Alan Kay, who coined the term "object-oriented" a little later, intensively studied both *Simula* and *Sketchpad* before developing his own language, *Smalltalk*. He recognized that both systems functioned in a very similar way. See Casey

Alt, "The Materialities of Maya: Making Sense of Object-Orientation," *Configurations* 10, no. 3 (2002): 409–10, and Ole-Johan Dahl and Kristen Nygaard, "SIMULA: An ALGOL-Based Simulation Language," *Communications of the ACM* 9, no. 9 (1966).
31. For a comprehensive explanation of various procedural programming approaches, see Casey Alt, "Objects of Our Affection. How Object Orientation Made Computers a Medium," in *Media Archaeology. Approaches, Applications, and Implications*, ed. Erkki Huhtamo and Jussi Parikka (Berkeley, Los Angeles: University of California Press, 2011), 288–91.
32. Sutherland, "Sketchpad" (2003), 82.
33. Sutherland, "Sketchpad" (2003), 142, emphasis in original.
34. See Sutherland, "Sketchpad" (2003), 142.
35. In the 3D graphics software *Autodesk Maya*, the concept of instances is still used today. The function is also similar to Sutherland's program: "The Duplicate and Duplicate Special commands let you create either a complete duplicate or a lightweight instance of the original. For example, you could create armies and forests full of duplicate objects without needing the memory or computing power to handle that much actual geometry. An instance is like an alias or shortcut or symbolic link in a file system: it's a visual pointer back to the original. However, each instance has its own transform node so it can have its own position, rotation, and scaling. An instance stays linked to the original, so when the original changes, the instance changes too. If you move a control point on the original, all instances automatically update. Instances do not have their own control points." "Copies vs. instances," Autodesk Maya, accessed December 11, 2021, https://help.autodesk.com/view/MAYAUL/2022/ENU/?guid=GUID-2851AE11-C3EF-4AE1-B7C5-8773E2068BB9
36. Sutherland, "Sketchpad" (2003), 47.
37. I use the term here in the sense of philosopher Sybille Krämer. In German she uses the word *Spur*. Krämer has a specific definition of it and emphasizes an essential characteristic of traces: "Traces tell us nothing, but show us something. Above all, however, what they show us must have arisen incidentally, i.e. unintentionally – otherwise it would not be a trace, but a sign consciously staged as a trace." Sybille Krämer, "Das Medium als Spur und Apparat," in *Medien, Computer, Realität: Wirklichkeitsvorstellungen und Neue Medien*, ed. Sybille Krämer (Frankfurt am Main: Suhrkamp, 1998), 79.
38. Sutherland, "Sketchpad" (2003), 77, emphasis in original.
39. Sutherland, "Sketchpad" (2003), 77.
40. Even today, the *Autodesk Maya* software still contains this term and a related concept: "Constraints let you constrain the position, orientation, or scale of an object to other objects. Further, with constraints you can impose specific limits on objects and automate animation processes. [...] Note that other software packages use the term 'animation controllers' to refer to what Maya calls *constraints*." "Constraints," Autodesk Maya, accessed December 11, 2021. https://help.autodesk.com/view/MAYAUL/2022/ENU/?guid=GUID-7665A291-FAA7-44C0-BDEB-A6C83482116C, emphasis in original.
41. Sutherland, "Sketchpad" (2003), 141, emphasis in original.
42. Sutherland, "Sketchpad" (2003), 17.
43. Sutherland, "Sketchpad" (2003), 24–25.
44. Sutherland, "Sketchpad" (2003), 17.
45. Sutherland also considered settings that could be used to display lines in different styles and thicknesses, for example, to display underlinings as dotted or dashed lines. See Sutherland, "Sketchpad" (2003), 71.
46. Sutherland, "Sketchpad" (2003), 25.
47. Sutherland, "Sketchpad" (2003), 28, emphasis in original.
48. Sutherland, "Sketchpad" (2003), 9.
49. Sutherland, "Sketchpad" (2003), 72–73, emphasis in original.
50. Sutherland, "Sketchpad" (2003), 107–10.
51. See Sutherland, "Sketchpad" (2003), 99–116.
52. Sutherland, "Sketchpad" (2003), 9.
53. Sutherland, "Sketchpad" (2003), 75.
54. Sutherland, "Sketchpad" (2003), 75–76.
55. Sutherland, "Sketchpad" (2003), 99.
56. See Sutherland, "Sketchpad" (2003), 99–100.
57. For example, he shows the drawing of a delay line, which can occur in the representation of circuits and is made up of a repetitive staircase pattern. Another example is the coding of a digital clock, which is similar in appearance to an analog clock face. Other sections also deal with the dimensioning of technical drawings or the graphical representation and calculation of the loading conditions of bridges. See Sutherland, "Sketchpad" (2003), 100–2 and 104–7.
58. Sutherland, "Sketchpad" (2003), 102.
59. In one example, he uses still images to show a schematic representation of a driving lever, a mechanical component with several interlocking joints and rotational movements, which he has set in motion using *Sketchpad*. He points out that it is difficult to physically build such a linkage. See Sutherland, "Sketchpad" (2003), 102–4.
60. See Sutherland, "Sketchpad" (2003), 102.
61. Sutherland, "Sketchpad" (2003), 107.
62. Blackwell and Rodden, "Preface," 5.
63. Without further explanation in his report, he gives the depicted girl the name Nefertite, with which Sutherland implicitly establishes a reference to the ancient Egyptian queen Nefertiti. He does not use the name again in the title of the picture of the girl. Here he merely writes "winking girl and components." There is no outward

resemblance to the traditional depictions of the ancient Egyptian queen. See Sutherland, "Sketchpad" (2003), 107–9.

64. Sutherland, "Sketchpad" (2003), 107.
65. Sutherland, "Sketchpad" (2003), 107.
66. Sutherland, "Sketchpad" (2003), 107.
67. Sutherland, "Sketchpad" (2003), 107. The project to which Sutherland refers here, which also made use of the fax machine, was a parallel research project carried out at MIT by Lawrence G. Roberts, the aim of which was to display three-dimensional objects on a two-dimensional screen as a spatial projection using line drawings. See Lawrence G. Roberts, "Machine Perception of Three-Dimensional Solids" (PhD diss., Massachusetts Institute of Technology, 1963), MIT Libraries, DSpace@MIT (33959125).
68. Sutherland, "Sketchpad" (2003), 107/10.
69. Sutherland, "Sketchpad" (2003), 72.

CHAPTER 4

Parallel Developments

The Computer in the Fine Arts and Design of the 1960s

THIS CHAPTER SERVES TO focus on Sutherland's contemporaries who were also concerned with the question of how the computer could be used to create images or even for artistic purposes. My decision to include artistic approaches in this chapter arises from the fact that Sutherland himself opened up this category of "art" in order to demonstrate that he saw great versatility in his program. A comparison with the production processes of Frieder Nake from Germany, for example, who was doing pioneering work as a computer artist at around the same time, could also have been a suitable choice for the purpose of the following sections. The images he produced bear no resemblance to Sutherland's experimental approaches, either in terms of visual aesthetics or production aesthetics (Figure 4.1).[1] Although this stark contrast would most likely have provided meaningful insights into Sutherland's conception of pictoriality, it seemed more fruitful, instead of contrasting Sutherland with Nake, to choose a parallel development, which, in a sense, initially shows greater similarities to Sutherland's ideas and is thus indeed comparable with his work but in the end led to completely different production methods and pictorial results. The works of US artist Charles A. Csuri, who began experimenting with early forms of computer technology in the 1960s after having previously worked mainly with painting techniques,[2] are suitable for such a comparison. Csuri's computer-based artistic work was comprehensively examined and contextualized in 2006 in the exhibition *Charles A. Csuri: Beyond Boundaries, 1963 – Present.* The exhibition was organized jointly by the *Special Interest Group on Computer Graphics* (SIGGRAPH), one of the leading conferences in the field of computer graphics,

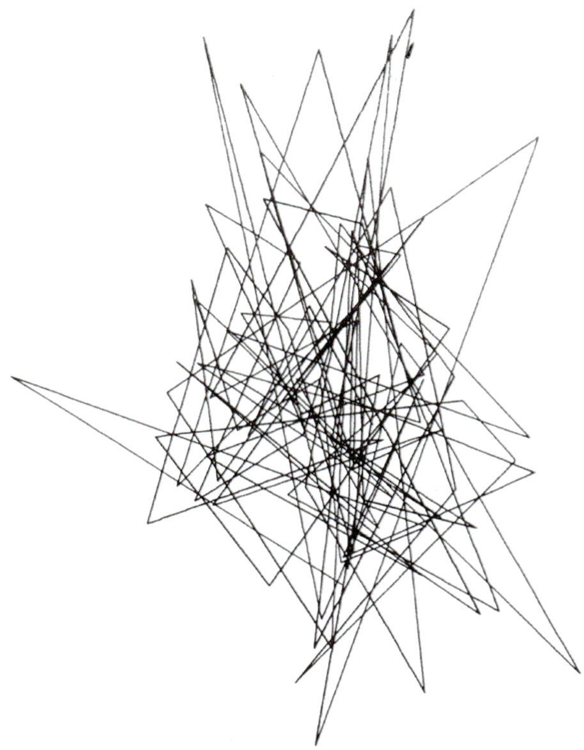

FIGURE 4.1 Frieder Nake, *6/7/64 Nr. 20 Zufälliger Polygonzug*, 1964, computer generated, ink on paper, 8.3 in × 5.9 in (21.1 × 15.1 cm). (© Frieder Nake. Reprinted with permission from Frieder Nake.)

DOI: 10.1201/9781003649861-6

and the *Advanced Computing Center for the Arts and Design* (ACCAD), which Csuri founded at the *College of Arts and Sciences* at *Ohio State University* (OSU) in 1986.[3] In the introduction to the exhibition catalog, art historian Janice M. Glowski emphasizes in her role as editor of the catalog, "[i]t's easy to look at the history of computer graphics and to note Charles Csuri's role as the 'father of digital art and animation.'"[4] With Csuri's works it can be demonstrated how Sutherland's desire to open up creative processes on the computer could also have been realized. Looking at Csuri provides a very vivid perspective on the fact that software development is always dependent on a certain mindset in terms of creativity, design or art. Or to put it the other way round: Had Csuri had the opportunity to incorporate his computer graphics research into the development of today's commercially available computer graphics software on a larger scale, it might have reflected different creative or artistic parameters than those that I attempt to make visible with my study.

Following on from Csuri and as a transition to Coons, William A. Fetter, another artist who worked in the field of computer graphics parallel to Sutherland, is introduced. His way of working shows points of contact as well as considerable differences to Csuri's approach.

4.1 CHARLES A. CSURI – CREATIVE WORK ON THE COMPUTER BETWEEN ART AND SCIENCE

> I feel like an old-fashioned expressionist painter who got caught in some kind of time warp that included the computer. My spirit and temperament is that of a romantic who is involved in symbols and icons representing humanistic values which may belong in another era.[5]
>
> *CHARLES A. CSURI (1989)*

In Chapter 3 it was demonstrated that Sutherland developed an approach with *Sketchpad* and the object-oriented programming paradigm that would make it possible in the long term to enable a larger group of people to work with the computer in a more comprehensive way than would be likely with procedural programming processes. With this goal in mind, it was central to the programming activity to anticipate and program certain functions for a potential user in advance so that they would only have to call them up at a later point in time. Another special feature of the object-oriented paradigm was that these functions could be used to make subsequent changes to a result. Therefore, results always became intermediate results. Sutherland considered his new approach to be less restrictive than the procedural programming process. At the same time, I pointed out that the procedural approach nevertheless allowed greater creative freedom as long as the object-oriented paradigm influenced the way of working with pre-programmed functions. This created a paradox.

If one wanted to get out of this paradox and combine the advantages of the object-oriented approach with the freedom of the procedural paradigm, one would have to have the ability to code one's own control elements. As a result of this deficit, operating systems, computer programs and interfaces have been developed with which everyone can work freely and openly, although they are always bound to the decisions of others. The artist Charles A. Csuri can serve as a striking example of having escaped this paradox. His works show that his creative freedom was not restricted by the procedural process. Rather, it was precisely his understanding of programming processes – and this is the main proposition for this section – that enabled him to express himself freely in his art.

The aspect of freedom of expression now also serves as the starting point for a comparison between Sutherland and Csuri. For although ultimately Csuri's approach to production and visual aesthetics can only be brought into agreement with Sutherland in certain areas, Csuri articulated a similar claim to artistic production as Sutherland in principle and thus provides a decisive basis for comparison: "The creative process works when I am able to live in a space of psychological uncertainty. I'm comfortable with the notion that I don't know where I'm going. It is a journey to somewhere, and I can not anticipate where it will end."[6] Csuri's description here initially appears to be completely in line with Sutherland's idea that art requires an openness in the work process without having to define a potential goal in advance. Nevertheless, it is only with regard to the use of the computer that it becomes clear that the two pioneers had very different ideas of how this open process could be realized.

The difference between Sutherland and Csuri therefore lies in their respective self-conceptions with which they approached working with the computer. While Sutherland speaks of artistic processes, he also emphasizes that he is not an artist.[7] Csuri was just as much a computer pioneer as Sutherland, but unlike Sutherland, Csuri's artistic training made him first and foremost an artist. Or put differently: His technological achievements in the field of computer graphics all took place against the backdrop of an artist's perspective.

The aim of this section is to answer the question of how Csuri was able to fulfill this demand on his artistic process with the help of the computer. To this end, his artistic career will first be briefly traced in order to be able to understand which concepts he ultimately translated into his work with the computer. As the main basis for the results presented in this section serve, on the one hand, the exhibition catalog for the 2006 exhibition *Charles A. Csuri: Beyond Boundaries, 1963 – Present*, and, on the other, two interviews with Charles A. Csuri, both conducted as part of different oral history projects, the first in 1989 at the *Charles Babbage Institute* of the *University of Minnesota*,[8] and the second in 2003 at OSU.[9]

In the interview conducted in 1989, Csuri describes himself as an "artist and computer graphics researcher."[10] He illustrates impressions of his artistic training, which he completed in the 1940s at OSU, where he eventually, before the age of 40, also became a full-tenured art professor – a position that strongly helped with his artistic interest in pursuing research on computer graphics.[11] Regarding his time as a student, Csuri particularly highlights some of his professors, such as James Hopkins, who worked as a young artist in Paris and told his students in the United States about his encounters with Edgar Degas and Auguste Renoir.[12] Recalling these stories, Csuri summarizes, "his experiences offered to us a very romantic view of the artist."[13] Together with his fellow student Roy Lichtenstein, who also became a close friend of Csuri, he studied as well under Hoyt L. Sherman. With his concepts of perception theory and his idea of the visual structuring of colors and forms Sherman had – as Csuri explains – a great influence not only on Lichtenstein but also on Csuri himself. He describes his relationship with his professor as conflictual, but at the same time dynamic and progressive for the time.[14] Looking back, Csuri remembers, for example, a teaching method in which the students were shown a slide projection in a completely darkened room for a tenth of a second to then trace the image shown in the dark within a minute using charcoal on a large sheet of paper based on the afterimage that remained in their perception. Csuri describes the type of images shown as "abstract shapes in a variety of combinations representing formal concepts of visual structure."[15] In his monograph *Image Duplicator: Roy Lichtenstein and the Emergence of Pop Art*, US art historian Michael Lobel dedicates a chapter to the art professor and the influence he had on Lichtenstein. In addition to the "Flash Drawing Technique,"[16] Lobel describes others of Sherman's teaching methods that complement and illustrate Csuri's explanations. For example, Sherman had set up a so-called "Visual Demonstration Center"[17] for his teachings in the field of human perception, which was a room in which Sherman exhibited graphics and models to illustrate "various principles of visual perceptions, particularly optical illusions."[18] Lobel refers specifically to a model labeled "Distorted Room." This was a room with a distorted perspective that evoked the illusion of a square floor plan, although the rear wall was not at right angles to the other walls, i.e. not parallel, but at an angle to the viewer. From the viewer, technically, the left-hand corner of the room was much further back than the right-hand corner, although this distortion could visually not be perceived. For the viewer, an inconspicuous central perspective representation of a room appeared. In this context, Lobel refers to an illustration created by Sherman, which visualizes the effect of the distorted space. The drawing shows that two windows were set into the diagonal rear wall of the model, side by side, which were themselves distorted to give the impression of flawless rectangles. When two people looked through the two panes at the same time, one of them appeared considerably smaller than the other due to the greater distance to the viewer (Figures 4.2 and 4.3).[19] Lobel deduces from Sherman's preference for optical illusions that the art professor did not want to explain in a positive sense how the human perceptual apparatus works, but in a deficient sense how fallible our perceptual apparatus is:

> Sherman intended to show the viewer how various components of the perceptual process

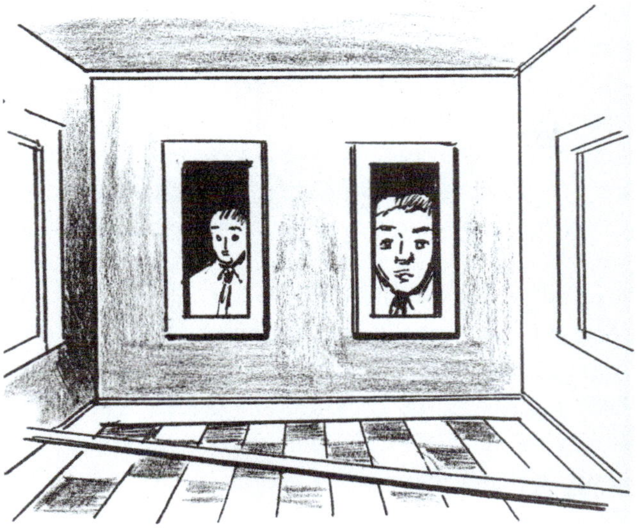

FIGURE 4.2 Hoyt L. Sherman, *Visual Demonstration Center* in *A Manual for Operation: Second Draft*, 1951, drawing. (© The Ohio State University.)

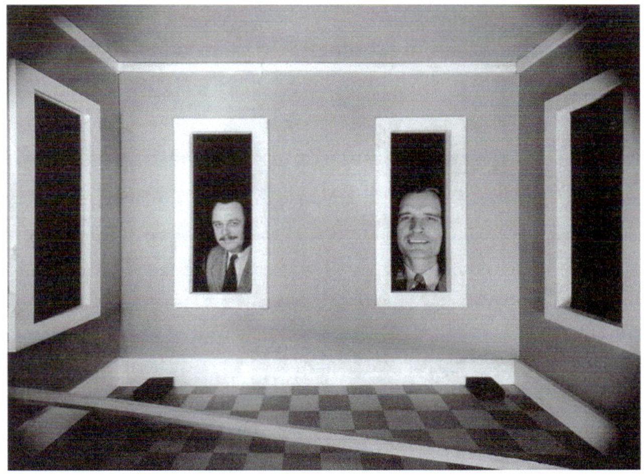

FIGURE 4.3 Hoyt L. Sherman, *Visual Demonstration Center* in the *Vision to Action* catalog, undated, photography. (© The Ohio State University.)

> (such as binocular vision or the individual's prior knowledge of objects in the world) infringed on the possibility of an ostensible pure – that is to say, immediated – perception of the visual field.[20]

Csuri does not explicitly refer to the "Distorted Room" in his remarks, but he makes general reference to Sherman's interest in theories of Gestalt psychology.[21] Although Csuri emphasizes that he does not consider himself to belong to the school of Gestalt psychology, he confirms at the same time that he considers the principles expressed in it to be self-evident phenomena: "I think that it's just the nature… Things are never really quite simple."[22] Csuri was therefore sensitized by his academic teacher to adopt a critical and questioning attitude toward his own perception. He explains how the concepts taught by Sherman remained the subject of dialogue with Lichtenstein long after they graduated together. During their studies, the following had long been clear to both of them: "Three dimensional space, perspective and chiaroscuro did not exist for us. Everyone who did not agree with us, of course, were simply romantics and fools."[23] It is evident to what extent Csuri was exposed to completely different influences during his artistic training than Sutherland at MIT or even before that in his electrical engineering studies. The later reflections on Steven A. Coons will ultimately shed light on the visual concepts that surrounded Sutherland in contrast to Csuri.

So where did Csuri's technical interest come from? He did not receive the impetus for this in any way from the artistic environment of the university. By the time he fully immersed himself in working with computers, he was already a tenured art professor for painting, which is why he had achieved a secure status as an artist at the time – also thanks to exhibitions in New York.[24] Nevertheless, the people in this artistic environment were not open to his interest in computer technology. Sherman in particular rejected his turn to the computer: "Sherman and I simply had no dialogue. Once I got involved with the computer, that simply dissolved whatever relationship we had."[25]

Csuri himself refers to 1955 as the year in which he first came into contact with computer technology. In this context, he mentions a personal friend, Jack Mitten, who was also a professor at OSU, but in the field of mechanical engineering. Mitten introduced Csuri to the essential features of computer technology and its possible applications. In his remarks, Csuri explicitly recalls that at that time computers were not yet connected to graphic output devices that could have been used to visualize calculations. Plotters, i.e. automated output devices for drawings, were also not yet available. Nevertheless, Csuri and Mitten speculated in private conversations about whether computer technology might one day be suitable for artistic purposes: "During the cocktail hour, we would talk about computers, and as the martinis began to flow more freely, so did our ideas about computers and art."[26]

The catalog, which was published along with the Csuri exhibition held in 2006, reveals that Csuri's access to technical knowledge was already established earlier due to his deployment in the Second World War. In one of the catalog's contributions titled *A Record of Decisions: Envisioning Computer Art*, German art historian and media artist Margit Rosen explains this. With her accounts she aims to trace Csuri's creative process, placing particular emphasis on highlighting aspects of his artistic mindset that were already apparent before his work with the computer, but which subsequently continued to shape his creative decisions and artistic spirit.[27] After presenting key milestones in Csuri's artistic development, Rosen also mentions the exchange with Jack Mitten that began in 1955.[28] Her reference to Csuri's military service provides a plausible explanation as to why the artist followed developments in the field of computer technology with such great interest in the first place, or why he was able to comprehend his friend's professional point of view:

> Csuri brought with him prior knowledge to the topic. In 1943, he had been drafted into the Army to fight in Europe during World War II. Before he was transferred, the Army sent him to the Newark College of Engineering, where he passed a one-year program of algebra, trigonometry, analytic geometry, calculus, physics, chemistry, and engineering drawing.[29]

Csuri himself does not refer to this historical detail in either interview; he merely mentions that his studies were interrupted by a three-year deployment in the Second World War before he completed his bachelor's degree. When asked which schools he attended, he only mentions OSU.[30] In an interview published in 1990 in the journal *IEEE Computer Graphics and Applications*, there is also no mention of his education at *Newark College*.[31] He bases his technical affinity for computer technology and his understanding of it solely on the exchange with his friend and colleague Jack Mitten: "Because of the dialogue over 10 years with my engineer friend, it all made sense to me."[32] In the context of this statement, he refers to a specific event that directly motivated him to use the computer as a medium of artistic expression around ten years after the beginnings of his conversations with Jack Mitten. In 1964,[33] Csuri discovered a computer-generated image in a scientific publication from the *Department of Electrical Engineering* at OSU, which was created using an automated electric typewriter, a so-called Flexowriter. The image, which showed a female face in profile, was a digitized copy of a photograph that had previously been divided into several shades of gray. The different shades of gray were then entered into a computer to be printed on a new sheet of paper using a typewriter (Figure 4.4–4.6).[34] For this task, the Flexowriter fulfilled the necessary requirement of being able to output shades of gray in different strengths.[35] Csuri attached great importance to the discovery of this image for his own artistic development: "All it took for me was to see that one picture produced by computer and everything just simply came together for me. And I knew instantly, I literally knew instantly that this is what I had to do."[36]

After his discovery, Csuri immediately enrolled in a programming course at OSU to pave the way for his own artistic endeavors on the computer.[37] The conversations with his friend Jack Mitten had prepared him well: "At least at a conceptual level, I had a pretty good idea of what I was getting into."[38] This conceptual level that Csuri is referring to here can already be recognized in artistic works that he produced shortly before he began to use the computer as a medium of expression. I want to focus on these works now in order to demonstrate how Csuri's purely conceptual understanding of computer technology influenced his artistic practice. This step serves to subsequently discuss how Csuri succeeded in utilizing the peculiarities of the computer for his own purposes without losing control over his creative decisions.

Csuri's statement about his computer skills becomes particularly vivid against the background of his work *She's Watching Superman*, created in 1963 and 1964, which is an inked portrait of an old woman supporting her head on her left hand, her hair wrapped in a cloth. While Csuri depicted the body and the cloth merely with fine contours, he drew the hand and the face with a more detailed type of flat

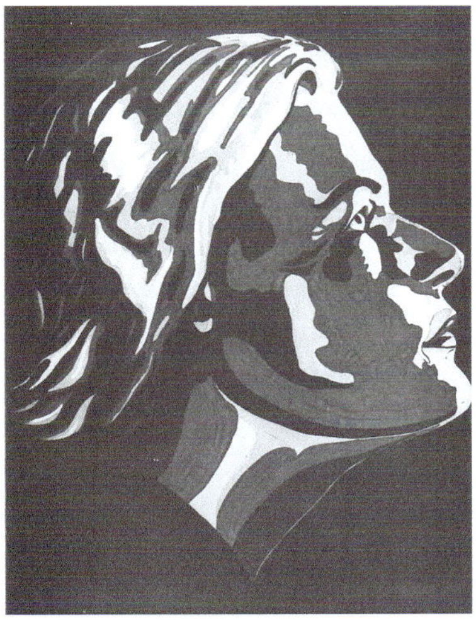

FIGURE 4.4 Juris G. Raudseps, *Picture after quantizing by artist*, 1963, color on paper.

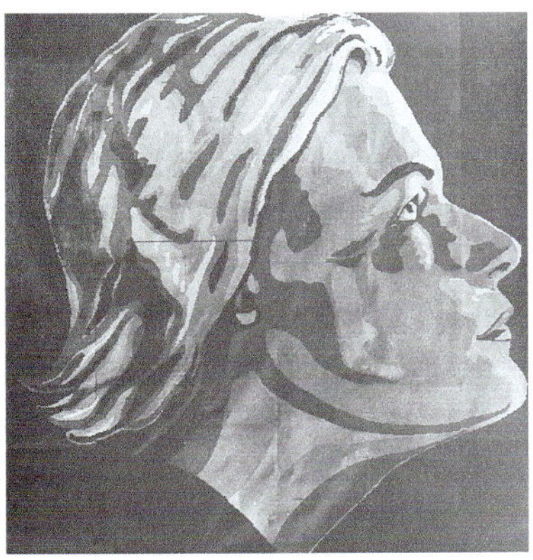

FIGURE 4.5 Juris G. Raudseps, *Quantized picture produced from scan data for checking purposes*, 1963, produced with Flexowriter.

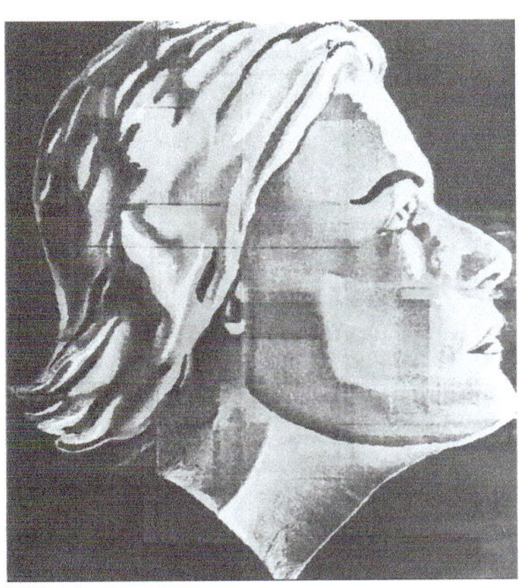

FIGURE 4.6 Juris G. Raudseps, *Picture smoothed on basis of both horizontal and vertical scans*, 1963, produced with Flexowriter.

shading (Figure 4.7). Csuri's engagement with computer technology is not communicated on a visual level, but the way in which he proceeded and his own statements on the production process make the reference explicit. The techniques he learned in art school, such as Sherman's "Flash Drawing Technique,"[39] appear in a new light for him:

> I began questioning the role of a tactile-kinesthetic approach to painting and drawing. What is the relationship between the mind and the hand? As an experiment, I made this drawing, one dot at a time, with a pen. It was a procedural approach in which I worked mechanically like a machine. I also wondered if words and comments could attribute to and become part of an art object. I was curious to see if in the end, there would still be an aesthetic quality.[40]

Here, Csuri unequivocally describes the nature of the procedural programming paradigm, which, as discussed in the chapter on Sutherland, was used as the standard in the field of computer technology at the time. Around the same time as this creative phase of Csuri, Sutherland developed the first approaches of the new object-oriented programming paradigm with *Sketchpad*, even if the term itself did not emerge until a few years later. Csuri's statement that he proceeded like a machine initially appears to be related to those intellectual approaches in which the idea of an artistically expressing subject was rejected. However, Rosen aptly points out that Csuri cannot be classified within this movement. As the quote at the beginning of this section indicates, in his own view Csuri represented a humanist attitude which – as he himself states – possibly did not fit in with his time[41]:

> Charles Csuri's concept of art only *seemed* to resemble the militant ideas of "the computer as an artist." Csuri never called into question the authority of the human artist. He did not cultivate the rhetoric of the extinction of the subject, of a transhuman art. As much as he explored the computer, the machine itself as a symbol of rationality and discipline never stood in the center of his reflection.[42]

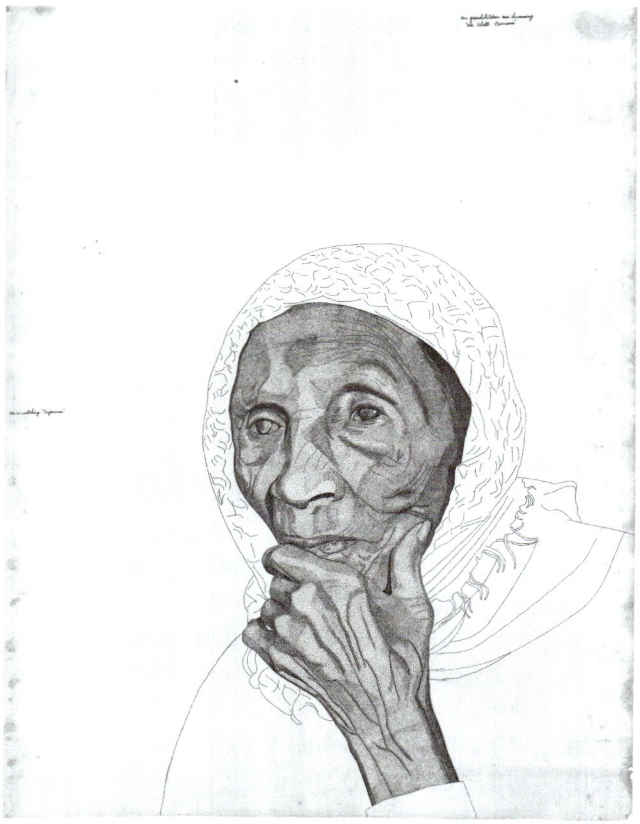

FIGURE 4.7 Charles A. Csuri, *She's Watching Superman*, 1963–1964, ink on paper, procedural drawing, 41 × 58 in (101.14 × 147.32 cm). (Reprinted with permission from Caroline Csuri.)

Another of Csuri's works, which he also produced shortly before he turned completely to the computer, can illustrate his intellectual horizon as explained by Rosen here. Between 1963 and 1964, he developed a series of nine drawings, which he entitled *After the Artist*. As the title of the series suggests, Csuri's aim in the drawings was to recreate works by other artists.[43] To do this, he used a pantograph, a drawing device that allows a drawing to be duplicated either in its original size or on a different scale.[44] However, Csuri was not content with simply reproducing images; instead, his interest was in *transforming* images with an automated procedure, i.e. a computer, in a sense. He thus made structural changes to the pantograph so that it could be used to create highly distorted copies of the other artists' works. In this way, he combined several views of another person's work of art within one drawing. Figure 4.8 shows an example in which Csuri refers to the German painter Paul Klee.[45] Not only the reproduction of other artists' works but also the title of the series suggest that Csuri felt an appreciation for the quoted colleagues and their subjective expression. Although he referred to his pantograph as an "analog computer," for him the automation of the artistic process is not at odds with the notion of an artistic subject. As Rosen emphasizes, Csuri even continued his *After the Artist* series with Leonardo da Vinci's *Vitruvian Man* on a digital computer in 1966 (Figure 4.9).[46]

As Rosen's comments on Csuri's series show, his way of working is contrary to the idea of rejecting an artistically working subject. She describes how Csuri was able to develop his artistic ideas on the computer precisely *because* he studied the artistic processes of other artists in advance:

> Constructing a tool presupposes the analysis of the production process. Csuri, the artist, was prepared. He followed up an aesthetic interest rooted in his study with impressionist painters John Hopkins and Hoyt Sherman, who taught him to understand Monet, Cézanne, Braque, and Picasso – an interest in the structure of artworks and the decision-procedures involved in their production.[47]

As becomes clear here, Csuri was therefore not primarily interested in the automation of artistic processes, but rather in understanding the production steps and techniques used. Rosen points out in

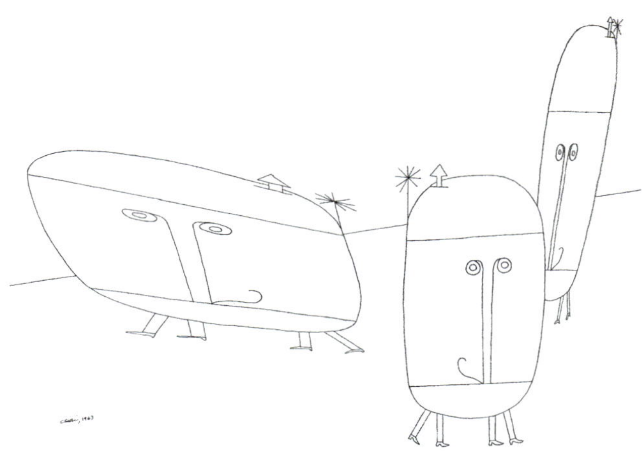

FIGURE 4.8 Charles A. Csuri, *After Paul Klee*, from the series *After the Artist*, 1963, ink on paper, drawn with pantograph/analogue computer, 26 × 20 in (66 × 51 cm). (Reprinted with permission by Caroline Csuri.)

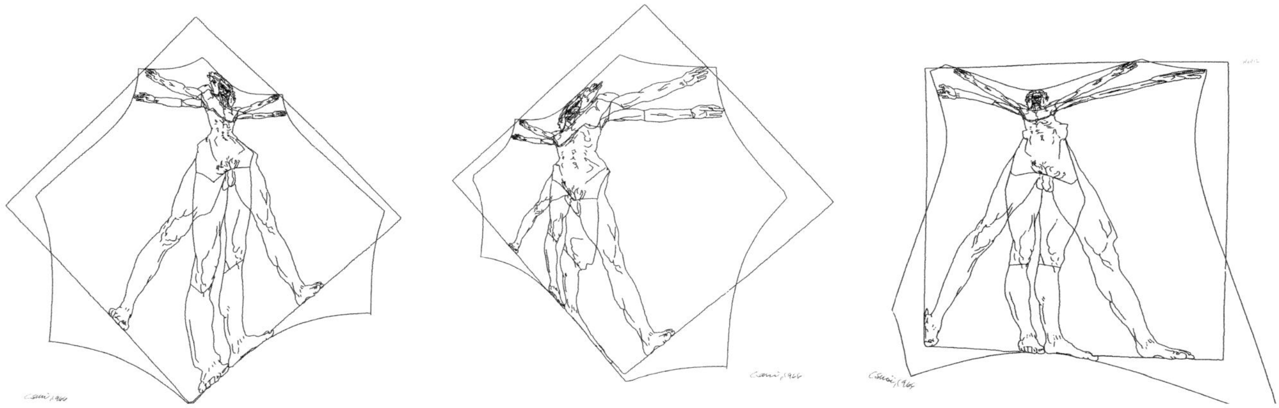

FIGURE 4.9 Charles A. Csuri, *Leonardo da Vinci Series*, 1966, ink on paper, IBM 7094 and drum plotter, 20 × 60 in (51 × 152 cm). (Reprinted with permission from Caroline Csuri.)

her accounts that this interest in the artistic process even formed the core of one of Csuri's research projects as expressed in a research proposal developed in 1967. According to Rosen, Csuri thus picked up on something that was also widespread among other pioneers who dealt with the production of computer graphics from an artistic perspective. Rosen explicitly mentions, for example, A. Michael Noll from the United States or the German philosopher Max Bense, "who sought to detect within the framework of his 'information aesthetics' the elements and rules of artworks."[48] To Rosen a key difference between Bense and Csuri's interest, however, was that Bense analyzed finished works of art, while Csuri rather focused on the production processes of artworks. As Rosen explains, Csuri's interest can in turn be reconciled with the conceptual approaches of the German computer artist Frieder Nake, which he presented in his 1968 article *Die Kunstproduktion als Entscheidungsprozeß* (Art Production as a Decision-Making Process) for the second issue of the magazine *bit international 2*.[49] Although with his ideas, Nake developed a possibility of how artistic decision-making processes can be modeled with the computer, he optimistically adds, "there is not the slightest danger that mathematicians or even computers could completely take over image-making. A strong intrusion of exact science – i.e. discursive thinking – into the productive area of intuitive thinking will not abolish it but rather provoke it to advance."[50] This intuitive approach to art, as Rosen emphasizes, was Csuri's main interest. It reflects his view that not every aspect of an artistic production process can be left to the computer.[51] It is striking that Csuri, despite his fundamentally comparable attitude to Nake, strived for completely different image aesthetics in his early works. While Nake's paintings are abstract compositions (see Figure 4.1), Csuri's works always feature figurative elements. Rosen also observes that

> [m]ost of the artists and scientists producing images and movies with the computer in the 1960s designed abstract imagery. They inquired in a nonfigurative way about variability, randomness, and complexity – aspects that represented the potential of the new medium. Csuri never focused his imagination on the visualization of the structure of the computer itself. Neither did he entertain a mythical relation to the eternal world of mathematics. Rather, Csuri used mathematics as a means of representation. He did not seek to represent the idea of mathematics itself.[52]

In the interview conducted in 1989, Csuri himself also provides a possible explanation for his lack of interest in abstract compositions. Referring to his work *Sine Curve Man* from 1967 (Figure 4.10), he is asked whether he had always been interested in figurative expression. Csuri confirms the question and emphasizes that he had always been interested in Rembrandt's or Frans Hals' painting and portraiture in general. He also points out that even his own abstract compositions usually refer to human figures. He summarizes

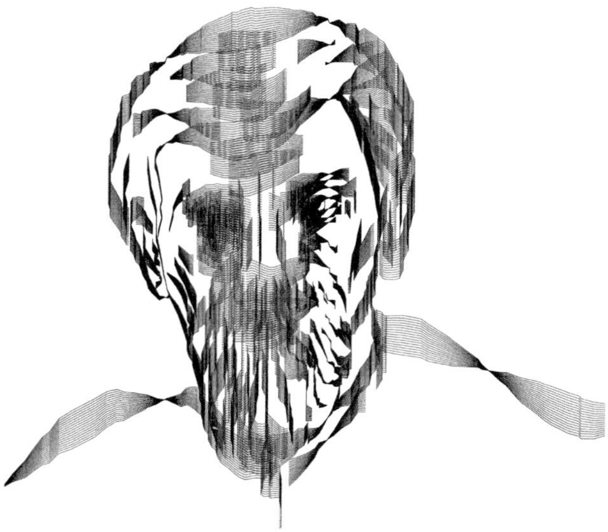

FIGURE 4.10 Charles A. Csuri, *Sine Curve Man*, 1967, ink on paper, IBM 7094 and drum plotter, 40.9 × 40.9 in (104 × 104 cm). (Reprinted with permission from Caroline Csuri.)

his attitude to abstraction in art succinctly: "While I think I know a fair amount about visual organization and abstraction, that as an end is not very interesting to me. I just find it kind of boring."[53]

This statement gives an idea of the kind of tools Csuri was looking for in the computer. They had to be ones that corresponded to his research into other artistic processes on the one hand and his own artistic ideas on the other. At the same time, Csuri was faced with the task of combining these requirements with the properties that computer technology itself offered.

So how did he go about it? Csuri's decision to first analyze other artistic processes when developing "computer tools" illustrates an aspect that Sutherland also hinted at and which is particularly relevant for my study: The features that are developed for the computer are often oriented toward already-existing and familiar work processes. Software development is therefore also very often – like my own study – carried out against the background of production-aesthetic analyses (this is explained in more detail in Section 5.2). However, as noted earlier, Csuri obviously analyzed different production processes than Sutherland. So, although both pioneers were interested in an openness to the artistic process, it is now clear that Csuri, unlike Sutherland, was not only familiar with artistic processes through his own practice, but that he had also analyzed the artistic production processes of other artists in detail. Sutherland's argument that his program was also designed to be particularly open due to the artistic application possibilities loses its impact against the background of Csuri's artistic and computer-technological considerations. In the long term, however, Sutherland's ideas have survived in later software developments, whereas Csuri's ideas receded somewhat more in the background – although merely in the context of commercial software. The object-oriented approach, which made the computer easier to use, played a part in this. Although Csuri did not initially make use of such developments, he succeeded in maintaining openness in his artistic process according to his own ideas. But how so? Csuri, like Sutherland, eventually went on to develop his own software, and both had fundamentally similar demands on the performance of this software. However, the following statement by Csuri demonstrates that for him the starting point was always an artistic goal, in contrast to Sutherland, who regarded the artistic use of his program as an additional argument for its application:

> When I began working with the computer, I had to look closely at how it could be used within an artistic context. How might I work with this new medium in a way that would offer me greater freedom? Where is the sense of play and fun in this universe of linear logic? Is there something new buried in this logic or is the innovation within me? Over many years, I have shaped a software environment that offers me methods and strategies that allow me to work more freely. I realized early on that I preferred an approach to making art that allowed for multiple solutions to a problem. The software was designed to reflect this idea. As a consequence of this choice, an art object becomes many statements about the same thing.[54]

This description of Csuri's fundamental approach to working with the computer shows that, from the very beginning, he was looking for ways not to surrender to technological developments, but to help shape them. For Csuri, therefore, the distinction between the procedural and object-oriented programming paradigm was initially completely irrelevant, unlike for Sutherland. What was decisive, however, was Csuri's sense of collaboration, because his artistic expression with the help of the computer was always characterized by cooperation with computer scientists and mathematicians. Here, too, there is a decisive difference to Sutherland's approach in the development of his graphics software – he did not seek a dialogue with artists as proactively as Csuri did the other way around with mathematicians and programmers. I will now examine the way in which Csuri organized this collaboration.

As I have noted, the automated elements in the production process Csuri made use of from the early 1960s onward changed his view on his own artistic process. The unpredictability of the results became increasingly important to him. For example, Rosen describes, "[a]lready while he was using the pantograph, Csuri started playing with the notion that he could not anticipate or imagine the result of the rules he had set up."[55] He himself noticed changes in his production process, particularly in relation to painting – the medium of expression with which he had previously mainly worked and which formed the main subject of his teaching[56] for a period of almost 20 years during his work as an art professor:

> When I did a traditional painting, I was thinking in terms of start, beginning, and some end point – a painting, a drawing. Today I don't have the expectation in the same way. I explore the computer as a search engine for art. I am hoping that when I set up that environment, there will be something I cannot think of.[57]

From the moment Csuri turned to the computer, his previous connection to painting faded into the background. He also realized that this new means of expression was very expensive for him and that he would need financial support if he wanted to bring his own artistic ideas to life. Between 1965 and 1968, he was still mainly concerned with experimenting artistically with computer graphics, creating his own approach to it, as can be demonstrated, for example, with his work *Sine Curve Man* from 1967, which was, incidentally, like others of his first computer graphics presented in the exhibition *Cybernetic Serendipity* at the Institute for Contemporary Art in London in 1968. From the late 1960s onward, he was increasingly involved in promoting research in the field of computer graphics and computer animation and raising funds for it.[58] As he had not yet made a name for himself in a scientific context and, as a professor of art, especially not in the field of natural sciences, it was ultimately friends of his, including mathematicians and physicists, who inspired and encouraged him to develop a research project from his artistic ambitions and present it to the *National Science Foundation*.[59] A lot of the motivation for this step also came from a rejection letter by *Artforum* in 1967, in which Philip Leider, one of the editors of the journal, expressed how he "cant [*sic*] imagine ARTFORUM ever doing a special issue on electronics or computers in art [...]."[60] Therefore, Csuri followed his colleagues' suggestion and, contrary to his expectations, was eventually granted research funding. This event led to ongoing funding for Csuri's work from the *National Science Foundation* for a period of over 20 years. Although the organization initially supported Csuri's artistic ideas, in the long term his success was only possible because he no longer overtly presented his artistic ambitions as the subject of his research in the subsequent applications and instead focused on computer technology developments.[61] While he was still pursuing the goals of his artistic practice in purely conceptual terms with his research, the production of his own works was completely pushed into the background during this time: "As I understood the broader implications of computer graphics, I became very involved in basic research and set aside my attempt to produce art. I shifted my emphasis because it was the only way I could acquire the necessary resources to develop some of my ideas."[62]

It was not until the end of the 1980s that Csuri resumed his work as an artist. Painting also played a greater role in his artistic expression again at this time. In her contribution *Exploration and the Artist's Tools* for the exhibition catalog published in 2006, Maria Palazzi, then in her role as director of ACCAD, explains that during this phase Csuri not only generally reintroduced his own drawings and paintings into his production process, but that he also began to integrate them into his work on the computer.[63] As Palazzi notes, Csuri systematically expanded his collaboration with computer scientists during this period. The aim of this collaboration was to develop customized software for his artistic ideas.[64] Numerous features that are very characteristic of Csuri's work emerged during this creative phase, including those that Palazzi describes as "fragmentation, ribbon, and colormix."[65] As mentioned, Csuri often worked with figurative representations, and he continued to pursue this approach in this later creative phase at the end of the 1980s. In the 1990s and 2000s, for example, he often depicted human figures, objects or animals in the form of a kind of cloud, composed either of a ball of thread or of particles (Figure 4.11), a mode of expression whose origins are explored in more detail in the last part of this section. Palazzi notes: "Works from this and subsequent periods demonstrate increased mastery and subtle use of his core programming scripts, or 'tools' as the artist often refers to them. Csuri speaks of a greater sense of freedom as his familiarity with these programs deepened."[66] Csuri therefore achieved his artistic ideas and his freedom of expression by always maintaining a continuous and, above all, interdisciplinary dialogue with colleagues and, as Palazzi points out, also with master's and doctoral students from the field of computer science.[67] A separate chapter in the exhibition catalog is dedicated to Csuri's working methods. It is written by Wayne Carlson, a former colleague of Csuri, himself a computer scientist and also a former director of ACCAD. In his contribution *Dialogue and Creativity: The Faces of Collaboration*, he takes a comprehensive look at Csuri's collaborative and interdisciplinary approach and the dialogue he constantly maintained with people from other disciplines. Carlson's remarks demonstrate once again that Csuri's work processes were characterized by an exchange with other disciplines long before this later creative phase focused on by Palazzi. When Csuri began working with the computer, his production process began to develop a dynamic that Rosen, referring to Bruno Latour, describes in her essay as reciprocal:

> The computer was a tool, which he tried to master and enhance. Foremost in his mind was that the relationship between man and machine was always, to a certain degree, reciprocal, and that in the process of taming, so to speak, the one who tames is transformed as well.[68]

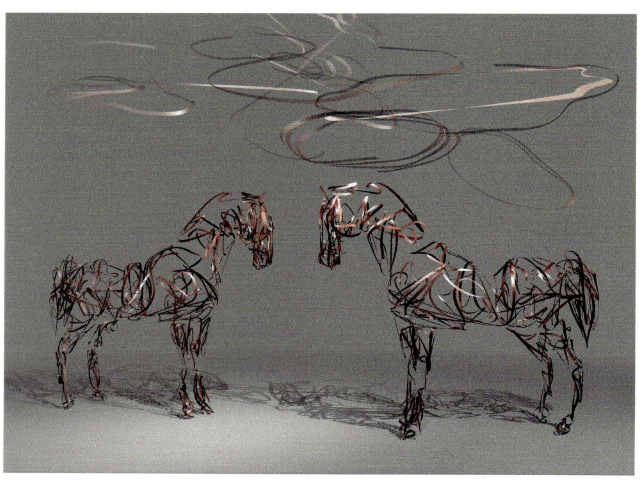

FIGURE 4.11 Charles A. Csuri, *Horse Play*, 1999, Unix environment, LightJet on paper with laminate, 30 × 40 in (76 × 102 cm). (Reprinted with permission from Caroline Csuri.)

Although it is true that Csuri's production process was altered by the machine, Carlson also opens up a perspective that allows Csuri's work process, characterized by interactions, to be seen less as a reciprocal encounter with the machine and more as a reciprocal encounter with other people. For although Csuri trained himself in programming in order to "tame" the machine, as Rosen puts it, he was only able to develop his artistic visions completely freely and openly by seeking dialogue with like-minded computer scientists and mathematicians, as mentioned above. Rosen also refers to this collaboration in her remarks. For example, she highlights Csuri's teamwork with the mathematicians Leslie Miller and James Shaffer, who supported Csuri between 1965 and 1972 in the development of a code to realize his artistic ideas.[69]

A particularly pivotal example of this collaboration is Csuri's 1968 experiment with a computer-driven milling machine. Miller wrote a code for it that Csuri explored the parameters of to create "what might be the first 3D sculpture."[70] This incident was pivotal as it encouraged Csuri to envision further possibilities of many different types of 3D art. Thus, in a way, his three-dimensional interactive art object from 1971 can be seen as a logical next step. With the help of, again, Leslie Miller, among others, Csuri was able to realize one of the first projects that made it possible to interact on a screen and also with a light pen with what appeared to be solid and colored virtual 3D objects, such as butterflies and planes.[71] Vita Berezina-Blackburn, creative technologist and teacher at ACCAD, describes the type of influence these achievements had on today's applications for the creation of procedural and generative imagery: "What we now see as core capabilities for abstraction and visualization in Houdini, Touchdesigner, some AI applications at the very least echoes Csuri's research if not source some inspiration and methodology from it."[72]

Rosen emphasizes that Csuri's colleagues from the field of mathematics were very helpful to him because he did not want to devote his creative energy primarily to programming, even though he continued his education in this area as described above. Thus, as Rosen notes, the implementation of Csuri's ideas depended not only on his own engagement with the machine, but above all on the collaboration with experts in the field of computer technology: "Csuri's vision was brought ever-closer through the process of interdisciplinary discussion and collaborative realization."[73]

Carlson also opens his accounts by discussing the collaboration between Csuri and Shaffer, emphasizing that Csuri was an artist with a pronounced interest in computers and that Shaffer was a mathematician with a pronounced interest in computer-aided image generation: "Together, these two started what would turn out to be a legacy of two divergent backgrounds coming together to press the boundaries of their research areas, and to make art with a computer."[74] Carlson thus paints a picture that can illustrate not only the collaboration between Csuri and Shaffer, but more generally the kind of collaboration that Csuri always maintained in his work with many different people. Although he trained himself technically, Carlson explains, Csuri recognized that the greatest creative potential could arise when experts from different disciplines came together.[75]

Unlike Rosen, Carlson does not use the concept of reciprocity. However, his writings on Csuri also make it evident that Csuri's production process was deeply characterized by interaction. Carlson offers a perspective that clearly shows the extent to which this interaction was present not only in Csuri's work with the computer, but above all in the collaboration with other people:

> Csuri, as an artist, would have an idea about how he wished to represent something. He would approach the scientists and make inquiries. When engaged with requests for computer code that could transform Csuri's mental images into reality, a dialogue between artist and scientist would ensue. Csuri would press on with questions. The scientist would attempt to envision his words and to explain to him the current state of technological capabilities. After numerous discussions, it was time for the scientists to explore the creative boundaries of technology within the realm of their skills and knowledge base. Through such ongoing dialogue, creativity exploded within the different disciplinary spheres, eventually coming together in the form of artistic tools that allowed computer art to be made.[76]

To illustrate this still abstract depiction of Csuri's working method, Carlson highlights the development of the "ribbon" tool from Csuri's later creative phase in the 1990s – the tool that Palazzi also lists in her chapter as one of the "signature elements in his artwork."[77] Csuri approached one of his students with a very precise idea of this tool. The student was Steve May who was then a doctoral student in computer science at OSU, and who is today the Chief Technology Officer at Pixar, where he has been employed for over 25 years.[78] Csuri was, back then, looking for a way to bring drawings from the surface into space. He no longer wanted to be able to draw on a two-dimensional plane, but instead directly in three dimensions: "Where I may have a brush mark going around your face, that blocks part of your face, but I can see the back of the brush mark behind your head."[79] According to Carlson, he was inspired by the Japanese artist Kitagawa Utamoro, who mainly worked with calligraphy and woodcut techniques in the 18th century. The quality of the lines in Utamoro's calligraphy was particularly influential on Csuri's ideas. He told May that he wanted to draw in space with lines that correspond to those of Utamoro's. Csuri imagined these lines as spatial structures in which they could develop their own depth and width and move in any direction. He also wanted his spatial lines to become objects that, unlike their two-dimensional counterparts, could reflect light and cast shadows. Carlson's account of the collaboration between Csuri and May clearly characterizes the determination with which Csuri wanted to realize his artistic ideas on the computer. He always insisted on finding a way in which it would not be him who would fulfill the demands of the computer, but a way in which the computer would fulfill *his* demands:

> May noted, as any competent computer scientist of the time would, that a line, by definition, is a two-dimensional concept, with no breadth or depth and, therefore, no ability to interact with a light source in three-dimensional space. Csuri pressed on with his inquiries, in his usual fashion, asking "But what if it could? What if line had depth and could be rendered in three-dimensional space?" Then came the familiar request, "I want to be able to do this. Can you help me?"[80]

May used the programming language *Scheme*[81] to develop a code that Csuri could use repeatedly and whose parameters he could adjust in every new situation. The width, length and movement of the lines could be set individually.

Csuri explicitly acknowledged the role his collaborators played in his artistic process. Palazzi is not the only one to emphasize this aspect;[82] in the 1989 interview, he also comments on it himself. When asked if the starting point for his work is always a meeting with a mathematician or programmer and if he therefore considers his work as a kind of group effort similar to film production, Csuri confirms this impression. However, he notes that this observation applies more to the past than to the future. With the advent of commercial software, the focus shifted much more quickly to the artist using the software than to those who developed it. He transfers this thought to the process of writing a novel: "[M]aybe this is an oversimplification, but if I'm typing a novel do I credit everybody who manufactured the typewriter?"[83] With regard to his own work, however, he emphasizes, "[b]ut in my case because I was so involved in basic research, it involved many graduate students and staff, that indeed credit had to be shared."[84] Yet, he clarifies that this applies primarily to the early phase of his career and is less relevant to the present, i.e. 1989.[85]

On the one hand, Csuri's statements about the more recent software environment contradict one of my main concerns, as I do seek to identify the influence of individuals on current computer graphics applications. On the other hand, he can also be drawn upon to legitimize my approach, because he acknowledges that the creation of computer graphics is a collaborative process. His own work is particularly well-suited to demonstrate how a certain personal background can shape the development of software. Especially in the case of commercial software, it is therefore relevant from a practical perspective to ask which people were involved in the production process and what intentions they were pursuing.

Csuri continued to create by expanding the coding he co-developed with Steve May and others in the early 1990s until the age of 99. In the 2006 interview, Csuri's perspective on the further development of commercial software and his attitude toward these developments play a central role. By that time, an industry standard had already been established in the field of 3D computer graphics. Against this background, Csuri expresses his regret at the tendency for students in the study program he developed to rarely pursue their own artistic ambitions with the technology and that they instead try to adapt to the standard in order to find employment after graduation.[86] Interviewer Robert Butche contrasts this with Csuri's own way of working. It was, as Butche describes, always about using algorithms in such a way that previously designed artistic concepts were then ultimately realized by the computer. Butche's description leads him to the question of whether Csuri expects this form of algorithmic art to die out. Csuri rejects this prediction, believing instead that it could be a long time before many more people turn to this type of art.[87] He emphasizes here that for one's own artistic expression it is crucial to have knowledge of programming or three-dimensional computer graphics, rather than simply relying on predefined software. In confirmation of Butche, he adds:

> I might mention one other thing, is that a friend of mine observed that the software that I use is not that sophisticated. [...] It's not the state of the art. But it's the way that I use it, I think that makes the difference. And there are much more powerful tools out there that one could use.[88]

When asked whether he had considered what might happen to his way of working if he included these newer, more powerful tools in his repertoire, Csuri replies that he faces an inner resistance in this regard. He is worried about turning to contemporary developments for fear of being taken over by technology.[89]

Matthew Lewis, another colleague of Csuri who supported him in the development of codes in the 1990s, provides in his own contribution to the exhibition catalog a comprehensive insight into Csuri's working methods in his so-called *Infinity series* from the 2000s (Figure 4.12). He used generative codes with which the computer independently produced image results based on parameters that were set at a starting point. Lewis describes that, according to Csuri, the series had already begun conceptually in 1966 and 1967 with the works *Feeding Time* and *Random War* (Figures 4.13 and 4.14). Both can be viewed as early forms of generative or procedural drawings, as Csuri used the computer to automatically generate these images according to a random principle.[90] While *Feeding Time* simulates the movement patterns of houseflies, *Random War* deals with the generation of different combat situations between soldiers, all in the same motionless pose but in different colors – red or black – applied to a sheet of paper using a plotter. The figures are rendered with simple outlines and modeled after a toy figure that was widely used in the United States at the time, the "little green army man,"[91] which depicts the soldiers of the Vietnam War in various poses. *Random War* is a work that is highly self-reflexive and layered with meaning as it comments not only on the arbitrariness of war but also on the use of the machine in the context of art, as well as the context of war. In addition to the depiction of the combat situations and to discuss the arbitrariness of war, a series of names of real people are listed above the "battlefield," including both Csuri's colleagues and his own name as well as numerous prominent people such as, for instance, Ronald Reagan or John F. Kennedy. Anticipating computer games, the names are, in this artwork, each assigned a status in a randomized manner, such as "wounded," "missing" or "surviving." Against the backdrop of the Vietnam War, art historian Glowski examines the level of meaning of the computer used by Csuri for this work in her examination of *Random War*:

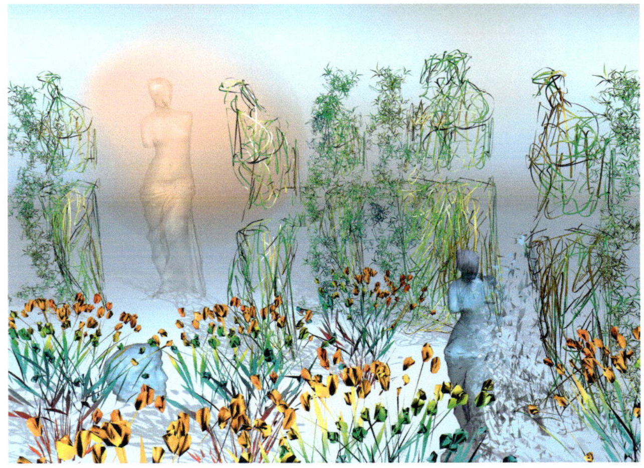

FIGURE 4.12 Charles A. Csuri, *Venus in the Garden* Frame 73, *venus series*, 2005, Unix environment, color ink on canvas, 38 × 52 in (97 × 132 cm). (Reprinted with permission from Caroline Csuri.)

> Technology was enthusiastically embraced in suburban households and touted by many as the savior of countless social and medical ills. Simultaneously, many perceived it as a demonic force that introduced chaos, depersonalizing and degrading human beings. To many in the art community, creating art with a computer was an act of evil in itself.[92]

That *Random War* was important for Csuri can be seen by the fact that he returned to it and its comment on the phenomenon of war using his newer tools from the 1990s until 2016.[93] The themes of "randomness, game-like playfulness and innovation in his digital art creation,"[94] i.e. his conceptual approach to generating images on the computer, were always maintained. This was still the case when the visual aesthetics changed to a three-dimensional space at a later stage, like, for example, in the *Infinity series* from the 2000s. In terms of visual aesthetics it differs considerably from the two works from the 1960s. The images of the *Infinity series* no longer depict merely black or red outlines on a sheet of paper; instead, they resemble other contemporary computer graphics in their appearance, in which three-dimensional geometric objects are arranged in a virtual space, each reacting to light and casting shadows. However, Lewis confirms once again that Csuri's conceptual approach has not changed significantly since the 1990s:

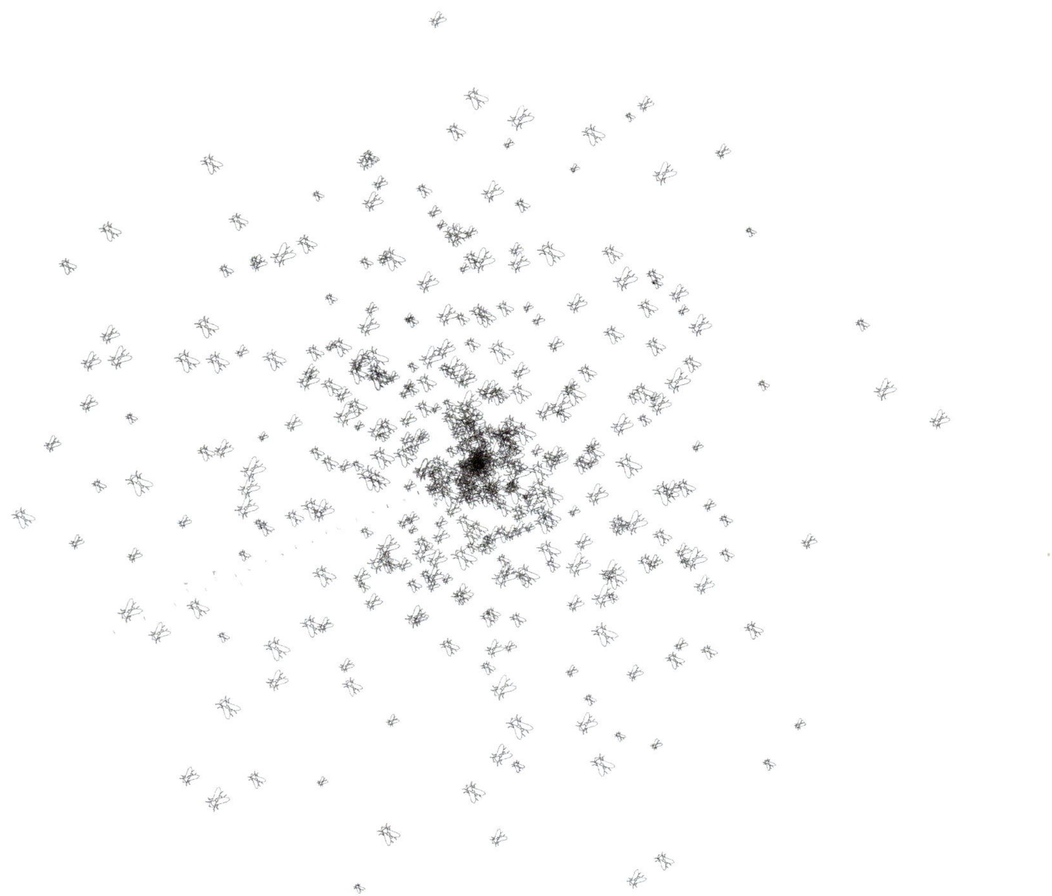

FIGURE 4.13 Charles A. Csuri, *Feeding Time*, 1966, ink on paper, IBM 7094 and drum plotter, 30 × 50 in (76 × 127 cm). (Reprinted with permission from Caroline Csuri.)

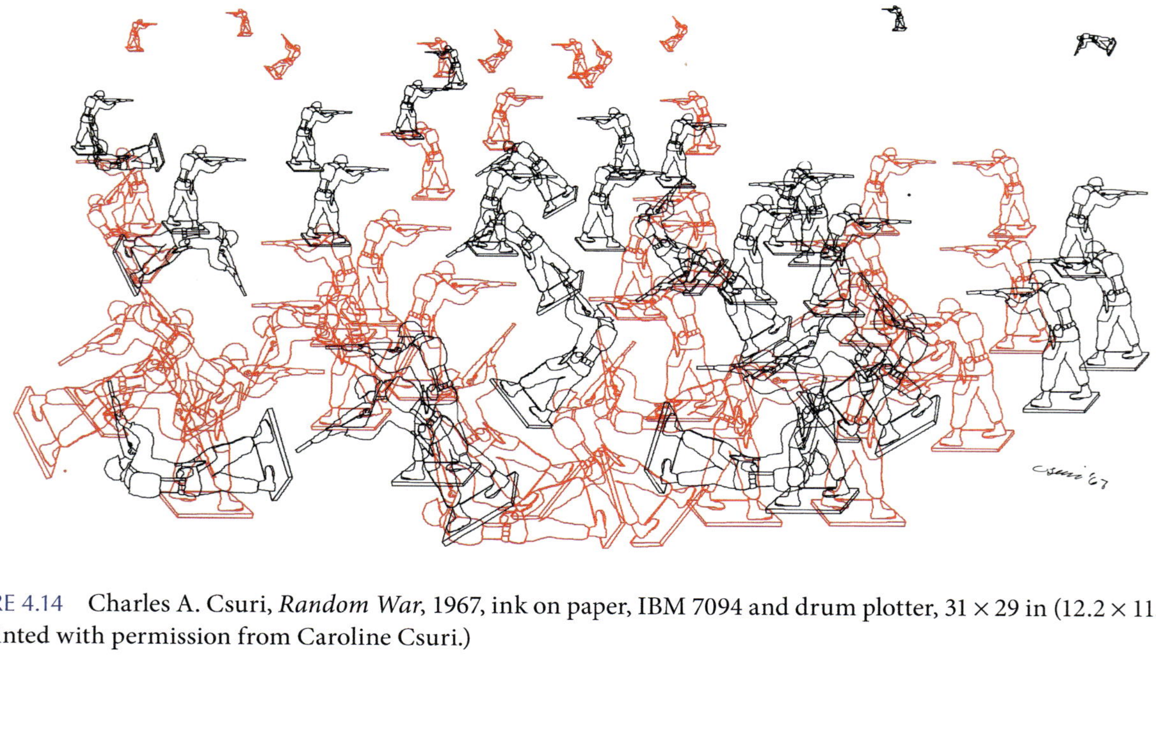

FIGURE 4.14 Charles A. Csuri, *Random War*, 1967, ink on paper, IBM 7094 and drum plotter, 31 × 29 in (12.2 × 11.4 cm). (Reprinted with permission from Caroline Csuri.)

> While most three-dimensional computer graphics images are created by artists using highly interactive commercial computer graphics software packages, Csuri composes his scenes primarily by writing short programs in an environment built upon the old but well-respected computer language Scheme. The code is assembled in an ancient text editor on what was once a very expensive workstation. Csuri rarely sculpts geometry using direct interactive modeling. He creates designs more commonly by intuitive selection from computer-generated options, exploring the results of numerical parameter changes and exchanging procedures.[95]

In his description of Csuri's approach, Lewis notes that the conceptual background of the individual images is never visible in the finished result. Rather, the way in which the depicted scenery takes on a new appearance by changing individual parameters can only be explored by experimenting with the code used by Csuri. As a rule, Csuri spent several weeks designing virtual environments in order to later "wander" through the landscapes, some of which were automatically generated using the various parameters. He would then have the computer calculate individual sections as single images. During each of these walks, individual "viewpoints" were saved as images in a kind of series, which also contained metadata about the exact location in the virtual space so that it could later be determined where the virtual image was taken. Lewis refers to these cached viewpoints as a "metadrawing."[96] These viewpoints were never visible in this form; they were only implicitly depicted as part of an image sequence, which Csuri rarely exhibited in its entirety. As a rule, he selected individual stills from a sequence that he found particularly interesting, "sometimes the final destination, but more often an image discovered along the way."[97] Occasionally, Lewis reports, Csuri let the computer take the walks and select images while he himself was asleep.[98] The image *Festive Frame 47* from the *Leo series*, for example, was found – as Csuri wrote on his website – by his "virtual me"[99] (Figure 4.15). He analyzed this find in critical self-reflection:

> I'm told there may be a way to give the image an aura of complexity. Maybe even a niche for my work. I need to bring attention to the algorithms I use. Make the code part of the aesthetic. I might find a home with generative art, artificial life, or even multi-agent systems. But these are procedures and processes or recipes which have little to do with art. So how do we tell if its [*sic*] art?[100]

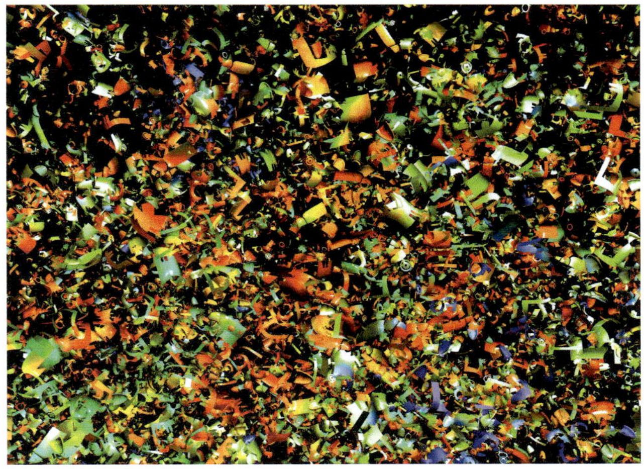

FIGURE 4.15 Charles A. Csuri, *Festive Frame 47, leo series*, 2006, Unix environment, LightJet on paper with laminate, 72 × 96 in (183 × 244 cm). (Reprinted with permission by Caroline Csuri.)

In addition to this approach, in some cases Csuri not only selected images or had them selected but also changed the virtual environment even further after a find. Lewis explains that Csuri used this option particularly when the computer took different paths than Csuri had originally foreseen.

Two insights can be derived from these descriptions by Lewis: First, it becomes clear once again that Csuri's pictures from different creative phases cannot necessarily be connected with each other based on image aesthetics. Rather, as has been noted, they can be connected on a conceptual level in terms of how he made use of the computer. They are therefore similar in regard to *production aesthetics*. Second, Lewis can also be interpreted in such a way that this production-aesthetic level contributed significantly to the aesthetic value of Csuri's works. After all, especially in the later works from the 1990s onward, it only becomes clear through the examination of the production of the images that Csuri did not utilize the commercially available software that was beginning to be established at that time.

An important interim conclusion of this section is that Csuri was able to maintain openness in his artistic process on the computer because he remained true to the codes that he developed or had developed according to his own artistic ideas until the end. He also used codes that surprised him, where he would always find something new. Openness was therefore also intended from the outset in his approach to developing the codes. He confirms this impression in the 1989 interview:

> I mean with computer graphics you can end up doing what every traditional painter has ever done, or what photographers do. But I think the more interesting challenge is really to do things that one would not ordinarily think of. I think from my point of view, I sort of have a rule. I ask myself a question: "Can I do this by conventional means?", then I'm on the wrong track.[101]

Once again, his self-assessment makes evident that for him the artistic intention always took precedence over the technological aspect of his art. Csuri's works are often even described as organic. As Palazzi explains, he also used this term himself to characterize the pictures he produced in the late 1980s and early 1990s.[102] Bonnie Mitchell, the curator of the exhibition organized in 2006, even presents the organic appearance of the works as a contradiction to the means of expression used by Csuri. She refers to a panel discussion entitled *New Methods, New Artforms*, which took place in 1990 as part of a SIGGRAPH event. Csuri was one of the panelists and in the discussion he expressed the idea, as I also present it in this section, that he did not see the computer as a control instance with which he wanted to plan the entire process in advance, but rather that he used it to be surprised by chance results.[103] Looking back, Mitchell says, "I was inspired by Csuri's ability to communicate human spirituality using tools that were so inorganic in nature."[104] Accordingly, the computer remains external to Csuri's work in the sense of John Dewey[105] or, as Csuri himself put it in 1989, "[i]t doesn't matter whether it's a keyboard or a brush, it's all the same."[106]

One question is now still unresolved: Why have Csuri's concepts made only little direct contribution to shaping the 3D software available today and thus the contemporary commercial practice of synthetic image generation, even though he was involved in the development of 3D graphics software not only as an artist but also as part of his financially supported research for over 20 years, and even though he always endeavored to expand the expressive possibilities on the computer with new codes? While some of the commercial software Csuri and his colleagues did develop – as will be described below – was, in fact, passed on to big tech companies, his artistic tools, which were really the ones that carried his artistic signature, were not commercialized – nor were they meant to.[107] Wayne Carlson's discussion of Csuri's interdisciplinary way of working provides further insight on these questions. In his chapter, Carlson focuses on Csuri's vision of developing, on the one hand, an academic program in which art and technology were to be a central component of teaching in an interdisciplinary way, and exploring, on the other hand, the potential of computer graphics expression in business terms. In 1971, Csuri founded the *Computer Graphics Research Group* (CGRG) at OSU. This research unit evolved into the ACCAD in 1986,[108] which was then incorporated into the *College of Arts and Sciences* as an independent department. After several years of research in computer graphics at CGRG, Csuri, with the support of investor Robert Kanuth of *The Cranston Companies*, founded *Cranston/Csuri Productions, Inc.* (CCP) in 1981 to commercialize the new technical possibilities in computer graphics for both the film industry and television. In the course of this development, the employees of the newly founded production company modified the software designed by the research group to make it more user-friendly. During this time, the software was expanded to include modules that made it easier to animate characters or interactively model virtual objects. A function for procedural effects and a render engine were also added. The software was used until the company was dissolved in 1987 and was subsequently acquired by the Minneapolis-based production company *Lamb and Company*.[109]

Over a period of a few years, Csuri's company achieved certain success in the market, which is why he developed the desire to invest part of the income in experimental exploration of the field. In the long term, this idea was not compatible with the views of the company's board of directors and investors, which is why Csuri left the production company in 1985 and returned to OSU to work there full-time. Parallel to his work at the company, he had continued to pursue his artistic research there.[110] The company ultimately closed their doors due to massive changes in computer hardware and software. Carlson explains,

> [w]hile CCP was directing much of its investment capital to the mainframe technology that was available at the time, the computer hardware industry was introducing the workstation, and the per-cycle cost was dropping dramatically. In addition, while the conversion from the lab-oriented software base to dependable commercial software was eating its share of the company assets, the computer software industry was introducing licenses for integrated CG software that was designed from the contributions we and other pioneers made, but it was also built on very significant and ongoing research efforts of others.[111]

Former software developer at CCP, Flip Phillips, who later also worked for Pixar and who is now professor of Motion Picture Science at the *School of Film and Animation* at *Rochester Institute of Technology*, adds a few details to Carlson's accounts, indicating that Csuri did anticipate that instead of mainframe technology, workstations would be the future. This becomes evident in Phillips' remark that Csuri actively pursued that his workstations would be continuously upgraded after his retirement. He also agreed to the wish of CCP's management to sell modified software that was in use at the company for commercial purposes, but it was, according to Phillips, in the end mostly a question of intellectual property rights that led to problems in the further distribution of the full software. Yet, although it was difficult to differentiate who had ownership of which part of the software, eventually, some of the code was repackaged and taken up by large corporations such as Pixar, Adobe and Lego.[112]

Based on these accounts by Phillips and Carlson, it is now possible to understand that it was external influences beyond Csuri's control that made it difficult for him to exert more influence on the software available today. In the 1989 interview, Csuri states that he is convinced of the superiority of the software developed in Ohio over the applications developed by others. When asked, for example, which software Csuri and his colleagues had developed that he himself regarded as particularly influential, he simply replied that they had developed all the components of the software for generating 3D computer graphics themselves from the outset and rarely used commercial products.[113] In the interview he describes a project he was involved in at the time that dealt with the subsequent image processing of digital photographs. He emphasizes a special feature of the program that allowed users to operate the computer with icons instead of code. Behind each icon a function was hidden – for example a tool with which the contrast of an image could be changed or one that could give digital photographs a painterly appearance: "[T]he code will make it work and then it's almost like pushing buttons."[114]

Csuri mentions features here that are now taken for granted in image editing programs such as Photoshop or apps like Instagram. Although he notes that using the program he describes requires little knowledge of the computer technology behind it, he stresses that it is always advantageous to have a basic understanding of computer technology and the underlying processes. In this particular context, he does not explain again why he holds this opinion. He ends his answer to the question of how his work is influential with a reference to the interdisciplinary working environment in which he and his colleagues developed software such as the image processing program. He acknowledges this as a unique quality that distinguishes it from other environments in which graphics software was developed:

> In this environment, you would have a very good relationship between the technical and the art people. So there's a great deal of interaction and an influence on the way that software is often put together, and some of the features in software that will need some fine arts requirements that you're not going to find in commercial software.[115]

Csuri's interviewer, Kerry Freedman, also asks him about the developments of other people, for instance, the technologies of texture and bump mapping, which were particularly central to Csuri's way of working at the time. In reaction to Freedman he mentions the name Jim Blinn, who developed bump mapping at the *Computer Science Department* of the *University of Utah* in the 1970s. In response to Freedman's assumption that Blinn had influenced Csuri's own research, he replies, "[y]es. But we did it as early as anybody else. In fact, we're probably doing it better."[116] In this context, he also refers to Pixar's rendering algorithm *RenderMan*, which was co-developed by Edwin Catmull and very advanced at the time. Csuri emphasizes that he and his team were also working in parallel on a rendering algorithm that was supposed to be much more efficient. His comments indicate that he did perceive his approach as unique among all the others and if one considers his artistic background, it most likely was. For example, Csuri explains in the interview that the development of the algorithm at OSU was driven by artistic interests – unlike, for instance, in his opinion, the development of *RenderMan*: "The scientists are perfectly happy with what they have now, but we want to do something that's better for the artist."[117] Csuri was just as much a scientist, but the separation that he makes here between "artists" and "scientists" against the background of software development is of particular interest for my discussion, because – unless one programs an image from scratch – for today's practice of synthetic image generation the path that the "scientists" have created is much more influential. If one follows Csuri's separation in terms of terminology, then from today's perspective, the "scientific" approach to synthetic image generation, as he calls it, is what mostly prevails in commercially available software. Pixar's *RenderMan*, for example, is used worldwide in film production, both for the creation of computer-animated films and for effects sequences in live-action films as has also been pointed out in Section 2.1. And, to put it bluntly, since the rendering process represents (at least in simplified terms) the final stage in synthetic image creation and is therefore responsible for the final image aesthetics, it can be said in retrospect that from a production-aesthetic perspective the images that largely characterize popular culture today bear the signature of Pixar much more than that of Csuri. With regard to the entire 3D graphics software, i.e. the part of the application that is required *before* the rendering process, other people besides Edwin Catmull and Pixar also played a role, but here too, Csuri's contributions to their software did not shift the entire aesthetic goal that was pursued by the "scientists." The separation that he creates between himself and the other researchers explains this observation.

Csuri saw one of the greatest differences between his own approach and that of the "scientists" in relation to the idea of what synthetic image production must be able to achieve in terms of image aesthetics. As he pointed out himself, the motivation behind his own creation of such images differed greatly from the interests of the "scientists." They were mainly interested in creating photorealistic images, a possibility that even Csuri regarded as particularly revolutionary,[118] but which did not inspire him from an artistic perspective:

> The kind of issues that researchers deal with are so basic, like how do I develop a technique to make something look like this table or this woodgrain? There's a preoccupation with realism, photo-realism. Or in the case of animation they're trying to [...] come up with algorithms to determine how the body should move. [...] Well, I'm interested in that, but I'm much more interested in the algorithms and the techniques, and I don't want to do realistic people moving. I want to do some abstract shapes that are in motion. I want to think of it in a more expressive way. But in order to do that I need to understand the technology. So I suppose in that regard it stimulates my thinking. I mean it's important that I understand the graphics algorithms and how they work, and as I understand them, then I can think of ways of using them artistically that the researcher would never think of.[119]

Although with my study I do not aim to assess whether the scientists' ambitions can be considered artistic, I do agree with Csuri's observation about the stylistic choices of this group of developers from whom he so decisively differentiates himself. I view the endeavors toward computer-generated photorealism as an aesthetic phenomenon that, just like Csuri's visual language, has a cultural origin and emerged from a specific motivation. Csuri's differentiation provides a significant justification for why I chose to present him as a parallel phenomenon within the historiography I pursue here. It is because the history I try to trace with my investigation refers to these very photorealistic endeavors and to their origin. Csuri himself is not – at least not directly – one of them.

So, how can these findings be used to return to the path of the historiography I want to pursue here and how can they help to describe the relation between Sutherland's and Csuri's work? As indicated, Sutherland can be counted among the group of scholars from whom Csuri differentiated himself. The *Smithsonian Magazine*, which dedicated its cover story to the artist in 1995, even reports on a meeting between the two pioneers. The account of this meeting illustrates particularly vividly how differently Sutherland and Csuri approached their respective tasks of creating computer graphics. The other – "scientific" – side also seemed to notice the difference to Csuri, here called Chuck:

> Lee [Csuri's wife] recalls a conference where Csuri met Ivan Sutherland, an engineer who pioneered in developing the graphics for pilot-training simulators. "He was disparaging towards Chuck, yet he seemed selfconscious about doing art with an engineering background. And Chuck was feeling that engineers were so much smarter than he was. So one night after the meeting, as we were all sitting around drinking and feeling no pain, I told Ivan, when you go home tonight you should stand in front of the mirror and say, 'I am an artist! I am an artist!' And I'm going to stand Chuck in front of the mirror and he's going to say, 'I am a scientist! I am a scientist!' They started laughing, and got along fine after that."[120]

This anecdote from Csuri's wife Lee Csuri confirms the assumption that Sutherland did not seek a dialogue with artists for his developments in the same way that Csuri did with scientists. In any case, Sutherland obviously had a different view of what art or even what a picture should achieve than Csuri. The extent to which the two were opposed in their mindsets is therefore very aptly expressed here. The comparison between Sutherland and Csuri that I set up at the beginning of this section was rooted in the fundamentally comparable attitude of both: Artistic processes should be able to proceed openly without a goal having to be defined in advance. Both were aware that the unpredictability of the work process did not correspond to the way of working on the computer at the time, which is why both considered it desirable if the computer, when used for artistic purposes, could nevertheless enable an open work process. Having reached the end of this section, it is now clear that, beyond this starting point, there are only a few other points of contact between Csuri and Sutherland. The essential difference between the two pioneers remains that Sutherland originally pursued a different goal with his research than Csuri. Although both found a plausible way to configure the computer in such a way that it could be used freely, it must be emphasized here that both pursued this task with completely different motivations. Both understood the concept of freedom differently. While Sutherland wanted to facilitate interaction with the computer in general and, in doing so, developed a tool that could also be used for artistic work, Csuri's artistic background was always the starting point and driving force behind his computer technology developments. Margit Rosen confirms this observation, although she does not explicitly refer to Sutherland. Like Csuri, she also makes a distinction between artists and scientists, although she does not adopt his terminology:

> It should be remembered that it was primarily the military, automotive, and the aviation industries that had been defining the goals for interactive graphical systems and computer simulation. Now, an artist appeared on the scene, defining different goals. He wanted to develop tools for artists – software and hardware – that would enable them to subject drawings to mathematical transformations, to construct multidimensional pictorial spaces, to virtually render sculptures that then could be milled automatically, and to draw objects that could move in these spaces and be manipulated in real time.[121]

Once again, it becomes clear that the freedom that Sutherland discovered in the computerized work process merely existed against the background of certain requirements and only within the framework of the operating features he developed. Given Rosen's description, it can therefore be assumed that Sutherland's *Sketchpad* program would probably not have been free enough for Csuri, despite the open working structure. In other words, it is possible that the program would even have restricted him. Additionally, this section could demonstrate that even before the paradigm shift in the programming process brought about by Sutherland, Csuri had already succeeded in using the computer as an artistic tool that would turn his artistic process in an open, more unpredictable direction. Completely independently of Sutherland and at a time when goal-oriented procedural programming was still standard, computer technology triggered a rethinking in Csuri, so that he no longer understood his artistic process as something that had an end, as in painting, but as something fundamentally open. Sutherland's realization that the change in the programming process he had brought about with *Sketchpad* would completely renew work processes, especially with regard to the subsequent changeability of a work result – a realization that Sutherland considered to be very far-reaching at the time – was therefore initially irrelevant for Csuri. Ultimately – as I have described several times already – it took a few more years until the object-oriented programming paradigm was established, or until it was even labeled as such by Alan Kay. Csuri also ended up working with programming languages that supported the object-oriented approach, and in the 2006 interview, he even explicitly comments on the advantages of object-oriented languages such as C++.[122] But again, it should be noted that he never fully relied on pre-programmed functions when using the object-oriented paradigm, unless he had co-developed them himself or used them in a way they were not designed for.[123] With regard to Csuri, the production-aesthetic distinction between the two paradigms is therefore of little importance. For him, the paradox I described at the beginning of this section does not apply, i.e. that the object-oriented programming paradigm can open up processes, on the one hand, but can have a restrictive effect, on the other, if operating steps are predefined. Due to Csuri's knowledge of the technical implications, it was not insignificant for him, but much less decisive, whether he could subsequently change a result or not.

So if, according to Csuri's own conviction, it was necessary to interact directly with the device in order to work freely on the computer, then it can be concluded that, even from a purely hypothetical point of view, a computer program containing Csuri's artistic ideas as prefabricated control elements would appear completely contradictory. Although Rosen highlights that Csuri wanted to create tools for artists on the computer, it must also be noted that it would be fundamentally contrary to his mindset if he had pursued this goal on a large scale and marketed commercial graphics software with his artistic tools. After all, as I have indicated, he himself emphasized that it is always advantageous to be able to operate more than just buttons. This central point is one of the most substantial differences to Sutherland, as his main concern when developing *Sketchpad* was to enable non-experts to operate the computer. Against this background, it seems almost like a logical consequence that, in the long term, the approach of the scientists, including Sutherland, has predominantly prevailed in commercially available software packages. Here, the interest was not primarily in art, but in commercial success, and this in turn can only be achieved if the entry barriers for operation are as low as possible.

One question that has yet to be answered in this context, however, is the origin of photorealism in the images of the "scientists." Although Rosen reminds us that the interactive graphics programs available today originated in the military, aviation and automotive industries, and thus indicates a genealogy that at least hints at a possible context of meaning, this is not yet sufficient to explain the realistic-figurative style of the images originating in these areas. With his choice of the term "photorealism," Csuri himself provides explicit image aesthetic indications that I will focus on in later chapters of this study. In contrast to Csuri's description, I do not consider the interest in photorealistic computer graphics to merely be a necessity of scientific accuracy. I rather view it as a cultural phenomenon that needs to be understood in greater depth. The question still remains as to why this interest has developed. My study is based on the fundamental assumption that scientific accuracy is not dependent on an impeccably photorealistic visual aesthetic when it comes to the representation of physical conditions, for example.[124] Nevertheless, it was precisely this aesthetic – as also Csuri observed – that was mainly pursued by the "scientists." The research project at the *University of Utah* under the direction of Dave Evans and Ivan E. Sutherland also fit into this category.

If William A. Fetter is now introduced as a further representative of developments parallel to those at MIT, through him a first approximation of this visual phenomenon can be provided. Fetter can be seen as a bridge between Csuri and Coons. Rosen refers to Fetter among numerous other pioneers as one of Csuri's contemporaries who, like Csuri, was interested in reproducing the visible world using new technical processes.[125] He did not pursue the goal of developing software or hardware himself to make this possible, which sets him apart from both Csuri and Sutherland. The proximity to Coons and, consequently, to Sutherland can be derived from the visual aesthetics Fetter was aiming for and from his understanding of images. And on a more superficial level, this proximity can also be established by the fact that Fetter – like Coons and Sutherland – was interested in the graphic depiction of airplanes.

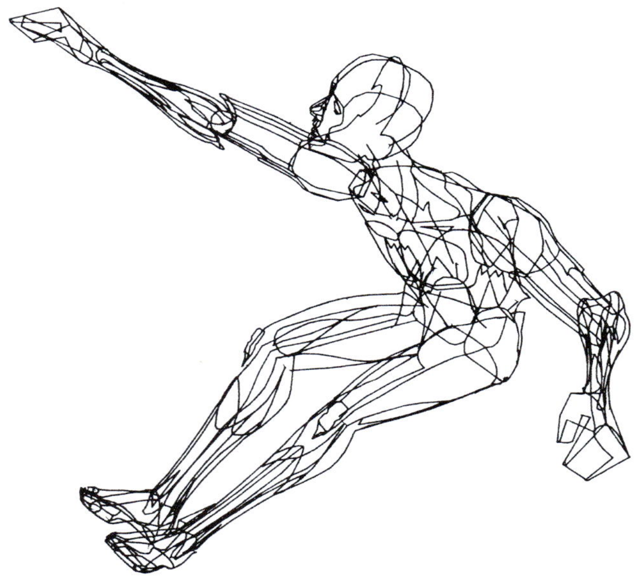

FIGURE 4.16 William A. Fetter, *First Boeing Man*, 1966–1969, ink on paper, IBM 7094 and CDC 6600, Gerber plotter, 7.2 × 9.4 in (18.2 × 24 cm). (Copyright © 1966–1969 Boeing. All rights reserved. Licensing Terms and Conditions.)

4.2 WILLIAM A. FETTER – THE COMPUTER AS A MEANS TO AN END

> Computer Graphics [...] make it possible to have the results available in a form that is understandable by the engineer and the non-technical observer as well.[126]
>
> *WILLIAM A. FETTER (1966)*

William A. Fetter is regarded as one of the first persons to produce perspective computer graphics and also as the first person to generate perspective views of a human in this manner in the mid-1960s.[127] Figure 4.16 shows one of these first graphics, which aims to show the maximum reach of a person in the cockpit of an airplane. Fetter pursued the task of creating images like this in his role as a graphic designer for the aircraft manufacturer Boeing. He was convinced that the technical details of aircraft production can be communicated particularly well with the help of perspective illustrations, "rather than in verbal or numerical form alone."[128] This proposition also forms the basis of his monograph *Computer Graphics in Communication*, published in 1965. He was convinced that the task of creating designs for airplanes and components is divided into two different areas: The production of components required, on the one hand, true-to-scale technical drawings without perspective and, on the other, perspective illustrations that could be used to visualize the components in an accessible way – an access that, according to Fetter, technical drawings could not provide. Additionally, visualizing the aircraft in operation, such as the simulated landing process from the cockpit's perspective, was, for Fetter, a useful variation of the perspective illustrations.

The prerequisites for the precise technical construction drawings were completely different from those for the illustrative designs. The distinction between these two types of drawings is of central importance in this section. Fetter's aim was to automate the production of both types of drawings with the help of a computer. In the 1966 issue of *Design Quarterly* entitled *Design and the Computer*, Fetter published the essay *Computer Graphics*, in which he outlined the computer graphics achievements he had been pursuing since the early 1960s. Fetter is introduced in the issue as "supervisor of Computer Graphics at Boeing in Seattle Washington"[129] with an additional reference to the fact that the aircraft manufacturer is regarded as the birthplace of computer graphics. According to the introduction of the essay, Boeing first made the technology available as a tool for the production of airplanes. In the article Fetter himself notes that the term "computer graphics" has been in use since 1960 and originated at the Boeing Company. He also states that in the same year he developed a new concept for perspective drawings, which replaced the approaches that had been common in the field of design drawing up to that point. Similar to Csuri's interdisciplinary approach, Fetter collaborated with mathematicians and programmers to translate his concepts into mathematical principles and then into programming language commands.[130] Using the commands for the computer, which followed the procedural programming paradigm common at the time, a plotter was instructed to produce black-and-white line drawings on a sheet of paper. Fetter did not, initially, make use of a CRT screen as a graphic output device like, for instance, Sutherland did.

In his essay, Fetter attempts to define what the phenomenon of computer graphics actually is. Indirectly, it can be drawn from his reflections that the idea of interdisciplinarity can characterize the technology particularly aptly, although he emphasizes how difficult it is to positively describe the characteristics of computer graphics. He therefore takes the opposite approach and attempts to define what it is not:

> It is not a machine. It is not a computer, nor a group of computer programs. It is not the know-how of a graphic designer, a programmer, a writer, a motion picture specialist, or a reproduction specialist.
>
> Computer graphics is all these – a consciously managed and documented technology directed toward communicating information accurately and descriptively.[131]

With his description that computer graphics are "consciously managed," Fetter provides initial clues that make it possible to place him within the historiography I pursue here: For him, computer graphics are an imaging technique that requires elaborate and meticulous planning. In direct comparison to Sutherland, a considerable difference becomes apparent here right at the beginning, because for Sutherland the exact opposite was the goal of his developments. He no longer wanted to meticulously plan what would come out in the end when working with the computer. However, despite their different approaches to making use of computers, I propose that they had similar ideas of what a computer graphic should be able to achieve. Implicitly, this hypothesis underlines my general point of view that the openness proclaimed by Sutherland in the design process was at the same time tied to clear and therefore, in a way, limiting ideas, just as it is true for today's software applications. The main focus of this section is the difference between the two pioneers in their use of the computer. Yet, their comparable understanding of images remains relevant as well, although it should be mentioned here again that Sutherland's understanding of images can only be fully comprehended when Steven A. Coons also comes into the focus of the investigation. Fetter can therefore also be understood as a preparation for the examination of Coons and consequently Sutherland's concept of pictoriality.

With his description of the two different types of drawing, for design purposes on the one hand and technical on the other, Fetter articulated a concept that already hints at the context of meaning of today's computer graphics, although Fetter, as a historical figure, did not himself actively contribute to the introduction of this context of meaning into the software. While I comparatively drew upon Csuri's work process to show which alternative concepts of art and imagery can influence software development, the focus is now on Fetter to show that a certain idea of imagery does not *have* to become part of the computer or the software. In Fetter's case, the machine remained practically untouched by his understanding of imagery. In this respect, he differs from both Sutherland and Csuri. Clarifying why this statement applies to Fetter but not Sutherland (or Csuri, for that matter) sheds light on how Sutherland actually "programmed" an understanding of images into his software.

To explore these observations in depth, this section is divided into two parts. The first part discusses Fetter's approach to his work with the computer, in order to then analyze his graphic concepts in the second part and thus create a bridge to Coons. At the center of my examination of these two aspects of Fetter's work is his 1965 monograph *Computer Graphics in Communication*.[132] In it, he explained in detail how he proceeded in the creation of computer graphics and which graphic ideas he pursued.

Before I introduce his own remarks, I will first place Fetter in a historical context by drawing on Rebecca Perry's accounts in her study *Rigging the World: 3D*

Modeling and the Seduction of the Real. I will occasionally refer to Perry in the chapters on Fetter and Coons because, as was discussed in the section on the state of research, she also traces key historical milestones in the development of 3D computer graphics. Perry's investigation provides a possible explanation as to why Fetter's approach to working with computers did not influence the software in the same way as Sutherland's but nevertheless appears informative for the context of meaning of today's 3D graphics. According to Perry, the current practice of creating virtual models in digital space for the entertainment industry can be divided into two interconnected strands of development:

> the creation of computer hardware and software in military-funded academic research centers, and the evolution of digital objects as analytical and communication tools. The first is connected to the invention of calculating machines and their application to the manufacture and analysis of physical objects, and the second is connected to the production of virtual objects-visual representations that connect technical and non-technical audiences, performed in the spaces of the computer.[133]

Perry does not yet name any particular people in regard to the individual strands of development she presents. Nevertheless, according to the findings of my own study so far, Sutherland can be categorized in the first and Fetter in the second strand. From a historical perspective, Sutherland was, after all, initially interested in the machine and its operating options, while Fetter was concerned with producing computer-aided drawings of airplanes and components for communication purposes – the title of his above-mentioned monograph *Computer Graphics in Communications* also indicates this.

For the historical accounts of the 3D model, which is her focus, Perry makes a further distinction between three historical waves of development. It is also suitable for my focus on the production of synthetic images and the historical categorization of Fetter. In addition, the other contributors I present in this study can be categorized according to Perry's classification as well. In the course of the first wave, Perry describes, computer-generated models were primarily depicted in the form of outlines. Perry explains, this early approach corresponded to the long-established concepts underlying the creation of diagrams and plans. In the second wave, which she dates from the early to late 1960s and in which she categorizes Fetter,[134] among others, efforts were made to expand the outline drawings of the objects depicted to include surface information and to lend them a dimensionality. The third wave finally led to the elaboration of the surfaces and materials of the depicted objects, their texturing and the way in which they react to light and reflections. Perry refers to the shift in the computer-aided representation of objects using outlines to the representation of objects with surface information that occurred with the second wave in the 1960s as the "geometric turn."[135] On the basis of this historical structure developed by Perry, it can be deduced to what extent Sutherland and Fetter can be regarded as part of a common historical context, although they approached the subject of computer graphics with completely different interests in mind. In addition, Perry's structure can also explain why Csuri appears as a marginal figure in this structure: He was not involved in the "geometric turn" in the same way as Sutherland and Fetter, which is shown by his lack of interest in the emerging photorealistic tendencies in the field of computer graphics.

In a separate chapter section, which Perry calls "The Digital Shadow of Real Objects," she first turns her attention to Fetter and Pierre Bézier, who worked for the French car manufacturer Renault in a similar capacity to Fetter for Boeing. She emphasizes, "[f]or both Fetter and Bézier, the ability to think broadly and collaborate outside of their own departments was key to their achievements."[136] One detail that is not relevant to Perry's study, but which proves to be quite interesting for my own, is that, unlike Fetter, Bézier is still encountered today in graphical computer applications in both 2D and 3D. In the latter field, the Bézier curves he developed are a way of modeling virtual objects. They can be seen as an alternative to polygon-based modeling, which, as explained in Section 2.1, is widely used in large parts of the entertainment industry. Bézier functions are primarily applied in cases where graphical information requires a high degree of mathematical precision, for example in the field of industrial design when it comes to the production of components. Since it is not important to Perry why Fetter's work does not characterize today's production process compared to Bézier's, she does not address the question why this might be the case. To find possible reasons for this, Fetter's own notes, in which he meticulously documented his working methods and particularly his use of the computer, are suitable. His monograph *Computer Graphics in Communication* provides insightful clues.

As indicated at the beginning of this section, when comparing Sutherland with Fetter, it is noticeable that Fetter's work with the computer was always preceded by a working goal, whereas this was not the case with Sutherland. The mere fact that Fetter was employed by an aircraft manufacturer predetermined the general direction of his computer-generated drawings,[137] but as he himself describes in his publication, not only was this overriding goal predetermined for him, but he also began each individual computer graphical image with a concrete objective:

> Steps towards producing simple or complex communications by Computer Graphics are (*1*) Aims Definition, a careful examination of the requirement; (*2*) Communication Design, a mental image or a careful plan of the desired end result; (*3*) Data Transcription, putting data in a form acceptable to the computer; (*4*) Computer Programing, a careful preparation in machine language of the generalized mathematical capabilities necessary to calculate any projection; (*5*) Automatic Drawing, the actual production of the image; (*6*) Final Rendering, any treatment of the drawing such as adding shading and coloring for a conventional communication media; and (*7*) Reproduction, a repetitive processing to increase the total number of copies, as in the process of photoprocessing and printing.[138]

It is clear from this description that, unlike Sutherland, Fetter worked with the procedural programming paradigm. In addition to his previously expressed objective, this description also reveals that, unlike Sutherland, Fetter was not interested in designing the use of the computer itself. For Sutherland, computer graphics were first and foremost a means to an end, a way of operating the computer using graphical commands. For Fetter, on the other hand, the creation of computer graphics was the goal from the outset. The motivation to use the computer was, for Fetter, solely linked to this goal. This once again confirms my observation that the creation of computer graphics is based on completely different motivations in each case.

The fact that Fetter was aware of Sutherland's alternative working approach proves to be particularly insightful. Fetter's reflections also suggest that he not only consciously chose his approach but also consciously decided against Sutherland's. In other words, he actively chose a different course of action. He refers to *Sketchpad* in several places in his monograph. For instance, the bibliography lists both *Sketchpad* and *Sketchpad III* (this version is discussed in more detail in Chapter 7) and Coons is also cited. However, in a comment on his bibliography, Fetter generally points out that his own developments occurred independently of the titles mentioned: "While references were not used directly in the development of Computer Graphics, the following may be of value to the reader in understanding engineering graphics and perspective theory."[139] Although Fetter provides this comment along with his bibliography, references to *Sketchpad* can be found in two places in his book. In the first passage, one can only indirectly deduce from the way he presents his argument that he is referring to Sutherland's *Sketchpad*, or at least to its research context:

> In the developments of computer-related graphics there appear to be two major avenues of effort. One avenue is the use of generally available digital equipment and trained computer programers. The other is the development and use of new equipment by means of which the designer draws with a light pen directly on a cathode ray tube (CRT) screen with virtually immediate response in the form of drawings, dimensions, computations, and views at his request. While the techniques described here may be useful and complementary to the CRT approach, this monograph concentrates on the digital computer-programer approach only.[140]

Fetter does not give a reason why he does not want to follow the approach pursued by Sutherland. One possible explanation is that the two approaches he describes here were too different and it would have meant considerably more effort for him to familiarize himself with a different method first, when he knew that he would also achieve his predetermined goal with his procedural approach. In addition, the hardware equipment available to Sutherland was not yet generally available but was largely restricted to research at MIT's *Lincoln Laboratory*. This can be confirmed by the second passage in which Fetter explicitly mentions *Sketchpad* this time. Although Fetter still does not refer to *Sketchpad* in the main text, he lists it in a schematic diagram, which he uses to illustrate his own approach. The overview shows several developments in the form of a list, of which *Sketchpad* is in last place. The diagram and its explanation clearly show the extent to which Fetter differentiated himself from them:

> The next figure shows the equipment near the top of the diagram which has been used within the Computer Graphics technology and the equipment near the bottom which is expected to be significantly productive in a reoriented approach that falls outside the scope of this monograph [...].[141]

Fetter's commentary demonstrates that he was not only aware of Sutherland's approach but also that he even considered it to be very promising. In his publication, Fetter does not go into detail about the exact programming innovations that Sutherland's *Sketchpad* offered. Fetter merely mentions the use of the pen and the possibility of using it to draw on a screen. The paradigmatic shift from procedural to object-oriented programming had not yet taken place in a widespread form at that time. The concept of the object-oriented paradigm was only introduced by Alan Kay in the 1970s, as I have explained elsewhere. Consequently, Fetter does not address the fact that Sutherland has fundamentally changed the way we work with computers. Nevertheless, Fetter's descriptions of the programming process provide insights into the differences between his and Sutherland's approach. Fetter's discussion of his colleague's work even makes the innovations that Sutherland brought about particularly clear. Fetter explains the work steps with the computer as follows:

> Many basic tasks must precede the arrival of the subject data cards prepared for the computer. These are (*1*) direction, the accurate definition of a distinct graphic need; (*2*) research, the basic solution to mathematically treating the graphic need; (*3*) programing, the translation of these mathematical advances in the form of workable subroutines; and (*4*) production programing, the placing of a number of programing routines in a form which allows conventional solutions to recurring Computer Graphics needs.[142]

According to this description, Fetter also had in mind – like Sutherland – that certain subroutines could be reutilized for other graphical purposes. However, it was not possible for Fetter to subsequently change his finished results. If he had wanted to make a later change to a graphic element of a drawing, he would have been forced to start again at his work step labeled with the number (1). He would have needed to develop a new, precise definition of his goal. This description by Fetter therefore aptly demonstrates what effects the changes in the programming approach brought about by Sutherland had on working with computers in general, but also on creative work with computers. Against the backdrop of Fetter's explanations, it becomes particularly evident how it is Sutherland's influence that shapes today's way of working with graphic applications. Fetter's approach would be unthinkable today.

Fetter's process confirms once again that the computer remained to a certain extent external to his goal. In the sense of John Dewey, for Fetter the computer was less a medium that significantly characterized the result and more a means that would have been interchangeable had there been alternatives.[143] Fetter himself was presumably convinced that he was using the computer not only as a means but also as a medium in Dewey's sense, because for him the computer represented an entity that facilitated and expanded the designer's ability to create complex designs and communicate his ideas. In this respect, Fetter also refers to abstract representations of data sets, for example the three-dimensional visualization of aerodynamic acoustic signals.[144] Nevertheless – as can be deduced from

Fetter's own description of the process – the planning for both abstract visualizations and concrete, perspective designs always preceded the use of the computer. The machine was only used afterward to carry out the meticulous – or in Fetter's words "tedious"[145] – work of the precise drawing process. Conversely, however, Fetter's work steps show that it would also have been possible – with a great deal of effort – to produce these drawings by hand. In his paper *Computer Graphics*, Fetter even explains that the computer does not necessarily have to be used if the concept to be presented could be communicated in another way:

> In Computer Graphics, three aspects have to be understood: first, the communicator who has an idea or message to communicate; second, the communication specialist who decides whether the problem should be solved graphically, verbally or as a combination of both; third, the computer specialist who selects the computer equipment and interprets the problem so that the computer can act upon it.[146]

Fetter's starting point was always the idea of communication, and although he had a device at his disposal that he could have instructed to do anything using procedural programming – as Csuri's artistic approach proves – Fetter persisted in merely having the computer execute something that he could have realized manually with great effort. As shown in the quote, according to Fetter, an existing concept for implementation on the computer must even first be interpreted in such a way that the machine can be used at all. In comparison to Csuri, it is now apparent that Fetter did not utilize the freedom of procedural programming in the same way. Csuri transferred part of the responsibility for the artistic results to the computer itself and thus involved the machine much more closely in his creative processes than Fetter. Csuri thus utilized the computer and the procedural programming paradigm in the sense of Dewey as a medium. This statement applies to Sutherland in a similar way. He also recognized that the computer had the potential to permanently change work processes so that they could not have been imitated manually in the same way. For him, too, the computer left its own new medial traces in the finished product, but Sutherland also helped to shape these traces in a more lasting way. The manner in which he used the computer in new ways, on the one hand, and steered it in his own direction, on the other, forms the actual intersection with Fetter – Sutherland used similar graphic parameters for the prefabricated program modules as Fetter defined for his work. I will now present and analyze these parameters.

What was a successful graphic representation for Fetter? As explained at the beginning of the section, he divided the activity of creating graphics into two areas, each of which was based on different requirements. On the one hand, his task was to produce technical drawings that had to be precise and comprehensible for production, while on the other hand, he also needed illustrations that could make his ideas accessible to those who did not have the ability to read technical drawings. The problem of communicating concepts was therefore always at the heart of Fetter's graphic interest – this applies equally to both forms of drawing, although the type of communication is defined differently for the two forms. In the introduction to Fetter's monograph, Edward C. Wells, then Vice President of Product Development at Boeing, provides an initial characterization of the more comprehensible variant of drawings. He explains why it makes sense for engineers to use the non-specialist field of "graphics" instead of specialist terms and concepts for the purpose of better communication: According to Wells, graphics are "among the most universal means of depicting phenomena or solving engineering problems."[147] He explains further that computer technology is particularly suitable for organizing these drawing processes economically. The distinction he makes here between the field of graphics and the field of computer technology sheds light on two aspects: First, it shows once again that in this way of thinking the computer is still a means to an end, so it plays a different role here than it does to Sutherland; second, however, the idea of a universal mode of expression establishes a direct connection to Sutherland, because he also believed that universal design principles exist, as was demonstrated in Chapter 3. Furthermore, it is even clearer here than in Sutherland's work that not only did the idea of a universal form of graphic expression exist in Fetter's environment, but that this was also linked to perspective forms of representation. Analyzing Fetter's concept of imagery can help explain how this link came about. To illustrate his communicative aims, he refers right at the beginning of his monograph to Étienne-Jules Marey, who had at the end of the 19th century also developed with his chronophotographs a new technical process to visualize and communicate a subject matter graphically or rather *photo*graphically – in his case, they were motion sequences. Fetter prefaces his own text with a quote from Marey in which he explains his view of the potential of graphic visualization methods:

> The graphic method, with its various developments, has been of immense service to almost every branch of science, and consequently many improvements have of late been effected. Laborious statistics have been replaced by diagrams in which the variations of a curve express in a most striking manner the several phases of a patiently observed phenomenon, and, further, a recording apparatus which works automatically can trace the curve of a physical or physiological event, which by reason of its slowness, its feebleness, or its rapidity, is otherwise inaccessible to observation.
>
> Language is as slow and obscure a method of expressing the duration and sequence of events as the graphic method is lucid and easy to understand. As a matter of fact, it is the only natural mode of expressing such events; and, further, the information which this kind of record conveys is that which appeals to the eyes, usually the most reliable form in which it can be expressed.[148]

Marey mentions a whole series of aspects here that indicate the context of meaning of synthetic 3D computer graphics – for example his phrasing that the graphic method is the only "natural" way to visualize the duration or sequence of a given situation. The concept of "naturalness" can be compared with the concept of "universality" introduced by Wells above. How did Wells and Marey interpret these concepts? With Fetter, the meaning can be narrowed down somewhat, but he also does not question whether there is a natural or universal approach to creating or reading images.

One aspect that Fetter particularly highlights in his own comments in response to Marey's statement is the idea of reliable communication. Although Marey's statement was already outdated in Fetter's time, it is, according to him, still valid or is just becoming valid again, against the background of new computer graphics methods. He even takes up this aspect in the summarizing thoughts at the end of his monograph: "An aim of Computer Graphics is to improve the directness with which the engineer communicates and each new generation of equipment furthers this aim."[149] Although Fetter categorized Marey's technical "equipment" as belonging to a previous generation, he considered the demands on their images comparable: "His [Marey's] work provided science with descriptive tools that were both technically valid and strikingly descriptive."[150]

Fetter also sought a process to create images that could reliably and vividly provide information about a subject matter. With reference to Marey, Fetter mentions two aspects at the very beginning of his monograph that play a central role for him in the creation of computer graphics and that he then frequently revisits: Technical precision on the one hand and the immediate comprehensibility of a drawing on the other. The two criteria reflect the two types of drawings, i.e. the true-to-scale technical drawings, on the one hand, and the illustrative perspective design drawings, on the other. To describe the requirements for the two types of drawings, Fetter uses the term "measurability" for the first type and the term "clarity" for the second, explicitly linking the concept of clarity to perspective design principles.[151] He also provides a justification for the connection he has made:

> Central projections or perspectives, common in production illustrations, are most valuable for the clarity of the elements and the true appearance of the subject, since they are presented just as they are seen by the eye. Each addition of shading, color, and movement enhances the degree of realism and special clarity in the drawing. A principal advantage of Computer Graphics is the ability to produce any projection in this spectrum from a single set of data.[152]

Fetter does not provide more detailed definitions for the terms "clarity," "true appearance" and "realism." He merely explains that perspective representation can do justice to all these criteria: the aforementioned clarity, a true appearance and the way our visual apparatus works. The technical drawing, on the other hand, cannot achieve this. For Fetter, the two ways of producing designs are therefore opposites. He illustrates his definition of the two forms of design work using two schematic representations. Each contains a graph. The first is called "Ease of measuring drawings" and the second is called "Ease of understanding drawings."[153] In both diagrams, Fetter combines the two different types of representation on the X-axis by gradually increasing the degree of perspective distortion from left to right. The gradations, of which the first stage forms one extreme and the last stage the other, are labeled by Fetter as "orthographic," "oblique," "isometric," "dimetric," "trimetric" and "perspective."[154] The term "orthographic" is used in engineering to describe representations that have no perspective distortion. Depth information is not represented using vanishing points; instead, in the case of a cube, for example, the front and rear sides would have the same dimensions. All further steps denote forms of perspective representations that have varying degrees of foreshortening and distortion up to the last step. The two diagrams differ on the Y-axis. In the first diagram, Fetter indicates the value of the measurability of the different forms of representation. Using a curve that slopes downwards from left to right, he illustrates that an orthographic projection is most suitable for the purpose of measurability and that no reliable measurements can be obtained from a drawing with increasing perspective distortion (Figure 4.17). The Y-axis of the second graph shows the value of the comprehensibility of the different forms of representation. Here he works with four curves, each of which refers to a different stage of refining the perspective representation: Fetter differentiates between a simple line drawing, a drawing with additional shading, then a colored graphic and finally a colored illustration in motion. According to Fetter, this last form, an animated sequence, provides the greatest clarity. Ultimately, however, all four curves increase from left to right, thus expressing the fact that the degree of comprehensibility increases with the increase in perspective distortion. In his paper *Computer Graphics*, published a year later in 1966, he does not show the two diagrams, but he reiterates the proportionality shown in them and summarizes the key ideas they illustrate:

> Since perspective projections represent objects just as the eye sees them, *measuring* becomes difficult while *understanding* increases. With the addition of shading, color and especially motion to the perspective projection, the graphic effect can be most effective and thus facilitate communication.[155]

Once again, Fetter refers to the human perceptual apparatus here – a reference that will become relevant again at the end of this section. However, to understand Fetter's descriptions and their impact on his computer-aided practice even more comprehensively, it is helpful to remember that of the four aspects of perspective drawing – lines, shading, coloring and movement – only the first stage, the line drawing, could be realized with the aid of the computer. Various perspective views of an object could fairly rapidly be generated automatically by the computer and output using a plotter. The line drawings could also be transferred to film in a sequence for moving images, but every form of

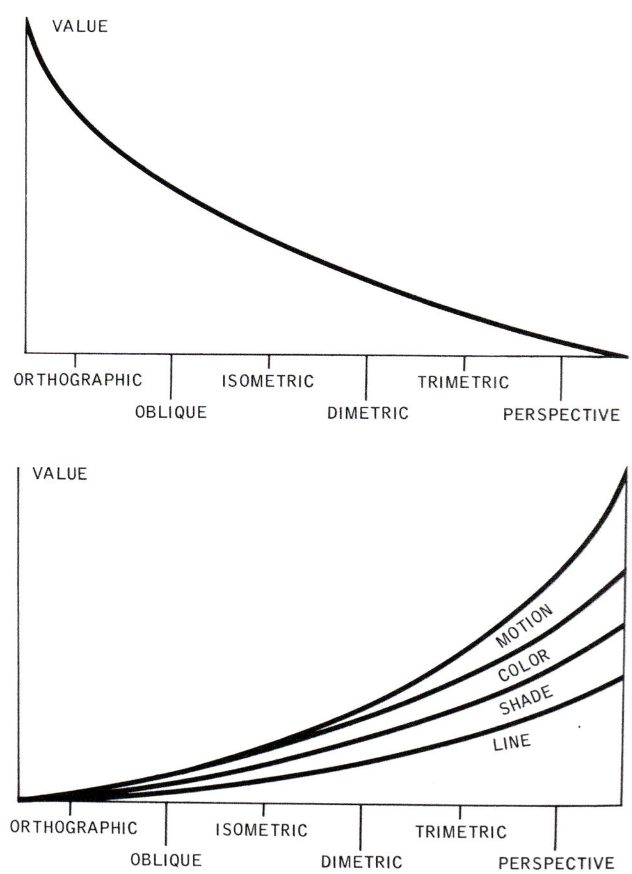

FIGURE 4.17 William A. Fetter, (a) *Ease of measuring drawings* and (b) *Ease of understanding drawings*, 1965. (Copyright © 1965 McGraw Hill.)

shading or coloring had to be done manually both on the sheets of paper and for the creation of a film after the computer had finished its work. As listed in the overview of the individual work steps, Fetter calls this fine-tuning of the computer-generated line drawings "Final Rendering."[156] He defines the term as follows:

> [Final Rendering] involves final preparation of the computer-produced drawings. The range of activity in this step can be wide.
>
> In some cases no further work need be done if the initial planning took all possible end uses into account. For plots intended as standardized engineering drawings, documents, or films, the Final Rendering may be resolved by arranging the line weight, scaling, number of data, and other factors from a format predesigned to be compatible with the current graphic design and reproduction requirements. In specialized drawings, brochures, documents, and film, considerable art work may be required for clarity or realism.[157]

In one of the last chapters of his monograph, Fetter lists numerous typical examples of the application of his computer graphics process. The large number of examples illustrates the scope of the term "final rendering" – some of the finished pictures use only simple contours to depict different flight situations (Figure 4.18), while others pay particular attention to the surface texture of the materials and are generally depicted with great detail. Their appearance is stylistically reminiscent of the photorealistic painterly movement that was establishing itself in the United States at the same time[158] (Figures 4.19 and 4.20). Fetter comments on the graphic shown in Figure 4.19: "For one illustration need, an artist heightened realism by carefully rendering the view of a low approach angle [...]."[159]

The term "final rendering" is still occasionally used today in the field of computer graphics and also describes a process similar to that described by Fetter in his day. A parallel between the "final renderings" of that time and today's finished 3D computer graphics can be established as follows: In order for an artist to create such an image back then, they first had to determine from the computer's line drawing which areas in the graphic are in the foreground and which are in the background. The parallel perspective line drawing of a cube in Figure 4.21 illustrates this problem. In the depiction on the left the two square surfaces could potentially each represent the front or back of the cube. However, in the center and right-hand depictions the cut-outs in the corresponding lines immediately

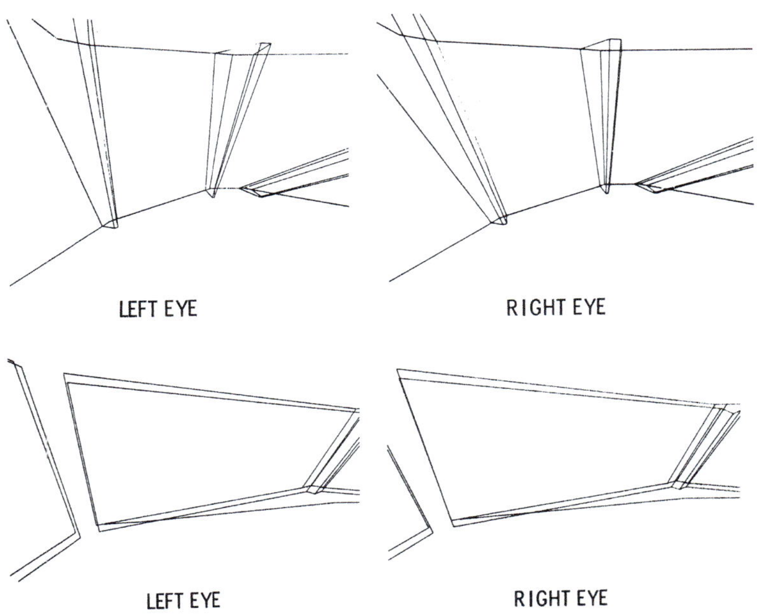

FIGURE 4.18 William A. Fetter, *Stereo views of two transport aircraft windshield designs*, 1965. (Copyright © 1965 Boeing. All rights reserved. Licensing Terms and Conditions.)

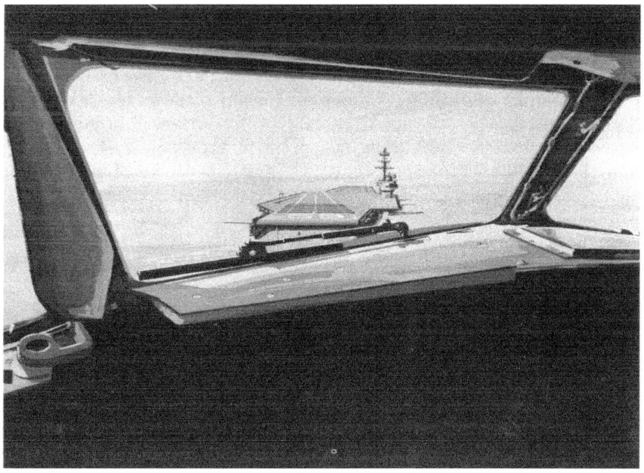

FIGURE 4.19 William A. Fetter, *Illustration of CV A-59 landing rendered by an artist from computer plots*, 1965. (Copyright © 1965 Boeing. All rights reserved. Licensing Terms and Conditions.)

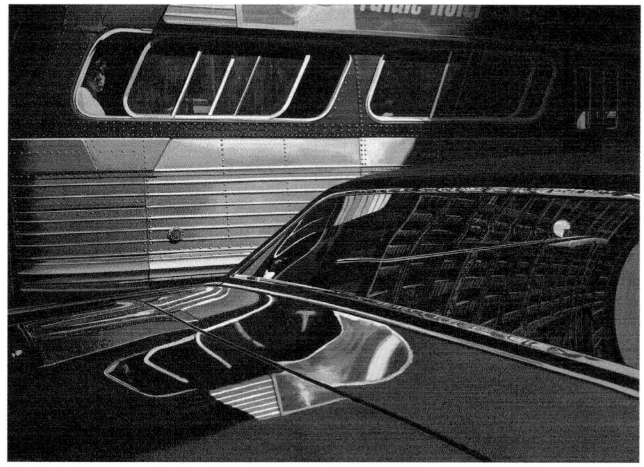

FIGURE 4.20 Richard Estes, *Bus with Reflection of the Flatiron Building*, 1966–1967, oil on canvas, 36 × 48 in (91.4 × 121.9 cm). (Photography by Luc Demers. © Richard Estes. Courtesy Schoelkopf Gallery.)

clarify how the cube behaves differently in space and which square forms the front, depending on which surface is defined as the foreground. The different perspective representation of the center and right-hand cube is achieved solely by deciding which of the three diagonal lines should remain in the image, the three at the top right or the three at the bottom left. For a "final rendering," it was therefore first necessary to decide which lines were actually required for the visualization of the objects and their surface properties. Fetter explains in his paper *Computer Graphics*: "The hidden contour lines, also drawn by the computer, had to be removed manually."[160] As discussed in the section on the state of research, this problem led to the development of various "hidden line algorithms" – also in Utah – in order to automate the decision-making process about which surfaces form the foreground and which form the background, as well as to enable computers to automatically hide the lines. The "final renderings" created in Utah a few years later also often made use of the photorealistic visual language. Chapter 7 deals with this development in detail.

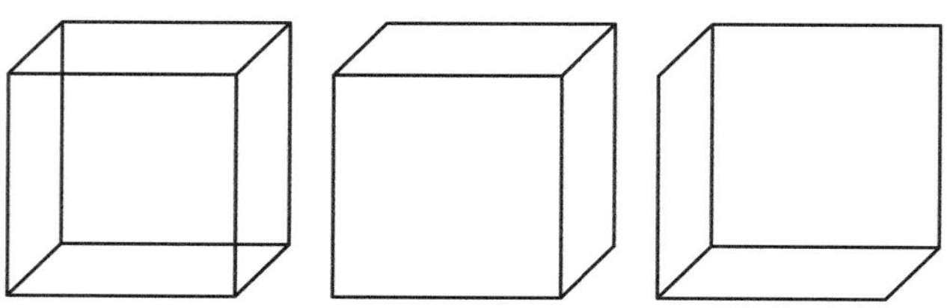

FIGURE 4.21 Drawing by the author, *the hidden line problem illustrated using a cube*, 2021.

Fetter's historical contribution to the development of computer graphics clearly illustrates where the two forms of representation, the "wireframes" and the "solids," originated. With the cube, it was also possible to illustrate why Fetter considered the elaborate illustrations with surface information and realistic visual language to be "clear," even though they are not suitable for taking measurements. Fetter's juxtaposition of the two forms of drawing – the perspective and "clear," on the one hand, and the technical and precise, on the other – appears convincing at first glance. However, considering the terms he used to describe perspective graphics, it becomes evident that the choice of words appears paradoxical. For example, it is not clear from Fetter's own written documentation why a technical drawing that is measurable is not, in his opinion, also truthful. In this context, he always bases his argument on the human visual apparatus. The abstract-looking technical drawings, which in fact only become legible with the help of prior training, may not correspond to the way our eyes see, but in principle they can also fulfill the claim of truth *precisely* because of their accurate and true-to-scale presentation – regardless of whether the concept of "truth" appears to be even viable as such. A similar conclusion could be drawn for each of the other terms used by Fetter to describe the colorful perspective illustrations. In addition to "clarity" and "reliability" borrowed from Marey, he also speaks of "realism"[161] and "credibility."[162] It is only against the backdrop of the aspect of communication, which has the highest priority for Fetter as a graphic designer, that it is possible to understand why he does not consider technical drawings to be reliable or credible. The fact that Fetter does not provide a definition for most of the terms proves to be problematic. Only with regard to his choice of the word "realism" can we guess what type of meaning he associates with it. In relation to the depiction of an airplane landing, he describes,

> [f]urther, a new approach was to be added to improve realism. It was felt that, the closer the display came to recreating the actual visual experience, the more the attention of the audience would be focused on the subject, rather than their being asked to interpret a more symbolic representation.[163]

The term "realism" consequently refers to images that require no interpretation and are immediately understandable. Technical drawings cannot be described with this definition. Fetter's reference to the human visual apparatus is therefore obviously oriented toward this idea of direct perception, which requires no training. It can be assumed that Fetter closely links his concept of realism with the idea of credibility for the same reason. According to Fetter, color photography combines both concepts in their purest form: "Color photography from a landing aircraft could provide a high degree of realism plus credibility."[164] From today's perspective – especially against the background of digital images – it is questionable whether photographs can always or ever fulfill the claim of credibility. However, statements like this make it possible to understand why a photorealistic method of representation was pursued from the outset with the new computer graphics. Compared to the difficult-to-grasp technical drawings, photorealistic image design offered more effective communication possibilities, especially for those people who were not involved in the technical aspects of a production process. However, Fetter's conclusions seem plausible only in contrast to the technical drawing – without this contrast they lose their validity.

In summary, Fetter's two graphs, that illustrate the measurability and legibility of images, give the concepts of "realism" and "credibility" a new interpretation, allowing an initial attempt to define the context of meaning of synthetic images. With the graphs, Fetter admits that the principle "true to scale" is for him not a criterion for the "realism" of a representation. His schematic overview thus reveals that the perspective images are constructions, but ones that we humans are familiar with. The question of where this idea of familiarity could come from and to what extent this is a cultural development will become relevant again in connection with Coons. Like Fetter, Coons also simply presupposes the familiar way of seeing. Both are convinced that there are universally understandable images, and thus they share an intellectual mindset similar to that presented by Edward C. Wells, then production manager of the Boeing Company, in the introduction to Fetter's volume. Paradoxically, Fetter lends the constructed perspective images – solely due to the familiarity of their appearance – the attribute of credibility. It is therefore astonishing that he opted for illustrations rather than technical representations to convey "reliable" information in the field of engineering. From his own artistic perspective, Charles A. Csuri could not attach any particular value to this photorealistic visual language, which he clearly deemed scientific. Although he did not comment on the hand-made photorealistic graphics that Fetter shows as examples, it can be assumed that they would have been just as uninteresting to him as the later graphics produced entirely on the computer, comparable to those created in Utah. Based on these statements by Csuri and the discussion of Fetter's approach, it can be seen that today's computer graphics do not correspond to Csuri's visual language, but rather to Fetter's "maxim of believability" which is closely linked to central perspective. According to this maxim, illustrations in science or at least in engineering should be used to convey new technical phenomena in a tangible, accessible manner, although they do not represent a correct representation of the phenomenon from a purely technical point of view. Truthfulness is linked solely to the degree of familiarity, but not to measurability. Computer graphics are therefore images that should be understandable on an intuitive level.[165]

With Fetter and the principle of the maxim of believability, essential characteristics of the context of meaning of synthetic 3D computer graphics could be identified. The problem with this analysis, however, is that Fetter himself did not contribute to software development, which is why his ideas presented here do not yet directly characterize today's software and thus also not today's images. The question of how his idea of imagery, the maxim of believability, ultimately found its way into the software as a cultural artifact and thus also into all images generated with it, is therefore still open. One clue can be found by looking back at *Sketchpad*: Fetter's working method demonstrates that Sutherland was responding to creative needs that initially emerged from the field of technical drawing and did not primarily reflect the working methods of fine artists. Unlike for Csuri, the use of *Sketchpad* would have been particularly suitable for Fetter's creative work. However, since Fetter cannot be linked to Sutherland on a historical level, the question of how Fetter's pictorial ideas have survived must be answered differently, and that is by examining Steven Coons' contribution to the developments in computer graphics. Like Fetter, he was originally a technical draftsman in aircraft construction, which is why it is not surprising that similar graphic principles can be identified in his work. The maxim of believability is apparent in his work as well and again closely linked to central perspective. One level that is new in Coons' work is the way he thought about the use of the computer. Examining his kind of thinking, allows me to clarify the background against which the paradigm shift in programming took place in Sutherland's *Sketchpad*. Coons can be used to illustrate that this change was conceptualized before Sutherland developed his program. In addition, the concepts of visual language become much clearer with Coons than with Sutherland himself. In Coons' work, the paradigmatic technological changes are linked for the first time with the graphic ideas that, for example, also characterized Fetter's work. Coons is thus a particularly central figure who essentially characterizes the context of meaning of today's 3D computer graphics. Sutherland's *Sketchpad* is ultimately merely a practical manifestation of a development that had previously taken place on a conceptual level in Coons' work.

NOTES

1. A comprehensive analysis of computer art in the 1960s was undertaken by Christoph Klütsch, for example. See Christoph Klütsch, *Computergrafik. Ästhetische Experimente zwischen zwei Kulturen. Die Anfänge der Computerkunst in den 1960er Jahren* (Vienna: Springer, 2007).
2. See, for example, Margit Rosen, "A Record of Decisions: Envisioning Computer Art," in *Charles A. Csuri: Beyond Boundaries, 1963–Present*, ed. Janice M. Glowski and SIGGRAPH (Columbus: The Ohio State University, College of the Arts, Advanced Computing Center for the Arts and Design, 2006), 25.
3. The ACCAD emerged from the *Computer Graphics Research Group* (CGRG) founded in 1971, a research unit also set up by Csuri at OSU. See Janice M. Glowski and SIGGRAPH, eds., *Charles A. Csuri: Beyond Boundaries, 1963–Present* (Columbus: The Ohio State University, College of the Arts, Advanced Computing Center for the Arts and Design, 2006), 173–74.
4. Janice M. Glowski, "Introduction to the Catalogue," in *Charles A. Csuri: Beyond Boundaries, 1963–Present*, ed. Janice M. Glowski and SIGGRAPH (Columbus: The Ohio State University, College of the Arts, Advanced Computing Center for the Arts and Design, 2006), 17. Tom Sito also highlights Csuri in his historical accounts of computer animation. He refers to Csuri's work *Hummingbird* from 1967 with the following statement: "The film is considered one of the landmarks of CG, because it is the first time someone attempted to move a living thing rather than geometric shapes." Tom Sito, *Moving Innovation: A History of Computer Animation* (Cambridge: MIT Press, 2013) 58. See also *Hummingbird*, directed by Charles Csuri (1967).
5. Charles A. Csuri, "Oral history interview with Charles A. Csuri," interview by Kerry J. Freedman, October 23, 1989, transcript, Charles Babbage Institute, University of Minnesota, https://hdl.handle.net/11299/107236, 6. An explanation of the *Charles Babbage Institute* can be found in endnote 8.
6. Charles A. Csuri, "Beyond Boundaries," in *Charles A. Csuri: Beyond Boundaries, 1963–Present*, ed. Janice M. Glowski and SIGGRAPH (Columbus: The Ohio State University, College of the Arts, Advanced Computing Center for the Arts and Design, 2006), 22.
7. See Ivan E. Sutherland, "Sketchpad: A Man-Machine Graphical Communication System" (technical report, ed. Alan Blackwell and Kerry Rodden, University of Cambridge, 2003), Computer Laboratory (UCAM-CL-TR-574), 110.
8. The *Charles Babbage Institute*, named after the English mathematician of the same name, is an institution associated with the *University of Minnesota* that pursues the initiative of compiling archival material on the history of information technology

and, for example, using interviews to generate and make available additional primary sources in this specialized field. See "About CBI," Charles Babbage Institute, College of Science and Engineering, accessed December 11, 2021, https://cse.umn.edu/cbi/about.

9. See Csuri, interview by Freedman, and see Charles A. Csuri, "Interview of Charles A. Csuri by Robert Butche," interview by Robert W. Butche, June 10, 2003, transcript, The Ohio State University Oral History Project, Ohio State University Archives, http://hdl.handle.net/1811/5928.
10. Csuri, interview by Freedman, 3.
11. See Csuri, interview by Freedman, 3, 14.
12. See Csuri, interview by Freedman, 3.
13. Csuri, interview by Freedman, 3.
14. See Csuri, interview by Freedman, 14.
15. Csuri, interview by Freedman, 3.
16. Csuri, interview by Freedman, 3.
17. Michael Lobel, *Image Duplicator: Roy Lichtenstein and the Emergence of Pop Art* (New Haven: Yale University Press, 2002), 77.
18. Lobel, *Image Duplicator*, 77.
19. See Lobel, *Image Duplicator*, 77–78.
20. Lobel, *Image Duplicator*, 78.
21. See Csuri, interview by Freedman, 3.
22. Csuri, interview by Freedman, 12.
23. Csuri, interview by Freedman, 3.
24. From 1955 to 1966, Csuri's works were exhibited in New York in both solo and group exhibitions. See Csuri, interview by Butche, 35, and see Glowski and SIGGRAPH, *Charles A. Csuri*, 173. See also Rosen, "A Record of Decisions," 26.
25. Csuri, interview by Butche, 36. On the relationship with his artistic environment at OSU, see also Csuri, interview by Butche, 36, 35.
26. Csuri, interview by Freedman, 4.
27. The editor of the volume also summarizes Rosen's intention in a similar way in her introduction. See Glowski, "Introduction to the Catalogue," 17, and see Rosen, "A Record of Decisions," 25–46.
28. Rosen dates the beginning of the exchange with Jack Mitten to 1954. Csuri himself dates it to 1955 in the 1989 interview. See Csuri, interview by Freedman, 4, and see Rosen, "A Record of Decisions," 26.
29. Rosen, "A Record of Decisions," 26.
30. See Csuri, interview by Freedman, 13–14.
31. See Charles A. Csuri, "An Interview with Charles Csuri," interview by John Staudhammer, Tom Culviner and Margaret Neal, *IEEE Computer Graphics and Applications* 10, no. 1 (1990): 5–9.
32. Charles A. Csuri, interview by Staudhammer, Culviner and Neal, 7.
33. In the interview, Csuri himself refers to the year 1965, whereas Rosen cites 1964 as the year of discovery, which seems plausible as Csuri began the first computer graphics experiments in 1964. See Csuri, interview by Freedman, 14–15; see Rosen, "A Record of Decisions," 26.
34. In order to subdivide the gray tones, a painting was first created based on the photograph, in which the gray shades were reduced. In this way, the image was divided into zones, each of which was assigned a gray value. These zones with their respective gray tones could then be entered into the computer so that the information could be passed on to the Flexowriter. See Juris G. Raudseps, "Picture Regeneration from Quantised Data" (Technical Report, The Ohio State University, 1963), The Ohio State University Libraries Archives, 4–9.
35. See Csuri, interview by Staudhammer, Culviner and Neal, 3. See also Csuri, interview by Freedman, 4, and Rosen, "A Record of Decisions," 26.
36. Csuri, interview by Freedman, 15.
37. See Csuri, interview by Freedman, 15.
38. Csuri, interview by Freedman, 15.
39. Csuri, interview by Freedman, 3.
40. Glowski and SIGGRAPH, *Charles A. Csuri*, 48.
41. See Csuri, interview by Freedman, 6.
42. Rosen, "A Record of Decisions," 40, emphasis in original.
43. The artists he "copied" were Gentile Bellini, Paul Cézanne, André Derain, Albrecht Dürer, Francisco Goya, Jean-Auguste Ingres, Paul Klee, Piet Mondrian and Pablo Picasso. See Ariana Maki, "After the Artist Series," in *Charles A. Csuri: Beyond Boundaries, 1963–Present*, ed. Janice M. Glowski and SIGGRAPH (Columbus: The Ohio State University, College of the Arts, Advanced Computing Center for the Arts and Design, 2006), 52–58.
44. Although the creativity theorist Friedrich Weltzien does not describe the pantograph as a computer – as Csuri does – he does categorize it as an autonomous pictorial practice that was used alongside other autopoietic processes in Romantic art. Weltzien describes the mechanism as follows: "The way the pantograph [in German he uses the word *Storchenschnabel*] works is simple in its mechanical principle: four slats have to be screwed together, *mobile,* to form a parallelogram that can be moved against each other. If one angle of this parallelogram is fixed, a pin can be attached to the neighboring angle so that its tip rests on a piece of paper [...]. If you then trace a contour with the angle opposite the pencil, the pencil will trace the same contour on the paper. According to the mathematical principle of the theorem of intersecting lines, the pantograph can be adjusted by shifting the length ratios of the slats so that this drawing enlarges or reduces the model. In any case, however, all ratios are retained." Friedrich Weltzien, *Fleck – das Bild der Selbsttätigkeit. Justinus Kerner und die Klecksografie*

als experimentelle Bildpraxis zwischen Ästhetik und Naturwissenschaft (Göttingen: Vandenhoeck & Ruprecht, 2011), 296, emphasis in original.

45. See Rosen, "A Record of Decisions," 32.
46. See Rosen, "A Record of Decisions," 32. Rosen also explains what inspired Csuri to create the series and refers in this context to the biologist and mathematician D'Arcy Thompson and his 1917 book *On Growth and Form*: "Thompson sought a tool to deduce from a particular animal the ideal form, similar to the Aristotelian genus, as well as the laws of evolution. Csuri reversed Thompson's enterprise. Rather than seeking the laws of transformation, he created them. He did not seek to reduce variety, but to produce it."
47. Rosen, "A Record of Decisions," 30. The painter referred to here as John is James Hopkins.
48. Rosen, "A Record of Decisions," 36.
49. See Rosen, "A Record of Decisions," 36.
50. Frieder Nake, "Art Production as a Decision-Making Process," in *bit international*, vol. 2, ed. Boris Kelemen and Radoslav Putar (Zagreb: Galerije grada Zagreba, 1968), 49.
51. See Rosen, "A Record of Decisions," 36–37.
52. Rosen, "A Record of Decisions," 40.
53. Csuri, interview by Freedman, 7.
54. Csuri, "Beyond Boundaries," 21.
55. Rosen, "A Record of Decisions," 33.
56. See Maria Palazzi, "Exploration and the Artist's Tools," in *Charles A. Csuri: Beyond Boundaries, 1963–Present*, ed. Janice M. Glowski and SIGGRAPH (Columbus: The Ohio State University, College of the Arts, Advanced Computing Center for the Arts and Design, 2006), 94.
57. Quoted from Rosen, "A Record of Decisions," 33. Rosen does not cite a source for this statement by Csuri in her own essay. In her bibliographical references, she refers to conversations she had with Csuri on the occasion of her essay. I assume that she is quoting from one of these conversations.
58. See Csuri, interview by Freedman, 5.
59. See Csuri, interview by Butche, 38, and see Csuri, interview by Freedman, 5 and 20.
60. Philip Leider, letter to Matthew Baigell, October 30, 1967, in the collection of Caroline Csuri. See also "Research," Charles Csuri, accessed on June 11, 2025, https://www.charlescsuri.com/research.
61. See Csuri, interview by Butche, 38, and see Csuri, interview by Freedman, 5 and 20. In the interview conducted by the *Charles Babbage Institute*, Csuri provides a detailed insight into the politics behind the application process and his role in it: "There's a kind of politics involved, too, in that you really need to get to know who are the top researchers, because you know, only too well, that they're going to be your reviewers on your next grant, and they know I'm going to be their reviewer, you see? I don't have any proposal spending, but right now I'm very involved with the 30 most credible people… I'm part of the group. I'm on the advisory board of a prestigious publication, IEEE Computer Graphics and Applications, and I'm on the Board of Directors for the National Computer Graphics Association." Csuri, interview by Freedman, 21.
62. Csuri, interview by Freedman, 5.
63. See Palazzi, "Exploration and the Artist's Tools," 93 The integration of Csuri's painterly activity often took place using two interrelated functions: On the one hand, he utilized the possibility of adding texture to virtual objects and, on the other, he used the function of bump mapping to give his objects a surface structure. For example, he translated the color values of the used texture into height values so that the painted texture does not appear smooth but as a relief. See Palazzi, "Exploration and the Artist's Tools," 94.
64. See Palazzi, "Exploration and the Artist's Tools," 93.
65. Palazzi, "Exploration and the Artist's Tools," 94.
66. Palazzi, "Exploration and the Artist's Tools," 93.
67. See Palazzi, "Exploration and the Artist's Tools," 94–95.
68. Rosen, "A Record of Decisions," 40. Rosen refers here to Bruno Latour, "Mixing Humans and Nonhumans Together: The Sociology of a Door-Closer," *Social Problems* 35, no. 3 (1988), https://doi.org/10.1525/sp.1988.35.3.03a00070.
69. See Rosen, "A Record of Decisions," 35.
70. Charles Csuri, "Research."
71. See Charles Csuri, "Research."
72. Vita Berezina-Blackburn, Email to author, May 12, 2025.
73. Rosen, "A Record of Decisions," 35.
74. Wayne E. Carlson, "Dialogue and Creativity: The Faces of Collaboration," in *Charles A. Csuri: Beyond Boundaries, 1963–Present*, ed. Janice M. Glowski and SIGGRAPH (Columbus: The Ohio State University, College of the Arts, Advanced Computing Center for the Arts and Design, 2006), 85.
75. See Carlson, "Dialogue and Creativity," 86.
76. Carlson, "Dialogue and Creativity," 86.
77. Palazzi, "Exploration and the Artist's Tools," 93.
78. See "Steve May," Pixar Animation Studios, accessed June 12, 2025, https://www.pixar.com/may.
79. Csuri, interview by Freedman, 22.
80. Carlson, "Dialogue and Creativity," 87.
81. The *Scheme* programming language was developed in 1975 by Gerald Jay Sussman and Guy Lewis Steele Jr. It is a dialect of the *Lisp* language. Both languages do not correspond in principle to the object-oriented programming paradigm but can be extended to this end. See Ronak K. Dybvig, *The Scheme Programming Language*, 4th ed. (Cambridge: MIT Press, 2009), ix, 381.
82. See Palazzi, "Exploration and the Artist's Tools," 94–95.

83. Csuri, interview by Freedman, 15.
84. Csuri, interview by Freedman, 16.
85. Against the background of Palazzi's descriptions, this statement by Csuri seems contradictory. As she describes, the 1980s represent a high point in his collaboration with computer scientists, with whom he developed his tools. What he is presumably referring to here is that the development of these tools at that time can no longer be clearly attributed to a single person, but to a group of many.
86. See Csuri, interview by Butche, 73.
87. See Csuri, interview by Butche, 74.
88. Csuri, interview by Butche, 75.
89. See Csuri, interview by Butche, 75.
90. See Matthew Lewis, "Randomness, Chance, Process: The Infinity Series," in *Charles A. Csuri: Beyond Boundaries, 1963–Present*, ed. Janice M. Glowski and SIGGRAPH (Columbus: The Ohio State University, College of the Arts, Advanced Computing Center for the Arts and Design, 2006), 147.
91. Janice M. Glowski, "Random War," in *Charles A. Csuri: Beyond Boundaries, 1963–Present*, ed. Janice M. Glowski and SIGGRAPH (Columbus: The Ohio State University, College of the Arts, Advanced Computing Center for the Arts and Design, 2006), 76.
92. Glowski, "Random War," 76.
93. See "Charles Csuri 'Random War,' 1967," Charles Csuri, accessed June 12, 2025, https://www.charlescsuri.com/historic/random-war.
94. Charles Csuri, "Charles Csuri 'Random War,' 1967."
95. Lewis, "Randomness, Chance, Process," 148.
96. Lewis, "Randomness, Chance, Process," 149.
97. Lewis, "Randomness, Chance, Process," 149.
98. See Lewis, "Randomness, Chance, Process," 149.
99. "Complexity," Charles A. Csuri, accessed December 12, 2021, http://www.csurivision.com/index.php/2008/10/complexity/.
100. Charles A. Csuri, "Complexity."
101. Csuri, interview by Freedman, 8.
102. See Palazzi, "Exploration and the Artist's Tools," 94.
103. See Barbara Mones-Hattal, Ken Snelson, Sally Weber, Charles Csuri and Tony Longson, "New Methods, New Artforms (panel session): 3D Applications in Sculpture," in *ACM SIGGRAPH 90 Panel Proceedings*, ed. ACM (New York: ACM Press, 1990), 904.
104. Bonnie Mitchell, "Introduction to the Exhibition," in *Charles A. Csuri: Beyond Boundaries, 1963–Present*, ed. Janice M. Glowski and SIGGRAPH (Columbus: The Ohio State University, College of the Arts, Advanced Computing Center for the Arts and Design, 2006), 13.
105. In his monograph *Art as Experience*, Dewey develops the definition of an artistic medium. For this purpose, he distinguishes between a means and a medium and, at first glance, for Csuri the computer is merely a means: "There are two kinds of means. One kind is external to that which is accomplished; the other kind is taken up into the consequences produced and remains immanent in them. There are ends which are merely welcome cessations and there are ends that are fulfillments of what went before. [...] Such external or *mere* means, as we properly term them, are usually of such a sort that others can be substituted for them; the particular ones employed are determined by some extraneous consideration, like cheapness. But the moment we say 'media,' we refer to means that are incorporated in the outcome." John Dewey, *Art as Experience* (New York: Perigee, 1980), 197, emphasis in original. At the same time, Dewey's definition also demonstrates that the computer nevertheless characterizes Csuri's artistic work and that, contrary to his own assumption, it is more than just a means to an end. Dewey would therefore probably have disagreed with Csuri and perhaps even criticized him: "Even bricks and mortar become a part of the house they are employed to build; they are not mere means to its erection. Colors *are* the painting; tones are the music. A picture painted with water colors has a quality different from that painted with oil. Esthetic effects belong intrinsically to their medium; when another medium is substituted, we have a stunt rather than an object of art." Dewey, *Art as Experience*, 197, emphasis in original.
106. Csuri, interview by Freedman, 10.
107. See Flip Phillips quoted after Caroline Csuri, email to author, May 21, 2025. See also Caroline Csuri, email to author, May 11, 2025.
108. In the institute's own overview of the history of ACCAD, the year 1987 is given as the year of foundation, while the year 1986 is mentioned in the timeline of significant events in Csuri's biography in the exhibition catalog. See "ACCAD History," ACCAD, accessed February 18, 2021, https://accad.osu.edu/about/accad-history, and see Glowski and SIGGRAPH, *Charles A. Csuri*, 174.
109. See ACCAD, "ACCAD History." Like the film studio Pixar, *Lamb and Company* produced computer-animated short films in the 1990s. Particularly noteworthy is the production *The Incredible Crash Dummies*, directed by Mark Mariutto (Lamb & Co. and Nelvana, 1993), the first computer-animated television production created for children with a length of 22 minutes, which was considerable at the time. See Wayne E. Carlson, *Computer Graphics and Computer Animation: A Retrospective Overview* (Columbus: The Ohio State University, 2017), 367.
110. See ACCAD, "ACCAD History," and Carlson, "Dialogue and Creativity," 88–89.
111. Carlson, "Dialogue and Creativity," 89.
112. See Flip Phillips quoted after Caroline Csuri, email to author.

113. At the same time, however, he admits that this development was beginning to change at the time of the interview, i.e. in 1989. See Csuri, interview by Freedman, 24. His attitude to commercial software products has already been discussed in this chapter.
114. Csuri, interview by Freedman, 25.
115. Csuri, interview by Freedman, 25.
116. Csuri, interview by Freedman, 27.
117. Csuri, interview by Freedman, 28.
118. He describes in detail which aspects of this process appear revolutionary in his eyes: "[T]he algorithms where you can create objects, that's one aspect. But then where people have come up with solutions that deal with perspective, with lighting models, with color, with transparency, material types, things of that nature, where we have the ability to literally represent a physical universe very realistically. I think that has to be a very significant development in computer graphics." Csuri, interview by Freedman, 23.
119. Csuri, interview by Freedman, 22–23.
120. Paul Trachtman, "Charles Csuri is an 'Old Master' in a New Medium (Cover Story)," *Smithsonian* 25, no. 11 (1995): 62/64.
121. Rosen, "A Record of Decisions," 27.
122. Csuri expresses a similar vision here as Alan Kay originally did for his *Smalltalk* language. Both share the idea of being able to develop one's own tools and programs on the computer in a modular way using object-oriented approaches. See Csuri, interview by Butche, 70; see Casey Alt, "Objects of Our Affection. How Object Orientation Made Computers a Medium," in *Media Archaeology. Approaches, Applications, and Implications*, ed. Erkki Huhtamo and Jussi Parikka (Berkeley, Los Angeles: University of California Press, 2011), 299.
123. Csuri often used digitized versions of his oil paintings as textures for virtual objects, but in such a way that texture and object do not belong together. His work *A Child's Face* from 1989 is an example of this. See Palazzi, "Exploration and the Artist's Tools," 94.
124. In this basic assumption, I follow Birgit Schneider and her references to scientific images, as noted in my methods chapter. See Birgit Schneider, "Wissenschaftsbilder zwischen digitaler Transformation und Manipulation. Einige Anmerkungen zur Diskussion des 'digitalen Bildes,'" in *Logik des Bildlichen*, ed. Martina Heßler and Dieter Mersch (Bielefeld: transcript, 2015).
125. See Rosen, "A Record of Decisions," 40.
126. William A. Fetter, "Computer Graphics," *Design Quarterly* 66, no. 67 (1966): 19.
127. Fetter introduced computer drawings of humans, for example, in his 1966 paper *Computer Graphics*. See Fetter, "Computer Graphics."
128. William A. Fetter, *Computer Graphics in Communication. Written for the Course Content Development Study in Engineering Graphics, supported by the National Science Foundation* (New York: McGraw-Hill, 1965), ix.
129. Fetter, "Computer Graphics," 15.
130. See Fetter, "Computer Graphics," 15.
131. Fetter, "Computer Graphics," 15.
132. See Fetter, *Computer Graphics in Communication*.
133. Rebecca A. Perry, "Rigging the World: 3D Modeling and the Seduction of the Real" (PhD diss., Massachusetts Institute of Technology, 2014), MIT Libraries, DSpace@MIT (900615015), 17.
134. See Perry, "Rigging the World," 95–96.
135. Perry, "Rigging the World," 37.
136. Perry, "Rigging the World," 96.
137. Parallel to his work at Boeing, Fetter was a member of the *Experiments in Art and Technology* (EAT) association founded in New York in 1967, a group of artists and engineers who explored the graphic possibilities of the computer technology of the time in an experimental way. The founding members were the artists Robert Rauschenberg and Robert Whitman and the engineers Billy Klüver and Fred Waldhauer. See "History," Patricia Failing and Robin Oppenheimer, *University of Washington*, last modified September 16, 2002, http://courses.washington.edu/eatreun/html/history/h_intro.html. Fetter himself was involved in founding an EAT group in Seattle, where he worked for Boeing. He was inspired to do so by a meeting with other computer graphics pioneers in 1965, organized by *Bell Telephone Laboratories*. In his perception, almost everyone who was experimenting with creating images using computers at the time gathered there, and he realized, "I was the only one with an art background and an art degree. Surprisingly, I was still the only one of this group doing perspective images. Some present were Ken Knowlton and Ed Zajac of Bell Laboratories, George Michaels and Bob Crowley of Lawrence Livermore National Laboratories, myself from Boeing and others. E.A.T. was first described to me during a meeting in New York at a conference and I felt the rich mix of art and technology interactions already in progress in the Northwest might benefit by tying in with that group. I contacted Dr Kluver [*sic*], obtained a film about their show at the Armory in New York, and called a meeting of like-minded people [in Seattle]." "Northwest Chapters. William Fetter (1928–2002)," Patricia Failing and Robin Oppenheimer, *University of Washington*, last modified September 16, 2002. http://courses.washington.edu/eatreun/html/history/h_nw.html. In 1969, works by Fetter (as well as by Charles A. Csuri and Frieder Nake, among others) were presented at the *Galerija suvremene umjetnosti* (Gallery of Contemporary Art) in Zagreb in the exhibition *tendencies 4. computers and visual research*. The exhibition was part of a series of events and magazines produced by a movement called *New*

Tendencies, which emerged in Yugoslavia in 1961. A jury, including, among others, Umberto Eco, decided which works would be included in the exhibition. In addition to Fetter's perspective computer images, which he had designed for Boeing, contributions by employees of *Bell Telephone Laboratories Inc.* including Leon O. Harmon, Kenneth C. Knowlton, A. Michael Noll and Manfred R. Schroeder were also exhibited. The jury justified its decision as follows: "The works that were produced by Boeing Computer Graphics and the Bell Telephone Laboratories exhibit, in our opinion, the best developed technology and programming of visual phenomena." Umberto Eco, Karl Gerstner, Vera Horvat-Pintarić, Boris Kelemen and Martin Krampen, "Program Information 13. tendencije 4/tendencies 4. Computers and Visual Research. Decision of the Competition Jury," in *A Little-Known Story about a Movement, a Magazine, and the Computer's Arrival in Art: New Tendencies and Bit International, 1961–1973. Bit International. [Nove] tendencije. Computer and Visual Research Zagreb 1961–1973, exhibitions Neue Galerie Graz am Landesmuseum Joanneum April 28–June 17, 2007, ZKM, Center for Art and Media Karlsruhe February 23, 2008–January 18, 2009*, ed. Margit Rosen, Darko Fritz, Marija Gattin and Peter Weibel (Karlsruhe, Cambridge: ZKM Center for Art and Media; MIT Press, 2011), 369. The members comment on the decision criteria as follows: "In our opinion, in view of the experimental nature and completely open domain represented by the materials exhibited, it is not possible at the present time to establish criteria for judging the entries, for example, aesthetic quality, complexity of programming, or mathematical ingenuity. This holds particularly if we consider the fact that the goal of computer-aided aesthetic research is to suggest new aesthetic parameters for the future. It would be 'authoritarian' to submit such research to judgement in terms of traditional parameters. Furthermore, early individual work should be considered in terms of our own human and technical premises. As a whole, the exhibited materials can be treated from different points of view, and the interesting characterizations of individual works can be highlighted from these viewpoints." Eco, Gerstner, Horvat-Pintarić, Kelemen and Krampen, "Program Information," 368.

138. Fetter, *Computer Graphics in Communication*, 8.
139. Fetter, *Computer Graphics in Communication*, 105.
140. Fetter, *Computer Graphics in Communication*, 5.
141. Fetter, *Computer Graphics in Communication*, 9.
142. Fetter, *Computer Graphics in Communication*, 17.
143. See Dewey, *Art as Experience*, 197. See also endnote 105.
144. See Fetter, "Computer Graphics," 15.
145. Fetter, "Computer Graphics," 15.
146. Fetter, "Computer Graphics," 15.
147. Edward C. Wells, "Introduction," in *William A. Fetter: Computer Graphics in Communication. Written for the Course Content Development Study in Engineering Graphics, Supported by the National Science Foundation* (New York: McGraw-Hill, 1965), vii.
148. Quoted from Fetter, *Computer Graphics in Communication*, 1. Fetter quotes Marey from his monograph *Movement* from 1895, but without giving a page number. A closer look at the source reveals that the first paragraph is from the preface, the second from the first chapter. See Étienne-Jules Marey, *Movement*, trans. Eric Pritchard (New York: D. Appleton and Company, 1895), vii, 2.
149. Fetter, *Computer Graphics in Communication*, 100.
150. Fetter, *Computer Graphics in Communication*, 2.
151. See Fetter, *Computer Graphics in Communication*, 5–7.
152. Fetter, *Computer Graphics in Communication*, 7.
153. Fetter, *Computer Graphics in Communication*, 6.
154. Steven A. Coons and John T. Rule also explain the rules for creating these different types of design drawings in their handbook *Graphics*. See John T. Rule and Steven A. Coons, *Graphics* (New York: McGraw-Hill, 1961) 78, 231. The terms become relevant again in the discussion of Coons, which is why they are explained in detail there. See Section 5.1 in this study.
155. Fetter, "Computer Graphics," 17, emphasis in original.
156. Fetter, *Computer Graphics in Communication*, 8; see also Fetter, *Computer Graphics in Communication*, 23–24.
157. Fetter, *Computer Graphics in Communication*, 23.
158. Examples include Richard Estes and Ralph Goings.
159. Fetter, *Computer Graphics in Communication*, 59.
160. Fetter, "Computer Graphics," 19.
161. Fetter, *Computer Graphics in Communication*, e.g. 23 and 62.
162. Fetter, *Computer Graphics in Communication*, e.g. 50.
163. Fetter, *Computer Graphics in Communication*, 62.
164. Fetter, *Computer Graphics in Communication*, 50.
165. In his biography of the pixel, computer scientist Alvy Ray Smith also makes the observation that there is a preference for central perspective in the field of synthetic image generation and therefore establishes the term "Central Dogma" in his monograph. Alvy R. Smith, *A Biography of the Pixel* (Cambridge: MIT Press, 2021), 7. He attributes the use of central perspective solely to Euclidean geometry. Additionally, the images of the Central Dogma were later, according to Smith, also characterized by the simulation of physical reality, which for him can be traced back to the laws of Newtonian physics. He recognizes one of the main reasons for the realistic visual language in the early military demands to create images of outer space for the field of space travel, which were to be perceived as a reproduction of the actual conditions. He does not cite any other cultural references for the image design but explicitly points out that the

computer could also generate any other image aesthetic. At the same time, however, he is convinced – like Fetter and many other historical protagonists to follow – that the Central Dogma has prevailed because it is familiar to us due to our retinal image. In his monograph, he also expresses his astonishment that no one has ever explicitly reflected on the emergence of this norm. However, my examination of Coons and my in-depth investigation of individuals at the *University of Utah* can show that in the historical development of synthetic images, different possibilities for representing perspective were repeatedly reflected upon. Coons' ideas, for example, deliberately do not go back to Euclid. At the same time, like Smith, all the people involved always came to the conclusion that the retinal image predetermined the central perspective. See Smith, *Pixel*, 279, 327. See also, for example, Section 5.1 and Section 7.1 in this study.

CHAPTER 5

Steven A. Coons

A New Confluence between Man and Machine

> Man is quite good at inventing and organizing ideas, making associations among apparently unrelated notions, recognizing patterns and stripping away irrelevant detail; he is creative, unpredictable, sometimes capricious, sensitive to human values. The computer is almost exactly what man is not. It is capable of paying undivided attention to unlimited detail; it is immune to distraction, precise and reliable; it can carry out the most intricate and lengthy calculation with ease, without a flaw and in much less than a millionth of the time that would be required by its human counterpart. It is emotionless, or so we suppose. It suffers from neither boredom nor fatigue. It needs to be told only once; thereafter it remembers perfectly until it is told to forget, whereupon it forgets instantly and absolutely.[1]
>
> *STEVEN A. COONS (1966)*

In her study *Rigging the World: 3D Modeling and the Seduction of the Real*, Rebecca Perry particularly emphasizes Steven Coons' influence on the development of three-dimensional (3D) computer graphics. Not only does she introduce her entire study with a reference to Coons, but in one section she even specifically addresses the links between Sutherland's and Coons' respective research – she calls it "Steven Coons, Ivan Sutherland and Sketchpad."[2] Perry describes Coons as an "important but somewhat overlooked figure in computer graphics history."[3] This assessment is consistent, as Cardoso Llach, who dealt with Coons in great detail with regard to today's architectural software, published his study a year after Perry.[4] As I have shown in the state of research, Coons forms a kind of fork in the road from which developments in architecture and in the field of 3D computer graphics can be traced. Although Perry highlights important links between Coons and today's 3D graphics, her findings on this historical protagonist, which relate primarily to the process of virtual modeling, can be supplemented in a significant way with regard to the imagery of 3D graphics and the software environment in which they are created.

There are several reasons why Coons had such a low profile in the history of computer graphics for so long. Even his friend and colleague Bertram Herzog wrote in a eulogy that he gave on the occasion of Coons' death in 1979: "His nature was such that many details about Steve Coons are not readily accessible for this occasion."[5] Little was known about Coons, even within his own circle. Herzog also paints a picture of Coons that leaves an overall reserved or inconspicuous impression. As described in Section 2.2, Coons had been working in the *Mechanical Engineering Department* at MIT since the late 1940s. After initially contributing to university teaching as a faculty member, he was promoted to associate professor in 1961.[6] In this role, he was also a member of Sutherland's dissertation committee while the latter was developing his *Sketchpad* program. That Coons would be part of an academic environment in this

DOI: 10.1201/9781003649861-7

way is surprising given that he had never completed a university degree. As Herzog explains, Coons himself had only spent a short time at MIT as a student and dropped out after about a year.[7] Herzog emphasizes that many people were unaware of this biographical detail about Coons: "This was always most surprising to those of us who first met him under professional circumstances. He was often and mistakenly introduced as Dr Coons. Steve would then quietly chuckle with close friends about his 'flunking' out of MIT and reentering degreeless."[8] Although he did not have a degree, he worked as an engineer for the *Vought-Sikorsky Aircraft Corporation* from 1940 to 1948 before returning to MIT. According to Herzog, Coons specialized there in graphically illustrating complex components and surfaces, which caught the attention of John T. Rule from MIT and motivated him to bring Coons back to his former educational institution as a university lecturer. Rule had been the head of the *Graphics Department* since 1938, initially as an associate professor and from 1947 with a full professorship.[9] Coons remained at MIT until 1969, almost 20 years, and later took up a position as professor at *Syracuse University*. His employment at these two universities was extended by many shorter research stays at numerous other US universities. He gave guest lectures at the *University of Michigan*, spent a year at *Harvard University* and another at the *University of Utah*. As I explore the developments there in the following part, the connection between Coons and Utah, hinted at here, is particularly interesting for the further course of my discussion. Finally, Herzog also refers to Coons' work as a "photographic illustrator and color consultant"[10] for the publishing house *Ginn and Company*, which he also carried out during his employment at MIT.

The insights that Herzog provides into Coons' life in his eulogy offer valuable information for this study. Coons' less than straightforward career suggests that he shaped his life according to his own ideas, using his creative energy to bring them to fruition rather than following social conventions or the ideas of others. So, if Coons was instrumental in shaping the way 3D computer graphics are produced today, it is now becoming apparent that he has left his own mark on this development. The aim is to find out which of the aspects that still exist today are possibly based on Coons' fundamental ideas and conceptions.

From a content-related angle, another possible reason for Coons' inconspicuous role in the history of computer graphics may be that his contribution only becomes apparent when viewed from the perspective of production aesthetics. Both Perry and Cardoso Llach choose such a perspective for their investigations, although they do not use the term production aesthetics. While Perry focuses primarily on the discipline of modeling, I examine in this chapter the role Coons plays for the common context of meaning of today's 3D computer graphics in a broader sense. Initially, my following examination of Coons picks up some of Perry's insights, as she also ascribes a central or – to use her words – emblematic role to Coons for 3D computer graphics:

> Coons' approach is emblematic of the productive bridge between engineering and art that evolved and became a defining characteristic of the field of computer graphics. Coons' thinking combined tacit knowledge and a tactile understanding of materials – an understanding acquired when he worked in an aircraft manufacturing company, and which augmented his formal training in draftsmanship at MIT. Evidence suggests that this type of thinking was critical to the path that computer graphics and 3D modeling took – the creation of interactive digital objects that combine virtual and physical realities.[11]

In her statement, Perry speaks of a concept of art that I will explore in this chapter, but rather than assessing whether Coons had a valid artistic concept, I focus on finding out what cultural ideas he had when he started working with the computer and how he influenced later developments.

Despite the prominent position she assigns him, Perry's discussion of Coons is nevertheless brief. From the outset, she does not focus on the question of *why* computer graphics developed the way they did – in other words, she does not ask about its context of meaning. Instead, Perry focuses on the question of *how* individual stages of development took place. She presents the historical steps as if they had been natural and necessary to reach the point where we find ourselves today.[12] According to Perry, Coons' greatest contribution to the phenomenon of virtual models, which is her focus of investigation, was, above all, the fact that – as indicated in her previous comment – he had such a comprehensive and tactile understanding of the physical nature of objects:

> His most valuable contribution to problems of digital representation may have been a tactile understanding of physical materials, possibly gained through his work on aircraft surfaces. Coons added his voice, his drawings and his understanding and tacit knowledge of the craft of constructing physical objects to the discussion in the early days of 3D modeling and computer graphics research as it took shape in the 1960s.[13]

In this statement Perry attributes his sense of surface textures primarily to his work as a draftsman in aircraft construction, but she does not offer any suggestions as to how he passed on this knowledge. It can, however, be assumed that she considers his handbook *Graphics*, which he co-authored with his colleague John T. Rule in 1961, to be one of the channels of communication. Although computer technology does not yet play a prominent role in it, she explicitly highlights this handbook because, in her opinion, it characterizes Coons' contribution to the history of computer graphics in a special way. In contrast to the other textbooks of the time, this book also promoted the practice of freehand sketching techniques as part of engineering studies. To illustrate this special characteristic of the handbook, Perry shows a page where the authors give instructions for a "realistic" drawing style (Figure 5.1). However, she points out that there is no indication in the book as to which of the two authors produced the drawings. Nevertheless, Perry assumes

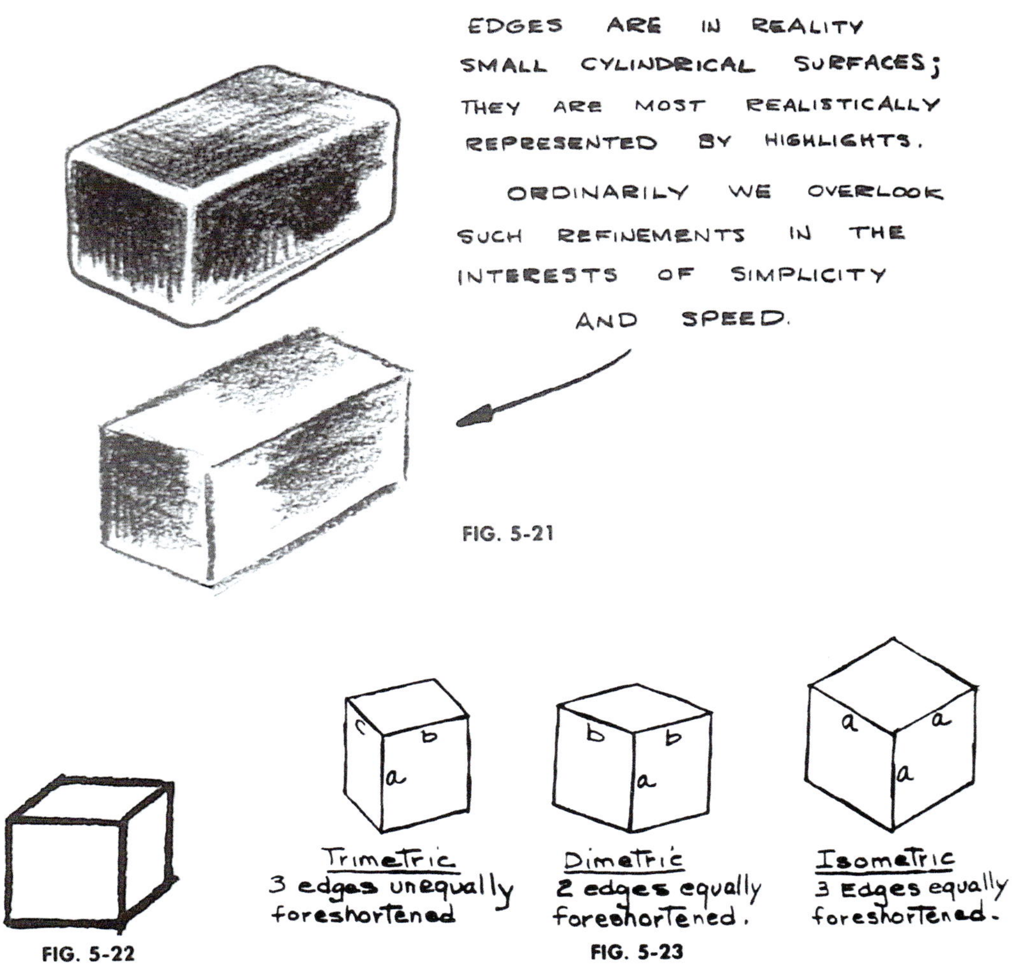

FIGURE 5.1 John T. Rule and Steven A. Coons, *Fig. 5-21–5-23*, 1961, drawing. (Courtesy of HathiTrust.)

that they reflect Coons' thinking.[14] She bases her argument on the fact that the manuals Rule had previously published independently on the same subject had a completely different character than the one he developed in collaboration with Coons.[15] She rediscovers in the handbook an aspect that she also mentions at the beginning of her study and which she links directly to Coons. As noted, her introductory thoughts start out with him – she even opens her entire study with a quote from a paper published by Coons. In doing so, she gives him a central position and expresses that this quote aptly illustrates his thinking:

> The design process begins with a graphical description of a proposed device or system to satisfy a human need. To say that the description is graphical is to assert that at the very inception of an idea the designer's understanding of his creation is almost visceral instead of intellectual. He perceives his idea at first not in the perfection of a well-turned English word description, nor in the precision of a mathematical formula, but in some nebulous assembly of building blocks of structure, vaguely beheld; he "feels" his creation. The sketch forms the natural bridge between these vague stirrings of the imagination and the subsequent precise statement of the refined details of the concept.[16]

The image that Coons draws here with his phrasing of the "natural bridge" is taken up again by Perry at various points in her study.[17] Her examination of the virtual model is based on what Coons calls the transformation of a vague idea into a tangible object. To further strengthen her argument that Coons' thinking had a decisive influence on the graphics manual, she quotes a passage from it that makes a very similar statement to the one expressed by Coons above. In fact, a comparison of the quotes leads to the conclusion that it is not Rule but Coons who is largely responsible for the content of the following statement, or at least that both authors were very much in agreement in their thinking:

> When an association is first made in the mind (when we get the first glimmer of an idea) it is usually vague and not clearly perceived. It is at this early stage in the creative process that mankind has learned to use the sketch and the written symbol as aids to the thinker's memory and imagination. These graphic devices, whether pictorial, diagrammatic, or abstract (like words or algebraic symbols), enable us to make solid and tangible the shifting images of our minds, so that we may examine them at our leisure. Through this recording art we free ourselves of the effort to hold ideas in memory, an effort that we must constantly sustain lest as in a dream they change form and fade away.[18]

Similar to the previous text excerpt, this one also expresses that Coons ascribes a certain power to the graphic means of expression,[19] which, in his view, few other means of expression possess. However, Coons also had very clear ideas about how to draw in order to make use of this power. Perry does not take into account these specific instructions for her own analyses. Although Coons' image of the "natural bridge" between idea and design already conveys a certain idea of his thinking, Perry does not clarify the specific features that Coons considered essential for a successful design drawing. For example, she does not examine his or Rule's drawing instructions in her own pictorial example. Her description of the drawing is limited to the following observation: "Coons and Rule present abstract mathematical constructs such as cones, cubes and spheres sketched with an artist's lively line, as if drawn from life."[20] The following section therefore explores what Perry might have understood by a "lively" artistic drawing style, or what criteria Coons considered to be a "good" drawing.

Another aspect that Perry explicitly mentions in addition to the manual, which also particularly characterizes Coons' influence, is the so-called "Coons Surface Patch" that he developed. This is a mathematical model that enables a more precise and simplified description of curved surfaces of virtual objects.[21] The "Coons Surface Patch" makes Coons' influence somewhat clearer than his graphical approaches, which he expressed in the manual. In 1983 – four years after his death – the ACM SIGGRAPH, one of the largest conferences on computer technology, established an award named after him, which is presented every two years to those who have made special achievements in the field of computer graphics.[22] In light of this award, it is surprising that Coons has hardly been considered in histories of early computer graphics developments – with the exception of Perry's and Cardoso Llach's studies. Several people who play a central role in my own study have received the award – for example, Sutherland, who was the first in 1983, followed by Pierre Bézier in 1985 and Edwin Catmull in 1993.[23] However, the awards themselves, of course, say nothing about the direct influence that Coons had on the work of Sutherland and Catmull. Although I will not be focusing on Catmull until later, it can nevertheless be highlighted again here that in his own dissertation in 1974, he explicitly and particularly mentions Coons in the first sentence of his acknowledgments: "I express my appreciation to Steve Coons who gave me considerable help in writing this report."[24] In his dissertation, Catmull's mathematical calculations were not only based on the "Coons Surface Patch," Coons was obviously also actively involved in the development of Catmull's project.[25]

In her own argument that Coons influenced Sutherland's work on *Sketchpad*, Perry relies primarily on the fact that Sutherland mentions Coons several times in the *Sketchpad* report. To strengthen her observation, she quotes Sutherland's text:

> Evidence suggests that Coons' and Rule's approach, of thinking with physical objects such as aircraft parts, influenced Sutherland's design thinking. In the introduction to his dissertation he thanks, "…Members [*sic*] of the Mechanical Engineering Department, notably Professor Stephen [*sic*] A. Coons, who agreed to serve on my thesis committee [and who] suggested mechanical design problems and applications." A discussion of dimensioning and conics in the "Examples" section also reflect Coons' contributions.[26]

As with the examples of Coons' drawing style that Perry presents, she does not elaborate in any depth on the ideas and concepts with which Coons approached his work. Although the text passages she cites here clearly show a connection between Sutherland and Coons in terms of content, Perry ultimately does not clarify how this connection took shape.

In a footnote, Perry provides a reference that can make the connection between Coons and Sutherland a lot clearer. She quotes from the above-mentioned eulogy on the occasion of Coons' death. In it, Herzog lets Sutherland speak for himself by quoting him from a letter they had previously exchanged. What Perry omits is that Sutherland's statement refers to his collaboration with Coons at *Harvard University*, where Sutherland conducted research as an associate professor between 1965 and 1968 following his time at MIT:

> We are deeply saddened by the passing of our teacher and friend Steven Coons. We recall with joy the days sepnt [*sic*] with Steve at Harvard: his work was central to our activity in three-dimensional computer graphics; his enthusiasm was fundamental to our progress; his openness and approachability provided a rare cameraderie [*sic*] between generations; we still feel his influence.[27]

Sutherland's research on *Sketchpad* had taken place 15 years prior to this statement of his. The fact that Herzog let Sutherland, of all people, contribute to his eulogy on Coons' death indicates that his influence obviously extended far beyond their time together at MIT. Although Sutherland does not mention his time there and any possible influence from Coons in this passage from the letter, the connection between the two is still evident in the eulogy. Herzog himself addresses it and thus provides a decisive indication of the collaboration between Coons and Sutherland at MIT. In a passage that Perry does not refer to, Herzog describes,

> [a]bout 1962 it became apparent that computers would be able to produce graphical images and, more important, to receive instruction from humans in human ways, i. e., one could sketch pictures which a computer could understand. Steve Coons was an important member of the thesis committee of Ivan Sutherland. The thesis is entitled Sketchpad – a scheme which clearly demonstrated this concept. Steve Coons advised on this hallmark achievement. More important, however, was Steve's ability to perceive, and perceive very sharply, the significance of this achievement.[28]

In the eulogy, Herzog does not reveal which aspect of *Sketchpad* he or Coons considered to be so significant. Herzog merely mentions that Coons, with remarkable eloquence, praised the potential of the then newly emerging computer graphics in speeches at home and abroad. Instead of focusing on how to describe this potential, Herzog chooses to highlight Coons' ability to have been very persuasive linguistically: "His keen sensitivity could rapidly appraise the background of an audience. Then he would quickly relate the kernel of the notion of computer graphics to that audience in terms they easily understood."[29] My discussion of Coons aims to determine what, for him, characterized this "kernel" of computer graphics, as Herzog puts it. I assume that the resulting findings contribute significantly to the Blumenbergian context of meaning of today's 3D computer graphics.

To illustrate Coons' ability to eloquently demonstrate the potential of computer graphics, a television program produced by MIT for *National Educational Television* in 1963 is well-suited.[30] At the same time, this television program and the statements made by Coons in it can be used to derive how I structure the following sections on him in order to make his concepts accessible. The subject of the television report is the *Sketchpad* program, although Sutherland is only mentioned and does not speak himself. Two people are central to the television program; they present the system developed by Sutherland: Steven Coons and Timothy Johnson. At the time, Johnson was a master's student at MIT who developed a 3D version of Sutherland's two-dimensional (2D) application that could be used to draw and display not only two-dimensional drawings but also three-dimensional objects. However, *Sketchpad III*, as Johnson called the program, will only play a secondary role in the following discussion of Coons. Although Johnson developed numerous features in his version of the program that are still relevant in 3D applications today, it becomes clear in the investigation of Coons' concepts that Johnson was guided by ideas that already existed before he implemented them into the computer.[31] It is therefore more expedient to derive the concepts directly from Coons rather than from Johnson (nevertheless, Johnson's work is examined in more detail in Chapter 7).

In the TV report, the journalist approaches Coons to find out more about the research project on communication between man and machine being pursued at MIT's *Lincoln Laboratory*. He introduces Coons as an associate professor and co-director of the so-called *Computer-Aided Design Project*.[32] In the short conversation between the reporter and Coons, numerous points central to this study and this chapter are addressed. In his speech, Coons provides a general and conceptual introduction to how *Sketchpad* works. He refers to Sutherland as the initiator of *Sketchpad* in this context. At the same time, Coons takes the opportunity to announce what he sees as *Sketchpad's* main innovative contribution. His statement helps to understand what Herzog might have meant when he praised Coons in his eulogy for his ability to precisely describe the innovative power of Sutherland's work. While Herzog does not mention what it is that Coons considered as innovative, Coons himself provides information about this in the television report:

> And you'll see a designer, effectively, solving a problem step by step and he will not at the outset know precisely what his problem is. Nor will he know exactly how to solve it. But little by little he will begin to investigate ideas, and the computer and he will be in cooperation, in the fullest cooperation in this work.[33]

In light of this statement, the results from the Sutherland chapter can be revisited. There, it was made clear that Sutherland brought about a rethinking in the programming process that simultaneously opened up and restricted the work process on the computer, as for the first time someone else defined program features that only had to be called up later. In the television report, Coons also discusses how people had previously worked on the computer. His description is reminiscent of how Fetter described his approach:

> Well, the conventional way, the old way of solving problems with the computer, has been to understand the problem very, very well indeed and moreover to know at the very outset just exactly what steps are necessary to solve the problem. So, the computer has been in a sense nothing but a very elaborate calculating machine, but now we're making the

> computer be more like a, almost like a human assistant and the computer will seem to have some intelligence. It doesn't really, only the intelligence that we put in it. But it will seem to have intelligence.[34]

The discussion of Coons in this chapter will demonstrate what the ideas Sutherland expressed with his *Sketchpad* program were based on. It will become clear that he brought to life and made visible something that Coons had previously anticipated. So even if Sutherland brought about a comprehensive change in terms of programming, I argue that he actually realized a concept that ultimately cannot be attributed to him, but rather to Coons and others. This is discussed further in the second section of this chapter when Coons' software-related considerations are the focus.[35] It can therefore be assumed that Sutherland was also guided by the concepts of images and the worldviews of those who had previously approached the question of how to communicate with the machine in a new way. Therefore, with his pre-programmed features, Sutherland technically inscribed not only Coons' concept of imagery but also his worldview into the machine. As this worldview is communicated through Coons' graphic ideas and continues to be updated today in the form of 3D images, it is necessary to now present these graphic ideas. In analyzing them, it becomes clear that parallels can be drawn with Fetter's understanding of images.

As with Fetter, the following remarks on Coons are divided into two main subject areas. The first section will deal with the importance Coons attached to graphic expression and the criteria he considered necessary for successful graphic representation. The second section will focus on Coons' research contributions in the field of *computer-aided design* (CAD). In this context, Coons' understanding of the use of the computer, and how he brought his idea of graphics into his work with the computer will become clear. Conversely, the following discussion will also shed light on how he brought his idea of the computer into his work with graphic methods. Connecting both fields provides insight into his understanding of the world, which subsequently found its way into the visual landscape of synthetic 3D graphics through people like Sutherland or Edwin Catmull. Coons' worldview largely shapes the common context of meaning of 3D computer graphics. The aim of this chapter on Coons is therefore to establish a foundation on which all subsequent historical developments presented in this study can be built and to which its fundamental line of argumentation can be linked, that is, to overcome the historical leaps to gain insight into what the common context of meaning of 3D graphics could be.

5.1 GRAPHICS AS AN INSTRUMENT OF THOUGHT

The purpose of this section is to get to know and analyze Coons' understanding of successful graphics and his concept of imagery in greater depth. The handbook *Graphics*, co-authored with Rule in 1961 and mentioned in the introduction to this chapter, is a suitable source for this. I base my examination of Coons' criteria for successful graphics on the assumption that these criteria still essentially characterize the context of meaning of computer graphics today. The results of this chapter therefore make it possible to explore how Coons' convictions have found their way into computer technology in the parts following this one.

Rule and Coons take a similar stance to Fetter in their handbook – like him they are convinced that graphics are particularly suitable for communicating ideas and concepts. This becomes clear from a guiding principle that the authors present at the beginning of their manual. They describe graphic drawing as an instrument of thought.[36] This aligns with an aspect that Perry defined as the core of Coons' thinking, as explained above. According to Perry, Coons was deeply interested in transforming a feeling or a vague idea into a concrete and tangible concept in order to capture unshaped and diffuse thoughts. This impulse is also expressed in the handbook written together with Rule:

> Just as we use pencil and paper and set down figures to aid us when we multiply two large numbers, so the sketch is an aid to the mind, a tangible record of an idea, at first perhaps elusive and only dimly perceived. We fix the idea and make it permanent in the sketch, and we can then marshal our critical forces to test it and our creative forces to refine and develop it.[37]

Based on this understanding of drawing, the authors also refer to the sketch as a "memory device"[38] as an alternative to their term "instrument of thought." While, for example, Fetter believes that graphic communication is often much more effective and clearer than written communication, Rule and Coons regard language as an equally important means of expression. It is just as much an instrument of thought as graphics. According to the two authors, there are actually three different such instruments – the "extended symbols" of language, the "compact symbols" of mathematics and the area that they simply call "graphics."[39] The same goal can be pursued with all three – albeit in different ways:

> Each of these instruments permits three modes of manipulation of ideas: creation, or the formation of an initial concept; analysis, or the systematic evaluation and criticism of the concept; and communication, or the comprehensible transmission of the refined and elaborated concept to others. These three instruments are equally powerful and equally necessary, and the scope of the intellect is limited in proportion to limitations in any one of them.[40]

Although the authors emphasize with this statement that all three instruments of thought are equally suitable for expressing concepts and communicating them, their handbook aims to highlight the specifics and advantages of the third field, graphics. A key aspect here is the concept of "tangibility" mentioned by the authors in the previous quote. At the end of this section, there is a precise discussion of the significance that the term has for Rule and Coons.

Before diving into their instructions, they point out that their handbook is not intended to provide students with an all-encompassing training in drafting, but rather to give prospective engineers an idea of the type of thinking required for the job of a draftsman. They explain that each industry has different demands, which is why the automotive industry, for example, requires different detailed knowledge than the aerospace industry.[41] At the same time, however, the graphics that are created for different specialist areas have, to Rule and Coons, fundamental similarities. Knowing them is essential for the authors. Particularly, the last sentence in their foreword explicitly states the central conceptual theme on which they base their book:

> The ultimate educational goal of this text is to provide the student with an awareness of and some familiarity with the third instrument of thought, graphics. Then, when in later professional life he is confronted with an entirely new unsolved problem, he will have an augmented advantage over nature.[42]

Even though they do not work with this term, the authors express here their conviction that the instrument of thought of graphics is based on a common context of meaning, regardless of its subject-related form. A very central element of this context of meaning, which can be derived from this statement made by Rule and Coons, is the fundamental attitude they take toward the process of "thinking." For the authors, thinking means gaining an advantage in an unknown situation, and they see the discipline of graphics as a particularly suitable means of doing this. Although it is not possible to fully decipher what it means for Rule and Coons to have an "extended advantage over nature" and they do not define the concept of nature, the interpretation of their statement can nevertheless be summarized to the effect that the authors regard human thinking as something that lies outside of nature and can therefore be placed above it. The idea of tangibility can also be linked to this: The term implicitly characterizes a process by which something diffuse and untamed – such as nature – is made manageable. The question for this section is therefore how this mindset is translated into Rule and Coons' graphic expressions.

As can be seen from the structure of their book, they use the term "graphic" to summarize very different types of drawing – here too, parallels to Fetter can be seen, because like him, Coons and Rule also make a fundamental distinction between precise technical drawings and perspective illustrations. Since they serve a different target group with their handbook than Fetter with his documentation, Rule and Coons are much more thorough when it comes to discussing which criteria both forms of representation must fulfill. Unlike their colleague, they also provide practical instructions for the production of the various drawings, which prove to be particularly fruitful for my investigation. The authors also supplement their instructions with a meta-reflexive level, explaining why they establish certain rules – they attach great importance to emphasizing that they do not see their instructions as dogmas. They recognize this as their unique selling point compared to other textbooks:

> In the past most graphics texts concentrated on the communication phase, as though the design of a machine consisted only in drawing it in final form according to established rules and conventions. This is an incomplete treatment of graphics and leaves a good two-thirds of the subject submerged. In this volume, the chapters devoted to the formalities of communication – that is, the chapters on dimensioning, sectioning, fasteners, and the like – set forth only the most important rules but with an explanation of the reasons for these rules. Rules by themselves seem entirely arbitrary to a beginner, and since this book will be read by critical and inquiring minds, it is essential that the rules be explained on a logical basis (so far as one exists) and not merely stated as elements of dogma.[43]

As the authors clarify in this statement, they offer meta-reflexive comments mainly in those chapters that address formal rules for creating technical drawings. However, even in the second field, that of the perspective illustration, which – as Fetter would say – is more comprehensible, it is apparent that the authors have clear ideas about the graphic design process. They consider adhering to these ideas essential for the purpose of communication. Yet, for this type of drawing they hardly ever explicitly disclose the reasons for these ideas. Therefore, when the authors describe the rules for the technical drawings as "arbitrary,"[44] as long as they are not explained, their ideas for the perspective illustrations, which they base on no explanations at all, appear particularly arbitrary in contrast. Some of their comments even allow the interpretation that they are aware of this inner contradiction in their conceptual approach:

> Perhaps the hardest concept for the beginner to grasp is the need of adhering to conventions in drawing. In any form of symbolic communication, we depend strongly upon well-established forms which are familiars of our experience. Drawings have a grammar (or perhaps more accurately, an idiom) which is better established and more filled with implicit meaning than we might suspect at the beginning. When we study the details of these conventions, we should carry in mind the reader and his needs. He is by long experience (as we have said before) trained to read and interpret not only *what* is put on the drawing, but *how* it appears there, and a substantial part of the meaning of the drawing is conveyed in this implicit way.[45]

Without specifically distinguishing between the two basic types of drawings – the technical or the illustrative – they clearly characterize the graphic method of representation here as a symbolic form of expression. The rules for this symbolism are, according to them, based on conventions, and although Rule and Coons indicate that they reflect on the traditions handed down, they also find it important to adhere to the rules because of the recipients. New approaches would stand in the way of successful communication. Their scope to really scrutinize these conventions in depth and possibly even question them to create new rules is therefore limited. However, the authors do not see this circumstance of having to adhere to a symbolic level of communication as an obstacle, but rather as a requirement. The authors' own awareness of the symbolism of the graphics is reminiscent of Erwin Panofsky's essay *Perspective as Symbolic Form*.[46] However, since the authors view the symbolism as a requirement rather than a contingent phenomenon, their position at the same time clearly contradicts Panofsky's in his essay. Later in this section, this discrepancy will be addressed again by specifically examining some of Rule and Coons' graphic instructions against the backdrop of Panofsky.

According to Rule and Coons, graphics should therefore be created that not only adhere to conventions but also explicitly express them to function particularly reliably in terms of communication. Thus, their explanations refer not only to the role of the draftsman but also to the role of the recipient. For this reason, Rule and Coons also explicitly underline that it is not only fundamentally important for the draftsman to know the conventions of drawing, but that this should also apply to all other persons involved in the communication process. They justify this consideration with an example from the everyday work of an engineering draftsman:

> As the work progresses, the designer will have on paper an increasingly clear and more and more detailed study of the device. When he is quite certain of its form, a conference is usually called in which representatives of management, sales, engineering, and styling (if such a division exists in the company) get together to discuss the merits and shortcomings of the proposed design. It is, of course, necessary for the drawings and pictures of the machine to be clear and understandable, and for various conferees to be able to visualize the machine from these drawings. This naturally makes it desirable for everyone concerned to have some training in graphics.[47]

With this statement, the authors address a similar problem that was also central to Fetter. As was demonstrated in the section on him, he also attached such great importance to perspective illustrations. In accordance with the maxim of believability he was convinced that they would be easier and more intuitive to understand than technical drawings. Comprehending those requires training. Rule and Coons' statement thus definitively shows that graphic communication can fail in their eyes if not everyone shares the experience of the same rules. They do not question the rules as such in any way.

Every graphic that is created according to the instructions of Rule and Coons therefore reproduces the conventions anew and thus also the "implicit meaning" that the authors speak of. Taking this idea further, it is now possible for me for the first time to deduce that 3D computer graphics, since they can be linked historically to Coons, also perpetuate the conventions he considered valuable with each new image. To understand more precisely which conventions are carried forward and manifest themselves as a common context of meaning in today's computer graphics, a main concern of the further discussion in this section is to gain a deeper understanding of both the conventions and the implicit meaning the authors express. Like Rule and Coons, I am assuming that the images are easier to read if the recipient also has at least a basic knowledge of the conventions. Or to be more precise and refer this thought to the main purpose of this study, I argue that the context of meaning of today's 3D computer graphics can *only* be fully grasped if the tradition from which the graphics originated is known. Therefore, I will now focus primarily on those instructions that the authors provide for the field of illustrative freehand sketches, i.e. for those drawings to which the particularly arbitrary, implicit rules apply. As it is more difficult for the authors to question their rules for this field, I base the following discussion in this section on the assumption that particularly the perspective illustrations are characterized by a worldview or cultural influences that still characterize the context of meaning of 3D graphics today. These influences cannot be identified and justified as directly as the rules for technical drawings, which are primarily intended to ensure that a component or object can be manufactured precisely. To understand the context of meaning of today's 3D images, it therefore seems more relevant to focus not primarily on the rules for producing such technical drawings, but rather on the symbolically charged drawing conventions that Rule and Coons draw upon for perspective illustrations. This focus can also be justified from a visual-aesthetic angle, as today's graphics generally follow principles of perspective. Nevertheless, it should be noted that the context of meaning of today's 3D graphics is fed by both fields – that of perspective illustration and that of technical drawings. While, on the surface, the perspective instructions are of particular interest for the visual aesthetics of today's and former graphics, the technical instructions also play a significant role on a production-aesthetic level of these graphics. Numerous instructions for the production of technical drawings survive in today's software, as will also be discussed in the third part of this study.

For the precise examination of the drawing conventions that Rule and Coons follow and which they want to convey in their handbook, two chapters from their comprehensive manual are focused on in particular: Chapter 5 "Freehand Sketching" and Chapter 16 "Pictorial Drawing."[48] Both are thematically related, as they respectively deal in different ways with various possibilities of creating perspective drawings. The overarching aim of both chapters is to convey an additional illustrative representation method alongside the technical drawing processes that must ensure the production of components. Those more artistic sketches can either be used – as mentioned at the beginning – to graphically support the ideation phase or to illustrate the design of a component in addition to the often abstract technical drawings: "Projections which permit easy visualization of objects are called *pictorial views*."[49] The authors often use several terms for the same phenomenon. They therefore occasionally also refer to "pictorial views" as "space sketches"[50] or as "pictorial projection."[51]

In the introduction to their fifth chapter, the authors explain, "[t]his book, and particularly this chapter, is devoted to the diagrammatic and pictorial aspects of the graphic art."[52] It should be noted here that the authors only use the term "diagrammatic" in two places in their handbook, both in Chapter 5.[53] In the context of other sections of the manual, however, the authors frequently use the term "diagram."[54] Examples show that the authors refer to diagrams when they are used to depict relationships in schematic representations, on the one hand, or when they are used to represent measurements, on the other. In numerous images, both forms of representation are used in combination. In those cases it is particularly the diagrams used for illustration purposes that often also contain elements drawn in perspective.[55] The "pictorials," on the other hand, are produced without exception in perspective. Various perspective methods are available for this purpose, which will be referred to again in the following paragraph. As noted, the illustrations serve to visualize technical designs. They are often more refined than the perspective diagrams, as shown for example in Figure 5.2, in which Rule and Coons demonstrate the production of an isometric drawing using a rectangular component. The intention for the perspective illustrations is therefore more elaborate and also similar to that described by Fetter with his two graphs (Figure 4.17). In their Chapter 5, Rule and Coons establish their ideas and concepts for the production of the different types of drawings; it is therefore particularly informative for my discussion. Chapter 16, on the other hand, focuses on concrete practical exercises. Here, precise drawing instructions are given step by step. Some insights can also be gained from these practical examples.

The authors summarize all the forms of representation featured in the two chapters under the term "pictorial projection."[56] They use this term to describe different drawing methods, each of which pursues a different approach to perspective projection. Rule and Coons basically divide the various methods into two categories, on the one hand, those that are created using parallel perspective and, on the other, those that are created using central perspective. The first category includes the "*oblique pictorial*,"[57] which can be seen on the left in Figure 5.3, as well as the so-called trimetric, dimetric and isometric drawings. These types of representation do not have a vanishing point, which is why any lines that are intended to indicate the depth of an object do not converge within this first category (Figure 5.3). It thus builds a contrast to the drawing type of the second category, the so-called "perspective pictorial."[58] Like Fetter, Rule and Coons also comment on the degree of realism of the different forms of representation. They consider the tri-, di- and isometric drawing methods to be "[s]omewhat more realistic"[59] than, for example, the "*oblique pictorial*."[60] Again in agreement with Fetter, Rule and Coons also describe the last type, the "perspective picture," as "most realistic."[61] In their Chapter 5, they refer with this statement to a drawing with two vanishing points, and in Chapter 16 to a drawing with only one vanishing point.[62] From these two references, it can be deduced that the second category of "perspective pictorials," in which both perspective foreshortening and tapering of the vanishing lines occur, allows for the most realistic type of representation of objects for Rule and Coons as well as for Fetter. In Chapter 16, however, it is also pointed out that perspective representations are often not used at all for the purpose of visualization because they are not measurable in any way:

> Judicious orientation of an object can yield an orthographic projection which is not only an acceptable pictorial view, but is also easier to construct and to measure than a perspective projection. Such projections are consequently much more commonly used in engineering practice than are perspectives when pictorial views are desired.[63]

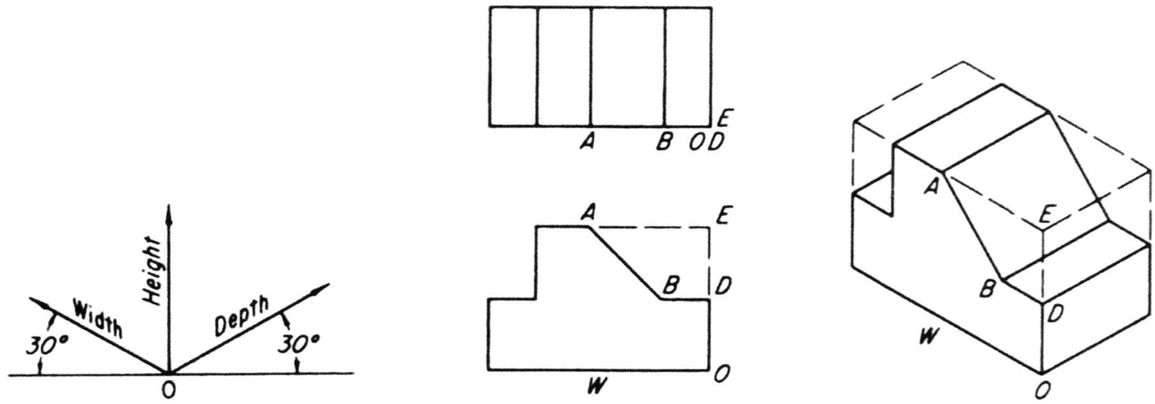

FIG. 16-7

FIG. 16-8

FIGURE 5.2 John T. Rule and Steven A. Coons, *Fig. 16-7–16-8*, 1961, technical drawing. (Courtesy of HathiTrust.)

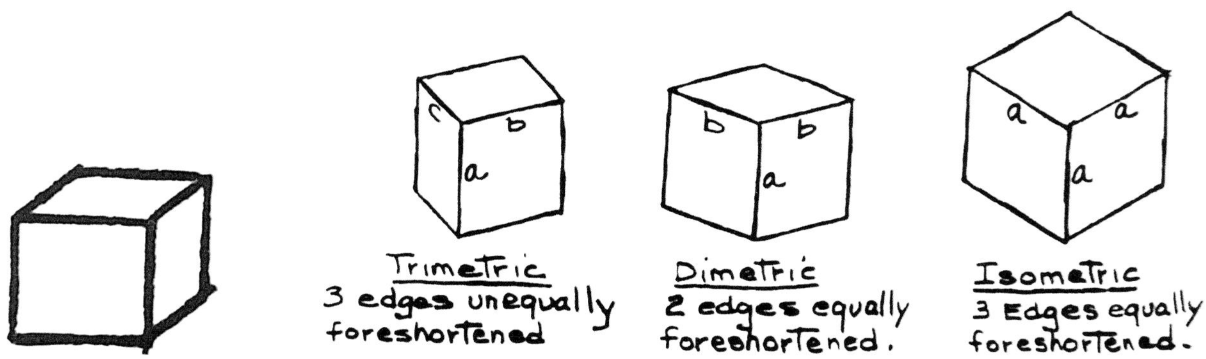

FIG. 5-22

FIG. 5-23

FIGURE 5.3 John T. Rule and Steven A. Coons, *Fig. 5-22–5-23*, 1961, drawing. (Courtesy of HathiTrust.)

The orthographic views Rule and Coons refer to here are the oblique, iso-, di- and trimetric drawings explained above, all of which can be constructed without a vanishing point. Like Fetter, the authors conclude that these orthographic views are somewhat more measurable than the representations with perspective distortion. At the same time, their wording indicates that they are aware of the extent to which all these forms of drawings are merely constructions. Nevertheless, like Fetter, they closely tie their concept of realism to the perspective representations based on vanishing points. For them, the basis for this argument is the human visual apparatus, just as it is for Fetter and his maxim of believability. While Fetter provides no information about how he arrived at this insight, Rule and Coons' conviction can be deduced from their handbook. Although they can be brought into alignment with Fetter, Rule and Coons approach their assertion in a much more comprehensive and self-critical manner than their colleague. This can be illustrated by their section "What we know and what we see"[64] in Chapter 5 of the handbook. In it, Rule and Coons explicitly address the human vision from a physiological and perceptual perspective, taking drawing conventions into account. In short, they deal with the question of learned vision, which Panofsky also explores in his essay *Perspective as Symbolic Form*. The section "What we know and what we see" contains key insights on the above-mentioned "grammar" of graphics and their "implicit meaning," as defined by Rule and Coons.

They open the section with the question of what a child would draw if it were asked to depict a house or a glass of water. They even make their own drawing suggestions as to what such sketches might look like (Figure 5.4) and comment on their attempts as follows:

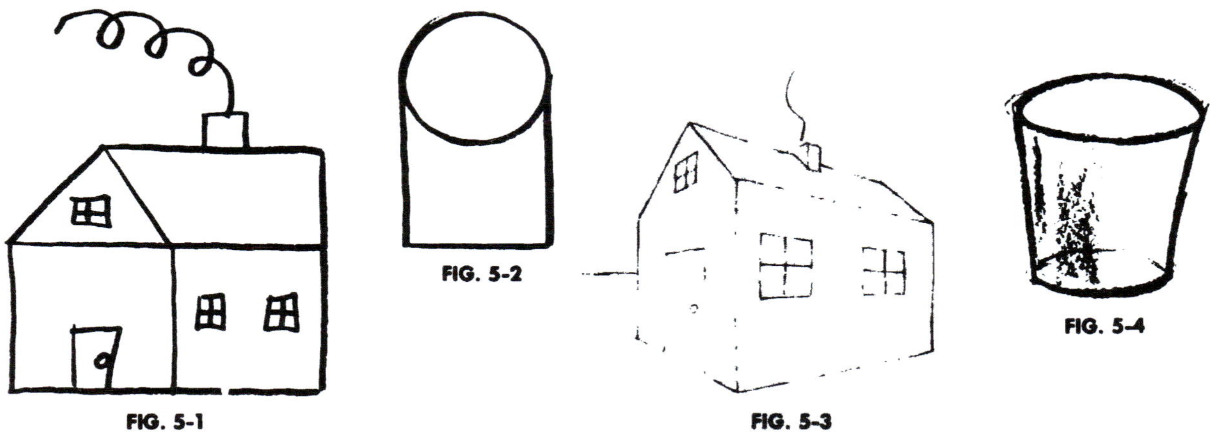

FIGURE 5.4 John T. Rule and Steven A. Coons, *Fig. 5-1–5-4*, 1961, drawing. (Courtesy of HathiTrust.)

> At first glance, these drawings seem distorted, as in truth they are. But upon examination, we see that they are mixtures of what the child sees and what he thinks (or knows) about the true shapes of the two objects. He draws the front of the house as though he were standing in front looking at it and seeing what he knows to be the true shape of angles and true proportions of lines; then the side of the house also has a true shape, and it is only natural to try to tell the truth by drawing it so. Paradoxically, a good drawing is more naïve and at the same time more sophisticated than the drawings made by a child.[65]

Here, it becomes particularly clear that the authors are concerned with a claim to truth that needs to be captured in graphic representations and which they specifically attribute to perspective drawings. For although they show that even a child considers what it draws to be truthful, they believe that the perspective drawing is the correct realization. It is, in their view, a "good drawing." They even admit that such a representation is in principle more "naïve" than a child's drawing. Yet, they use two such "good drawings" to show how to do it "correctly." One depicts a house with two vanishing points, while the other is a simple freehand sketch of a glass distorted in perspective, with the base and opening shown as an ellipses (Figure 5.4). Finally, they point out that neither of the two approaches – the child's and the "correct" one – represent the actual geometry of a house or glass.

But why is perspective representation easier for the human perceptual apparatus to understand, according to Rule and Coons, and why do the authors consider it more advanced than children's drawings? They justify their hypothesis by assuming that we have learned to translate the perspective distortions in our minds into geometric shapes that we can perceive in space:

> For instance, the retinal elliptical image of the top of the drinking glass is interpreted quite automatically into a circle. It is "seen solid." The geometrical interpretation into three dimensions is so well learned, so unconscious, and so instantaneously automatic that it is difficult to produce on paper the halfway point of perception, the copy of the retinal image that occurred before our minds took over and interpreted the image into an intellectual space concept of reality in agreement with what we have learned to know.[66]

As can be seen from this statement, the authors describe an intellectual and learned process of seeing. In doing so, they align the symbolic concept of central perspective with our retinal image and thus remain true to the above-defined maxim of believability. In his essay *Perspective as Symbolic Form*, Panofsky also includes considerations on central perspective and a possible connection of it to our retinal image. However, he comes to the opposite conclusion:

> In order to guarantee a fully rational – that is, infinite, unchanging and homogenous – space, this "central perspective" makes two tacit but essential assumptions: first, that we see with a single and immobile eye, and second, that the planar cross section of the visual pyramid can pass for an adequate reproduction of our optical image. In fact these two premises are rather bold abstractions from reality, if by "reality" we mean the actual subjective optical impression. For the structure of an infinite, unchanging and homogenous space – in short, a purely mathematical space – is quite unlike the structure of the psychophysiological space […].[67]

In his essay, Panofsky aims to explain the extent to which central perspective is only one of many ways of constructing a pictorial representation. With his statement on psychophysiological perception and the title of his essay, Panofsky refers to Ernst Cassirer's *Philosophy of Symbolic Forms, II (Mythical Thought)* and his comparison of mathematical space with the "space of immediate perception"[68] expressed therein. Cassirer argues that the way in which we subjectively perceive spaces cannot be brought into alignment with the mathematical description of spaces. While these can be described as homogeneous, immediate perception is inhomogeneous. Cassirer therefore concludes,

> [h]ence homogeneous space is never given space, but space produced by construction; and indeed the geometrical concept of homogeneity can be expressed by the postulate that from every point in space it must be possible to draw similar figures in all directions and magnitudes.[69]

Cassirer's view contradicts Rule and Coons' description above, as Cassirer emphasizes that in the "space of immediate perception […] there is no strict homogeneity of position and direction […]."[70] Comparing his line of argument with Coons and Rule's assumptions therefore leads to the conclusion that the technical draftsmen – including Fetter – prematurely equate central perspective with our retinal image. Even the claim to truth that they attach to such drawings no longer holds against the background of Panofsky and Cassirer. Thus, the maxim of believability on which the central perspective illustrations are based has no foundation; it is a pure construction. Panofsky additionally takes Cassirer's observations a step further. Panofsky points out that the mathematical construction of central perspective always assumes that we look at our surroundings with just one eye, which also remains still. However, the fact that our eyes are always in motion is just as little taken into account by the homogenized mathematical central perspective as the fact

> that this retinal image – entirely apart from its subsequent psychological "interpretation," and even apart from the fact that the eyes move – is a projection not on a flat but on a concave surface. Thus already on this lowest, still prepsychological level of facts there is a fundamental discrepancy between "reality" and its construction. This is also true, of course, for the entirely analogous operation of the camera.[71]

Rule and Coons do not consider the fact that the retinal image is curved, in contrast to the flat surface of a perspective drawing, and for them the subjective "psychophysiological" perception of space plays no role either. Their mindset clearly contradicts that of Panofsky, who even points out that an awareness of the "discrepancy between retinal image and perspectival representation"[72] already existed in the Renaissance. Panofsky also notes that due to "the curvature of the retina […] our eye perceives them [straight lines] (from the center of projection) as convex curves."[73] With their considerations, Rule and Coons primarily refer to the homogeneous, mathematical space – to make use of Cassirer's choice of words here. This applies to all the forms of drawings they present. For Rule and Coons, the human perception and its mathematical translation into an image show no differences, or to put it the other way round, they do not regard human perception as a subjective phenomenon, but rather as one that can be described with mathematical precision. As noted above, this mindset leads them to the conclusion that the "perspective pictorial" is the most realistic. It would correspond not only to the retinal image but also to that of the camera:

> The best visual picture is given by a photograph which is a perspective projection. Such a perspective produces exactly the same retinal image, geometrically speaking, if the eye is placed at the center of projection, as the object itself would have produced. Thus a perspective projection is as nearly as possible the same as viewing the object itself in space.[74]

Cassirer would criticize Rule and Coons for ignoring the "psychophysiological" aspect with their mathematical view of human perception. However, it is precisely this mathematical viewpoint that leads Rule and Coons to attribute a claim to truth to the central perspective. The argument that viewing a central perspective drawing hardly differs from viewing a physically present object can only be made if the psychophysiological characteristics of human vision are ignored. At least, the authors acknowledge that their conclusions are drawn from a geometric perspective. However, whether they would reach a different conclusion, if they were to adopt a different point of view, remains open.

Although it has now been possible to clarify why Rule and Coons considered the "perspective pictorials" to be particularly realistic, their views can be called into question with Panofsky's and Cassirer's arguments. Interestingly, Rule and Coons themselves even provide reflections in numerous text passages that align with Panofsky and Cassirer, which is why the authors – to put it bluntly – contradict their own convictions at these points. For example, regarding the perspective drawings, they point out themselves that in order to actually achieve the impression of an object physically present in space, our eye must remain still. To illustrate their argument, they once again relate human vision and the camera lens to each other: "You will achieve a perspective pictorial if you keep your eye fixed (at one point only) and trace the object on the glass. Note that this is the sort of picture a camera takes."[75] In addition to the instruction to keep the eye still for a successful perspective drawing, the authors also speak of just one single eye. It cannot be assumed that they wanted their readers to actually cover one of their eyes, but regardless of how exactly the authors imagined the process, it is clear that they are describing a formalized and not an intuitive way of seeing. Their sterile instructions on how to use our eyes to create a successful perspective drawing are at odds with their idea of sketching as an intuitive instrument of thought. For the authors, however, there is no contradiction here. For them, the geometric view seems to fulfill their own demands on human intuition.

Also in other instructions, they continuously take no notice of the fact that our vision is generated by the interaction of two eyes. Instead, their instructions are reminiscent of Alberti's visual pyramid or the workings of a camera obscura:

> The rays of light from an object to the eye are in effect projectors which pass through the optical center of the eye's lens and are focused on the retina. Imagine looking at a scene through a glass window. If you photographed the scene from the position of the eye, you could enlarge the picture to the proper size and paste it on the window so that the projectors from every point in the scene would pass through the image of the same points on the picture and into the eye. Thus geometrically, the picture would produce exactly the same image on the retina as the scene itself. Obviously such a projection is the most realistic of all forms of pictorial projections.[76]

Once again, it can be deduced that Rule and Coons link their concept of realism to a mathematical image model, which, from their perspective, applies equally to the human eye and to the camera lens. However, connecting the retinal image to central perspective not only appears contradictory against the backdrop of Panofsky, it is also inconclusive against the background of the children's drawings mentioned by the authors. With those they admit that the process of drawing in central perspective does not come naturally to us. They try to resolve this contradiction by reasoning that people constantly forget what their own retinal image actually looks like, as our brain would translate everything directly into spatial impressions. As a solution, they therefore suggest remembering that everything in our eye is depicted as a flat surface in order to learn to draw from there. Rule and Coons claim that even with a flat perspective drawing, one must first remember that we are not dealing with three-dimensional objects and that spatial perception only occurs in our mind: "This, and not manual skill, is the most difficult obstacle for the beginner to overcome."[77] For Rule and Coons, drawing in central perspective is therefore not primarily linked to a learning process of the craft, but to a learning process that concerns one's own vision. Neither a beginner nor a child would therefore have an awareness of these processes. It can therefore be concluded that the authors assume all people have the same intuitive visual behavior – provided they have developed an awareness of their own intuition. With their references to children's drawings, however, they undermine their own line of argument, because this example could also be used to derive the opposite argument: The intuitive vision of each person is very individual and children do not produce their drawings according to specific principles of drawing construction, but rather according to their individual perception of the world, precisely for the reason that they have not yet internalized – in this case Western – drawing conventions. Rule and Coons apparently rule out the possibility that the human perceptual apparatus is influenced by learned concepts, such as perspective drawings, or by traditions transmitted through culture. Therefore, they do not believe that our perception can change or that we can unlearn these conventions, even though they speak of conventions and traditions themselves.

In contrast to their instructions regarding the *production* of perspective sketches, inconsistencies in Rule and Coons' argumentation are also evident in their remarks on the *observation* of perspective drawings. At first glance, their position seems almost entirely consistent with Panofsky's, but they draw completely different conclusions and consequences from it:

> In a perspective picture it is possible to look along all projectors at once. This happens when the eye is placed in the position from which the picture was drawn – the center of projection. In this position there is no distortion of the object at all. By this we mean simply that the retinal image is the same as it would be if we were actually looking at the object. As we move to some other viewing position, the image becomes more and more distorted, but we are not greatly aware of this distortion over an acceptably large area around the center of projection, because the geometrical differences between the retinal images made by the incorrectly viewed picture and retinal images made by real objects are second-order differences that do not easily catch the attention of the mind.[78]

Once again, the authors draw a connection to the retinal image here and once again they provide clues according to which the supposed retinal image actually only appears under very specific conditions – for example, when we do not move our eyes and only when we adopt a very specific viewing angle to the image. They use a schematic diagram to illustrate their ideas about viewing an image (Figure 5.5). A bird's eye view of a cube is shown, as well as a point slightly below it that marks the location of a potential viewing position. A horizontal line drawn between this point and the cube indicates the area where a drawing of the object would be located from the observer's perspective. To the left and right of the cube, two vanishing points are marked on the line, which would be used for a drawing of the cube from this specific observation position. Below this representation is an example of what the drawing of the cube would look like from the perspective of the person depicted if the vanishing points were used for construction as planned. Not only the cube is shown here but also the vanishing lines. Finally, the authors point out that if a viewer of this drawing wanted to get a true impression of the cube, they would theoretically have to take the distance between the viewer and the cube marked in the bird's eye view and thus place themselves about 2 in. in front of the book page. At the same time, they admit that this would only be possible if we had a lens with the correct focal length at our disposal that could compensate for the short distance between the observer and the image. Without a lens, at a viewing distance of around 8–10 in. from the book page, the cube would appear somewhat deeper than it is, "but even so its appearance is quite realistic."[79] Due to the difficulties that arise when viewing such perspective drawings, they conclude that small-format presentations are not as satisfactory as somewhat larger-format ones. At a viewing distance of around 10 in. from the perspective image, it would therefore be optimal if the vanishing points were around 20–24 in. apart.[80] While Panofsky would conclude here that central perspective is in no

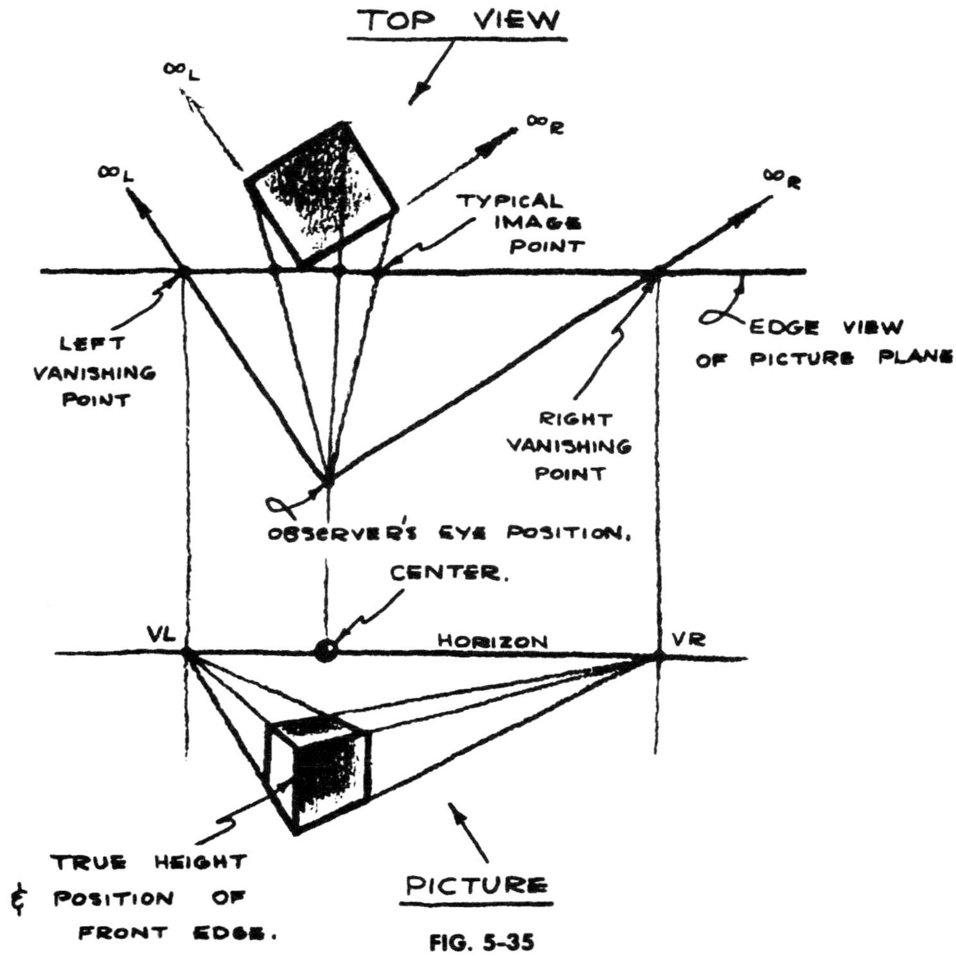

FIGURE 5.5 John T. Rule and Steven A. Coons, *Fig. 5-35*, 1961, drawing. (Courtesy of HathiTrust.)

way compatible with our "psychophysiological" perception of space, Rule and Coons and even William A. Fetter came to the opposite conclusion. Given that all three were familiar with much more precise methods of construction drawings, which could also be considered "true" depictions of "reality," it is surprising that they placed so much trust in perspective illustrations for the visualization of concepts and ideas.

The question therefore remains as to why Rule, Coons and Fetter nevertheless concluded that perspective illustrations of all things correspond to "truth" or "reality." Ultimately, all three have obviously experienced empirically that the perspective illustrations can be intuitively grasped by many people, even those who are not deeply trained in graphic drawing – and I do not deny this perception. The perspective drawings were certainly well suited to the three engineers' communication needs. However, if their respective reasons for their conclusions seem contradictory, why does their drawing approach still work for their purposes? Panofsky again offers possible clues to answer this question:

> And indeed, if even today only a very few of us have perceived these curvatures, that too is surely in part due to our habituation – further reinforced by looking at photographs – to linear perspectival construction: a construction that is itself comprehensible only for a quite specific, indeed specifically modern, sense of space, or if you will, sense of the world.[81]

Panofsky's theory explains why Rule and Coons' communication through perspective illustrations was so successful and above all intuitive. With their understanding of graphics they tap into a "sense of the world" and both the draftsmen as well as those to who view the graphics are united in this "sense of the world." However, and I am again following Panofsky and Cassirer here, this does not guarantee that a central perspective drawing also fulfills the claim of reality. Against this intellectual background, it seems particularly contradictory that Rule and Coons speak of a long-standing convention on which their teachings are based, as they are initially implying at least an awareness of the *possibility* of other conventions. However, by establishing a close connection between the convention of central perspective and "reality" or "truth," they ultimately express that there is *no* other possibility of representation that could be used to depict the world truthfully. For the authors there is no conflict in this respect. For them, their own references to a symbolic and implicit meaning, which is perpetuated in the form of graphic conventions, in no way contradict the idea of a claim to truth or reality. On the contrary, for Rule and Coons the concept of truth is an essential element of this symbolic level. Thus, when they speak of a grammar of images, they are completely convinced that this grammar contains not only reality but also truth. They derive their legitimization for the perspective images solely from this conviction, but not from the idea of habituation offered by Panofsky. For them, the photographic lens, for example, is merely proof that the "truth" of our human vision can also be imitated by an apparatus. For Panofsky, on the other hand, photography serves as proof that our learned conventions of central perspective merely continue to manifest themselves in the apparatus. While for Rule and Coons the idea of truth lies in what they call the "implicit meaning" of graphics, with Panofsky this implicit meaning could instead be described as a particular "sense of the world." Based on a truth that, according to Rule and Coons, applies to everyone, and a concomitant uniform perceptual behavior, the authors would most likely consider Panofsky's sense of the world also to be a universal principle. This preliminary result forms the basis for my further investigation.

In the final step of this section, Panofsky's essay is drawn upon to derive a further concept, which – in addition to the "sense of the world" – is essential for the following parts of this study. In retrospect, William A. Fetter's concept of perspective illustrations can also be included in this "sense of the world," even though he did not make a direct contribution to today's software. And with the help of Fetter, it is also possible to further sharpen the idea of what this sense of the world stands for. As was noted, he too – like Rule and Coons – links the perspective image to the human visual apparatus. In this context, he makes use not only of the term "realism," as explained above, but also of the term "credibility."[82] In line with what I call the maxim of believability, for Fetter, a perspective construction is therefore not only particularly realistic but also particularly credible – in contrast, for example, to a technical representation of a phenomenon that is not drawn in perspective and is therefore measurable. Rule and Coons do not use the term credibility in their handbook but instead work with the term "tangibility," as mentioned at the beginning of this section. Their concept of "tangibility" will now be related to Fetter's choice of the term "credibility" and analyzed with Panofsky. This step serves to create a link between all three engineers, so that Fetter's contribution can also be made fruitful for my further investigation. Although references to this have already been made throughout this chapter, the conceptual proximity to Fetter finally clarifies that the maxim of believability also continues in the historical narrative thread of Rule and Coons.

In their introduction, the two authors make use of the term "tangibility" for the first time. As stated at the beginning of this section, they repeatedly refer to the power of the sketch to make a fleeting idea tangible. They use the term and the concept behind it again in a chapter called "Graphics and Accuracy"[83] that deals with geometric drawing methods for mathematical purposes. Although the authors do not focus here on representational drawing methods and therefore not on the communicative aspect of a drawing, but instead on schematic representations of, for example, force ratios, the introduction to the chapter allows me to derive a more precise idea of the concept of tangibility from the two authors. In the chapter, Rule and Coons differentiate between two methods of visualizing mathematical problems and contrast them with each other. On the one hand, they are concerned with the discipline of Euclidean geometry and, on the other, with a field that they refer to as graphical geometry. Although both approaches are in their opinion suitable for the visualization of mathematical problems, they show considerable differences in their respective implementation. The main difference, as the title of the chapter suggests, lies in the aspect of precision of both methods. This distinction is of particular importance for my discussion, as the authors attribute the concept of tangibility only to the second method of graphical geometry. To close this section, I will now explain how they arrived at this conclusion.

As indicated, the two methods place different demands on the finished visualization. The authors characterize Euclidean geometry as a method that is theoretically always perfect, but at the same time very complex and therefore also prone to errors.[84] It is particularly suitable

> to establish true theorems about relationships of ideal geometric elements – points, lines, planes, circles, curves, surfaces – under severely restricted postulates of constructibility [*sic*] and with the use of only certain tools. Euclid permitted the use of the unmarked straightedge and the compass only.[85]

In their discussion of the two approaches, Rule and Coons emphasize that the Euclidean method is not intended for a drawing process used to produce designs for engineering or construction. Rather, it is intended to approach mathematical issues in an abstract, theoretical way. The authors therefore explain, "[t]o a student who prides himself on his practical-mindedness, these efforts may seem artificial."[86] However, only those who do not know the principles and requirements behind the Euclidean approach will, according to Rule and Coons, come to this conclusion.

In their chapter on graphic precision, the authors distinguish between two groups of people: The "geometers,"[87] on the one hand, and the "draftsmen,"[88] on the other. According to the authors' descriptions, the latter group primarily draws on the principles of graphic geometry. For various reasons, Rule and Coons say it is more intuitive than the Euclidean method. For example, with graphic geometry, any tool can be used to achieve a drawing goal immediately.[89] At the same time, the method is much less prone to errors due to its less stringent specifications. However, the authors do not consider its lack of precision to be a disadvantage. As a rule, the graphical method merely pursues a different goal – one in which the loss of precision is insignificant:

> The central purpose of graphics [...] is to deal with tangible physical elements of our real world. For example, graphics deals with lines which may not be perpendicular or parallel in the precise mathematical sense, but which are for some immediate purpose sufficiently perpendicular or parallel to satisfy immediate requirements of accuracy. These matters have been discussed at length in the chapter on line and circle constructions. Notably the construction of parallels and the construction of tangents to a curve or circle by graphical means allow operations which can be made as accurate as the immediate purpose may require but which, not being theoretically exact, cannot be tolerated by geometers. This merely means that the purposes of the draftsman and the purposes of the geometer are different.[90]

Although the authors remain thematically focused on mathematical problems, it nevertheless becomes clear that for them graphic geometry is directly related to our "real" life – or in their own words: To the "real world."[91] Similar to their reflections on the sketch, which can serve to capture a fleeting idea into a tangible representation, here too, they use the concept of tangibility to demonstrate that graphic geometry – in contrast to Euclidean geometry – is primarily suited to making the events of our real environment visually palpable. The authors take their thoughts one step further with a significant clarification: Although they distinguish between the more precise Euclidean geometry and the less precise graphical geometry, they also recognize that the concept of precision refers not to the world we live in, but rather to the units of measurement we use to measure it. In essence, Rule and Coons question the principle of precision as such, because the world was already present before we created units for all phenomena:

> We can make the case for graphics somewhat stronger if we consider the assumption of absolute precision. A problem stated in an

> arithmetic text is indeed composed of data of an absolutely precise nature, but in the real universe no such precision exists; all we know about the universe is what we can measure, and since measurement is inherently graphical, we are forced to the conclusion that data can only be known to a certain imperfect degree of accuracy.[92]

By linking graphics to the real world and at the same time arguing that the real world is not precise anyway, the authors demonstrate that the graphic method cannot and should not fulfill the demand for precision. With this argument that graphics must not or cannot be precise, yet still fulfill – for this exact reason – the requirement of tangibility, Rule and Coons share a similar mindset with William A. Fetter. He, too, linked the maxim of believability not to precise drawings that could be used to measure an object's dimensions, but to images distorted in perspective. According to Fetter, those images are especially vivid and possibly also intuitively closer to the "real world," even if they are completely unsuitable for the production of a component. All three authors therefore did not make mathematical accuracy a prerequisite in order to fulfill the maxim of believability or tangibility. For Rule and Coons, the idea of precision even contradicts their claim to tangibility. For them, precision is not at all desirable when it comes to grasping the world.

Although Rule and Coons base their discussion in their chapter "Graphics and Accuracy" on mathematical problems rather than the field of perspective drawing, their fundamental division into "Euclidean" and "graphic" geometry in this chapter demonstrates that any graphic instructions in their handbook that do not explicitly follow Euclid's principles belong in the second category. Against the background of this distinction made by the authors between the two fields, it is now possible to understand the meaning they attach to the concept of graphics and why they do not regard Euclidean geometry as an instrument of thought. The title of their handbook – *Graphics* – can also be understood more precisely having the distinction between the two fields in mind. The authors' comments on the relationship between precision and tangibility can now be understood as part of the maxim of believability. Therefore, this maxim can now also be applied to Rule and Coons' perspective illustrations, which are of particular relevance to the development of 3D computer graphics and, consequently, also to my overall analysis.

Thus, if Rule and Coons assumed that an idiomatic symbolism is implicitly communicated through the grammar of a graphic, then it can be argued that both their concept of tangibility and Fetter's concept of credibility are essential elements of this symbolic level of meaning. Fetter even linked his concept of credibility directly to the central perspective. However, since Rule and Coons also placed great importance on perspective illustrations believing them to be the most likely to fulfill a claim to truth, it is accurate to say that mathematical precision was not essential for a truthful representation in the context of perspective drawing for all three of them. Given that Rule, Coons and Fetter were familiar with various other, even mathematically more precise drawing processes, it is now particularly clear that their decision to use perspective graphics to represent "reality" was intentional yet arbitrary – even though it may have been without alternative for all three. This conclusion also leads to a contradiction – especially against the background of Cassirer's remarks on psychophysiological perception: All three authors argue with a mathematically calculable model of human visual behavior and link their concept of truth to it, while at the same time they make mathematical inaccuracies a criterion for drawings that are supposed to be particularly tangible or credible. To understand this contradiction Panofsky can be consulted again. With him, the symbolic meaning that central perspective harbors can be precisely understood, although it cannot be legitimized from either a mathematical or psychophysiological point of view:

> But if perspective is not a factor of value, it is surely a factor of style. Indeed, it may even be characterized as (to extend Ernst Cassirer's felicitous term to the history of art) one of those "symbolic forms" in which "spiritual meaning is attached to a concrete, material sign and intrinsically given to this sign." This is why it is essential to ask of artistic periods and regions not only whether they have perspective, but also which perspective they have.[93]

To borrow Panofsky's phrasing, it is therefore essential to ask of Rule, Coons and Fetter's perspective illustrations not *whether* they have perspective, but rather *which* perspective they have. Based on what could be learned in this chapter about their understanding of perspective, it seems that they consider it to be an appropriate and truthful representation of their perception of reality. Accordingly, illustrations that follow isometric, trimetric or even central perspective principles, also have *some* type of perspective, but it can, for each type, be asked *which* one it is and what symbolic meaning it might carry. It is clear now that, on the one hand, Rule and Coons followed a similar line of thought as Panofsky. For them, too, it made a difference which perspective they chose in order to fulfill the maxim of believability, although it was not decisive whether it was executed with mathematical precision. On the other hand, the major intellectual difference between Panofsky and them lies in their belief that there is only *one* single way to credibly and tangibly express "reality." Although Panofsky would therefore disagree with Rule and Coons, his statement here also offers a way of viewing any decision in favor of a particular perspective without judgment. I intend to adopt this mindset for my further discussion. So, if the computer-graphic images that were gradually developing at that time reflect Rule and Coons' sense of the world, it is indeed essential to know *which* type of perspective those early graphics have. However, this realization does not necessarily serve as the basis for a judgment on these images. For now, my intention is merely to recognize that the 3D images are part of a tradition not only in terms of production aesthetics but also stylistically. This can be suitably demonstrated through an art historical investigation. Thus, Panofsky provides the decisive legitimization to expand my study with a style-historical excursus. The question of whether art is produced using computer graphics is ultimately irrelevant to my approach. It is, however, essential to understand the common context of meaning of today's 3D computer images, and to this end, it is relevant to know *which* perspective, or *which* "sense of the world," was adopted in the development of computer graphics software. The aim of the following chapters is therefore to show the extent to which Rule and Coons' approaches and the maxim of believability remain anchored and are perpetuated in the further development of 3D graphics.

5.2 THE COMPUTER AS AN AUGMENTATION OF THE INTELLECT

In order to examine Coons' contributions to advancements in computer technology and specifically to the field of computer graphics in this section, I will once again highlight Sutherland's *Sketchpad*. Coons' impact can be illustrated particularly clearly through Sutherland's research and the innovations that *Sketchpad* brought about in the use of computers. The Sutherland chapter therefore serves as a starting point for the following remarks. An essential insight from the Sutherland chapter for the subsequent considerations lies in the paradox that first appeared in practical terms with Sutherland after he had fundamentally renewed the previously common approach to the programming process. Instead of working procedurally, he introduced an approach that was labeled object-oriented programming a few years later. The unique aspect of this approach was that it no longer required a predefined goal during the work process with the computer. Because it was a drawing program, it was no longer necessary to develop an idea of the finished drawing in advance, as *Sketchpad* made it possible to make changes to a finished drawing afterward. Sutherland's aim was to make the computer available to everyone. He intention was not only to open up the work process and thus make it less specific but also to expand the user group. For this purpose, he therefore designed a program that, thanks to its controls, could in principle be operated by virtually anyone after minimal training. However, these controls presented Sutherland with the problem that he now had to anticipate which features other people might need for their work process. The paradox of this approach is that, although it opens up the work process, it also restricts it at the same time – at least in the way that Sutherland designed it. Although he aimed to impose as few restrictions as possible, it is now clear that, despite a greater openness in the use of the computer, there was actually a focus on a specific way of using it. A prerequisite for this fundamental change was the analysis of work processes in order to be able to later translate them into the program. However, as it is not possible to anticipate an infinite number of work processes, the software developers were faced with the task of selectively deciding which ones to include. As a result of this selection process, specific convictions of these individual personalities entered the software landscape, because by opening up computers to a broader audience, they were virtually forced to define certain program features as relevant and others as irrelevant. The developers therefore set the tone for the way in which computers could be used – their signature is reflected in the software.

Understanding the impact of Sutherland's *Sketchpad* innovations lays the groundwork for appreciating Coons' role in these developments. With an in-depth examination of his computer technology ideas, it becomes evident that Coons had anticipated this paradox before Sutherland put it into practice for the first time with his *Sketchpad* program. In connection with Sutherland, I demonstrated that he was only partially aware of the paradox of his program. Sutherland was convinced of the existence of universal design principles, so that he did not recognize a problem in his selection of design parameters for the program. Coons took a much more nuanced view of the problem. His thoughts provide a much deeper understanding of why certain concepts have survived in software beyond Sutherland and the developments at the *University of Utah* to this day. With this in mind, I will now examine Coons' perspective in detail.

The relationship between Sutherland's *Sketchpad* and Coons' own positions now gives rise to several propositions for this section. In the introduction to this chapter, I referred to a eulogy on the occasion of Coons' death, written by his colleague Bertram Herzog. In it, Herzog claims that Coons not only always recognized the importance of Sutherland's *Sketchpad* program, but that Coons was also able to present the innovations precisely and eloquently. Herzog even emphasizes that Coons knew "the kernel of the notion of computer graphics."[94] As Herzog himself did not explain this "kernel" in his eulogy, I have instead referenced a television report in which Coons presented the *Sketchpad* program. His explanations reveal what this "kernel" could have been for him and why he was able to convey it so eloquently. If Herzog was convinced that Coons was able "to perceive, and perceive very sharply, the significance of this achievement,"[95] then the premise of this chapter is that Coons not only possessed the talent to recognize the significance of Sutherland's contribution but also that Coons was able to describe it so aptly because he had played a decisive role in shaping the changes that Sutherland presented – changes Coons had already conceptualized in advance. The explanations in this chapter are therefore based on the assumption that the essential concepts that have survived to this day within the 3D software landscape are in its "kernel" not attributable to Sutherland, but to Coons and other of his contemporaries. It should be emphasized here that Coons himself did not contribute to comprehensive software solutions, but his concepts actually made the survival of cultural artifacts in the software landscape possible in the first place. At the same time, unlike Sutherland, Coons did not pursue the goal of making the use of computers available to everyone – instead, he focused specifically on creative fields of activity. Nevertheless, it can be assumed here that for Sutherland – despite a somewhat different objective – Coons' concepts were not only fruitful, but that Sutherland also carried them forward with the practical realization of his program. The problem inherent in Coons' thinking thus found practical expression for the first time in Sutherland's work, and – foreshadowing the hypothesis for this book's third part – was further intensified in the continuing developments that took place in Utah.

However, I will first focus on Coons. The significance of his role for the subject of this study is that he integrated both a graphic and a design interest into his computer technology achievements. With these interdisciplinary interests, he shares similar prerequisites with Csuri, who ultimately became even more actively and concretely involved in software development than Coons. Unlike with Csuri, with whom it was possible to demonstrate that his ideas of pictoriality have barely, if at all, survived in today's commercially available software, it now becomes a question of how Coons' graphic ideas, despite not directly being practically realized by him in software development, were ultimately passed on. Even if Coons, unlike Csuri, did not actively attempt to translate his graphic ideas into the language of the computer, I argue that it was mainly a mindset that Coons contributed. It has survived to this day and characterizes both his graphic and computer-technological ideas. With this mindset, Coons offered a way of thinking about the use of the computer that aligned naturally with his ideas on graphics. This approach – particularly in the context of democratizing computer use – proved more enduring than those of Csuri or Fetter. Both Csuri's and Fetter's approaches will be referenced at relevant points throughout the chapter to illustrate this. Coons' mindset also ties in with a discourse that was being conducted by other engineers at the time. For this reason, this section will also selectively draw on the positions of Douglas C. Engelbart, an engineer Coons explicitly referred to. Engelbart's contribution to computer technology, however, took place on a more wide-ranging level and therefore often does not refer directly to the field of computer graphics applications, but rather to the future of interaction between man and machine in general. Engelbart's 1962 publication *Augmenting Human Intellect: A Conceptual Framework*[96] is particularly central here. In it, he presented a concept that he believed could be used to expand and support human intelligence and intellect. He followed the intention "to [improve] the intellectual effectiveness of the individual human being."[97] Under certain conditions he saw the computer as a particularly suitable tool for this purpose. Engelbart's considerations will be taken up in the course of this section in order to illustrate Coons' positions.[98]

However, Coons' own contributions serve as the main basis for this section, primarily his paper *An Outline of the Requirements for a Computer-Aided Design System*,[99] which he presented at the *Spring Joint Computer Conference* held in Detroit, Michigan, in May 1963. In it, he illustrated a research project based at MIT that dealt with the question of how design processes can be supported by computers. His research goal, described in the paper, aimed to investigate how humans and machines can work together effectively in relation to design tasks – similar to Sutherland with *Sketchpad* or Dave Evans a few years later on a more wide-ranging level at the *University of Utah*. In order to explain his research process as a whole in his paper, Coons begins by describing the key elements of the design process as he sees them. He then discusses the requirements that a computer system would need to fulfill in light of these design challenges. His explanations of the design process take up numerous aspects in a very abbreviated manner that are familiar from his graphics handbook. In the outlook at the end of his paper, Coons cites Sutherland's *Sketchpad* and Timothy Johnson's *Sketchpad III*. He considered both programs to be practical solutions for his theoretically elaborated concept, which is why he concludes with reference to Sutherland's and Johnson's respective contributions: "We have already come quite a way toward accomplishing some of the desired ends as outlined."[100] Once again, Coons' outlook shows that he was ahead of Sutherland's and Johnson's efforts with his insights and considerations.

In the introduction to his paper, before he delves even deeper into his reflections, Coons emphasizes one aspect of particular relevance to my research interest, as it reveals the differences in thought to Csuri and Fetter. On the one hand, he was convinced that the design process can be optimized and simplified by the computer, while on the other hand, as a by-product of this research he thought "new computer techniques and an enriched understanding of the creative thought process"[101] would also emerge. His findings on the extent to which the use of a computer provides insights into creative thought processes indicate that he not only anticipated the paradox that arose with Sutherland but also offered considerations on how to deal with it. At the same time, his conception of new computer technologies indicates that he believed the computer to have a certain autonomy. In this respect, Coons differs considerably in his thinking from both Fetter and Csuri, albeit for different reasons. While Fetter only used the computer to automate very complex drawing tasks and did not allow it to work independently in any way, Csuri took up the peculiarities of a computer's algorithmic way of "thinking," but at the same time ensured that as an artist he still maintained sovereignty over how the computer works. Csuri also rejected the idea of handing over processes completely to the computer without knowing how they were created. Coons' idea that the computer should expand the creative work process with new, independent techniques is therefore contrary to the approaches of Fetter and Csuri. The computer no longer remains external to creative work; in Coons' view, it works on the design tasks itself as a creative partner: "The different powers of man and machine are complementary powers, cross-fertilizing powers, mutually reinforcing powers. It is becoming increasingly clear that the combined intellectual potential of man and machine is greater than the sum of its parts."[102] In other words, while neither Fetter nor Csuri was prepared to delegate the intellectual work to the computer, it becomes clear here that Coons was not only convinced that the machine could make an independent and complementary contribution to human intellectual work, but that he also actively pursued this potential. In the television report in which the *Sketchpad* program was presented, Coons also emphasized that with Sutherland's project, the computer would no longer be just a very complex calculating machine, but that it would almost develop into a "human assistant" that also possesses its own intelligence. At the same time, he noted, "it doesn't really, only the intelligence that we put in it. But it will seem to have intelligence."[103] Although he was still cautious with his predictions, Coons not only clearly emphasized his idea of the computer's autonomy with this statement but also addressed the problem that arises from this autonomy: How does the computer learn and apply the new techniques? This is therefore the problem that also underlies Sutherland's *Sketchpad*. While Sutherland believed he had found an approach that, on the one hand, required no programming knowledge and, on the other, was as complex as a programming language, Coons recognized that this discrepancy cannot actually be overcome. However, for my research interest it is particularly relevant that he established a legitimization in his essay that allowed him to resolve the problem. Since Coons cited Sutherland's *Sketchpad* himself, he included the program in his legitimization. So how did Coons arrive at his solution to the problem?

The fundamental prerequisite for Coons to begin with the idea of a computer-aided design is explained historically at the beginning of his paper. The term for this discipline emerged at the end of the 1950s from a collaboration between two departments at MIT: The *Computer Applications Group* and the *Design Division* of the *Mechanical Engineering Department*. At an initial meeting of individual representatives of the two groups, they aimed to develop a system in which the strengths or essential characteristics of both fields would come together: "[T]he creative and imaginative powers of the man and the analytical and computational powers of the machine [...]."[104] The attribution of the different qualities that man and machine bring to the joint work on design tasks indicates that both Coons and his colleagues had a clear idea of which tasks were "human" and which were rather "technical" or mechanical:

> We envisioned even then the designer seated at a console, drawing a sketch of his proposed device on the screen of an oscilloscope tube with a "light pen," modifying his sketch at will, and commanding the computer slave to refine the sketch into a perfect drawing, to perform various numerical analyses having to do with structural strength, clearances of adjacent parts, and other analyses as well.[105]

First of all, Coons' description very obviously indicates that Sutherland realized, at least in part, a vision that had already been shaped in this form four years earlier. In particular, the aspect of editing a result, one of the main features of Sutherland's new programming paradigm, is expressed here, although at that time only the procedural paradigm was available. Coons' paper also indicates that he was aware of the extent to which this shift in working with computers was changing the way we design and work. Coons even reflects that his idea of letting the computer work independently requires the definition of individual operations:

> A computer system, to work in partnership with a designer, must have several clearly definable capabilities. It must be able to accept, interpret, and remember shape descriptive information introduced graphically. When such a graphical input capability is properly designed, the man-computer combination can manipulate the elements of a drawing in an entirely new way, with a freedom and precision far surpassing what is possible with pencil and paper.[106]

In addition to the enthusiasm that Coons shows for the collaboration between designer and computer, his phrasing expresses that he considered the input of graphic commands to be suitable for all design processes – this is therefore a function that Coons would define equally for every design discipline. His confidence in the computer also confirms once again that by defining certain tasks in the computer, he not only wanted to automate design processes but also wanted to change and redesign creative processes. However, a contradiction emerges in his wording, as he himself initially emphasized in his paper that the computer should only be assigned tasks that are supposedly less dependent on human decisions. To this end, he undertook a comprehensive analysis of the design processes he was familiar with in the field of engineering in order to differentiate between creative and less creative tasks. The decisive insight for my study lies in this analysis, because with his differentiation he legitimized delegating tasks to the computer. Coons' decision to make computer-aided processes dependent on a prior analysis of the design process is reminiscent of Csuri, as he also wanted to recreate artistic processes with his algorithms. With Coons, however, a clear reciprocal cycle emerges, even more so than with Csuri. In this cycle human working methods were first analyzed and examined in order to then recreate them algorithmically, ultimately resulting in independent, new processes that only resemble the original human actions. Csuri would presumably have avoided this final step in the cycle. With Coons, the original human processes are dialectically sublated (German: aufgehoben) in the Hegelian sense, as they are transferred to the computer, on the one hand, but also renewed, on the other.

In order to better understand the reciprocity underlying Coons' concept, the engineer Engelbart mentioned at the beginning of the section will now be drawn upon for a brief but informative excursus for this study. His ideas demonstrate that the development of the computer was also conceived reciprocally on a larger scale and by other contemporaries of Coons. The way in which we generally work on computers today (extending beyond the use of graphical applications) can be derived from these very early concepts. I will then examine the results of Coons' analysis, in which he explained which tasks he defined as creative and which he did not.

Coons referred to Engelbart in a very specific context, which initially involved the consideration of organizing work functions on the computer graphically. This step was according to Coons suitable for visually emphasizing the parallelism and interconnectedness of different commands, as verbal commands would tend to follow a "one-dimensional" logic, which would mean that cross-connections between functions may not be clearly emphasized.[107] As Coons did not refer to any specific text passage in his citation of Engelbart, it is assumed here that he was also generally familiar with Engelbart's ideas and incorporated aspects of his thinking. In addition, Coons' fundamental idea of using computers to make people's work more efficient indicates a proximity to Engelbart, because – as explained in the introduction to this section – Engelbart also assumed that the computer is suitable for augmenting people's intellect. For his proposition, he presented his ideas on how this augmentation could succeed in a comprehensive concept. To do this, he first defined in a very basic manner what he understood by the augmentation of the intellect:

> By "augmenting human intellect" we mean increasing the capability of a man to approach a complex problem situation, to gain comprehension to suit his particular needs, and to derive solutions to problems. Increased capability in this respect is taken to mean a mixture of the following: more-rapid comprehension, better comprehension, the possibility of gaining a useful degree of comprehension in a situation that previously was too complex, speedier solutions, better solutions, and the possibility of finding solutions to problems that before seemed insoluble.[108]

As Engelbart subsequently explains, his considerations apply to many different fields of activity, such as diplomacy, physics, law and design. He also focused on the idea that he was looking for a technical solution that would merge with the way people work and think, so that intuitive behavior, feelings or even alleged wrong turns would remain part of thought processes.[109] This suggests an intellectual parallel to Coons, who also spoke of intuitive and vague thought processes, which for him had to be captured and concretized – for example with the help of graphics as one of the "instruments of thought."

In order to design suitable technical means that would intervene in this way to support human intellectual labor, Engelbart started by refining the means that we already use, i.e. "all of which appear to be but extensions of means developed and used in the past to help man apply his native sensory, mental, and motor capabilities [...]."[110]

He was convinced that "[i]ndividuals who operate effectively in our culture have already been considerably 'augmented.'"[111] For the development of new procedures, Engelbart therefore proposed as a first step, on the one hand, to find out in which situations the effectiveness of individuals is limited[112] and, on the other hand, to precisely analyze which previous procedures individuals used to achieve their "present level of effectiveness."[113] He defined these means in the broadest sense as symbolic forms of communication, be they languages, pictograms, logic or mathematics. By conceptually building on such concepts, he assumed that people who already communicate or approach tasks in these ways would benefit significantly from his augmentations.[114] As a starting point for his analysis, he therefore developed four categories in line with his assumption, according to which he classified the "augmentation means" used by people up to that point:

> (1) Artifacts--physical objects designed to provide for human comfort, for the manipulation of things or materials, and for the manipulation of symbols.
> (2) Language--the way in which the individual parcels out the picture of his world into the concepts that his mind uses to model that world, and the symbols that he attaches to those concepts and uses in consciously manipulating the concepts ("thinking").
> (3) Methodology--the methods, procedures, strategies, etc. with which an individual organizes his goal-centred (problem-solving) activity.
> (4) Training--the conditioning needed by the human being to bring his skills in using Means 1, 2, and 3 to the point where they are operationally effective.[115]

Against the backdrop of these four "augmentation means," Engelbart attempted to understand in minute steps how people learn and how they make decisions. When analyzing his concept, it becomes clear that he considered a certain body of knowledge to be valuable or at least particularly efficient, while he dismissed other forms of knowledge as non-progressive. This judgment becomes clear, for example, when he used in a comparative manner the life and knowledge strategies of Indigenous peoples such as the Aborigines to illustrate his ideas. For example, he described how an Aborigine, who has the same sensorimotor prerequisites as someone from "our" culture, nevertheless did according to him not have the "indirect knowledge"[116] to anticipate the respective action steps that would be required, for example, to cope with a traffic situation in a car, borrow a book, make a phone call or type a letter on a typewriter.[117] His justification for this assumption provides an initial insight into one of the results of his analysis:

> While an untrained aborigine cannot drive a car through traffic, because he cannot leap the gap between his cultural background and the kind of world that contains cars and traffic, it is possible to move step by step through an organized training program that will enable him to drive effectively and safely. In other words, the human mind neither learns nor acts by large leaps, but by steps organized or structured so that each one depends upon previous steps.[118]

Engelbart therefore assumed that the human brain learns processes step by step and is not in a position to overcome omitted developmental steps in one big leap. Interestingly, his choice of words is strongly reminiscent of Hans Blumenberg's wording that humans want to progress by leaps with the technization of the world (see Section 1.1). However, while Blumenberg concluded that we need to clarify the history of a mechanized object in order to counteract excessive leaps, Engelbart evidently assumed that even in the case of mechanized processes, too great a leap can no longer be overcome. He would therefore not have shared Blumenberg's concern that technologies might spread in cultures which have not experienced the individual steps in the development of technology, unless they have dealt with them retrospectively. For Engelbart, the "augmentation means" were also suitable for presenting and depicting the individual steps in the human work process in an orderly manner,[119] but based on his statements about the Aborigines, it can be inferred that this hypothesis did not account for the behavior of Indigenous peoples. This can be illustrated by his use of phrases such as "representative human" and also "characteristically 'human' activities,"[120] which he links to tasks such as producing texts, drawings, diagrams or lists, as well as activities like driving a car. By defining these activities as representative, he effectively judges which tasks are considered characteristically human, excluding others in a way that assumes these are universal values. This notion, which implies that only those who perform such tasks are "normal" humans, is highly problematic. He overlooked the possibility that the four classes of "augmentation means" defined by him may also have developed in Aboriginal culture – albeit with different results.

If we now focus on Engelbart's proposed overall concept in front of the backdrop of his fundamental attitude about humans, a paradox also becomes evident. This is a similar contradiction to the one identified by Coons, because Engelbart on the one hand assumed humans approach tasks step by step, but on the other hand he expressed a vision in which humans no longer have to carry out all the steps themselves and instead are supported by the machine. Both Coons and Engelbart somewhat recognized and valued every human step of action, yet at the same time, they speculated that many of these steps can be replaced by the computer. Engelbart and Coons thus actively contributed to the problem that Blumenberg described, because they both had nothing other in mind than to support people in making leaps forward – even if only people from a certain cultural background, if one follows Engelbart's explanations. However, this contradiction is, if nothing else, the reason for the reciprocity with which processes were first modeled and then redesigned on the computer. With Engelbart it can be illustrated that this dynamic did not occur inadvertently, but that – on the contrary – it was an explicit goal to bring about changes in people's behavior with technology-supported optimization:

> A concept structure often grows as part of a cultural evolution – either on a large scale within a large segment of society, or on a small scale within the activity domain of an individual. But it is also something that can be directly designed or modified, and a basic hypothesis of our study is that better concept structures can be developed – structures that when mapped into a human's mental structure will significantly improve his capability to comprehend and to find solutions within his complex-problem situations.[121]

With this statement, Engelbart reveals that certain ways of thinking were deliberately incorporated into technology-supported processes in order to predetermine and steer behavior. With his phrasing he thus legitimizes my general aim to find out which cultural artifacts shape production processes on the computer – especially as it is now clear that these artifacts do not survive by chance but were used deliberately to shape the computer and software landscape.

With regard to the development of computer graphics software, Coons now moves back into the center of attention. Looking at Coons' approach, one gets the impression that he directly followed Engelbart's advice in his own analysis of previous design processes:

> To redesign a structure, we must learn as much as we can of what is known about the basic materials and components as they are utilized within the structure; beyond that, we must learn how to view, to measure, to analyze, and to evaluate in terms of the functional whole and its purpose. In this particular case, no existing analytic theory is by itself adequate for the purpose of analyzing and evaluating over-all system performance; pursuit of an improved system thus demands the use of <u>experimental</u> methods.[122]

Engelbart uses the term "structure" here to describe the step-by-step manner of a human action. The question that remains for this section is which experimental path Coons took for his analyses. Both Engelbart's and Coons' analyses are reminiscent of the production-aesthetical investigative approach of my own study: In order to make progress by leaps and to identify the points at which the computer could come to use, individual action steps and decisions first had to be closely traced. Engelbart's concept thus legitimizes not only the concern of this study but also its method, because in order to be able to retrospectively overcome the leap and retrace the entire production process, it makes sense – as Engelbart suggests – to analyze the individual steps and decisions that were taken into account in the development of the technology. This approach serves as the foundation for understanding how Coons described the design process in his paper and what he derived from it for a computer-aided design process.

As we know from the previous section, for Coons the design process began with a vague idea that is gradually developed into a concept with the help of initial sketches. In this context, Coons mentioned the idea that Perry emphasized several times in her study because, in her eyes, it characterizes Coons' thinking in a particular way: "The sketch forms the natural bridge between these vague stirrings of the imagination and the subsequent precise statement of the refined details of the concept."[123] Coons describes how qualitative decisions are initially made in the design process as to whether to keep a design or change the overall concept or specific details. In feedback loops, a first draft would gradually evolve toward a final idea. Once this refinement occurs, more precise processing steps of the design could then further be developed for the production of components. In aircraft construction this final step of the process would contain analyses of the physical behavior of the component, including tasks such as aerodynamic or stress calculations. Coons defined the first steps in this process, which he describes as "qualitative," as highly creative. While only a few engineers would be involved in this early phase, a large number of technical draftsmen would also work very early on to visualize the ideas graphically. As this area of responsibility also includes mathematical and physical analyses, Coons concluded that they are "not in themselves of a creative nature,"[124] unless new mathematical models would be developed specifically for this purpose. Furthermore, other tasks in the design process can, according to him, be characterized as purely mechanical:

> [F]or example, a detail draftsman does nothing creative whatever. At the worst, he merely traces the outline of a part from the layout drawing, and adds the dimensions. Usually this drawing goes directly to some machinist or patternmaker in the shop, but sometimes it is used by a part programmer and converted by him into symbolic information for use by a computer to prepare punched tape for automatic fabricating machinery. These are all essentially mechanical operations, however, and it is quite clear that at least in principle, the computer can be made to deal with them all.[125]

Based on his distinction between the creative and non-creative tasks in the design process, Coons arrived at a proposal as to how the computer could be integrated in the individual steps. For him, it was particularly the non-creative tasks that legitimized allowing the computer to work independently, as Coons assumed that they would apply equally to everyone who works with the computer. Coons further differentiated here into task areas that were to him very fundamental and that would equally be necessary for all design tasks. He rejected a comprehensive computer program that would handle every design task with its respective specifications. He was not convinced that a sufficient number of different functions could be stored in the computer to fulfill all possible work situations in the design process, because

> [i]f the assembly of such a library of special routines could be made complete enough, then the system would exhibit to the user on the outside an appearance of complete flexibility and generality. This would be satisfactory so long as the designer never called for a capability not already rigidly imbedded in the mechanism. But the process is unpredictable. Indeed part of the design process consists in designing new ways to perform the design function itself. This is a higher order of design activity, a sort of meta-design [...] that clearly is outside the scope of any rigid set of special processes that can be anticipated at the beginning.[126]

Against the background of his work as a draftsman, it becomes particularly clear here that Coons was convinced of the partnership between humans and computers with regard to design issues, but that he also saw clear limits in this collaboration. To address this problem of not being able to anticipate all design steps, he therefore suggested that instead of developing a large number of individual specific programming routines, only a few should be designed, "perhaps indeed only one,"[127] which would be conceptualized to be so general that a designer could quickly and easily expand and adapt them for their own purposes:

> Finally, the system will be so general that it will be applicable to any creative activity. For example, the *general* problems of the architect, the machine designer, and the electronic

> designer are the same, but the *specific* details of their problems bear scant resemblances one to another. Yet an appropriately designed system will be so flexible that it will enable each discipline to modify the structure to fit its purpose.[128]

The graphical input option mentioned at the beginning, which Coons and his colleagues had expressed as a vision, was for Coons, for example, one of the basic functions that would be equally useful for every design discipline. He also listed other features that he would have liked to see as part of the design process, which only the computer could help with – for example, saving results in order to continue working on them at a later date, or displaying the movement of objects instead of showing them schematically and statically, as was customary for design drawings up to that time.[129] His way of reasoning is reminiscent of the approach in the graphics manual. As shown in the previous section, the priority for him and his colleague Rule in their textbook was not to present the discipline of design drawing in detail for all specialist areas, such as the automotive or aircraft industry. Instead, they concentrated on the areas that apply equally to all fields. Against the background of his conviction that there are fundamental commonalities regardless of the respective discipline, it becomes clear why he also came to the conclusion that in the development of potential computer applications there would be a common and universal starting point for all design disciplines. In contrast to the handbook, which no one is obligated to consult, Coons' idea of a common starting point in design processes becomes much more significant in the context of computer applications. While it is possible to pick up a book, question it and put it back down, this is not possible with a computer – at least not for a layperson. They are limited by and dependent on the functions available on the computer. Coons himself conceptualized the effects that this dynamic can develop:

> There is considerable evidence that our intellectual tools influence to a very great extent the form and scope of our intellectual works. It is quite certain that when the computer replaces pencil and paper in this very real way, it will bring about a truly miraculous chance in man's intellectual potential.[130]

What is significant about Coons' insight is that he viewed the influence on people's intellect caused by a given way of working on the computer as an opportunity, rather than a problem. In comparison to Sutherland, it is now clear that Coons' concept dealt much more fundamentally and self-reflexively with the implications of including the computer in creative work processes *in a certain way*. Although Coons did not problematize the dynamics, he did at least still engage in a process of reflection. Sutherland, on the other hand, did not. Rather, it seems as if he took the legitimization that Coons derived from his own concept for granted and then continued to work with it quite naturally. With *Sketchpad*, Sutherland thus offered a straightforward solution to Coons' ideas. Similar to what Coons himself suggested, Sutherland asserted that he had developed a basic program that could be extended for any task. Thanks to Coons' intellectual groundwork and at least also self-reflexive engagement with the problem of influencing creative processes, Sutherland could pursue his actual goal of making the computer available to everyone. He no longer had to deal with the limits of the computer or the influence it has on intellectual work – as long as he adhered to Coons' ideas of designing the program in a sufficiently general way. The problem with this development is that Sutherland has introduced a different nuance into his program development that no longer aligned with Coons' process of reflection. Unlike Coons, Sutherland started from even more uniform design principles. If Engelbart is consulted again here, it becomes clear that there is even a strong contradiction between Coons and Sutherland at this level. Engelbart phrased a similar view to Coons:

> There are, of course, the explicit computer processes which we use, and which our philosophy requires the augmented man to be able to design and build for himself. A number of people, outside our research group here, maintain stoutly that a practical augmentation system should not require the human to have to do any computer programming--they feel that this is too specialized a capability to burden people with.[131]

Sutherland, who completed his work on *Sketchpad* shortly after Engelbart's report, explicitly expressed the aspiration to develop a program that would maintain complexity without requiring programming skills (see Section 3.1). It can therefore be argued that although Sutherland tried to live up to Engelbart's and Coons' ambitions, i.e. to maintain a high degree of diversity and complexity, Coons' reasoning clearly shows that this goal could ultimately not be achieved through Sutherland's approach in designing his program.

As a result, it can now be stated that a level of reflection has been lost in the developmental steps from Coons to Sutherland. I therefore hypothesize for the next chapters in this study that this loss is largely responsible for the fact that computer graphics have developed further with a specific understanding of images. In the continuing research on human–machine interaction, it was no longer considered necessary to gauge whether creative decisions are excluded by the translation into the computer. The part that Coons still described as individual and not definable is entirely gone and with it the part in which Coons still attributes creative decision-making power to the human being. In the further development of the software, the machine is therefore fundamentally designed to work independently – the goal of contributing as a human being with one's own free concepts is reduced to a minimum.

Coons did not intend this development in this form, but he did conceptualize an intellectual framework in which the further development, as it ultimately occurred, was laid out. Finally, the question remains as to how his graphic ideas found their way into the software without his direct developmental contributions. Instead, he supplied two building blocks: One relating to the graphics and one relating to the computer. The way in which these building blocks came together will be analyzed in the following part of this study. However, it can be summarized that in a very fundamental aspect, his graphic ideas and his computer-technological considerations arose from a common mindset, which is why it is almost inevitable that both building blocks would later come together. It becomes clear both in the examination of his graphic principles and his reflections on computer technology that he granted the human mind a central position in both fields. If graphics – alongside language and mathematics – represented an instrument of thought for him, with which an "augmented advantage over nature" could be achieved, then it now becomes clear why he also saw the computer as an instrument with which the intellectual thought process could be optimized. All in all, the narrative continued in the ongoing historical developments focusing on using the computer to make the world accessible by thinking graphically. The fourth and fifth parts of this study will explore the cultural roots of this way of thinking. Before this cultural-historical background is explored, further computer graphical developments at the *University of Utah* will be presented in order to determine to what extent the previous concepts and principles have been continued.

NOTES

1. Steven A. Coons, "The Uses of Computers in Technology," *Scientific American* 215, no. 3 (1966): 177.
2. See Rebecca A. Perry, "Rigging the World: 3D Modeling and the Seduction of the Real" (PhD diss., Massachusetts Institute of Technology, 2014), MIT Libraries, DSpace@MIT (900615015), 5.
3. Perry, "Rigging the World," 10.
4. Cardoso Llach's acknowledgments show that he exchanged views with Perry. See Daniel Cardoso Llach, *Builders of the Vision: Software and the Imagination of Design* (New York: Routledge, 2015), xxi.
5. Bertram Herzog, "Eulogy Delivered at the Memorial Service of Steven A. Coons (22.08.1979)," *Syracuse University Clipping Files, Steven A. Coons-Folder*, 1979. Syracuse University Libraries, Special Collections Research Center, 1.
6. See The Tech, ed., "28 Faculty Members Receive Promotions," *The Tech* 81, no. 6 (1961): 1.
7. Herzog does not give any dates for this period. Coons was born in 1912, which is why it can be assumed that he began his studies at MIT at the end of the 1920s and either dropped out before the change to the new decade or shortly afterwards.
8. Herzog, "Eulogy," 1.
9. Rule himself had graduated from MIT in 1921 with a degree in "science." In 1936, he was hired at MIT as an assistant professor for technical drawing. Two years later, in 1938, he was promoted to associate professor, also for the fields of technical drawing and descriptive geometry. He received a full professorship in 1947. Rule's research interests centered on the development of three-dimensional representations, in particular the creation of stereoscopic drawings, photographs and films. During the Second World War, he applied

his research findings on stereoscopic processes to the field of combat simulation. See The Tech, ed., "Killian Names Rule to Head Course IX. Will Still Administer Graphics Department," *The Tech* 70, no. 15 (1950): 1, 4.

10. Herzog, "Eulogy," 1.
11. Perry, "Rigging the World," 11.
12. Her following statement confirms this impression: "The evolution of representational forms from diagrams and plans into visual displays of three-dimensional objects was prompted by the search for improved manufacturing methods. But it soon became evident that interactions that evoked the objects themselves, using compelling visualizations, were engaging on multiple levels, and involved many different modes of thought." Perry, "Rigging the World," 67. Perry gives the impression here that the search for improved production processes automatically evoked the development of "compelling visualizations." She evidently regards the visual aesthetic that has gradually developed as having no alternative. In a further thought, Perry differentiates between two fields that have contributed to the development of computer graphics processes. On the one hand, there are those who have specifically searched for graphic display methods on the computer, and on the other hand, there are those for whom images were only created as an accessory, as they were actually looking for methods that would make the computer easier to use. Nevertheless, she does not raise the question of why a certain idea of imagery has developed in this field. See Perry, "Rigging the World," 67.
13. Perry, "Rigging the World," 58.
14. See Perry, "Rigging the World," 56.
15. Perry merely refers to this fact in a footnote. See Perry, "Rigging the World," 57.
16. Steven A. Coons, "An Outline of the Requirements for a Computer-Aided Design System," In *Proceedings of the Spring Joint Computer Conference – AFIPS '63*, ed. E. Calvin Johnson (New York: ACM Press, 1963), 300.
17. See Perry, "Rigging the World," 10–11 and 57.
18. John T. Rule and Steven A. Coons, *Graphics* (New York: McGraw-Hill, 1961), 66.
19. In their handbook, Coons and Rule also categorize written symbols – such as words or mathematical symbols – as graphic forms of expression. In their eyes, they represent an abstract form of graphic expression. See Rule and Coons, *Graphics*, 66.
20. Perry, "Rigging the World," 57.
21. See Perry, "Rigging the World," 57. Coons developed the concept as part of a research project entitled *Surfaces for Computer-Aided Design*. See Steven A. Coons, *Surfaces for Computer-Aided Design of Space Forms* (Cambridge: Massachusetts Institute of Technology, 1967). His study is often referred to as the *Little Red Book*. See Perry, "Rigging the World," 257; see Jacob Gaboury, *Image Objects. An Archaeology of Computer Graphics* (Cambridge: MIT Press, 2021), 94.
22. See "Steven Anson Coons Award," ACM SIGGRAPH, accessed December 12, 2021, https://www.siggraph.org/about/awards/steven-anson-coons-award/.
23. See "Steven Anson Coons Award."
24. Edwin Catmull, "A Subdivision Algorithm for Computer Display of Curved Surfaces" (PhD diss., University of Utah, 1974), J. Willard Marriott Library (712681), [i].
25. Robert Rivlin also comments on the influence of Coons' mathematical model on Catmull's research in his historical accounts on the developments of 3D computer graphics. See Robert Rivlin, *The Algorithmic Image: Graphic Visions of the Computer Age* (Redmond: Microsoft Press, 1986), 55. See also Catmull, "A Subdivision Algorithm," [i].
26. Perry, "Rigging the World," 66. Perry quotes here from Ivan E. Sutherland, "Sketchpad: A Man-Machine Graphical Communication System" (technical report, ed. Alan Blackwell and Kerry Rodden, University of Cambridge, 2003), Computer Laboratory (UCAM-CL-TR-574), 30.
27. Herzog, "Eulogy," 3. The letter from which Herzog quotes was written by Sutherland together with his colleague Robert F. Sproull. A historical review on the website of *Harvard University*'s AR/VR Studio (AR stands for augmented reality, VR for virtual reality) also reports on the time Sutherland spent at Harvard. See "AR/VR Studio. Harvard's Role in the History of AR/VR," Harvard Innovation Labs, accessed May 13, 2021, https://innovationlabs.harvard.edu/arvr-studio/.
28. Herzog, "Eulogy," 2.
29. Herzog, "Eulogy," 2.
30. See Fitch, *MIT Science Reporter*, "Computer Sketchpad," directed by Russell Morash (Boston: National Educational Television, 1964).
31. See Timothy E. Johnson, "Sketchpad III: Three Dimensional Graphical Communication with a Digital Computer" (Master's thesis, Massachusetts Institute of Technology, 1963), MIT Libraries, DSpace@MIT (33828890).
32. See Fitch, "Computer Sketchpad."
33. Fitch, "Computer Sketchpad."
34. Fitch, "Computer Sketchpad."
35. See for example Douglas C. Engelbart, *Augmenting Human Intellect. A Conceptual Framework* (Menlo Park: Stanford Research Institute, 1962).
36. See Rule and Coons, *Graphics*, v.
37. Rule and Coons, *Graphics*, vi. To always be ready to capture an idea in the way described in the quote and make it tangible, the authors recommend always carrying a pen with you – be it a pencil, a ballpen or even a fountain pen. According to Rule and Coons, it is also important to learn to draw without an eraser. Further instructions such as these follow, including help on how to sharpen the pencil correctly. See Rule and Coons, *Graphics*, 67.
38. Rule and Coons, *Graphics*, vi.
39. Rule and Coons, *Graphics*, v.

40. Rule and Coons, *Graphics*, v.
41. See Rule and Coons, *Graphics*, v–vi.
42. Rule and Coons, *Graphics*, vii.
43. Rule and Coons, *Graphics*, v.
44. For example, the following description demonstrates that the authors not only lay down certain rules, but that they also meticulously explain why the guidelines they are concerned with exist: "The assembly drawing (and copies of the original layout drawing, too, if necessary) are next turned over to detailers, who make separate drawings of each of the constituent parts, excluding, of course, the standard items that may be purchased. These detail drawings are for the use of machinists (and in the case of castings, for the use of patternmakers), and they must contain accurate dimensional information. Machinists and patternmakers are accustomed by years of experience to having this information presented to them in a certain formal and conventionalized way. Since these conventions are rather complicated, we shall devote a chapter to them later on." Rule and Coons, *Graphics*, 4.
45. Rule and Coons, *Graphics*, 8, emphasis in original.
46. See Erwin Panofsky, *Perspective as Symbolic Form*, trans. Christopher S. Wood (New York: Zone Books, 1991).
47. Rule and Coons, *Graphics*, 3.
48. See Rule and Coons, *Graphics*, 66–91 and 231–46.
49. Rule and Coons, *Graphics*, 231, emphasis in original.
50. See e.g. Rule and Coons, *Graphics*, 39.
51. Rule and Coons, *Graphics*, 78.
52. Rule and Coons, *Graphics*, 67.
53. See Rule and Coons, *Graphics*, 66 and 67.
54. Rule and Coons also occasionally differentiate between sub-genres of diagrams when they use terms such as *alignment diagram* or *nomogram*. This pair of terms refers to the same type of diagram, for which, however, two common terms are available. See Rule and Coons, *Graphics*, e.g. 314.
55. See Rule and Coons, *Graphics*, e.g. 223 and 292.
56. Rule and Coons, *Graphics*, 78.
57. Rule and Coons, *Graphics*, 78, emphasis in original.
58. Rule and Coons, *Graphics*, 79.
59. Rule and Coons, *Graphics*, 78.
60. Rule and Coons, *Graphics*, 78, emphasis in original. In a cube drawn in this way, one side of the cube would be shown frontally, while the back of the cube would be shown with the same dimensions but placed slightly to the side and upward, for example. The respective corner points of the front and back are connected with lines running parallel to each other. As the front and back of the cube have the same dimensions, the vanishing lines do not taper, which is why, strictly speaking, they are not vanishing lines. (See also Figure 4.21 in this study.)
61. Rule and Coons, *Graphics*, 78.
62. See Rule and Coons, *Graphics*, 78–79 and 240.
63. Rule and Coons, *Graphics*, 231.
64. Rule and Coons, *Graphics*, 67.
65. Rule and Coons, *Graphics*, 68.
66. Rule and Coons, *Graphics*, 68.
67. Panofsky, *Perspective*, 28–30.
68. Ernst Cassirer, *The Philosophy of Symbolic Forms. Part Two: Mythical Thought*, trans. Ralph Manheim (New Haven: Yale University Press, 1955), 84.
69. Cassirer, *The Philosophy of Symbolic Forms*, 84.
70. Cassirer, *The Philosophy of Symbolic Forms*, 84.
71. Panofsky, *Perspective*, 31.
72. Panofsky, *Perspective*, 32.
73. Panofsky, *Perspective*, 32.
74. Rule and Coons, *Graphics*, 231.
75. Rule and Coons, *Graphics*, 79. They point out in several places in their manual that the gaze must not move in order to successfully draw a central perspective image – as in the following instructions: "If we stand on the ground and place our glass window in front of us, our view to the distant horizon at ground level is substantially horizontal, and holding our eye still, we can trace this horizon on the glass or picture plane at eye level. We can also trace the scene on the glass, and the retinal image produced by the drawing will, geometrically, exactly coincide with the image produced by the scene itself [...]." Rule and Coons, *Graphics*, 85.
76. Rule and Coons, *Graphics*, 240.
77. Rule and Coons, *Graphics*, 69.
78. Rule and Coons, *Graphics*, 80.
79. Rule and Coons, *Graphics*, 88.
80. See Rule and Coons, *Graphics*, 88.
81. Panofsky, *Perspective*, 34.
82. William A. Fetter, *Computer Graphics in Communication. Written for the Course Content Development Study in Engineering Graphics, supported by the National Science Foundation* (New York: McGraw-Hill, 1965), e.g. 50.
83. See Rule and Coons, *Graphics*, 247–58.
84. They already discuss the two methods in the introduction to their manual and also emphasize the difference in approach here: "We shall refer to them as *Euclidean* and *graphical* constructions. The draftsman performs Euclidean constructions under the rigorous restrictions of plane geometry, using as tools only the compass and unmarked straight edge, and using as principles only the axioms of construction of Euclidean plane geometry. In performing graphical constructions, on the other hand, the draftsman employs many other axioms of construction and uses many other tools. For example, in the preceding chapter on instruments we saw that by using a pair of triangles we could construct parallels and perpendiculars to given lines very easily and quickly. This is a typical graphical construction, very different from and much more accurate than

the corresponding Euclidean construction. [...] The Euclidean method, although theoretically perfect, has too many steps and therefore too many chances for error; the graphical method, on the other hand, is self-checking, and we can see at a glance the precision of the result." Rule and Coons, *Graphics*, 23–24, emphasis in original.

85. Rule and Coons, *Graphics*, 247.
86. Rule and Coons, *Graphics*, 247.
87. Rule and Coons, *Graphics*, e.g. 248.
88. Rule and Coons, *Graphics*, e.g. 248.
89. To illustrate this, they list examples of which tools would be suitable for the graphical method: "In graphics, there is no restriction on tools. We may use marked straight edges, transparent overlays, triangles, T squares, and any other device that serves a useful purpose. There is no restriction on permissible constructions, as long as these constructions produce results of acceptable accuracy. We may draw curves through points, slide or roll curve on curve, draw tangents to curves by eye, use methods of successive approximation, and even compare small areas by eye, so long as we are aware of the ultimate accuracy of the operation." Rule and Coons, *Graphics*, 248.
90. Rule and Coons, *Graphics*, 248.
91. Rule and Coons, *Graphics*, 248.
92. Rule and Coons, *Graphics*, 251.
93. Panofsky, *Perspective*, 40–41. In the German original Panofsky quotes Ernst Cassirer, *Wesen und Wirkung des Symbolbegriffs*, 8th ed. (Darmstadt: Wissenschaftliche Buchgesellschaft, 1994), 175.
94. Herzog, "Eulogy," 2.
95. Herzog, "Eulogy," 2.
96. See Engelbart, *Augmenting Human Intellect*.
97. Engelbart, *Augmenting Human Intellect*, ii. Engelbart was of the opinion that "man's problem-solving capability possibly represents the most important resource possessed by a society," which is why he believed it makes sense to expand the human intellect. Engelbart, *Augmenting Human Intellect*, 131.
98. Engelbart is also regarded as the inventor of the computer mouse, although the *Computer History Museum* points out on its website that Telefunken also introduced a mouse at around the same time. See "The Mouse," Computer History Museum, accessed December 12, 2021, https://www.computerhistory.org/revolution/input-output/14/350.
99. See Coons, "Requirements for a Computer-Aided Design System."
100. Coons, "Requirements for a Computer-Aided Design System," 302.
101. Coons, "Requirements for a Computer-Aided Design System," 300.
102. Coons, "Requirements for a Computer-Aided Design System," 300.
103. Fitch, "Computer Sketchpad."
104. Coons, "Requirements for a Computer-Aided Design System," 300.
105. Coons, "Requirements for a Computer-Aided Design System," 300. The term "slave," which Coons uses here, has survived in computer technology to this day. Due to the associated connotations, particularly in relation to the term "master," which is also frequently used, efforts are currently being made to establish new terms for the relationships between hierarchical structures within computer technology. See Elizabeth Landau, "Tech Confronts Its Use of the Labels 'Master' and 'Slave,'" Wired, 2020, accessed June 14, 2021, https://www.wired.com/story/tech-confronts-use-labels-master-slave/. For Cardoso Llach, the word is a key concept. For him, it expresses one of two positions that he believes emerged in the 1960s in relation to the use of computers. That is, the machine was seen by some as a facilitator for automatable and tedious work steps, while others saw it as an equal creative partner. Cardoso Llach recognizes, like I do, traits of both approaches in Coons. See Cardoso Llach, *Builders of the Vision*, e.g. 54.
106. Coons, "Requirements for a Computer-Aided Design System," 301.
107. The description given here attempts to reproduce Coons' very specialized explanations in a more generally understandable way. In the original, he phrases his idea as follows: "Beyond shape description, such a graphical facility should be an extension of language in general. It should be possible, as has been indicated earlier, to use such a graphical mode to structure abstractions. This has been brought out with great force and clarity by Engelbart, where he remarks in effect that the essentially one-dimensional nature of symbolic language is not wholly adequate to exhibit the interconnections of ideas." Coons, "Requirements for a Computer-Aided Design System," 301.
108. Engelbart, *Augmenting Human Intellect*, 1. In his report, Engelbart presented, for example, a "writing machine" which, from the description, is reminiscent of today's word processing programs. Both functions such as "copy" and the possibility of loading and further processing old drafts were conceptualized here by Engelbart as a vision. See Engelbart, *Augmenting Human Intellect*, 13–14.
109. See Engelbart, *Augmenting Human Intellect*, 1.
110. Engelbart, *Augmenting Human Intellect*, 2.
111. Engelbart, *Augmenting Human Intellect*, 15.
112. See Engelbart, *Augmenting Human Intellect*, 6.
113. Engelbart, *Augmenting Human Intellect*, 8. Engelbart's way of thinking also gives an idea of the background against which large tech companies today carry out usage analyses and document user behavior in order to further refine their products based on the data generated.

114. See Engelbart, *Augmenting Human Intellect*, 6.
115. Engelbart, *Augmenting Human Intellect*, 9, emphasis in original.
116. Engelbart, *Augmenting Human Intellect*, 8.
117. See Engelbart, *Augmenting Human Intellect*, 8. Another example he listed also refers to the ability to convene a committee meeting to discuss preliminary planning.
118. Engelbart, *Augmenting Human Intellect*, 9–10.
119. See Engelbart, *Augmenting Human Intellect*, 10.
120. Engelbart, *Augmenting Human Intellect*, 16.
121. Engelbart, *Augmenting Human Intellect*, 34–35. Engelbart assumed that people follow a certain pattern of individual action steps in a hierarchical manner, some of which could be optimized: "Increasing the effectiveness of the individual's use of his basic capabilities is a problem in redesigning the changeable parts of a system. [...] To redesign the system's capability for performing these processes means redesigning all or part of the repertoire hierarchy." Engelbart, *Augmenting Human Intellect*, 16. The "concept structure" mentioned in the quote is one of five so-called structures that, according to Engelbart, humans develop in order to acquire complex abilities: "Tentatively we have isolated five such types–although we are not sure how many we shall ultimately want to use in considering the problem of augmenting the human intellect, nor how we might divide and subdivide these different manifestations of physical-process structuring. We use the terms 'mental structuring,' 'concept structuring,' 'symbol structuring,' 'process structuring,' and 'physical structuring.'" Engelbart, *Augmenting Human Intellect*, 32.
122. Engelbart, *Augmenting Human Intellect*, 15–16, emphasis in original.
123. Coons, "Requirements for a Computer-Aided Design System," 300.
124. Coons, "Requirements for a Computer-Aided Design System," 301.
125. Coons, "Requirements for a Computer-Aided Design System," 301.
126. Coons, "Requirements for a Computer-Aided Design System," 301
127. Coons, "Requirements for a Computer-Aided Design System," 302.
128. Coons, "Requirements for a Computer-Aided Design System," 302, emphasis in original.
129. See Coons, "Requirements for a Computer-Aided Design System," 302.
130. Coons, "Requirements for a Computer-Aided Design System," 302.
131. Engelbart, *Augmenting Human Intellect*, 93. In a fictitious forecast, which had not yet materialized in this form at the time but was expressed by Engelbart as a vision of the future, it also becomes clear that he did not expect to be able to make full use of the many facets of the computer unless you had your own programming skills: "It is true that the more of the sophisticated tricks you learn the more computer power you can harness and the more powerful you become--but very significant and personally thrilling practical problem-solving capabilities have been developed by quite few subjects who were given only fifteen hours of training at one of these stations." Engelbart, *Augmenting Human Intellect*, 107. In his vision, he also anticipated a program in which there is a tool with which computer tools can be designed themselves if a function is missing. See Engelbart, *Augmenting Human Intellect*, 103.

III

University of Utah

The Cradle of Contemporary 3D Computer Graphics

CHAPTER 6

A Common Goal

3D Computer Graphics between Credibility and Realism

> Sutherland and Dave Evans [...] were magnets for bright students with diverse interests, and they led us with a light touch. Basically they welcomed us to the program, gave us workspace and access to computers, and then let us pursue whatever turned us on. The result was a collaborative, supportive community so inspiring that I would later seek to replicate it at Pixar.[1]
>
> *EDWIN CATMULL (2014)*

In 1988, Ivan Sutherland received the prestigious Turing Award for his pioneering work in the field of computer graphics.[2] The award has been presented by the *Association for Computing Machinery* (ACM) every year since 1966 to honor those individuals who have advanced and shaped the field of computer science in a special way. Some of the award recipients have already been mentioned in the context of this study, such as Douglas C. Engelbart, who received the award in 1997, or Edwin Catmull, who was more recently honored with the award in 2019 and will play a central role in this third part of this study. On the occasion of Sutherland winning the award, an interview with him was published in June 1989 in *Communications of the ACM*, a journal published by the ACM. The interview provides crucial clues to derive the central question for this chapter.

Various topics are covered in the conversation, such as programming, Sutherland's later work at the *California Institute of Technology*[3] and robotics. Another talking point is the field of computer graphics, in which the research project at the *University of Utah* is also addressed. At the beginning of the interview, Sutherland is first asked about his career in general, how he got into the field of computer science and specifically into the field of graphics. Although he mentions individual people who had an influence on him by name,[4] he does not mention Steven A. Coons again in this interview, 26 years after his development of *Sketchpad*. When asked where he got the idea for his program back then, he replies, "[w]here do ideas come from? I haven't a clue as to where ideas come from. Ideas just come around."[5] However, Sutherland's interest in graphics came early on, as his father worked as a civil engineer and familiarized his son with the process of technical drawing at a young age.[6] While it should not be assumed that Coons is directly responsible for Sutherland's later career steps or concrete ideas, it becomes clear in the course of the interview that Coons' understanding of graphic communication has survived or is at least recognizable in Sutherland's thinking. Fetter's related ideas of graphic communication can also be found in the section of the interview on computer graphics. Based on these references, which will now be explained, the central question for this and the following chapters can subsequently be framed.

First of all, it is remarkable that, in the interview, intellectual connections between Coons and

DOI: 10.1201/9781003649861-9

Sutherland, or between Fetter and Sutherland, can be identified at all, as Sutherland expressed his thoughts a long time after he worked with Coons and during a time when computer graphics were well-established and no longer subject to any fundamental reconsiderations – an aspect that I will refer to again at the end of this chapter. With her questions, Sutherland's interviewer Karen A. Frenkel also addresses the particularly influential research at the *University of Utah*. In this context, she refers to an issue that characterized computer graphics research in general early on, but also specifically the research at the *University of Utah*, and which continues to drive developments in the field today: It is about the tension between "photorealism versus fast image processing,"[7] i.e. two potentially conflicting aspects of computer graphics. Particularly in the early days of computer images, a fundamental decision often had to be made as to whether the images should be generated efficiently in terms of time or whether they should have a finely elaborated appearance, which in these cases could be described as photorealistic. Although it will be shown later in this part that this fundamental decision is mentioned in many of the research reports written in Utah, Sutherland reacts dismissively to the topic: "I mean, you're making a dichotomy that I don't understand very well."[8] It can be assumed that Sutherland was satisfied with the appearance of the graphics and the amount of time it took to calculate them back then. Nevertheless, it is a dichotomy whose further dissolution is still given great weight by, for instance, today's gaming industry.[9]

For me, the contrast that Frenkel opens up with her question is not all that important. What is essential, however, is her reference to photorealistic imagery. Sutherland also comments on this but initially emphasizes that photorealism was not even relevant at the beginning. In Utah in the mid-1960s, at the beginning of computer graphics research there, the main focus was, according to him, rather on opaque representations of three-dimensional objects, in contrast to the line drawings that were common at the time. I addressed this problem previously under the keyword "Hidden Surface Problem," both in connection with Gaboury's study in the state of research and in Section 2.1. Sutherland particularly refers to Evans in this context and describes that his colleague not only made a significant technical contribution to being able to work graphically on the computer but also created a place in Utah where many different players in the research field came together, resulting in a great density of approaches and ideas that advanced the development of computer graphics.[10] Sutherland does not mention in this interview that he himself made the funding of the project possible as an employee of the *Advanced Research Projects Agency* (ARPA), as was also described in the historical overview at the beginning of this study. Although Sutherland places Evans in the foreground and was only involved in his research project two years after it started, Sutherland had a significant influence on the computer graphics developments at the *University of Utah*. This becomes evident when considering both his *Sketchpad* program and his connection to Coons.

In the interview with Frenkel, Sutherland shows more interest in answering questions about the purpose of the representational images. He states that although it was now – in 1989 – possible to create very successful representative graphics, some images were technically very sophisticated but were missing an "underlying meaning."[11] More important to him than simply exhibiting the technical possibilities, however, was the question of how the technology could be used to visualize abstract scientific phenomena:

> How do I make a beautifully realistic photograph of an atom? Well, atoms are smaller than the wavelength of light, so no one's ever seen one. So I don't know what an atom looks like. Any picture that I make of an atom is going to be a representative picture that may be beautifully rendered with the most gorgeous techniques and have shiny globular parts, shiny electrons and shiny neutrons. That may be very impressive, but it may not correspond to good physics. The important underlying question is, does it convey a meaning that's of some importance? So I don't see the realism *per se* as being controversial.[12]

Although Sutherland describes an abstract situation in his example, his statements not only provide a link to Coons and Fetter, but their positions can even be intensified with Sutherland's considerations. As previously noted, both Coons and Fetter were concerned not only with the use of representational modes of perspective illustration to visualize concepts, it was also important to them that the drawing processes were capable of conveying an idea in a credible and tangible way. Both associated this requirement with a mode of representation that they described as realistic. It is striking that all three, Coons, Fetter and Sutherland, do not place primary importance on whether the drawing or the photorealistic computer image is physically correct, as long as the maxim of believability is adhered to. Sutherland even addresses this aspect explicitly in the interview by explaining that the aim of depicting the atom is not to present its properties in a physically flawless way, but rather to create an image with an "underlying meaning." His phrasing is reminiscent of the way Rule and Coons speak of an "implicit meaning,"[13] which in their view is inherent in drawing conventions. For Sutherland, photorealism is not absolutely necessary in order to lend the pictures a deeper level of meaning, but it does not present an obstacle for him either. However, what Sutherland aims for in any event is a representational depiction. Regardless of how he imagines such a representation in relation to an atom, it becomes clear that his line of reasoning is very similar to that of Coons and Fetter. They also link their idea of a credible and tangible representation not to the technical construction drawings, but always to the perspective, representational illustrations. Interestingly, Fetter and Coons still refer to drawings that depict concrete physical objects or those that are to exist in the future, while Sutherland suggests to use a representational mode of expression even for phenomena that always remain abstract in origin – such as an atom. As he explains in the interview, this is clearly where he sees the greatest benefit for computer-generated images: "The most exciting power of computer graphics is to make abstract concepts real, and that's also the hardest because it involves visualizing new ideas."[14] Sutherland also establishes a link between "realism" and perspective or representational modes of expression. To him these are as well the ones that best adhere to the maxim of believability. This observation now raises the question of how, to what extent and, above all, for what reason Coons' and Fetter's convictions have become more firmly established in further developments in the field of computer graphics. As has now been established, Sutherland offers a possible starting point for pursuing this question. At the *University of Utah*, he made a decisive contribution to advancing Coons' ideas. At the same time, the following chapters are based on the assumption that the actual development of a context of meaning underlying 3D graphics has been completed with the developments in Utah.

Although this study is the first to comprehensively analyze overarching cultural artifacts in the history of the development of 3D computer graphics, my observation that the research of the 1970s was trend-setting for the development process and thus essentially complete is not new. The animation historian Tom Sito, for example, confirms this impression:

> Ever since the 1960s, when pioneers like John Whitney, Ivan Sutherland, Ken Knowlton, and Charles Csuri set out the basic principles, CG technology had been slowly building. The 1970s were about creating the basic tools, and the 1980s mostly about improving the power of these tools and making them user-friendly enough that creative minds could be free to explore. The development of CG had been advanced by governments, scientists, engineers, game makers, architects, motion picture visual effects studios, and university academics. As the 1980s moved into the 1990s, all these diverse strands, operating on heretofore separate tracks, began to merge into one grand convergence.[15]

Sito's overview provides several points of reference for the further course of this study. On the one hand, his statement that the tools were essentially finished being developed in the 1970s justifies my decision to focus primarily on the developments in that decade in the further course of my discussion. I will do so to determine the extent to which the "basic tools" adopt the values previously identified in Coons', Fetter's and Sutherland's work. On the other hand, Sito's phrase "grand convergence" suggests that there is a kind of consensus about what characterizes computer graphics and how it works. His descriptions are reminiscent of Gaboury's suggestion that research needed an overarching vision for its progress.[16] So the question is, what characterized this common idea for developing a technique that could be used to create 3D computer graphics?

The researchers at the *University of Utah*, among them Sutherland, Evans, Romney, Catmull, Phong,

Blinn and Gouraud, contributed significantly to this pioneering development. Although, as explained in the state of research, Gaboury finds the developments there neglected to date, the *University of Utah* is consistently highlighted as a central research institution in various historiographies. In her study, Rebecca Perry is not the only one to acknowledge Utah's pivotal role describing the research conducted there as the "foundation for computer graphics."[17] In his 1986 monograph *The Algorithmic Image*, Robert Rivlin also points out Utah's significant role. Although he refers to other research institutions as well where the development of computer graphics was advanced – for example *Ohio State University*, MIT, *Cornell*, *New York Institute of Technology*, *Carnegie Mellon* and *Stanford* – he particularly singles out the *University of Utah* among all institutions: "Virtually every modern concept in computer graphics either had its origin or received significant further development at the University of Utah in the late 1960s and early 1970s."[18] In order to pursue the question of a common goal, I will first focus on the research project at the *University of Utah* under the direction of Dave Evans (which was, a few years later, under the direction of Evans *and* Sutherland). In the following chapters I will thus present key developments and relate them to the aspects previously discussed. Initially, in this part of my book, I will focus on *how* these aspects found their way into computer graphics developments. In Part V, I will eventually address the question of *why* they have survived. To do justice to this last concern, a visual-aesthetic or rather style-historical discussion will be added to the discussion in Part IV, which up to this point has been mainly production-aesthetic. In this style-historical analysis a special focus will be placed on Catmull, a graduate of the computer science department at the *University of Utah*. My decision to explicitly take into account the visual surface level of computer graphics in the context of Catmull's contributions is based on the assumption that in his imagery, especially in the Pixar films, the production history of synthetic computer graphics finds a visual-aesthetic expression that not only makes the common context of meaning of synthetic computer graphics describable, but even explicitly visible. This visual-aesthetic examination therefore includes a look at US visual culture to clarify more profoundly *why* the graphic applications for the computer were developed in a certain way. In order to get there, the following explanations now trace the developments in Utah chronologically. Edwin Catmull forms the end point here.

NOTES

1. Edwin Catmull and Amy Wallace, *Creativity, Inc. Overcoming the Unseen Forces That Stand in the Way of True Inspiration* (New York: Random House, 2014), 12.
2. This event was also referred to in Chapter 3.
3. Sutherland was involved in the founding of the *Computer Science* program at the *California Institute of Technology* in 1975. See "History and Facts," Caltech Computing | Mathematical Sciences, accessed December 13, 2021, https://cms.caltech.edu/about/history.
4. Sutherland explicitly mentions, for example, Wesley A. Clark and Claude E. Shannon, who were mentioned in Chapter 3. See Ivan E. Sutherland, "An Interview with Ivan Sutherland," interview by Karen A. Frenkel, *Communications of the ACM* 32, no. 6 (1989): 712, https://doi.org/10.1145/63526.63531
5. Sutherland, interview by Frenkel, 712.
6. See Sutherland, interview by Frenkel, 713.
7. Sutherland, interview by Frenkel, 713.
8. Sutherland, interview by Frenkel, 713.
9. Alvy Ray Smith, who was involved in the founding of *Pixar Animation Studios* together with Edwin Catmull, also points this out: "We were certainly limited to low-resolution displays in the old days (nominally 512x512). We knew that film required much higher resolution, but the computers weren't up to it yet. We designed for higher resolution, however, and also for vastly more computational power. My brilliant colleague Loren Carpenter suggested that we set our sights on 80 million polygons per picture (NOT per second, but per frame). This was in the 1980s. Our mantra was (and I said this in public often): Reality begins at 80 million polygons. In other words, scenes start to reach a level of verisimilitude there where people stop paying close attention to the details (and pay attention instead to the characters). We were just guessing really, but the estimate turned out to be a good one. One of the results was that none of our code would fail when numbers as large as 80 million polygons were thrown at it, even in the bad old days of exceedingly slow machines. By free association, I came up with this quote as perhaps the one you remember. The quote is silly, of course, because reality is of far far higher resolution, but it served to set the stage for us and our code. [Just this last year, the Unreal engine has achieved this level of shaded, lit, polygons, with hidden surfaces removed, IN REAL TIME! It had to happen, but it still astonishes me.]" Alvy R. Smith, email to author, September 27, 2021, square brackets and emphasis in original.

10. Sutherland describes Evans' research contribution as follows: "The man who figured out the basic techniques that made modern graphics possible was David Evans. He had come out of a whole collection of early computing experiences in which incremental computing was used simply because that was all that could be done with the available equipment. He knew that incremental computing was a powerful way to get more results for less work. He suggested to a collection of his students, and to me, that we make use of all of the information that we'd computed for one pixel in doing the computations for the adjacent pixel – that we try never to recompute *ab initio*, but rather to compute on the basis of nearby changes." Sutherland, interview by Frenkel, 713, emphasis in original.
11. Sutherland, interview by Frenkel, 713.
12. Sutherland, interview by Frenkel, 713, emphasis in original.
13. John T. Rule and Steven A. Coons, *Graphics* (New York: McGraw-Hill, 1961), 8.
14. Sutherland, interview by Frenkel, 714.
15. Tom Sito, *Moving Innovation: A History of Computer Animation* (Cambridge: MIT Press, 2013), 253.
16. See Jacob Gaboury, *Image Objects. An Archaeology of Computer Graphics* (Cambridge: MIT Press, 2021), 32–33.
17. Rebecca A. Perry, "Rigging the World: 3D Modeling and the Seduction of the Real" (PhD diss., Massachusetts Institute of Technology, 2014), MIT Libraries, DSpace@MIT (900615015), 26. She also emphasizes that "anyone with a serious interest in computer graphics was drawn to Utah, whose graduates began to decisively shape the field." Perry, "Rigging the World," 73. With this statement, she is referring, for example, to the fact that influential companies such as *Adobe* and *Pixar Animation Studios*, or even the development of the laptop driven by Alan Kay, can be traced back to alumni of this research hub in Utah. See Perry, "Rigging the World," 73, footnote 106. Against the background of this central position of the *University of Utah* and the knowledge that the research carried out there in the field of computer graphics was subsidized by government and military funds, it is surprising that the professor of queer and gender studies Jack Halberstam places in his monograph *The Queer Art of Failure* computer graphics developments in general and Pixar in particular within his theory of failure. He wants to open up a space for alternative academic approaches and narrative strands that do not correspond to the heteronormative performance requirements of society and academia: "[T]he computer scientists who pioneered new programs to produce computer-generated imagery (CGI), as many accounts of the rise of Pixar have chronicled, were academic rejects or dropouts who created independent institutes in order to explore their dreams of animated worlds. These alternative cultural and academic realms, the areas beside academia rather than within it, the intellectual worlds conjured by losers, failures, dropouts, and refuseniks, often serve as the launching pad for alternatives precisely when the university cannot." Judith/Jack Halberstam, *The Queer Art of Failure* (Durham: Duke University Press, 2011), 7. Halberstam refers here to the historiography of *Pixar Animation Studios* by David A. Price without citing more specific passages. Price traces the development of the company very comprehensively but does not set himself the task of contextualizing or evaluating the historical facts with regard to a larger cultural framework. Halberstam's interpretation is therefore presumably based on a self-interpretation by the people involved in the founding of the animation studio. See David A. Price, *The Pixar Touch: The Making of a Company* (New York: Vintage Books, 2009).
18. Robert Rivlin, *The Algorithmic Image: Graphic Visions of the Computer Age* (Redmond: Microsoft Press, 1986), 27.

CHAPTER 7

Opacity, Light and Animation

A Strategy for Realizing the Common Goal

In the examination of Steven Coons' conception of graphics, one area has so far been completely omitted. Instead of focusing on the engineering drawings, I have up to this point merely discussed why Coons, Rule and also Fetter, attached such great importance to the illustrative perspective drawings. In this part, which deals with the further development of computer graphics in Utah, I will now also focus on the technical aspects, which have received little attention so far. Numerous principles that Coons developed for drawing on paper and which were already established for the production of engineering drawings were later integrated into the computer to enable the computer-aided generation of representational and perspective images. The "Coons Surface Patch" developed by him, a mathematical calculation model for the precise determination of curved surfaces, was also adopted and further developed in Utah.[1]

Regarding Coons and Fetter, I identified a divergence between the orthographic, abstract technical drawings and the perspective illustrations. While both engineering draftsmen considered the latter form of representation to be more credible or tangible, they attested greater precision to the technical drawings. What is interesting for this part is that both approaches were integrated in later computer applications. Today's computer representations thus oscillate between the technical and the perspective approach, whereby the orthographic views are generally only encountered in the production process, while the perspective and thus also symbolic views manifest themselves primarily in the finished images. Even before these two contrasting approaches were merged into computer technology at the *University of Utah*, this development was already apparent in Timothy Johnson's 1963 master's thesis *Sketchpad III*, developed under the supervision of Steven Coons at MIT. Johnson worked on his thesis while Sutherland was still developing the *Sketchpad* program for the creation of two-dimensional drawings. Unlike Sutherland's approach, Johnson's was the first to allow for the creation of three-dimensional perspective drawings of objects directly on a screen using a computer. What is particularly significant about Johnson's work for my analysis is that the problems he encountered with his approach and the solutions he proposed anticipated key aspects that would later also characterize the research in Utah.[2] I therefore want to discuss his preliminary work at the beginning of this part, as numerous research topics pursued in Utah can thus be illustrated in advance.

Sutherland, who played a central role in the research project in Utah, also referred to Johnson's 3D version *Sketchpad III* in his 1963 technical report, which he wrote as part of his work on *Sketchpad*:

> The methods outlined in this report generalize nicely to three dimensional drawing. In fact, work has already been begun to make a complete "Sketchpad Three" which will let the user communicate solid objects to the computer. A forthcoming thesis by Timothy Johnson of the Mechanical Engineering

DOI: 10.1201/9781003649861-10

> Department will describe this work. When Johnson is finished it should be possible to aim at a particular place in the three dimensional drawing through two dimensional, perspective views presented on the display. Johnson is completely bypassing the problem of converting several two dimensional drawings into a three dimensional shape. Drawing will be directly in three dimensions from the start. No two dimensional representation will ever be stored.[3]

Here, Sutherland is referring to a feature that Johnson developed for his version of the program, and which has survived in this form to this day. Instead of generating individual two-dimensional views of an object, the computer directly stores the mathematical description of a virtual three-dimensional model. To be able to display different views of this model, Johnson integrated four viewports into his program, "one in each quadrant of the CRT screen. A perspective view of the object appears in the upper right quadrant, and three orthogonal views in the remaining quadrants: top view–upper left, front view–lower left, and side view–lower right."[4] As is still the case today, all four views therefore show the same object from different perspectives, so that a change in one of the four screen quadrants occurs simultaneously in all four views.[5] Interestingly, Johnson's approach is based on the same drawing principles used in the analog process for producing technical engineering drawings. As Coons explains together with Rule, the different views from the side, from above and from the front are primarily required "to describe objects accurately and unambiguously so that there can be no question concerning their size and shape in even the smallest detail."[6] Coons' influence on Johnson is immediately apparent here. While Coons still reflects on why he considers an additional perspective drawing to be necessary despite its lack of precision in the design work, Johnson no longer engages in such a discussion. He merely notes, "[b]ecause the screen is two-dimensional and the objects are three-dimensional wire frames, several viewing conventions were adopted to aid in visualizing the object in three-dimensional space."[7] For him, the idea of being able to visualize depth information of an object is essential.[8] He even addresses the fact that a perspective drawing, especially one of a completely unknown object, can be misleading. With this statement, Johnson is primarily referring to "wire frame" representations, i.e. line drawings that show an object in a type of grid. According to Johnson, the other views are therefore required for the unambiguous representation of an object. This demonstrates again the arbitrariness with which also Johnson relies on the perspective visualization.[9] He discusses various options that would facilitate the clear legibility of a perspective representation in the computer. Based on his considerations, it is now possible to deduce which research questions were also in the main focus in Utah: For example, Johnson emphasizes that being able to move the object itself or move around it is central to better comprehending a perspective line drawing,[10] a possibility that he had already implemented.[11] He proceeds by explaining that it would also be helpful if the lines on the back of an object were hidden, so it could be depicted opaquely and react to light and shadow.[12] Although the engineer Lawrence G. Roberts was also conducting research on the hidden line problem of three-dimensional objects at MIT at the same time, Johnson initially excluded this still very computationally intensive approach for his own purposes.[13] Instead, he concentrated his research exclusively on the

> graphical description of straight-edged objects – in hopes that the experience gained in this restricted area would indicate a way to a solution of the general problem. The term straight-edged object means that the intersections of all surfaces are straight lines, although the object does not necessarily have plane surfaces.[14]

Overall, Johnson saw his program – similar to Sutherland – as suitable for universal use, although he was aware that many work steps would still have to follow in order to perfect graphic communication with the help of the computer.[15] However, even at that time, he pointed to design work and the possibility of achieving "entirely new artistic effects"[16] as a particular area of application for *Sketchpad III.* With this phrasing, he was referring to the design of a chair in which the backrest can be interactively displayed at different angles using his program (Figure 7.1).[17] It is clear from Johnson's introduction that all of his

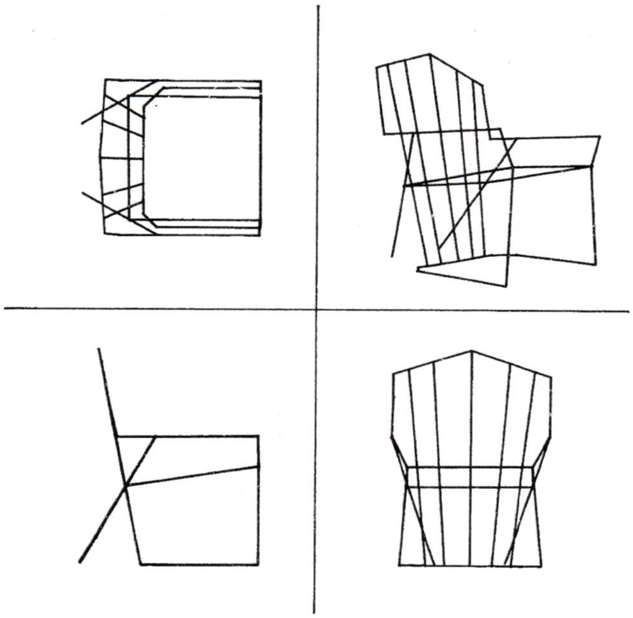

FIGURE 7.1 Timothy E. Johnson, *Wrought Iron Chair Design*, 1963, *Sketchpad III* drawing.

thoughts on the production of designs were directly influenced by Coons. At the beginning of his descriptions, Johnson explains that the first drawings in the design process are "not a precise statement of refined detail, but [...] a vague stirring of the imagination."[18] He repeats Coons here – without citing him – almost word for word: "The sketch forms the natural bridge between these vague stirrings of the imagination and the subsequent precise statement of the refined details of the concept."[19] Johnson sees his program as a means of refining these initial sketches into precise drawings.[20] *Sketchpad III*, which is technically based on Sutherland's *Sketchpad*, is therefore a direct realization of Coons' visions.

The interests that Johnson pursued can now be used to illustrate the concerns that were ultimately focused on in Utah. The overarching goal of the research project at the *University of Utah* aligns with Johnson's, Coons' and Fetter's objectives, as is evident in Evans' descriptions from 1966 in the first retrospective research report, six months after the start of the project:

> A major objective of the project is to develop a method which will produce synthetic video signals representing two-dimensional projections of three-dimensional objects described only in the data structure of the computer. It is considered that such a representation of the object is of basic value, because it corresponds to the representation of the real world on the human retina.[21]

The central starting point for Evans – just as it was for Coons and Fetter – is human vision. Similar to how Coons and Fetter independently related perspective illustrations to human vision, this line of argument is repeated here by Evans. He also assumes that two-dimensional projections of three-dimensional objects are a suitable way of creating images that best reflect human vision. The research report quoted here is the first of a total of 11 reports that Evans produced every six months over the entire duration of the funding period (see also endnote 25 in Section 2.2). The project took place in two phases: The first research period ran from June 1966 to June 1970, the second from January 1971 to December 1972.[22] My following remarks are structured chronologically along these reports. In them, Evans also mentions the publications of research papers that were produced as part of the research project. Throughout this chapter, I will also refer to these publications occasionally. Although the project's objectives gradually became more differentiated over the following years,[23] the perspective Evans presented at the beginning remained the guiding principle. In contrast to Coons' statements, it becomes apparent that Evans no longer reflected on his considerations. While Coons and Rule compared their work to children's drawings to explain why they considered perspective projections to be the more coherent graphic constructions, no such level of meta-reflection can be found in Evans' reports. With his desire to create two-dimensional projections of three-dimensional objects using a computer, he simply set a standard. He did not deviate from this goal until the end of the research project. As will become clear in the following sections, the reports of individual authors contain some reflections on human perception and the reproduction techniques that respond to it. However, as I have emphasized at the end of Section 5.2, Evans' introductory objective shows that in his research project there was no longer a fundamental need to negotiate which alternative principles should be used to create computer-aided images. Thus, the maxim of central perspective believability continued unreservedly from this point onward.

The solutions developed in Utah between 1966 and 1972 for the comprehensible representation of two-dimensional projections using computer graphics became the industry standard. Yet, the research objectives to reach this point resemble the three proposals that Johnson presented as early as 1963: Thus, the following explanations will show that within the framework of the research project at the *University of Utah*, solutions were developed to (1) supplement the wireframe display of objects with an opaque representation of the models, (2) stage the models with the aid of light to make them even more vivid; and (3) set the models in motion. Regarding this last point, both of Johnson's suggestions were realized. On the one hand, the objects were animated or rotated in the view, and, on the other hand, early types of virtual glasses were used to move around the objects.[24] During this time, the fields that are still central to the creation of computer graphics today were developed: Modeling, shading, texturing and animation as well as virtual reality glasses as an extended display method. Like animation, this particular field is not the focus of my study. I view both rather as an extension of the desired realism of the images. The spatial impression of virtual objects is still created using two-dimensional images. In the case of the glasses, however, as with the stereoscopes established in the 1920s, two images are combined by the human brain to be seen as one. The area of modeling, i.e., describing objects purely technically in a computer, is also – at least today – not ultimately decisive for the appearance of finished graphics. Nevertheless, some modeling approaches are presented in the following section because, at that time, modeling had an influence on the finished appearance of the 3D graphics. Yet, the focus below is primarily on the areas of shading and texturing, as these fields are crucial to understanding how computer graphics gradually achieved the maxim of believability envisioned by Coons and Fetter.

7.1 SHADING ALGORITHMS AND THE PERFECTION OF 3D COMPUTER GRAPHICS

When attempting to trace the history of shading, it is noticeable that although Evans' research project in Utah is not solely responsible for the entire development of this discipline, the features that still play a role today in the creation of 3D computer graphics from a production-aesthetic perspective can be almost entirely traced back to the achievements made in Utah.[25] In addition, it is particularly the first steps taken in the historical development of shading that reveal an intellectual affinity to Coons' and Fetter's concepts of pictoriality. The ideas expressed in the first year of the research project in 1966 regarding the direction in which 3D graphics should develop in terms of visual-aesthetics came to fruition in the early 1970s with the first easier-to-use shading algorithms.

With his aim of using the computer to generate "two-dimensional projections of three-dimensional objects,"[26] Evans was referring specifically to the creation of so-called halftone images. It is a term that originates from the field of printing or reproduction technology. As can be seen from early 1968 examples by Evans and his graduate students Gordon W. Romney and Gary S. Watkins, the appearance of halftone images Evans had in mind contrasted with the previously common computer graphics that were mostly line drawings. The first computer graphics Romney, Watkins and Evans presented in the form of halftone images contained letters and primitive shapes such as a cone (Figure 7.2).[27] The interest in creating computer graphics as halftone images emerged, because – in contrast to line representations – virtual models could this way be displayed as opaque objects, including their surface information. In short, they could be provided with "shading." Romney can be considered the first person to realize these types of 3D renderings as he was the first graduate student that was recruited by Evans to work on this goal.[28]

However, due to its origins in printing technology, the term halftone image is misleading. Three years after the start of the project in Utah, Romney explained in his dissertation *Computer Assisted Assembly and Rendering of Solids*, completed in 1969, why he considered the term unsuitable for computer images and did not want to use it:

> The word halftone has undergone an evolutionary transition as far as its semantic definition is concerned. Halftone was often used to refer to the shades of grey that occur between the highlights and the shadows in photographs. Thus, the term was used to name

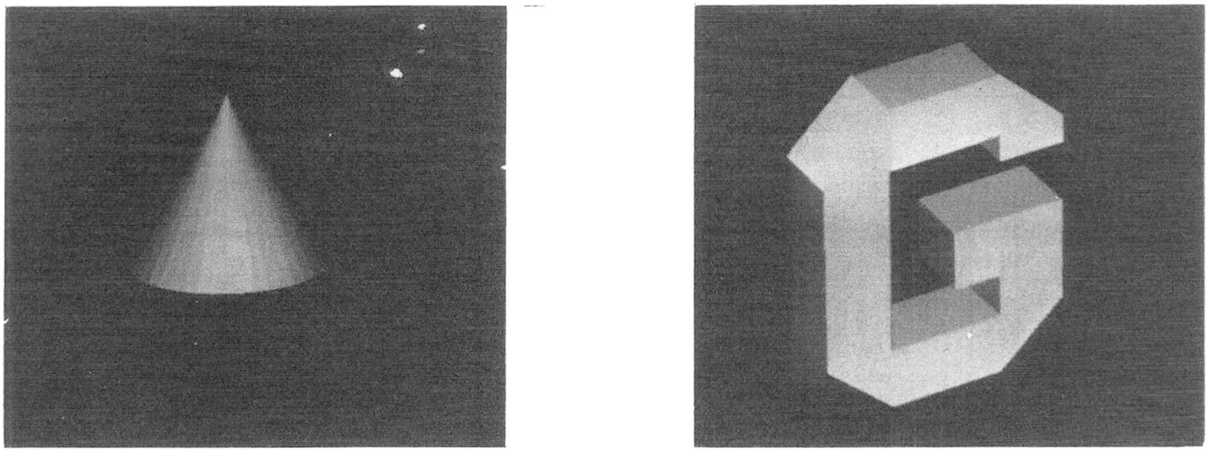

FIGURE 7.2 Gordon W. Romney, Gary S. Watkins and David C. Evans, *Cone* and *Letter 'G'*, 1968, computer rendering recorded on film (here reproduced as a halftone image). (© 1968 Gordon W. Romney.)

> the first practical process to reproduce photographs by a printing technique. Ever since, halftone has taken on a dichotomous nature referring to both a continuous (photography) and discontinuous (printing) distribution. For this reason, photographic terminology has switched to midtone or tone and relegated halftone to the realm of the discontinuous.
>
> Consequently, computer renderings are halftone only in the sense of shaded representation. The fact that they are produced by a raster technique that displays individual points of intensity should not be interpreted as being analogous to the halftone printing process [...]. It is for this reason that this author [Romney] has avoided the use of the word halftone when referring to computer generated images – they are shaded renderings, not halftone.[29]

It is interesting to note that apart from Romney, none of the other researchers commented on the choice of terms. Although the words "shading" and "rendering" were gradually becoming more common in the context of computer graphics at that time, they were generally used in parallel with the term "halftone image." I will refer to Romney's research several more times throughout this chapter and examine it in more detail, as along with his early rendering solutions the author's meta-reflexive approach provides, for my production-aesthetic angle, fruitful insights into the aesthetic values on which the creation of 3D graphics was based at the time.

Regardless of Romney's assessment, Evans still worked with the term "halftone image," although he did not refer to a printing process with his choice of words, but rather to the representation of solid objects, including shading in real time on a display. Very early on, photography served as an explicit point of orientation in terms of image aesthetics, as becomes clear in the descriptions of the research intentions within the second report from May 1967. In it, Evans already expressed the desire "to produce photograph quality pictures of objects illuminated by incident light showing appropriate shading and shadows."[30] At the end of 1967, in the third report, Evans expressed his satisfaction with the developments to date, even before the shading algorithms that are still in use today had been developed: "Good progress has been made in the development of techniques for producing halftone photograph like pictures of three dimensional objects whose descriptions are stored in the computer memory."[31] He returns to this success again later in the report and also stresses that there is an "urgent need for realistic pictures,"[32] a phrase which demonstrates that for him the concept of realism was closely linked to photography. In the report, he does not specify from where the need for such images originates, but he does refer to a 1967 research paper he co-authored entitled *Half-tone perspective drawings by computer*,[33] in which the specialist areas he believed would benefit from 3D visualizations are pointed out.

This paper generally provides a deeper understanding of the initial research steps taken in Utah. Romney was also involved in the paper, even before completing his independent doctoral thesis. The authors specify the predicted areas of application as follows:

> For example, it is important for a designer or architect to quickly describe a three-dimensional object and view it immediately; not as an endless set of engineering drawings, but as if he were viewing the three-dimensional object itself. He should be able to take a distant look at a complicated object, and then view, in detail, any subsection of the object. In other words, he would like to quickly and cheaply simulate and view the thing he is designing.
>
> The goal of this project is to provide a system which will display images that a person can "feel," as contrasted with images that he must laboriously interpret (e. g. the engineering drawings of an air-plane).[34]

Like Coons and Fetter, the authors distinguish here between technical drawings, which are complex to read and have to be interpreted, and perspective representations, which are intuitively understandable and can be "felt." This choice of words is particularly reminiscent of Coons, who used the term "feeling" in relation to design work, for example. Coons employed this term to describe the moment when an idea first takes shape and becomes perceptible to the senses with the help of a sketch.[35] In the paper, Evans, Romney et al. also define factors that they believe support the ability to actually "feel" such an image – these are almost identical to the criteria mentioned by Johnson in his report and presented at the beginning of this chapter. They list four options: (1) a stereo representation of the objects; (2) a possibility to hide the lines and surfaces that are covered by the front of the object; (3) lighting and shading of the virtual models and (4) the ability to move objects in real time.[36]

In their endeavor to develop a calculation model that conceals hidden lines, the authors – like Johnson – refer to Lawrence G. Roberts in their paper, who had dealt with this problem four years earlier at MIT. However, Roberts' approach could only generate simple models made of cuboids and prisms, which is why Evans, Romney and their colleagues decided to describe models made of triangular polygons. This method can generate any possible shape. They demonstrate this using a sphere as an example (Figure 7.3).[37] Furthermore, Roberts was not yet working with a method that could show shaded objects. Despite the elimination of excess lines, his objects were still presented in the form of line drawings.[38]

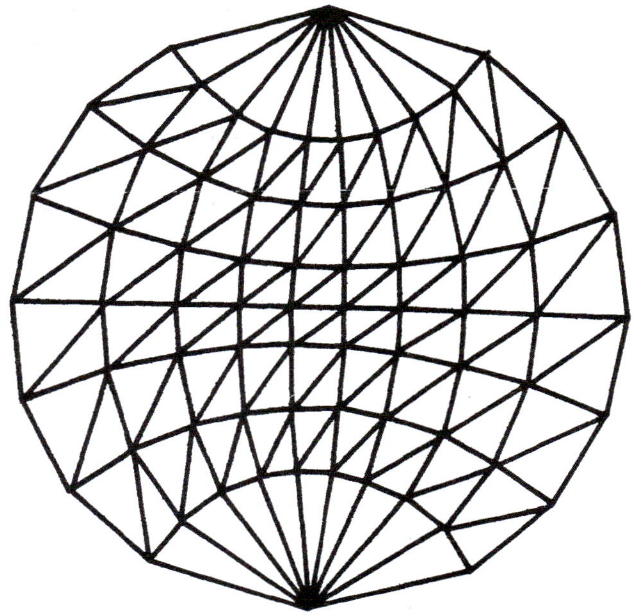

FIGURE 7.3 Chris Wylie, Gordon W. Romney and David C. Evans, *Line-drawn Sphere Approximated by Planar Triangles*, 1967. (© 1967 Gordon W. Romney.)

In his above-mentioned 1969 dissertation *Computer Assisted Assembly and Rendering of Solids* – supervised by Evans and Sutherland – Romney independently elaborated on the approach that he developed with Evans and colleagues in 1967 and builds on it directly.[39] Romney's report reveals much more comprehensively than the previous paper the ideas of pictoriality with which the research on computer-generated renderings was carried out. After Romney's work, none of the subsequent and related research projects dealt with a possible justification for the chosen approach in such detail. The basic idea of what a computer graphical image should look like, which emerged in connection with these initial steps in Evans' research project, was merely further developed and refined in Utah in the following years but has not fundamentally changed to this day.[40] This development is evident in Evans' biannual research reports. While Evans noted in his fourth report, published in November 1968, that there had been no significant innovations in the field of "halftone images,"[41] the fifth report, published in May 1969, also only briefly describes further developments in this area.[42] It was not until the sixth report, in November 1969, six months before the end of the first four-year research period, that Evans reported extensive innovations, including also Romney's contribution.[43] The following sub-sections will therefore take a closer look at this.

7.1.1 Gordon W. Romney's Objective Design Criteria for Computer Graphics

This sub-section is divided into two steps. First, aspects are addressed that again deal with questions about the perspective representation of objects. This establishes links to the previous parts of this study and traces a line of development. Second, Romney's approach to shading is discussed in more detail. Romney begins his report with an extensive overview of parallel or preceding developments at other research institutions that were pursuing similar goals to his own and his colleagues' in Utah. In this context, he first refers to research at MIT in the early 1960s, explicitly mentioning Sutherland work on *Sketchpad* and Johnson's 3D version of the program, *Sketchpad III*. He also mentions Roberts' hidden line algorithm in this context.[44]

According to Romney, Johnson's desire to have perspective drawings be generated by the computer and Roberts' goal to hide unnecessary lines in such drawings were based on objective goals for the generation of computer graphics. This is why, as Romney argues, similar efforts could therefore also be observed elsewhere, for example, in a NASA-funded project at *General Electric* or in a project at *Mathematical Applications Group, Inc.* (MAGI).[45] Both companies facilitated the possibility of computer-aided generation of halftone images on a display at around the same time as Evans, Romney et al. in 1967. The NASA-funded project at *General Electric* even established a way of displaying images in real time and in color. In terms of the production-aesthetic angle of my study, however, the NASA project is of little relevance, as the approach to image generation it pursued was not continued.[46] The methods developed at the *University of Utah* often served as the basis for further research into the production of "halftone images." These approaches were continued not only at the same institution, for example – parallel to Romney – by his colleague John E. Warnock[47] but also at other universities, such as the *University of Illinois*. There, W. Jack Bouknight, with reference to Warnock, developed an algorithm that could display 3D models as shaded objects.[48] Working in parallel, Warnock and Romney were the first in Utah to create 3D graphics in color. Figures 7.4 and 7.5 show their respective initial results. While Romney chose a soma cube as the motif for his example, Warnock opted for the depiction of a molecule.[49] The findings that can be drawn from Romney's explanations about his shading approach are representative of all the other parallel approaches that were developed at the *University of Utah*, including Warnock's, as his research intention also followed Evans' overarching research objective. The parallel research therefore also falls into Romney's category of the "objective" criteria for image creation, as do the research sites outside the *University of Utah*. So which principles did he regard as objective?

With reference to the physicist Loyd A. Jones, Romney derives the "objective" design principles from so-called psychophysiological aspects of human perception. Romney therefore assumes that

> [h]uman judgement must be relied upon to determine image quality. The criterion of quality, or whether something is good or bad, depends significantly upon psychological attributes. With images, however, certain objective attributes such as perspective and contrast-range can be quantitatively determined. The interaction of the psychological and physical realms and their relative importance is known as the discipline of psychophysics. Psychophysics has played an important role in the improvement and perfecting of both the photographic and video processes. Also, the discipline has helped significantly in the development of computer-generated images.[50]

Based on this line of argument, Romney concludes that the historical development of 3D computer graphics is nothing more than an attempt to recreate the process of human vision. Unlike Rule and Coons, Romney initially even takes into account the

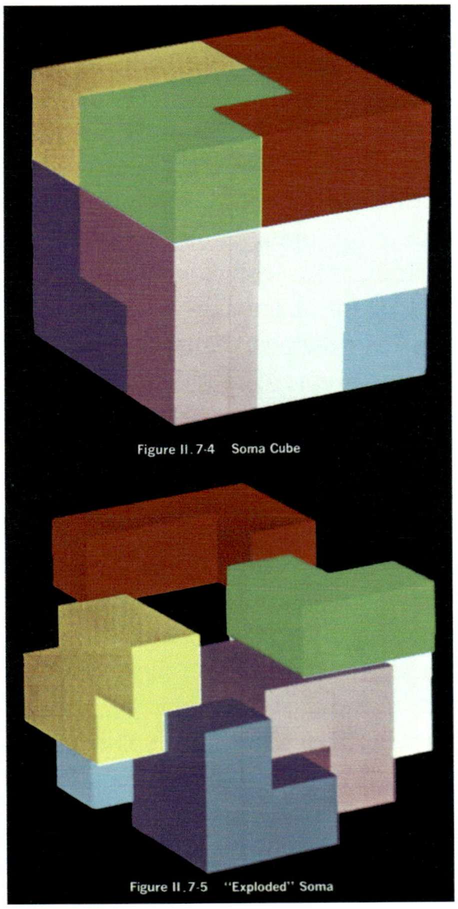

FIGURE 7.4 Gordon W. Romney, *Colored Pieces Assembled Soma Cube* and *Colored Pieces Expanded, Rotated Soma Cube*, 1969, computer rendering recorded on polaroid film (here reproduced with halftone four color process). (© 1968 Gordon W. Romney.)

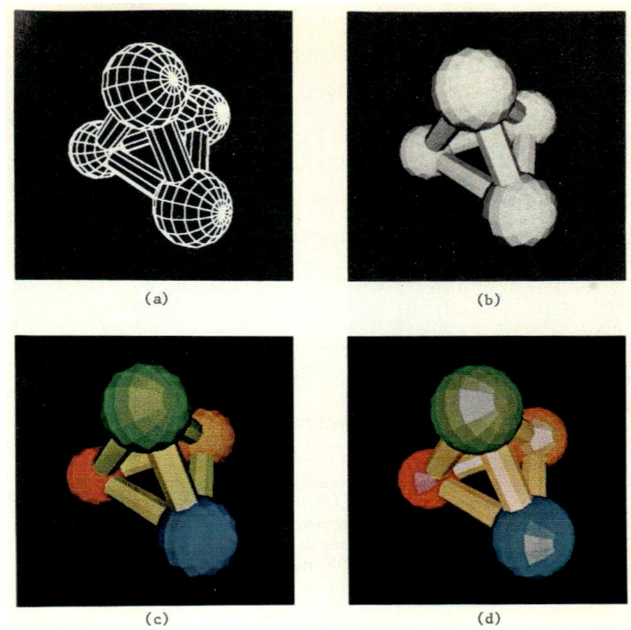

FIGURE 7.5 John E. Warnock, *Fig. 5*, 1969, raster scan image (here reproduced as a halftone image).

aspect that people usually see with two eyes, because – according to his explanation – the process of seeing comprises monocular characteristics that affect each eye individually and spatial vision, which only results from the interaction of both eyes. The most important monocular characteristics are "1) perspective, 2) object overlay, 3) shading and color, 4) motion and subjective factors of experience and proprioception (muscle tension)."[51] In order to generate 3D computer graphics, Romney concludes, the aim must therefore be to transfer these objective aspects into the computer-aided imaging process.

In a separate and extensive chapter, Romney therefore turns to the subject of "projection." He defines it as any form of translation of a three-dimensional environment onto a two-dimensional surface and emphasizes that artists and photographers as well as draftsmen are always bound by this limitation. He then presents a variety of different projection possibilities and distinguishes between two types in particular: Perspective projections, which include central perspective and other forms of projection, and parallel perspective projections. As the second form of visualization is much easier to create using drawing tools, it is to him the preferred method for developing engineering designs. Nevertheless, Romney clearly emphasizes, "[p]erspective projections [...] are those always encountered in the real, visual world."[52] Like the previous individuals I discussed in this study, Romney justifies this statement with the retinal image. While, as Romney describes, the eye lens produces central perspective projections, the "oblique perspective," which uses two vanishing points, is, alongside the central perspective, also common in camera technology:

> Oblique perspectives are often employed by the artist in order to achieve special effects. The photographer, also, often uses oblique perspective to compensate for image distortion. [...] The draftsman, however, encounters considerable difficulty in achieving the particular oblique perspective he desires.[53]

The system Romney created for his computer graphics could realize both parallel perspective and central perspective projection as well as the "oblique perspective" with two vanishing points. It appears contradictory that Romney clearly distinguishes between different projection methods and thus demonstrates that these are graphic constructions and conventions, yet nevertheless concludes that perspective drawings with vanishing points and foreshortening are best suited for the realistic reproduction of our surroundings. He places this thought in the introductory sentences of his entire study: "The problem of all imaging processes, consequently, is how to incorporate dimensionality or spatial relationship into the image."[54] The fact that *other* established approaches exist in the field of art which – *instead* of working exclusively with perspective constructions – discuss aspects such as dimensionality and spatial relationships on the two-dimensional surface, is irrelevant to Romney. This is interesting as he himself selectively refers to alternative approaches to transferring the three-dimensional world onto a two-dimensional surface. Consequently, the maxim of believability based on the central perspective continues with him. For him, too, perspective construction, and above all central perspective, is a substantial element of pictoriality. Recalling Panofsky's remark that it is essential *which* perspective one chooses for their pictorial representations,[55] it is evident now to what extent the development of software and hardware for generating computer graphics is also strongly characterized by very specific pictorial ideas. It was not, for instance, cubist painterly approaches that found their way into the software landscape. In Cubism spatiality is also transferred to the two-dimensional surface. Rather it was a realistic visual language orientated primarily toward optical principles that was implemented into the algorithms emerging at the time. The visual aesthetic or style Romney aimed for is thus clearly linked to perspective projection, as it was for Coons and Fetter. The goal of Romney's research project did not primarily follow artistic standards – after all, the overarching research project in Utah was guided by military interests. Nevertheless, Romney occasionally references artistic work, as Sutherland did in his work on *Sketchpad*. Romney's belief that the perspective constructions can be objectively derived from human vision also shows that he, like Sutherland, assumed a universality that should characterize the 3D graphics. How did this mindset affect the development of shaded renderings?

According to Romney, the central task of shading was "to provide picture understandability. In other words, to convey to an observer the intended information in an unambiguous manner."[56] His idea of what shading can achieve is familiar against the background of the discussion of Coons and Fetter. Continuing his previous argument, Romney claims that the surface representation of objects presented in central perspective is also based on objective principles. Like the aspects of optics, these principles have, as he explains, their origin in physics and can "produce a meaningful rendering."[57] These "meaningful" criteria include, for example, the manner in which the light reflection is displayed on the material surface, for instance whether the materials are matt or reflective, or whether reflective materials themselves emit light into the surroundings. The topic of light reflection therefore encompasses not only possible direct light sources but also indirect light sources. Lastly, in the continued logic of this physical approach, the question arose as to how shadows could be rendered by the computer.[58]

The calculation of shaded objects was one of the main factors that created the dichotomy between "good" and "fast" images at the time. Thus, although Romney listed extensive criteria for shading, compromises were still made in many cases due to the computing power available at the time. For instance, Romney worked with a light source located at the observer's point of view, as is also described in the paper published with Evans et al. This way, the shadows always fall behind the displayed objects and do not have to be calculated. Only the surfaces evoke the impression of a light source through different gradations of brightness. Evans also describes this method in the third interim report in 1967:

> Halftone shading computations have been made reasonable by assuming only first order illumination from a single light source located at the eye of the viewer. This illumination is not the most artistic, but pictures produced have been pleasing to look at. The illumination is similar to the single flash illuminations of many press photographs.[59]

Two years later, Romney was still following this approach and also used the phrase "flash photography quality"[60] to describe the aesthetics of the images he produced. Figure 7.6 shows one of these early attempts using a sphere formed from triangular polygons with a strong reflection in the center, as would be typical for flash photography. The example is an image from the collaboration with Evans. Romney initially ignored the calculation of reflections, such as those that occur on smooth surfaces. All of the objects he depicted in his example images are shown with matt surfaces that only reflect light diffusely.[61]

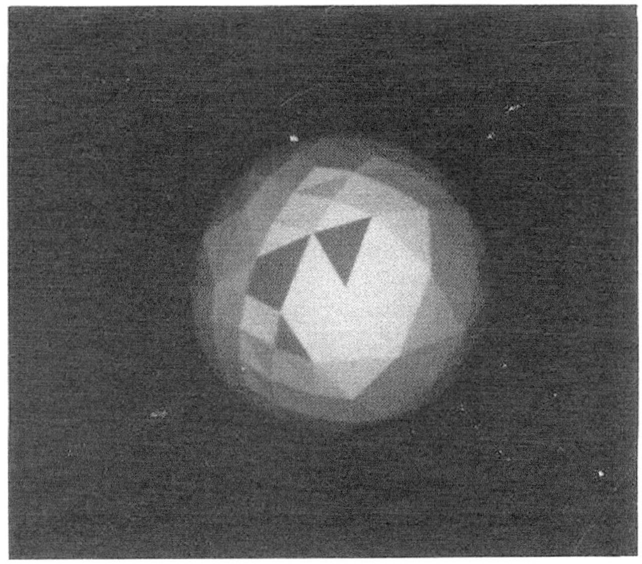

FIGURE 7.6 Gordon W. Romney, Gary S. Watkins and David C. Evans, *Sphere*, 1968, computer rendering recorded on film (here reproduced as a halftone image). (© 1968 Gordon W. Romney.)

Finally, the images were output or rather recorded in an analog photographic process. To display and then save an image, Romney used an oscilloscope. All the values needed for the appearance of the surfaces and lighting were calculated and displayed on the oscilloscope screen, line by line. This gradual build-up of the image was recorded photographically under long exposure, as not all lines could be displayed at the same time.[62] Any duplication of the computer-generated images then took place via reproductions of the resulting photographs, which is one reason why Romney occasionally used the term "photograph" for the finished computer-generated images.[63] Although photography, as an imaging technique, was not primarily an aesthetic model for Romney, but rather a practical part of the production process at that time, his examination of the reproduction process reveals that photography was also an important reference for the appearance of the 3D graphics:

> Tone reproduction with computer-generated images is not "reproduction" work in any sense of the word. Consequently, the previous definition of photographic quality is not applicable – or is it? The observer definitely has not seen the original. However, as a result of accumulated experience with similar objects, he has acquired a definite impression that is the result of stored memory records of previous visual stimuli. This impression, in turn, is used to evaluate the quality of the photographic reproduction although the observer has never seen that particular object.[64]

Evans' desire to produce "half-tone photographs like pictures of three dimensional objects,"[65] that was quoted above, can now be better understood against the background of Romney's considerations. Romney ultimately applied his findings on the viewing habits associated with photographs to the production of color images. With reference to engineer David L. MacAdam, Romney points out that objective criteria for the production of black-and-white images had already been empirically determined through studies and would be repeatedly used in reproduction. However, such comprehensive criteria for the reproduction of color images did not yet exist.[66]

Romney used color film to create the color images, although the oscilloscope could not display any colors. This is why Romney had to transfer the color information using color foils, which he placed between the camera and the oscilloscope. He worked with the three primary colors red, green and blue, as other colors can be mixed from these three colors when exposed to light. In preparation for the three channels, Romney generated an image on the computer in three individual passes – one for each color. Specifically, this means that he had to output an image once with all the red components, once with all the green components and once with all the blue components. To reassemble the three channels, he first exposed the film with the red parts of the computer image, then the green parts and finally the blue parts.[67] As this process was very time-consuming and did not allow for any direct and interactive manipulation of the displayed object, Romney refers in his study to his colleague Alan Erdahl, who was working in Utah on a parallel approach that allowed color images to be displayed on a color television.[68]

With regard to Romney's work, it can now be summarized that his considerations and ideas for the implementation of his approach indicate the topics and problems that were the focus of the further development of Evans' research project at the *University of Utah*. Although Romney was not yet in a position to implement all his criteria for creating what he considered to be objective 3D computer graphics, his reasoning clearly shows the logic behind the making of the images: The creation of the first computer-graphic images, for example, is based on photographic parameters as well as on parameters of perceptual psychology. It can be said that these initial endeavors by Romney and Evans resulted in further goals and needs, but these were merely improvements to the fundamental objective of creating realistic 3D graphics with photographic quality. One such "new" goal would be to be able to place light sources anywhere in the virtual space instead of just from the observer's point of view. As a result, this goal would in turn be linked to the need to be able to display shadows.[69] Fundamentally new approaches to visual aesthetics were no longer explored from this point onward.

But why was this approach further continued and established at all? To answer this question, it is helpful to revisit Romney's statement that the creation of 3D graphics is nothing more than a simulation of human vision. In this context, the importance he attaches to the concept of objectivity should also be examined more closely. Examining the sources Romney draws on from the fields of optics as well as film and television technology reveals that the meaning the original authors attributed to the terms "subjective" and "objective" differs from the logic on which Romney bases them. He adds his own interpretation of the terms. This deviation makes Romney's use of the words seem paradoxical, if not misleading. Romney's decision to work with these sources is based on the question of which parameters from photography or the field of moving images could also be informative for the creation of computer graphics. In the above-mentioned sources by Jones and MacAdam, to which Romney refers to derive his objective criteria, greater importance is placed on the intuitive perception of humans in the production of images than on physical parameters alone. If one thinks back to Coons and Rule or Fetter, this way of thinking seems familiar – and in their 1967 paper Evans, Romney et al. also aimed for images that can be "felt." Regarding the reproduction of photographic images, for example, MacAdam emphasizes, "[w]ithout psychophysical relationships, the results of optical measurements tell little about the quality of tone reproduction."[70] As MacAdam explains, the criteria for reproduction are, because of this, determined empirically based on subjective perception using a test group of people. Concerning this aspect, MacAdam refers to Jones, whom Romney also cites. Jones explains why a physically correct image is often unsatisfactory on a psychophysical level:

> From the physical point of view, a *perfect* reproduction, that is perfect *objective* photographic quality, is obtained when the brightness and brightness differences in the illuminated positive are identical with those in the object or scene photographed. However, such a positive would, in general, fail to reproduce with satisfactory fidelity the subjective impression of the original because of the difference (usually very great) between the visual field environment of the original and that of the reproduction.[71]

Against this background, it seems contradictory that Romney speaks of objective criteria that are used to generate 3D computer graphics, because the field of research that he cites in support of this is conversely concerned with the question of why purely objective and physically correct criteria for reproducing the real environment are not satisfactory for human perception. Consequently, the criteria that Romney describes as objective could be defined as subjective perception criteria. These criteria are only objective in the sense that they can be used to repeatedly produce images of the same quality and according to comparable standards, similar to what MacAdam and Jones sought to achieve for photography.

Although central features of early computer graphic image aesthetics can be traced back to the simulation of physical phenomena, such as the relationship between light and shadow or the functioning of a camera, including the perspective distortions generated in the lens, an essential component of image-aesthetic criteria is based on these so-called psychophysical insights. When Romney uses the term objective, he merges the interaction of these two areas: The physical phenomena, on the one hand, and the human perception of them, on the other. The coupling of these two aspects has emerged in the form of what I call the maxim of believability in the work of Coons and Fetter as an essential aesthetic characteristic of the production of graphics and computer graphics, and it also remains an essential component of the visual-aesthetic approach at the *University of Utah*, as can be seen in Romney's work.

7.1.2 Smooth Shading – Henri Gouraud and the Bridge to Today's 3D Software

Another major success occurred at the end of the first research period in June 1970. It made the subsequent investigations in the second research period between January 1971 and December 1972 much faster and easier to progress: As part of his dissertation, Gary S. Watkins developed a new algorithm that was designed to be implemented in a processor as a stand-alone hardware component and which could then be coupled with any computer system to calculate surface and color information of virtual objects on a display in real time.[72] Evans' second report of the new research period shows that Watkins completed the processor by the end of 1971.[73] He directly optimized the previous methods, achieving one of Evans' key objectives: developing a computer graphics system that not only displays images but also allows the user to work interactively with the displayed objects. This objective remained central to the second research period.[74]

Although Watkins was able to improve upon previous methods with his algorithm, and the graphics produced by the existing methods were satisfactory for those involved in the research project, all available shading approaches produced an angular appearance as soon as the models contained curved surfaces. If the polygons were only used to represent flat surfaces, this visual phenomenon was not visible (see Figures 7.4–7.6). To overcome this problem, the French mathematician Henri Gouraud[75] developed a new algorithm as part of Evans' research project, which made it possible to display surfaces with smooth color gradients in a simple way. Evans explains the problem in the first report of the new research period as follows:

> The shading techniques previously developed at the University of Utah by Romney [1], Warnock [2], and Watkins [3] *seemed* to be "the way to go," but introduced two problems:
>
> 1. Hidden parts suppression for curved surfaces is not easily done;
> 2. Approximation of the surface with small planar polygons, although better than the line drawing method, still conveyed some undesirable visual effect caused by the artificial texture brought about by the parameter spacing.[76]

Until then, the only way to visualize curved surfaces was to approximate their actual shape with a larger number of polygons. While this approach made the individual polygonal surfaces much smaller, it also resulted in larger amounts of data. Consequently, this significantly increased the computing time for an image.[77] The method that Gouraud developed to solve the problem of angular surfaces is still relevant from a production-aesthetic perspective, as has already been pointed out in Section 2.1. For example, his approach is still used today in the 3D graphics software *Cinema 4D*. To further investigate the developments at the *University of Utah*, Gouraud's research contribution and his underlying intentions will now be presented first, followed by a brief look at other protagonists whose work also still significantly characterizes the production of 3D graphics today. The focus here is on Bui Tuong Phong, Edwin Catmull and James F. Blinn. This concluding production-aesthetic discussion prepares the ground for the next part of this study, in which I will explore the question of where the visual ideas that might have guided all these researchers' work originated. Catmull and his company Pixar will come into focus again there.

Further developments at the *University of Utah* continue to focus on the pursuit of a realistic visual language. Gouraud also links his research directly to a specific form of realistic visual aesthetics. In the abstract he notes,

> [t]he research describes a method for producing shaded pictures of curved surfaces. It uses a small polygon approximation of the surface to solve efficiently the hidden parts detection, and then computes the shading on each polygon in such a way that visual discontinuities between adjacent polygons disappear, thus restoring the apparent smoothness of the surface and increasing greatly the realism of the pictures produced.[78]

Even in this final shaping phase of 3D graphics, the concept of realism retains its familiar meaning in accordance with the maxim of believability. What characterizes Gouraud's statement here is the concept of "restoring." Since smooth surfaces could not be displayed as halftone images with the polygon approximation until his approach was developed, Gouraud's method does not, strictly speaking, *restore* a soft surface but *produces* it in the first place. This observation raises the question of what state Gouraud was actually referring to when he spoke of a restoration process. It can be assumed that he was referring to a pictorial aesthetic that existed only theoretically, in the imagination, but which had not yet been realized. As computer graphics came closer to this ideal, researchers became more certain that they could achieve a level of realism that had previously only existed in the imagination. This demonstrates that the technology was based on a pictorial concept from the outset and that it was not the technological limitations that dictated the image aesthetic. This dynamic can also still be observed in current developments in the field of 3D graphics – today, the goal is still to bring the visual concept conceived at that time to life using available technology or by developing the necessary new technology. Examples of this will be given later.[79]

Gouraud presented his idea in a conference paper in 1971. The starting point for his approach was also the hidden line problem. He points out in the paper that models with curved surfaces are particularly difficult to understand when presented as line drawings if the lines in the back of an object are also visible. As he explains in his dissertation, this is especially true "when the surface is not a well known shape – sphere, cone, torus – that the pattern recognition aptitude of our mind recognizes more easily."[80] This statement illustrates that, like his previous colleagues, Gouraud started with human perception. The definition for the field of shading he provides in his conference paper continues this line of thought: "In attempting to represent a scene, the shading technique is subject to all the psychological illusions present in the visual process."[81] Specifically, Gouraud's statement refers to a physiological phenomenon of the human visual apparatus described by Ernst Mach that affects the perception of color gradients. According to Mach, when uniformly colored surfaces are aligned next to each other and together produce a brightness gradient, the human eye perceives a gradient on each surface individually. This phenomenon occurs with colored surfaces as well as with black, white or gray values. Each uniformly colored surface appears darker toward the edge of the next lighter surface and lighter toward the edge of the next darker surface. Thus, the overall contrast between the individual colored surfaces increases significantly (Figure 7.7).[82] For Gouraud and his 3D models with

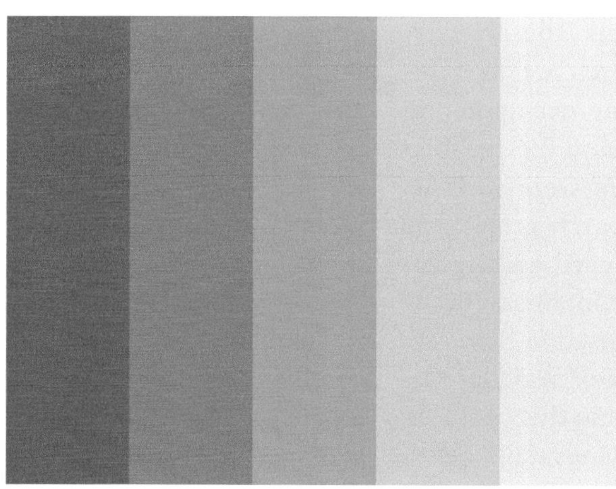

FIGURE 7.7 Illustration by the author, *Mach bands*, 2025, 2D graphic.

curved surfaces made up of individual polygons with different gray values, the so-called Mach bands posed a particular challenge.[83] As Gouraud describes, even a higher number of polygons and the resulting reduction in the size of the individual surfaces could not solve the problem described by Mach.[84] It was this limitation that motivated Gouraud to develop a smoothing algorithm. Until then, for the purpose of shading, a color value was calculated for each point on the image surface where a virtual object was located. Gouraud suggested changing this color value to create a smooth appearance (Figure 7.8).[85] This new color value would then not reflect the actual physical appearance of the polygons, but rather an imaginary uniform surface of the object.[86] It is therefore an illusion. To justify this approach, Gouraud refers to painting:

> In fact artists have known for a long time how to create a three-dimensional illusion on a flat canvas by painting it with the appropriate shade. By giving to each small polygon approximating our surface some appropriate shade, we might restore the illusion of the smooth surface we were originally trying to display.[87]

Gouraud's approach once again raised the question of the dichotomy between efficient images, on the one hand, and appealing, realistic images, on the other. He points out in his paper that the previous reason for the flat presentation of the individual polygons was that they could be calculated more efficiently in this way.[88] At the same time, he notes that his own approach only incurs minimal time losses for improved realism. He presents his findings by making a direct comparison between his own and Watkins' method. The comparison with Watkins is well suited for Gouraud, as he built directly on his colleague's approach, designing his own algorithm so that it could later be implemented in Watkins' processor.[89] To illustrate the differences between the two methods, Gouraud presented two pairs of images, each with identical content. In both cases, one can see rectangular curved surfaces; however, he

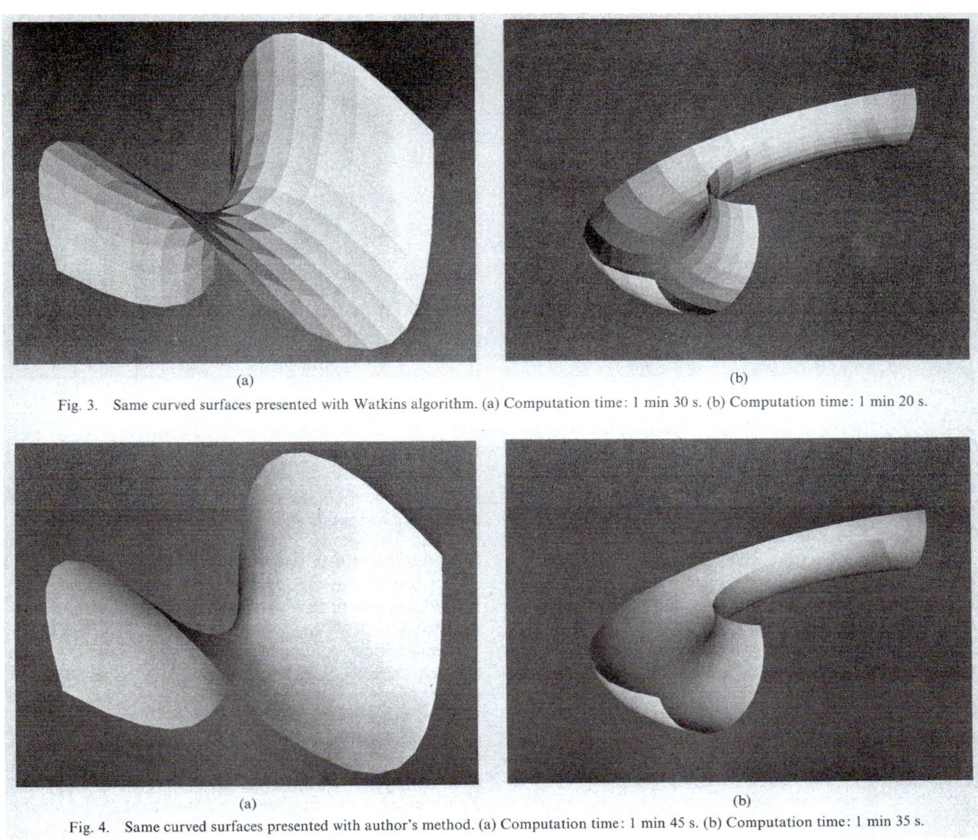

FIGURE 7.8 Henri Gouraud, *Same curved surfaces presented with Watkins algorithm* and *Same curved surfaces presented with author's method*, 1971, computer rendering. (Reprinted with permission from IEEE Transactions on Computers.)

generated one image with his own calculation model and the other with Watkins' calculation model. While Watkins' algorithm produced an angular appearance, Gouraud's method produced a smooth surface. As Gouraud also notes in the caption, his approach took only 15 seconds longer (Figure 7.8).[90]

Overall, Gouraud's work clearly shows that he maintained the logic of Evans' and Romney's earlier reflections, as well as those expressed previously by people such as Coons. His concept of realism can be related to this, but apart from the physiological aspects observed by Mach, Gouraud offered no additional explanations as to why he believed the pictorial aesthetic he was striving for was adequate. Only the application examples he provided for his algorithm suggest that he followed a similar line of reasoning, for example, to that of Sutherland in his development of *Sketchpad*. Sutherland attested a universality to his program, and Gouraud recognized the same potential in his algorithm: "The generality and the simplicity of the smooth shading technique presented here makes it possible to represent with great realism a large new class of objects."[91] He saw specific application examples in the field of flight simulation, for instance, or in the field of industrial design, particularly in automotive design.[92] However, Gouraud legitimized the universality of his algorithm with experimental examples that are completely outside the aviation or automotive industry. In the conclusion of his dissertation, he therefore summarizes,

> we might examine the different areas where the smooth shading technique could be applied. Quite obviously, these areas will be found in the world of simulation, but the drastic improvement in the realism of the pictures produced does open to the computer simulation some new domains. One of them, which is under study at the University of Utah, is the simulation of a dancer. In order to make this simulation acceptable for a choreographer, it is quite important to reproduce with realism not only the movements of the body, but also the shape of this body.[93]

Like Sutherland, Gouraud also presents here an artistic-experimental application of his algorithm to prove the generality of his approach. He does not address the possibility of creative approaches that work with different aesthetic standards – approaches that could not be reconciled with his algorithm. Rather, he provides a recreation of his wife's face on the computer in preparation for the dance project (Figures 7.9–7.11) as particular proof of the comprehensive utilization possibilities of his approach. However, he admits that "[a]lthough it is true that in most respects this model is far from the original, the likeness between the two, compared with the results obtained with previous methods, constitutes the best example of the qualities of the smooth shading technique."[94]

In summary, Gouraud's approach is similar to those of Coons, Fetter and Sutherland in that for him, the concept of realism coincides with a notion of universality. Although Gouraud's approach brought him significantly closer to this goal of achieving realism, he points out problems and necessary further research in his dissertation's outlook that would better realize the imagined pictorial ideal. Notably, many of his suggestions were accomplished within a few years. For example, his proposal to be able to color polygons across borders and give them a surface structure was implemented just a few years later by Edwin Catmull and James Blinn. At the same time, Gouraud expressed the concern that any innovation should not result in a loss of real-time calculation, once again addressing the problem of the dichotomy between "beauty" and "efficiency."[95] The realization of the pictorial concept, especially the pursuit of a specific type of realism capable of achieving the maxim of believability, essentially ended with Gouraud's introduction of the possibility to represent objects with curved surfaces. The individual developments that have taken place since Gouraud, or even those that are taking place today, can therefore be seen as a direct continuation of this achievement, as all progress conceptually strives toward the same goal. For the first time, the common context of meaning of 3D graphics is becoming somewhat clearer. Although firmly established in technological means, it actually exists outside of technology, even before the mechanisms to express it were available. When I present Phong, Blinn and Catmull's contributions to this history below, this step serves to confirm this impression and at the same time to lead into the style-historical part of the investigation.

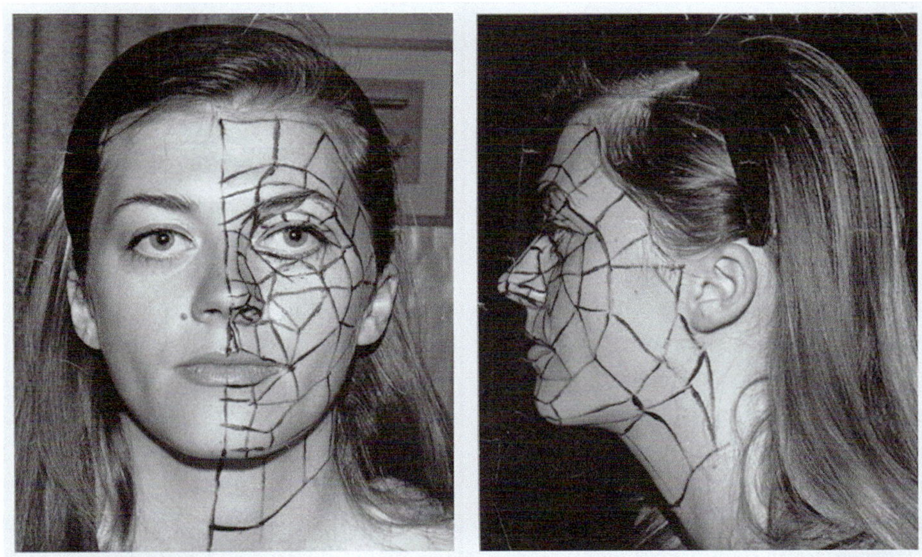

FIGURE 7.9 Henri Gouraud, *Fig. 26 – Two orthogonal views of the author's wife which have been used to input the data of figures 28 and 29 into the computer*, 1971, photography. (Reprinted with permission from Henri Gouraud.)

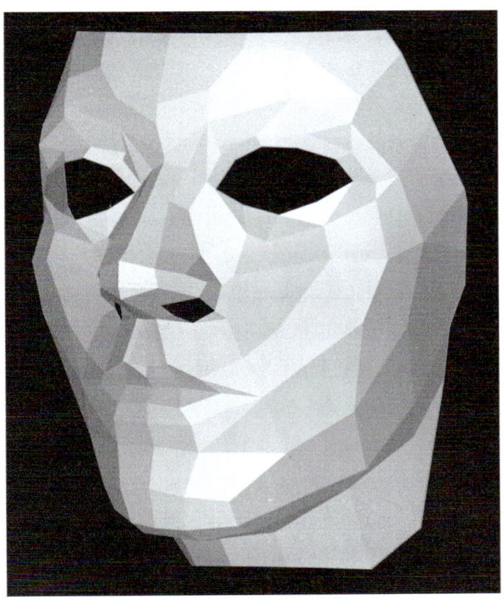

FIGURE 7.10 Henri Gouraud, *Fig. 28 – Polygon approximation of figure 27* (reference to portrait of his wife), 1971, computer rendering. (Reprinted with permission from Henri Gouraud.)

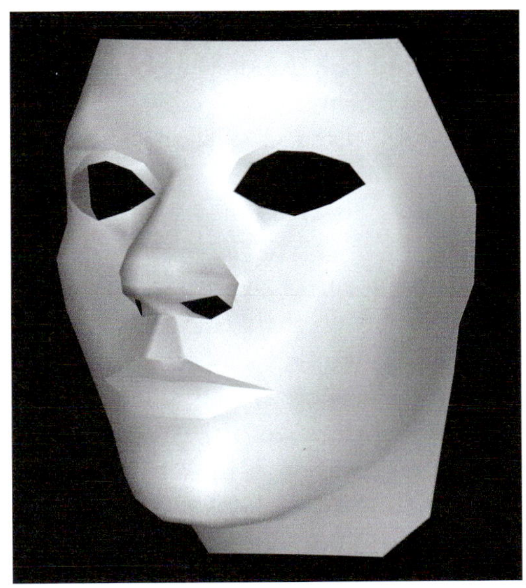

FIGURE 7.11 Henri Gouraud, *Fig. 29 – The smooth shading technique applied to the same geometric data as in figure 28* (reference to portrait of his wife), 1971, computer rendering. (Reprinted with permission from Henri Gouraud.)

7.1.3 Texture and Structure – The Goals after the Goal

Consistent with the results of the previous sub-section, Evans notes in the second report of the new research period, dated December 1971, that the primary components in the graphics area had been finalized.[96] From then on, the focus shifted to improving the technical realization of the achievements made in the field of computer graphics – a point he also reiterates in the last two subsequent reports. The aim was to work more interactively with the virtual environment and models, and to display the images more smoothly.[97]

Goals for the final year of the research period included improving display errors in digital image reproduction[98] and coloring polygons beyond or across their edges: "This results in an unlimited range of colors and patterns, thus allowing a more realistic imitation of the real world."[99] Additionally, computer animation became an increasingly relevant topic in the context of the reports, as demonstrated, for example, by the deformation and animation of computer-generated models and the movement of objects in space.[100] Catmull has also contributed to the topic of animation – his research on the subject is mentioned in Evans' last report.[101] However, as animation-related developments are not my area of focus, I will not explore this topic in depth here. Instead, my focus remains on image generation, a field in which Catmull has also made significant contributions. He will now be presented alongside Phong and Blinn. After the completion of Evans' research project in December 1972, all three continued conducting research at the *University of Utah*. The individual projects were still supported by military funds[102] and generally continued to take place under the supervision of Evans and Sutherland. Steven Coons was also consulted as a supervisor for some of the projects, including Edwin Catmull's dissertation, which he completed in 1974.[103]

What was the focus of the three colleagues' work and to what extent do their research interests from that time still play a role today? One answer can be found in Gouraud's work, as his results had significant limitations in terms of the engineers' common goal. For instance, although his algorithm provided a solution to represent surfaces in a largely smooth manner (and it still does today), it did not take into account the edges of the objects (and it still does not today). As can be seen in Figure 7.11, for example, the silhouette of the models still revealed their actual polygonal and therefore angular structure. All three of the research projects discussed below addressed this issue.[104] Additionally, they are directly linked to Gouraud's predictions in his dissertation regarding further research questions, such as texturing models and giving them a surface structure.[105] While Phong focused on improving Gouraud's shading algorithm, Catmull worked on an approach to enable textures. Blinn aimed to provide objects with a surface structure.[106] The projects will now be presented, starting with Phong's approach. Subsequently, Catmull's and Blinn's projects will be put in relation to Phong's.

As the title of Phong's 1973 dissertation *Illumination for Computer Generated Images* suggests, he aimed to study the behavior of light when it hits virtual objects. Gouraud's approach was not yet mature enough for Phong in this respect, as Gouraud's algorithm could only calculate light reflections at the edges of the polygons and not at any point on an object's surface.[107] Although Phong wanted to develop a new mathematical solution for Gouraud's calculation model, the motive that Phong had for his intention is still reminiscent of Gouraud's. In a 1975 paper presenting his algorithm, Phong states, "[h]uman visual perception and the fundamental laws of optics are considered in the development of a shading rule that provides better quality and increased realism in generated images."[108] Phong also built on Romney's line of argument, because like Romney, Phong assumed that the decision as to whether an image is successful and looks appealing lies in the eye of the observer:

> Unlike a photograph of a real world scene, a computer generated shaded picture is made from a numerical model, which is stored in the computer as an objective description. When an image is then generated from this model, the human visual system makes the final subjective analysis. Obtaining a close image correspondence to the eye's subjective interpretation of the real object is then the goal. The computer system can be compared to an artist who paints an object from its description and not from direct observation of the object. But unlike the artist, who can correct the painting if it does not look right to him, the computer that generates the picture does not receive feedback about the quality of the synthetic images, because the human visual system is the final receptor.[109]

Phong adds that, to do justice to these subjective perception criteria, "[w]e must at the outset define the degree of realism we wish to attain, and fix certain goals to be accomplished."[110] He mentions three goals for creating realism to illustrate his ideas, even though he acknowledges that they are not comprehensive:

(1) the ability to calculate computer images in color and in real time, (2) the representation of objects with smooth surfaces and (3) the reduction of digital artifacts that arise during image calculation.[111] Phong demonstrates the realism of his computer graphics by comparing his computer-generated images with photographs showing the same motif. For his comparisons he used representations of spheres, cylinders and cones (Figures 7.12–7.17).[112] Similar to Romney, Phong's visual aesthetics are thus orientated toward photographic parameters, but here too with the restriction that it is not photography that is the model for image creation, but human perception. Unlike Romney, Phong does not address the parameters used to create photographs at that time. Nevertheless, by imitating the aesthetics of photographs with his 3D graphics, Phong also ultimately reacted to the perceptual parameters on which the reproduction methods of the time were based in order to do justice to people's subjective visual perception.

Although Phong's algorithm produced much more precise results than Gouraud's preliminary work – Phong used Warnock's algorithm and his molecule to illustrate this (Figure 7.18)[113] – Phong was also unable to completely solve the problem of the angular appearance of the polygons at the edges of the objects. For Figures 7.12–7.17 he found a calculation model that could generate an almost flawless representation of the round edges. However, in his dissertation Phong pointed out that this required a very extensive data set, which would also be computationally intensive to handle.[114] And although his algorithm is still used in various graphics applications today, work on this and other problems continued after Phong. The subsequent developments responded directly to some of Phong's predictions as expressed in the final sentence of his conclusion: "Finally a greater improvement in the quality of the synthetic pictures will be obtained when shadows and the texture of the objects can be simulated. When solutions to these problems are found, a new world will be opened in the domain of the computer-generated images."[115] In line with Phong's prediction, two areas of today's work with 3D graphics that were also developed in Utah in the following years are the creation of textures and the calculation of unevenness in an object's surface. Similar to Phong's reference to Gouraud's preliminary work, both Catmull in 1974 and Blinn in 1978 refer to Gouraud's and Phong's previous approaches.[116] Both, Catmull and Blinn, emphasize the respective advantages and disadvantages of the shading methods to build on them in their own work. In his dissertation, Catmull develops the aim "to produce high quality computer-generated images of surfaces and curved

FIGURE 7.12 Bui Tuong Phong, *Figure 4.19 Real spheres with different light orientations* (here only image (a) can be seen), 1973, photography.

FIGURE 7.13 Bui Tuong Phong, *Figure 4.20 Spheres rendered with improved shading technique* (here only image (a) can be seen), 1973, computer rendering.

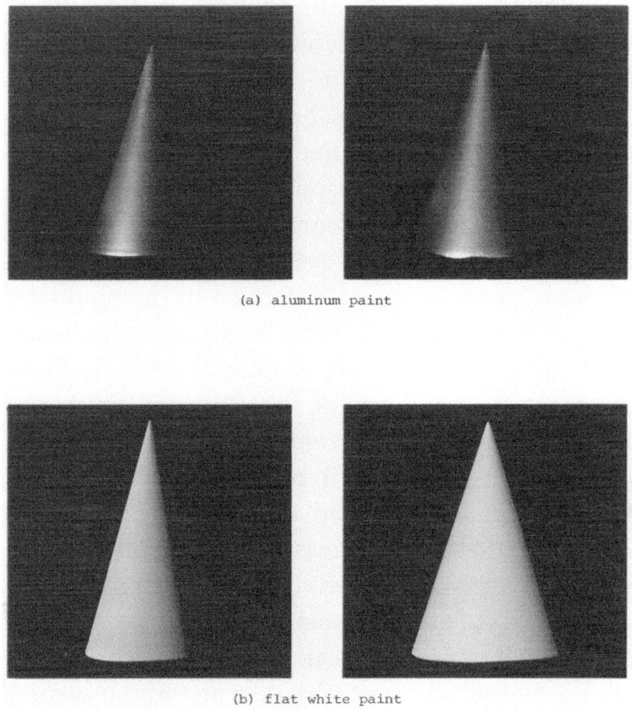

FIGURE 7.14 Bui Tuong Phong, *Figure 4.15 Real cones with different light orientations and surface finishes*, 1973, photography.

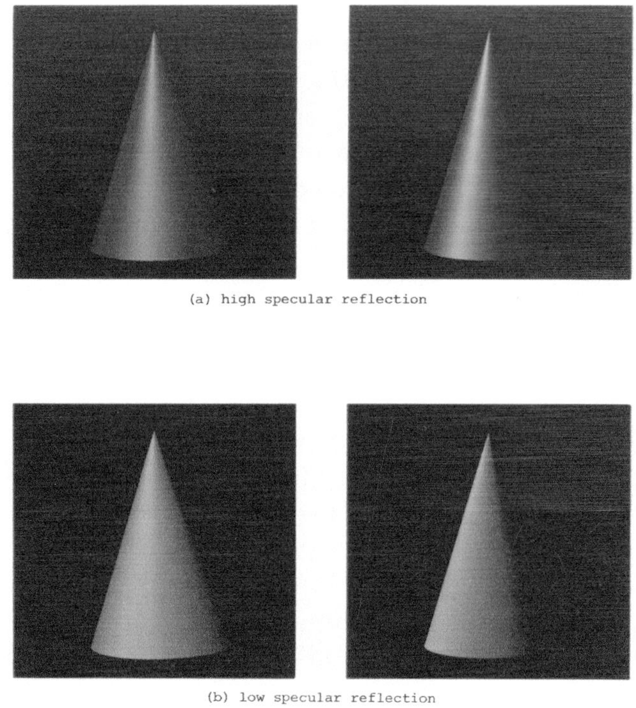

FIGURE 7.15 Bui Tuong Phong, *Figure 4.16 Cones rendered with improved shading technique*, 1973, computer rendering.

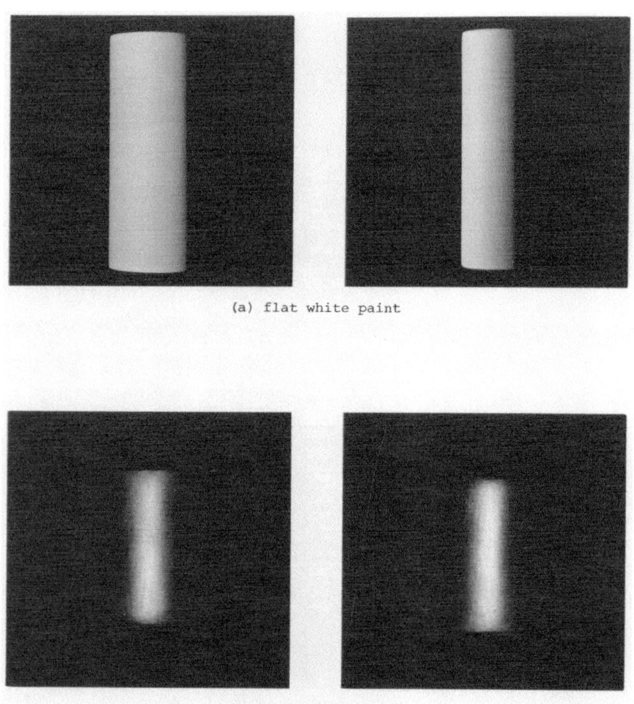

FIGURE 7.16 Bui Tuong Phong, *Figure 4.17 Real cylinders with different light orientations and surface finishes*, 1973, photography.

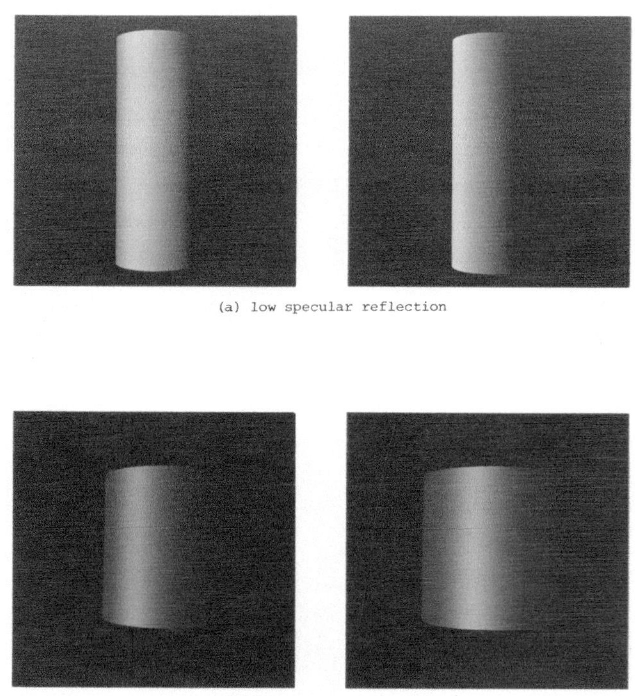

FIGURE 7.17 Bui Tuong Phong, *Figure 4.18 Cylinders rendered with improved shading technique*, 1973, computer rendering.

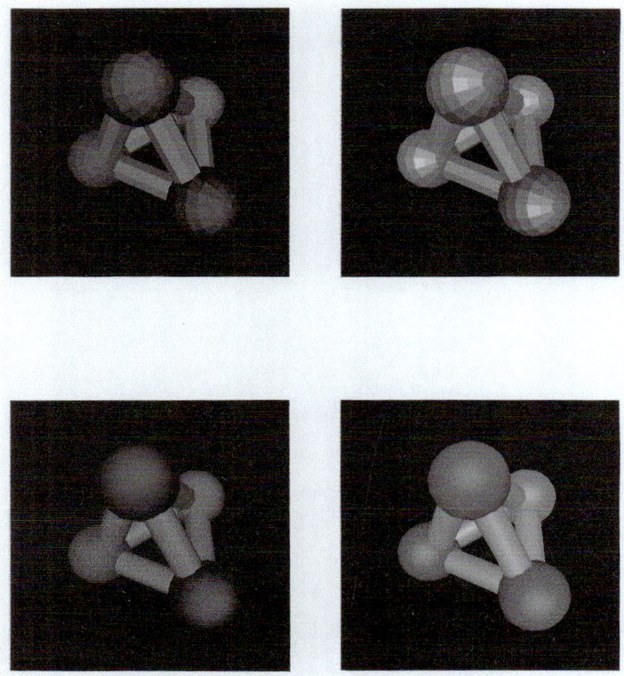

FIGURE 7.18 Bui Tuong Phong, *Figure 4.12 Molecule with different shading techniques* (t. l.: Warnock shading, t. r.: Warnock shading with highlight, b. l.: Gouraud shading, b. r.: Phong shading), 1973, computer rendering.

objects."[117] His project can therefore also be linked to a description by Blinn, which he wrote four years after Catmull's work. Once again this description confirms Evans' statement that no new developments were being made: "In the branch of computer graphics known colloquially as 'hidden surface elimination' the goals have traditionally been to generate more and more realistic pictures of three dimensional objects and to produce them at greater and greater speed."[118]

According to Catmull, what were the characteristics that made it possible to create what he called "high quality computer-generated images"? Catmull only explicitly addresses the criteria that, in his opinion, characterize a good image in a few places in his dissertation. Like many of his contemporaries, he no longer fundamentally negotiated what kind of imagery he was striving for. Although he implies in his dissertation that he also associated a realistic visual language with perspective distortion,[119] his ideas of adding textures or images to virtual objects, as well as using the same method to create shadows and reflections, suggest that his research merely aimed to improve upon previous developments. His image examples of transparent objects can also prove this.[120]

Despite the few references to visual aesthetics in his dissertation, Catmull had a very clear idea of imagery, as demonstrated by his development of rendering algorithms a few years later and his role in founding the *Pixar Animation Studios*. As also explained in Section 2.1, rendering involves transferring a virtual scene into a two-dimensional image. The rendering algorithms and Pixar are closely linked in terms of company history, because Pixar was initially a hardware manufacturer that enabled the creation and processing of images with the *Pixar Image Computer*. These initial steps later gave rise to rendering software and, subsequently, an animation studio. The company still markets its rendering system *RenderMan* today.[121] However, Catmull's dissertation already focused specifically on "how to model objects and then how to render them."[122] The project can therefore be seen as the foundation for his later work, which will be discussed in more detail in the next chapter.

Regarding the creation of 3D models, Catmull developed a method that made it possible to generate virtual objects using mathematical functions and also to texture them, giving them a more complex coloring than had previously been possible. He illustrated his concept by applying a wall texture to various objects (Figure 7.19). Catmull also used the so-called "Coons Surface Patch" to calculate the models,[123] which explains why he mentions Coons in the first sentence of his acknowledgments and why Coons was also a member of his dissertation committee together with Evans and Sutherland. With his approach, Catmull decided against the use of polygon-based models, which he justified with the fact that the problem of the angular silhouette does not occur with the mathematical model of the surface patch. At the same time, he acknowledged that calculating surfaces using mathematical functions offers less freedom in the creation of models:

> Polygons, and sometimes quadric patches, are used to model objects in current shaded-picture methods. There are some difficulties with using these simple pieces to model or approximate free-form curved surfaces. Approximation with polygons gives a faceted effect and a silhouette made up of straight-line

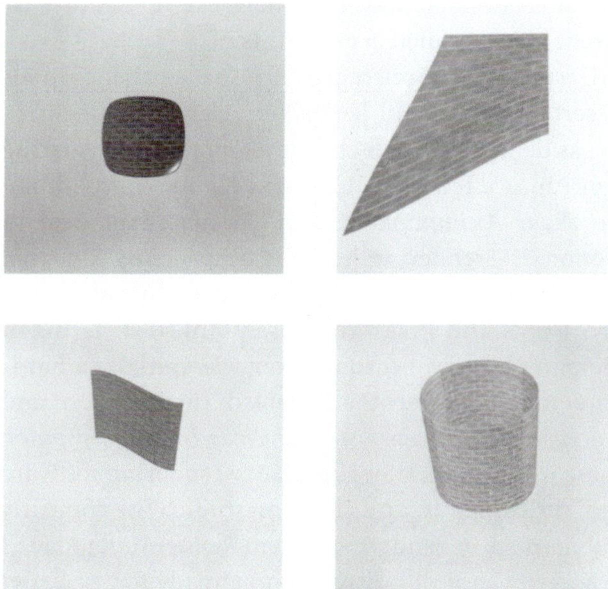

FIGURE 7.19 Edwin Catmull, *Picture 18 – The brick image mapped respectively onto a single rounded patch, a stretched patch, an S curved patch, and a cylinder of four patches*, 1974, computer rendering. (Reprinted with permission from Edwin Catmull.)

> segments. Quadric patches, while smooth in appearance, are not suitable for modeling arbitrary forms, since they don't provide enough degrees of freedom to satisfy slope continuity between patches.[124]

With the possibility of texturing the mathematical patches, Catmull developed one of the most essential functions for 3D graphics, even though polygon models can also be textured.[125] Blinn's approach of creating so-called bump maps built directly on Catmull's preliminary work. Blinn expanded on the concept of textures, including information that allowed a model to be displayed with surface irregularities in addition to its color. He illustrated this with the example of an orange peel (Figure 7.20). In his dissertation Blinn explains how his approach builds on Catmull's:

> Even with a very accurate lighting model the rendered surfaces tend to look artificial due to their extreme smoothness. What is needed is a means of simulating the surface irregularities

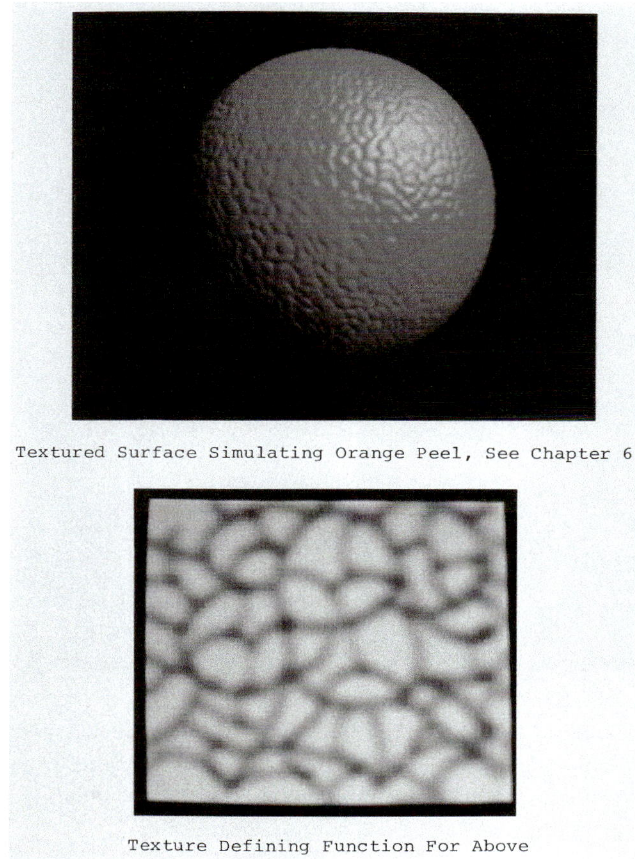

FIGURE 7.20 James F. Blinn, top: *Textured Surface Simulating Orange Peel*, 1978, computer rendering; bottom: *Texture Defining Function For Above*, 1978, texture patch with hand drawn pattern. (Reprinted with permission from James F. Blinn.)

> that are characteristic of real surfaces. These could, of course, be generated by explicitly modelling each wrinkle and fold. Hopefully, there are methods for avoiding this. Catmull introduced the idea of using the patch parameter values to index into a texture definition function which scales the intensity of the reflected light.[126]

According to Blinn, his method therefore offers "extensions to the texture mapping approach to modulate other surface properties to simulate roughness more realistically."[127] Catmull's first priority when working on the textures was to display the models, including their colored surfaces, appropriately on a screen, which is why rendering was such a central issue for him. When outputting to the screen, the screen grid also had to be considered. This means that the mathematically calculated "images," which initially only existed as a description in the computer, had to be translated into the screen's grid. In his dissertation, Catmull explains that the display is made up of individual lines, which in turn are made up of individual rectangular "raster elements," or what is commonly referred to as pixels today.[128] The resolution determines how many of these raster elements an image is composed of. The display available to Catmull had 512 lines and 512 raster elements per line. In order to be able to output a mathematical calculation of an image in the computer in the form of these raster elements, a color value had to be determined for each raster element.[129] This translation process is known as sampling and often produces undesirable artifacts in the finished image that have to be circumvented at great expense. One of these problems associated with the sampling process is aliasing, which remains relevant today. It is the staircase effect that appears on the contours of image elements that are not perfectly horizontal or vertical (as was also addressed in Section 2.1). Catmull explains the phenomenon as follows: "Aliasing occurs because we are sampling an image which has information that the raster-display cannot possibly reproduce."[130] He adds a footnote to the term "image" here, which is particularly interesting for my discussion, as it provides at least a glimpse into Catmull's understanding of images: "This image we are sampling exists only as a high resolution description in the computer, as contrasted with an actual photograph."[131] This statement shows that Catmull was talking about an image even before it could be seen. Therefore, it can be concluded that he perceived an image as such already once it had been fully calculated according to all the predetermined criteria. The process of displaying it was of secondary importance. This observation aligns with my conclusion from the previous sub-section on Gouraud. The examination of his research also revealed that his idea of the images to be created with the computer always existed first, and only afterward was an attempt made to bring this idea to life with the available technology. And if that technology did not yet exist, it would be developed with the desired image aesthetic in mind. Catmull implicitly took up this idea by speaking of an image that cannot yet be seen. In a sense, he merely presented the technical fact that, from a purely mathematical perspective, images could be produced with much higher resolutions than the screens available at the time were capable of displaying. However, it was precisely these technical limitations, which meant that engineers like Catmull had to rely on their imagination to create the images.

The visual-aesthetic criteria that Catmull had in mind can be explored by placing his later work in connection with Pixar at the center of the investigation. In the following part I will therefore analyze the image aesthetics and stylistic history of the image criteria used by Pixar. This will provide a deeper understanding of the production of all computer-graphic images stemming from this genealogy. What essential results can be summarized from this part for the following part? Of particular importance is the fact that at the beginning of the research carried out at the *University of Utah*, a common goal was established: Most central to this was to find an efficient solution to the hidden line problem in order to move away from the wireframe representation of virtual objects in the long term and to be able to show them as opaque image elements that react to light and show shading. The motivation behind this common goal was to create images that could be intuitively understood or even felt. A purely objective approach to the topic of computer-based imagery is therefore not evident in the researchers' work, although they considered their images to be objective, as they believed that how an image feels to someone is an objective criterion. To achieve their goal, the researchers not only examined the technical aspects of improving the representation of opaque objects – such as displaying curved surfaces, textures and structures – but also how to improve the quality of computer-generated images from a psychophysiological point of view. To this end, findings that were originally communicated for the field of reproduction technology, such as photography, were particularly taken into account. As previously at MIT, the guiding principle remained the maxim of believability, in other words, the idea of a central perspective image of our surroundings created in the human eye. Comparisons with the functioning of the camera lens also remain a reference point at the *University of Utah*.

The final parts of this study no longer put emphasis on the question of *how* the computer images are created, but rather *why* they have been developed as described in this and the previous parts. Thus, the focus shifts from the motive of individuals to an overarching motive that all pursue together and which as I propose characterizes the common context of meaning of computer graphics on a more profound level.

NOTES

1. See Steven A. Coons, *Surfaces for Computer-Aided Design of Space Forms* (Cambridge: Massachusetts Institute of Technology, 1967).
2. Gaboury also lists the research interests that I analyze in this chapter, but he attributes them solely to the research project in Utah and not to Johnson. In addition, Gaboury describes the criteria he highlights as "base conditions for any contemporary graphical system." Jacob Gaboury, *Image Objects. An Archaeology of Computer Graphics* (Cambridge: MIT Press, 2021), 34. This is a statement that I can confirm with my study, but that I at the same time link to the question of *why* these approaches have shaped the development of 3D computer graphics from the very beginning.
3. Ivan E. Sutherland, "Sketchpad: A Man-Machine Graphical Communication System" (technical report, ed. Alan Blackwell and Kerry Rodden, University of Cambridge, 2003), Computer Laboratory (UCAM-CL-TR-574), 110, 114.
4. Timothy E. Johnson, "Sketchpad III: Three Dimensional Graphical Communication with a Digital Computer" (Master's thesis, Massachusetts Institute of Technology, 1963), MIT Libraries, DSpace@MIT (33828890), 3.
5. In his own words, Johnson explains the function of the four views as follows: "The four projections viewed on the scope are not four independent displays of stored two-dimensional information; rather, space coordinates in a single data structure are transformed into two-dimensional images for display. Rotating, translating, magnifying, and changing the perspective does not affect the data structure, (local transformation excluded). A line being drawn in any one view is simultaneously seen in the three other views; lines are in effect drawn in three-dimensions and simultaneously fed back for display." Johnson, "Sketchpad III," 5.
6. John T. Rule and Steven A. Coons, *Graphics* (New York: McGraw-Hill, 1961), 35. To achieve this unambiguous representation, Rule and Coons suggest using the orthographic projection method, a method with which the individual top views from different sides of an object can be determined in order to be able to draw the object from above, from the side and from the front. The individual views are therefore the width, height and depth of an object. See Rule and Coons, *Graphics*, 36, 39. Although this is a standardized procedure, Rule and Coons themselves point out the arbitrary nature of the method: "The front, top, and right side views of an object related in the manner shown have been agreed upon as standard views. The names are quite arbitrary since we could have oriented the object to make any of its faces the front face, and in so doing, we would have obtained a different set or a different order of views. The names therefore can be said to apply only to the positions of the views on the paper." Rule and Coons, *Graphics*, 38. Johnson finally transfers the standardized procedure to the computer and also explains why he believes that four views are necessary in his application: "Clearly, at least two views are necessary, a top and front view, for instance, with one of the views convertible to perspective. Depth checking and continuity problems would be eliminated. But two views are not enough. A third independent view must be added to give the necessary micro-macro viewpoint feature. [...] A fourth view, as in Sketchpad III, offers the luxury of an additional viewpoint which aids visualization." Johnson, "Sketchpad III," 41.
7. Johnson, "Sketchpad III," 2.
8. In this context, he also explains that he considered various technological approaches for this requirement, such as stereoscopic visualization using two displays, but decided against this as the technical conditions were not yet satisfactory. In order to still be able to visually display depth information of an object, he chose the option of integrating four views into his program. See Johnson, "Sketchpad III," e.g. 2 and 16.
9. See Johnson, "Sketchpad III," 3–4, 16.
10. See Johnson, "Sketchpad III," 17.
11. See Johnson, "Sketchpad III," 24.
12. See Johnson, "Sketchpad III," 16.
13. See Johnson, "Sketchpad III," 17. See also Lawrence G. Roberts, "Machine Perception of Three-Dimensional Solids" (PhD diss., Massachusetts Institute of Technology, 1963), MIT Libraries, DSpace@MIT (33959125).
14. Johnson, "Sketchpad III," 17. He also points out here that it makes sense to work with straight lines because they do not change their shape after any transformation, but only their length – unlike curves, for example. See Johnson, "Sketchpad III," 17.
15. See Johnson, "Sketchpad III," 2, 9.
16. Johnson, "Sketchpad III," 37.
17. See Johnson, "Sketchpad III," 37.
18. Johnson, "Sketchpad III," 1.
19. Steven A. Coons, "An Outline of the Requirements for a Computer-Aided Design System," In *Proceedings of the Spring Joint Computer Conference – AFIPS '63*, ed. E. Calvin Johnson (New York: ACM Press, 1963), 300.
20. See Johnson, "Sketchpad III," 1.
21. David C. Evans, "Graphical Man/Machine Communications: November 1966" (research report, University of Utah, 1966), J. Willard Marriott Library (703452), 3.

22. The dates are derived from the reports. See endnote 25 in Section 2.2 in this study.
23. The research interests expressed in the reports relate to various possible applications for 3D computer graphics. A particular focus developed, for example, for use in the field of architecture or medicine, especially for cardiological examinations. See e.g. David C. Evans, "Graphical Man/Machine Communications: May 1967" (research report, University of Utah, 1967), J. Willard Marriott Library (704511), 3. In the later course of the project, further fields of investigation also developed, for example from 1968 onward the field of signal processing, which dealt with the translation of analog into digital signals and vice versa, both with regard to images and with regard to sounds. See David C. Evans, "Graphical Man/Machine communications: November 1968" (research report, University of Utah, 1968), J. Willard Marriott Library (703204), 7. A further achievement resulting from this research project was the ARPANET in 1970, the first type of the Internet. See David C. Evans, "Graphical Man/Machine Communications: May 1971" (research report, University of Utah, 1971), J. Willard Marriott Library (703517), 35. The report was not published until 1971.
24. See David C. Evans, "Graphical Man/Machine Communications: June 1972" (research report, University of Utah, 1972), J. Willard Marriott Library (702817), 18.
25. Gaboury also notes that the shading algorithms written by Gouraud and Phong in Utah at the time have hardly been further developed to this day: "While one might presume that these illusionistic algorithms are simply small steps on the road to a more accurate model for material effects such as curvature or smooth surfaces, in fact they have remained largely unchanged for the past forty years." Gaboury, *Image Objects*, 100.
26. Evans, "Graphical Man/Machine Communications: November 1966," 3.
27. See Gordon W. Romney, Gary S. Watkins and David C. Evans, "Real-Time Display of Computer Generated Half-Tone Perspective Pictures," in *Information Processing '68. Proceedings of IFIP Congress 1968. Volume 2 – Hardware, Applications*, ed. A. J. H. Morell (Amsterdam: North-Holland, 1969), 976. This early paper was later republished in Rosalee Wolfe's volume *Seminal Graphics: Pioneering Efforts That Shaped The Field*. See Gordon W. Romney, Gary S. Watkins and David C. Evans, "Real-Time Display of Computer Generated Half-Tone Perspective Pictures," in *Seminal Graphics: Pioneering Efforts That Shaped The Field, Volume 1*, ed. Rosalee Wolf (New York: ACM, 1998).
28. In the historical overview of *Kahlert School of Computing* at *University of Utah* special attribution to Romney is made in regard to these early renderings. See "History," University of Utah, accessed June 19, 2025, https://www.cs.utah.edu/resources/history/. See also "Ivan Sutherland – Complete Biography, History, and Inventions," History Computer, accessed June 20, 2025, https://web.archive.org/web/20220107123638/https:/history-computer.com/ivan-sutherland-complete-biography/. See also Gordon W. Romney, email to author, June 19, 2025.
29. Gordon W. Romney, "Computer Assisted Assembly and Rendering of Solids" (PhD diss., University of Utah, 1969), ProQuest (7003776), 155–56. Romney also points out that the computer-generated graphics on the paper of the physical final version of his thesis were actually printed using a halftone reproduction process. See Romney, "Rendering of Solids" (1969a), 156. Romney's dissertation was published again in two further editions, one of them written in a text format for use in computer graphics courses. See Gordon W. Romney, "Computer Assisted Assembly and Rendering of Solids," (technical report RADC-TR-69-365, Griffiss Air Force Base, 1969). Defense Technical Information Center (AD0753673); see also Gordon W. Romney, "Computer Assisted Assembly and Rendering of Solids," (technical report 4-20, University of Utah, 1970); see also Gordon W. Romney, email to author, June 19, 2025.
30. Evans, "Graphical Man/Machine Communications: May 1967," 1.
31. David C. Evans, "Graphical Man/Machine Communications: February 1968" (research report, University of Utah, 1968), J. Willard Marriott Library (707101), 1.
32. Evans, "Graphical Man/Machine Communications: February 1968," 6.
33. See Chris Wylie et al., "Half-Tone Perspective Drawings by Computer," in *Proceedings of the Fall Joint Computer Conference – AFIPS '67*, ed. ACM (New York: ACM Press, 1967). A technical report with the same name was also published at University of Utah by the same authors. See Chris Wylie et al., "Half-Tone Perspective Drawings by Computer," (technical report 4-2, University of Utah, 1967). Defense Technical Information Center (AD0761965). It was a few months later followed by another technical report by the same authors, except Alan Erdahl. See Gordon W. Romney et al., "Computer Generated Halftone Perspective Pictures," (technical report 4-3, University of Utah, 1968). These early renderings were also patented by Romney and his colleagues. See Gordon W. Romney et al., *Electrically-Generated Perspective Images*, U.S. Patent No. 3621214, 1970.
34. Wylie et al., "Half-Tone Perspective Drawings" (1967a), 49.
35. See Coons, "Requirements for a Computer-Aided Design System," 300.
36. See Wylie et al., "Half-Tone Perspective Drawings" (1967a), 49.

37. See Wylie et al., "Half-Tone Perspective Drawings" (1967a), 49.
38. See Roberts, "Machine Perception of Three-Dimensional Solids," 2, 54–55.
39. With reference to the paper, on which Evans, among others, collaborated, Romney notes, "[a] major portion of this thesis is a detailed description of an improvement over the initial algorithm used by this author to produce the first shaded renderings in February, 1967. Partial disclosures of the technique have been published previously, and the technique has been referred to in this thesis as the Romney algorithm. In the remainder of the thesis the algorithm will be referred to as RENDER." Romney, "Rendering of Solids" (1969a), 10–11.
40. This statement does not refer to different approaches and algorithms, but to the way in which different approaches and calculation models have repeatedly been used to try to realize a specific goal and come closer to it on the technical side.
41. Instead, the focus of the six-month research period was on the use of graphical methods to solve partial differential equations, the development of medical applications for the field of cardiology and the further development of an architecture program for modeling objects. In the latter sub-project, Douglas C. Engelbart from the *Stanford Research Institute*, who I have previously mentioned in this study, was consulted for support. See Evans, "Graphical Man/Machine Communications: November 1968," 1–7.
42. Reference is made, on the one hand, to a conference paper in which Evans, Romney and Watkins further developed the approaches from the earlier paper from 1967, and on the other hand, to an internally published technical report in which another colleague, John E. Warnock, presented a new calculation model for hidden lines. Evans also cites another paper on the implementation of a new programming language in the field of computer graphics. In addition, he mentions, for the first time, the company *Evans & Sutherland*, founded together with Sutherland, but only in relation to a processor they developed there and not in relation to computer graphics endeavors on which the company was also working. See David C. Evans, "Graphical Man/Machine Communications: May 1969" (research report, University of Utah, 1969), J. Willard Marriott Library (702679), 5–6.
43. Warnock, mentioned in the previous note, also completed his dissertation in the course of this six-month period. His work will be taken up selectively in the sub-section on Romney. See David C. Evans, "Graphical Man/Machine Communications: November 1969" (research report, University of Utah, 1969), J. Willard Marriott Library (706332), esp. 12 and 15.
44. See Romney, "Rendering of Solids" (1969a), 3–5.
45. See Romney, "Rendering of Solids" (1969a), 4–5.
46. While reports were produced on the NASA project, which were also available as research material, MAGI's own research was only documented for internal communication purposes. According to his list of references, Romney apparently had access to an internal MAGI document. James F. Blinn, on the other hand, who continued the research in Utah in the late 1970s, states in his dissertation: "A detailed description of their [MAGI's] algorithms has never been published." James F. Blinn, "Computer Display of Curved Surfaces" (PhD diss., University of Utah, 1978), J. Willard Marriott Library (105596), 42. See also Romney, "Rendering of Solids" (1969a), 164. The MAGI project was at least briefly presented in the journal *Datamation*. See MAGI, "3-D Simulated Graphics Offered by Service Bureau," *Datamation* 14, no. 2 (1986): 69. Two interim reports on the NASA project have been archived. Unfortunately, my request to NASA for access to the final report remained unanswered. See General Electric, "Modifications to Interim Visual Spaceflight Simulator. Sixth Quarterly Report. 12 April to 12 July 1966" (technical report, NASA Manned Spacecraft Center, 1966), NASA Technical Reports Server (19660030678); see General Electric, "Modifications to Interim Visual Spaceflight Simulator. Ninth Quarterly Report. 12 January to 12 April 1967" (technical report, NASA Manned Spacecraft Center, 1967), NASA Technical Reports Server (19670023039). Information on the NASA project is also provided by another *General Electric* report published in 1969 on a follow-up project that was financially supported by the *Air Force* instead of NASA. The technology used in this project was based on the infrastructure developed in 1967. Similar to the NASA project, the aim was to create a way for pilots or astronauts to learn their task of controlling an aircraft or spaceship in a simulated environment. For the simulated flights and landings, it was therefore desirable to be able to present corresponding scenarios in real time. See Robert A. Schumacker, et al., "Study for Applying Computer-Generated Images to Visual Simulation" (technical report, General Electric Company, 1969). Defense Technical Information Center (AD0700375).
47. See John E. Warnock, "A Hidden Surface Algorithm for Computer Generated Half-Tone Pictures" (PhD diss., University of Utah, 1969). J. Willard Marriott Library (1602152). Warnock was later involved in the founding of *Adobe Systems*. See David A. Price, *The Pixar Touch: The Making of a Company* (New York: Vintage Books, 2009), 12.
48. In his state of research, Bouknight explains why he did not use NASA's approach as a starting point for his research, but rather an algorithm developed at the *University of Utah* by John E. Warnock: "At General

Electric, a system which combines both hardware and software to produce color half-tone images in real time was developed for NASA for space rendezvous, docking and landing simulation studies. The output medium is a 525 line three-color television tube display and up to 240 edges (as many as 40 planes with 6 edges per plane) may be processed at a given time. The algorithm was developed with a heavy hand from the hardware designers and is not desirable for implementation in software on a digital computer in light of other algorithms which have been reported." W. J. Bouknight, "An Improved Procedure for Generation of Half-Tone Computer Graphics Presentations" (technical report, University of Illinois at Urbana-Champaign, 1969). Defense Technical Information Center (AD0707403), 3–4. Martin E. Newell, also a graduate of the *University of Utah*, comments on the NASA-funded *General Electric* project from 1969 and the lack of practicability of the approach developed there: "The third major limitation found with existing techniques is concerned with restrictions on the scene. This has several aspects, the first of which involves constraints on the scene resulting from assumptions or simplifications in the algorithm. Examples of such constraints include non-intersecting objects, convex polygons, and a limit on the number of edges allowed per polygon. The constraints imposed by Schumaker's [*sic*] algorithm are unusually severe, although they are acceptable in simulation applications involving fairly static scenes." Martin E. Newell, "The Utilization of Procedure Models in Digital Image Synthesis" (PhD diss., University of Utah, 1975. J. Willard Marriott Library (1507175), 20–21.

49. Phong explains in 1973 that Bouknight "worked on systems for shaded picture display with shadows and movable light sources," while Warnock not only dealt with the display of color, but also for the first time with the calculation of "hue, brightness, and specular reflection of light, applied to computer-generated images." Bui T. Phong, "Illumination for Computer-Generated Images" (PhD diss., University of Utah, 1973), J. Willard Marriott Library (1602050), 3.
50. Romney, "Rendering of Solids" (1969a), 4. See also Loyd A. Jones, "Psychophysics and Photography," *Journal of the Optical Society of America* 34, no. 2 (1944): 66.
51. Romney, "Rendering of Solids" (1969a), 5.
52. Romney, "Rendering of Solids" (1969a), 116.
53. Romney, "Rendering of Solids" (1969a), 118. Romney uses the term "oblique perspective" differently from Rule and Coons. In their illustrations, this specific perspective uses no vanishing points. See Figure 5.3 in section 5.1.
54. Romney, "Rendering of Solids" (1969a), 1.
55. See Panofsky, *Perspective as Symbolic Form*, trans. Christopher S. Wood (New York: Zone Books, 1991), 108.
56. Romney, "Rendering of Solids" (1969a), 130.
57. Romney, "Rendering of Solids" (1969a), 131.
58. With regard to the objective criteria that he believed should be taken into account for successful shading Romney also refers to the aspects of "[r]etinal spectral response as a function of intensity" and "[h]aziness as a function of distance." Romney, "Rendering of Solids" (1969a), 130.
59. Evans, "Graphical Man/Machine Communications: February 1968," 7.
60. Romney, "Rendering of Solids" (1969a), 131. Parallel to the approaches developed at the *University of Utah*, Arthur Appel from the *IBM Research Center* worked on a method that made it possible to cast more complex shadows on virtual objects. Appel did not place the light source at the observer's point of view, so that the shadows did not remain hidden behind the objects, but became visible to the side of the objects or on their surface. However, the graphics he created were neither designed for use in real time nor for use in moving images. His approach related exclusively to images that were intended for print. Furthermore, his method was limited to virtual objects composed solely of flat surfaces. See Arthur Appel, "Some Techniques for Shading Machine Renderings of Solids," in *Proceedings of the Spring Joint Computer Conference – AFIPS '68*, ed. ACM (New York: ACM Press, 1968).
61. See Romney, "Rendering of Solids" (1969a), 134.
62. Romney precisely describes the process as follows: "An entire picture is rendered by sequentially displaying on a cathode-ray tube the intensity information for each scan-line in the frame. The frame is made up of M scan-lines where M ≤ 1024. A slow transmission rate requires that a time-exposure photograph of the screen be made. [...] The computation for RENDER [the name for his rendering algorithm] is performed by a UNIVAC 1108 computer. The intensity information is determined by the Shader [...], and transferred to a PDP-8 computer. The PDP-8 generates the raster that drives the oscilloscope beam at a constant rate across a scan-line. Consequently, a picture is 'painted' by modulating the z-axis with the computed intensity values." Romney, "Rendering of Solids" (1969a), 145, 147. The images were already recorded and "stored" in this way in 1967, two years prior to Romney's dissertation. Evans, Romney, et al. describe, "[e]ach scan line [...] is stored in the PDP-8 memory and then transmitted through a digital to analog (D-A) converter to a Tektronix 453 oscilloscope. The scan position is dictated by ten bit x and y registers in the D-A converter. The intensity of the beam at each point in the scan is controlled by a six bit z register. Due to storage and 1108 – PDP-8 transmission-rate limitations we have been forced to take time exposure photographs of the scope trace. As soon as a scan

line is completed, the PDP-8 requests information for the next scan line." Wylie et al., "Half-Tone Perspective Drawings" (1967a), 55–56.

63. In a description of the process that ends with the creation of the photograph, the use of the term is misleading. Romney could be understood here to mean that he understood the finished 3D graphics as photographs, although – as is clear from the context – he actually meant photographic Polaroids here: "A stick-drawing of the object appears on the IDI. The user then decides that he likes the view and pokes the tablet to initiate a rendering. A shaded image of the assembled object is computed and transmitted to a display oscillograph and a photograph is produced." Romney, "Rendering of Solids" (1969a), 84. He comments on the use of photographic film as follows: "The black and white photographs were made on Polaroid Positive-Negative film and reproduced by a halftone printing process [...] with a screen of 150 lines/inch." Romney, "Rendering of Solids" (1969a), 81.
64. Romney, "Rendering of Solids" (1969a), 144.
65. Evans, "Graphical Man/Machine Communications: February 1968," 1.
66. See Romney, "Rendering of Solids" (1969a), 144. In his essay *Quality of Color Reproduction*, MacAdam, who is taken up again later in this sub-section, deals with the question of whether the criteria according to which photographs are produced can be transferred to moving images in the field of film and television. In his discussion of the question, he first presents the approach used to determine the quality of black-and-white photographs, before moving on to the question of whether the method used to measure the quality of black-and-white images is also suitable for determining the quality of color images. MacAdam's conclusion leads to his realization that the process of determining the quality of color photographs would be considerably more complex than for black-and-white photographs, as far fewer parameters play a role in the creation of those. For both processes, however, it would be equally necessary not to rely solely on physical parameters that attempt to faithfully recreate the real environment. It would be more important to interview people and find out empirically which images are perceived as pleasant. Only when the quality of a black-and-white or color photograph would have been determined in this way would it make sense to document the technical parameters in order to be able to reproduce images with the same settings. See David L. MacAdam, "Quality of Color Reproduction," *Journal of the Society of Motion Picture and Television Engineers* no. 56 (1951).
67. While in printing technology all colors are created using the primary colors cyan, magenta and yellow as well as black in a subtractive color mixing system, in light-based image creation processes, such as camera technology, this process takes place using an additive color mixing system and the three colors red, green and blue. In both processes, primary colors are mixed in different degrees of saturation and brightness gradations, but in printing, the superimposition of several colors produces a darker color tone, while the superimposition of the three primary colors in the light-based, i.e. additive, process produces white light. In order to create colored 3D images, Romney therefore worked with the additive process, athough at that time he could only color entire polygons with which the models were virtually described. For the red channel, all the polygons that did not contain any red components were then hidden. A red color filter was placed between the camera and the oscilloscope to color the bright light from the oscilloscope, which is always the same color, before it falls on the long-exposure film. This process was then repeated for the green and blue channels. It was also taken into account that, strictly speaking, the oscilloscope did not output pure white light: "Good color mixing is possible only if the oscilloscope phosphor, the film and filters are all selectively matched. The CRT (Appendix F.6) used to record the computer generated images has a P4 phosphor that emits both a blue and a yellow component of light." Romney, "Rendering of Solids" (1969a), 150.
68. See Romney, "Rendering of Solids" (1969a), 114, and see Alan Erdahl, "Displaying Computer Generated Half-Tone Pictures in Real Time" (technical report, University of Utah, 1969), Defense Technical Information Center (AD0753672). Evans also emphasizes Erdahl's approach in his sixth semi-annual research report as one of the results of the research period. See Evans, "Graphical Man/Machine Commu nications: November 1969," 5.
69. Romney also refers to these goals, for example. See Romney, "Rendering of Solids" (1969a), 114.
70. MacAdam, "Color Reproduction," 498.
71. Jones, "Psychophysics and Photography," 76, emphasis in original. MacAdam quotes Jones with a similar statement from a more recent essay from 1951: "In fact, there are many cases where we know that the perfect objective reproduction, although obtainable, is not the one the majority of judges will choose as of best photographic quality." Loyd A. Jones, "The Psychophysical Evaluation of the Quality of Photographic Reproductions," *PSA Journal* 17, no. 12 (1951): 754.
72. See Evans, "Graphical Man/Machine Communications: May 1971." See also Gary S. Watkins, "A Real Time Visible Surface Algorithm" (PhD diss., University of Utah, 1970), J. Willard Marriott Library (703562).
73. See David C. Evans, "Graphical Man/Machine Communications: December 1971" (research report, University of Utah, 1971), J. Willard Marriott Library (702292), 1.

74. Evans expresses this concern again in the first report of the new research period. See David C. Evans, "Graphical Man/Machine Communications: June 1971" (research report, University of Utah, 1971), J. Willard Marriott Library (702407), 2.
75. Gaboury attributes Gouraud's motivation to relocate from France to the United States to Sutherland, who considered research in the field of mathematics in France to be particularly advanced. He therefore campaigned to recruit young researchers for the project at the *University of Utah*. Phong, whose family had originally emigrated to France during the Vietnam War, had also left France for the United States as a result of this dynamic. See Gaboury, *Image Objects*, 97–99. Gaboury describes Gouraud's "adaptation process" to research in Utah: "On arriving Gouraud had no experience with computer graphics, and had only worked in Fortran and numerical computation as part of his training at the École Centrale. Nonetheless, he quickly took to the culture of problem solving that defined the Utah program, and began developing tools for the shading and display of complex objects." Gaboury, *Image Objects*, 98.
76. Evans, "Graphical Man/Machine Communications: June 1971," 3, emphasis in original. Evans reproduces Gouraud's phrasing from his dissertation almost word by word. See Henri Gouraud, "Computer Display of Curved Surfaces" (PhD diss., University of Utah, 1971), ProQuest (7127878), 1. With the term "parameter spacing," Gouraud refers to the parameters that are necessary to describe a surface. Here he refers in particular to the arrangement of the polygons on the surface, which was always visible in the previous shading methods. His approach was intended to conceal these previously visible parameters. For a definition of the term "parameter spacing," see Gouraud, "Computer Display of Curved Surfaces," e.g. 26.
77. See e.g. Evans, "Graphical Man/Machine Communications: June 1971," 4–5.
78. Gouraud, "Computer Display of Curved Surfaces," iii.
79. The state of research at the beginning of this study has shown that Gaboury also describes this impression, although he refuses to make the ideas expressed by the computer scientists the starting point of his investigation. Instead, he assumes that the technology provided the scope for the development of 3D graphics. See Gaboury, *Image Objects*, 4–5, and 27.
80. Gouraud, "Computer Display of Curved Surfaces," 4.
81. Henri Gouraud, "Continuous Shading of Curved Surfaces," *IEEE Transactions on Computers* C-20, no. 6 (1971): 624.
82. See Ernst Mach, *Über die Wirkung der räumlichen Vertheilung des Lichtreizes auf die Netzhaut* (Vienna: K. k. Hof- und Staatsdruckerei, 1865).
83. Under certain conditions, this effect even occurred with the smooth surfaces simulated by Gouraud. This becomes clear, for example, in his acknowledgments: "Without the numerous discussions I have had with Dr. T. G. Stockham, Mach bands would still destroy the smoothness of curved surfaces. Thanks to him, the cathode ray tube display device I used was properly calibrated, which made possible the quality of the pictures contained in this document." Gouraud, "Computer Display of Curved Surfaces," i. In his later dissertation in 1974, Edwin Catmull also refers to the fact that Mach bands occur with Gouraud's algorithm. See Edwin Catmull, "A Subdivision Algorithm for Computer Display of Curved Surfaces" (PhD diss., University of Utah, 1974), J. Willard Marriott Library (712681), 2.
84. See Gouraud, "Computer Display of Curved Surfaces," 12.
85. See Gouraud, "Computer Display of Curved Surfaces," 16.
86. He developed a mathematical function with which he was able to determine the normals of the individual vertices between the polygons. From there, a linear color interpolation could be calculated between the normals so that the individual boundaries of the polygons and the different color values arising there could be overcome in this way. See Gouraud, "Computer Display of Curved Surfaces," 19–23. In his conference paper, Gouraud describes the calculation process of the normals as follows: "At a particular vertex common to several polygons, one might compute a normal for each polygon as a vector perpendicular to the plane of that polygon. To achieve continuity of the shading we have to have only one possible normal at any particular vertex. This normal could be computed as, for example, the average of the normals to each polygon associated with this particular vertex; but in the examples described in this paper an analytical description of the surface is available and it is possible to compute an exact normal at each vertex of the grid of polygons approximating the surface. Each polygon has a different shading for each of its vertices, and the shading at any particular point inside the polygon has to be computed as a continuous function of the shading at the vertices of the polygon." Gouraud, "Continuous Shading of Curved Surfaces," 626.
87. Gouraud, "Computer Display of Curved Surfaces," 9.
88. See Gouraud, "Continuous Shading of Curved Surfaces," 623–24.
89. Watkins had created the decisive technical prerequisites for Gouraud's algorithm, as Watkins made it possible for the first time to calculate images using polygons that are not flat in themselves. The use of triangular polygons also resulted from the necessity that the polygons always had to be a flat surface in order to be recognized by the algorithms. Romney and Warnock were also still dependent on this. With

Watkins' algorithm, it was now possible for Gouraud to develop curved surfaces for his algorithm that did not necessarily consist of flat polygons. Gouraud used the mathematical calculation model developed by Coons, the so-called "Coons Surface Patch," to calculate his surfaces. However, no polygons are created with this approach, as it belongs to the class of alternative modeling methods that do not work with approximation by polygons, but with precise mathematical calculations. However, as Gouraud's algorithm only worked in connection with polygons, he interpreted the individual mathematically described grid elements within the "Coons Surface Patch" as polygons. This step meant that the polygons were not flat, but uneven. However, the Watkins processor was able to handle this, so that by combining Watkins' preliminary work with the "Coons Surface Patch," Gouraud was able to realize his goal of displaying curved surfaces smoothly. See Evans, "Graphical Man/Machine Communications: June 1971," 4.

90. See Gouraud, "Continuous Shading of Curved Surfaces," 628.
91. Gouraud, "Computer Display of Curved Surfaces," 1.
92. See Gouraud, "Computer Display of Curved Surfaces," 60.
93. Gouraud, "Computer Display of Curved Surfaces," 55.
94. Gouraud, "Computer Display of Curved Surfaces," 2.
95. See Gouraud, "Computer Display of Curved Surfaces," 60.
96. See Evans, "Graphical Man/Machine Communications: December 1971," 4.
97. See Evans, "Graphical Man/Machine Communications: June 1972," 2, and see David C. Evans, "Graphical Man/Machine Communications: December 1972" (research report, University of Utah, 1972), J. Willard Marriott Library (706529), 27.
98. See Evans, "Graphical Man/Machine Communications: December 1971," 1.
99. Evans, "Graphical Man/Machine Communications: December 1971," 6.
100. See e.g. Evans, "Graphical Man/Machine Communications: December 1971," 11.
101. See Evans, "Graphical Man/Machine Communications: December 1972," 50. Catmull developed a virtual model of his left hand for his animation by first creating a plaster cast of it, which he then coated with latex. On this setup, he manually drew the polygons with which the virtual model was to be described in the computer. The aim was to make the virtual hand move by closing it into a fist and opening it again. See Edwin Catmull, "A System for Computer Generated Movies," in *Proceedings of the ACM Annual Conference – ACM '72*, ed. John J. Donovan and Rosemary Shields (New York: ACM Press, 1972).
102. In the individual dissertations, reference is made to research funding on the cover page. See e.g. Catmull, "A Subdivision Algorithm."
103. See Catmull, "A Subdivision Algorithm," [i].
104. Phong's references to this are discussed more extensively in this chapter, see also, for example, Catmull, "A Subdivision Algorithm," 1–2, and see Blinn, "Computer Display of Curved Surfaces," 107.
105. See Gouraud, "Computer Display of Curved Surfaces," 64.
106. Blinn also developed a refined shading algorithm that is so closely linked to Phong's approach that the "Blinn-Phong" calculation model is still often referred to today in the field of shading. See e.g. Renee Dunlop, ed., *Production Pipeline Fundamentals for Film and Game* (Burlington: Focal Press, 2014), 150. Blinn basically adopted Phong's algorithm for his new calculation model but changed individual parameters in the mathematical function so that even fine unevenness on the surface is simulated, as real-life surfaces are never completely smooth. He based this on studies by Kenneth E. Torrance and Ephraim M. Sparrow, who had previously investigated the behavior of light on surfaces using real objects. See also James F. Blinn, "Models of Light Reflection for Computer Synthesized Pictures," in *Proceedings of the 4th Annual Conference on Computer graphics and Interactive Techniques – SIGGRAPH '77*, ed. ACM (New York: ACM Press, 1977).
107. See Phong, "Illumination for Computer Generated Images," 52.
108. Bui T. Phong, "Illumination for Computer Generated Pictures," *Communications of the ACM* 18, no. 6 (1975): 311.
109. Phong, "Illumination for Computer Generated Pictures," 311.
110. Phong, "Illumination for Computer Generated Pictures," 311.
111. Phong speaks of the "effects of digital sampling techniques." Phong, "Illumination for Computer Generated Pictures," 311. In his dissertation, Phong explains what he means by this phrase. With the display devices available at the time and their resolution, it was extremely difficult to display contours in the image that ran almost horizontally or vertically. Instead, the display of such lines appeared as a sequence of several parallel lines. When displaying particularly elongated polygon elements, it could also happen that they disappeared completely if they were narrower in one direction than the resolution of the screen. To give an example, Phong speaks of lane markings applied in the center of roads. See Phong, "Illumination for Computer Generated Images," 77–78.
112. See Phong, "Illumination for Computer Generated Images," 62–67.

113. The basic idea of changing the appearance of a polygon object in the final output so that a smooth surface appears instead of individual polygons with different shades of gray was identical for Gouraud and Phong. However, the implementation was based on two different aspects. While Gouraud used the values of the normals at the corners of the polygons in order to be able to calculate a linear color gradient between them, Phong also calculated the normals relative to the face of each polygon and relative to each of the polygon edges. See Phong "Illumination for Computer Generated Pictures," 315.
114. He describes his approach as follows: "At the present time, when a smooth profile of the object is desired, as in the case of the pictures made for comparison with pictures of real objects, a large numerical data base is required." Phong, "Illumination for Computer Generated Images," 77.
115. Phong, "Illumination for Computer Generated Images," 78.
116. See Blinn, "Computer Display of Curved Surfaces," vii; see Catmull, "A Subdivision Algorithm," 2.
117. Catmull, "A Subdivision Algorithm," 1.
118. Blinn, "Computer Display of Curved Surfaces," 1. With this he also describes his own goal, as he announces in the abstract: "This thesis attacks the problem of generating computer synthesized images both more rapidly and more realistically." Blinn, "Computer Display of Curved Surfaces," iv.
119. See Catmull, "A Subdivision Algorithm," 5.
120. See Catmull, "A Subdivision Algorithm," 38.
121. The *Pixar Image Computer* was originally designed to combine camera footage with recordings of animated effects. However, it was also used for medical and military purposes. The device was not profitable in the long term, which is why Pixar decided to specialize in rendering software. The first algorithm developed for this was called *Reyes* (Renders everything you ever saw), but the product was later renamed *PhotoRealistic RenderMan* and finally *RenderMan*. See Edwin Catmull and Amy Wallace, *Creativity, Inc. Overcoming the Unseen Forces That Stand in the Way of True Inspiration* (New York: Random House, 2014), 29–30, and see Price, *Pixar Touch*, 43, 88–89, 95–99, 295.
122. Catmull, "A Subdivision Algorithm," 1.
123. Catmull explicitly addresses the "Coons Surface Patch" in his appendix, in which he precisely explains the exact procedure of his calculations of surfaces. See Catmull, "A Subdivision Algorithm," 58, 66.
124. Catmull, "A Subdivision Algorithm," 1.
125. To date, still only individual polygons can be colored when working with polygon-based models. Coloring beyond the boundaries of a polygon is also currently only possible with a texture.
126. Blinn, "Computer Display of Curved Surfaces," 4–5.
127. Blinn, "Computer Display of Curved Surfaces," 5.
128. The term "raster element" is a predecessor of the term "pixel." As the computer scientist Alvy Ray Smith notes in his biography of the pixel, other terms have also been used before, such as "spots," "point arrays," "picture points" and "picture elements." In his monograph, Smith deals with the historical origins of the pixel but points out that the mathematical basis of what is referred to as a pixel is usually not anchored in the general public's consciousness, which is why the idea of what a pixel is differs greatly from what it actually means mathematically. The term is therefore not usually used precisely: "Pixels are *not* little squares! This may surprise you because *very* often they're represented that way – so often, in fact, that many people *equate* pixels with little abutting squares of color – which is perhaps the most widespread misunderstanding of the nascent digital age. The word *pixelation* has even institutionalized the misconception. In fact, pixels have *no* shape. They're just samples taken on a regular grid [...]. They exist only at a point, so they have no extent, no width, zero dimensions. You can't see them, and they have no visible color. They just have a number *representing* a shade of gray, or three numbers *representing* a color." Alvy R. Smith, *A Biography of the Pixel* (Cambridge: MIT Press, 2021), 51, emphasis in original.
129. See Catmull, "A Subdivision Algorithm," 4–5.
130. Catmull, "A Subdivision Algorithm," 41.
131. Catmull, "A Subdivision Algorithm," 41.

IV

Realism in US Visual Culture

CHAPTER 8

Pixar's Realism

Edwin Catmull as a Bridge between Production Aesthetics and Visual Aesthetics

> He has "something in mind." "It takes a long time for an idea to strike," he said. "Then I have to think about it for a long time. I don't start painting until I have it all worked out in my mind. I'm all right when I get to the easel."[1]
>
> *EDWARD HOPPER IN CONVERSATION WITH SUSANNE BURREY (1955)*

What idea of imagery did Catmull and his predecessors as well as his contemporary colleagues draw on when they developed their technologies for synthetic image generation in the way described in this study? To find possible answers, I will turn to US visual culture in this part. To begin, it is worth taking a look at the preceding statement by US painter Edward Hopper. His relevance will become clearer later in this part, but the description of his artistic process provides an initial indication of possible parallels between computer-graphic endeavors and realistic-figurative painting in the United States: Just as Catmull or Gouraud had an image in mind *beforehand* for the development of their technologies, Hopper also states here that he only begins painting when he has finished conceiving it in his mind. Although this statement alone does not establish whether there is a conceptual relationship between Hopper's and Catmull's ideas, an analogy to the developments in computer technology can nevertheless be immediately identified. This analogy will inform the following remarks: Like Catmull, Hopper pursues a figurative-representational reproduction of his environment with his images and for him, too, the expression of light plays a special role, which is also central to every shading and rendering algorithm. However, as this observation alone is not very informative, it will be explored in greater depth below.

An understanding of the development of visual culture in the United States is particularly insightful to be able to contextualize the computer-technological endeavors in terms of cultural history and to make their common context of meaning comprehensible. The further course of this study follows the hypothesis that the idea which Catmull, but also individuals such as Coons, had of the images to be generated by the computer is anchored in the cultural history of a worldview that developed in the United States, and which is also closely linked to a technology-driven concept of progress.

Why it can be useful to pursue this assumption can first be illustrated on a purely visual-aesthetic level using the Pixar films as an example. They can largely be traced back to Edwin Catmull, and before I turn my attention to the computer graphic image-generation process in a more general sense in Part V, I will now deduce from the Pixar films why the following chapters of this study deal with US visual culture from an art-historical perspective.[2] The aim is to synthesize all the results of this study in Part V, drawing on the findings from the examination of US visual culture in Part IV. To this end, in Part V, insights into visual aesthetics are placed within a broader cultural-historical

DOI: 10.1201/9781003649861-12

framework, which also encompasses developments in computer technology. The following image-aesthetic focus of the study thus serves to delineate overarching production-aesthetic motifs in US visual culture that greatly characterize the development of 3D computer graphics and can be identified independently of individual protagonists.

To understand why the Pixar films are a suitable introduction to this topic, it is helpful to take a general look at the commercial computer-animated films produced today. It is striking that they all have a rather uniform visual language – even if they were created in very different countries and cultures. Only quite recently have studios begun to deviate from this visual aesthetic.[3] The origins of this "visual order" can initially be traced back to Pixar, as the company was the first to release a feature-length computer-generated animated film with their production *Toy Story*[4] in 1995.[5] The Pixar films can therefore be ascribed a role model status similar to that attributed to the Disney studios by animation theorist Paul Wells: In his study *Animation and America*, he assumes that Disney set a kind of standard for the animation film industry with its first feature-length film *Snow White and the Seven Dwarfs*.[6] Wells also discusses Pixar films in the context of his animation theory, although he focuses on John Lasseter rather than Catmull. Lasseter was the first animator hired by Pixar, and he subsequently played a central role alongside Catmull in the company's history.[7] This chapter's examination of the visual culture of computer graphics at Pixar is intended to bring Catmull and thus also the historical events and individuals presented in this study into focus. Considering the previous findings from this study, I argue that Lasseter plays, at most, a secondary role in the visual aesthetics of the Pixar films. It can also be deduced from the historical origins of the Pixar company that the visual aesthetics of Pixar films had already taken a specific direction before John Lasseter joined the young company. In his 2014 monograph *Creativity, Inc.*, Catmull describes his first encounter with Lasseter in 1983. The book is intended to explain Pixar's corporate history and the approaches as well as creative techniques pursued there. After graduating from the *University of Utah*, Catmull first transferred to the *New York Institute of Technology* (NYIT) in 1974 and then to George Lucas' production company *Lucasfilm* in 1979.[8] It was here where Catmull and Lasseter first met, before Pixar existed as an independent production company. Catmull was the head of the computer department that George Lucas had established to explore how computer technology could be used in the feature film industry. Although the developments made by Catmull and his team were not well received by the film editors at *Lucasfilm*, external filmmakers regularly visited the department to familiarize themselves with the new technology and possibly use it for their own productions. On one of these visits, John Lasseter, an animator at Disney at the time, came with a group of other Disney employees. Catmull presented the group with the "one-frame movie"[9] *Road To Point Reyes*, which had recently been created in his department by colleagues, including Alvy Ray Smith, with whom Catmull founded Pixar a few years later. The picture shows the course of a road along a coastline under a bright blue sky with a double rainbow. The road bends to the left at the center of the image, while a seascape dotted with green mountains stretches into the distance (Figure 8.1). Catmull describes Lasseter's reaction to the presentation as follows:

> When I showed everyone a computer-animated image that we were so proud of we'd given it a name – "The Road to Point Reyes" – he just stood there, transfixed. I told him we'd developed the image of a gently curving road overlooking the Pacific Ocean using a software program we'd developed called Reyes (for Renders Everything You Ever Saw), and the pun was intended: Point Reyes, California, is a seaside village on Route 1, not far from Lucasfilm. Reyes represented the cutting edge of computer graphics at the time. And it bowled this John guy over.[10]

Although Catmull himself was not actively involved in the creation of this particular image, it can be deduced from this early computer graphics work that it was Catmull and his colleagues at *Lucasfilm*, not Lasseter, who set the visual-aesthetic tone before Lasseter joined Catmull and Smith.

Due to the frequent focus on Lasseter in animation theory, as is the case with Wells, Pixar films are often analyzed in the context of Disney films. Although the two companies are closely intertwined historically, my focus on the computer-technological origins of the

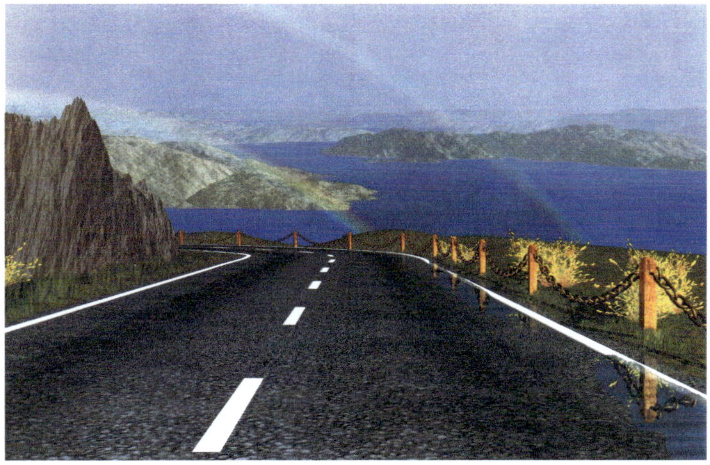

FIGURE 8.1 Loren Carpenter, Rob Cook, Tom Porter, Bill Reeves, David Salesin and Alvy Ray Smith, *Road To Point Reyes*, 1983, computer rendering. (© 1983 Disney/Pixar.)

Pixar films allows me to detach them from the Disney context and examine them independently of the traditional animation studio.[11] The following question is now in the foreground: What visual order have the Pixar films and – based on this – many other commercial computer-animated films followed for the large part of their fairly young history? This question arises from the observation I expressed at the beginning of this study that an infinite number of different appearances can be realized with the 3D software. It is also noticeable that Disney's 3D-animated films often have a very inconsistent visual aesthetic compared to those of Pixar, even though Disney productions such as *Zootopia*[12] also exist that adhere to the visual order of the Pixar films.[13]

What visual-aesthetic criteria can be identified as examples to describe this visual order? Similar to the work *Road To Point Reyes*, in Pixar films the sun often shines under a bright blue sky. Most of the time, the sun is rather low in the sky, as it is typical of a summer afternoon, casting long shadows on the sun-drenched artificial worlds. The afternoon mood often manifests itself in warm bluish-yellow color hues.[14] Due to the fact that the technology could enable so many different appearances, it can be concluded that Pixar "assigned" a distinct visual aesthetic to the young computer graphics technology with their debut film *Toy Story* in 1995. In contrast to the photorealistic graphics, in which the technology is almost completely transparent and cannot be recognized as means of imaging, Pixar and the popular cultural dissemination of the films made the new imaging process recognizable for the first time with its "own aesthetic."[15]

Before I place the Pixar films in the context of US painting in the following steps, it should first be noted that the productions often thematize their own visual aesthetics in a self-reflexive manner. The film *Inside Out*[16] is a good example of this. In one scene, for instance, the characters explicitly negotiate the fact that an abstract visual language is dangerous and alien, while a figurative visual language is safe and familiar.[17] Through this form of self-reflexivity, Wells identifies a tradition in the Pixar films that represents the origins of animation, when the genre still had an avant-garde and subversive character – something that, according to Wells, was lost with Disney's first animated feature film.[18] Wells argues that this avant-garde characteristic of animation lies, for example, in bringing things to life that are usually unable to move independently. Wells particularly discerns a meta-reflexive approach in the early animations of Winsor McCay, a pioneer of animated films. McCay often reveals the moment in which he brings a character to life and incorporates it into the story.[19] Wells also recognizes such self-reflexive moments in the themes of the *Toy Story* films, because the characters constantly have to deal with the question of whether they are "just" toy figures or whether they lead an independent "real" life. Interestingly, Wells sees the technology as the driving force behind this self-reflexive approach to animation.[20] According to the animation theorist, technology played a role in Pixar's return to the origins of animation. By pursuing a self-reflexive approach, Wells states, the *Toy Story* films are able to counter the determinism of technology and utilize the aesthetics of 3D technology to their advantage.[21] However, the films' frequent self-reflexive comments on their own appearance clearly contradict Wells' argument, because in the meta-reflexive film scenes, the producers always show that they could actually pursue a different visual aesthetic. This aligns with the variety of appearances of the computer graphics I presented at the beginning of this study. The visual aesthetic of the Pixar films is therefore not determined by the technology. Rather, it was a conscious and independent creative decision.[22] Nevertheless, Wells' fundamental observation of the films' uniform visual aesthetic must be recognized: According to the above conclusions, however, this aesthetic does not stem directly from the technology, but from an underlying common cultural background. Consistent with the main premise of this study, the visual aesthetic of the Pixar films can therefore be traced back to individuals who designed the technology against this cultural backdrop.

Although Wells frequently refers to Lasseter, who was as a director significantly involved in designing the look for the *Toy Story* films, the previous findings of this study reveal that, with their first computer-animated feature film, Lasseter and Catmull created a *visual*-aesthetic implementation of those *production*-aesthetic principles that had also driven the software development. Thus, Wells' view that the software predetermined a visual aesthetic can be confirmed to a certain extent, although in this larger context it becomes evident that the visual aesthetic was not fundamentally determined by the technology but was actively anticipated based on specific visual ideas. I will now discuss which pictorial ideas these could have been.

A first indication was already mentioned at the beginning of this chapter with Edward Hopper. The visual-aesthetic similarities between the Pixar films and Hopper's paintings are perhaps not very surprising and will only be hinted at here (Figures 8.2 and 8.3), as Hopper will be discussed in more detail in the following chapters. In order to set the direction for the further examination of US visual culture, in a brief comparison I will now focus instead on US landscape painting of the 19th century.[23]

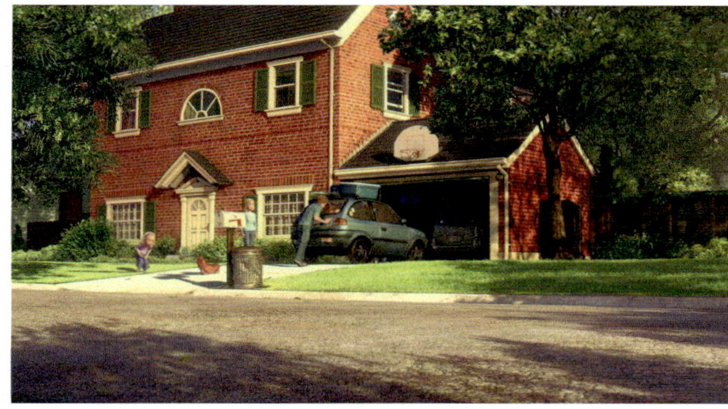

FIGURE 8.2 Lee Unkrich, director, still from *Toy Story 3*, 2010, 3D computer graphic. (© 2010 Disney/Pixar.)

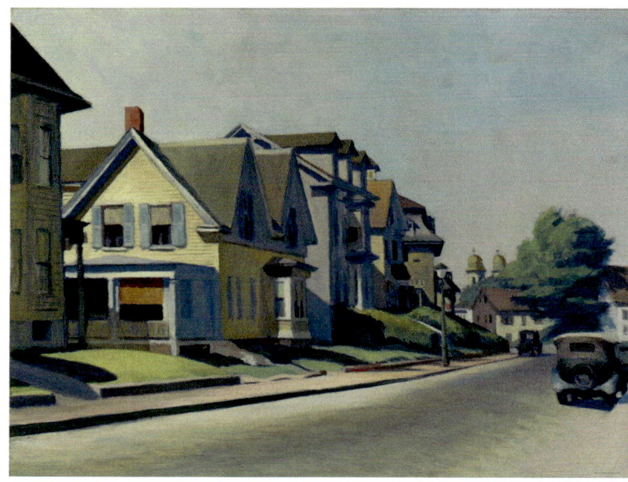

FIGURE 8.3 Edward Hopper (1882–1967), *Sun on Prospect Street (Gloucester, Massachusetts)*, 1934, oil on canvas, 28 × 36 1/4 in (71.1 × 92.1 cm), Cincinnati Art Museum, The Edwin and Virginia Irwin Memorial, 1959.49. (Reprinted with permission from Cincinnati Art Museum. © Heirs of Josephine N. Hopper/VAGA at ARS, NY/VG Bild-Kunst, Bonn 2025.)

A pair of images that can be used to highlight links between the Pixar films and landscape painting includes a still from the Pixar film *The Good Dinosaur*[24] and the painting *The Oxbow*, created in 1836 by the US painter Thomas Cole (Figures 8.4 and 8.5). Both paintings depict a river from an elevated perspective, extending diagonally into the depths of a green wooded valley. However, the two pictures can be related to each other not only in terms of visual aesthetics, but also in terms of production aesthetics as soon as individual production details are uncovered: For both Cole and Pixar, the composition of a picture is preceded by intensive research phases, which

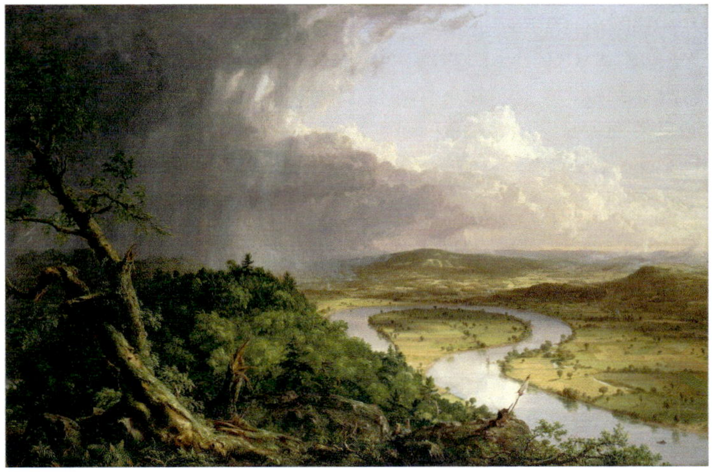

FIGURE 8.4 Thomas Cole, *View from Mount Holyoke, Northampton, Massachusetts, after a Thunderstorm – The Oxbow*, 1836, oil on canvas, 51 1/2 × 76 in (130.8 × 193 cm), Gift of Mrs. Russell Sage, 1908, The Metropolitan Museum of Art. (© CC0.)

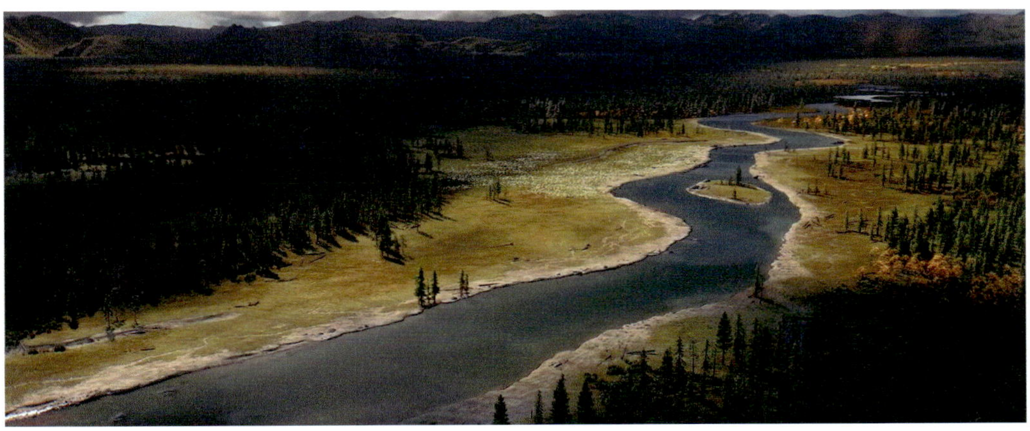

FIGURE 8.5 Peter Sohn, director, still from *The Good Dinosaur*, 2015, 3D computer graphic. (© 2015 Disney/Pixar.)

subsequently lead to the creation of a picture by arranging the researched surroundings in a new way, while, at the same time, strictly adhering to found elements.[25] Not only Catmull talks about this approach,[26] Lasseter also expresses himself in a similar way. In comparison of two statements by Thomas Cole and John Lasseter on the general approach to image creation, the intellectual relationship becomes particularly clear. Cole describes his approach to image composition as follows:

> If the imagination is shackled and nothing is described but what we see, seldom will any thing truly great be produced, either in painting or in poetry. [...] But a departure from nature is not a necessary consequence in the painting of compositions: on the contrary the most lovely and perfect parts of nature may be brought together and combined in a whole that shall surpass in beauty and effect any pictures painted from a single view.[27]

Lasseter's position becomes evident, for example, in Pixar's own publication *To Infinity and Beyond*: "Lasseter calls computer animation 'the mystical science': give the computer the right set of instructions to carry out, and you can create the impossible in a world with a physicality and seamlessness no other medium can."[28] Both statements express that Cole and Lasseter aim to merge physical realities with imagined scenes or, conversely, to depict imagined scenes with great physical precision in their images. Thus, both Cole and Lasseter create their images as idealized versions of a found reality, but without disregarding the physical laws of the environment.[29] As US art historian Barbara Novak points out, Cole was even criticized for this approach, as he detached himself too much from nature created by God in his approach to painting.[30] This contradiction expressed by Cole between the appreciation of nature, on the one hand, and the "improvement" of nature in painting, on the other, is addressed again in Chapter 11, while the art-historical background to which Novak refers here will be discussed in greater detail in Sections 9.1.2 and 10.2.

To consider the pictorial motif of the river in the comparison of the two images, the cultural circumstances in which Cole developed his position can also be explained in a somewhat broader context. As US art historian John Wilmerding explains, waterways had a special significance for the "young nation" at the time. They provided access to the impassable natural environment and thus also played an important role in forming national identity. Rivers enabled the expansion of territory and the creation of a new national self-confidence.[31] The theme of self-discovery is also present in the protagonist of the film *The Good Dinosaur*, which is why it seems logical that the film incorporates an important motif from US landscape painting: the river. According to Wilmerding, this historical development gave rise to the *Hudson River School*, to which Cole belonged, and which became the first comprehensive movement in landscape painting. Similar to Pixar's approach in the film *The Good Dinosaur*, the artists in the group of painters adopted the river as a "key component of their pictorial repertoire."[32]

Luminism, another movement in US landscape painting from the 19th century, provides additional evidence that can be used to demonstrate the links between the painterly traditions and computer-technological approaches to image creation at Pixar. Similar to the representatives of the *Hudson River School*, the luminist painters often adopted an elevated perspective.[33] Referring again to Wilmerding, this production-aesthetic detail can be linked to transcendentalist tendencies in the mid-19th century. As the name of the movement suggests, light played a central role in the composition of images in Luminism. Wilmerding describes the connection between Transcendentalism and luminist painting by referring to one of its representatives, Fitz Henry Lane as well as to the founder of Transcendentalism Ralph Waldo Emerson and his friend Henry David Thoreau:

> As with Lane and Emerson, we feel with Thoreau too the desire for full immersion in nature. Thoreau seeks to take nature's pulse as much as his own. He records his delight in the sensations of touch, as with water on the skin; of hearing, as with birds on a telegraph wire; or of sight, as in the autumnal tints on a red maple. The total union of artist and subject is a central aspect of pure luminism; with Lane's *Brace's Rock* still in mind, we can see the same aspiration of the transcendentalists to achieve both the spaciousness of the horizon and the immediacy of observed phenomena. [...] Distance, therefore, both measured and mental, is a significant element in the imagery of nature at this time. On one walk Thoreau urged climbing a tree to elevate our vantage point and gain the broader, deeper view. It is noteworthy that quite frequently the luminist painter sought out vistas from unusually high points of view.[34]

In his monograph *Fitz Hugh Lane* Wilmerding comprehensively analyzes Lane's painting technique. He points out that Lane had himself hoisted to the top of a sailing boat mast at least once in order to be able to adopt a certain perspective for one of his compositions.[35] The findings about the connection between luminist painting and the transcendentalist tendencies that were extremely widespread at the time can be related to various still images of completely different computer-animated productions on a purely visual-aesthetic level. While Lane's visual aesthetic is apparent in *WALL-E*,[36] for example, Frederic Edwin Church's painterly approach, whose use of light was even more intense, can be found not only in *WALL-E* but also, for example, in the European-animated film *Richard the Stork*[37] (Figures 8.6–8.10). With Novak, it can be reasoned why individual visual-aesthetic features of 19th century US landscape painting still survive in the films:

> A concomitant mode, practiced by many Hudson River men, as well as by such luminists as Lane

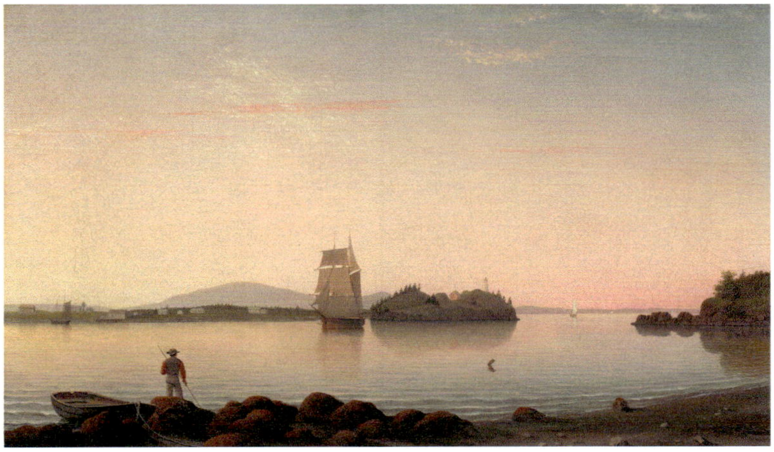

FIGURE 8.6 Fitz Henry Lane, American, 1804–1865, *Owl's Head, Penobscot Bay, Maine*, 1862, oil on canvas, 15 3/4 × 26 1/8 in (40 × 66.36 cm), Museum of Fine Arts, Boston, Bequest of Martha C. Karolik for the M. and M. Karolik Collection of American Paintings, 1815–1865, 48.448. (Photograph © 2026 Museum of Fine Arts, Boston.)

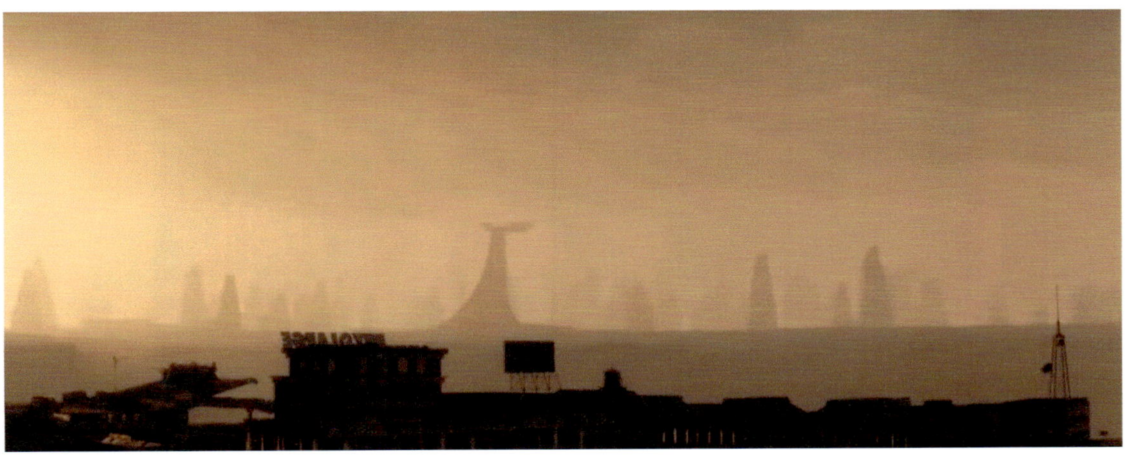

FIGURE 8.7 Andrew Stanton, director, still from *WALL-E*, 2008, 3D computer graphic. (© 2008 Disney/Pixar.)

> and Heade, was quietistic, precise and conceptual. [...] It is remarkable how these attitudes persist in the twentieth century, though disguised under new styles and associated with different ambitions and intentions.[38]

With this statement, Novak is not referring to synthetic computer images; rather, she occasionally recognizes the characteristics she describes in representatives of Abstract Expressionism, for example. And yet Novak's suggestion that the conceptual and precise approach of the luminists or the *Hudson River School* survived into the 20th century could also be applied to computer-animated films.[39]

How can the findings on the painterly references in Pixar be brought together with the previous technical-historical analyses and made fruitful for the overarching aim of this study? This introduction to the examination of US visual culture is, at best, a prelude to the goal of determining a common context of meaning for all computer graphics. While references to the luminists' worldview allow for initial attempts at interpreting *why* the software was developed in a certain way, this development can be comprehended and substantiated much more profoundly if the visual culture of the United

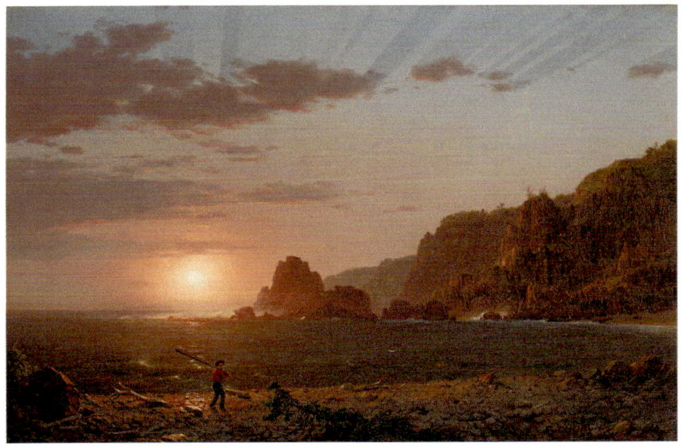

FIGURE 8.8 Frederic Edwin Church, American, 1826–1900, *Grand Manan Island, Bay of Fundy*, 1852, oil on canvas, 21 13/16 × 31 15/16 in (55.4 × 81.1 cm), Wadsworth Atheneum Museum of Art, Hartford, CT, Gallery Fund, 1898.6. (Photograph by Allen Phillips/Wadsworth Atheneum.)

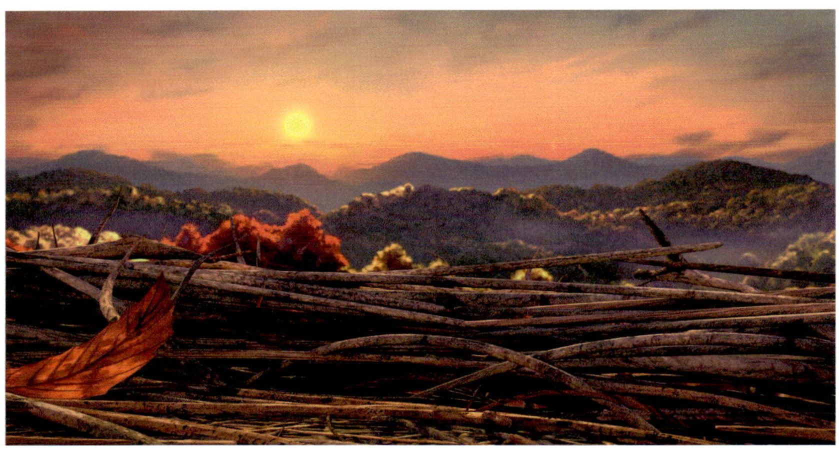

FIGURE 8.9 Toby Genkel and Reza Memari, directors, still from *Richard the Stork*, 2017, 3D computer graphic. (© 2017 Knudsen & Streuber Medienmanufaktur, Ulysses Filmproduktion, Walking The Dog, Mélusine Productions, Den siste skilling – License TELEPOOL GmbH, Munich.)

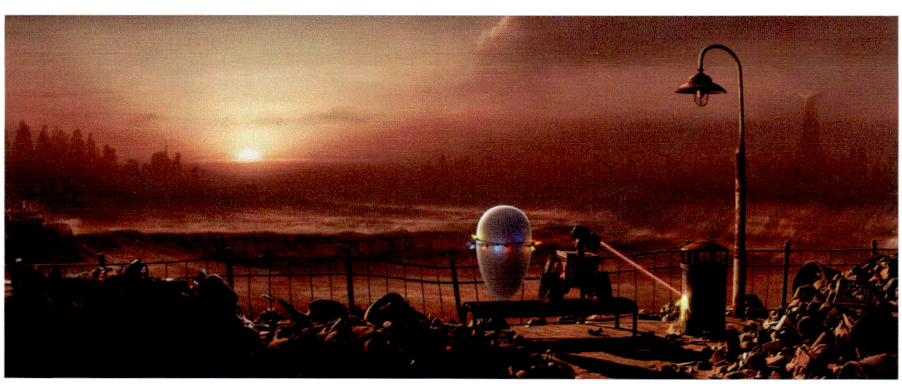

FIGURE 8.10 Andrew Stanton, director, still from *WALL-E*, 2008, 3D computer graphic. (© 2008 Disney/Pixar.)

States is systematically scrutinized. The focus here is on realistic painterly tendencies, which is why in the following chapter I will examine concepts of "American Realism." Based on this, it will also be possible to relate the role of technology in the cultural development of the United States to computer graphics developments in general. The historical analysis carried out in the first half of this study makes it possible to move away from the purely visual-aesthetic level toward the end of the study and explain how a specific understanding of the world and images can still characterize the production of computer images today, even if the visual aesthetic of the Pixar films is not strived for.

NOTES

1. Suzanne Burrey, "Edward Hopper: The Emptying Spaces," *Arts Digest* 29, no. 13 (1955), 8.
2. This chapter introduction is based on the author's 2021 essay *Der bildsprachliche Kosmos im computeranimierten Kinofilm* (The Pictorial Cosmos in Computer-Animated Films), but it expands on the theses expressed there. See Carolin Scheler, "Der bildsprachliche Kosmos im computeranimierten Kinofilm," in *Piktogrammatik: Grafisches Gestalten als Weltwissen und Bilderordnung*, ed. Annette Geiger and Bianca Holtschke (Bielefeld: transcript, 2021).
3. The most prominent example from popular culture indicating this change in visual aesthetics is perhaps the computer-animated movie *Spider-Man: Into the Spider-Verse*, directed by Bob Persichetti, Peter Ramsey and Rodney Rothman (Columbia/Marvel/Sony, 2018). Rather than making use of computer graphics to produce photorealistic visuals or the type of stylized realism that the Pixar films show, the 2018 *Spider-Man* film follows a "visual order" that is reminiscent of comic books and graphic novels. It can thus be said that with this film the software developers' conceptions of what an image is supposed to be and the worldviews that are inscribed into the software were overcome.
4. *Toy Story*, directed by John Lasseter (Disney/Pixar, 1995).
5. See Scheler, "Der bildsprachliche Kosmos," 137/39.
6. *Snow White and the Seven Dwarfs*, directed by William Cottrell, David Hand and Wilfred Jackson (Disney, 1937). See Paul Wells, *Animation and America* (Edinburgh: Edinburgh University Press, 2002), 48–49.
7. See Edwin Catmull and Amy Wallace, *Creativity, Inc. Overcoming the Unseen Forces That Stand in the Way of True Inspiration* (New York: Random House, 2014), 32–37.
8. Catmull developed an early interest in harnessing the possibilities of computer graphics for the production of films. As he explains, he was pursuing a goal that spurred few other in developing their ideas. However, his focus on this possible application of computer graphics attracted the attention of entrepreneur Alex Schure in 1974, who set up a research center at NYIT to produce the first computer-graphic feature film. Catmull eventually transferred to NYIT but emphasizes that Schure's goal was not a realistic one at the time. Nevertheless, Catmull's new job gave him the financial and creative freedom to pursue his own vision. Knowing that a computer-animated feature film could ultimately not be realized there, as no one was involved in the process who actually belonged to the film industry, Catmull began to look elsewhere. He observed that there had been little interest in the new computer graphics methods in the feature film industry, but in George Lucas he finally met a representative of the industry who was more open to the new technical processes. Catmull then transferred to *Lucasfilm* together with his colleague Alvy Ray Smith, where they developed their *Pixar Image Computer* (see Section 7.1.3 in this study, especially endnote 121) and marketed it as hardware. Ultimately, the computer-aided methods developed by Catmull and his team for film editing, for example, were not accepted by the individuals involved in film production. The financing of the department was therefore, in fact, even dependent on the marketing of the computer. For financial reasons, Catmull and Smith eventually left *Lucasfilm* and founded the animation studio Pixar in 1986 with the support of Steve Jobs. See Catmull and Wallace, *Creativity, Inc.*, 13, 16–31, 37–44.
9. "pt.reyes," Alvy R. Smith, accessed December 16, 2021, http://alvyray.com/Art/PtReyes.htm. The computer scientist Alvy Ray Smith chooses this description for the image on his website. He explains that the still image was a team effort. According to him, the colleagues involved in the production were Loren Carpenter, Rob Cook, Tom Porter, Bill Reeves and David Salesin. Catmull, then the chairman of the group, is not mentioned by Alvy Ray Smith, at least not on this project page of his website.
10. Catmull and Wallace, *Creativity, Inc.*, 33.
11. See Scheler, "Der bildsprachliche Kosmos," 141.
12. *Zootopia* directed by Byron Howard, Rich Moore and Jared Bush (Disney, 2016).
13. In addition to *Zootopia*, the Disney productions *Dinosaur*, directed by Ralph Zondag and Eric Leighton (Disney, 2000) and *Tangled*, directed by Nathan Greno and Byron Howard (Disney, 2010) can be mentioned, both of which explore further visual aesthetic possibilities of 3D technology in different ways. See Scheler, "Der bildsprachliche Kosmos," 141–42.

14. See Scheler, "Der bildsprachliche Kosmos," 137/39. The color moods of the Pixar films are elaborately planned along the storyline in the pre-production of the films. A so-called color script is therefore designed in advance for each animated film, which identifies the color scheme of the individual scenes that later make up the film. Depending on the dramaturgy of each film, its basic color mood can therefore change in individual scenes. The color script for the Pixar film *Inside Out*, for example, has a predominantly bluish-purple color scheme, in which, however, clear yellow accents are set at the same time. See Pete Docter and Amy Poehler, *The Art of Inside Out* (San Francisco: Chronicle Books, 2015), 170–71.
15. See Scheler, "Der bildsprachliche Kosmos," 141.
16. *Inside Out*, directed by Pete Docter (Disney/Pixar, 2015).
17. See Scheler, "Der bildsprachliche Kosmos," 149–51.
18. See Wells, *Animation and America*, 23, 48–49, 154. See also Paul Wells, *Understanding Animation* (London: Routledge, 1998), 24–26.
19. See Wells, *Animation and America*, 29–33.
20. See Wells, *Animation and America*, 160.
21. See Wells, *Animation and America*, 169.
22. See Scheler, "Der bildsprachliche Kosmos," 148–49.
23. See Scheler, "Der bildsprachliche Kosmos," 151–57.
24. *The Good Dinosaur*, directed by Peter Sohn (Disney/Pixar, 2015).
25. See Scheler, "Der bildsprachliche Kosmos," 153.
26. See Catmull and Wallace, *Creativity, Inc.*, 198.
27. Thomas Cole, "Letter to Robert Gilmor," dated December 25, 1827, *Thomas Cole Papers, Letters of Robert Gilmor to and from Thomas Cole – 1826–1837*, New York State Library Digital Collections, Manuscripts, 74–75, accessed March 18, 2022, https://nysl.ptfs.com/data/Library5/All%20Special%20Collections/Manuscripts/Thomas%20Cole%20Papers/Correspondence%2C%201820-1855/Cole%20and%20Gilmor%2C%201826-1837/pdf/SC10635-B3-F8-complete.pdf.
28. Karen Paik and Leslie Iwerks, *To Infinity and Beyond! The Story of Pixar Animation Studios* (San Francisco: Chronicle, 2007), 8.
29. See Scheler, "Der bildsprachliche Kosmos," 154.
30. See Barbara Novak, *American Painting of the Nineteenth Century. Realism, Idealism, and the American Experience*, 3rd edition (Oxford: Oxford University Press USA, 2007), 43.
31. See John Wilmerding, *American Views: Essays on American Art* (Princeton: Princeton University Press, 1991), 49, 51.
32. Wilmerding, *American Views*, 51. See also Scheler, "Der bildsprachliche Kosmos," 155.
33. See Scheler, "Der bildsprachliche Kosmos," 156.
34. Wilmerding, *American Views*, 72, emphasis in original.
35. See John Wilmerding, *Fitz Hugh Lane* (London: Praeger, 1971), 50.
36. *WALL-E*, directed by Andrew Stanton (Disney/Pixar, 2008).
37. *Richard the Stork*, directed by Toby Genkel, Reza Memari (Knudsen & Streuber Medienmanufaktur, Ulysses Filmproduktion, Walking The Dog, Mélusine Productions, Den siste skilling – License TELEPOOL GmbH, Munich, 2017).
38. Novak, *American Painting*, 233.
39. See Scheler, "Der bildsprachliche Kosmos," 156–57.

CHAPTER 9

The Tangibility of Things

Feeling and Precision in Painting

> No other style of painting appeals so naturally to the great majority of people, and in this sense it is a truly democratic style, offering no barrier of technique between the artist and the untrained eye. Now, after periods of impressionist, abstract and expressionist art, it is once again of interest to the cultivated taste, as it has always been to the general public.[1]
>
> – *DOROTHY C. MILLER (1943)*

This chapter aims to identify aesthetic categories that characterize visual culture in the United States in a particular way. The starting point for this endeavor is the term "American Realism," which refers to a cultural phenomenon primarily visible in literature and the visual arts in the United States. The main focus here is on the visual expression of this phenomenon. This chapter is based on the assumption that the combination of the adjective "American" and the noun "realism" results in a very specific meaning. In the following explanations, I will therefore not only explore the motivation behind the concept of "realism" and what could characterize the "American," but also how the conscious pairing of these two components could be described in order to make the insights that can be drawn from this fruitful for understanding the common context of meaning of 3D images, the overarching concern of this study.

The next section explains the variety of uses of the term "American Realism." In the two ensuing sub-sections, I focus specifically on possible meanings that emerge when the two terms are paired. To this end, in the first sub-section, I will describe the historical development of realist tendencies within the United States and the connections with the European debate on realism. Although the historical lens clarifies the development of realist trends, it can also lead to an overly rigid categorization. While this chapter aims to trace the historical and thus also social relevance of these movements, I ultimately search within US visual culture for overarching themes and motifs that transcend the historical context and express an "American worldview" both then and now. To break free from historical rigidity, in the second sub-section, I therefore consider realism as an aesthetic category. This perspective allows the exploration of the "American" to take center stage. In the second sub-section, taking into account the question of what meaning possibly emerges from pairing the terms "American" and "realism," it is possible to identify, primarily with reference to the art historian Barbara Novak, pictorial and production-aesthetic characteristics that transcend historical epochs. These characteristics exist independently of a temporal context in the manifestations of representational art in the United States. In the final step, in Part V, I will connect these aesthetic categories with the historical contexts of computer graphics developments described previously.

DOI: 10.1201/9781003649861-13

9.1 ON THE CATEGORIZATION OF "AMERICAN REALISM"

There is no clear definition of "American Realism" in art-historical literature. Regardless of its manifestation in the United States, the term "realist" is here used to describe a figurative mode of representation.[2] In his study *American Silences. The Realism of James Agee, Walker Evans, and Edward Hopper* literary scholar Joseph Anthony Ward attempts to synthesize the fields of literature, photography and the visual arts through aesthetic characteristics. He addresses the general difficulty of defining the concept of "realism" in his introduction:

> Most definitions agree that a realistic work of art is a true representation of men or things, but an absolute restrictive, and exclusively aesthetic definition of the concept is an impossibility. The most convincing definitions have always indicated not what realism is, but what it is not. [...] Nearly all realist theory insists on the priority of an objective or nearly objective fidelity to the phenomena of common social experience.[3]

With the justification that "[r]ealism has always been strongly ingrained in the American tradition,"[4] the *Museum of Modern Art* (MoMA) created its first exhibition in 1943, which focused programmatically on realist tendencies within US art. Titled *American Realists and Magic Realists*, it was the first MoMA exhibition to use the term "American Realists." Additionally, the exhibition introduced the term "Magic Realists"[5] for a previously untitled movement. Along with a retrospective of 19th century US painters, the curators primarily focused on contemporary artists of the time.[6] Edward Hopper and Charles Sheeler, who had already then been regarded as pioneers of the "new direction" 20 years earlier,[7] were also included. However, the accompanying exhibition catalog does not provide a clear definition of the terms. Although the curators differentiate between the "American Realists" and "Magic Realists," the selection of the artworks shown from *both* groups depended on a common aesthetic principle:

> The exhibition does not begin to cover all the varieties of painting which might be described by the term, realism. It is limited, in the main, to pictures of *sharp focus and precise representation*, whether the subject has been observed in the outer world – *realism*, or contrived by the imagination – *magic realism*.[8]

Around 50 years after the exhibition at MoMA, British art historian Edward Lucie-Smith also pairs the terms "American" and "realism" for the title of his monograph *American Realism*. However, he places the "Magic Realists" in a line with other realist movements. In his view, there is no "absolute value"[9] with which "realism" can be concretely understood. Instead, he recommends understanding each realist movement in relation to its time, as the representational art of the 20th century might not have met the "realist" requirements of 19th-century painting.[10] His overview begins in the 18th century with John Singleton Copley, "[t]he first fully professional painter in the United States,"[11] and ends in the 1990s. To narrow down the concept of "American Realism," Lucie-Smith emphasizes two aspects in particular: On the one hand – in reference to a social aspect of realist movements – the prevalent, historically founded relevance of democracy in the United States, and, on the other, the related role of photography. Lucie-Smith states that if one considers that, apart from the Indigenous population, US citizens have consisted of immigrants since the first colonization of the "new world" – people who deliberately left Europe in order to escape the firmly established hierarchies and social structures – a "democratic"[12] visual language that captures this new, "free" life seems logical. Not only was photography particularly well suited to this purpose, but it also significantly influenced the work of many US artists.[13] Lucie-Smith therefore emphasizes that "it has played a more prominent role in American visual culture than in that of Europe, where it originated."[14]

Lucie-Smith presents another possibility of categorization – independent of what the term "American" might imply – by discussing two different ways of understanding realism in general: On the one hand, as "conceptual realism" and, on the other, as "perceptual realism." The first is fundamentally dependent on our viewing habits: "[I]t can be defined as a kind of inventory of what the observer believes to be in front of him at a given moment."[15] At the same time, however, Lucie-Smith explains that the pioneers of photography brought about a change in our viewing habits by, for example, making things visible that could not be seen with the naked eye.[16] This is why they had an influence on "conceptual realism." Lucie-Smith describes "perceptual realism" as "seeing things without preconceptions, as innocently as possible."[17] But here, too, it is true that an objective, "innocent" perception is ultimately not possible, because the pioneers of photography had already changed the perception. To prove his point, Lucie-Smith mentions Jan Vermeer as an example. The painter intended to use the camera obscura to capture as objectively as possible a representation of his surroundings, but actually only received *one* possible concept of representation by looking through the lens.[18]

US art historian Barbara Novak takes a similar position in her study *American Painting of the Nineteenth Century. Realism, Idealism, and the American Experience*. She also differentiates between two painterly approaches: One based on conception and knowledge, and the other based on perception. For her, the use of the camera obscura also opens up a conceptual approach to the image,[19] but, at the same time, she seems to acknowledge an objective and perceptual approach for some painters who have made use of it. Her view of "perceptual realism" therefore differs from Lucie-Smith's. For Novak, the perceptual and objective approaches are directly related to plein air painting. In her view, the process of observing seems to be possible without any mediation.[20] She does not address a general change in viewing habits. For her, on the one hand, there is an academic and *conceptualizing* approach that was traditionally anchored in art and "which seems to be much the older of the two,"[21] as Lucie-Smith also emphasizes. On the other hand, Novak describes a second approach, plein air painting, which is known to have developed in the second half of the 19th century both in the United States and in Europe. The use of a mobile studio, which allowed artists to capture the light and atmosphere directly in nature, is for Novak unreservedly representative of "perceptual realism."[22]

The discussion of categorizing realistic tendencies in art can be supplemented by asking why MoMA, Lucie-Smith and Novak each developed their own concepts of realism. One possible answer is provided by Americanist John I. Baur, former director of the *Whitney Museum of American Art*. In his 1951 study *Revolution and Tradition in Modern American Art*, he explains *his* approach to categorizing artistic movements:

> [A] painter like Sheeler is discussed, for instance, both in the chapters on abstraction and on realism. [...] And classification is surely necessary if we are to perceive the order underlying the great diversity of modern art. Yet here a further danger arises: that in defining this order we may oversimplify it and thereby seriously falsify the truth. I have tried to guard against this by keeping my categories as elastic as possible, by frequently indicating the points at which they blend into one another, and by admitting freely that much art lies in these overlapping zones and could be considered with some justice under more than one heading.[23]

In contrast to the other studies presented, Baur explicitly communicates the necessity of using "elastic" categories for his research purpose. At the same time, it becomes implicitly clear that ultimately each of the studies presented so far uses its own categorization model. Therefore, it can be inferred that *each* new perspective from which artistic movements are viewed requires its own flexible categories. This is the only way to counter the danger of obscuring connections and blocking insights through rigid categorization. Although it might perhaps make more sense to talk about several realisms,[24] I will use the term "American Realism" in this chapter and throughout the study. Following Lucie-Smith, it can be understood as an umbrella term that in Baur's sense, unites numerous "elastic" categories. My aim is to identify these categories in the following sub-sections.

9.1.1 Realism as a Historical Phenomenon

The following presentation of the historically motivated development of realist trends in the United States is mainly based on the research of two authors: German art historian Boris Röhrl provides a systematic overview of realist trends and tendencies in his 2013 study *Realismus in der bildenden Kunst: Europa und Nordamerika 1830 bis 2000* (Realism in the Visual Arts. Europe and North America 1830–2000).[25] In the following I will describe his findings in relation to the United States and supplement them with viewpoints presented by US cultural historian David Shi in his 1995 monograph *Facing Facts: Realism in American Thought and Culture, 1850–1920.*[26] In it, Shi provides an interdisciplinary overview of various cultural areas such as the visual arts, literature and architecture. In contrast to Röhrl, who compares realism in the United States with European realist movements, Shi examines cultural developments within the United States. He derives the emerging realist tendencies of the mid-19th century directly from the idealism of the pre-war period, because "[u]nderstanding the rise of realism requires first understanding what it rose up against."[27] Röhrl's and Shi's positions are continually expanded to include other viewpoints from research on realism.

9.1.1.1 Bataille Réaliste

At the beginning of his study, Röhrl describes how "realism emerged as a natural consequence of the cultural development between 1830 and 1850 as a new direction in literature, painting and graphic art" and how it "strived for a factual and prosaic mode of representation."[28] Röhrl chooses the four basic positions of the French *bataille réaliste* as a historical point of reference. The first position – similar to the concept of photography at the time – advocated for a neutral depiction of nature, while the second strived for the representation of contemporary reality. The last two positions took a more socially critical stance and showed great similarities: The third pursued a critical realism that – for example through the depiction of poverty – sought to bring about a *reform* of conditions, and the fourth defended a realism that was intended to bring about a *radical transformation* of existing conditions.[29] Although Röhrl views "realism primarily from these four positions,"[30] he admits that some realist movements – such as magic realism and regionalism in the United States – cannot be reconciled with them.[31] Röhrl's perspective is often oriented toward the last two positions of the *bataille réaliste*, and he also attempts to reconcile painterly tendencies with them that pursued a different intention. In addition, he occasionally refers to US art historian Linda Nochlin, who, according to him, believes that realism in the United States is documentary and stands in the tradition of Dutch genre painting.[32] In her essay *The Realist Criminal and the Abstract Law*, in which Nochlin discusses the juxtaposition of realism and anti-realism within modernism, she does indeed refer to Dutch painting of the 15th and 17th centuries but uses the term "documentary" merely with reference to Rosalind Krauss. Nochlin emphasizes very clearly that, in addition to the historical phenomenon of realism within the second half of the 19th century, realist tendencies can be identified long before and even after this epoch.[33]

Röhrl's study is divided into four time periods – 1830–1917, 1918–1959, 1960–1989 and 1990–2000 – each of which contains individual chapters on realist movements in different countries, including France, Germany, England, Russia and the United States. Although Röhrl clearly points to a social aspect of US realism, he also speaks of a "separate line of development" that

> has several different roots: local traditions of genre painting, the influence of French realism (especially Millet), the Düsseldorf school of painting, the English influence, French naturalism in its commercial and socially critical forms. Social realism had already existed in the United States several decades before the *Ash Can School* at the turn of the century.[34]

According to Röhrl, the greatest influence on painting in the United States was French art – particularly the "naturalism of the 1870s"[35] – and the Düsseldorf School from Germany. Although Röhrl points to the idealistic influences of German painting, he insists that "the idealistic depiction of reality [...] remained alien to the Americans."[36] In Röhrl's view, Winslow Homer is a particularly apt example of a US painter who stands in the tradition of French naturalism. Like Thomas Eakins, Homer is regarded as one of the best-known representatives of realism in the United States in the second half of the 19th century – both artists are often associated with each other.[37] To give an example of their respective painterly approaches, Figures 9.1 and 9.2 present the paintings *Eagle Head, Manchester, Massachussetts (High Tide)* by Homer and *Baby at Play* by Eakins. Both paintings depict an everyday scene and both show, for instance, a comparable treatment of harsh light and the resulting strong dark shadows. Shi also highlights Homer as one of the most important realists, but at the same time emphasizes his

> potent strands of romantic idealism. His preference for the country over the city, his self-imposed isolation and his fascination with the essential loneliness of the human condition, his brooding preoccupation with nature's

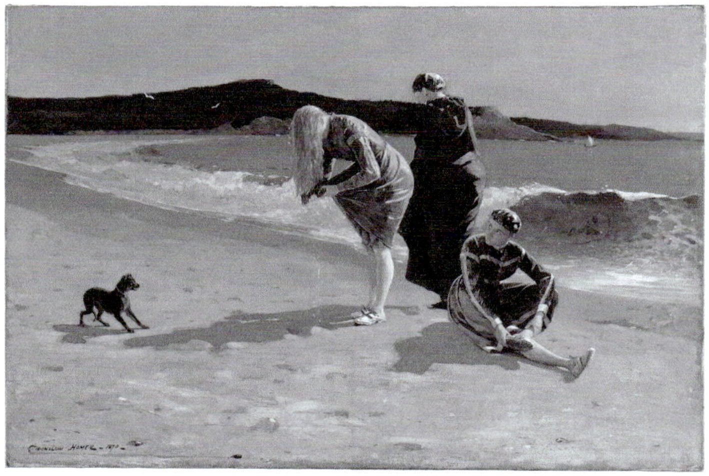

FIGURE 9.1 Winslow Homer, *Eagle Head, Manchester, Massachussetts (High Tide)*, 1870, oil on canvas, 26 × 38 in (66 × 96.5 cm), The Metropolitan Museum of Art, gift of Mrs. William F. Milton, 1923. (© CC0).

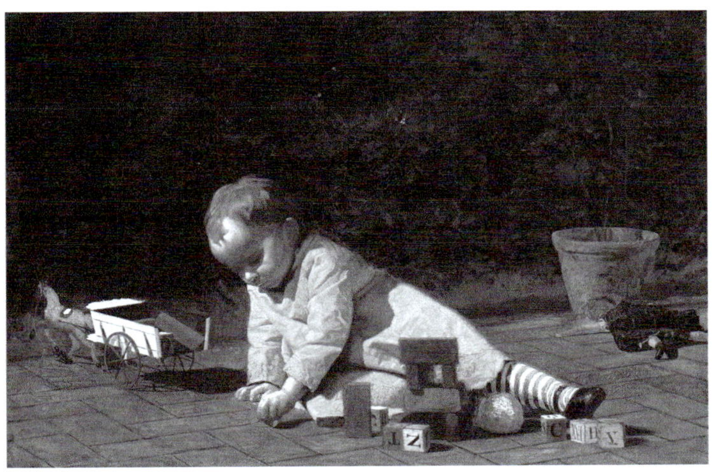

FIGURE 9.2 Thomas Eakins, *Baby at Play*, 1876, oil on canvas, 32 1/4 × 48 3/8 in (81.9 × 122.8 cm), National Gallery of Art, Washington, DC, John Hay Whitney Collection. (© CC0).

> dramas rather than those of the human community, his intoxicated awe in the face of the crashing sea [...] attest to his complex character and mixed motives. Homer's tangy blend of romantic realism gave his work its invigorating originality. Like Whitman he displayed virtues of a synthetic vision; he respected the dignity of facts but probed beneath them to explore deeper levels of feeling and meaning, rendering the transitory eternal.[38]

In his observations, Shi takes into account the idealistic tendencies of the early 19th century, which puts his argument in contrast to Röhrl's view that an idealistic representation of reality was foreign to US artists.

9.1.1.2 Ash Can Realism

Another movement that Röhrl considers within the first period discussed by him is the *Ash Can School*, which was active in New York in the early 20th century. His descriptions of this group of artists, initially also known as *The Eight*,[39] largely coincide with those of Shi. However, Röhrl's statement that "social realism had already existed in the United States several decades before the *Ash Can School* at the turn of the century"[40] proves to be contradictory. Although the group made a clear reference to society, its representatives did not pursue any political intentions. On the contrary, as Shi describes it, they were

> more concerned with expressing the charm of city life than with kindling social indignation or exploring the causes of poverty and injustice. Their vision of society was organic and inclusive, and their tone was more upbeat than strident, more descriptive than prescriptive, more enthusiastic than fearful.[41]

With this statement, Shi is referring to a text by Everett Shinn, a member of the group.[42] The working methods of the *Ash Can School* are well documented: John Sloan, another member, describes his mindset and methods in the volume *Gist of Art*, which he wrote with the support of his wife Helen Farr Sloan. He explains that "[m]y subjects were chosen with an illustrative point of view, literary, poetic motives."[43] Shi characterizes the attitude of Sloan and the entire *Ash Can School* as a "romantic fallacy"[44] because, according to him, they understood poverty and the suffering associated with it as a kind of virtue. Sloan, who was an active socialist from 1909 until the outbreak of the First World War, clarifies in his notes that he rejected the pictorial depiction of inhumane conditions: "I have never liked to show human beings when they are not themselves. I think it is an insult to their human dignity….One of the things I so dislike about most socially conscious pictures, is that the artist is looking down on people."[45] Röhrl himself describes Sloan's realism as illustrative[46] and emphasizes that there is a consensus in the literature that the *Ash Can School* was not socially critical. According to him, it developed as an independent style that was not influenced by European tendencies.[47] Röhrl and Shi both quote a statement by Robert Henri, who was the initiator of the artist group. In the statement, he expresses the desire to use art to capture the "American way of life" and the spirit of the times:

> As I see it, there is only one reason for the development of art in America, and that is that the people of America learn the means of expressing themselves in their own time and in their own land. In this country we have no need of art as culture; no need of art as a refined and elegant performance; no need of art for poetry's sake, or any of these things for their own sake. What we do need is art that expresses the spirit of the people of today.[48]

Henri's statement can be illustrated, for instance, by Sloan's painting *Six O'Clock, Winter*, in which he documents the hustle and bustle of New York commuters. The silhouette of an elevated railway station, into which a train has just pulled, is depicted against an evening sky. The dark iron frame of the station towers over the heads of numerous passengers, who are streaming in all directions (Figure 9.3). It is a snapshot

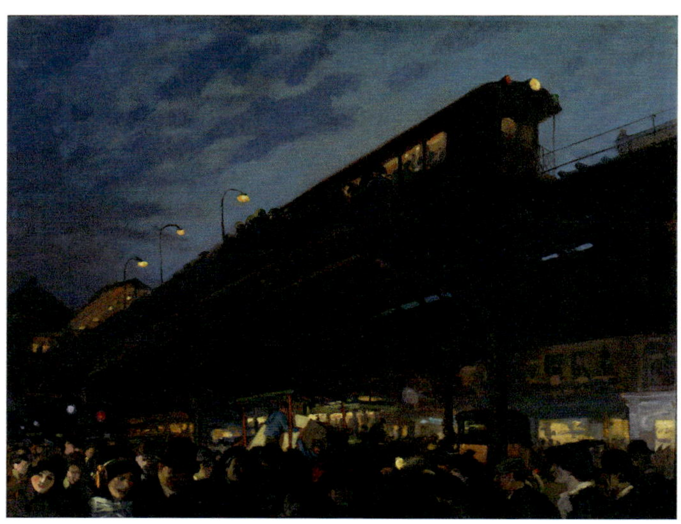

FIGURE 9.3 John Sloan, *Six O'Clock, Winter*, 1912, oil on canvas, 26 1/8 × 32 in. (66.36 × 81.28 cm), The Phillips Collection, Washington, DC, Acquired 1922.

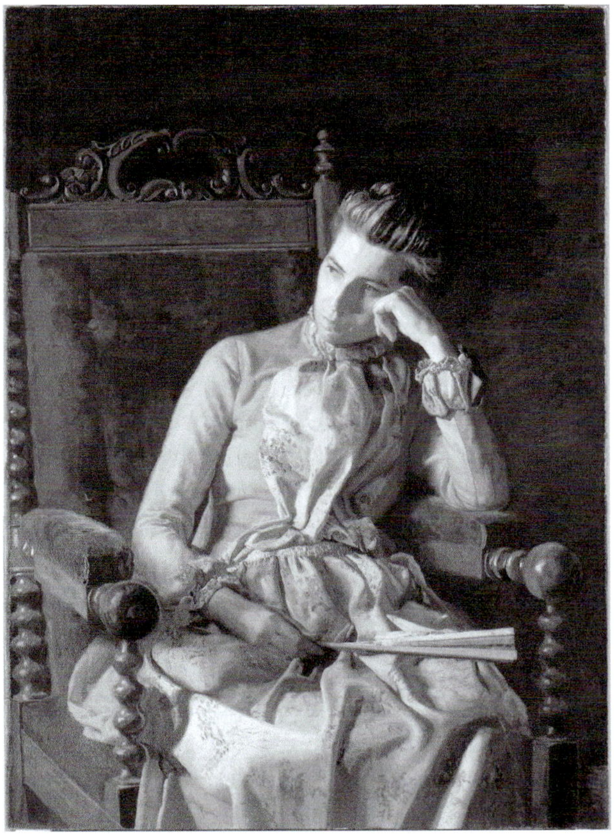

FIGURE 9.4 Thomas Eakins, *Miss Amelia Van Buren*, ca. 1891, oil on canvas, 45 × 32 in. (114.3 × 81.28 cm), The Phillips Collection, Washington, DC, Acquired 1927.

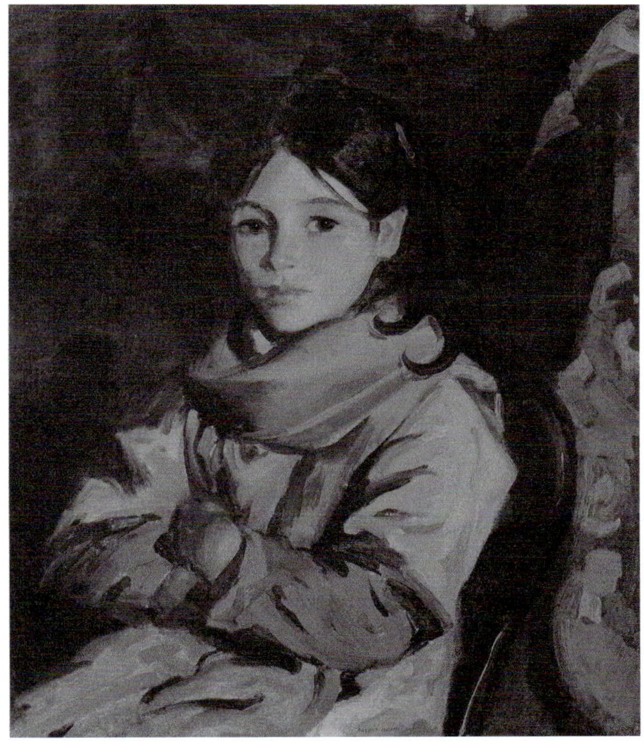

FIGURE 9.5 Robert Henri, *Mary Agnes*, 1924, oil on canvas, 24 × 20 in. (61 × 50.8 cm).

of an everyday situation and a mood that seems to be typical of the place depicted. In their endeavor to create an "indigenous American art,"[49] Homer and Eakins are regarded as central role models for Henri. Shi also describes Henri's view that, in contrast to a "factual reality," painting should strive for an "inner reality" in order to express one's feelings about what is perceived.[50] The depiction of "inner reality" also characterized Eakins' later creative phase at the turn of the century. However, during this period, he mainly produced portraits that expressed the state of mind of the people he portrayed rather than his own perception.[51] Although the painterly approaches differ greatly, comparing Eakins' painting *Miss Amelia Van Buren* with Henri's portrait *Mary Agnes* reveals the intellectual kinship between the two artists. The people portrayed are not posed for the viewer but shown in their respective states: Miss Amelia Van Buren looks thoughtfully to the side, turning away from the viewer. Mary Agnes looks directly at the viewer, but her facial expression and her folded arms indicate that she is also emotionally uninvolved in the portrait and is turning inward to her own thoughts (Figures 9.4 and 9.5).

Unlike Röhrl, Shi points in his study also to "the end" of the *Ash Can School*, which for him coincides with the *Armory Show* in 1913. The exhibition presented contemporary European art in the United States for the first time. In his 1955 monograph *American Painting from the Armory Show to the Depression*, art historian Milton Brown addresses the impact of the exhibition on US art: "It was a period in which newer concepts of art developing in Europe displaced an older tradition of 'realism' that had established itself in America in the first decade of this century."[52] He also emphasizes that "[a]fter the Armory Show American art was never the same again."[53] Although Henri's group was initially involved in the organization of the exhibition, according to Shi, their artistic expression also lost importance in direct comparison to the tendencies of the European avant-garde: "Henri and the other New York Realists were virtually forgotten amid the furor over the European modernists at the Armory Show."[54]

Shi concludes his account of realist movements in art with remarks on the *Ash Can School*. In the summary of his study, he offers an outlook and lists various positions on realism. He begins with a presentation of "anti-realist" arguments and emphasizes in this context that realism is a "bygone era."[55] However, he then transitions to an argument that attributes continued relevance to realism:

> Today realism retains its artistic appeal as the United States struggles to embody its ideal as a nation proud of its diversity and just in its social transactions. Painter Willard Midgette [...] clung tenaciously to the belief that realistic representation possesses a peculiar ability to intensify and extend a sense of social communion. For this reason alone, the creation of an "aesthetic of the common" and a "beloved community" remains a beckoning goal.[56]

Since Shi's observations end with the year 1920, his study offers no room for cross-references to later realist tendencies. Although Röhrl is also rather cautious with cross-references, he places Edward Hopper in the tradition of the *Ash Can School*, who – as Lucie-Smith describes it – plays a central role in the history of realist painting in the United States.[57]

9.1.1.3 Social Realism

Röhrl's second chapter on the United States, which covers the period from 1918 to 1959, particularly focuses on the *Social Realism* of the 1930s because, in contrast to the other realist movements,[58] it has, according to him, received little attention in art-historical research to date.[59] His discussion mainly takes place in the context of the economic crisis and the Roosevelt era, but he emphasizes that there were already socially committed artists in the United States before the actual development of *Social Realism*. This can be confirmed by Shi's comments on the developments within literature and in photojournalism[60] of the 19th century: Shi describes an emerging social attitude before 1850 that reacted to industrial growth and the associated consumer culture. According to Shi, this attitude continued throughout the rest of the 19th century, reaching its peak at the turn of the century.[61] Röhrl presents Rockwell Kent as an example, whose work also began before the 1930s. His works are to Röhrl a prototype of social realism: "His writings form the 'credo' of American *Social Realism*. The aim was to bring about change through evolution."[62] However, Röhrl contradicts his social perspective when he emphasizes Kent's love of "wild nature" and a related connection to Winslow Homer. Röhrl himself concludes that it is "difficult to connect his [Kent's] art with social realism."[63]

Although I try to avoid strict art historical categories, and rather keep them "elastic" in Baur's sense, US *Social Realism* of the 1930s can in fact be considered a nearly isolated historical phenomenon. The artist David Shapiro offers a comprehensive overview of the social realism of the 1930s with his volume *Social Realism: Art as a Weapon*. He argues that social realism was the predominant painterly style in the United States during that decade.[64] It is the only art movement in the United States that was clearly left-wing. This development can be attributed, at least in part, to the economic crisis. However, Franklin D. Roosevelt also established state support programs for artists to make them independent of the private, economically weakened art market.[65] The main idea was to provide access to art for everyone, which is why the funding programs particularly supported murals on public buildings. An example is Martin Fletcher's 1938 mural *Mail Transportation* (Figure 9.6). In Shapiro's view, "the single greatest element in the development of this explicitly political and social art may very well have been the United States government itself."[66] Abstract painters were excluded from the program because "it was assumed that their art was not comprehensible to the general public."[67] Edward Hopper deliberately did not take part in the art promotion programs, despite his realistic style of expression, because in his eyes they merely promoted mediocrity.[68]

The Mexican muralists also served as a model for this left-wing movement, although Röhrl describes the US representatives as more "restrained"[69]: "[I]ts content is neither revolutionary nor provocative." It merely documents "[t]he world of labor [...]. The working person is depicted anonymously. It is the same anonymity that is already present in Millet's genre paintings."[70] Alongside the US mural painting programs, Röhrl mentions the three Soyer brothers, Raphael, Moses and Isaac, who, according to both Röhrl and Lucie-Smith, also fall into the category of *Social Realism*. Like the other members of the

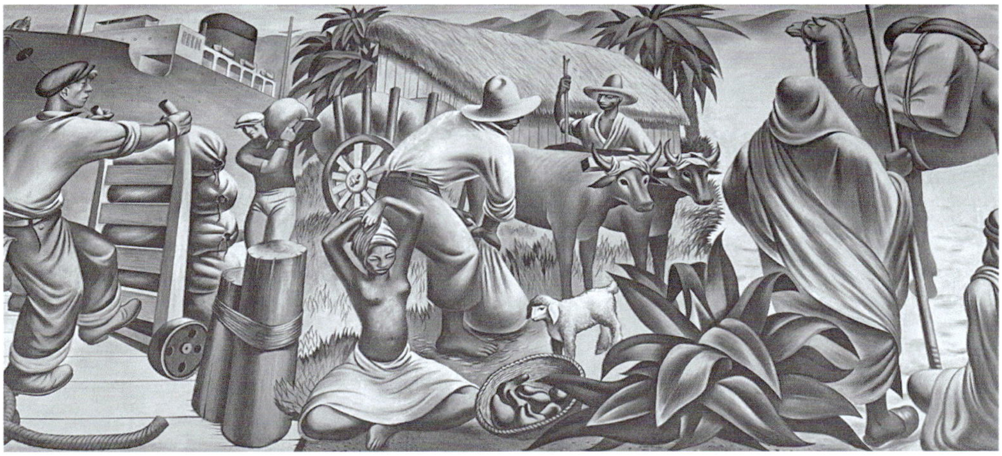

FIGURE 9.6 Martin Fletcher, *Mail Transportation* (detail), 1938, mural in post office, San Pedro, CA. (Photograph by Natalie McDonald. © Creative Commons 2024.)

so-called *Fourteenth Street Group*, they documented the lives of New York's poorer population in their paintings (Figures 9.7 and 9.8). Lucie-Smith therefore also speaks of *Urban Realism*, and although the Soyer brothers showed a particular sensitivity to the political developments of the 1930s and 1940s due to their own Jewish ancestry, Lucie-Smith also emphasizes that this did not apply to all *Urban Realists*:

> Any painter whose subject matter is chiefly urban is apt to find himself or herself characterized as a social realist. This is misleading in the case of a number of prominent American artists of the 1930s and 1940s. Their subject was the city and its environs – specifically New York – but what they painted was seen in a relatively neutral way, leaving social and moral commentaries to others.[71]

Among the members of the *Fourteenth Street Group*, some of whom were classified by Röhrl as *American Scene painters*,[72] were also artists such as Kenneth Hayes Miller and Isabel Bishop. Their paintings made the Depression visible, but they did not intend them to be explicitly political.[73] It therefore seems logical that a few years later – in the early 1950s – Raphael Soyer initiated the publication of the magazine *Reality: A Journal of Artists' Opinions*, which advocated for the "promotion of what were called human qualities in painting"[74] and consciously spoke out *against* a political stance.[75]

The British art historian Brendan Prendeville places Bishop and the Soyer brothers in the tradition of the *Ash Can School*. In his study *Realism in 20th Century Painting* he makes a decisive *aesthetic* differentiation between the *Social Realists* and the members of the *Fourteenth Street Group*:

> The work of Philip Evergood, a friend of the 14th Street painters, showed a still deeper social involvement. It is notable that of the painters associated with Social Realism those whose work was most sharply political were not realists in the naturalistic sense; Evergood himself, Jacob Lawrence (b. 1917) and Ben Shahn (1898–1969) were each quite independent of the Ashcan tradition, unlike Bishop, Marsh and the Soyer brothers [...].[76]

Prendeville describes Evergood as an activist and a "leading spirit" of various artists' initiatives, including the left-wing *American Artists Congress*.[77] It was formed in 1936 due to the political conditions in Europe, particularly Germany. Röhrl describes the event as a "milestone" and as "resistance against the imminent threat of war and against fascism and racism in one's own country [...]."[78]

According to Röhrl, the left-wing attitude of *Social Realism* began to dissolve at the start of World War II due to a newly emerging national sense of unity. Consequently, the mural painting programs were also discontinued in 1939.[79] Röhrl additionally describes

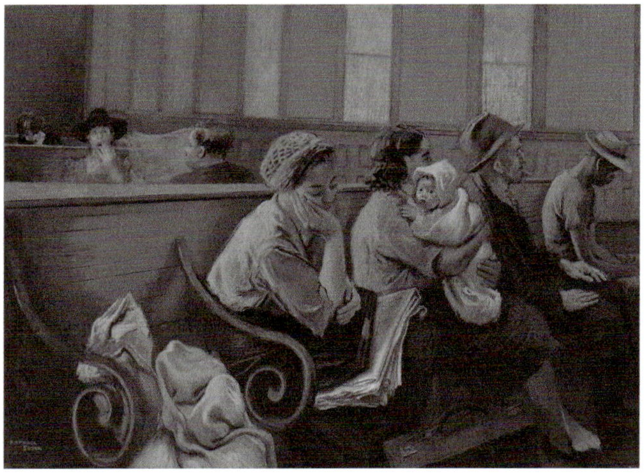

FIGURE 9.7 Raphael Soyer, *A Railroad Station Waiting Room*, 1940, oil on canvas, 34 1/4 × 45 1/4 in. (87 × 114.94 cm), National Gallery of Art, Washington, DC, Corcoran Collection (Museum Purchase, William A. Clark Fund). (Photograph by NGA. Reproduced with permission of the Estate of Raphael Soyer.)

the gradual emergence of *Abstract Expressionism* as related to this shift. However, by the start of the Cold War, "the political climate had [...] changed significantly."[80] Röhrl concludes by emphasizing that the *Social Realism* of the 1930s developed independently of the19th-century French *bataille réaliste*.[81]

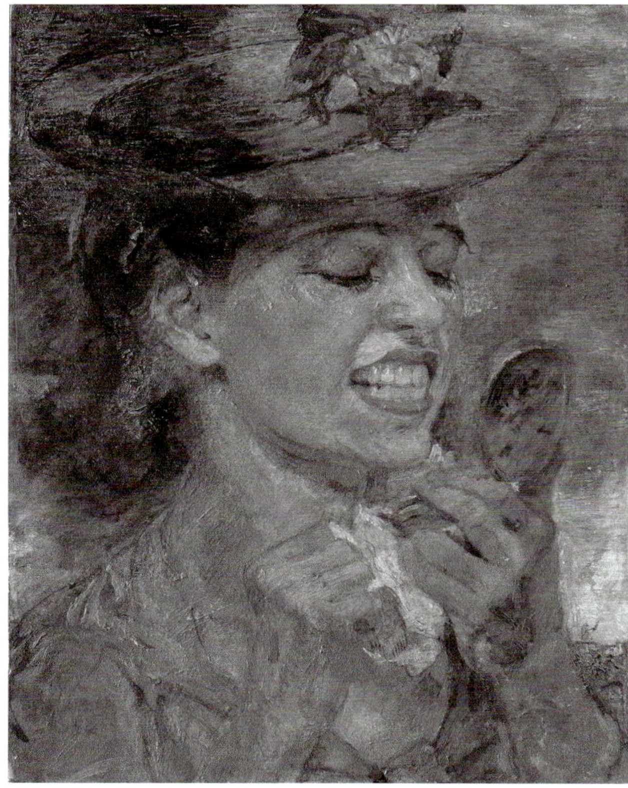

FIGURE 9.8 Isabel Bishop, *Tidying Up*, 1941, oil on Masonite, 15 × 11 1/2 in., collection of the Indianapolis Museum of Art at Newfields, Delavan Smith Fund, 43.24. (© Estate of Isabel Bishop. Courtesy of DC Moore Gallery, New York.)

9.1.1.4 The Trends of the Late 20th Century

Röhrl's third main chapter, which covers the period from 1960 to 1989, contains sections on *Pop Art*,[82] *Photorealism*,[83] *New Realism*[84] and *Critical Realism*[85] as well as on new forms of *Social Realism*.[86] Röhrl begins by questioning whether Pop Art and Photorealism should be included in a study of "realism," since they "were not connected to the *bataille réaliste* in terms of either their external form or their theory and [...] in some cases even represented aggressive counter-concepts."[87] For him, the starting point for answering this question is Edmond Duranty and his concept of a realistic and also critical realism. Due to the emerging prosperity in Western countries from the 1950s onward, *art critique* no longer seemed to be needed. Röhrl even speaks of a "slow disappearance of realism in art [...]."[88] Despite his strictly historical argumentation, he decides to include Pop Art and Photorealism in his discussions. In doing so, he aligns with the current state of research, which largely considers both movements.[89]

Röhrl summarizes the last period from 1990 to 2000 very briefly. He explains that the realist manifestations within the United States during this period can be attributed to the educational institutions there, which still primarily teach art techniques of academic realism, and to certain galleries that primarily exhibit representational paintings. In this context, he speaks of a "romantic impulse" that seems to characterize this representational mode of painting.[90] He also mentions the continuation of *Social Realism* through mural painting programs in various large US cities, such as the *Mural Arts Program* (MAP) in Philadelphia (see also endnote 70 in this chapter).[91]

Overall, Röhrl's comments on realism in the United States demonstrate his view that it is a predominantly independent development, as he himself also explains at the beginning of his study. His references to the French *bataille réaliste* occasionally create argumentative contradictions regarding realist tendencies in the United States, as he often has to depart from this perspective to be able to present deviating facts appropriately. In his comments above on *Ash Can Realism* this also became evident. Therefore, his approach contrasts sharply with Shi's. While both follow historical developments, Shi presents numerous approaches in his study that defy rigid categorization. For instance, unlike Röhrl, Shi addresses with greater ease the occasional fusion of realism and idealism within the United States' realistic tradition. Shi also refers to a particular sensitivity to scientific facts, which, in his view, had already developed in the United States before the Civil War, at the time of pre-war idealism. The progress of science "across every field of knowledge helped inspire and legitimize the realistic movement in thought, literature, and the arts."[92] However, although Shi thus opens up an overarching approach, he considers his own account to be purely historical. An aesthetic approach, on the other hand, is in his view insufficient:

> I do not offer any startling new thesis about realism as a conceptual or aesthetic category. No overarching interpretation can adequately encompass the diverse motives and methods associated with the realistic impulse. Instead, I use the era's preoccupation with "facing facts" as an organizing frame within which to examine the emergence of various realistic sensibilities […].[93]

Nevertheless, his study provides numerous points of reference for considering realism as an "aesthetic category." While I also do not aim to provide an all-encompassing interpretation of realist tendencies in this sub-section, I will, however, attempt to identify overarching motifs independent of their historical context in the following sub-section. This methodological decision can be understood in the sense of US literary scholar Ward, who also juxtaposes the historical and aesthetic approaches and recommends looking beyond a purely historical perspective:

> The indispensable substance of realism is observable phenomena; historically, the emphasized phenomena in both literary and visual realism are public activities and individuals in social situations. But these phenomena – so a variety of conflicting theories maintain – must subserve or at least accommodate an ideology, an aesthetic, or an attitude toward experience that sometimes organizes and always transcends the "mere" play of phenomenal energies.[94]

9.1.2 Realism as an Aesthetic Category

Building on the questions posed at the beginning of this chapter, in this sub-section I will now turn to the "American" and explore the influence it has on the phenomenon of "Realism." As noted, my focus here is on identifying overarching themes and parameters that characterize the "American" and through which the various forms of "American Realism" can be aligned. After a brief review of the 18th century, the main focus will be on the art-historical developments in the United States during the 19th century. These will be expanded upon with developments in the 20th century. Two aspects are of particular relevance in the following: First, the early sensitivity to scientific facts mentioned by Shi, and second, a strongly pronounced idealism that is even visible in Homer's realistic genre painting, as also described by Shi. Therefore, I argue, that the "American" synthesizes the opposing positions of realism and idealism and expresses itself in a visual language that shows a high degree of technical precision.

The following descriptions are based on the study *American Painting of the Nineteenth Century. Realism, Idealism, and the American Experience* by US art historian Barbara Novak. It contains essential points of reference for my discussion, as it is also in search of the "American" and therefore mainly looks at developments *within* the United States:

> [I]f it [the study] appears to raise the old question "What is American in American Art?" it does so with an awareness that *what* is American is sometimes not as apt as *how* is American. For we are dealing not only with indigenous properties but with processes of transformation of European traditions. […] What makes them indigenous is not their uniqueness to America but rather the *frequency or constancy of their occurrence within continuing American traditions to which they*

> *also contribute*. Certain concerns, qualities of form, and modes of procedure seem to occur again and again, though time and circumstances may have changed.[95]

What is problematic about Novak's approach is that she uses the term "indigenous" as well as the term "American" not in relation to the actual Indigenous population and their traditions, but rather – as becomes clear from her statement – only for those cultural traditions that have developed since the colonization of the continent. Although I distance myself from her use of these terms, Novak's observations provide valuable insights that can also be applied to computer graphics. This significantly helps to determine their common context of meaning, because she presents essential features that paradigmatically characterize the visual culture of the United States. Accordingly, when Novak discusses indigenous or native traditions, the terms must be understood in this context.

As the title of her study suggests, Novak's main focus is on the developments of the 19th century. Although she structures her accounts along a rough timeline, beginning with the end of the 18th century and extending into the 20th century, she makes it her agenda to establish references and cross-references in order to be able to present the "qualities of form" and "modes of procedure" in a comprehensive manner. To this end, she deliberately ignores commonly used art-historical categories "as, unfortunately, the historian with his necessity for labels often cannot."[96] She thus pursues an unusual and radical methodological approach within US art history.

Most of her chapters focus on individual artists who exemplify certain aspects of production aesthetics, while three chapters deal with specific topics instead of specific artists: (1) Luminism, which Novak considers particularly central; (2) a European-influenced painterly tradition in the United States; and (3), in the epilogue, the developments of the 20th century with a special focus on the 1960s, taking into account movements such as Abstract Expressionism and Pop Art.

9.1.2.1 The Significance of Things

Novak's depictions begin, like Lucie-Smith's, with John Singleton Copley (1738–1815). In his paintings from 1765 to 1774 she recognizes for the first time an ongoing "American vision," a tradition that has endured ever since: "In Copley's art of this period, the unique relation of object to idea that characterizes so much American realism from colonial times to the present assumes forceful and explicit form."[97]

Novak introduces the term "American realism" at the beginning of her study, although she only uses it rarely throughout her book. She traces her concept of realism back to the Limner tradition in the United States. This term describes self-taught artists and craftspeople without academic training during the initial colonization of the American continent. The Limner tradition was, as Novak describes, characterized by the need to make the "new world" comprehensible through a representational visual language, a mindset that has been deeply rooted in the US visual tradition ever since.[98] Novak explains that Copley emerged from this Limner tradition, even though he also spent several years in Europe to improve his technical skills.[99]

A defining characteristic of the Limner tradition is that all the depicted objects or figures are given equal importance. This means that the experiences to be captured in the paintings are transferred to a two-dimensional surface without any prioritization and in a strictly conceptual manner.[100] According to Novak, Copley also produced his paintings against this background. She describes his style as a "specific kind of ideal or conceptual realism,"[101] which she illustrates with his 1771 portrait of *Mrs Ezekiel Goldthwaith* (Figure 9.9). She recognizes this specific type of realism, which expresses a unique relationship between object and idea, for the first time in Copley's work. She also identifies a special cultural significance in this relationship that, to her, is emblematic of the "American experience."[102] With reference to the theologian Jonathan Edwards (1703–1758), she argues that, in addition to the word or the intellect, great importance was already attached to "things" in the United States in the 18th century.[103] As Novak explains, this mindset continued with Ralph Waldo Emerson in the 19th century, with nature being the main focus of his reflections. The significance of nature to Emerson is discussed in more detail in the following part of this study. The central aspect here is that Emerson believed the sensual experience of nature revealed a deeper truth. Spending time in nature meant connecting with the unity of the world.[104] As Novak explains,

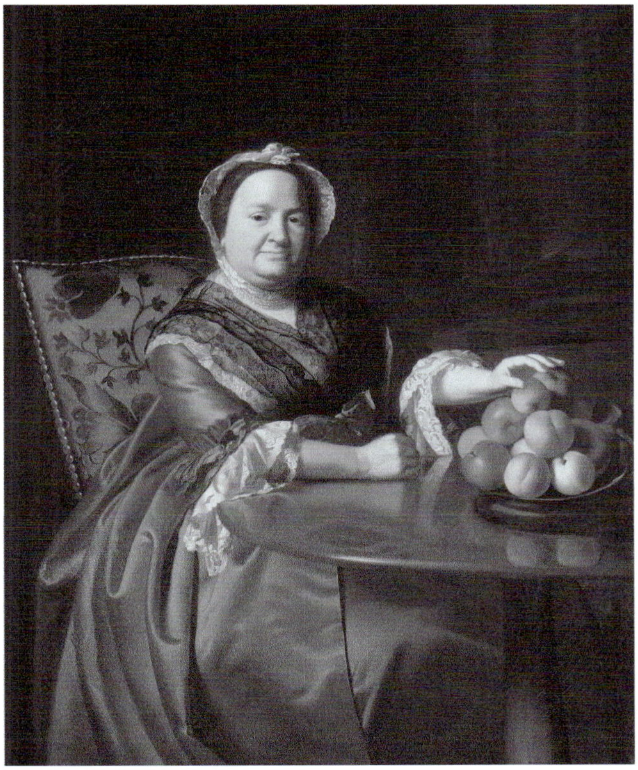

FIGURE 9.9 John Singleton Copley, American, 1738–1815, *Mrs. Ezekiel Goldthwait (Elizabeth Lewis)*, 1771, oil on canvas, 50 1/8 × 40 1/8 in. (127.32 × 101.92 cm), Museum of Fine Arts, Boston, Bequest of John T. Bowen in memory of Eliza M. Bowen, 41.84. (Photograph © 2026 Museum of Fine Arts, Boston.)

the physical presence of nature therefore held special significance for the transcendentalists:

> To the transcendental mind, object and idea were one, and all matter was an extension of God. Thus the landscape artists, and especially the luminists after Copley, could value the smallest fact in nature – the leaf, the pebble in the foreground of a Heade landscape – and embrace also the larger equivalence of God with nature through the infinite space of a Kensett distance or the other-worldly light of a Bierstadt sky.[105]

Overall, the appreciation of God-given nature was particularly influential in the United States during the 19th century when it came to the aesthetic examination of the environment. According to Novak, artistic expression at the time was therefore less characterized by romanticist tendencies. It refrained from imagining the world created by God completely freely and changing it too much. It was to be depicted as it is.[106] At the beginning of this part, this dynamic was addressed in connection with Thomas Cole. He, too, had to justify himself for occasionally deviating too far from the reality he found. According to Novak, romanticist elements appeared in the 19th century – if at all – in the form of "super-real techniques,"[107] similar to those that characterize Surrealism in the 20th century, for which the imaginary was one of the central starting points. Although the religious and moral concepts no longer apply today, Novak notes that the special relationship to things has survived in the United States to this day:

> Americans are still uniquely aware of *things*. For the need to grasp reality, to ascertain the physical *thereness* of things seems to be a necessary component of the American experience. […] From the very beginning, artists in America have tried to create measurable certainties and have utilized scientific, mathematical, and mechanical aids to achieve their aims.[108]

In Copley's paintings, this highly technical approach to his portraits manifested itself in the fact that, as Novak explains, he met the people to be portrayed many times before attempting to translate their personalities into a painting using strictly conceptual methods.[109]

The relevance of things and the related connection between "object" and "idea" or "concept" now provide an initial answer to the question of what characterizes the "American" in "American Realism." Consistent with my hypothesis that the typically "American" visual language unites realism and idealism and is expressed with a sensitivity for technical precision, David Shi aptly describes the merging of factual realism and transcendental idealism. Although he deems a purely aesthetic examination of the phenomenon of realism to be insufficient, he notes that

> [t]his romantic celebration of the actualities of common life, however tentative, vicarious, or celestial, greatly expanded the range of cultural expression. By embracing the aesthetic

> significance of their everyday surroundings, the Transcendentalists nudged the boundary of idealism towards the border of realism.[110]

As Shi expresses here, the transcendental appreciation of ordinary things is reminiscent of historically motivated realism, which was also concerned with depicting everyday life. At the same time, Shi's description also demonstrates that, especially in Transcendentalism, the objects contain an idealizing statement, because each object stands as an idea for the entirety of the universe. Novak also notes this. Shi recognizes a contradiction in this merging, which is why he reasons:

> [W]hat makes the Transcendentalists so compelling – and baffling – are their contradictory impulses. While searching for a mystical union of their souls with the Universal Being, they also celebrated the essential dignity and beauty residing in common things and common experiences. They believed it possible to unite the common and the divine, to produce a fertile synthesis of the real and the ideal.[111]

The synthesis of realism and idealism mentioned here by Shi will be examined in more detail below. Shi frequently refers to this synthesis in his study, for example in regard to Walt Whitman, who closely followed Emerson's philosophy.[112] Shi thus establishes a line of argument comparable to Novak's, although he does not pursue it systematically, like she does. She titles the chapter on Thomas Cole, who aimed to capture the "characteristic spirit" of nature, "The Dilemma of the Real and the Ideal," because "[he] was anticipating a concept of synthesis, in which form clothes idea [...]."[113] The dilemma refers to Cole's problem that critics and patrons, on the one hand, demanded that he not be too imaginative, while, on the other hand, they demanded more than mere imitations of "God's work."[114]

9.1.2.2 The Synthesis of the Real and the Ideal

According to Novak, it was the representatives of the *Hudson River School* – especially Asher B. Durand – who developed a particularly characteristic "hybrid aesthetic of the real-ideal."[115] In relation to Durand's technique, she mentions for the first time the plein air approach emerging in America. For her, as described earlier, this approach represents a form of "perceptual realism" involving the "objective" capture of nature, such as the weather and the mood of the light. In this context, she draws a line to the parallel developments in France, specifically to Gustave Courbet: "[Durand's] studies from nature in the 1850s are as vanguard in realistic observation as are Courbet's at the same time or slightly later in France."[116] Like Courbet in France, she considers Durand a harbinger of Impressionism in America. At the same time, however, she emphasizes that Durand, despite his "objective" and "realistic" approach, mainly produced "cliché compositions"[117] in the sense of the *Hudson River School*. Novak even sees parallels between Durand's painting and Luminism, which emerged somewhat later, as his use of light was often "poetic rather than analytic."[118] In his painting *Study from Nature, Stratton Notch, Vermont*, he combines, according to Novak, impressionist and luminist characteristics with an impasto style in the foreground and a very linear style in the background (Figure 9.10).[119] Although light plays a decisive role in both forms of expression, Novak makes a crucial distinction: "If we say that Impressionism is the *objective* response to the *visual* sensation of

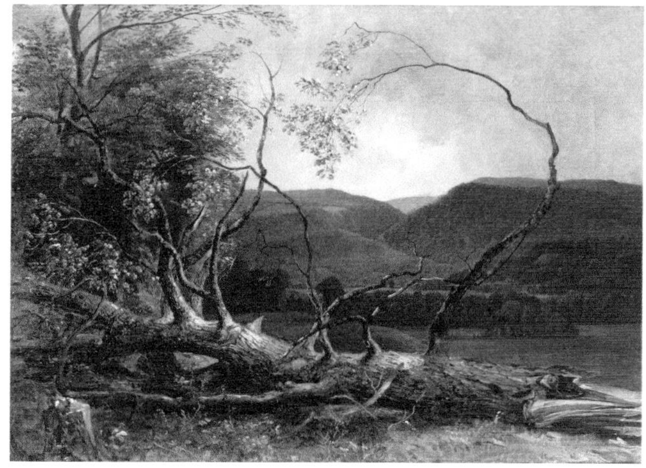

FIGURE 9.10 Asher Brown Durand, *Study from Nature, Stratton Notch, Vermont*, 1853, oil on canvas, unframed: 18 × 23 3/4 in. (45.7 × 60.3 cm), framed: 27 1/2 × 33 1/2 × 3 5/8 in. (69.9 × 85.1 × 9.2 cm), gift of Mrs. Lucy Maria Durand Woodman, New-York Historical Society, 1907.21. (Photography © New-York Historical Society.)

light, then perhaps we can say that luminism is the *poetic* response to the *felt* sensation."[120] Novak then refers to the different developments of Impressionism and the associated approach to light in both regions. In the United States, as in Europe, the sense of the "real" had gradually replaced the need for "idealism," but in the United States, the sense of both had always survived:

> The American necessity for the ideal, for "sentiment," which needs but a touch of profundity to become "lyricism," militated against an objective, analytic dissection of God's world. Sunlight, as a divine attribute, could hardly be broken down into the light rays of the spectrum. God's rocks could not be dissolved (the conceptual integrity of form had to be maintained), nor could they really lose their local color. The road to Impressionism as coloristic analysis and dissection was, despite all atmospheric observations, blocked to American painters.[121]

For Novak, it therefore seems logical that – instead of a pronounced US Impressionism – it was Luminism which developed from this mindset. In terms of thought, the movement was close to Emerson's Transcendentalism. Similar to Copley's work in the 18th century, in Luminism the artist recedes into the background leaving barely any brushstrokes. People are only depicted in miniature and take on the same importance as the nature that surrounds them.[122] Fitz H. Lane's painting *Owl's Head, Penobscot Bay, Maine* combines all these qualities (see Figure 8.6). It synthesizes the real and the ideal by combining an analytical acumen to render the depicted scenery as precisely as possible with a luminosity that, on the one hand, reflects the physical properties of light and, on the other, has an inherent mystical power.[123]

9.1.2.3 Luminism

Novak ascribes a central role to Luminism within US art history. Although the movement is primarily concerned with landscape painting, she also recognizes its influence on other painterly traditions. She describes the movement as "one of the most truly indigenous styles in the history of American art, a way of seeing so intimately related to the artist's idea of world and his relation to it that it can be identified not only in landscape painting but also in still life, genre, and portraiture."[124] In this context, she refers to Baur, whose definition of Luminism in his 1954 essay *American Luminism* is still valid according to Novak. In Baur's view, Luminism developed a sense not only for light, but also for the "things" in nature. The luminist artist becomes a "transparent eyeball" in Emerson's sense[125] and remains completely anonymous. The artist merely acts as a mediator by transferring one's feeling directly to a depicted object. Novak summarizes Baur's thoughts on Luminism as follows: "It is thus a realism that goes far beyond 'mere' realism, to be touched, in some instances, with super-real overtones and, in others, to register that magnified intensity that turns realism into a form of impersonal expressionism."[126]

Novak describes the horizontal composition of many Luminist paintings as an almost mathematical approach. Often the arrangement of individual picture planes is offset in perspective, which creates depth parallel to the surface of the canvas. The artist becomes a "clarifying lens"[127] that allows the viewer to experience the painting directly. As the particular sensitivity for dimension and technical precision is an essential characteristic of Luminism, it cannot be ruled out that mechanical aids were used in the composition of the paintings. Researchers assume that the "purest luminist,"[128] Fitz H. Lane, made use of a camera obscura or camera lucida. In this context, Novak also mentions Thomas Eakins, whose rowing pictures essentially correspond to luminist characteristics as well. Both Lane and Eakins used photographs and technical drawings as aids for their paintings to lend scientific precision to their already conceptual images. For instance, a central perspective grid can be seen in Eakins' *Perspective Studies for "John Biglen in a Single Scull,"* which Eakins used to meticulously plan the depth planes in his painting (Figures 9.11–9.13). Novak also lists numerous painters who worked as inventors alongside their artistic activities.[129] In this context, she refers to the Americanists John A. Kouwenhoven and Leo Marx, as both have extensively explored the role of technology within the United States.[130] In his monograph *Made in America: The Arts in Modern Civilization*, Kouwenhoven contrasts the developments in the United States with European ones, discussing the

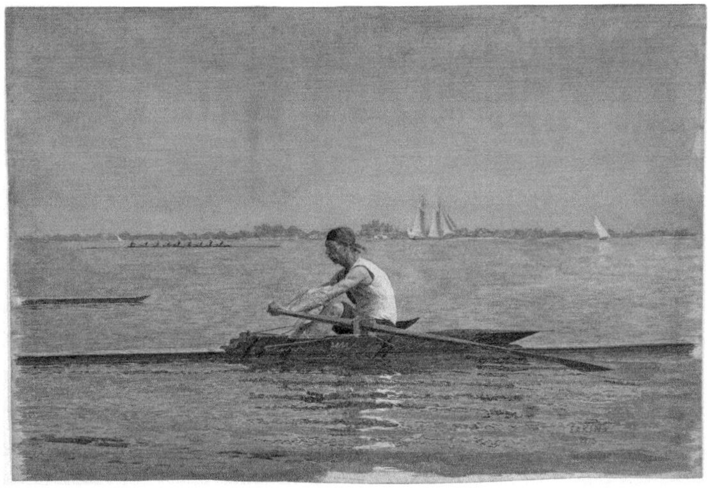

FIGURE 9.11 Thomas Eakins, *John Biglin in a Single Scull*, ca. 1873, watercolor, sheet: 16 7/8 × 23 15/16 in. (42.9 × 60.8 cm), Yale University Art Gallery, gift of Paul Mellon, B.A. 1929, LHDH 1967, in honor of Jules D. Prown, the first Director of the Yale Center for British Art. (© CC0.)

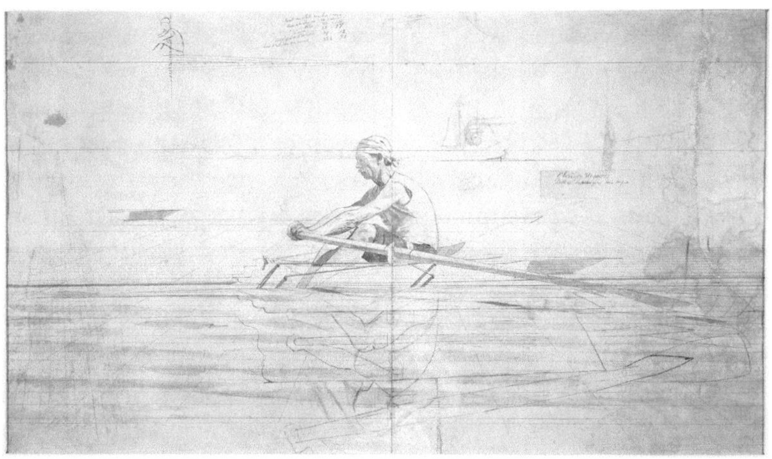

FIGURE 9.12 Thomas Eakins, American, 1844–1916, *Perspective Studies for John Biglen in a Single Scull*, about 1873, graphite, pen and brown ink, and brush with brown wash on two sheets of buff paper, sheet: 27 3/8 × 45 1/4 in. (69.5 × 114.9 cm), Museum of Fine Arts, Boston, Gift of Cornelius V. Whitney 60.1130. (Photograph © 2026 Museum of Fine Arts, Boston.)

significant influence of technology on the development of art in the United States:

> Their importance [that of US arts] lies in the fact that because they are American, and because America is [...] the only major world power to have taken form as a cultural unit in the period when technological civilization was spreading throughout the world – because of both these facts the arts in America reveal, more clearly on the whole than the arts of any other people, the nature and the meaning of modern civilization.[131]

The influence of technological and scientific progress on US art is clearly visible in Luminism. As Novak recognizes the movement as the first truly "indigenous" artistic tradition, the question arises as to whether and to what extent the connection between technology and art has survived in art beyond Luminism. According to one of Novak's main arguments, many typical Luminist qualities are still visible in later movements:

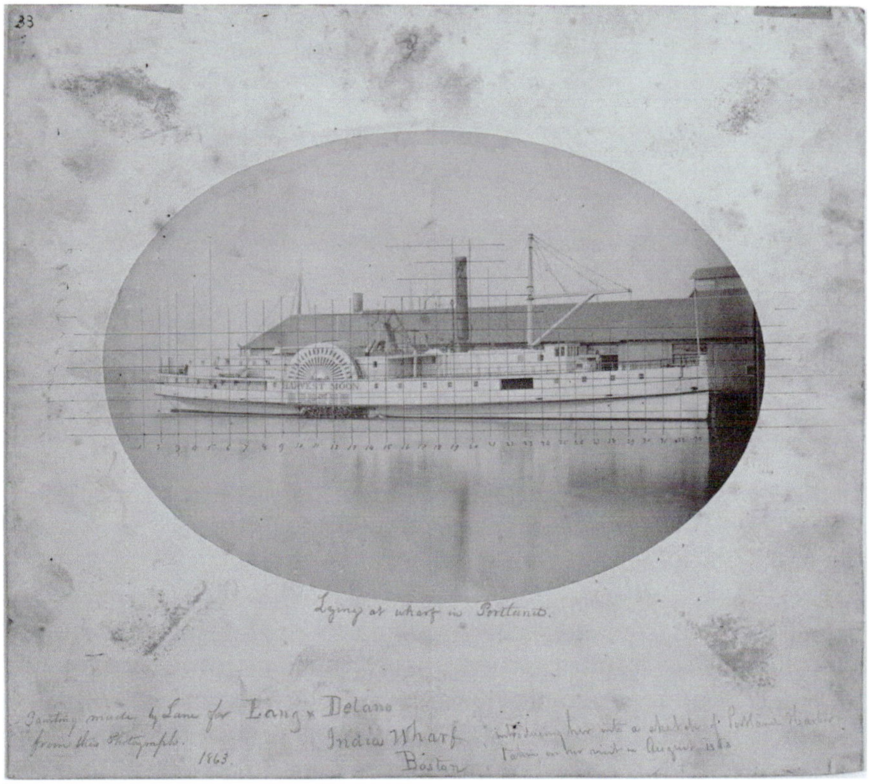

FIGURE 9.13 Fitz Henry Lane (1804–1865), *Steamer "Harvest Moon," Lying at Wharf in Portland*, 1863, graphite over photograph on paper, 9 3/4 × 10 1/2 in. (24.8 × 26.7 cm), collection of the Cape Ann Museum, Gloucester, MA. (Gift of Samuel H. Mansfield, 1927 (485.33).)

> Throughout the history of American painting, from Copley to the present, aspects of this luminist vision have endured. The quality of artistic anonymity, the concern with the fact of the physical object, with its thingness and thereness, are continuous right up to the bland surfaces of much art in the 1960s.[132]

Upon closer inspection, the "scientific idealism" that characterized Luminism is made up of individual, more differentiated characteristics. I will list these characteristics below as overarching aesthetic elements and illustrate them using examples. For the conceptual approach of this study and to be able to determine more clearly the common context of meaning of computer graphics, this is of central importance. The previously mentioned aspects of "light" and "photography" are supplemented below by the themes of "nostalgia" and "silence." They have hardly been mentioned so far, but are closely linked to the first two aspects.

9.1.2.4 The Aesthetic Survival of Luminism

The desire of many US artists "to create measurable certainties" with the help of "scientific, mathematical, and mechanical aids"[133] meant that the invention of photography had a completely different effect in the United States than in Europe. While it "liberated" European painting from its original purpose and thus steered it in a new direction,[134] it was, as described at the beginning of the chapter, used in the United States as a tool to create "objective truths" within art.

Thomas Eakins' intensive anatomical studies and the use of photography as an aid are particularly exemplary of the pronounced affinity for facts in the 19th century. Like Eadweard Muybridge, Eakins carried out movement studies in which Novak recognizes the need for a "fixed reality,"[135] which, according to her, was original to the United States. The measures Eakins took to capture reality were even increasingly perceived as rebellious, for example because in his role as a teacher, he confronted his female students with male nude models or even undressed himself.[136]

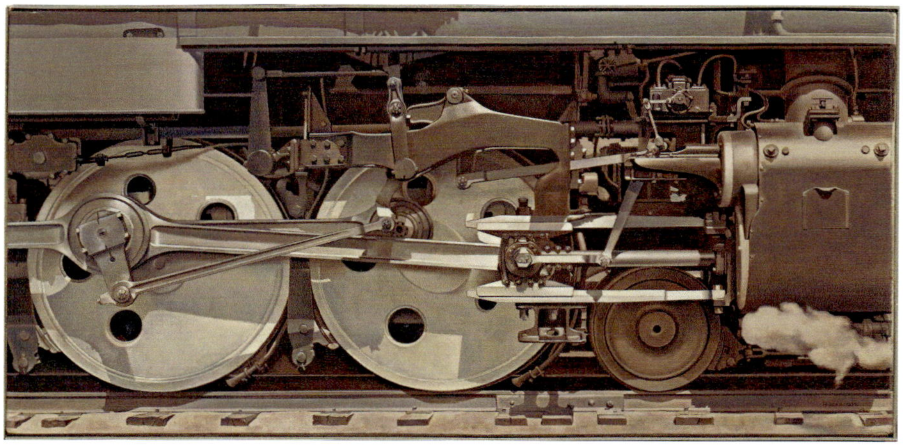

FIGURE 9.14 Charles Sheeler, *Rolling Power*, 1939, oil on canvas, frame: 22 5/8 × 37 5/8 × 2 3/4 in. (57.4 × 95.5 × 7 cm); stretcher: 15 × 30 in. (38.1 × 76.2 cm), purchased with the Drayton Hillyer Fund, Smith College Museum of Art, Northampton, Massachusetts, SC 1940.18.

Even beyond the 19th century, photography has a special significance, as Lucie Smith explains: "American art of the twentieth century has conducted a long and complex dialogue with the camera."[137] In the United States, numerous important movements in representational painting have made use of the camera. In addition to the members of the *Ash Can School*, who used "new snapshot cameras" for their designs at the beginning of the century,[138] the Precisionists, especially Charles Sheeler and Georgia O'Keeffe, can also be highlighted (Figures 9.14 and 9.15):

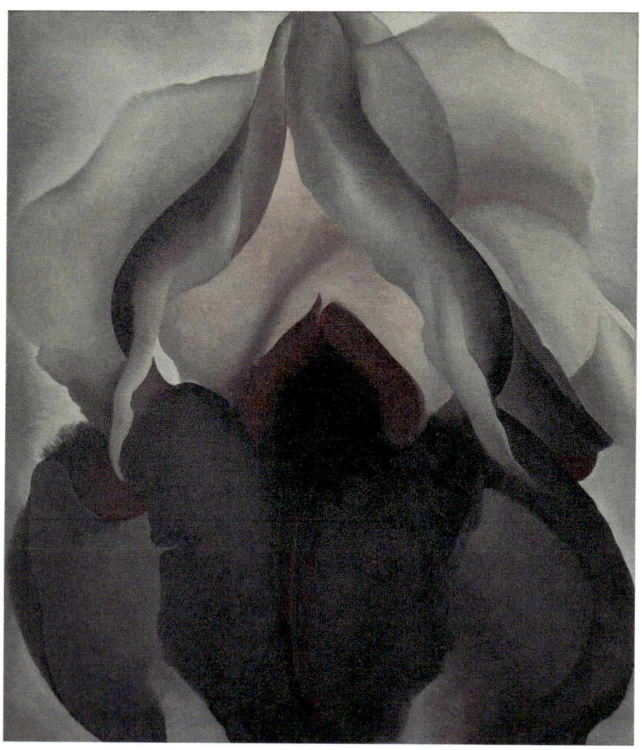

FIGURE 9.15 Georgia O'Keeffe, *Black Iris*, 1926, oil on canvas, 91.4 × 75.9 cm (36 in. × 29 7/8 in.), Alfred Stieglitz collection, 1969. bpk/The Metropolitan Museum of Art/ Malcolm Varon. (© Georgia O'Keeffe Museum/VG Bild-Kunst, Bonn 2025.)

> Sheeler's compositions, among them the famous *Rolling Power*, are based directly on his own photographs. Georgia O'Keeffe, closely allied to the Precisionist group, was influenced by the work of her husband Alfred Stieglitz (1864–1946), one of America's most celebrated photographers. Her close-up images of flowers [...] clearly owe much to photographic exemplars.[139]

The affinity for technological progress within US culture not only had a great influence on the development of art, but it also characterized the lives of the people in a more general sense. Kouwenhoven shows that even before the Industrial Revolution, the development of the "untouched" continent was closely linked to technological progress:

> Many people, including a good many historians, like to think of the United States as having been a nation of farmers and handicrafters, relatively untouched by the so-called Industrial Revolution, during a great

> part of its formative period. And it is, of course, true that until about the time of the Civil War the nation's economy was predominantly based upon agriculture. But it is easy to overestimate the agrarian aspects of our early history, and it is well to be reminded that in significant respects our civilization has from the beginning been dependent upon technology.[140]

Technological ingenuity was therefore a basic prerequisite for the development of a civilization in the "new world." In addition to this opportunity to make a fresh start on a new continent, this circumstance also resulted in a departure from the original European tradition. As a country of immigration, the task of creating a new culture was thus imposed on the population from the time of the first colonization. As German historian Volker Depkat recounts, this process was not yet complete in the 19th century. He describes the cultural development following the migration movements in 1848 and 1849:

> The various immigrant groups retained many elements of their home cultures, sometimes over several generations. [...] At the same time, as time went on, they also adopted many elements from their new North American environment. This gave rise to specific German-American, Swedish-American or Iro-American subcultures in the United States, which had less and less to do with the lifestyles of their home countries, but in many cases reinvented this "home" in the first place.[141]

These historical circumstances also correlate with an aesthetic development, which can be illustrated, for example, when considering the painter William M. Harnett, who was born in Ireland in 1848 and emigrated with his family to Philadelphia in the United States at the age of one.[142] He can therefore be counted among the generation described by Depkat, who had to reinvent their home country. Novak recognizes a sense of nostalgia in Harnett's paintings, which she attributes to this reinvention. In her opinion, the depiction of patina and wear in US visual culture is a development unique to the United States, which is why the "ruined object" – "[q]uite apart from similar

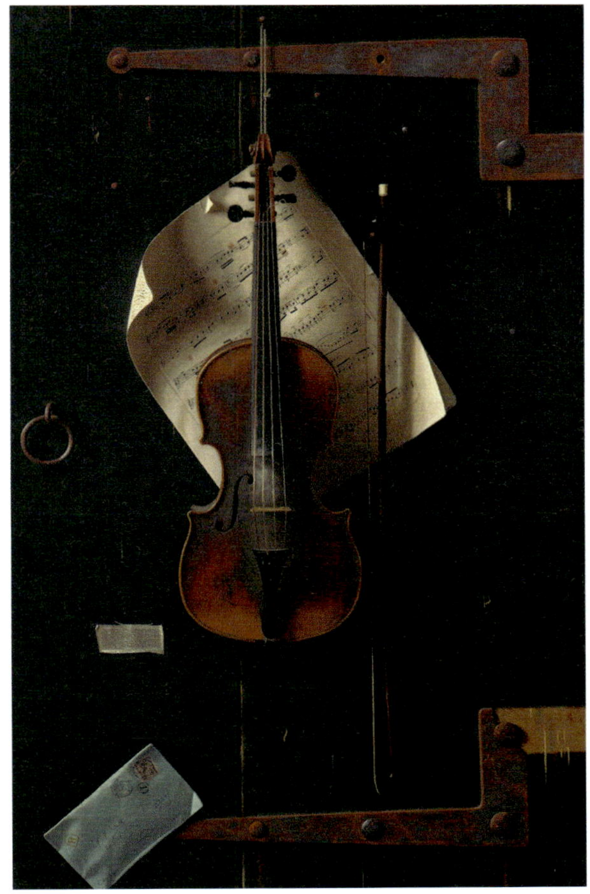

FIGURE 9.16 William M. Harnett, *The Old Violin*, 1886, oil on canvas, 38 × 23 5/8 in. (96.5 × 60 cm), National Gallery of Art, Washington, DC, gift of Mr. and Mrs. Richard Mellon Scaife in honor of Paul Mellon. (© CC0.)

European practices"[143] – was particularly prevalent in US tradition. This mode of expression is also characteristic of William M. Harnett's still lifes, as can be seen in his painting *The Old Violin*, for example. The painting shows a violin hanging on a wooden wall or door. It partially conceals a sheet of music attached behind it and is otherwise framed by rusty hinges and an envelope below the instrument on the left. Some of the varnish on the door is scratched and peeling, and the various paper elements are torn and creased. Additionally, some of the hinges are broken. Harnett is thus also staging an artificial nostalgia in his painting (Figure 9.16):

> Nostalgia is a way of civilizing the past, especially interesting in America, a country "without a past," since it involves inventing

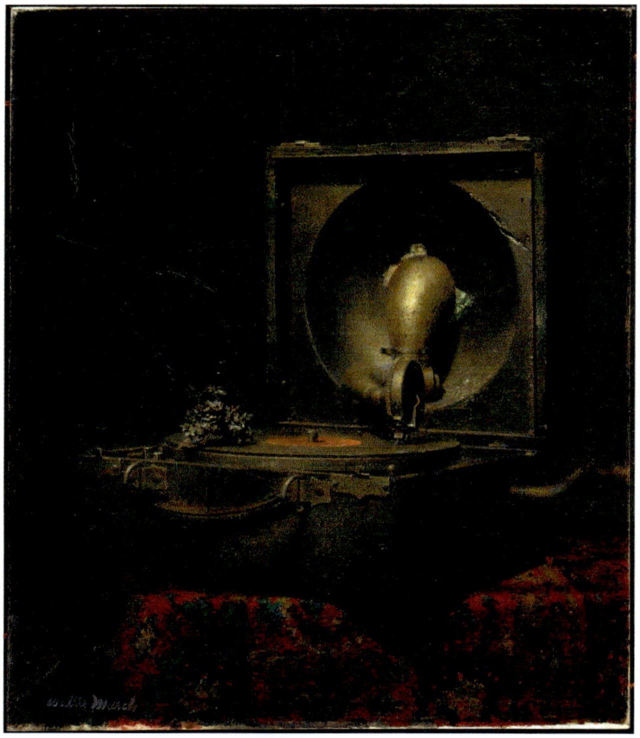

FIGURE 9.17 Walter Tandy Murch (American, born Canada, 1907–1967), *The Circle*, ca. 1948, oil on canvas, 26 × 22 in. (66 × 55.9 cm), frame: 37 × 32 9/16 × 2 3/4 in. (94 × 82.7 × 7 cm). Brooklyn Museum, Dick S. Ramsay Fund, 49.7. (© Walter Tandy Murch Estate.)

> that missing past. Initially, as with Cole, nostalgia took the conventional form of grafting onto the limited repertory of American subjects the traditions of Greece and Rome. Ultimately, that nostalgia transferred itself to America's own past. [...] But [...] the taste for the picturesque eventually extended from the antique ruin to the ruined *thing*, so that a whole syntax of nostalgia was available for still life and, ultimately, for assemblage.[144]

The difference between these developments in the United States, as described here by Novak, and the European practices to which she is referring can be illustrated by a line of reasoning pursued by German art historian Thomas Lange in his examination of the Romantic tradition of ruin paintings. It also originated in the 19th century but was rooted in Germany. Lange develops an aesthetic of ruins against the backdrop of autopoietic practices. Through his approach he demonstrates that the ruins depicted in paintings by artists such as Caspar David Friedrich (1774–1840) exist in a dialectical state between art and nature. The man-made cultural artifacts, interwoven with natural processes of decay, therefore developed a "new aesthetic meaning that emerges by itself."[145] This "by itself" no longer applies to the aesthetics of decay in US paintings. Here, on the contrary, it is central to merely give objects the *appearance* of having emerged from an autopoietic aesthetic process.

This theme persisted in US art well into the 20th century. Walter Tandy Murch (1907–1967), who also produced still lifes, creates a nostalgic reference to the past in *The Circle* (1948), for example. Unlike Harnett, however, he does not imitate objects exposed to decay, but the changing aesthetics of an ageing photograph (Figure 9.17). Lucie-Smith describes his preference for the

> special qualities possessed by old photographs, and in particular to the way in which their very defects – fading, scratches and stains – made them expressive by demonstrating how the moment frozen by the camera was, despite all efforts to retain it, inexorably vanishing into the past.[146]

Lucie-Smith draws another connection between Murch and John F. Peto, who, like John Haberle, was active during Harnett's time and produced similar still lifes, primarily so-called letter racks.[147] Comparable to the luminists, these artists disappear behind their illusionistic style of depiction, ultimately giving their paintings an abstract quality. Novak continues her idea of the "taste for the picturesque" and the "assemblage" by referring to the concept of reality in Cubist collage and Dada. She illustrates her thought with Harnett's technique:

> He so exactly superimposes reality and abstraction that they obscure one another. [...] Harnett, it seems, received a complete reciprocal system, in which his objects depend for their reality on abstraction, and abstraction depends for its perfection on objects. This is another way of saying that he made such distinctions irrelevant, and speaking of his pictures in terms of either reality or abstraction

does them violence. They are both and neither; that is, at their best, they are perfect pictures.[148]

Although the term "perfect picture" is debatable, Novak's classification of Harnett's paintings as abstract compositions shows once again how the representational painterly tendencies anchored in the United States can often only be "captured" with what Baur calls "elastic categories." Consequently, it is quite convincing that Novak also identifies a continuation of the luminist tradition in Harnett's technique:

> The perception of objects is similarly intense, the hermeticism invokes a similar silence, the removal of the artist is as radical and complete. The distant wall of light in luminism is replaced in Harnett's work by the boards and doors from which the objects hang. But the mode of vision, in its tonal sophistication, is similar enough to speak of a constant style.[149]

The aspects of silence and light that Novak addresses here are recurring features within US visual and written culture, both individually and in combination. Their significance will now be presented, bringing this chapter to a close.

In his monograph *American Silences*, the literary scholar Ward, whom I referenced at the beginning of this chapter, turns to the motif of silence. Comparable to Novak's approach, and as indicated earlier, he also sets out to identify overarching aesthetic qualities that unite realist tendencies in various forms of expression.[150] It is therefore not surprising that, although Ward focuses on 20th-century realism, he makes a clear reference to 19th-century Transcendentalism:

> These artists form a body of twentieth-century American realists who in complementary ways extend the familiar nineteenth-century tension between a realistic valuation of common experience and a transcendental (or otherwise mystical) passion for enduring meaning.[151]

Before turning to the motif of silence, he narrows down the concept of realism. I will discuss his line of thought in more detail here to better comprehend the aspects of silence that he mentions. According to Ward, literary and visual realism was, historically speaking, concerned with the depiction of individuals in social contexts. However, he also emphasizes that these phenomena must ultimately be based on a consistent aesthetic or ideology.[152] He therefore argues that no realist movement exists that does not also want to make a statement. In principle, every realist classification – including Marxist Realism, Christian Realism, Formalist Realism, Romantic Realism, Humanist Realism and Existentialist Realism – attempts to distinguish itself from a "naïve realism":

> In a sense all of these are realisms that challenge the presumed dominance of what each regards as a shallow or simply naïve realism. The antagonism towards an absolute realism generally follows the argument that objectivity in art is both a pointless and an impossible achievement.[153]

Conversely, Ward's statement means that every – non-naïve – realism ultimately pursues an intention. Thus, according to Ward, there is no realism that merely endeavors to depict "reality" as it is. His argument aligns with the previously quoted statement by painter Thomas Cole, who offered a similar perspective on the representation of reality: "If the imagination is shackled, and nothing is described but what we see, seldom will anything truly great be produced, either in Painting or Poetry."[154]

Finally, Ward examines how the artists he analyzed express the motif of silence. However, he notes right from the start that silence is actually a contrary concept to most of the "conventional categories of realism," as these usually attempt to generate attention almost *noisily*:

> The fervor for silence cannot be fully assimilated to the rationalizing and normalizing impulses of realism, and in this respect the artists I discuss are comparable to those novelists [...] who locate protagonists of an Emersonian or Nietzschean disposition in the center of otherwise realistic fictions.[155]

Ward uses the term "silence" but adds the word "stillness" to his definition. For him, "silence" is expressed, on the one hand, through the silence of

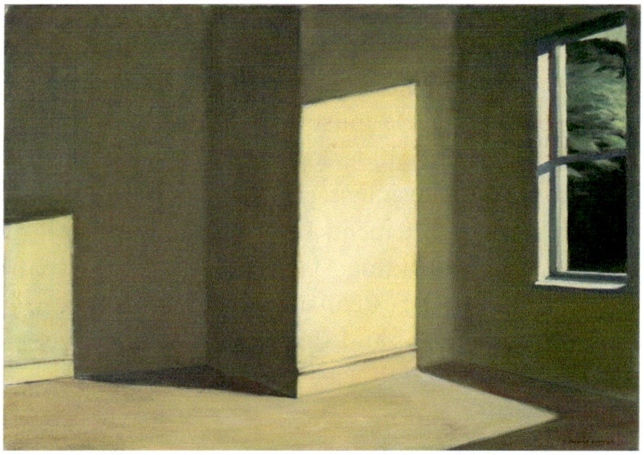

FIGURE 9.18 Edward Hopper, *Sun in an Empty Room*, 1963, oil on canvas, 28 3/8 × 40 1/4 × 1 1/2 in. (72.1 × 102.2 × 3.8 cm), courtesy Crystal Bridges Museum of American Art, Bentonville, Arkansas. (Photography by Edward C. Robison III. © Heirs of Josephine N. Hopper/VAGA at ARS, NY/VG Bild-Kunst, Bonn 2025.)

mute protagonists or static objects, and, on the other, through stillness deliberately created through "artistic modes"[156] by excluding sound and movement in unusual and radical ways. With these "artistic modes," Ward can align the authors and visual artists he discusses. This methodological approach is reminiscent of Novak's when she speaks of artistic "modes of procedure."[157] In terms of content, however, Ward's argument can also be linked to Leo Marx's description of Sheeler's works: "On closer inspection, we observe that Sheeler has eliminated all evidence of the frenzied movement and clamor we associate with the industrial scene. The silence is awesome."[158]

To illustrate how the concept of silence is expressed within painting, Ward discusses the work of Edward Hopper, whose paintings feature silence particularly prominently. The paintings are, according to Ward, "uniquely silent, conveying a sense of unnatural stillness."[159] Hopper deliberately excluded pictorial elements that could evoke the association of a source of noise.[160] This phenomenon is particularly evident in the painting *Sun in an Empty Room* (Figure 9.18), which is why Ward states, it is probably his

> barest, most silent painting; there is room, window, forest, light, shadow, and nothing else. Its silence and emptiness completely achieve what many of Hopper's other works hint at or anticipate – the complete annihilation of human life. Put another way, *Sun in an Empty Room* is Hopper reduced to his essence, rather achieving his essence.[161]

In her remarks on the 20th century, Barbara Novak also refers to Hopper's stillness and, like Ward, links it to the depiction of "deserted" scenes. She attributes this overarching quality to the aesthetics of Luminism, a connection that Ward does not make, although it would be fundamentally consistent with his stance:

> Hopper […] emphasized overtones of luminist mystery still further in dealing with the almost depopulated city. Into the silent world of luminism, now transposed to grim urban architecture, he introduced the weighted geometries of Homer and the unsettling spatial shifts from classic parallelism found throughout the nineteenth century. He also shared luminism's concern with unbroken light […].[162]

The stillness in Hopper's paintings is strongly linked to his use of light, which is why he is often more closely associated with light than the luminists are. Hopper precisely modeled the light, and, as Lucie-Smith writes, he was "always very skilful in using light to suggest times of day, which in turn help to set a mood."[163] As Hopper's biographer Gail Levin explains, objective and subjective perception of light overlap in his work: "'Light,' he said, was 'important, a means of conveying the structure of reality, a valuable weapon that allows the artist to convey his vision without having to fall short through lack of technical ability.'"[164]

These different accounts clearly demonstrate the importance of light for both Hopper and the luminists. More than any of the other overarching aesthetic qualities, light is able to unite mystical qualities with physical precision. I therefore argue that light is one of the main characteristics of the "American," thus creating an intellectual bridge to Novak's argument that aspects of Luminism survived into the 1960s.

Hopper can be used to illustrate the survival of light within the figurative tradition in the United States,

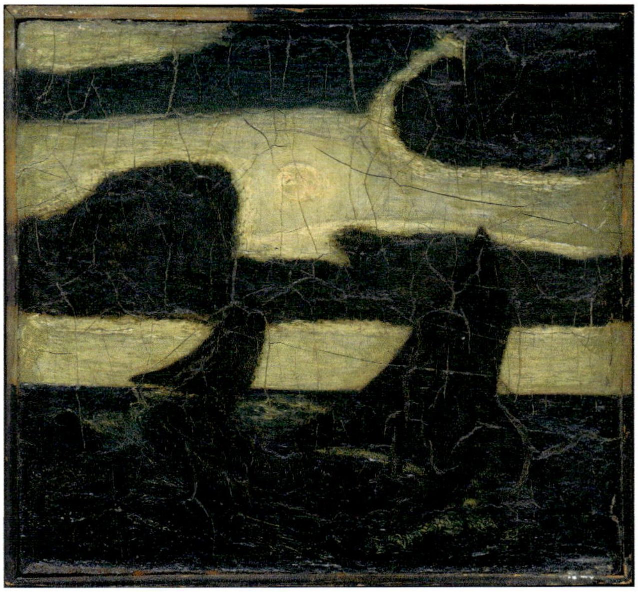

FIGURE 9.19 Albert Pinkham Ryder, *Moonlight Marine*, 1870–1890, oil and possibly wax on wood panel, 11 1/2 × 12 in. (29.2 × 30.5 cm), The Metropolitan Museum of Art, Samuel D. Lee Fund, 1934. (© CC0.)

FIGURE 9.20 Mark Rothko, *Untitled*, 1968, synthetic polymer paint on paper, 17 7/8 × 23 7/8 in. (45.4 × 60.8 cm). Gift of The Mark Rothko Foundation, Inc. Acc. n.: 463.1986. Digital image, The Museum of Modern Art, New York/ Scala, Florence. (© 1998 Kate Rothko-Prizel & Christopher Rothko/VG Bild-Kunst, Bonn 2025.)

but its overarching qualities can also be seen in Albert Pinkham Ryder's painting, which stands between figuration and abstraction, as well as in Mark Rothko's complete and two-dimensional abstractions. Novak contends that Ryder's *Moonlight Marine* and other of his moon paintings are reminiscent of the "luminist modes" due to their clear horizon line and the static ships (Figure 9.19): "They are shapes imprinted on and becalmed in this stillness. The constant subject of the 'lonely boat' becomes ideographic and neutral, and sea and sky some abstract void that Ryder wished to invent."[165]

Novak herself subsequently establishes a connection with Rothko's painting, describing it "as carefully measured, in its amounts of light, color and geometry, as that of the luminists […]."[166] Her characterization can be illustrated by his painting *Untitled* from 1968 (Figure 9.20). She attributes a mediating power and the ability to express a condition that stands for far more than just the self to the painting, with its bright yellow in the upper half and the strong orange in the lower half.[167] Novak bases her thoughts on a statement by Rothko, which, according to her, Emerson would have fully agreed with: "The progression of a painter's work, as it travels in time from point to point, will be toward clarity: toward the elimination of all obstacles between the painter and the idea, and between the idea and the observer."[168]

Whether and to what extent Rothko operated out of a spiritual mindset remains a topic of debate in the research on the artist. Although James Breslin mentions the personal acquaintance between Novak and the artist in his biography of Rothko,[169] Breslin insists that Rothko did not imply any transcendental aspects with his statement about "clarity." According to Breslin, Rothko was merely expressing his desire to break down any barriers between the artist and his work and between the work and the viewer. However, Breslin also mentions a possible spiritual aspect of Rothko's art: "If someone praised the sensual beauty of his paintings, Rothko pointed to their spirituality; but if someone else hinted at spiritual properties, he defined himself as an earthy materialist. It is as if almost any verbal response, any naming of his work, made Rothko uneasy."[170] Regardless of the speculation about Rothko's spiritual intentions, it can be stated with some certainty that the "American" in his paintings is expressed through light, or a "Wall of Light," in reference to the announcement of an exhibition Rothko planned for December 1954 at the *Art Institute Chicago*.[171]

In summary, the four aesthetic categories of light, silence, nostalgia and photography offer answers to the initial question of what might characterize the "American" in "American Realism," even if they are not exhaustive. Not only are they closely linked to the transcendentalist tendencies of the 19th century, but they are also frequently expressed in images "caught" in what Novak calls the dilemma between realism and idealism. This blending of two actually contradictory trends is characterized, on the one hand, by a high degree of technical precision, which often pushes the author of a picture into the background, and, on the other hand, by the simultaneous attempt to express the true feeling about a given situation. In US culture, this often results in pictorial worlds that exist precisely *between* a physical and a perceived understanding of the experienced environment.

NOTES

1. Dorothy C. Miller, "Foreword and Acknowledgement," in *American Realists and Magic Realists. Exhibition Catalogue*, ed. Dorothy C. Miller and Alfred H. Barr Jr. (New York: The Museum of Modern Art, 1943), 6.
2. In the introduction to his study *Kunsttheorie des Naturalismus und Realismus* (Art Theory of Naturalism and Realism), German art historian Boris Röhrl presents various alternative terms within the theory of realism that have developed in research outside of Germany, such as the English term "representational art." See Boris Röhrl, *Kunsttheorie des Naturalismus und Realismus: Historische Entwicklung, Terminologie und Definitionen* (Hildesheim: Georg Olms, 2003), 2.
3. Joseph A. Ward, *American Silences: The Realism of James Agee, Walker Evans, and Edward Hopper*, 2nd ed. (New Brunswick: Transaction Publishers, 2010), 1–2.
4. Miller, "Foreword," 5.
5. See also Seymour Menton, *Magic Realism Rediscovered, 1918–1981* (Philadelphia, London: Art Alliance Press; Associated University Presses, 1983), 9.
6. The retrospective included the following artists: Henry Alexander, John James Audubon, George Caleb Bingham, Thomas Cole, Thomas Eakins, Erastus Salisbury Field, Richard La Barre Goodwin, William M. Harnett, Edward Hicks, Winslow Homer, John Frederick Kensett, William S. Mount, Raphaelle Peale, Harry W. Watrous. Aside from Edward Hopper and Charles Sheeler the contemporaries include: Ivan Le Lorraine Albright, John Atherton, Peter Blume, Audrey Buller, Paul Cadmus, Clarence Holbrook Carter, Ferdinand Cartier, Jared French, Louis Guglielmi, Hananiah Harari, Z. Vanessa Helder, Peter Hurd, Lawrence Kupferman, Edmund Lewandowski, Louis Lozowick, Theodore Lux, Fred Papsdorf, Charles Rain, H. D. Rothschild, Patsy Santo, Ben Shahn, Miklos Suba, Patrick J. Sullivan, Stow Wengenroth, Andrew Wyeth, Malvin Marr (Zsissly) Albright. See Dorothy C. Miller and Alfred H. Barr Jr., eds., *American Realists and Magic Realists. Exhibition catalogue* (New York: The Museum of Modern Art, 1943).
7. See Miller and Barr Jr., *American Realists and Magic Realists*, 9.
8. Miller, "Foreword," 5, emphasis in original.
9. Edward Lucie-Smith, *American Realism* (London: Thames & Hudson, 2003), 13.
10. See Lucie-Smith, *American Realism*, 13.
11. Lucie-Smith, *American Realism*, 19.
12. One reason that Lucie-Smith gives as an example to explain why photography is a democratic imaging process is that, as soon as it became available, it revolutionized the genre of the portrait. With the new photographic technology of the time, it was no longer reserved for the wealthy to have portraits made. These new possibilities opened up by photography corresponded to the ideal of an egalitarian society that had developed since the colonization. See Lucie-Smith, *American Realism*, 14.
13. See Lucie-Smith, *American Realism*, 13–14.
14. Lucie-Smith, *American Realism*, 14.
15. Lucie-Smith, *American Realism*, 9.
16. See Lucie-Smith, *American Realism*, 10.
17. Lucie-Smith, *American Realism*, 11.
18. See Lucie-Smith, *American Realism*, 12.
19. See Barbara Novak, *American Painting of the Nineteenth Century. Realism, Idealism, and the American Experience*, 3rd edition (Oxford: Oxford University Press USA, 2007), 163.
20. See Novak, *American Painting*, 62, 120.
21. Lucie-Smith, *American Realism*, 9.
22. See Novak, *American Painting*, e.g. 156.
23. John I. H. Baur, *Revolution and Tradition in Modern American Art*, 2nd ed. (New York, London: Praeger, 1967), viii.
24. Linda Nochlin, like Baur, opens the discussion about the demarcation between different movements and suggests speaking of several realisms: "Yet, while realism may be a perennial phenomenon, one might do better to talk about 'realisms' rather than a single unitary 'realism.' A wide range and variety of

stylistic possibilities are subsumed under the general category. Indeed, it might be fruitful to think of realism as a country on a map, surrounded by other countries, whose borders often merge imperceptibly with it." Linda Nochlin, "The Realist Criminal and the Abstract Law," *Art in America* 61, no. 5 (1973): 55.

25. See Boris Röhrl, *Realismus in der bildenden Kunst. Europa und Nordamerika 1830 bis 2000* (Berlin: Mann, 2013).
26. See David E. Shi, *Facing Facts. Realism in American Thought and Culture, 1850–1920* (Oxford: Oxford University Press, 1995).
27. Shi, *Facing Facts*, 13. Shi uses the term "Antebellum Idealism" to refer to romantic idealism, which was largely characterized by authors such as Ralph Waldo Emerson and Henry David Thoreau before the Civil War (1861–1865) and is based on a deep connection to nature, on the one hand, and on the philosophical idealism of Plato and Immanuel Kant, on the other. See Shi, *Facing Facts*, 15–25.
28. Röhrl, *Realismus*, 1.
29. In his concluding remarks on the entire study, he combines the last two positions and simply calls them "realism as critique." See Röhrl, *Realismus*, 1, 296.
30. Röhrl, *Realismus*, 1.
31. See Röhrl, *Realismus*, 2.
32. See Röhrl, *Realismus*, 296–97.
33. Nochlin draws a distinction between "realist" art, on the one hand, and "anti-realist" art, on the other, under which she categorizes idealism, symbolism or abstract art, for example. Although in her essay *The Realist Criminal and the Abstract Law*, she discusses the juxtaposition of realism and anti-realism within modernism, she points out that the debate about what is ideally represented through art goes back to antiquity and Plato's conception of the idea. While Clement Greenberg describes the representational art of modernism as "impure," it was Michelangelo in the 16th century who spurned Flemish painting, which even then captured everyday situations in pictures, motivated by a similar mindset. In her essay, Nochlin defends the depiction of "everyday" circumstances typical of historical realism by pointing out that many modernist movements, such as New Objectivity or Surrealism, are completely excluded by the concept of "pure" art as Greenberg would like to see it. On the other hand, she emphasizes that realistic depictions are definitely selective and by no means naively create a simple mirror image of a scene. See Nochlin, "The Realist Criminal," 56–60.
34. Röhrl, *Realismus*, 75, emphasis in original.
35. Röhrl, *Realismus*, 76.
36. Röhrl, *Realismus*, 76. In her chapter on the artist Washington Allston (1779–1843), Barbara Novak also addresses the influence of German Romanticism on cultural development within the United States, for example on Transcendentalism. See Novak, *American Painting*, 29.
37. Lucie-Smith, for example, discusses both their works in relation to each other in the chapter "Thomas Eakins and Winslow Homer." See Lucie-Smith, *American Realism*, 29–39.
38. Shi, *Facing Facts*, 137. In her comments on Homer, Barbara Novak also points out that his works are repeatedly accompanied by romantic tendencies. She calls this phenomenon "a pictorial concomitant to the final hermetic romanticism of his own withdrawal from society, as he lived out the icy winters at Prout's Neck, Maine […]." Novak, *American Painting*, 148.
39. The name *The Eight* is derived from the eight artists who turned away from the previously prevailing "academic realism" and formed their own group: Robert Henri, who brought the group together in this form, John Sloan, William J. Glackens, George Luks, Everett Shinn, Ernest Lawson, Arthur B. Davies and Maurice B. Prendergast. See e.g. Röhrl, *Realismus*, 79, and see Shi, *Facing Facts*, 260.
40. Röhrl, *Realismus*, 75.
41. Shi, *Facing Facts*, 254.
42. See Everett Shinn, "Recollections of The Eight," in *The Eight: Exhibition Catalogue*, ed. The Brooklyn Museum (New York: Brooklyn Museum Press, 1943), 11–12.
43. John Sloan, *John Sloan on Drawing and Painting: Gist of Art* (Mineola: Dover Publications, 2000), 3.
44. Shi, *Facing Facts*, 264.
45. Helen Farr Sloan, *John Sloan's New York Scene* (New York: Harper & Row, 1965), xx.
46. See Röhrl, *Realismus*, 79.
47. See Röhrl, *Realismus*, 81.
48 Robert Henri, "The New York Exhibition of Independent Artists," *The Craftsman* XVIII, no. 2 (1910): 161.
49. Shi, *Facing Facts*, 254.
50. In this context, Shi thematizes a fundamental conflict between Henri and William Merrit Chase, who was an advocate of "academic realism" and strove for an art that should primarily show life's beautiful aspects, while Henri wanted to capture the spirit of the times in its positive and negative facets in his paintings. Shi attributes Chase's attitude to the "art for art's sake principle" and thus makes a statement that contrasts with Röhrl's view. Conversely, Röhrl attributes Henri's realism to the "l'art pour l'art principle" and quotes him: "Great works of art should look as though they were made in joy." Robert Henri, *The Art Spirit*, 3rd ed. (New York: Basic Books, 2007), 174. Röhrl describes this attitude as "social indifference." Although both he and Shi use the term in a similar way, they attribute it to one of the two opposing artists. Röhrl's argumentation appears conclusive if

complete autonomy is attributed to the l'art pour l'art principle, because then Henri would not have intentionally produced political art, but at the same time would not have been able to prevent it from exerting political influence quite independently, whereby this line of argumentation would then also apply to Chase. See Shi, *Facing Facts*, 257–58, and see Röhrl, *Realismus*, 82.

51. See Novak, *American Painting*, 171–73.
52. Milton W. Brown, *American Painting from the Armory Show to the Depression* (Princeton: Princeton University Press, 1955), vi.
53. Brown, *American Painting*, 47.
54. Shi, *Facing Facts*, 290.
55. See Shi, *Facing Facts*, 303–4. Shi explains this development, on the one hand, with the fact that political circumstances such as war and corruption meant that mimetic representations were no longer desirable. On the other hand, he presents the position of the structuralists, post-structuralists and deconstructionists, who, referring to Kant, Nietzsche and Heidegger, claim that the arts are never capable of representing the "actual" world, as "reality" is merely a linguistic construction. Shi also describes the opinion of a group he calls "anti-realists," who believe that the entire external world is fundamentally an illusion, which is why works of art ultimately "deconstruct" themselves.
56. Shi, *Facing Facts*, 307. Shi quotes Willard Midgette after Willard Midgette, "Illusionistic Portraiture," *Allan Frumkin Gallery Newsletter*, no. 3 (1977): 5.
57. See Lucie-Smith, *American Realism*, 126.
58. Röhrl describes the parallel realist movements in the United States as "sub-concepts." He lists the following: *Regionalism*, *Magic Realism*, *Superrealism* (meaning *Surrealism* in the 1930s) and *American Scene painting*. See Röhrl, *Realismus*, 197.
59. See Röhrl, *Realismus*, 196. The other sections contain brief overviews of Regionalism, see Röhrl, *Realismus*, 216–17, on Magic Realism, see Röhrl, *Realismus*, 218–19, and on social documentary photography, within which Walker Evans is particularly highlighted. See Röhrl, *Realismus*, 219–21. Röhrl describes Magic Realism "as indeed socially related. A statement should be made. In this respect, American Magic Realism reveals a proximity to Social Realism." Röhrl, *Realismus*, 218. In his study Rediscovering Magic Realism, Seymour Menton opens up an opposite view of the trend: "The movement flourished in post-World War I and post-World War II Germany in response to the tremendous despair caused by the crushing defeats and a series of concomitant factors. In the rest of the Western world a similar longing for peace and tranquility steered artists and writers in the same direction." Menton, *Magic Realism*, 10.
60. Shi focuses here on the photographer Jacob Riis, who emigrated from Denmark to the United States and whose photographs can be described as photojournalistic. Riis' explicit intention was to draw attention to grievances. See Shi, *Facing Facts*, 188–93.
61. See Shi, *Facing Facts*, 98–100. However, Shi also emphasizes a recurring Romantic attitude at the end of the 19th century, which was mainly noticeable in literature. See Shi, *Facing Facts*, 181–211.
62. Röhrl, *Realismus*, 200.
63. Röhrl, *Realismus*, 200.
64. See David Shapiro, *Social Realism: Art as a Weapon* (New York: Ungar, 1973), 4.
65. See Röhrl, *Realismus*, 200.
66. Shapiro, *Social Realism*, 9.
67. Röhrl, *Realismus*, 201.
68. See Gail Levin, *Edward Hopper: An Intimate Biography*, 2nd revised ed. (New York: Rizzoli, 2007), 271.
69. Röhrl describes, for example, an incident that took place in connection with Diego Rivera's mural *Crossroads*. This was a work intended for the Rockefeller Center in New York that was destroyed before it was completed due to its political content. See Röhrl, *Realismus*, 202. Röhrl does not address who instigated the destruction. An audio contribution by MoMA on a sketch Rivera made in preparation for the fresco reveals that the Rockefeller family itself was responsible for it. Rivera juxtaposed communism with capitalism in his planned painting and decided to integrate an image of Vladimir Lenin into the mural based on a photograph. The reason for the Rockefeller family's decision to remove the painting was that Rivera did not want to follow Nelson Rockefeller's wish to change Lenin's face and instead depict an anonymous person. See "Diego Rivera, Man at the Crossroads, 1932," The Museum of Modern Art, accessed March 03, 2022, https://www.moma.org/collection/works/34635.
70. Röhrl, *Realismus*, 202. Although he stresses that Roosevelt's politics were not the sole cause of the development of Social Realism, Röhrl often makes a connection between a social attitude and politically motivated art programs, because, according to him, also with new mural programs in the 21st century, "[t]he social realism has found a continuation." See Röhrl, *Realismus*, 286–87.
71. Lucie-Smith, *American Realism*, 130.
72. Röhrl uses a different categorization than Lucie-Smith. While Röhrl categorizes the somewhat more political Soyer brothers as "Social Realism," he assigns the less political Isabel Bishop and Edward Hopper to the "American Scene." He lists the movement parallel to "Social Realism" and describes it as "a modern form of genre painting" that "demonstrates the *American way of life*." Röhrl, *Realismus*, 212–16, emphasis in original.

73. See Lucie-Smith, *American Realism*, 129–31.
74. Lucie-Smith, *American Realism*, 144.
75. See Röhrl, *Realismus*, 214.
76. Brendan Prendeville, *Realism in 20th Century Painting* (New York: Thames & Hudson, 2000), 87.
77. See Prendeville, *Realism in 20th Century*, 87.
78. Röhrl, *Realismus*, 204.
79. See Röhrl, *Realismus* 208.
80. Röhrl, *Realismus*, 208. As an example, Röhrl mentions the discussion at the time about the potential destruction of Anton Refregier's post-office frescoes.
81. See Röhrl, *Realismus*, 211.
82. See Röhrl, *Realismus*, 263–65.
83. See Röhrl, *Realismus*, 265–69.
84. See Röhrl, *Realismus*, 269–70. Röhrl's conception of New Realism is oriented towards the lines of argumentation of Philip Pearlstein, Sidney Tillim and Linda Nochlin. Although Röhrl later places "New Realism" in the context of photorealism, he identifies some aspects that allow "New Realism" to be regarded as an "independent movement." For Röhrl, it is characterized by the fusion of a style imitating photography with "traditional painting techniques," which he does not, however, differentiate further. He mentions the painter Fairfield Porter as one of the main representatives of the movement. Lucie-Smith, on the other hand, does not work with this category at all. Instead, he recognizes socially critical traits in Porter's figurative style and his depiction of US class structures. See Lucie-Smith, *American Realism*, 161.
85. See Röhrl, *Realismus*, 270–71.
86. See Röhrl, *Realismus*, 271–72.
87. Röhrl, *Realismus*, 261.
88. Röhrl, *Realismus*, 261.
89. See Röhrl, *Realismus*, 262.
90. See Röhrl, *Realismus* 286.
91. See Röhrl, *Realismus* 287.
92. Shi, *Facing Facts*, 73.
93. Shi, *Facing Facts*, 4.
94. Ward, *American Silences*, 5.
95. Novak, *American Painting*, xiii, emphasis in original.
96. Novak, *American Painting*, 217.
97. Novak, *American Painting*, 1.
98. See Novak, *American Painting*, 1. Novak explains the term in a footnote: "The limner style was rooted not only in an indigenous craft tradition, which included such skills as sign-making, but in the linear traditions of Tudor and Jacobean England, in late sixteenth- and seventeenth-century Dutch art, and in the English seventeenth- and eighteenth-century country tradition, which perpetuated an increasingly rigid painterly convention through Van Dyck to Sir Peter Lely and Sir Godfrey Kneller, reaching the colonies largely via the mezzotint." Novak, *American Painting*, 239.
99. See Novak, *American Painting*, 11–18.
100. See Novak, *American Painting*, 1.
101. Novak, *American Painting*, 4.
102. Novak, *American Painting*, 6. Art historian John Wilmerding and art critic Karen Wilkin also address Copley's relationship to "things" in their biography of Fairfield Porter: "The paradox is that the determined realist Porter [...] not only belonged to the generation of America's most radical modernist painters of the time, the abstract expressionists, but also counted some of its leading exponents among his friends and neighbors. Like them, he embraced a version of radical modernist values, yet, unlike them, his conception of what a picture could be allies him with a long American multidisciplinary tradition of fascination with the particulars of things as they are. Think of John Singleton Copley's orchestrations of meticulously rendered textures in the 18th century or of Thomas Eakins's uncompromising portraits in the 19th [...]." John Wilmerding and Karen Wilkin, *Fairfield Porter* (New York: Rizzoli, 2016), 33.
103. Edwards even made a threefold division. On the first level was the "idea," on the second the "thing" and on the third level the "sign" or also the "word," two terms that he uses predominantly synonymously. In his eyes, signs are often the only thing that is perceived, because "there is very often no actual idea of those things when we are said to think of them, and that the thought is not employed about things themselves immediately, or immediately exercised in the idea itself, but only some sign that the mind habitually substitutes in the room of the idea." Jonathan Edwards, "782. Ideas. Sense of the Heart. Spiritual Knowledge or Conviction. Faith," in *Works of Jonathan Edwards Online, Volume 18, The Miscellanies*, ed. Ava Chamberlain, Jonathan Edwards Center (New Haven: Yale University Press, 2008), 454, accessed September 29, 2017, http://edwards.yale.edu/archive?path=aHR0cDovL2Vkd2FyZHMueWFsZS5lZHUvY2dpLWJpbi9uZXdwaGlsby9nZXRvYmplY3QucGw/Yy4xNzo0OjI4Mi53amVv.
104. In his most important work, *Nature*, Emerson describes the "universe" as being made up of "nature" and the "soul." The soul is the immaterial "self" of every individual, while the human body – like all material things and art – belongs to nature. However, he also uses the term in relation to plants and animals. Emerson also makes use of the term "world," associating it with "beauty" by referring to the ancient Greek term *kósmos*, and frequently using it instead of "universe" and "nature." See Ralph W. Emerson, "Nature (1836)," in *The Collected Works of Ralph Waldo Emerson. Volume I: Nature, Addresses, and Lectures*, ed. Robert E. Spiller and Alfred R. Ferguson (Cambridge: Belknap Press of Harvard University Press, 1971), 8, 12. Emerson's comments on "beauty" make his understanding of universal unity particularly clear, because for him "beauty" is the connecting element between the most diverse properties of

nature: "Nothing is quite beautiful alone: nothing but is beautiful in the whole. A single object is only so far beautiful as it suggests this universal grace." As a medium, the artist reproduces this beauty, according to Emerson, which is why he continues: "The poet, the painter, the sculptor, the musician, the architect, seek each to concentrate this radiance of the world on one point, and each in his several work to satisfy the love of beauty which stimulates him to produce. Thus is Art, a nature passed through the alembic of man. Thus in art, does nature work through the will of a man filled with the beauty of her first works." Emerson, "Nature," 17.

105. Novak, *American Painting*, 6.
106. See Novak, *American Painting*, 7.
107. Novak, *American Painting*, 7.
108. Novak, *American Painting*, 7, emphasis in original.
109. See Novak, *American Painting*, 7.
110. Shi, *Facing Facts*, 20.
111. Shi, *Facing Facts*, 20.
112. See Shi, *Facing Facts*, 29, and see Catherine Tufariello, "'The Remembering Wine': Emerson's Influence on Whitman and Dickinson," in *The Cambridge Companion to Ralph Waldo Emerson*, ed. Joel Porte and Saundra Morris (Cambridge, UK: Cambridge University Press, 1999).
113. Novak, *American Painting*, 49.
114. See Novak, *American Painting*, 43.
115. Novak, *American Painting*, 59.
116. Novak, *American Painting*, 62.
117. Novak, *American Painting*, 62.
118. Novak, *American Painting*, 62.
119. Novak recognizes comparable characteristics in Winslow Homer's *The Bridle Path, White Mountains* (1868) as in Durand's painting: "Homer incorporates along with this painterly realism a luminist distance that radiates a diffused glare quite different in character from the palpable sun that strikes upon the horse and rider." Novak, *American Painting*, 144.
120. Novak, *American Painting*, 67–68, emphasis in original.
121. Novak, *American Painting*, 69. Novak makes a further comparison between Martin Johnson Heade, on the one hand, and Gustave Courbet and Claude Monet, on the other. In addition to some similarities, the Impressionist approach of these painters also exhibits decisive differences: "Monet's dissolution of the object, though abstract and conceptual in result, was the logical end point of impressionist analysis of the thing fragmented by light – an analysis that would, as we have said, have represented to American artists a basic disregard for matter." Novak, *American Painting*, 106–7.
122. See Novak, *American Painting*, 99.
123. See Novak, *American Painting* 83.
124. Novak, *American Painting*, 74.
125. Emerson establishes this phrase in his essay *Nature*, referring to the dissolution of the self within nature and the transformation into an all-knowing medium: "Standing on the bare ground, – my head bathed by the blithe air, and uplifted into infinite space, – all mean egotism vanishes. I become a transparent eye-ball. I am nothing. I see all. The currents of the Universal Being circulate through me; I am part or particle of God." Emerson, "Nature," 10.
126. Novak, *American Painting*, 76. See also John I. H. Baur, "American Luminism," *Perspectives USA* 9 (1954): 90, 98.
127. Novak, *American Painting*, 76.
128. Novak, *American Painting*, 86.
129. See Novak, *American Painting* 86.
130. See John A. Kouwenhoven, *Made in America. The Arts in Modern Civilization* (Garden City: Doubleday & Company, Inc., 1949); see Leo Marx, *The Machine in the Garden. Technology and the Pastoral Ideal in America* (Oxford: Oxford University Press USA, 2000).
131. Kouwenhoven, *Made in America*, 6.
132. Novak, *American Painting*, 76. In his study of the Luminist Fitz H. Lane, the art historian John Wilmerding also describes Novak's line of argument as provocative, but he expressly agrees with Novak: "Probably the most important recent scholarship devoted to Lane has been that of Barbara Novak in her book *American Painting of the Nineteenth Century*. She has raised some provocative and fascinating ideas about the meaning of measurement in Lane's painting; the self-trained, primitive qualities of some of his work; and his affinities to Emerson, especially with regard to the relationship of the physical and the spiritual in their respective views of nature." John Wilmerding, *Fitz Hugh Lane* (London: Praeger, 1971), 15, emphasis in original.
133. Novak, *American Painting*, 7.
134. Marshall McLuhan, for example, comments: "Perhaps the great revolution produced by photograph was in the traditional arts. The painter could no longer depict a world that had been much photographed. He turned, instead, to reveal the inner process of creativity in expressionism and in abstract art." Marshall McLuhan, *Understanding Media: The Extensions of Man* (London: Routledge & Kegan Paul Ltd, 1968), 194.
135. See Novak, *American Painting*, 163–65.
136. See Shi, *Facing Facts*, 144–45.
137. Lucie-Smith, *American Realism*, 15.
138. See Lucie-Smith, *American Realism*, 15.
139. Lucie-Smith, *American Realism*, 15, emphasis in original.
140. Kouwenhoven, *Made in America*, 5.
141. Volker Depkat, *Geschichte der USA* (Stuttgart: Kohlhammer, 2016), 100.
142. See Alfred V. Frankenstein, *After the Hunt: William Harnett and Other American Still Life Painters 1870–1900* (Berkeley: University of California Press, 1953), 4.
143. Novak, *American Painting*, 192.

144. Novak, *American Painting*, 192, emphasis in original.
145. Thomas Lange, "Orientierungen an den Leerstellen der Geschichte. Zum Verhältnis von Gewordenem und Gemachtem in Ruinenbildern der Romantik,"in *von selbst: Autopoietische Verfahren in der Ästhetik des 19. Jahrhunderts*, ed. Friedrich Weltzien (Berlin: Reimer, 2006), 81.
146. Lucie-Smith, *American Realism*, 159.
147. The art critic Alfred V. Frankenstein calls them "card racks" and refers to their long tradition, which goes back to the Belgian artist Wallerant Vaillant and his painting *A Board with Letters, Quill Knife, and Quill Pen behind Red Straps* (1658, oil on paper on canvas, 51.5 × 40.5 cm, Gemäldegalerie Alte Meister, Dresden). It is, according to Frankenstein, the first known painting of its kind. See Frankenstein, *After the Hunt*, 53. Lucie-Smith does not mention Vaillant but describes general content-related differences between US and European still life traditions. He provides an analysis that builds a bridge to Transcendentalism in the United States: "Recent commentators have been at pains to tease out the *Vanitas* theme in the American still-life and *trompe-l'oeil* painting of the late nineteenth century. This reference to mortality was inherent in the European still-life tradition, and Harnett at least was not averse to using traditional *Vanitas* symbols, such as the skull. Yet it can also be said that many of these works achieve their force because they eschew transcendental overtones. They are reflections of a new American materialism, barely mitigated by moments of sentimental nostalgia." Lucie-Smith, *American Realism*, 48, emphasis in original.
148. Novak, *American Painting*, 196.
149. Novak, *American Painting*, 193.
150. The foreword, written by the author Richard Goodman, indicates that Ward's approach is rather unusual for a US researcher: "The great gift J. A. Ward bestows on us is to bring these visual and verbal artists together, something that is all too infrequently done. We Americans are great categorizers and labelers, and we feel each type should be with its own, snug and safe. So we put writers with writers and painters with painters, and so on, and write about them within those boundaries." Richard Goodman, "Introduction to the Transaction Edition," in *Joseph Anthony Ward: American Silences. The Realism of James Agee, Walker Evans, and Edward Hopper*, 2nd ed. (New Brunswick: Transaction Publishers, 2010), xx.
151. Ward, *American Silences*, 7.
152. See Ward, *American Silences*, 5–6.
153. Ward, *American Silences*, 5–6.
154. Thomas Cole, "Letter to Robert Gilmor," dated December 25, 1827, *Thomas Cole Papers, Letters of Robert Gilmor to and from Thomas Cole – 1826–1837*, New York State Library Digital Collections, Manuscripts, 74–75, accessed March 18, 2022, https://nysl.ptfs.com/data/Library5/All%20Special%20Collections/Manuscripts/Thomas%20Cole%20Papers/Correspondence%2C%201820-1855/Cole%20and%20Gilmor%2C%201826-1837/pdf/SC10635-B3-F8-complete.pdf.
155. Ward, *American Silences*, 7. In this context, Ward draws on Henry James' descriptions of Émile Zola's works, in which James explicitly addresses background noise with the phrase "hubbub of voices." See Henry James, *Notes on Novelists: With Some Other Notes* (New York: Charles Scribner's Sons, 1914), 35.
156. Ward, *American Silences*, 7.
157. Novak, *American Painting*, xiii.
158. Marx, *The Machine in the Garden*, 356.
159. Ward, *American Silences*, 169.
160. See Ward, *American Silences*, 169.
161. Ward, *American Silences*, 200, emphasis in original.
162. Novak, *American Painting*, 230.
163. Lucie-Smith, *American Realism*, 124.
164. Levin, *Edward Hopper*, 407. Levin quotes from an article by Rafael Squirru, who interviewed Hopper about his approach to light and quotes him verbatim. Rafael Squirru, "Edward Hopper," *Américas* 17 (1965): 16.
165. Novak, *American Painting*, 183.
166. Novak, *American Painting*, 235.
167. See Novak, *American Painting*, 183.
168. Mark Rothko, "Statement on His Attitude in Painting," *The Tiger's Eye* 1, no. 9 (1949): 114.
169. See James E. B. Breslin, *Mark Rothko: A Biography* (Chicago: University of Chicago Press, 1993), 503.
170. Breslin, *Mark Rothko*, 247.
171. See Hubert Crehan, "Rothko's Wall of Light," *Arts Digest* 29, no. 3 (1954): 5, 19.

V

Retrieving 3D Computer Graphics' Lost "Context of Meaning"

> Let the powers be well directed, directed by love, and they would everywhere be greeted with joy and honor. [...] I call upon you, young men, to obey your heart, and be the nobility of this land. In every age of the world, there has been a leading nation, one of a more generous sentiment, whose eminent citizens were willing to stand for the interests of general justice and humanity, at the risk of being called, by the men of the moment, chimerical and fantastic. Which should be that nation but these States?[1]
>
> *RALPH WALDO EMERSON (1844)*

This part focuses on how the findings on computer graphics developments from Parts II and III of this study can be brought together with the findings on a possible concept of realism specific to the United States from Part IV. The goal is to create a synthesis of all these insights that will be useful in determining a common context of meaning for 3D graphics, which is the purpose of this study. The overarching question is therefore *why* the developments in computer technology have taken place in the way described in this study, and what it means for the practice of creating images on the computer when the available tool is characterized by a specific worldview and concept of images. In contrast to the previous accounts, my following remarks no longer concentrate primarily on the motives of individuals in the history of computer graphics. Rather, I will focus on the common cultural-historical background against which the protagonists acted. In other words, I will address the overarching context that might have motivated them to take their approaches. This overarching view is possible because many of the different protagonists actually pursued similar goals. When developing means to create computer graphics, the engineering draftsmen and computer scientists were each striving for a figurative-realistic visual language based on human intuitive perception, on the one hand, and on central-perspective construction or the functioning of optical and camera-technical processes, on the other. All of the protagonists presented these demands regarding the design of computer images because they assumed that phenomena, including fictional ones, could be depicted in a credible and tangible way with images that fulfill these criteria. To summarize all these characteristics into a manageable concept, I introduced the phrase "maxim of believability." The images created today with the help of 3D graphics programs therefore also oscillate between physical or photographic realism, on the one hand, and a perceptual ideal described as subjective, on the other. This reveals similarities to the dilemma between realism and idealism described by Novak as presented in the previous part. In purely visual aesthetic terms, this dilemma is not always expressed in today's computer graphics, but in terms of production aesthetics, these characteristics are also anchored in images that pursue an independent aesthetic, such as a two-dimensional cartoon aesthetic – provided these images are created with commonly available computer graphical software. In the following, I will discuss a cultural background which

DOI: 10.1201/9781003649861-14

presumably shaped the entire development of the software and, consequently, now shapes its use. I provided initial insights into the integration of cultural artifacts in computer graphics when I examined individual still images from various Pixar films in Chapter 8. However, I did not explicitly express the extent to which a particular understanding of images and the world is embedded in the software beyond Pixar or commercial animated films. Based on these reflections and the previous examination of pictorial tendencies in the United States, I will now explore how these cultural artifacts have influenced software development. Against the backdrop of Leo Marx's 1964 study *The Machine in the Garden*, I will also consider a broader cultural-historical context to ultimately situate both narrative strands – the computer-technological and the art-historical – within it.

NOTE

1. Ralph W. Emerson, "The Young American (1844)," in *The Collected Works of Ralph Waldo Emerson. Volume I: Nature, Addresses, and Lectures*, ed. Robert E. Spiller and Alfred R. Ferguson (Cambridge: Belknap Press of Harvard University Press, 1971), 238–39.

CHAPTER 10

Technological Progress and Image Practice in the United States

Examining the creative approach of the Belgian artist David Claerbout, who primarily uses digital imaging techniques for his works, can provide helpful introductory insight for these final considerations. His work *Travel* is particularly suitable for this purpose. It is a 12-minute photorealistic 3D-animated short film, realized between 1996 and 2013. In an extremely slow tracking shot, a dense forest is traversed in a uniform movement. Initially composed of European flora, the forest gradually and smoothly transforms into a tropical jungle. The shot begins outside the forest next to a park bench (Figure 10.1) and ends, also outside the forest, in an extreme bird's-eye view, making the forest appear as a small grove surrounded by meadows and fields. Although the floating journey through the woods is divided into individual sections by slow dissolves, and even though the vegetation is gradually changing, the flowing movement of the camera almost seems like a long sequence shot. A museum visitor discovering the film as part of an exhibition and unaware of how it might have been made would perhaps simply be confronted with calming but ordinary video footage of an unusual forest, especially as this impression is reinforced by the soundtrack. In fact, it is relaxation music, originally composed for the purpose of meditation, that inspired Claerbout's film project.[1]

This work is a suitable entry point for synthesizing all the previous findings from this study, because the artist began working with 3D computer graphics at a time when the software for creating such images had only been generally available for a few years. Although he had clear ideas for the film right from the beginning, he knew he was somewhat limited by the visual-aesthetic artifacts embedded in the software. In his preparatory sketches and drafts, Claerbout anticipated the technical implementation possibilities of the 3D software he used. In one of the sketches (Figure 10.2), he makes a marginal note about the planned lighting mood for the HD animation: "Opening to TRAVEL. 7 seconds of utter stillness with the Bench. Summer-light – late afternoon off [*sic*] course: Because that is the time we live in. And it certainly is the time of C. G. I. light."[2] Claerbout does not comment further on this statement in his sketch, and although from a purely mathematical point of view the virtual light could also be calculated differently and Claerbout could certainly give this command to the computer, the artist implicitly assumes that the 3D computer graphics predetermine a lighting mood to a certain extent. They harbor the light of the afternoon sun.

Claerbout also takes a stance on the photographic parameters within the software. He refers to the photographic process integrated within 3D software as "Dark Optics," contrasting it with "Light Optics," a term he uses for the camera technology dependent on physical light. He even describes "Light Optics" as the "enemy" of computer graphics, even though he relates it to the virtual technology by opening up this dichotomy.[3] Through these reflections, which are partly intuitive and partly very specific, Claerbout demonstrates that he is aware of the production-aesthetic aspects inherent in 3D applications and that these aspects inevitably influence his artistic expression. With his marginal note on the afternoon sun in

DOI: 10.1201/9781003649861-15

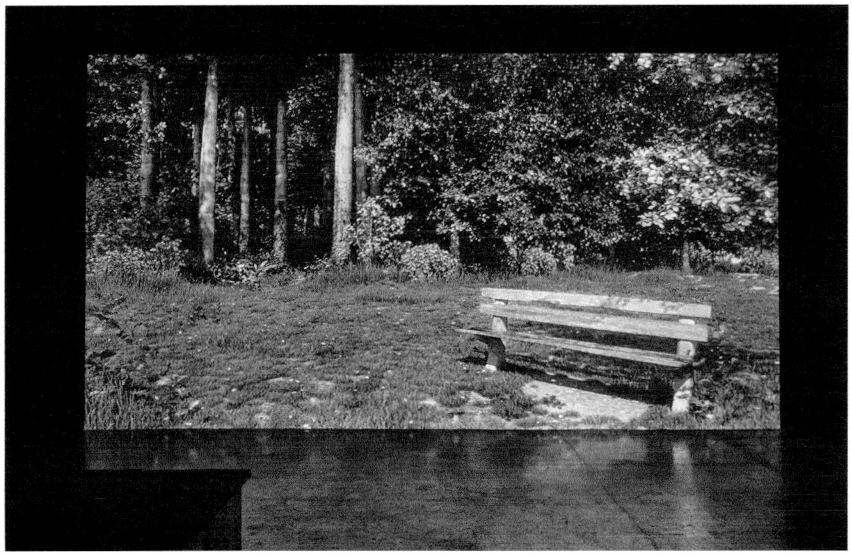

FIGURE 10.1 David Claerbout, *Travel*, 1996–2013, single channel video, stereo sound, 12 minutes, HD animation. (Photography by Ros Kavanagh. Reprinted with permission from David Claerbout's studio.)

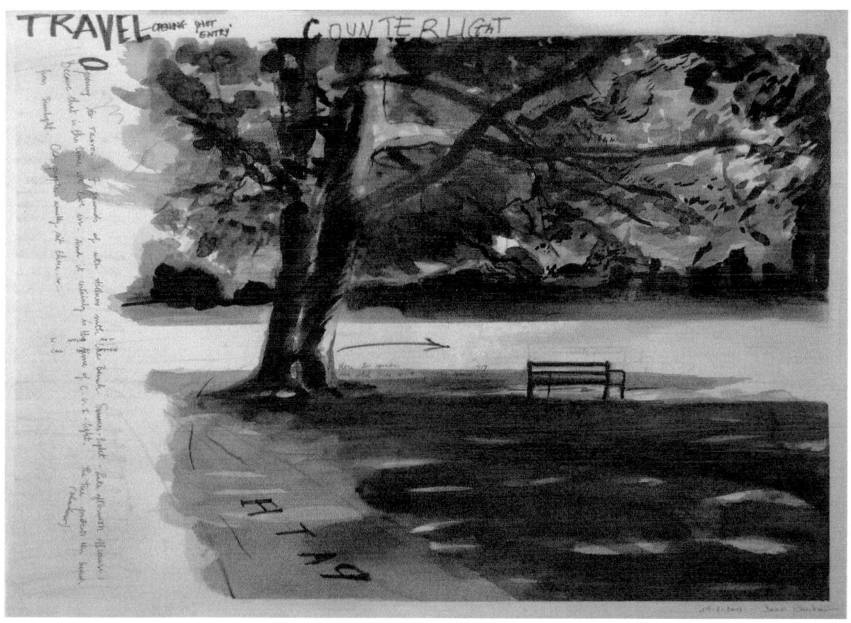

FIGURE 10.2 David Claerbout, *Travel (Entry Counter Light)*, 2013, washed ink and felt-tip pen on paper, 18.1 × 24 in. (46 × 61 cm). (Reprinted with permission from David Claerbout's studio.)

the sketch and his comments on the peculiarities of virtual camera technology, he therefore provides an indication that the aesthetic categories of "American Realism" identified in the previous part can still be detected in computer graphics practice. In his work, the cultural artifacts of light and photography are especially prominent. The key observation here is that this is the case even though Claerbout strives for a very specific, self-imposed, extremely photorealistic image aesthetic. Unlike Pixar, he deliberately pushes the imaging technology used into the background so that it is not immediately recognizable.

These insights raise the final question of this investigation: How are the aesthetic categories linked to the technology and why do they also affect the work of a Belgian artist? The decisive link between the developments in computer graphics and the aesthetic categories of "American Realism" can now be established. As noted earlier, the visual-aesthetic characteristics of light, photography, silence and nostalgia directly represent a very specific worldview that can often be traced back to transcendentalist tendencies. The software was thus conceived against the backdrop of a cultural heritage that can be placed in the luminist pictorial tradition I delineated above. With Sutherland's contribution to the development of computer graphics, I demonstrated how the creation of images with the computer is divided into two phases: one that concerns the development of the software and one that concerns the application of the software. Every possible application of the computer programs in the production process is always influenced, predetermined and shaped by the first phase. Therefore, if a transcendentalist worldview has become firmly established in this first phase during software development, it affects everyone who uses the software. This worldview plays a decisive role in shaping the common context of meaning of all 3D images – regardless of what happens in the second phase during the application of the software. Even when an independent visual aesthetic is sought, as in the case with Claerbout or the *South Park* series (Figure I.3), to which I referred at the beginning of this study, the aesthetic categories of "American Realism" are constantly reproduced anew with the virtual tools in the software. The software's features, such as shaders, modeling, lighting and rendering, thus represent a transcendentalist world view and a particular concept of pictoriality. In terms of production aesthetics – *regardless* of the visual aesthetics – in Claerbout's images or in those of the *South Park* series, the (possibly) unintentional trace of a common context of meaning can therefore always be found. I use the term "trace" here in the sense of philosopher Sybille Krämer, as has been briefly discussed in endnote 37 in Section 3.2.[4] My fundamental assumption for this study – that all 3D images possess this common context of meaning – is thus beginning to be confirmed.

To systematically substantiate this hypothesis in this last part, I will first draw concrete parallels between the findings on computer graphics and art. I will then revisit some of Pixar's production details and images to explain how the studio's visual worlds directly work with the aesthetic categories to create the visual aesthetics of their films.

10.1 COMPUTER GRAPHICS AS THE GUARDIAN OF THE TRADITION OF "AMERICAN REALISM"

What similarities in production aesthetics can be identified by directly comparing the developments in computer graphics with the art historical findings? Realist and idealist tendencies merge among many individual painters and movements. For instance, Shi attributes romantic-idealistic traits to Winslow Homer's paintings – one of the artists in the United States who can also be described as realistic in a historical sense. However, Shi also describes how the boundaries between idealism and realism were fluid among the transcendentalist luminists. Additionally, Shi argues that the realistic nuances of the luminist paintings can be traced back to a preference for depicting ordinary things and situations.[5] It is also notable that the realistic endeavors were rarely politically motivated, as was often the case with historically motivated European realism, for example. Like most representational forms of US painting, no political aspirations can be discerned in the early computer graphics experiments. Although they were made possible by military funding, the first 3D images mainly depicted everyday objects, such as an orange in Blinn's work[6] or glasses and bottles in Catmull's work.[7] Even the now famous "Utah Teapot" by Martin E. Newell[8] or John Lasseter's lamp, which is now Pixar's logo,[9] can be listed here as examples (Figures 10.3 and 10.4). Thus, like many realistic paintings, the early computer graphics illustrated everyday facets of life. Especially in the 19th century, the situations and objects depicted in paintings often represented a higher unity of all things, ultimately characterizing the idealistic features of the paintings. While these idealistic tendencies are not immediately apparent in computer graphics, they can still be identified by considering Barbara Novak's description of how this connection between realism and idealism was *technically* realized:

> From the limners on, American artists had held, in one way or another, to the adamant control of idea. Enlisting measure, mechanics, and technology as aids toward a certainty that was often as ideal as it was real, American artists guarded the unbroken integrity of the objects or things of this world, which became, very often, vessels or carriers of metaphysical meaning.[10]

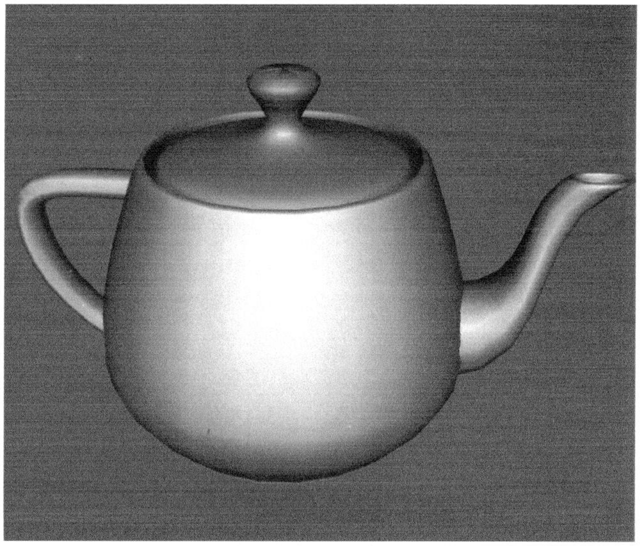

FIGURE 10.3 Martin E. Newell, *Figure 28 Various objects defined using Bézier patches* (here only one of four objects is shown), 1975, computer rendering. (Reprinted with permission from Martin E. Newell.)

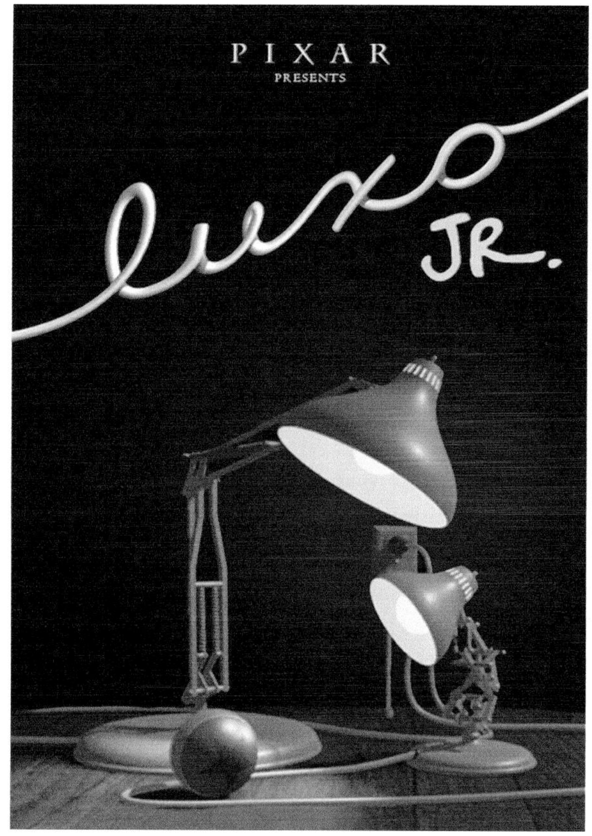

FIGURE 10.4 John Lasseter, director, *Luxo Junior*, 1986, film poster. (© 1999 Disney/Pixar.)

Although computer graphics cannot be explicitly linked to metaphysical concerns, Novak's description can be directly applied to their production. Here, too, the creation of images always oscillates between relying on technical aids and perspective construction while at the same time taking into account that the images should be credible and meaningful. As Sutherland emphasized in the interview with Karen Frenkel, the photorealism of computer images alone is not convincing as long as the image has no "underlying meaning."[11] Rule and Coons' phrasing of an "implicit meaning,"[12] which underlies perspective drawing conventions, also indicates that the early computer graphics endeavors were not only aimed at achieving technical precision, but also at creating meaningful images that represent more than can be seen with the naked eye. A description by Shi in relation to Homer's painterly style picks up on this aspect, and it can again be applied to the development of the computer graphics: for example when Evans, Romney et al. announce that they wanted to use the computer to create images "that a person can 'feel,' as contrasted with images that he must laboriously interpret,"[13] this attitude is reminiscent of Homer, who, according to Shi, "respected the dignity of facts but probed beneath them to explore deeper levels of feelings and meaning."[14] For the engineers analyzed in this study, the idea of images that can be "felt" is also linked to perspective and representational depictions with a photographic quality – fully in line with the maxim of believability. In the spirit of Transcendentalism, computer graphics have thus developed into what Shi describes as a "fertile synthesis of the real and the ideal."[15] This blending of realism and idealism, or the connection between feeling and technology as described by Evans, Romney et al., responds directly to the comparison Novak makes between luminist and impressionist painting quoted above: "If we say that impressionism is the *objective* response to the *visual* sensation of light, then perhaps we can say that luminism is the *poetic* response to the *felt* sensation."[16]

The link between luminist painting and computer graphics can be strengthened by revisiting Novak's use of the term "idea." Similar to what she describes for the transcendentalist painterly movement, Coons and Rule aimed to capture an idea with the help of perspective illustrations. Their description, "the sketch is an aid to the mind, a tangible record of an idea,"[17] communicates this just as much as Coons' independently expressed idea of the designer's work:

> He perceives his idea at first not in the perfection of a well-turned English word description, nor in the precision of a mathematical formula, but in some nebulous assembly of building blocks of structure, vaguely beheld; he "feels" his creation. The sketch forms the natural bridge between these vague stirrings of the imagination and the subsequent precise statement of the refined details of the concept.[18]

Coons' wording is very similar to Novak's description of US artists using technical aids to gain control over an idea: "American artists have always been makers. The artist now stands behind, as generating idea, his aim to have technology render his idea concrete and tangible. As in luminist classicism, the idea becomes the palpable thing."[19] Similarly to the luminist painters or even the Limners, who tried to make something indescribable tangible with their technical approach, Rule and Coons are also concerned with "[making] solid and tangible the shifting images of our minds, so that we may examine them at our leisure. Through this recording art we free ourselves of the effort to hold ideas in memory [...]."[20]

Novak considers Luminism to be the first genuinely "indigenous" art movement since the arrival of the first Europeans on the continent. Furthermore, she recognizes traits of this movement in many different US painterly approaches well into the 20th century. As previously illustrated by the connections between computer-animated films and US landscape painting, Novak's reflections on US painterly trends in no way refer to computer-graphic developments.[21] Nevertheless, based on her line of reasoning, it can now be precisely demonstrated that not only Pixar's imagery, but also computer graphics developments in general exhibit clear traits of the luminist tradition. Just as Novak describes the painting of the *Hudson River School* and the luminists as "quietistic, precise and conceptual,"[22] computer graphics are also not primarily concerned with depicting reality but with conveying a concept. And as far as the engineers were concerned, this concept was to be depicted with the precision of a camera so it could be understood particularly intuitively. The conceptual nature of computer graphics is evident not only in Fetter's and Coons' work, but also in Sutherland's. He assumed that the computer images should be representative and contain meaning to credibly illustrate something abstract, such as an atom, even if this image is not an accurate representation of what an atom looks like.[23] Also Gouraud and Catmull developed their graphics based on a concept. This is particularly evident in Catmull's work, as he uses the term "image" even before it can be displayed on a screen. For him, the conceptual, mathematical description in the computer is enough to speak of an image.[24]

One of Novak's remarks provides a deeper understanding of this conceptual approach to image creation. It deals with the paradox that both in Luminism, in which it was so central to depict objects in a particularly tangible way,[25] and beyond that – for instance, much later in Conceptual Art – the conceptual always took precedence over perception in image creation. In all these cases – including computer graphics – the creation of images remains an intellectual endeavor. Computer graphics even fulfill this requirement on several levels. For Rule and Coons, *graphics* are an instrument of *thought*. However, according to Coons, Engelbart, Johnson and Sutherland, the *computer* also serves as an augmentation of the *intellect*. In this sense, the computer is also an instrument of thought, or, as the authors put it, an equal working partner.[26] The merging of *graphics* and *computer* – *computer graphics* – thus corresponds to the standards of Luminism not only in terms of the engineers' understanding of computer technology, but also in terms of their understanding of image creation. While the painters were still dependent on technological *aids* for their intellectual and conceptual pictorial work, those who now create a picture with the computer are working *from the outset* in a completely mechanized environment designed to create images that embody these same specific pictorial ideas. The concepts embedded in the software therefore correspond to Novak's observation that US artists protect the "unbroken integrity of the objects or things of this world."[27] This statement can be read as a description of the overarching goal of computer graphics endeavors. It is not only in painting that things and objects are presented figuratively and with the aid of camera technology; Coons and Fetter also emphasized that the camera always produces the most realistic and reliable view in order to depict an object in a tangible and credible way.[28] Today, the camera is an integral part of the software, as was also discussed in connection with Claerbout. Additionally, photography has played a role in the development of shaders, but here primarily with regard to how surfaces and contrasts are perceived. Nevertheless, research in computer graphics also relied on findings from photographic reproduction technology quite generally. In Phong's case, this led to the creation of computer-graphic images that almost completely resembled photographs.[29] Fetter also explicitly addressed the aspect of integrity. With reference to Etienne-Jules Marey, Fetter expressed the idea that, compared to language, graphics are the most reliable means of representing concepts and also temporal sequences.[30]

It can therefore be said that the blending of idealism and realism, evident above all in Luminism and, in traces, in many other US painting movements, also characterizes the development of computer graphics. They are just as sensitive to scientific facts and – perhaps for this reason – rely on photography with the same special vigor as the painters did. Photography fulfills the maxim of believability for both artists and software developers alike because it is able to capture the perspective constructions familiar to human vision with technical perfection. The fact that the camera's images correspond only to *one* possible image concept,[31] as Lucie-Smith notes, is relevant neither for the painters nor for the engineers explored in this study. The only requirement that they have for their images is that they are generally understandable – they assume that the maxim of believability is equally valid for all people in the world. This idea of universality is also expressed in Sutherland's descriptions of his *Sketchpad* program and, in continuation of these initial approaches, today's software is designed in full capacity to generate images that correspond to the MoMA catalog's definition of the American Realists and Magic Realists: "No other style of painting appeals so naturally to the great majority of people, and in this sense it is a truly democratic style, offering no barrier of technique between the artist and the untrained eye."[32]

10.2 PIXAR AND 3D COMPUTER GRAPHICS' "CONTEXT OF MEANING" AS A VISUAL PHENOMENON

The aesthetic categories of photography, light, silence and nostalgia that I identified in Part IV – whose origins lie in the ideological convictions presented above – can be found to a significant extent in the images of the *Pixar Animation Studios* and also in other commercial productions that pursue a similar visual-aesthetic standard (see a more thorough discussion on this in Chapter 8). Computer graphics that do not *also* exhibit these production-aesthetic characteristics on a *visual-aesthetic* level – such as the images from *South Park* – are excluded from the following analysis.

Given Edwin Catmull's involvement in the development of algorithms central to today's 3D graphics, it is reasonable to assume that his thinking was influenced by the identified ideological tendencies. This would also explain why the Pixar films express their production-aesthetic characteristics so directly through their visual aesthetics. However, *past* algorithmic developments are not the only way to deduce the criteria that characterize the visual aesthetics of Pixar films; *more recent* algorithmic approaches can also demonstrate that a certain visual aesthetic is still the goal. The development of a new shading approach shows that the original motifs for creating computer graphics are – purely conceptually – being directly continued by the more recent developments at Pixar.

Pixar's new shading method, called *PxrDisney*, is based on a shading algorithm originally designed by Brent Burley for Disney's computer-animated films in 2012.[33] Pixar further developed the approach according to its own standards and describes it in the documentation of its own render engine *RenderMan* as a "'catch-all' shader, designed to be flexible and dynamic in a production shading pipeline. The shader is based on the Disney 'principled' BRDF by Brent Burley; it is 'principled' rather than strictly physical."[34] The wording in the *RenderMan* documentation is partly taken from Burley's paper, in which he presents the shader's development and key features. In the paper, Burley explains the principles on which he based his new development and lists five criteria. They are reproduced almost word for word in the *RenderMan* documentation:

1. Intuitive rather than physical.
2. As few parameters as possible.

3. Parameters are zero to one over their plausible range.
4. Parameters are allowed to be pushed beyond their plausible range where it makes sense.
5. All combinations of parameters should be as robust and plausible as possible.[35]

As subsequently explained in the *RenderMan* documentation, the implementation of adjustable parameters within the software differs somewhat from Disney's approach. For instance, while the original shader provides only one parameter for the coloring of an object, the modified *PxrDisney* shader offers an additional slider for an object's emitted color as well as more complex subsurface scattering color settings.[36] Pixar's use of the term "catch-all" also indicates that the new shader not only shows a connection to historical developments in computer graphics but also to developments in US art history. The shader is designed for an intuitive workflow and an intuitive conception of images – in short: for the fulfillment of the maxim of believability. If the parameters are "catch-all," then they are conceptualized to be as universal as Sutherland considered his *Sketchpad* program to be universal. From a purely technical standpoint, according to the descriptions quoted here, many of the requirements expressed from the beginning of computer graphics in terms of image quality can be implemented much more easily and intuitively with the shader. The fact that no new demands on the concept of imagery are being articulated here, but that software development is still driven by one specific idea of imagery, can be demonstrated particularly impressively by the first principle mentioned above: It states that working with the shader should be based on intuition rather than physical accuracy. The last three principles additionally address the concept of "plausibility," which can easily be related to the concept of "believability." Together these principles demonstrate that it is possible to push the shader's parameters beyond a certain limit – that is, to distort its physical properties, on which the shader is based, for one's own purposes. Nevertheless, the principles imply that it is not desirable to extend this limit too far. Plausibility – or integrity – should be maintained. This fine line, which is hinted at here and on which the pictorial design depends to remain credible, is reminiscent of the dilemma between idealism and realism, as described by Novak, in which, for instance, painter Thomas Cole found himself. Abstractly speaking, his mindset expresses something quite similar to the principles of the new shader. To Cole it was also important to closely study the real environment, although not to simply copy it, but to create a new scenery for a new painting based solely on what he observed, while at the same time designing an independent composition. As Cole's approach was already compared to Catmull's idea of creative work in Chapter 8, it is not surprising that the new shading algorithm is also based on similar principles.

Moving away from shading and examining the studio's other areas of activity reveals that this concept of image design is present there as well. Former longtime Pixar employee Kyoung Swearingen particularly impressively expresses this idea in an interview that I conducted for this study when she talks about her work in the field of lighting direction. Her accounts suggest that her work at the studio was also based on the maxim of believability. This becomes evident in her answer to the question of how she would describe Pixar's visual aesthetic or its overarching "signature look":

> [W]e try to achieve a believable look, instead of a realistic look. So, I would like to say, the […] image in my head about this cozy Christmas time in front of a fireplace, you know, that has the actual picture […] versus the actual, my aspired look, right? […] And I think what we are trying to more connect with this believability that we are imagining […] what it is like to be in that moment. And, I think that's why image becomes – if you're talking about signature look – I think that is more motive behind it, the overarching big motive on every single film that we're trying to make believable, so that we can transfer the audience into that spot, right into Paris, right into, you know, I don't know, Monster's University, or what, you know, […] this imaginative place that […] it's believable, I, I'm there kind of a feel.[37]

She then goes on to provide examples of how this mindset is realized in her professional field of lighting direction:

> So, for lighters, it's, you know, we have to kind of think about the balance between, the real,

> the realistic or realism and something that is more palatable or more [...] relatable. So, to create that [...] we fake all the time, right? Trying to make that. So sometimes we defy that [...] physics or we defy the, you know, things don't make any sense [...]. [T]here's a light behind me, therefore my face is going to be really dark, because it's a [...] back light, but we don't want that, we want to make sure that [...] it's. So there's a story, there is a, a, emotion, there is the, the believability and those kind of combine into, you know, certain look and I think that's more like an overarching kind of, I guess, kind of a drive [...].[38]

Further into the interview, Swearingen mentioned a specific case in which she altered the physical conditions of a scene to increase its credibility. She described a shot in which a character held a white cup, whose white surface was supposed to serve as an indirect light source. The cup was to illuminate the character's face with a faint glow of light. However, to have more control over the indirect light emitted by the cup, Swearingen placed an independent light source in proximity to the virtual object. This light source merely simulated indirect light but was actually a direct light source. Ultimately, this trick still did not result in the desired credibility. To eventually achieve the desired lighting mood on the character's face, Swearingen decided to place this new light source slightly away from the cup, where, from a purely physical point of view, no light had its origin.[39]

Swearingen then explicitly emphasized that the relationship between realism or physics and believability is merely a matter of visual-aesthetic requirements within a larger framework. The individual directors of Pixar's feature films generally pursue their own visual-aesthetic ideas.[40] Nevertheless, Swearingen's descriptions illustrate that the individual visual-aesthetic concepts are also shaped by the "dilemma" between idealism and realism. With this insight, the characters that populate the films and which cannot at all be reconciled with the US painterly tradition on a visual-aesthetic level, also find a place in the conceptual approach I pursue in this study: Just as the images of the *South Park* series and those by Claerbout are connected to each other purely in terms of production aesthetics via a common context of meaning, because they were created within the framework of the same software landscape, the characters in the Pixar films can also be understood as part of this common context of meaning.

So, while Claerbout takes a self-reflexive approach to the visual concepts embedded in the software in his work *Travel* and in the *South Park* series those visual concepts are almost completely ignored, the visual worlds presented in Pixar's films largely respond to the production-aesthetic criteria against which the software was developed. Pixar's imagery is characterized to a considerable degree by the overarching aesthetic categories of nostalgia, light, silence and photography, as discussed above. Since photography is now firmly anchored in the software as a means of expression, the images of the Pixar films are also "virtual photographs" – as are all other computer graphics from a purely production-aesthetic perspective, including the images of the *South Park* series. However, unlike the producers of *South Park*, for instance, Pixar also uses the algorithmic possibility to simulate lens blur, which is typically caused by the optical properties of the lens in photographic images. I have previously discussed this in Section 2.1. Claerbout also uses this option and neither he nor Pixar deviates from US painterly trends in this respect: Photographic depth of field was also imitated in photorealistic painting in the 1960s, as seen, for example, in Chuck Close's large-format portraits.

Swearingen's comments have already addressed the aspect of light. From a purely visual-aesthetic point of view, it is striking that the lighting moods of Pixar films often resemble the lighting moods of 19th-century US landscape painting. However, considering these final conclusions, the previously mentioned references to Edward Hopper's painting in the *Toy Story* films now become clearer as well. Hopper's style is emulated, for instance, by the afternoon sun also mentioned by Claerbout. Since Novak places Hopper in the tradition of the luminists, the connection between Pixar and Luminism is not lost, even in the visual references that Pixar makes to Hopper. At the same time, the animation studio also frequently incorporates the aspect of silence or stillness, which is closely linked to light. The technicized image environment is initially completely silent and almost sterile, which is why 3D artists pay particular attention to making computer graphics lively and *noisy*. However, silence can also be detected as a cultural theme in Pixar films, for example in the film *WALL-E*, named after the last inhabitant of Earth. He is a robot that cleans up humanity's trash while all remaining humans hold out on a spaceship until life is potentially possible again on the withered planet. The only sounds that characterize the apocalyptic landscape of this completely silent planet are those of the robot. The silence in *WALL-E* is no longer characterized by serenity compared to the tranquility of the luminist paintings; instead, it is extremely threatening. Nevertheless, there are scenes in which the combination of light and silence expresses peace, for example, when WALL-E looks into the sunset together with his partner Eve, another robot that has travelled to earth from the human spaceship (see Figure 8.10). But even apart from these individual scenes, the computer-animated film expresses a deep longing for and a connection to nature that is characterized by transcendentalist spirituality. Central elements of the plot revolve around desperate attempts to reverse the complete destruction of the planet's vegetation in the long term. This paradoxical situation, which arises from the fact that a film from a highly technological environment criticizes the loss of nature, is revisited in the conclusion of this study.

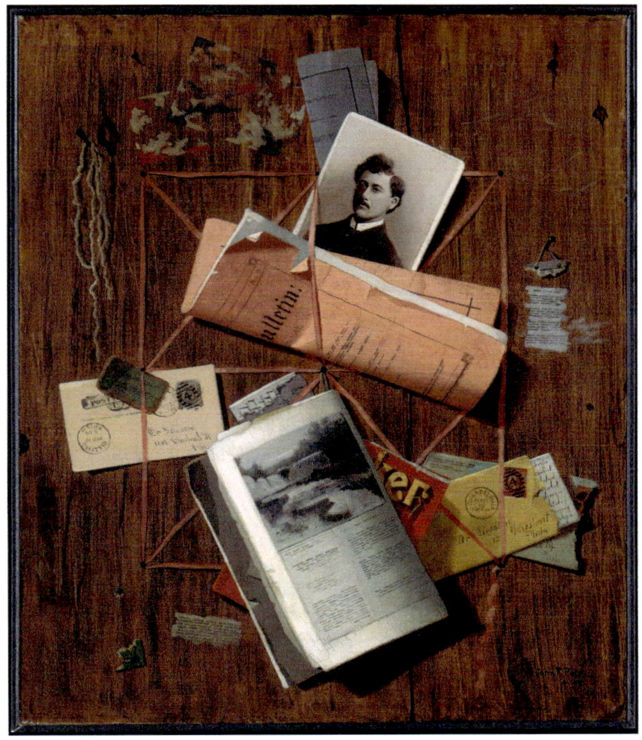

FIGURE 10.5 John F. Peto, *Office Board*, 1885, oil on canvas, 24 3/8 × 19 7/8 in. (61.9 × 50.5 cm), The Metropolitan Museum of Art, George A. Hearn Fund, 1955. (© CC0.)

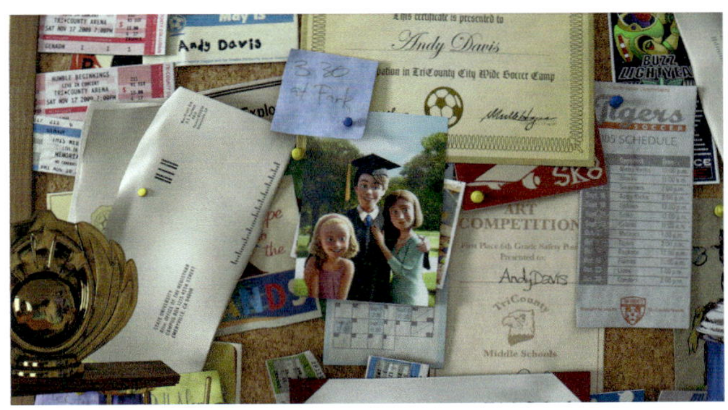

FIGURE 10.6 Lee Unkrich, director, still from *Toy Story 3*, 2010, 3D computer graphic. (© 2010 Disney/Pixar.)

The aesthetic category of nostalgia can be recognized most impressively in the Pixar films. One of the defining tasks of synthetic image generation is to make the artificial environments appear alive to convey a sense of credibility. In purely technical terms, this aesthetic category has been integrated into the realm of shading by Edwin Catmull with his textures and by James F. Blinn with his bump maps. These are the two functions which allow surfaces to be colored or given a structure as well as a patina. The desire to simulate a past – and thus, indirectly, a sense of liveliness – characterizes the synthetic images just as much as the work of painters such as William M. Harnett. Similar to how he invented the feeling for a non-existent past and created an aesthetic of decay with his paintings, depicting objects that appear old and have a history, a patina must also be artificially created in the computerized synthetic image generation, because the virtual objects, like the then-young nation, have no past that could have aged them. Against this background, it is not surprising that a pinboard can also be found in the Pixar films. It unmistakably resembles William M. Harnett's or John F. Peto's letter racks – and not only visually, but also in terms of production aesthetics, as is now clear (Figures 10.5 and 10.6). But even beyond the depiction of pinboards, the artificial aging of the scenes is a central aspect of image design at Pixar. As the studio's own publication *To Infinity and Beyond* reveals, the design of details took on a new significance with the 2006 production *Cars*.[41] The story takes place along Route 66, which is still lined with many abandoned and dilapidated villages.[42] The production team aimed to recreate the wealth of detail found during research trips in the film, but this task presented a particular challenge:

> Patina, of course, is directly contrary to the preferences of the computer for the simple and the perfect. "It takes so much effort," said Lasseter. "The design, the thought, the planning, the implementation, the art – every step until you get to the final screen. You're just battling with the computer the whole way to make things less perfect. The eye is so comfortable with the organic world – the moment that something isn't done to that level, it pops you out of the film. It ruins the suspension of disbelief."[43]

Eben Otsby, a colleague of Lasseter's, expands on his thoughts in his role as the film's technical director:

> We drove into the desert, to see the hills and cliffs and figure out how we could capture their essence and make it work in the film. We also took a lot of pictures of the way dirt piles up near roads, and the way paint peels off buildings, all these things that give the sense of an old, somewhat down-at-the-heels town. Bill Cone was so interested in the beautiful desert light; that came together with the town to create something really unlike anything anyone's ever done in CG before.[44]

Through the use of the term "essence," not only the themes of nostalgia and decay is again addressed here but also the desire or the idea of capturing the concept of a found environment.

As has now been demonstrated, the four aesthetic categories identified above can be traced not only in the software itself, but also in Pixar's stylistic history. The animation studio thus works with cultural artifacts in terms of both production aesthetics *and* visual aesthetics, which have also shaped the previously described painterly tendencies within the United States. While additional aesthetic categories could certainly be identified, this study has revealed a relationship between the historical development of computer graphics and US painterly traditions, particularly Luminism and, consequently, 19th-century Transcendentalism. Interestingly, Transcendentalism is characterized by a paradox similar to that expressed in the film *WALL-E*. I will elaborate on this paradox in the next chapter. It represents a worldview deeply rooted in US culture, that, I would argue, significantly characterizes 3D graphics software and thus also the practical use of it. Ultimately, this is the core of the common context of meaning of *all* 3D computer graphics, even those that *do not* express the production-aesthetic characteristics in terms of image aesthetics. Many of the aspects were previously mentioned in the art-historical discussion – they will now be revisited once more in the context of a broader cultural-historical background.

NOTES

1. See David Claerbout, "Travel, 1996–2013," in *David Claerbout*, ed. Kunsthaus Bregenz (Cologne: Walther König, 2018), 47.
2. Sean Kelly, ed., *David Claerbout: Drawings and Studies* (Ostfildern: Hatje Cantz, 2015), 102.
3. See Kunsthaus Bregenz, ed., *David Claerbout* (Cologne: Walther König, 2018), 15–16.
4. See Sybille Krämer, "Das Medium als Spur und Apparat," in *Medien, Computer, Realität: Wirklichkeit svorstellungen und Neue Medien*, ed. Sybille Krämer (Frankfurt am Main: Suhrkamp, 1998), 79.
5. See David E. Shi, *Facing Facts: Realism in American Thought and Culture, 1850–1920* (Oxford: Oxford University Press, 1995), 20, 137.
6. See James F. Blinn, "Computer Display of Curved Surfaces" (PhD diss., University of Utah, 1978), J. Willard Marriott Library (105596), [v].
7. Edwin Catmull, "A Subdivision Algorithm for Computer Display of Curved Surfaces" (PhD diss., University of Utah, 1974), J. Willard Marriott Library (712681), 69–74. Catmull also notes: "ARPA's administrators did not hover over the shoulders of those of us working on the projects they funded, nor did they demand that our work have direct military applications. They simply trusted us to innovate." Edwin Catmull and Amy Wallace, *Creativity, Inc. Overcoming the Unseen Forces That Stand in the Way of True Inspiration* (New York: Random House, 2014), 13.
8. See Martin E. Newell, "The Utilization of Procedure Models in Digital Image Synthesis" (PhD diss., University of Utah, 1975. J. Willard Marriott Library (1507175), 84, 86. In his study, Newell also shows a computer-graphic representation of a children's carousel. See Newell, "Digital Image Synthesis," 88. On the special significance of the "Utah Teapot," see also Jacob Gaboury, *Image Objects. An Archaeology of Computer Graphics* (Cambridge: MIT Press, 2021), 87–123. Perry also refers to a rabbit that, parallel

to the teapot, has a high degree of recognition in the 3D community as well: "The teapot, created at the start of 3D modeling and computer graphics development in the University of Utah's computer graphics group, and the bunny, created a few years later by Stanford University researchers, are two of the most salient examples of the standardized models that have evolved within the computer graphics research community and their circulation among the researchers." Rebecca A. Perry, "Rigging the World: 3D Modeling and the Seduction of the Real" (PhD diss., Massachusetts Institute of Technology, 2014), MIT Libraries, DSpace@MIT (900615015), 114.

9. See Karen Paik and Leslie Iwerks, *To Infinity and Beyond! The Story of Pixar Animation Studios* (San Francisco: Chronicle, 2007), 58–62.
10. Barbara Novak, *American Painting of the Nineteenth Century. Realism, Idealism, and the American Experience*, 3rd edition (Oxford: Oxford University Press USA, 2007), 217.
11. Ivan E. Sutherland, "An Interview with Ivan Sutherland," interview by Karen A. Frenkel, *Communications of the ACM* 32, no. 6 (1989): 713, https://doi.org/10.1145/63526.63531
12. John T. Rule and Steven A. Coons, *Graphics* (New York: McGraw-Hill, 1961), 8.
13. Chris Wylie et al., "Half-Tone Perspective Drawings by Computer," in *Proceedings of the Fall Joint Computer Conference – AFIPS '67*, ed. ACM (New York: ACM Press, 1967), 49.
14. See Shi, *Facing Facts*, 137. Shi also attributes to Walt Whitman this quality in the literature.
15. Shi, *Facing Facts*, 20.
16. Novak, *American Painting*, 67–68, emphasis in original.
17. Rule and Coons, *Graphics*, vi.
18. Steven A. Coons, "An Outline of the Requirements for a Computer-Aided Design System," In *Proceedings of the Spring Joint Computer Conference – AFIPS '63*, ed. E. Calvin Johnson (New York: ACM Press, 1963), 300.
19. Novak, *American Painting*, 238.
20. Rule and Coons, *Graphics*, 66.
21. See Carolin Scheler, "Der bildsprachliche Kosmos im computeranimierten Kinofilm," in *Piktogrammatik: Grafisches Gestalten als Weltwissen und Bilderordnung*, ed. Annette Geiger and Bianca Holtschke (Bielefeld: transcript, 2021), 156–57.
22. Novak, *American Painting*, 233.
23. See Sutherland, interview by Frenkel, 713–14.
24. See Catmull, "A Subdivision Algorithm," 41.
25. See Novak, *American Painting*, 238
26. See Rule and Coons, *Graphics*, vii; see Steven A. Coons, "The Uses of Computers in Technology," *Scientific American* 215, no. 3 (1966): 177; see Douglas C. Engelbart, *Augmenting Human Intellect. A Conceptual Framework* (Menlo Park: Stanford Research Institute, 1962); see Timothy E. Johnson, "Sketchpad III: Three Dimensional Graphical Communication with a Digital Computer" (Master's thesis, Massachusetts Institute of Technology, 1963), MIT Libraries, DSpace@MIT (33828890), 1; see Ivan E. Sutherland, "Sketchpad: A Man-Machine Graphical Communication System" (technical report, ed. Alan Blackwell and Kerry Rodden, University of Cambridge, 2003), Computer Laboratory (UCAM-CL-TR-574), 17.
27. Novak, *American Painting*, 217.
28. See Rule and Coons, *Graphics*, 231; see William A. Fetter, *Computer Graphics in Communication. Written for the Course Content Development Study in Engineering Graphics, supported by the National Science Foundation* (New York: McGraw-Hill, 1965), 50.
29. See e.g. Bui T. Phong, "Illumination for Computer Generated Pictures," *Communications of the ACM* 18, no. 6 (1975): 317.
30. See Fetter, *Computer Graphics in Communication*, 1.
31. See Edward Lucie-Smith, *American Realism* (London: Thames & Hudson, 2003), 12.
32. Dorothy C. Miller, "Foreword and Acknowledgement," in *American Realists and Magic Realists: Exhibition Catalogue*, ed. Dorothy C. Miller and Alfred H. Barr Jr. (New York: The Museum of Modern Art, 1943), 6.
33. See Brent Burley, *Physically Based Shading at Disney* (Burbank: Walt Disney Animation Studios, 2012).
34. "PxrDisney," RenderMan Documentation, accessed December 20, 2021, https://renderman.pixar.com/resources/RenderMan_20/PxrDisney.html. BRDF stands for "bidirectional reflectance distribution function," i.e. a mathematical function.
35. RenderMan Documentation, "PxrDisney."
36. See RenderMan Documentation, "PxrDisney." Subsurface Scattering is used when shading skin, for example, as it is slightly translucent and the lower layers of skin influence the reflection of light and therefore the appearance of the skin. Due to the different coloring of the various skin layers, subsurface scattering shaders usually offer several color setting parameters so that the uppermost skin layer most closely corresponds to the main color tone of the skin, while lower skin layers are given a flesh-colored red tone in the shader, for example, so that the slightly translucent quality of skin can be simulated on the basis of these different color tones.
37. Kyoung L. Swearingen, interview by the author, February 11, 2020 transcript, Research Online/Data, 5, https://doi.org/10.25625/VBODBG.
38. Swearingen, interview, 5. Interestingly, when asked, both Swearingen and the previously mentioned 3D artist Dominik Pott emphasize that they themselves would not describe the style pursued by Pixar

as their own. While Pott cannot clearly determine which aesthetic decisions he would make differently, Swearingen refers to her Asian cultural background, which strongly characterizes her aesthetic sensibility and her creative work. See Swearingen, interview, 7, and see Dominik Pott, interview by the author, August 16, 2020, transcript, Research Online/Data, 26, https://doi.org/10.25625/Z27EP6.

39. See Swearingen, interview, 8.
40. See Swearingen, interview, 5–6.
41. *Cars*, directed by John Lasseter (Disney/Pixar, 2006).
42. Route 66 was completed in 1926, providing a continuous connection from the north-east to the south-west of the United States for the first time. In the 1930s in particular, many residents from the Midwest and the southern Great Plains travelled to the western states via the new road in order to build a new life there – following the symbol of the "promised land." After the road was also used for military purposes during the Second World War and the towns along the route experienced an economic boom after the war, this development came to an end with the Federal-Aid Highway Act of then-President Dwight D. Eisenhower in 1956, as the new motorways were built parallel to Route 66. Route 66 eventually became superfluous as a transport route, which is why settlement along the road declined in the long term. See Michael Wallis, "Foreword: America's Road," in *A Route 66 Companion*, ed. David King Dunaway (Austin: University of Texas Press, 2012), ix–x.
43. Paik and Iwerks, *To Infinity and Beyond*, 268.
44. Paik and Iwerks, *To Infinity and Beyond*, 268. CG stands for Computer Graphics.

CHAPTER 11

On the Cultural-Historical Background of Synthetic Imaging

> Yet this twilight mood, a blend of sadness and repose, succeeds aesthetically. It is a virtual resolution. Like the middle landscape, or the ritual marriage at the end of a pastoral romance, this consolatory prospect figuratively joins what has been apart.[1]
>
> – *LEO MARX (1964)*

In his 1964 monograph *The Machine in the Garden* US cultural historian and Americanist Leo Marx examines in detail a paradox that was a decisive factor in the shaping of the identity of US cultural development: the desire for technological progress and the simultaneous appreciation of nature, two seemingly contradictory aspects. His study and the subject matter he dealt with emerged from his dissertation from 1949.[2] The year provides context for Marx's intellectual approach and makes it more accessible, as in many respects his thought processes do not correspond to those that form the basis of much research in American Studies today – a problem I briefly addressed in endnote 45 of Section 1.2. However, Marx's insights are highly topical in many other respects. They can be used to gain insights into not only political phenomena occurring in the United States today but also technical-cultural phenomena – such as the computer graphics discussed in this study.

Marx develops his observation that the United States' identity is formed not only by nature but also by technological progress, in three essential steps. He first examines the concept of the "garden," then that of the "machine," and finally, he synthesizes his findings on both phenomena. A series of historical documents from the founding period of the new states are central to his study. For example, he references Thomas Jefferson's 1785 treatise *Notes on the State of Virginia*. Jefferson later became the third president of the United States, serving from 1801 to 1809. In the final part of his study, Marx applies his findings to seminal US literature. He focuses in particular on authors such as Nathaniel Hawthorne, Herman Melville and Mark Twain, but also includes the transcendentalist authors Ralph Waldo Emerson and Henry David Thoreau in his observations. The insights he presents in this context are particularly revealing regarding the common context of meaning of 3D graphics.

To follow Marx's line of thought, it is first necessary to understand his concept of nature. Marx describes how nature, as a symbol, shifted between two opposing extremes in the perception of the first settlers. On the one hand, the "untouched" nature symbolized a retreat from the corrupt structures of European civilization. It represented a place of independence, regeneration, fertility and abundance. On the other hand, the settlers often experienced the exact opposite of this idealized vision, as the land often seemed uninhabitable, wild and threatening.[3] Using Jefferson's notes as an example, Marx illustrates that the life of the Indigenous inhabitants, who were just as much perceived as "wild, threatening nature" by the colonists, appeared admirable to the settlers in some ways, because – as Jefferson states – not only could they

DOI: 10.1201/9781003649861-16

handle the "wild" nature, they were also in complete harmony with it. In the passage to which Marx refers, Jefferson contrasts Indigenous life with the civilized and corrupt society of Europe and even concludes that he would prefer the way of life of the Indigenous population to European structures. However, as Marx points out, neither concept of life was an option for Jefferson: "Jefferson is not endorsing the Indian style of life here. What appears as a preference for the primitive actually is a rhetorical device: *were* it made a question, he says, he would prefer the Indian way, the whole point being that in the New World such questions need not arise."[4] According to Marx's main line of argument, a concept of life emerged from this dichotomy expressed by Jefferson, which lies precisely between the two extremes – something that Marx refers to in his study as the "middle landscape."[5] By this, he means that a concept of nature gradually developed that represented neither a threatening wilderness nor a naïve paradisiacal refuge for all those who wanted to escape the European way of life.

In this definition, nature was not simply a peaceful retreat but offered an opportunity to provide for oneself in a new and independent way. According to this logic, nature became a facilitator of self-realization, because it was seen as something that each inhabitant could farm and cultivate. In other words, nature could be *changed* for one's own benefit. Marx therefore also points out the violent connotation of this image of nature:

> To describe America as a hideous wilderness, however, is to envisage it as another field for the exercise of power. This violent image expresses a need to mobilize energy, postpone immediate pleasures, and rehearse the perils and purposes of the community. Life in a garden is relaxed, quiet, and sweet [...], but survival in a howling desert demands action, the unceasing manipulation and mastery of the forces of nature, including, of course, human nature. Colonies established in the desert required aggressive, intellectual, controlled, and well-disciplined people.[6]

In the 18th century, the new concept of nature was also linked to moral standards. Leading a good and exemplary life meant living and working as a farmer.[7] Marx even refers to a statistic in this context, stating that "[a]t the time nine out of ten Americans were farmers living in a virtually classless society [...]."[8] Nature was the essential foundation for this concept of life, which is why it became a central source of identity for the "new world." A specific affinity with nature emerged at that time, even though the focus remained on cultivating it.

Marx's fundamental concern was to explore how the machine could be integrated into this understanding of nature. Initially, the burgeoning industrialization in Britain and the working conditions prevailing in the factories did not appear to be compatible with the pastoral ideal.[9] However, Marx shows that the machine was gradually integrated into the image of this pastoral ideal. People began to justify the machine by claiming that it would make hard farm labor less straining and would thus help to achieve the goal of cultivating nature and one's own piece of land for self-realization. Once again, Marx illustrates his line of thought with Jefferson's beliefs:

> From Jefferson's perspective, the machine is a token of that liberation of the human spirit to be realized by the young American Republic; the factory system, on the other hand, is but feudal oppression in a slightly modified form. Once the machine is removed from the dark, crowded, grimy cities of Europe, he assumes that it will blend harmoniously into the open countryside of his native land. He envisages it turning millwheels, moving ships up rivers, and all in all, helping to transform a wilderness into a society of the middle landscape.[10]

Other, more radical voices also emphasized the importance of independence. While raw materials were initially transported to Europe to be processed into products there, it was realized that true independence could only be achieved if machines were included in this process that were used at home.[11] At the same time, the railroads were also believed to be able to live up to the values of democracy and dehierarchization on which the new nation was founded, as increased new mobility made it possible to distribute goods evenly instead of reserving them only for those living near processing sites. Thus, the railway was a symbolic "testament to the will of man rising over natural obstacles."[12] Marx further summarizes the symbolic power of the railway:

> Associated with what seemed a world-wide surge of the poor and propertyless, with democratic egalitarianism, the machine is used to figure an unprecedented release of human energy in science, politics, and everyday life. Armed with this new power, mankind is now able, for the first time, to realize the dream of abundance. The entire corpus of intoxicated prose seems to rest on the simple but irresistible logic of first things first: all other hopes, for peace, equality, freedom, and happiness, are felt to rest upon technology.[13]

Marx directly links his descriptions here with statements by Emerson, which also express the idea that human progress is closely linked to or made possible by technological developments.[14] Before Marx turns to the literary examination of this phenomenon, in which Emerson again plays a central role, he describes how the technologization of the nation was perceived and depicted in newspapers and magazines. Overall, these popular media also reflected euphoria about the country's advancing technologization. The basic tone of the time seemed to be that technological progress was perceived as a prerequisite for realizing one's own happiness. This is why, as Marx describes it, "Americans have seized upon the machine as their birthright."[15] Marx attributes what is specific to the United States in this experience to the fact that the transition from an agrarian to an industrial nation occurred quickly, with one extreme suddenly tipping into the other.[16]

Against this historical backdrop, Marx's line of argument becomes particularly clear when he explains that in the United States, the machine cannot be understood as something that is *opposed* to the garden. Rather, it must be understood as *part* of the concept of nature. It is therefore not a paradox in the true sense of the word, as described at the beginning of this chapter, but rather two closely interwoven elements that have become part of a common dynamic. It forms the core of what Marx calls the "pastoral ideal," because it is not simply a matter of describing the garden in isolation, but of always defining it against the backdrop of the industrialization that had been underway for a long time. This dynamic is frequently taken up as a motif in both literature and painting – especially in the 19th century. According to Marx, literature often depicts the pastoral ideal as a conflict between the garden and the machine, or "nature" and "art," only to then attempt to reconcile these extremes.[17] The conflict is often expressed, for example, by the protagonist's retreat into nature in reaction to his corrupt civilized living environment. However, the protagonist does not intend to stay in nature forever, rather he experiences a learning or growth process and finally returns to the civilized environment.[18] The disturbance caused by the machine often does not represent an external disturbance of nature, but rather an internal process to harmonize one's own idea of nature with the image of the machine.[19] This motif is particularly evident in Thoreau's *Walden*, for example, but Marx also recognizes it in Melville's *Moby Dick*, in various texts by Hawthorne and in Twain's *Huckleberry Finn*.[20] Marx devotes a significant portion in his study to Emerson's texts before turning to the other literary contributions. Although Marx notes in a footnote that Emerson became increasingly critical of technological progress in his later writings,[21] Marx shows that Emerson expressed similar enthusiasm about industrial progress in his major publications as the voices in popular magazines and newspapers: "Of American writers with authentic gifts, Emerson and Whitman pay the most direct, wholehearted tribute to this industrialized version of the pastoral ideal."[22] As Marx explains, Emerson's literary career began with his essay *Nature*, in which he first employed the "rhetoric of the technological sublime."[23] Like the other authors mentioned, *Nature* also begins with a retreat into nature. Nevertheless, Emerson did not completely turn his back on civilization or technology. Marx derives Emerson's mindset from Immanuel Kant's concepts of "understanding" and "reason." What Marx describes as "the dualistic theory of mind"[24] is formative for the romantic ideal of landscape, as also expressed by Emerson: "Although the prudent, sensible Understanding may be trained in schools and cities, the far-ranging, visionary Reason requires wild or rural scenes for its proper nurture."[25] This mode of thought suggests that Emerson preferred rural life but also advocated for urban civilization. Like Jefferson, Emerson believed that scientific knowledge and technology could fundamentally support the concept of a rural life.[26] As Marx demonstrates, even in Emerson's view, the machine could contribute to human self-realization: "In the decade before 1844 Emerson repeatedly draws upon the facts of technological progress to illustrate his exultant sense of human possibilities. For him, new inventions are evidence of man's power to impose his will upon the world."[27]

Overall, it can be said of Emerson that he believed technology produced by humans is just as much a part of nature as humans themselves. This is why he did not see technology as conflicting with nature.[28] Instead, in his view, technology even created an identity for the young nation. In his lecture *The Young American*, for instance, Emerson describes the machine, especially the railway and the steamship, as an "instrument of national unity."[29] In light of these insights into Emerson's thinking, it is not surprising that Barbara Novak describes Luminism, which was closely related to Emerson's Transcendentalism, as one of the first truly "indigenous" painterly movements in the United States. This is because the combination of a sense of nature and a sense of technological progress is firmly anchored in large parts of US culture. Not only painting is often characterized by this but also literature, as Marx illustrates with numerous works. The common context of meaning of 3D graphics can now also be traced back to this cultural heritage, as demonstrated by the aesthetic categories of US realist painting. So, how can a concrete link be established between the historical developments in computer graphics and Leo Marx's observations toward the end of this study?

Numerous themes that Marx mentions, particularly in the context of Emerson, can also be found in the technical descriptions of the engineers presented in this study. Both components of computer graphics – the graphics *and* the computer – fully align with Emerson's ideas when Rule and Coons describe the graphics as an instrument of thought and when Engelbart envisions the computer to be an augmentation of the intellect. All three authors show a proximity to Emerson's appreciation of the human mind and its capacity to think. However, Engelbart's comments on the Aborigines particularly stand out. He contrasts their way of life with his own ideas of progress. These comments appear in a new light against the background of Marx's concept of the "middle landscape": For Engelbart, the Aborigines are just as "savage" as Jefferson deemed the Indigenous population encountered by the first settlers in the "new world," even though Engelbart made his comments around 177 years after Jefferson. Neither for Engelbart nor for Jefferson it is an option to recognize the way of life of the Indigenous people as it is. Both are driven by the idea of self-realization, which in turn means not putting oneself in the hands of nature but taking nature into one's own hands. And this task is an intellectual achievement that can be further enhanced by the machine. Rule and Coons' statement that graphics are an instrument of thought that can be used to gain an "augmented advantage over nature"[30] corresponds directly to this kind of thinking. They even use the term "nature," although they do not contextualize their sentence in any way. This is why it is not at all clear in the context of their graphics manual what they actually want to express with this sentence. However, against the backdrop of the "middle landscape" Rule and Coons' phrasing strongly evokes the image of the cultivated landscape. If we take the two authors at their word, they also seem to assume that nature should not be left to its own devices. Instead, it should be tamed. As they literally put it, it is about gaining an advantage over nature.

Notably, Timothy Walker, one of the early, more radical advocates of industrialization, with whom Marx engages in his study, also wrote a book on geometry.[31] Marx mentions this detail about Walker's mathematical knowledge merely in a side note to explain his very stringent argumentative behavior. Walker worked professionally as a lawyer but also saw himself as "America's attorney."[32] In this role, he propagated the position that technology would replace the animalistic traits of humans and free the mind.[33] According to Marx, Walker was therefore convinced that "[w]ithout technology there would be no culture."[34]

Like Emerson, Walker viewed technology as a means of realizing the egalitarian aspirations and ideals envisioned for the young nation. In particular, Emerson's idea that technology contributed to the unity of the population can be linked to Walker's attitude. However, Marx also emphasizes a level of consciousness in relation to Emerson that does not apply to Walker in the same way, because "Emerson's attitude follows from the assumption of philosophical idealism. What we do with instruments of power depends, finally, upon the way we perceive them."[35] Marx uses the phrase "instruments of power" to refer to technological developments. Although he illustrates that Emerson was aware of the connection between progress and power, it also becomes clear that Emerson was optimistic about this power rather than skeptical. This optimistic attitude can be explained by his conviction that technology, being human-made, is also part of nature. Furthermore, he believed that any form of progress did not happen by itself. This is why Emerson appealed to society in his speeches, such as in *The Young American*, to actively promote the nation's development. In his own words, Emerson ascribes a special responsibility to artists in this task:

> There is no feature of the old countries that more agreeably and newly strikes an American, than the beautiful gardens of Europe; such as the Boboli in Florence, the Villa Borghese in Rome, the Villa d'Este in Tivoli, the gardens at Munich, and at Frankfort on the Maine: works easily imitated here, and which might well make the land dear to the citizen, and inflame patriotism. It is the fine art which is left for us, now that sculpture, and painting, and religious and civil architecture have become effete, and have passed into second childhood.[36]

As explicitly addressed here by Emerson, his thoughts are based on a deep patriotism. In the speech, Emerson also expresses his conviction that there should be leaders in every group and community and that this role comes naturally to some. In continuation of this idea, the quote at the beginning of this part likewise suggests that he saw the "States" in this leadership role on a larger scale – that is, in relation to other nations.[37]

At the beginning of this part, I asked *why* the development of commercial computer graphics occurred as described in this study. With Marx there is now a possible answer. The context of meaning of the imaging technique becomes particularly clear against this cultural backdrop. 3D computer graphics unite the two areas of technology and image culture brought together in this fifth part of the study. Both the technological *and* the image-cultural endeavors have developed against this background described by Marx. It is precisely through their union in 3D computer graphics that an "original US means of expression" has emerged, which could be seen as a paradigmatic distillation of the country's cultural development since colonization: Reproducing the natural environment in an idealized way with technical tools, without straying too far from the original physical reference, corresponds directly to Marx's description of cultivating wild nature. Using technical tools is appropriate, but this act of civilization should not be taken too far. Nature should not be fully destroyed. In the technological environment of 3D computer graphics, the two concepts are combined: The synthesis of realism and idealism, on the one hand, and the "middle landscape," on the other. This cultural heritage thus culminates in this imaging technique, which not only *utilizes* technological aids but has been *relocated* entirely to a technical environment.

At Pixar, this historical context becomes *visually* apparent – the studio directly translates the ideological background that has led to this specific pictorial culture into visual aesthetics. However, the technology itself carries this ideological background within it – quite in the spirit of Emerson's desired leadership role. This is why artists such as the European David Claerbout are always confronted with these pictorial ideas, even if they want to pursue a completely different visual aesthetic. Their images are enclosed within the same historical context of meaning.

NOTES

1. Leo Marx, *The Machine in the Garden. Technology and the Pastoral Ideal in America* (Oxford: Oxford University Press USA, 2000), 31.
2. See Marx, *The Machine in the Garden*, 367.
3. See Marx, *The Machine in the Garden*, 36–41.
4. Marx, *The Machine in the Garden*, 121, emphasis in original. The passage from Jefferson to which Marx refers reads, "[i]mperfect as this species of coercion may seem, crimes are very rare among them: insomuch that were it made a question, whether no law, as among the savage Americans, or too much law, as among the civilized Europeans, submits man to the greatest evil, one who has seen both conditions of existence would pronounce it to be the last, and that the sheep are happier of themselves than under care of the wolves." Thomas Jefferson, *Notes on the State of Virginia: With Related Documents*, ed. David Waldstreicher (London: Palgrave Macmillan, 2002), 144.
5. Marx, *The Machine in the Garden*, e.g. 138.
6. Marx, *The Machine in the Garden*, 43
7. See Marx, *The Machine in the Garden*, 98–101. For Jefferson, this was also linked to the idea of self-sufficiency. See Marx, *The Machine in the Garden*, 126–27.

8. Marx, *The Machine in the Garden*, 115.
9. See Marx, *The Machine in the Garden*, e.g. 103–4.
10. Marx, *The Machine in the Garden*, 150.
11. Marx is referring here to the politician Tench Coxe, who campaigned intensively for the establishment of factories in the 18th century. See Marx, *The Machine in the Garden*, 153–59.
12. Marx, *The Machine in the Garden*, 191.
13. Marx, *The Machine in the Garden*, 191–92.
14. See Marx, *The Machine in the Garden*, 192.
15. Marx, *The Machine in the Garden*, 205. On the different views in journals, see Marx, *The Machine in the Garden*, 194–207. Marx also addresses critical voices but notes that these have not been disseminated in the same way as the more popular publication organs. Moreover, the criticism was by no means voiced from a homogeneous circle, as it was made up of defenders of slavery in the southern part of the Confederacy, on the one hand, and socialist, literary or religious groups, on the other. See Marx, *The Machine in the Garden*, 219.
16. See Marx, *The Machine in the Garden*, 203–4.
17. See Marx, *The Machine in the Garden*, 24–33.
18. See Marx, *The Machine in the Garden*, 71.
19. See Marx, *The Machine in the Garden*, 28.
20. Marx notes, however, that the protagonists' return to civilization often leaves the conflict in literature unresolved, for example because the main characters die at the end of the plot or because they are completely alienated from the rest of society. See Marx, *The Machine in the Garden*, 364.
21. See Marx, *The Machine in the Garden*, 263.
22. Marx, *The Machine in the Garden*, 220.
23. Marx, *The Machine in the Garden*, 230.
24. Marx, *The Machine in the Garden*, 233.
25. Marx, *The Machine in the Garden*, 233.
26. See Marx, *The Machine in the Garden*, 236.
27. Marx, *The Machine in the Garden*, 230.
28. See Marx, *The Machine in the Garden*, 242.
29. Marx, *The Machine in the Garden*, 234.
30. John T. Rule and Steven A. Coons, *Graphics* (New York: McGraw-Hill, 1961), vii.
31. See Marx, *The Machine in the Garden*, 185.
32. Marx, *The Machine in the Garden*, 181.
33. See Marx, *The Machine in the Garden*, 186.
34. Marx, *The Machine in the Garden*, 184. Cardoso Llach also refers to Walker in his study on architectural software. Cardoso Llach recognizes a connection in Walker's attitude to Coons' problematic idea of machines as slaves in order to relieve humans of monotonous and automatable tasks. See Daniel Cardoso Llach, *Builders of the Vision: Software and the Imagination of Design* (New York: Routledge, 2015) 65. The principle of "mind over matter" described by Cardoso Llach, which is addressed in the state of research in this study, can also be mentioned in this context. Here, too, it is expressed that intellectual work takes precedence over manual labor. See Cardoso Llach, *Builders of the Vision*, 1. See also the comments on Cardoso Llach's research in Section 1.3 in this study.
35. Marx, *The Machine in the Garden*, 241.
36. Ralph W. Emerson, "The Young American (1844)," in *The Collected Works of Ralph Waldo Emerson. Volume I: Nature, Addresses, and Lectures*, ed. Robert E. Spiller and Alfred R. Ferguson (Cambridge: Belknap Press of Harvard University Press, 1971), 227.
37. See Emerson, "The Young American," 238–39.

CHAPTER 12

Conclusion

> The ultimate effect of the object-oriented turn is difficult to predict, precisely because we are so actively immersed in it. How does one even begin to ask the question of outcomes when almost every tool of representation is itself increasingly object oriented? Perhaps the first step is an honest assessment of how we got to where we are in the first place, as a means for beginning to recode the system from within.[1]
>
> *CASEY ALT (2011)*

Part V demonstrated that the aesthetic categories of US visual culture described in this study have survived in the software environment of computer graphics applications to this day. While in some cases, such as with the artist David Claerbout or the television show *South Park*, they can only be demonstrated in terms of production aesthetics, in many commercial computer-animated films, they also appear on a visual-aesthetic level. In the final review with Leo Marx, I contextualized the historical development of the imaging technology as genuinely specific to the United States. Throughout US history technological progress has often been equated with democratic values and the idea of self-realization. The transcendentalist Ralph Waldo Emerson, who had clear ideas about the extent to which the United States played a leading role in its cultural and technological developments as well as in its democratic values, was particularly influential in shaping this worldview. This background now allows us to understand the common context of meaning of the 3D graphics in depth.

Emerson's idea of American supremacy is reminiscent of the backdrop against which computer graphics developments began. The military funding that made the research possible in the first place was a direct response to the Sputnik crisis. The reaction was, like Emerson's, based on democratic aspirations. The aim was to protect space from communism, which was perceived as a threat, and to put the new potential "territory" back into the hands of democracy. Therefore, in the 1950s, the United States continued to believe it was their responsibility to take on this task. The research project *Graphical Man/Machine Communications* at the University of Utah, still essentially a reaction to these events from a few years earlier, brought together numerous young researchers to fulfill this democratic aspiration and advance the nation in a way that Emerson – at least at the time of his lecture *The Young American* – would also have wished for. Sutherland employs this rhetoric in his documentation of his *Sketchpad* program as well, assuming that it fulfills universal and general needs.

Now, taking another look at what Emerson wanted art to achieve in the 19th century – I briefly discussed his understanding of art at the end of Chapter 11 – it is striking that he emphasized the aspect of imitation. He envisioned making the new land palatable for its inhabitants by basing it on European examples of landscape design.[2] Not only does Marx's "middle landscape" resonate with Emerson's ideas here, as he obviously assumed that the found land may be cultivated according to one's own ideas, but numerous features that characterize the computer-graphic endeavors can also be identified in Emerson's thoughts. The illustrations by Coons and Fetter are also based on this principle of imitation. The maxim of believability in their drawings was not linked to technical precision, but rather to perspective constructions that essentially

DOI: 10.1201/9781003649861-17

answered to the aesthetic of the camera lens. This was based on the belief that the camera captures the image that also appears on our retina and would thus be most familiar to us. While Coons and Fetter's drawings were still analog, their drawing concepts and methods were later translated into the computer. Nevertheless, here too, photography and the related perspectival construction remained the standard. The aim was always to create images that could be intuitively understood and even "felt." Interestingly, long-time Pixar employee Kyoung Swearingen also used the term "palatable"[3] to describe the studio's images. She thus articulates a similar aspiration for computer graphics at Pixar as Emerson expressed for landscape design in the "new world." Comparable to Emerson's suggestions, since the beginning of computer graphics, the engineers believed that images are only pleasing when they imitate something familiar to human perception. Not only the visual language of the camera, but also the references to light and shading or the ability to move around the objects to see them in motion were believed to be able to cultivate for everyone a familiar relationship with the surroundings depicted by the synthetic images – even imaginary ones. However, the concept of imitation is particularly evident in the artificially created patina, which was intended to lend not only paintings but also the 3D images a sense of tradition, age and home. This artificially created feeling of familiarity and nostalgia is thus, in spirit, exactly reflected in Emerson's idea to imitate European gardens.

The realism on which the computer graphics are based and which the engineers always set as the standard for their images is therefore symbolically closely linked to Marx's concept of the "middle landscape." Just as the "middle-landscape" can be located between idealism and realism with its connection to nature, but to *idealized* nature, the computer graphics' realism also moves between these two paradigms. Although technically it is possible to create a true depiction of the physical reality with 3D graphics technology, it is not *intended* for this purpose. Rather, it is intended to deliver an idealized, cultivated form of the "wilderness." Similar to what Emerson expressed, it is always important to orient oneself toward examples to ensure that the images are accepted – or put differently: to adhere to the maxim of believability. Free or even abstract expression that is too detached from physical reality is not the goal that engineers had in mind when developing computer graphics. At the same time, this approach reflects the merging of nature and technology, because for the developers of 3D graphics reproducing our natural environment in a familiar form using a highly technical imaging process is not a paradox; on the contrary, it is the technology which makes this approach possible in its purest form – an approach that US artists already aimed for in the 19th century. Like the "middle landscape," computer graphics were therefore conceived as an imaging process that reconciles two opposing states into a unity – a "natural," familiar one and a mechanical, technological one.

Emerson's claim to a leading role has therefore been fulfilled. Every common 3D graphics program today contains the cultural artifacts described here. They are closely linked to the history of the United States and, in particular, to a transcendentalist mindset. The design principles related to this, such as those used in Luminism, are firmly anchored in the software landscape. This is why every resulting image bears this signature in its production aesthetics. Or to return to Blumenberg: Every 3D computer graphic emanates from this context of meaning – regardless of its image aesthetics – and carries it within itself, because in the production of the images it is not possible to escape the worldviews and image concepts described by David Shi, Barbara Novak or Leo Marx – at least not when using the common graphics programs available, and not even when changing the workflow with self-written code. At the same time, the design principles on which today's software is based have long been considered universal. Only recently have commercial productions, such as the *Spider-Verse* films with their comic book aesthetic, started to "rebel" against these design principles. Yet, similar to Blumenberg's description of the technical facades, the pictorial concepts embedded in the software are still often taken for granted. As will be shown in the outlook of this study, these concepts are perpetuated even in the newer AI environments. Thus, when luminist painting is expressed on a *visual*-aesthetic level in Pixar's *WALL-E*, the animation studio reveals the cultural artifacts on which its imaging process is based. *WALL-E* therefore exposes the *production* aesthetics of computer graphics.[4]

How can these values, which are anchored in the software, be dealt with in practice? How can, in purely practical terms, the leaps Blumenberg speaks of be overcome in the technicized environment of 3D graphics software? How can the context of meaning of the technology be uncovered without recounting its entire history each time an image is produced? Paradoxically, Pixar itself can serve as a role model here, as the animation studio takes a self-reflexive approach to its own visual aesthetics.[5] Claerbout also addresses the peculiarities of the digital environment he uses for his artistic expression in a meta-reflexive way. Perhaps this attitude could serve as an example for the general use of computers, because as the history of computer graphics shows, US dominance is not limited to the field of graphics applications. Many of the features we use daily on computers and smartphones can ultimately also be traced back to functions Sutherland developed for *Sketchpad* and the subsequent development of object-oriented programming languages. While this has made computers accessible to everyone and made it fairly easy to create images with graphics software, this study shows that it is becoming increasingly relevant to examine *who* designed the technology and with *what intentions*.

In my analysis I have therefore made a conscious decision not to view the imaging technology as a self-sufficient "actor," as might be done from the perspective of, for instance, actor-network theory.[6] Instead, I focused on the people who shaped it. This decision is based on the assumption that, in a technologically advanced world, it is becoming increasingly crucial to learn about the history of the technologies that surround us every day. This knowledge is perhaps even more important than mastering the technologies themselves in depth. In many cases, mastering them means reproducing them, which ultimately applies even to those who have programming skills. However, understanding technologies and programming languages in their historical development means recognizing that they only ever represent *one* possible form of expression and a very specific context of meaning.

NOTES

1. Casey Alt, "Objects of Our Affection. How Object Orientation Made Computers a Medium," in *Media Archaeology. Approaches, Applications, and Implications*, ed. Erkki Huhtamo and Jussi Parikka (Berkeley, Los Angeles: University of California Press, 2011), 299.
2. See Ralph W. Emerson, "The Young American (1844)," in *The Collected Works of Ralph Waldo Emerson. Volume I: Nature, Addresses, and Lectures*, ed. Robert E. Spiller and Alfred R. Ferguson (Cambridge: Belknap Press of Harvard University Press, 1971), 227.
3. Kyoung L. Swearingen, interview by the author, February 11, 2020 transcript, Research Online/Data, 5, https://doi.org/10.25625/VBODBG.
4. In his research, the Americanist Dietmar Meinel deals intensively and extensively with the Pixar films and the US myths and symbols that appear in them. Meinel also considers Marx's *The Machine in the Garden* in his research. Not only does Meinel selectively address Marx in his monograph *Pixar's America: The Re-Animation of American Myths and Symbols*, but also in the essay *The Garden in the Machine: Myth and Symbol in the Digital Age*, Meinel systematically analyses the film *WALL-E* against the background of Marx's study. See Dietmar Meinel, *Pixar's America: The Re-Animation of American Myths and Symbols* (London: Palgrave Macmillan, 2016), e.g. 26; see also Dietmar Meinel, "The Garden in the Machine: Myth and Symbol in the Digital Age," in *Rereading the Machine in the Garden: Nature and Technology in American Culture*, ed. Eric Erbacher, Nicole Maruo-Schröder and Florian Sedlmeier (Frankfurt am Main: Campus, 2014). Both in his monograph and in the essay, Meinel's investigative approach refers primarily to the narrative aspects of the Pixar films, although he also addresses aspects of visual aesthetics at certain points, for example when he remarks in relation to the film *WALL-E*: "The depiction of two robots blissfully wandering the paradisiacal garden of Earth, then, seems to echo nineteenth-century popular versions of the assimilation of technological progress into the pastoral and what Leo Marx has described as the myth of the machine in the garden." Meinel, "The Garden in the Machine," 190. For Meinel, it is particularly significant that the logic of the machine in the garden is reversed in *WALL-E*, because here it is not the machine that has been integrated into the garden, but the garden into the machine. Meinel therefore concludes: "The garden is not threatened but manufactured by the machine – in the twofold sense of WALL-E fostering the creation of the garden and the computer (machine) producing the pastoral imagery in *WALL-E*." Meinel, "The Garden in the Machine," 205, emphasis in original. As the quoted passage demonstrates, Meinel only superficially considers aspects of production aesthetics, which is why his findings can be significantly supplemented by those of this study. The observations that Meinel makes with regard to the visuals and the narrative of the Pixar films are already anchored in the production of the films, which is

why their entire design reacts much more deeply to Marx's motif of the machine in the garden than even Meinel was able to point out when he notes, for example, with reference to Vivian Sobchack: "Although the film aims mostly for a photo-realistic depiction of its characters and mise-en-scène, the animated quality of *WALL-E* never vanishes from sight. Due to its digital aesthetics, then the film alludes to its production by an 'electronic technology that seems to, phantasmatically, often have a secret mind of its own.' Not only WALL-E but also *WALL-E* offers continuation in the shift from illusionary omnipotence to human interdependence as the digital imagery of the bucolic garden and the technologically outdated machine both refer to the modern technology essential for their production." Meinel, "The Garden in the Machine," 206, emphasis in original. Meinel quotes Vivian Sobchack, "Animation and Automation, or, the Incredible Effortfulness of Being," *Screen* 50, no. 4 (2009): 386. Meinel's references to the photorealistic visual language and the "digital aesthetic" or Sobchack's concept of "electronic technology," which she says leads a mysterious life of its own, provide little information about the production-aesthetic background of the film or the hardware and software environment from which it emerged. Although, as Meinel shows, the garden does to a certain extent penetrate the machine, the results of this study can show that the machine with which the garden in *WALL-E* was realized was ultimately itself developed against the background of a worldview that regards the computer as a natural part of the cultivated garden. The representation of the garden by the machine can therefore not be read as a reversal of the image of the machine in the garden, but rather as a continuation of it. If, as Marx describes, it was legitimate in the United States to cultivate nature with the help of the machine, then it is equally legitimate in this conception to shape nature through the machine as an image – similar to what happened in US painting, for which Meinel's reversal is just as inapplicable. This also shows that Pixar seamlessly translates the production-aesthetic characteristics of technology into visual aesthetics.

5. See Carolin Scheler, "Der bildsprachliche Kosmos im computeranimierten Kinofilm," in *Piktogrammatik: Grafisches Gestalten als Weltwissen und Bilderordnung*, ed. Annette Geiger and Bianca Holtschke (Bielefeld: transcript, 2021), 149–51.
6. The programmer and media theorist Alexander Galloway explains why it can be problematic to examine questions about programming paradigms with the help of contemporary philosophical approaches, such as speculative realism, which is about removing the human from the focus of investigation. In his essay *The Poverty of Philosophy: Realism and Post-Fordism*, he poses the question: "Why, within the current renaissance of research in continental philosophy, is there a coincidence between the structure of ontological systems and the structure of the most highly evolved technologies of post-Fordist capitalism? I am speaking, on the one hand, of computer networks in general and object-oriented computer languages (such as Java or C++) in particular and, on the other hand, of certain realist philosophers such as Bruno Latour, but also more pointedly Quentin Meillassoux, Graham Harman, and their associated school known as speculative realism. Why do these philosophers, when holding up a mirror to nature, see the mode of production reflected back to them? Why in short, is there a coincidence between today's ontologies and the software of big business?" Alexander R. Galloway, "The Poverty of Philosophy: Realism and Post-Fordism," *Critical Inquiry* 39, no. 2 (2013): 347.

CHAPTER 13

A Brief Outlook

But What about AI?

A STUDY THAT TALKS ABOUT synthetic imaging without discussing the newer artificial intelligence (AI) technology perhaps might seem rather wondrous. By using "AI" as a term here, I am basically referring to the hype and fear around it,[1] but what I, in fact, mean with the term in the following reflections, is the subfield of generative AI, i.e. an algorithm that "use[s] neural networks to identify the patterns and structures within existing data to generate new and original content."[2] If the content is always original is debatable, but in terms of wording and to keep it simple, I will use the terms "AI" and "generative AI" from here on. To stay in line with the interests of this study about visual culture and its manifestations in the "digital realm," I will, however, in this outlook narrow down my focus to text-to-image models. Other types of generative AI related to text or music will not be discussed below; they might also lead to a fully different line of argument.

A simple reason for initially "ignoring" AI in this book – although I briefly mention it in the first part – is that the research for this study has mainly taken place during a time when the inflationary rise of generative AI had not fully taken place yet. It was then merely a gimmick to play around with and the way it would change the creative industry had not risen to full awareness back then. Talking about AI in such a short chapter now can therefore only be an attempt, a snapshot of current events, and it can, above all, not be comprehensive in any way. This epilog should instead be understood as a thought experiment, inviting to engage in a discussion that might soon turn into quite different directions altogether, once the technological advancements will catch up and surprise us all again.

In a conversation with artist Alan Warburton, early in 2025, who also worked in the industry as a 3D artist for several years, he described how he expects that the industry is aiming to get to a point at which all those different fields of discipline of 3D graphics, such as modeling, texturing, shading, lighting and rendering, will eventually be replaced by basically one AI command.[3] He already observes what he calls a "'pipeline collapse' where each stage in the CG workflow is condensed to its most reduced form,"[4] even if this perhaps means something different for each of the respective fields. If all these still separate steps were to be further reduced to just one AI tool and once it will be possible to simply tell an AI engine what the outcome is supposed to be, all this manual labor and meticulous and sometimes tedious work that takes a lot of time and therefore costs a lot of money, would not be needed anymore. Warburton is probably right with his expectation, and yet students are still being taught all the commercial 3D and compositing software that is needed for the manual work steps to create computer graphics with – those that were discussed in this study.

In terms of the common and therefore unifying cultural context of meaning of computer graphics, as presented in this study, Warburton's remark raises the question, if this AI development might eventually lead to more diverse visual aesthetics in synthetic imaging.

DOI: 10.1201/9781003649861-18

Could this technology actually "liberate" synthetic imaging from what Alvy Ray Smith, in his words, calls the "central dogma"[5] or what I have similarly in this study referred to as the "maxim of believability," because it will easily and quickly be possible to try out different styles? And in accordance with this question, would this also mean that the cultural-historical background described in this study will become obsolete in the way images are designed on the computer with the help of AI? My assumption is, no. I propose that this context of meaning is in different ways perpetuated in the new technology and that AI is ultimately a logical consequence of the historical accounts I described in this study.

An anecdote by Daniel Cardoso Llach in the preface to his book *Builders of the Vision*, in which he traces the cultural-historical roots of CAD software infrastructure, can be used as an entry point to illustrate what is meant by AI being the logical consequence of computer graphics. He recalls,

> Many years ago, I had a conversation with an older friend who argued that the perfect art would only be possible when a machine was capable of translating ideas directly into objects, without any bodily interaction with materials or tools. With no brushes, canvas, or pigments polluting the creative flow, my friend's machine would enable a seamless transfer between the limitless and immaterial worlds of mental images and the earthy worlds of physical objects.[6]

In reaction to this memory, Cardoso Llach expresses strong doubts, if this is all there is to creative work, and legitimately so.[7] The same question is central for these concluding remarks on AI: How do creative processes work and can a tool like AI serve them? And how is this same question related to "old school" computer graphics, as they are here put in relation with AI? The latter technology answers quite directly to Cardoso Llach's anecdote. There is now a tool with which an idea in anybody's mind can almost immediately be translated into some type of "materialization." This can be an image, but even the "objects" mentioned in the quote are not far-fetched from here. There are already AI tools that can create 3D objects based on prompts,[8] so even if those "materializations" are not yet in our physical environment, they are, nevertheless, immediately there, and they can always be 3D printed to bring them into our physical surroundings.

What is interesting in terms of the previously presented historical accounts on the development of computer graphics, and also in regard to the art historical discussion on image conception and style, is that the same motivation and concept of creativity that is expressed in Cardoso Llach's anecdote has shaped not only the work of the discussed artists but also the ideas of the developers who were involved in creating commercial computer graphics. The previously quoted remark by Edward Hopper illustrates this quite strikingly as he expresses something rather similar: "I don't start painting until I have it all worked out in my mind. I'm all right when I get to the easel."[9] Without wanting to disregard his artistic talent, and to be a bit blunt, one could say that today, anyone would be able to work like this. You can have something in mind and simply have generative AI create just that. But to keep things on the ground, for Hopper there was probably more involved than just imagining an image – painting it, for instance – and, conversely, anyone who has tried prompting in different AI engines will know that this does not always create what one had in mind. Yet, in terms of the *idea* behind the technology, it really answers to a notion of creativity in which an intellectual *concept* of an idea or image counts more than the *process*, the manual labor, that leads to a final output of this idea. Cardoso Llach therefore also calls this attitude "mind over matter."[10]

In the analysis of computer graphics, this mindset could be identified, for instance, in Edwin Catmull's 1974 dissertation. Here he speaks of an image already in the moment in which it can be described in the computer. Being able to *view* the image on a screen as a next step was not even necessary for him to already understand it as such.[11] This approach to thinking of what an image is was in the style-historical analysis within this study related back to US painterly approaches in the 19th century. Here it was pointed out that camera technology has intensively shaped the approach to painting in the United States very early on.[12] Image-making practice has in large parts been supplemented by such technological tools and while with computer graphics this practice has been moved entirely into a technical environment, with AI it is now even possible for a human to leave out any type of creative process. With generative AI the concept of an image and its output have come closer to one another than ever before – for the human using it, that is; probably less so for the machine. Barbara Novak's summarizing remarks on the painterly approach of many different US artists since the 19th century is given an entirely new meaning by this new technological development: "The artist now stands behind, as generating idea, his aim to have technology render his idea concrete and tangible."[13]

AI can, therefore, easily be perceived as a logical consequence of the cultural-historical accounts described in this study, which is why Warburton's expectation does seem very plausible. The way images are being created with AI answers deeply to the computer graphics' cultural context of meaning that was described in this study. Considering this it does not seem very plausible, however, that AI will automatically stylistically "liberate" the creative process within a technological environment. For the longest time, computer-generated animated movies from very different studios had a rather uniform visual style,[14] and only more than 20 years after *Toy Story*, the first computer-animated feature film, a new visual style was pursued in 2018 with *Spider-Man: Into the Spider-Verse* – or rather an old style, in fact, as the aesthetics refer back to comic book culture.

While I do not propose here that computer graphics technology determines the aesthetics, this study was apt to demonstrate how the technology is culturally shaped and does not necessarily *invite* to explore modes of creativity and expression shaped by *other* cultural backgrounds or concepts of creativity and image creation. Essentially, one could say that the same is true for the newer AI tools. Not only can it be assumed that they are based on the same or a similar conception of how a creative process works, they also do not seem to invite the users of such technology to deviate from this conception. On the contrary, even though the AI gets to go through some type of process, it is designed to deliver a perfect outcome – whatever that may be. Even in models of reinforcement learning that rely heavily on a process of intensive exploring to autonomously gather data and make sense of it, the idea is "to improve its behavior,"[15] i.e. the AI is allowed to meander provided the outcome will be satisfying or useful – and no other goal would probably get any funding. In all these cases AI does not invite the user in any way to meander, to err or to doodle, even though it is often meandering and erring itself. It is essentially conceptualized to do the opposite – to learn from mistakes, so *not* to do them again.[16] And this is true regardless of whether the AI interpolates or extrapolates, i.e. if it "looks between the known examples" or "looks past them,"[17] because the goal always remains to search "for 'reasonable answers,' 'answers that work well in practice.'"[18] Philosopher Toby Ord therefore does not even consider extrapolation to be particularly creative, although he does introduce with what he calls "hyperpolation" a concept that could possibly provide generative AI with the capability to transcend the known data not only in a one-dimensional or linear manner (extrapolation), but in a multidimensional and multidirectional manner.[19] According to Ord, so far, generative AI has not been able to achieve this:

> Of course many great works by humans also involve remixing and extrapolating what we've seen already. But we also possess the ability to transcend everything that has come before — to take a step off the beaten path in a new direction, orthogonal to the subspace of existing works. Think of Marcel Duchamp's *Fountain*, Allen Ginsberg's *Howl*, or The Beatles' *Sgt. Pepper's Lonely Hearts Club Band*. And this kind of originality is something that hasn't yet been clearly demonstrated by even the best generative models. While it is hard to measure this to know for sure, one suggestive thing is the apparent lack of any examples of foundation models producing new results in maths or science.[20]

Hyperpolation could change this dynamic, and Ord even presents examples of generative AI that have, in fact, created results which could be considered as transcending extrapolation. He describes how there has been created a series of frames to build a moving image sequence from just one picture, i.e. predicting a series of following pictures, including the position and rotation of the depicted objects to create frame by frame motion. However, he also points out that this particular type of hyperpolation is still based on these image-to-video systems having learned how to generalize, it is not trained to produce something arbitrary: "So [these systems] are not hyperpolating the training data (a set of images with their associated videos) but are hyperpolating the input (a 2D grid of pixels with their associated colours)."[21] In any case, creative or not, interpolating, extrapolating or hyperpolating, generative AI is always on the lookout for quality, not *any* output would suffice, it does need to meet some type of standard.

Compared to generative AI models and their processes, computer graphics applications are less hermetic – unless one would stop the AI in mid-creation and pull some unfinished result from the middle of the process. The creation of computer graphics still offers a type of manual labor and therefore more room for human errors and detours. This is why here, again for the human who uses it, a creative process can actually unfold and evolve. It is here a lot easier, to resist the cultural codes of the algorithm, even if this sometimes calls for a creative solution to make an idea work – for *Spider-Man: Into the Spider-Verse* the workflow of the "Physically Based Rendering" anchored in computer graphics technology was, for example, circumvented with a complicated workaround in order to achieve the desired aesthetic of a comic book.[22] The film was therefore created with a sense of imperfection, with the "rebel spirit" of cartooning and comics. The work process with AI prohibits this kind of creative "nonsense" for the human who makes use of it – or tries to, anyway. Typing prompt after prompt is a way of exploring, but in its essence, as could be shown with Ord, AI is designed to output quality, to get it right, and that is true regardless of the way AI is brought to use. So even if one trains their own model, the basic idea of the technology is still to create a tool that will not err – at least in respect to the final outcome. Discovering the errors and detours the AI takes is only possible, if one disrupts the process of the AI and this is, for the general user of generative AI engines, hardly possible.

In this sense, AI answers to what sociologist Sherry Turkle calls "friction free."[23] It is a tool that is "better than nothing,"[24] an easy fix that allows us to be quick and effective without being uncomfortable – it is instead uncomfortable *for* us, if you will. Of course, it is only easy once it works well, the process of developing it is most likely highly creative and full of errors and detours. But, again, once it works well, the *idea* is that if one cannot paint or draw fast enough, AI steps in. Transferring Turkle's thoughts on how we try to avoid conflict and friction through our engagement with technology to the realm of creativity in the digital sphere, AI "frees" us from the errors and the dead ends in creative processes. But those can often be the most productive. Not knowing where to go allows us to create knowledge through the act of doing. Creativity is rarely linear,[25] but messy and, because of this, it can be insightful. In this sense, generative AI tools are not designed to foster human creativity. This is not to say that it could not be incorporated in a creative process to brainstorm or to generate ideas and inspiration, and also it can most likely be put to use in many creative ways, but its *production aesthetics* are very different from, let's say, setting a pencil on a paper and starting to draw a line in any possible direction without knowing what will happen – which is a fundamentally creative act as will be shown, or, in Ord's words, an act of transcending what is known. When we think back of the quality it is supposed to output, AI is, ultimately, about being in control. The creative process of doodling is on the contrary – as art historian and creativity theoretician Friedrich Weltzien describes – about *letting go* of control.[26]

In his remarks on doodling (German: kritzeln), he enters into his elaborations with anecdotes on different artists and writers from different periods who all needed to doodle in order to find the right ideas.[27] Aside from the field of art, doodling has, however, also had negative connotations since the 17th century. During that time, it was beginning to be brought into connection "with judgments of illegibility and ugliness, carelessness and speed, lack, primitiveness, the offensive/vulgar and subversion."[28] Yet, and maybe *because* of these qualities, doodling has always been a form of creative exploration most likely since humans have begun expressing themselves. Early doodles can be found in prehistoric caves, in ancient Egypt or Greek antiquity, but also in medieval marginalia. In the 18th century doodling is, for instance, beginning to be connected with the art of caricature.[29] This already hints at the typical characteristics of doodling: It is not normative, it is not attached to a purpose, it questions, disregards conventions, it is inherently, as was already pointed out, subversive.[30]

Weltzien also connects doodling to the body – it is a bodily gesture after all – which is why he is convinced that doodling cannot happen with any type of technical device, and that it can merely in spirit be imitated in software environments, naming the graphics software Alchemy as an example.[31] There could surely more examples be listed, but what this indicates is that software, or more generally, algorithms can indeed be "designed" with different mindsets. Charles Csuri's approach is a striking example of this. Like with a pencil, he used the computer in a way so he would be surprised, so he would create knowledge and insight through the process of doing. AI on the other hand is not initially designed to subvert; it is, conversely, designed to serve, to make things easier. Doodling, in a way, makes things more difficult; it is nonintentional;[32] it is not straightforward in any way. That is, again, not to say, that AI or any other type of software could not be *used* with this playful mindset.

Consequently, regardless of how AI is made use of, from a merely production-aesthetical perspective it will not imitate the spirit of doodling, of a creative path that is "out of control." Even if it does go through phases of exploration, it is – at least currently – designed to gain control over something to output a result of quality. Even Steven A. Coons who was in the 1960s promoting to create computer tools to enhance the design process, described how drawing or sketching answers to the "vague stirrings of the imagination,"[33] before a clear concept even emerges. Thus, he, too, describes sketching as an ideation tool with access to the "stirrings" that are not yet clear ideas. So even if one uses generative AI to create what *looks* like a doodle, like a quick drawing, and even if one's own set of training data were used as a basis, the AI would not only take this task completely seriously, it would also treat this prompt, this task, exactly the way it would treat a command to create, for instance, a photorealistic picture. If we doodle, this affords a very different creative process from taking a photograph. For a human, the production aesthetics therefore differ in these two processes. For the generative AI they do not. This becomes evident, again, when considering a perspective from creativity theory. Weltzien and Gundel Mattenklott, describe that, in a creative process

> [c]hance and criticism, lucky finds and discarding what has been worked out do not alternate in an orderly succession; rather, the process of creation is an inclusive action in which all these activities intermingle. Meanings are not yet fixed, genre decisions are open. The fleeting and the ephemeral are juxtaposed with meticulous plans that have been stubbornly pursued over a long period of time. This simultaneity of creative paths is recognizable right down to the individual sheet – the drawing, the text draft – as the interplay and intertwining of order and chaos in table and doodle, of writing, drawing and calculation.[34]

Generative AI evidently is not designed to work like this, as it is ultimately designed to make sense of something – even if it does, in a way, go through phases of chaos while creating the output. Also, generative AI is hardly trained to be "inclusive" when considering the bias in the labeled data it works with. Even if exploring is important for an AI during the process of its training, the technology always takes away this exploration phase from the human. AI is not designed to let the user find something in the making. Instead, the user needs to know the concept from the outset. With generative AI the user's idea is always supposed to be at the beginning, and during prompting quite literally so as the idea needs to be put into words, it needs to be intellectualized, not felt as a "vague stirring" and intuitively found – and even typing a series of prompts in order to explore an idea does not in essence change this process.

With the historical development of computer graphics it has been similar, here an idea of an image, an intellectual concept also preceded the technological implementation – ultimately even for Coons. Yet, as Weltzien and Mattenklott point out, in artistic or creative processes "[t]he concept does not necessarily have to be at the beginning."[35] With the historical accounts on computer graphics presented in this study, the close links with AI in the approach to image-making become quite visible. If having an idea in mind *first* is all that counts in creating an image, it makes sense to expect that all the computer graphical tools available until now can be replaced with AI. It perpetuates the same ethos, the same concept of creativity, and this might not even be surprising as since Aristotle it "has become the standard Western model of creative work processes as a generalized theory of artistic creative processes,"[36] that a sketch, a concept needs to precede any of the following work steps that will lead to the realization of this concept. Cardoso Llach's phrase "mind over matter" expresses this same attitude.

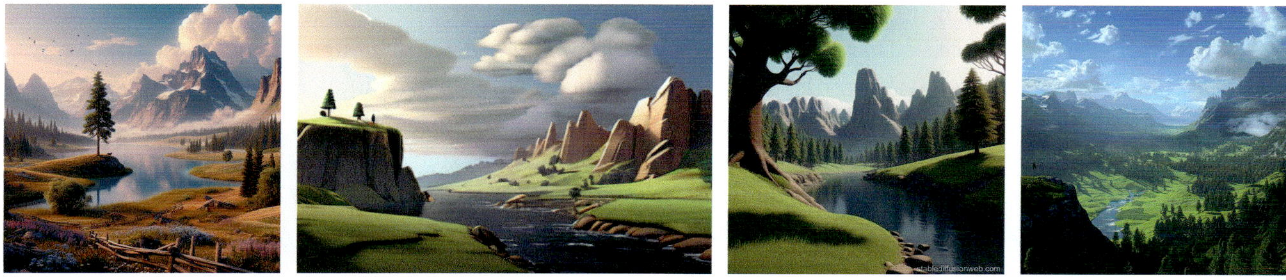

FIGURE 13.1 AI images from different generative AI engines using the same prompt: "create a still image of a landscape from a typical 3D animated movie," f.l.t.r.: DALL-E, Leonardo.Ai, Stable Diffusion, Midjourney.

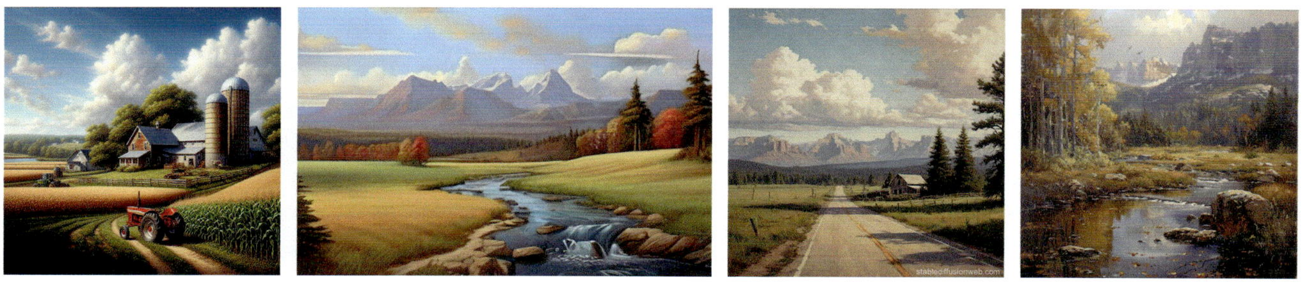

FIGURE 13.2 AI images from different generative AI engines using the same prompt: "create a typical American landscape painting," f.l.t.r.: DALL-E, Leonardo.Ai, Stable Diffusion, Midjourney.

So, in the sense of how AI is set up to be applied by a user, it does follow the tradition of computer graphics. It is a logical consequence. And this is true regardless of the aesthetics that a user aims for. Technically, to the AI a doodle is the same as any other type of image. But if one looks at actual engines and their output, it also becomes evident that AI, at least currently, also perpetuates the visual aesthetics, the style, of the computer graphical images – *and* the paintings, for that matter. This is in part due to how the technology functions, it is after all designed to find or react to patterns.[37] In other words, it is encouraged to compartmentalize and create stereotypes, if you will. Even more so it is, however, related to how it was trained, i.e. which data it has been fed – and this process has, as mentioned, in many cases not been inclusive toward different styles and cultures, and even skin colors.[38]

When asking four different engines to produce a typical image of a landscape from a 3D-animated movie and ask it in a different prompt to create an image of a typical landscape painting from the United States, a comparison of the results is striking. All outcomes have a remarkably overall similar visual style. The links between the 19th-century tradition of landscape painting and the computer graphical endeavors can thus, in a way, be empirically proven by AI.[39] It has been taught, on the one hand, what landscapes in animated movies look like and, on the other, what characterizes landscape paintings from the United States, but it has most likely not been told that they are connected or that they should appear similar. Yet, as Figures 13.1 and 13.2 show, they do.

I used each prompt only once and a result from the first batch of pictures, that were created with it, can be seen here. All images imitating a 3D landscape take up the motif of the river that was also typical for the *Hudson River School* – even the elevated perspective that also characterizes Thomas Cole's *The Oxbow* (see Figure 8.4) as well as the frame from Pixar's *The Good Dinosaur* (see Figure 8.5) is maintained in most of the images. The pictures imitating the landscape paintings pick up some different details: Instead of a river in two images a field and a road are depicted, respectively. Nevertheless, quite in line with the "maxim of believability," the images all use central perspective. Thus, aside from being created in a technical environment, they also visually answer to the "rule" to use central perspective construction to make the images be believable, so they can be felt immediately – as was always the goal with the first computer graphics. Additionally, many of the AI results use the "afternoon sunlight" that, as I have previously discussed in Chapter 10, artist David Claerbout also identified as the "native" light to computer-generated imagery.[40] AI vividly demonstrates that this light is in the "mind" of the AI also "native" to US painting, not just to computer graphics. Thus, the AI incidentally reveals the cultural links between computer graphics and painting – and, in a way, also its own link to both.

Yet, AI can also bring forward endless other styles. While this might be true for computer graphics as well, it could still be assumed that computer graphical algorithms have, more so than AI, been developed against the backdrop of a specific concept of imagery. The shaders, the rendering and all the other algorithms were written with a specific concept of imagery in mind. With generative AI it is, instead of a visual aesthetic idea, for the user mostly the approach to creation that indicates a relatedness to the painterly styles. In other words, the user always needs a concrete idea for an outcome at the beginning of a process in the form of a prompt. The visual style will here always be dependent on the training data and if this gets more diverse, then AI will also have the capability to become more diverse. But in the way the technology is set up to work currently, one could conclude that this training data will still not encourage surprises the same way they might come up in a process of doodling. This is why it can, at least at the moment, be questioned if the claim to originality mentioned at the start of this chapter can be confirmed. And while an interpolated synthesis or an extrapolated reinvention of different training materials might surprise us, make us laugh or irritate us, it is still only ever based on something that has been there before. And, more importantly, it always answers to the claim of success – quite unlike a crooked and unintentional line drawn across a piece of paper.

NOTES

1. See Alan Warburton, "The Wizard of AI," 2023, commissioned by Data as Culture at the Open Data Institute, https://culture.theodi.org/the-wizard-of-ai/; see also Sybille Krämer, "Zur Aisthesis des Maschinenlernens: Ein Kommentar zur zeitgenössischen Künstlichen Intelligenz," in *Ästhetik digitaler Medien: Aktuelle Perspektiven*, ed. Martina Ide (Bielefeld: transcript, 2022), 132.
2. "What is Generative AI?," NVIDIA, accessed June 5, 2025, https://www.nvidia.com/en-us/glossary/generative-ai/.
3. See Alan Warburton, video call with author, March 28, 2025.
4. Alan Warburton, email to author, June 6, 2025.
5. Alvy R. Smith, *A Biography of the Pixel* (Cambridge: MIT Press, 2021), 7.
6. Daniel Cardoso Llach, *Builders of the Vision: Software and the Imagination of Design* (New York: Routledge, 2015), xi.
7. See Cardoso Llach, *Builders of the Vision*, xi.
8. See for example 3D AI Studio, "Start page," 3D AI Studio, accessed June 5, 2025, https://www.3daistudio.com/.
9. Suzanne Burrey, "Edward Hopper: The Emptying Spaces," *Arts Digest* 29, no. 13 (1955), 8.
10. Cardoso Llach, *Builders of the Vision*, 1.
11. See Edwin Catmull, "A Subdivision Algorithm for Computer Display of Curved Surfaces" (PhD diss., University of Utah, 1974), J. Willard Marriott Library (712681), 41.
12. See Edward Lucie-Smith, *American Realism* (London: Thames & Hudson, 2003), 15.
13. Barbara Novak, *American Painting of the Nineteenth Century. Realism, Idealism, and the American Experience*, 3rd edition (Oxford: Oxford University Press USA, 2007), 238.
14. See Carolin Scheler, "Der bildsprachliche Kosmos im computeranimierten Kinofilm," in *Piktogrammatik: Grafisches Gestalten als Weltwissen und Bilderordnung*, ed. Annette Geiger and Bianca Holtschke (Bielefeld: transcript, 2021).
15. Susan Amin et al., "A Survey of Exploration Methods in Reinforcement Learning" (technical report, McGill University Montreal, University of Amsterdam, 2021), arXiv (2109.00157), 2.
16. See for example Krämer, "Zur Aisthesis des Maschinenlernens," 145–47.
17. Toby Ord, "Interpolation, Extrapolation, Hyperpolation: Generalising into new dimensions" (technical report, University of Oxford, 2024), arxiv (2409.05513), 2.
18. Ord, "Interpolation, Extrapolation, Hyperpolation," 3.
19. See Ord, "Interpolation, Extrapolation, Hyperpolation," 3. Ord draws his definition of creativity from Margaret Boden and Christopher Lucas et al. See Ord, "Interpolation, Extrapolation, Hyperpolation," 2.
20. Ord, "Interpolation, Extrapolation, Hyperpolation," 15.
21. Ord, "Interpolation, Extrapolation, Hyperpolation," 17.
22. See Edward Vega, "How 'Spider-Verse' forced animation to evolve," posted September 10, 2022, by VOX, YouTube, https://www.youtube.com/watch?v=l96IgQmXmhM.
23. Sherry Turkle, "Forgetting the Body in Digital Culture," in *A Psychoanalytic Exploration of the Body in Today's World*, ed. Vaia Tsolas and Christine Anzieu-Premmereur (New York: Routledge, 2017), 17.
24. Turkle, "Forgetting the Body," 17.

25. See Gundel Mattenklott and Friedrich Weltzien, "Einleitung," in *Entwerfen und Entwurf: Praxis und Theorie des künstlerischen Schaffensprozesses*, ed. Gundel Mattenklott and Friedrich Weltzien (Berlin: Reimer, 2003), 10.
26. See Friedrich Weltzien, "Kritzeln," in *Historisches Wörterbuch des Mediengebrauchs*, ed. Heiko Christians, Matthias Bickenbach and Nikolaus Wegmann (Cologne: Böhlau, 2014), 388.
27. See Weltzien, "Kritzeln," 382.
28. Weltzien, "Kritzeln," 383.
29. See Weltzien, "Kritzeln," 385.
30. See Weltzien, "Kritzeln," 388.
31. See Weltzien, "Kritzeln," 389.
32. See Weltzien, "Kritzeln," 383.
33. Steven A. Coons, "An Outline of the Requirements for a Computer-Aided Design System," In *Proceedings of the Spring Joint Computer Conference – AFIPS '63*, ed. E. Calvin Johnson (New York: ACM Press, 1963), 300.
34. Mattenklott and Weltzien, "Einleitung," 10–11.
35. Mattenklott and Weltzien, "Einleitung," 9.
36. Friedrich Weltzien, "Der 'nachgereichte Entwurf': Frühe Phototheorie und die Frage der Bildentstehung," in *Entwerfen und Entwurf: Praxis und Theorie des künstlerischen Schaffensprozesses*, ed. Gundel Mattenklott and Friedrich Weltzien (Berlin: Reimer, 2003), 173.
37. NVIDIA, "What is Generative AI?"
38. See for example Joy Buolamwini and Timnit Gebru, "Gender Shades: Intersectional Accuracy Disparities in Commercial Gender Classification," in *Conference on Fairness, Accountability and Transparency* (New York: ACM, 2018); see also Krämer, "Zur Aisthesis des Maschinenlernens," 143–44.
39. See Carolin Scheler, "Magnifying the Logic of Images: Artificial Intelligence and the Continuous Reproduction of Pictorial Codes," in *Pictologic: How images give form to our knowledge and imagination*, ed. Annette Geiger, Bianca Holtschke and Julia C. Ahrend (Bielefeld: transcript, 2026). In the original experiment I tested five engines. Due to copyright restrictions, the fifth engine, Prome AI, was left out here. The aesthetics it generated were fully in line with the other four engines – this is particularly interesting as this is an engine that was developed in Hongkong, thus not in a Western country. In other experiments, the results deviated slightly from the Western engines. It can be assumed that the training data was selected with a different cultural influence. This shows how the cultural background directly influences the technology we create.
40. See Sean Kelly, ed., *David Claerbout: Drawings and Studies* (Ostfildern: Hatje Cantz, 2015), 102.

Figures: Selected References

FIGURE I.3 *South Park. The Problem with a Poo*, directed by Trey Parker Comedy Central, 2018); "South Park TV Series," Alamy, accessed April 9, 2025, https://www.alamy.de/south-park-tv-series-1997-usa-creators-trey-parker-matt-stone-brian-graden-2018-saison-22-episode-3-das-problem-mit-einer-poo-animation-image383560210.html. 2

FIGURE I.4 *Toy Story*, directed by John Lasseter (Disney/Pixar, 1995). 2

FIGURE 1.2 "Steve," Paweł Somogyi, accessed February 14, 2023, https://www.artstation.com/artwork/8wbv2R. 6

FIGURE 1.3 "portrait of a middle aged black woman looking into the camera," neural.love, accessed January 23, 2023, https://neural.love/ai-art-generator/1ed9b0e2-bee8-6b30-bfe7-0198c651b5e0/portrait-of-a-middle-aged-black-woman-looking-into-the-camera. 6

FIGURE 2.6 "Billard ball," Pixabay, accessed January 31, 2022, https://pixabay.com/photos/pool-eight-ball-black-game-4306004/. 32

FIGURE 2.7 "Table tennis ball," Pixabay, accessed January 31, 2022, https://pixabay.com/photos/table-tennis-sports-game-ball-play-4040603/. 32

FIGURE 2.8 "Earth texture map," James Hastings-Trew, accessed February 1, 2022, http://planetpixelemporium.com/earth.html. 33

FIGURE 3.2 Ivan E. Sutherland, "Sketchpad: A Man-Machine Graphical Communication System" (PhD diss., Massachusetts Institute of Technology, 1963). MIT Libraries, DSpace@MIT (15036306), 11; "SketchpadDissertation-Fig1-2.tif," Wikimedia Commons, accessed June 21, 2025, https://commons.wikimedia.org/wiki/Category:Sketchpad#/media/File:SketchpadDissertation-Fig1-2.tif. 46

FIGURE 3.3 Ivan E. Sutherland, "Sketchpad: A Man-Machine Graphical Communication System" (PhD diss., Massachusetts Institute of Technology, 1963). MIT Libraries, DSpace@MIT (15036306), 14; "SketchpadDissertation-Fig1-4.tif," Wikimedia Commons, accessed June 21, 2025, https://commons.wikimedia.org/wiki/Category:Sketchpad#/media/File:SketchpadDissertation-Fig1-4.tif. 52

FIGURE 3.4 Ivan E. Sutherland, "Sketchpad: A Man-Machine Graphical Communication System" (PhD diss., Massachusetts Institute of Technology, 1963). MIT Libraries, DSpace@MIT (15036306), 10. 55

FIGURE 3.5 Ivan E. Sutherland, "Sketchpad: A Man-Machine Graphical Communication System" (PhD diss., Massachusetts Institute of Technology, 1963). MIT Libraries, DSpace@MIT (15036306), 133; "SketchpadDissertation-Fig9-8.tif," Wikimedia Commons, accessed June 21, 2025, https://commons.wikimedia.org/wiki/Category:Sketchpad#/media/File:SketchpadDissertation-Fig9-8.tif. 56

FIGURE 3.6 Ivan E. Sutherland, "Sketchpad: A Man-Machine Graphical Communication System" (PhD diss., Massachusetts Institute of Technology, 1963). MIT Libraries, DSpace@MIT (15036306), 134. 57

FIGURE 3.7 Ivan E. Sutherland, "Sketchpad: A Man-Machine Graphical Communication System" (PhD diss., Massachusetts Institute of Technology, 1963). MIT Libraries, DSpace@MIT (15036306), 135. 57

List of Films

Carpenter, Loren, Rob Cook, Tom Porter, Bill Reeves, David Salesin and Alvy Ray Smith, creators. *Road to Point Reyes.* Disney/Pixar, 1983. 1 frame.

Cottrell, William, David Hand and Wilfred Jackson, directors. *Snow White and the Seven Dwarfs.* Disney, 1937. 1 hr., 23 min.

Csuri, Charles, director. *Hummingbird.* 1967. 12 min.

Docter, Pete, director. *Inside Out.* Disney/Pixar, 2015. 1 hr., 35 min.

Genkel, Toby, and Reza Memari, directors. *Richard the Stork.* Knudsen & Streuber Medienmanufaktur, Ulysses Filmproduktion, Walking the Dog, Mélusine Productions, Den siste skilling – License TELEPOOL GmbH, Munich, 2017. 1 hr., 25 min.

Greno, Nathan, and Byron Howard, directors. *Tangled.* Disney, 2010. 1 hr., 40 min.

Howard, Byron, Rich Moore and Jared Bush, directors. *Zootopia.* Disney, 2016. 1 hr., 48 min.

Lasseter, John, director. *Luxo Jr.* Disney/Pixar, 1986. 2 min.

Lasseter, John, director. *Toy Story.* Disney/Pixar, 1995. 1 hr., 17 min.

Lasseter, John, director. *Cars.* Disney/Pixar, 2006. 1 hr., 36 min.

Mariutto, Mark, director. *The Incredible Crash Dummies.* Lamb & Co. and Nelvana, 1993. 22 min.

Morash, Russell, director. *MIT Science Reporter. Computer Sketchpad.* WGBH, 1964. 30 min.

Parker, Trey, director. *South Park. The Problem with a Poo.* Comedy Central, 2018. 22 min.

Persichetti, Bob, Peter Ramsey and Rodney Rothman, directors. *Spider-Man: Into the Spider-Verse.* Columbia/Marvel/Sony, 2018. 1 hr., 57 min.

Sohn, Peter, director. *The Good Dinosaur.* Disney/Pixar, 2015. 1 hr., 33 min.

Stanton, Andrew, director. *WALL-E.* Disney/Pixar, 2008. 1 hr., 37 min.

Unkrich, Lee, director. *Toy Story 3.* Disney/Pixar, 2010. 1 hr., 43 min.

Zondag, Ralph, and Eric Leighton, directors. *Dinosaur.* Disney, 2000. 1 hr., 22 min.

Bibliography

3D AI Studio. "Start Page." Accessed June 5, 2025. https://www.3daistudio.com/.

ACCAD. "ACCAD History." Accessed February 18, 2021. https://accad.osu.edu/about/accad-history.

ACM SIGGRAPH. "Steven Anson Coons Award." Accessed December 12, 2021. https://www.siggraph.org/about/awards/steven-anson-coons-award/.

Aikens, Nick, Thomas Lange, Jorinde Seijdel and Steven ten Thije, eds. *What's the Use? Constellations of Art, History, and Knowledge: A Critical Reader.* Valiz, 2016.

Alt, Casey. "The Materialities of Maya: Making Sense of Object-Orientation." *Configurations* 10, no. 3 (2002): 387–422. https://doi.org/10.1353/con.2004.0002.

Alt, Casey. "Objects of Our Affection. How Object Orientation Made Computers a Medium." In *Media Archaeology: Approaches, Applications, and Implications*, edited by Erkki Huhtamo and Jussi Parikka. University of California Press, 2011. https://doi.org/10.1525/9780520948518-015.

Amin, Susan, Maziar Gomrokchi, Harsh Satija, Herke van Hoof and Doina Precup. "A Survey of Exploration Methods in Reinforcement Learning." Technical report, 2021. arXiv (2109.00157). https://doi.org/10.48550/arXiv.2109.00157.

Appel, Arthur. "Some Techniques for Shading Machine Renderings of Solids." In *Proceedings of the Spring Joint Computer Conference – AFIPS '68*, edited by ACM. ACM Press, 1968. https://doi.org/10.1145/1468075.1468082.

Maya, Autodesk. "Constraints." Accessed December 11, 2021. https://help.autodesk.com/view/MAYAUL/2022/ENU/?guid=GUID-7665A291-FAA7-44C0-BDEB-A6C83482116C.

Maya, Autodesk. "Copies vs. Instances." Accessed December 11, 2021. https://help.autodesk.com/view/MAYAUL/2022/ENU/?guid=GUID-2851AE11-C3EF-4AE1-B7C5-8773E2068BB9.

Maya, Autodesk. "Learning Maya." Accessed December 11, 2021. https://help.autodesk.com/view/MAYAUL/2022/ENU/?guid=GUID-4191EE54-4500-4FFC-BF29-BA6C1EAD9F58.

Baudrillard, Jean. *Agonie des Realen.* Translated by Lothar Kurzawa and Volker Schaefer. Merve, 1978.

Baur, John I. H. *Revolution and Tradition in Modern American Art.* 2nd edition. Praeger, 1967.

Baur, John I. H. "American Luminism." *Perspectives USA* 9 (Autumn 1954): 90–98.

Berezina-Blackburn, Vita. Email to author. May 12, 2025.

Blackwell, Alan, and Kerry Rodden. "Preface." In "Sketchpad: A Man-Machine Graphical Communication System." Technical report by Ivan E. Sutherland, edited by Alan Blackwell and Kerry Rodden. University of Cambridge, Computer Laboratory, 2003. Computer Laboratory (UCAM-CL-TR-574).

Blender. "History." Accessed December 8, 2021, https://www.blender.org/about/history/.

Blender. "Japanese Anime Studio Khara Moving to Blender." *User Stories*, August 15, 2019. https://www.blender.org/user-stories/japanese-anime-studio-khara-moving-to-blender/?utm_source=www-homepage.

Blinn, James F. "Computer Display of Curved Surfaces." PhD diss., University of Utah, 1978. J. Willard Marriott Library (105596).

Blinn, James F. "Models of Light Reflection for Computer Synthesized Pictures." In *Proceedings of the 4th Annual Conference on Computer Graphics and Interactive Techniques – SIGGRAPH '77*, edited by ACM. ACM Press, 1977. https://doi.org/10.1145/563858.563893.

Blumenberg, Hans. "Phenomenological Aspects on Life-World and Technization (1963)." In *History, Metaphors, Fables: A Hans Blumenberg Reader*, translated and edited by Hannes Bajohr, Florian Fuchs and Joe Paul Kroll. Cornell University Press, 2022. https://doi.org/10.1515/9781501748004-015.

Bolter, Jay David, and Richard Grusin. *Remediation: Understanding New Media.* MIT Press, 1999.

Bouknight, W. J. "An Improved Procedure for Generation of Half-Tone Computer Graphics Presentations." Technical report, Coordinated Science Laboratory, University of Illinois at Urbana-Champaign, 1969. Defense Technical Information Center (AD0707403).

Bréaud, Ondine. *Le Réalisme dans l'image informatique. Étude des années 1980 et 1990.* Harmattan, 2001.

Breslin, James E. B. *Mark Rothko: A Biography.* University of Chicago Press, 1993.

Bret, Michel. "Anyflo Philosophy." Accessed December 5, 2021. https://anyflo.com/distribution/distribution_eng/env/philosophie.htm.

Bret, Michel. "L'artiste et l'ordinateur." In *Les images numériques: Créations françaises*, edited by Daisy Hochart. Corlet-Télérama, CinémAction TV 10, 1994.

Bret, Michel. "Tools for Artists." In *Computer Animation '91*, edited by Nadia Magnenat Thalmann and Daniel Thalmann. Springer Japan, 1991. https://doi.org/10.1007/978-4-431-66890-9_13.

Brown, Milton W. *American Painting from the Armory Show to the Depression*. Princeton University Press, 1955.

Buolamwini, Joy, and Timnit Gebru. "Gender Shades: Intersectional Accuracy Disparities in Commercial Gender Classification." In *Conference on Fairness, Accountability and Transparency*. ACM, 2018.

Burley, Brent. *Physically Based Shading at Disney*. Walt Disney Animation Studios, 2012.

Burrey, Suzanne. "Edward Hopper: The Emptying Spaces." *Arts Digest* 29, no. 13 (1955): 8–10, 33.

Caltech Computing + Mathematical Sciences. "History and Facts." Accessed December 13, 2021. https://cms.caltech.edu/about/history.

Cardoso Llach, Daniel. *Builders of the Vision: Software and the Imagination of Design*. Routledge, 2015. https://doi.org/10.4324/9781315798240.

Carlson, Wayne E. *Computer Graphics and Computer Animation: A Retrospective Overview*. The Ohio State University, 2017.

Carlson, Wayne E. "Dialogue and Creativity: The Faces of Collaboration." In *Charles A. Csuri: Beyond Boundaries, 1963 – Present*, edited by Janice M. Glowski and SIGGRAPH. The Ohio State University, College of the Arts, Advanced Computing Center for the Arts and Design, 2006.

Cassirer, Ernst. *The Philosophy of Symbolic Forms. Part Two: Mythical Thought*. Translated by Ralph Manheim. Yale University Press, 1955.

Cassirer, Ernst. *Wesen und Wirkung des Symbolbegriffs*. 8th edition. Wissenschaftliche Buchgesellschaft. 1994.

Catmull, Edwin. "A Subdivision Algorithm for Computer Display of Curved Surfaces." PhD diss., University of Utah, 1974. J. Willard Marriott Library (2111909).

Catmull, Edwin. "A System for Computer Generated Movies." In *Proceedings of the ACM Annual Conference – ACM '72*, edited by John J. Donovan and Rosemary Shields. ACM Press, 1972. https://doi.org/10.1145/800193.569952.

Catmull, Edwin, and Amy Wallace. *Creativity, Inc.: Overcoming the Unseen Forces That Stand in the Way of True Inspiration*. Random House, 2014.

Charles Babbage Institute, College of Science and Engineering. "About CBI." Accessed December 11, 2021. https://cse.umn.edu/cbi/about.

Claerbout, David. "Travel, 1996–2013." In *David Claerbout*, edited by Kunsthaus Bregenz. Walther König, 2018.

Clark, Wesley A. "The Lincoln TX-2 Computer Development." In *Western Joint Computer Conference – IRE-AIEE-ACM '57*, edited by Morton M. Astrahan. ACM Press, 1957. https://doi.org/10.1145/1455567.14555902.

Cole, Thomas. "Letter to Robert Gilmor." Dated December 25, 1827. Thomas Cole Papers, Letters of Robert Gilmor to and from Thomas Cole – 1826–1837. New York State Library Digital Collections, Manuscripts. Accessed March 18, 2022. https://nysl.ptfs.com/data/Library5/All%20Special%20Collections/Manuscripts/Thomas%20Cole%20Papers/Correspondence%2C%201820-1855/Cole%20and%20Gilmor%2C%201826-1837/pdf/SC10635-B3-F8-complete.pdf.

Computer History Museum. "The Mouse." Accessed December 12, 2021. https://www.computerhistory.org/revolution/input-output/14/350.

Coons, Steven A. *Surfaces for Computer-Aided Design of Space Forms*. Massachusetts Institute of Technology, 1967.

Coons, Steven A. "An Outline of the Requirements for a Computer-Aided Design System." In *Proceedings of the Spring Joint Computer Conference – AFIPS '63*, edited by E. Calvin Johnson. ACM Press, 1963. https://doi.org/10.1145/1461551.1461588.

Coons, Steven A. "The Uses of Computers in Technology." *Scientific American* 215, no. 3 (1966): 176–191. https://doi.org/10.1038/scientificamerican0966-176.

Couchot, Edmond, and Norbert Hillaire. *L'art numérique. Comment la technologie vient au monde de l'art*. Flammarion, 2003.

Crary, Jonathan. *Techniques of the Observer: On Vision and Modernity in the Nineteenth Century*. MIT Press, 1992.

Crehan, Hubert. "Rothko's Wall of Light." *Arts Digest* 29, no. 3 (1954): 5, 19.

Csuri, Caroline. Email to author. May 11, 2025.

Csuri, Charles A. "Beyond Boundaries." In *Charles A. Csuri: Beyond Boundaries, 1963 – Present*, edited by Janice M. Glowski and SIGGRAPH. The Ohio State University, College of the Arts, Advanced Computing Center for the Arts and Design, 2006.

Csuri, Charles A. "Complexity." Accessed December 12, 2021. http://www.csurivision.com/index.php/2008/10/complexity/.

Csuri, Charles A. "Interview of Charles A. Csuri by Robert Butche." Interview by Robert W. Butche. June 10, 2003. transcript. The Ohio State University Oral History Project. Ohio State University Archives. http://hdl.handle.net/1811/5928.

Csuri, Charles A. "An Interview with Charles Csuri." Interview by John Staudhammer, Tom Culviner and Margaret Neal. *IEEE Computer Graphics and Applications* 10, no. 1 (1990): 5–9.

Csuri, Charles A. "Oral History Interview with Charles A. Csuri." Interview by Kerry J. Freedman. October 23, 1989. transcript. Charles Babbage Institute, University of Minnesota. https://hdl.handle.net/11299/107236.

Csuri, Charles A. "Charles Csuri 'Random War,' 1967." Accessed June 12, 2025. https://www.charlescsuri.com/historic/random-war.

Csuri, Charles A. "Research." Accessed June 11, 2025. https://www.charlescsuri.com/research.

Dahl, Ole-Johan, and Kristen Nygaard. "SIMULA: An ALGOL-Based Simulation Language." *Communications of the ACM* 9, no. 9 (1966): 671–678. https://doi.org/10.1145/365813.365819.

DARPA. "The Sputnik Surprise." Accessed December 10, 2021. https://www.darpa.mil/about-us/timeline/creation-of-darpa.

Depkat, Volker. *Geschichte der USA*. Kohlhammer, 2016. https://doi.org/10.17433/978-3-17-026744-2.

Dewey, John. *Art as Experience*. 23rd impression. Perigee Books, 1980.

Docter, Pete, and Amy Poehler. *The Art of Inside Out*. Chronicle Books, 2015.

Dunlop, Renee, ed. *Production Pipeline Fundamentals for Film and Game*. Focal Press, 2014. https://doi.org/10.4324/9781315858272.

Dybvig, Ronak Kent. *The Scheme Programming Language*. 4th edition. MIT Press, 2009.

Eco, Umberto, Karl Gerstner, Vera Horvat-Pintarić, Boris Kelemen and Martin Krampen. "Programme Information 13. tendencije 4/tendencies 4. Computers and Visual Research. Decision of the Competition Jury." In *A Little-Known Story about a Movement, a Magazine, and the Computer's Arrival in Art: New Tendencies and Bit International, 1961–1973. Bit International. [Nove] tendencije. Computer and Visual Research Zagreb 1961–1973, Exhibitions Neue Galerie Graz am Landesmuseum Joanneum April 28–June 17, 2007, ZKM, Center for Art and Media Karlsruhe February 23, 2008–January 18, 2009*, edited by Margit Rosen, Darko Fritz, Marija Gattin and Peter Weibel. ZKM Center for Art and Media MIT Press, 2011.

Edwards, Jonathan. "782. Ideas. Sense of the Heart. Spiritual Knowledge or Conviction. Faith." In *Works of Jonathan Edwards Online, Volume 18, The Miscellanies*, edited by Ava Chamberlain. Jonathan Edwards Center. New Haven: Yale University Press, 2008. Accessed September 29, 2017. http://edwards.yale.edu/archive?path=aHR0cDovL2Vkd2FyZHMueWFsZS5lZHUvY2dpLWJpbi9uZXdwaGlsby9nZXRvYmplY3QucGw/Yy4xNzo0OjI4Mi53amVv.

Emerson, Ralph Waldo. "Nature (1836)." In *The Collected Works of Ralph Waldo Emerson. Volume I: Nature, Addresses, and Lectures*, edited by Robert E. Spiller and Alfred R. Ferguson. Belknap Press of Harvard University Press, 1971.

Emerson, Ralph Waldo. "The Young American (1844)." In *The Collected Works of Ralph Waldo Emerson. Volume I: Nature, Addresses, and Lectures*, edited by Robert E. Spiller and Alfred R. Ferguson. Belknap Press of Harvard University Press, 1971.

Engelbart, Douglas C. *Augmenting Human Intellect: A Conceptual Framework*. Stanford Research Institute, 1962.

Erbacher, Eric, Nicole Maruo-Schröder and Florian Sedlmeier. "Introduction: Rereading *The Machine in the Garden*." In *Rereading the Machine in the Garden: Nature and Technology in American Culture*, edited by Eric Erbacher, Nicole Maruo-Schröder and Florian Sedlmeier. Campus, 2014.

Erdahl, Alan. "Displaying Computer Generated Half-Tone Pictures in Real Time." Technical report, University of Utah, 1969. Defense Technical Information Center (AD0753672).

Evans, David C. "Graphical Man/Machine Communications: November 1966." Research report, University of Utah, 1966. J. Willard Marriott Library (703452).

Evans, David C. "Graphical Man/Machine Communications: May 1967." Research report, University of Utah, 1967. J. Willard Marriott Library (704511).

Evans, David C. "Graphical Man/Machine Communications: February 1968." Research report, University of Utah, 1968. J. Willard Marriott Library (707101).

Evans, David C. "Graphical Man/Machine Communications: November 1968." Research report, University of Utah, 1968. J. Willard Marriott Library (703204).

Evans, David C. "Graphical Man/Machine Communications: May 1969." Research report, University of Utah, 1969. J. Willard Marriott Library (702679).

Evans, David C. "Graphical Man/Machine Communications: November 1969." Research report, University of Utah, 1969. J. Willard Marriott Library (706332).

Evans, David C. "Graphical Man/Machine Communications: May 1971." Research report, University of Utah, 1971. J. Willard Marriott Library (703517).

Evans, David C. "Graphical Man/Machine Communications: June 1971." Research report, University of Utah, 1971. J. Willard Marriott Library (702407).

Evans, David C. "Graphical Man/Machine Communications: December 1971." Research report, University of Utah, 1971. J. Willard Marriott Library (702292).

Evans, David C. "Graphical Man/Machine Communications: June 1972." Research report, University of Utah, 1972. J. Willard Marriott Library (702817).

Evans, David C. "Graphical Man/Machine Communications: December 1972." Research report, University of Utah, 1972. J. Willard Marriott Library (706529).

Evans & Sutherland, A Cosm Company. "About – Evans & Sutherland." Accessed December 09, 2021. https://www.es.com/about/.

Failing, Patricia, and Robin Oppenheimer. "History." *University of Washington*, last modified September 16, 2002. http://courses.washington.edu/eatreun/html/history/h_intro.html.

Failing, Patricia, and Robin Oppenheimer. "Northwest Chapters. William Fetter (1928–2002)." *University of Washington*, last modified September 16, 2002. http://courses.washington.edu/eatreun/html/history/h_nw.html.

Farr Sloan, Helen. *John Sloan's New York Scene*. Harper & Row, 1965.

Fetter, William A. *Computer Graphics in Communication: Written for the Course Content Development Study in Engineering Graphics, Supported by the National Science Foundation*. McGraw-Hill, 1965.

Fetter, William A. "Computer Graphics." *Design Quarterly* 66, no. 67 (1966): 14–23. https://doi.org/10.2307/4047328.

Fitch, John. *MIT Science Reporter*. "Computer Sketchpad." Directed by Russell Morash. National Educational Television, 1964.

Flusser, Vilém. *Into the Universe of Technical Images*. Translated by Nancy Ann Roth. University of Minnesota Press, 2011.

Flusser, Vilém. "Digital Apparition." in *Electronic Culture: Technology and Visual Representation*, edited by Timothy Druckrey. Aperture, 1996.

Flusser, Vilém. "Digitaler Schein." In *Digitaler Schein. Ästhetik der elektronischen Medien*, edited by Florian Rötzer. Suhrkamp, 1991.

Frankenstein, Alfred Victor. *After the Hunt: William Harnett and Other American Still Life Painters 1870–1900*. University of California Press, 1953.

Frankovich, John M., and H. Phillip Peterson. "A Functional Description of the Lincoln TX-2 Computer." In *Western Joint Computer Conference – IRE-AIEE-ACM '57*, edited by M. M. Astrahan. ACM Press, 1957. https://doi.org/10.1145/1455567.1455593.

Gaboury, Jacob. *Image Objects: An Archaeology of Computer Graphics*. MIT Press, 2021. https://doi.org/10.7551/mitpress/11077.001.0001.

Galloway, Alexander R. "The Poverty of Philosophy: Realism and Post-Fordism." *Critical Inquiry* 39, no. 2 (2013): 347–366. https://doi.org/10.1086/668529.

Geiger, Annette. *Andersmöglichsein. Zur Ästhetik des Designs*. transcript, 2018. https://doi.org/10.1515/9783839444894.

Geiger, Annette, and Bianca Holtschke. "Einleitung. Grafisches Gestalten als Weltwissen und Bilderord nung." In *Piktogrammatik. Grafisches Gestalten als Weltwissen und Bilderordnung*, edited by Annette Geiger and Bianca Holtschke. transcript, 2021. https://doi.org/10.1515/9783839457436-001.

General Electric. "Modifications to Interim Visual Spaceflight Simulator. Sixth Quarterly Report. 12 April to 12 July 1966." Technical report, NASA Manned Spacecraft Center, 1966. NASA Technical Reports Server (19660030678).

General Electric. "Modifications to Interim Visual Spaceflight Simulator. Ninth Quarterly Report. 12 January to 12 April 1967." Technical report, NASA Manned Spacecraft Center, 1967. NASA Technical Reports Server (19670023039).

Glowski, Janice M. "Introduction to the Catalogue." In *Charles A. Csuri: Beyond Boundaries, 1963 – Present*, edited by Janice M. Glowski and SIGGRAPH. The Ohio State University, College of the Arts, Advanced Computing Center for the Arts and Design, 2006.

Glowski, Janice M. "Random War." In *Charles A. Csuri: Beyond Boundaries, 1963 – Present*, edited by Janice M. Glowski and SIGGRAPH. The Ohio State University, College of the Arts, Advanced Computing Center for the Arts and Design, 2006.

Glowski, Janice M., and SIGGRAPH, eds. *Charles A. Csuri: Beyond Boundaries, 1963 – Present*. The Ohio State University, College of the Arts, Advanced Computing Center for the Arts and Design, 2006.

Goodman, Nelson. *Languages of Art: An Approach to a Theory of Symbols*. 3rd printing. The Bobbs-Merrill Company, Inc., 1976.

Goodman, Richard. "Introduction to the Transaction Edition." In *Joseph Anthony Ward: American Silences: The Realism of James Agee, Walker Evans, and Edward Hopper*. 2nd edition. Transaction Publishers, 2010.

Gouraud, Henri. "Computer Display of Curved Surfaces." PhD diss., University of Utah, 1971. ProQuest (7127878).

Gouraud, Henri. "Continuous Shading of Curved Surfaces." *IEEE Transactions on Computers* C-20, no. 6 (1971): 623–629. https://doi.org/10.1109/T-C.1971.223313.

Halberstam, Judith/Jack. *The Queer Art of Failure*. Duke University Press, 2011. https://doi.org/10.2307/j.ctv11sn283.

Harvard Innovation Labs. "AR/VR Studio. Harvard's Role in the History of AR/VR." Accessed May 13, 2021. https://innovationlabs.harvard.edu/arvr-studio/.

Heim, Michael. *Electric Language: A Philosophical Study of Word Processing*. Yale University Press, 1987.

Heim, Michael. "The Cyberspace Dialectic." In *Digital Dialectic: New Essays on New Media*, edited by Peter Lunenfeld. MIT Press, 1999.

Henri, Robert. *The Art Spirit*. 3rd edition. Basic Books, 2007.

Henri, Robert. "The New York Exhibition of Independent Artists." *The Craftsman* XVIII, no. 2 (1910): 160–172.

Herzog, Bertram. "Eulogy Delivered at the Memorial Service of Steven A. Coons (22.08.1979)." In *Syracuse University Clipping Files, Steven A. Coons-Folder*. Syracuse University Libraries, Special Collections Research Center, 1979.

History Computer. "Ivan Sutherland – Complete Biography, History, and Inventions." Accessed June 20, 2025. https://web.archive.org/web/20220107123638/https:/history-computer.com/ivan-sutherland-complete-biography/.

Huhtamo, Erkki, and Jussi Parikka. "Introduction: An Archaeology of Media Archaeology." In *Media Archaeology: Approaches, Applications, and Implications*, edited by Erkki Huhtamo and Jussi Parikka. University of California Press, 2011. https://doi.org/10.1525/9780520948518-003.

Husserl, Edmund. *Experience and Judgement: Investigations in a Genealogy of Logic*. Edited by Ludwig Landgrebe. Translated by Spencer Churchill and Karl Ameriks. Northwestern University Press, 1973.

Husserl, Edmund. *Die Krisis der europäischen Wissen schaften und die transzendentale Phänomenologie: Eine Einleitung in die phänomenologische Philosophie.* Edited by Walter Biemel. Nijhoff, 1976.

Husserl, Edmund. *The Crisis of European Sciences and Transcendental Phenomenology: An Introduction to Phenomenological Philosophy.* Translated by David Carr. Northwestern University Press, 1970.

James, Henry. *Notes on Novelists: With Some Other Notes.* Charles Scribner's Sons, 1914.

Jefferson, Thomas. *Notes on the State of Virginia: With Related Documents.* Edited by David Waldstreicher. Palgrave Macmillan, 2002.

Johnson, Timothy E. "Sketchpad III: Three Dimensional Graphical Communication With a Digital Computer." Master's thesis, Massachusetts Institute of Technology, 1963. MIT Libraries, DSpace@MIT (33828890).

Jones, Loyd A. "The Psychophysical Evaluation of the Quality of Photographic Reproductions." *PSA Journal* 17, no. 12 (1951): 751–764.

Jones, Loyd A. "Psychophysics and Photography." *Journal of the Optical Society of America* 34, no. 2 (1944): 66. https://doi.org/10.1364/JOSA.34.000066.

Kanna, Ahmed. *Dubai: The City as Corporation.* University of Minnesota Press, 2011. https://doi.org/10.5749/minnesota/9780816656301.001.0001.

Kelly, Sean, ed. *David Claerbout: Drawings and Studies.* Hatje Cantz, 2015.

Klütsch, Christoph. *Computergrafik. Ästhetische Experimente zwischen zwei Kulturen. Die Anfänge der Computer kunst in den 1960er Jahren.* Springer, 2007. https://doi.org/10.1007/978-3-211-39410-6.

Kouwenhoven, John A. *Made in America: The Arts in Modern Civilization.* Doubleday & Company, Inc, 1949.

Krämer, Sybille. "Das Medium als Spur und Apparat." In *Medien, Computer Realität. Wirklichkeitsvorstellungen und Neue Medien*, edited by Sybille Krämer. Suhrkamp, 1998.

Krämer, Sybille. "Zur Aisthesis des Maschinenlernens: Ein Kommentar zur zeitgenössischen Künstlichen Intelligenz." In *Ästhetik digitaler Medien: Aktuelle Perspektiven*, edited by Martina Ide. transcript, 2022. https://doi.org/10.14361/9783839453612-008.

Kunsthaus Bregenz, ed. *David Claerbout.* Walther König, 2018.

Landau, Elizabeth. "Tech Confronts Its Use of the Labels 'Master' and 'Slave.'" *Wired*, July 6, 2020. https://www.wired.com/story/tech-confronts-use-labels-master-slave/.

Lange, Thomas. "Constellating History – Introduction." In *What's the Use? Constellations of Art, History, and Knowledge: A Critical Reader*, edited by Nick Aikens, Thomas Lange, Jorinde Seijdel and Steven ten Thije. Valiz, 2016.

Lange, Thomas. "Orientierungen an den Leerstellen der Geschichte. Zum Verhältnis von Gewordenem und Gemachtem in Ruinenbildern der Romantik." In *von selbst. Autopoetische Verfahren in der Ästhetik des 19. Jahrhunderts*, edited by Friedrich Weltzien. Reimer, 2006.

Latour, Bruno. *Pandora's Hope. Essays on the Reality of Science Studies.* 2nd printing. Harvard University Press, 2000.

Latour, Bruno. "Mixing Humans and Nonhumans Together: The Sociology of a Door-Closer." *Social Problems* 35, no. 3 (1988): 298–310. https://doi.org/10.1525/sp.1988.35.3.03a00070.

Leider, Philip. Letter to Matthew Baigell. October 30, 1967. In the collection of Caroline Csuri.

Le Meur, Anne-Sarah. "Création artistique en image de synthèse: Expression de la corporéité." PhD diss., Université de Paris VIII, 1999.

Levin, Gail. *Edward Hopper: An Intimate Biography.* 2nd revised edition. Rizzoli, 2007.

Lewis, Matthew. "Randomness, Chance, Process: The *Infinity* Series." In *Charles A. Csuri: Beyond Boundaries, 1963 – Present*, edited by Janice M. Glowski and SIGGRAPH. The Ohio State University, College of the Arts, Advanced Computing Center for the Arts and Design, 2006.

Lobel, Michael. *Image Duplicator: Roy Lichtenstein and the Emergence of Pop Art.* Yale University Press, 2002.

Loomis, Herschel H. "Graphical Manipulation Techniques Using the Lincoln TX-2 Computer." Technical Report, Massachusetts Institute of Technology, 1960. MIT Libraries, Distinctive Collections.

Lucie-Smith, Edward. *American Realism.* Thames & Hudson, 2003.

Lunenfeld, Peter. *Snap to Grid: A User's Guide to Digital Arts, Media and Cultures.* MIT Press 2000.

MacAdam, David L. "Quality of Color Reproduction." *Journal of the Society of Motion Picture and Television Engineers* 56 (1951): 478–512. https://doi.org/10.5594/J06314.

Mach, Ernst. *Über die Wirkung der räumlichen Vertheilung des Lichtreizes auf die Netzhaut.* K. k. Hof- und Staatsdruckerei Wien, 1865.

MAGI. "3-D Simulated Graphics Offered by Service Bureau." *Datamation* 14, no. 2 (1986): 69.

Maki, Ariana. "After the Artist Series." In *Charles A. Csuri: Beyond Boundaries, 1963 – Present*, edited by Janice M. Glowski and SIGGRAPH. The Ohio State University, College of the Arts, Advanced Computing Center for the Arts and Design, 2006.

Mann, Robert W. "Computer-Aided Design – 1959 through 1965 – In the Design and Graphics Division of MIT's Mechanical Engineering Department." In *Fundamental Developments of Computer-Aided Geometric Modeling*, edited by Les A. Piegl. Academic Press, 1993.

Manovich, Lev. *The Language of New Media.* MIT Press, 2001.

Manovich, Lev. *Software Takes Command*. Bloomsbury Academic, 2013. https://doi.org/10.5040/9781472544988.

Manovich, Lev. "Synthetic Realism: The Mythology of Computer Graphics." *Afterimage* 20, no. 2 (1992): 12–14. https://doi.org/10.1525/aft.1992.20.2.12.

Marey, Étienne-Jules. *Movement*. Translated by Eric Pritchard. D. Appleton and Company, 1895.

Marx, Leo. *The Machine in the Garden: Technology and the Pastoral Ideal in America*. 2nd edition. Oxford University Press USA, 2000.

Mattenklott, Gundel, and Friedrich Weltzien. "Einleitung." In *Entwerfen und Entwurf: Praxis und Theorie des künstlerischen Schaffensprozesses*, edited by Gundel Mattenklott and Friedrich Weltzien. Reimer, 2003.

Maxon. "Phong." Accessed March 25, 2025. https://help.maxon.net/c4d/r23/de-de/Default.htm#html/TPHONG.html?Highlight=Phong.

Maxon. "Shading." Accessed March 25, 2025. https://help.maxon.net/c4d/s26/en-us/Default.htm#html/DBASEDRAW-BASEDRAW_GROUP_VIEW.html.

McLuhan, Marshall. *Understanding Media: The Extensions of Man*. 4th impression. Routledge & Kegan Paul Ltd, 1968.

Meinel, Dietmar. *Pixar's America: The Re-Animation of American Myths and Symbols*. Palgrave Macmillan, 2016.

Meinel, Dietmar. "The Garden in the Machine: Myth and Symbol in the Digital Age." In *Rereading the Machine in the Garden: Nature and Technology in American Culture*, edited by Eric Erbacher, Nicole Maruo-Schröder and Florian Sedlmeier. Campus, 2014.

Menton, Seymour. *Magic Realism Rediscovered, 1918–1981*. Art Alliance Press; Associated University Presses, 1983.

Miller, Dorothy C. "Foreword and Acknowledgement." In *American Realists and Magic Realists: Exhibition Catalogue*, edited by Dorothy C. Miller and Alfred H. Barr Jr. The Museum of Modern Art, 1943.

Miller, Dorothy C., and Alfred H. Barr Jr, eds. *American Realists and Magic Realists: Exhibition Catalogue*. The Museum of Modern Art, 1943.

Minsky, Marvin, and MIT. "Marvin Minsky." Accessed December 11, 2021. https://web.media.mit.edu/~minsky/.

MIT CSAIL. "Mission & History." Accessed December 11, 2021. https://www.csail.mit.edu/about/mission-history.

Mitchell, Bonnie. "Introduction to the Exhibition." In *Charles A. Csuri: Beyond Boundaries, 1963 – Present*, edited by Janice M. Glowski and SIGGRAPH. The Ohio State University, College of the Arts, Advanced Computing Center for the Arts and Design, 2006.

Mitchell, William John. *The Reconfigured Eye: Visual Truth in the Post-Photographic Era*. 4th edition. MIT Press, 2001.

Mones-Hattal, Barbara, Ken Snelson, Sally Weber, Charles Csuri and Tony Longson. "New Methods, New Artforms (Panel Session): 3D Applications in Sculpture." In *ACM SIGGRAPH 90 Panel Proceedings*, edited by ACM. ACM Press, 1990.

Nake, Frieder. "Das Doppelte Bild." In *BAND 3,2 Digitale Form*, edited by Katja Müller-Helle and Claudia Blümle. De Gruyter, 2006.

Nake, Frieder. "Die Kunstproduktion als Entscheidung sprozeß." In *bit international*, vol. 2, edited by Boris Kelemen and Radoslav Putar. Galerije grada Zagreba, 1968.

NASA. "Sputnik and the Dawn of the Space Age." Accessed December 10, 2021. https://history.nasa.gov/sputnik.html.

Newell, Martin E. "The Utilization of Procedure Models in Digital Image Synthesis." PhD diss., University of Utah, 1975. J. Willard Marriott Library (1507175).

Nochlin, Linda. "The Realist Criminal and the Abstract Law." *Art in America* 61, no. 5 (1973): 54–61.

Nooney, Laine. "A Pedestal, a Table. A Love Letter: Archaeologies of Gender in Videogame History." *Game Studies* 13, no. 2 (2013). http://gamestudies.org/1302/articles/nooney.

Novak, Barbara. *American Painting of the Nineteenth Century: Realism, Idealism, and the American Experience*. 3rd edition. Oxford University Press USA, 2007.

NVIDIA. "What is Generative AI?" Accessed June 5, 2025. https://www.nvidia.com/en-us/glossary/generative-ai/.

Ord, Toby. "Interpolation, Extrapolation, Hyperpolation: Generalising into New Dimensions." Technical report, 2024. arXiv (2409.05513). https://doi.org/10.48550/arXiv.2409.05513.

Paik, Karen, and Leslie Iwerks. *To Infinity and Beyond! The Story of Pixar Animation Studios*. Chronicle, 2007.

Palazzi, Maria. "Exploration and the Artist's Tools." In *Charles A. Csuri: Beyond Boundaries, 1963 – Present*, edited by Janice M. Glowski and SIGGRAPH. The Ohio State University, College of the Arts, Advanced Computing Center for the Arts and Design, 2006.

Panofsky, Erwin. *Perspective as Symbolic Form*. Translated by Christopher S. Wood. Zone Books, 1991.

Perry, Rebecca Ann. "Rigging the World: 3D Modeling and the Seduction of the Real." PhD diss., Massachusetts Institute of Technology, 2014. MIT Libraries, DSpace@MIT (900615015).

Pharr, Matt, Wenzel Jakob and Greg Humphreys. *Physically Based Rendering: From Theory to Implementation*. 3rd edition. Morgan Kaufmann, 2017.

Phillips, Flip. Quoted after Caroline Csuri. Email to author. May 21, 2025.

Phong, Bui Tuong. "Illumination for Computer-Generated Images." PhD diss., University of Utah, 1973. J. Willard Marriott Library (1602050).

Phong, Bui Tuong. "Illumination for Computer Generated Pictures." *Communications of the ACM* 18, no. 6 (1975): 311–317. https://doi.org/10.1145/360825.360839.

Pias, Claus. "Das digitale Bild gibt es nicht. Über das (Nicht-)Wissen der Bilder und die informatische Illusion." *zeitenblicke* 2, no. 1 (2003). https://mediarep.org/handle/doc/4845.

Pixar Animation Studios. "Steve May." Accessed June 12, 2025. https://www.pixar.com/may.

Pott, Dominik. Interview by the author. August 16, 2020. transcript. Research Online/Data. https://doi.org/10.25625/Z27EP6.

Prendeville, Brendan. *Realism in 20th Century Painting*. Thames & Hudson, 2000.

Price, David A. *The Pixar Touch: The Making of a Company*. Vintage Books, 2009.

Raudseps, Juris G. "Picture Regeneration from Quantized Data." Technical report, The Ohio State University, 1963. The Ohio State University Libraries Archives.

RenderMan Documentation. "PxrDisney." Accessed December 20, 2021. https://renderman.pixar.com/resources/RenderMan_20/PxrDisney.html.

Rivlin, Robert. *The Algorithmic Image: Graphic Visions of the Computer Age*. Microsoft Press, 1986.

Roberts, Lawrence G. "Machine Perception of Three-Dimensional Solids." PhD diss., Massachusetts Institute of Technology, 1963. MIT Libraries, DSpace@MIT (33959125).

Röhrl, Boris. *Kunsttheorie des Naturalismus und Realismus: Historische Entwicklung, Terminologie und Definitionen*. Georg Olms, 2003.

Röhrl, Boris. *Realismus in der bildenden Kunst: Europa und Nordamerika 1830 bis 2000*. Mann, 2013.

Romney, Gordon W. "Computer Assisted Assembly and Rendering of Solids." PhD diss., University of Utah, 1969. ProQuest (7003776). (1969a)

Romney, Gordon W. "Computer Assisted Assembly and Rendering of Solids." Technical report RADC-TR-69-365, Griffiss Air Force Base, 1969. Defense Technical Information Center (AD0753673). (1969b)

Romney, Gordon W. "Computer Assisted Assembly and Rendering of Solids." Technical report 4-20, University of Utah, 1970.

Romney, Gordon W., Gary S. Watkins and David C. Evans. "Real-Time Display of Computer Generated Half-Tone Perspective Pictures." In *Seminal Graphics: Pioneering Efforts That Shaped the Field*, vol. 1, edited by Rosalee Wolf. ACM, 1998. https://doi.org/10.1145/280811.281011.

Romney, Gordon W., Gary S. Watkins and David C. Evans. "Real-Time Display of Computer Generated Half-Tone Perspective Pictures." In *Information Processing '68: Proceedings of IFIP Congress 1968. Volume 2 – Hardware, Applications*, edited by A. J. H. Morell. North-Holland. 1969.

Romney, Gordon W., Gary S. Watkins and David C. Evans. "Computer Generated Halftone Perspective Pictures." Technical report 4-3, University of Utah, 1968.

Romney, Gordon W., David C. Evans, Alan Erdahl and Chris Wylie, *Electrically-Generated Perspective Images*, U.S. Patent No. 3621214, 1970.

Romney, Gordon W. Email to author. June 19, 2025.

Rosen, Margit. "A Record of Decisions: Envisioning Computer Art." In *Charles A. Csuri: Beyond Boundaries, 1963 – Present*, edited by Janice M. Glowski and SIGGRAPH. The Ohio State University, College of the Arts, Advanced Computing Center for the Arts and Design, 2006.

Rothko, Mark. "Statement on his Attitude in Painting." *The Tiger's Eye* 1, no. 9 (1949): 114.

Rubin, Peter. "Happy 30th Birthday to the Engine That Powered the CGI Revolution." *Wired*, December 17, 2018. https://www.wired.com/story/renderman-30th-anniversary/.

Rule, John T., and Steven A. Coons. *Graphics*. McGraw-Hill, 1961.

Scheler, Carolin. "Ein Atelier im virtuellen Raum. 3D als Ausdrucksmedium." Master's thesis, Hanover University of Applied Sciences and Arts, 2015.

Scheler, Carolin. "Der bildsprachliche Kosmos im computeranimierten Kinofilm." In *Piktogrammatik. Grafisches Gestalten als Weltwissen und Bilderordnung*, edited by Annette Geiger and Bianca Holtschke. transcript, 2021. https://doi.org/10.1515/9783839457436-006.

Scheler, Carolin. "Magnifying the Logic of Images: Artificial Intelligence and the Continuous Reproduction of Pictorial Codes." In *Pictologic: How Images Give Form to Our Knowledge and Imagination*, edited by Annette Geiger, Bianca Holtschke and Julia C. Ahrend. transcript, 2026.

Schneider, Birgit. "Wissenschaftsbilder zwischen digitaler Transformation und Manipulation. Einige Anmerkungen zur Diskussion des 'digitalen Bildes.'" In *Logik des Bildlichen*, edited by Martina Heßler and Dieter Mersch. transcript, 2015. https://doi.org/10.1515/9783839410516-007.

Schröter, Jens. *3D. History, Theory and Aesthetics of the Transplane Image*. Bloomsbury, 2014.

Schröter, Jens. "Das Ende der Welt. Analoge vs. digitale Bilder – mehr und weniger ‚Realität'?" In *Analog/Digital – Opposition oder Kontinuum? Zur Theorie und Geschichte einer Unterscheidung*, edited by Jens Schröter and Alexander Böhnke. transcript, 2004. *https://doi.org/10.1515/9783839402542-017.*

Schumacker, Robert A., Brigitta Brand, Maurice G. Gilliland and Werner H. Sharp. "Study for Applying Computer-Generated Images to Visual Simulation." Technical report, General Electric Company, 1969. Defense Technical Information Center (AD0700375).

Shapiro, David. *Social Realism: Art as a Weapon*. Ungar, 1973.

Shi, David E. *Facing Facts: Realism in American Thought and Culture, 1850–1920*. Oxford University Press, 1995.

Shinn, Everett. "Recollections of the Eight." In *The Eight: Exhibition Catalogue*, edited by The Brooklyn Museum. Brooklyn Museum Press, 1943.

Sito, Tom. *Moving Innovation: A History of Computer Animation*. MIT Press, 2013.

Sloan, John. *John Sloan on Drawing and Painting: Gist of Art*. Dover Publications, 2000.

Smith, Alvy Ray. *A Biography of the Pixel*. MIT Press, 2021.

Smith, Alvy Ray. "pt.reyes." Accessed December 16, 2021. http://alvyray.com/Art/PtReyes.htm.

Smith, Alvy Ray. Email to author. September 27, 2021.

Sobchack, Vivian. "Animation and Automation, or, the Incredible Effortfulness of Being." *Screen* 50, no. 4 (2009): 375–391. https://doi.org/10.1093/screen/hjp032.

Squirru, Rafael. "Edward Hopper." *Américas* 17 (1965): 11–17.

Sutherland, Ivan E. "Sketchpad: A Man-Machine Graphical Communication System." PhD diss., Massachusetts Institute of Technology, 1963. MIT Libraries, DSpace@MIT (15036306). (1963a)

Sutherland, Ivan E. "Sketchpad: A Man-Machine Graphical Communication System." Technical report, edited by Alan Blackwell and Kerry Rodden. University of Cambridge, Computer Laboratory, 2003. Computer Laboratory (UCAM-CL-TR-574).

Sutherland, Ivan E. "Sketchpad." In *Proceedings of the Spring Joint Computer Conference – AFIPS '63*, edited by E. Calvin Johnson. ACM Press, 1963. https://doi.org/10.1145/1461551.1461591. (1963b)

Sutherland, Ivan E. "The Ultimate Display." In *Information Processing 1965. Proceedings of IFIP Congress: Part 2*. 2 vols, edited by Wayne A. Kalenich. Spartan, 1965.

Sutherland, Ivan E. Oral history interview by William Aspray. May 1, 1989. transcript. University Digital Conservancy, Charles Babbage Institute, University of Minnesota. https://conservancy.umn.edu/handle/11299/107642.

Sutherland, Ivan E. "An Interview with Ivan Sutherland." Interview by Karen A. Frenkel. *Communications of the ACM* 32, no. 6 (1989): 711–718. https://doi.org/10.1145/63526.63531.

Swearingen, Kyoung L. Interview by the author. February 11, 2020. transcript. Research Online/Data. https://doi.org/10.25625/VBODBG.

The Museum of Modern Art. "Diego Rivera. Man at the Crossroads, 1932." Accessed March 8, 2022. https://www.moma.org/collection/works/34635.

The Tech, ed. "28 Faculty Members Receive Promotions." *The Tech* 81, no. 6 (1961): 1.

The Tech, ed. "Killian Names Rule to Head Course IX: Will Still Administer Graphics Department." *The Tech* 70, no. 15 (1950): 1–4.

Trachtman, Paul. "Charles Csuri Is an 'Old Master' in a New Medium." *Smithsonian* 25, no. 11 (1995): 56–65.

Tufariello, Catherine. "'The Remembering Wine': Emerson's Influence on Whitman and Dickinson." In *The Cambridge Companion to Ralph Waldo Emerson*, edited by Joel Porte and Saundra Morris. Cambridge University Press, 1999. https://doi.org/10.1017/CCOL052149611X.010.

Turkle, Sherry. "Forgetting the Body in Digital Culture." In *A Psychoanalytic Exploration of the Body in Today's World*, edited by Vaia Tsolas and Christine Anzieu-Premmereur. Routledge, 2017.

University of Utah. "History." Accessed June 19, 2025. https://www.cs.utah.edu/resources/history/.

Vega, Edward. "How 'Spider-Verse' Forced Animation to Evolve." Posted September 10, 2022. By VOX. YouTube. https://www.youtube.com/watch?v=l96IgQmXmhM.

Virilio, Paul. *War and Cinema: The Logistics of Perception*. Translated by Patrick Camiller. Verso, 1989.

Wallis, Michael. "Foreword: America's Road." In *A Route 66 Companion*, edited by David King Dunaway. University of Texas Press, 2012. https://doi.org/10.7560/726604-001.

Warburton, Alan. "The Wizard of AI." 2023. Commissioned by Data as Culture at the Open Data Institute. https://culture.theodi.org/the-wizard-of-ai/.

Warburton, Alan. Video call with author. March 28, 2025.

Warburton, Alan. Email to author. June 6, 2025.

Ward, Joseph A. *American Silences. The Realism of James Agee, Walker Evans, and Edward Hopper*. 2nd edition. Transaction Publishers, 2010.

Warnock, John E. "A Hidden Surface Algorithm for Computer Generated Half-Tone Pictures." PhD diss., University of Utah, 1969. J. Willard Marriott Library (1602152).

Watkins, Gary S. "A Real Time Visible Surface Algorithm." PhD diss., University of Utah, 1970. J. Willard Marriott Library (703562).

Wells, Edward C. "Introduction." In *William A. Fetter: Computer Graphics in Communication: Written for the Course Content Development Study in Engineering Graphics, supported by the National Science Foundation*. McGraw-Hill, 1965.

Wells, Paul. *Animation and America*. Edinburgh University Press, 2002.

Wells, Paul. *Understanding Animation*. Routledge, 1998.

Weltzien, Friedrich. *Fleck: Das Bild der Selbsttätigkeit. Justinus Kerner und die Klecksografie als experimentelle Bildpraxis zwischen Ästhetik und Naturwissenschaft*. Vandenhoeck & Ruprecht, 2011.

Weltzien, Friedrich. "Der 'nachgereichte Entwurf': Frühe Phototheorie und die Frage der Bildentstehung." In *Entwerfen und Entwurf: Praxis und Theorie des künstlerischen Schaffensprozesses*, edited by Gundel Mattenklott and Friedrich Weltzien. Reimer, 2003.

Weltzien, Friedrich. "Kritzeln." In *Historisches Wörterbuch des Mediengebrauchs*, edited by Heiko Christians, Matthias Bickenbach and Nikolaus Wegmann. Böhlau, 2014. https://doi.org/10.7788/boehlau.9783412217280.382.

Weltzien, Friedrich. "Produktionsästhetik als Methode." In *Praxis. Ausüben. Begreifen*, edited by Michael Corsten. Velbrück, 2021. https://doi.org/10.5771/9783748912583-220.

Wilmerding, John. *American Views: Essays on American Art*. Princeton University Press, 1991.

Wilmerding, John. *Fitz Hugh Lane*. Praeger, 1971.

Wilmerding, John, and Karen Wilkin. *Fairfield Porter*. Rizzoli, 2016.

Wylie, Chris, Gordon W. Romney, David C. Evans and Alan Erdahl. "Half-Tone Perspective Drawings by Computer." In *Proceedings of the Fall Joint Computer Conference – AFIPS '67*, edited by ACM. ACM Press, 1967. https://doi.org/10.1145/1465611.1465619. (1967a)

Wylie, Chris, Gordon W. Romney, David C. Evans and Alan Erdahl. "Half-Tone Perspective Drawings by Computer." Technical report 4-2, University of Utah, 1967. Defense Technical Information Center (AD0761965). (1967b)

Glossary

3D Artist: A 3D artist is a person who works in the entertainment industry in one of the computer graphics fields, for example as a modeler, shading artist or animator.

3Ds Max: 3Ds Max is a graphics software by Autodesk that is primarily used in the gaming sector.

Aliasing: Aliasing is a phenomenon caused by the rasterized display of images and graphics on screens. It is an artifact that appears in the form of a staircase effect on lines or edges of image elements if they are diagonal or curved. Only horizontal and vertical lines are not affected by Aliasing.

Antialiasing: Antialiasing attempts to counteract the problem of aliasing by "blurring" the edges of image elements or lines with the help of equalizing the colors between the adjacent areas. This makes the staircase effect of aliasing less visible.

Autodesk Maya: Maya is a comprehensive 3D computer graphics program by Autodesk that is primarily used in the feature film industry.

Blender: Blender is a comprehensive open-source 3D graphics program which, like its commercial counterparts, provides all the usual features, including in particular the basic areas of modeling, texturing, shading, rendering and animation.

Bug: Today, a "bug" refers to an error in a code when a command could not be completed correctly. Originally, the term refers to hardware errors, i.e. a problem that actually occurs physically. The reason for calling such an error a "bug" is associated with US computer pioneer Grace Hopper, who was able to trace a burnt-out circuit back to a moth in the 1940s.

Bump Map: Bump maps are used to give a virtual object with a completely smooth surface a surface structure. To make such a structure visible, however, unevenness is merely simulated through shading. In the example of a wall, the joints would cast shadows in a specific direction depending on the direction of light, and – unlike with a displacement map – without the stones actually being a relief. In profile, a surface provided with a bump map would still exhibit complete smoothness. The bump map is less computationally intensive than the displacement map and is used for image elements that are not visible in detail or are only visible in the background.

CG or CGI: CG stands for computer graphics, CGI stands for computer-generated imagery.

Cinema 4D: Cinema 4D is a 3D computer graphics program from the German software company Maxon Computer GmbH, which, like Blender and Autodesk, can be used to create computer-generated images and animations. It is also popular in the field of motion graphics, which is relevant for logo or title animations, for example.

Compositing: Compositing refers to a work step in which various digital image elements are combined, for example when a fantasy creature such as a dragon has to be inserted into a filmed footage. Compositing can also be used to add effects such as fire and smoke to filmed or artificially rendered scenes. In 3D images this work step can also be used to subsequently create a depth of field.

Constraint: Constraints are used in graphics programs such as Autodesk Maya to forward commands that are directed from an object to another object, for example in the sense of an if-then formula. If this object moves, the other object follows accordingly. There are different constraints, each of which creates different conditions.

Copy: A copy is a duplicated object that, unlike an instance, does not refer to an original but exists independently of it. While changes to an instance affect the original, a copy is not affected.

Displacement Map: Displacement maps are used to give a virtual object, which has a completely smooth surface, a surface structure similar to a bump map. The difference to a bump map is that with a displacement map, the surface actually becomes a relief and the unevenness can also be seen in the profile. In the example of a wall, the joints would cast shadows in a specific direction depending on the direction of light. In the profile, the stones would be raised, making the wall structure appear more realistic than with a bump map, where the surface remains flat in the profile. Displacement maps are much more computationally intensive than bump maps and are only used where a high level of detail is required.

Edge: See → Modeling.

Face: See → Modeling.

Grid: The grid refers to the coordinate system in a 3D graphics program. The X and Z-axes form a surface in space, with the Z axis usually representing the direction, which moves in the depth of the image space. The Y-axis is perpendicular to the other two and projects upward. The grid is a surface that extends around the zero point in all directions on the surface of the X- and Z-axes. In some programs the grid is displayed infinitely, in Autodesk Maya only a partial area of the grid is displayed.

Hidden Line Problem: The hidden line problem relates to the wireframe structure of the virtual 3D models. Without simulating a surface, objects would only be visible in this "wireframe view." However, this does not provide any information about which lines describe the front and which the back of an object. Shading was developed to counteract this problem (and to give objects generally a greater vividness and a higher degree of realism). It enables objects to be displayed as opaque solids. Shading is now generally used to simulate materials in order to give objects the appearance of different textures.

Hidden Surface Algorithm: As an alternative to the term "Hidden Line Problem," the term "Hidden Surface Algorithm" is also used. See → Hidden Line Problem.

Hidden Surface Problem: As an alternative to the term "Hidden Line Problem," the term "Hidden Surface Problem" is also used. See → Hidden Line Problem.

Instance: An instance is a duplicated object that refers to an original. If the original is changed, the instance also changes. It is therefore different from a copy, which exists independently as a new object and would not react when the original is changed.

Lighting: Lighting refers to the discipline of illuminating settings in virtual space. As a rule, light sources are set according to our physical reality. Unlike in reality, however, lights can also deviate from reality and be set with parameters and values in a way that would not work under the physical conditions of the real world. Negative light is also possible, for example to intentionally dim areas. People who are responsible for virtual light are also known as lighting artists.

Modeling: Modeling is one of the disciplines carried out by a 3D artist. It refers to the process in which virtual objects are created, i.e. modeled. While it is possible to shape any conceivable object from a basic geometry such as a cube, the process of procedural modeling is now also used, in which large sets are modeled and also textured using automated processes based on commands. This method is used in particular for the creation of landscapes and natural environments. There are basically two different ways of modeling: polygon-based modeling and a second approach based on the creation of curves. The latter is mathematically more precise but is used less frequently in the entertainment industry. The geometry of a virtual polygon model consists of a wireframe. This is made up of faces (also called polygons), their edges and vertices (plural for vertex). The polygons are usually either quadrangular or, if they are divided diagonally, triangular.

Object-oriented programming paradigm: The object-oriented programming paradigm describes a way of programming. In principle, this paradigm differs from the procedural programming paradigm. The latter was the standard until the 1970s. While the older approach was linear, in which a computer executed a series of commands one after the other step by step, the object-oriented programming paradigm enabled greater interactivity in working with the computer. Work processes and objectives no longer had to be known in advance and could now be executed in parallel.

Opaque: Opaque is a synonym for non-transparent. In computer graphics, the term is relevant in the field of shading. See also → Hidden Line Problem.

Physically Based Rendering / pbrt: Physically based rendering is a development in the field of computer graphics that attempts to standardize all previous methods used for shading and virtual light calculation and to base them on the principle of physical calculations. Provided that appropriately programmed shaders are used, lighting situations always remain stable across programs in physically based rendering. The process makes shading and lighting in virtual environments much easier. Before this standardized working environment was created, shaders were based on completely different calculation models, each of which reacted to light in a different way. For this reason, each shader previously had to be individually and effortfully adapted to the light settings.

Pipeline: A pipeline refers to the workflow in the creation process of computer-animated productions. As many, but not all, production steps run in parallel and others have to take place one after the other, it is necessary to coordinate the individual groups of people involved in production. There are also often positions that deal solely with the programming of pipelines. This special field of activity is concerned with how work results can be passed back and forth between the areas in the best possible way and how work steps can be automated in a sensible manner in order to make the pipeline particularly efficient.

Polygon: See → Face.

Primitive: In 3D programs, basic objects, so-called primitives, are initially available for the creation of models. These usually include a sphere, a cube, a cylinder, a torus and a cone.

Principled Shader: The principled shader is a shader developed by Brent Burley for Disney in 2012, which can be used to display a very wide range of materials. It has since been implemented in all common graphics applications. Before this new shader, different shaders often had to be used for different materials. The principled shader is suitable for physically based rendering and makes work processes much more efficient than with previous shaders due to a smaller number of adjustable parameters.

Procedural Programming paradigm: See → Object-oriented programming paradigm.

Render Engine: A render engine is a program or an external plug-in in 3D graphics programs with which the 3D scenes can be calculated as an image. In rendering, for example, properties can be set for the light or for antialiasing as well as the resolution of the images in which they are to be calculated. As rendering processes for 3D graphics are highly computationally intensive, especially if they aim for photorealism, precise and very technical knowledge is required for this work step in order to keep the computing time as short as possible without causing a loss of quality in the images.

Rendering: See → Render Engine.

RenderMan: RenderMan is a render engine developed by Pixar, which today represents an industry standard for animated films. It is also used for major Hollywood productions, for example for the calculation of effects.

Shading: See → Hidden Line Problem.

Solid: See → Hidden Line Problem.

Subsurface Scattering: Subsurface scattering is a property that can be set during shading. It is intended for materials that are slightly translucent, such as skin or cheese. A shader that has to calculate subsurface scattering can simulate the light refractions that occur on deeper levels instead of just on the surface. Some rays of light also penetrate the lower layers of human skin, which is why smaller limbs such as ears or fingers glow red against the light. This effect can be achieved with subsurface scattering.

Texturing: Texturing allows to add colors and patterns to polygon models. In principle, individual polygons can also be colored with a solid color, but texturing allows models to be colored independently of the boundaries of the polygon surfaces. For example, a cuboid surface consisting of four rectangular polygons of the same size can be given a small-scale wall texture or a sphere can be textured to give the appearance of a detailed globe.

Vertex, Vertices: See → Modeling.

Viewport (top, side, front, perspective): The viewport is the centerpiece of 3D graphics programs. This is where the virtual space is displayed in which objects can be modeled, textured and animated. Objects can either be displayed in central perspective or, more technically, in parallel perspective in the side, top or front view.

Wireframe: 3D models can be displayed either with shading or as a wireframe. The term wireframe refers to the wireframe structure of the models, which they have due to their composition of faces, edges and vertices. See also → Modeling. In the wireframe display, the individual faces, edges and vertices can be better controlled individually, which can be important when modeling, for example.

Index

Note: Page numbers followed by 'n./nn.' refer to notes.

S

T

Organizational Chart of the Historiography

The organizational chart on the following two pages provides an overview of the historical developments in 3D computer graphics. For the sake of clarity, it should be emphasized that the distances between the temporal markers do not correspond to the actual periods of time that have passed in between. In some cases, the markers of shorter time periods may have the same distance to each other as markers of longer time periods. It should also be noted that the perspective of this organizational chart was developed from the practical point of view of this study. The focus here is therefore on the developments of commercial 3D graphics programs. The entries labeled "parallel developments" in the right-hand column thus become merely side issues from the perspective of this study. From a different perspective this could all be the other way around. Finally, it should be emphasized that a few individuals were not included in the organizational chart as this would have made it too complex for it to serve the purpose of a simple overview. A few protagonists mentioned in the study are therefore not included in this organizational chart.

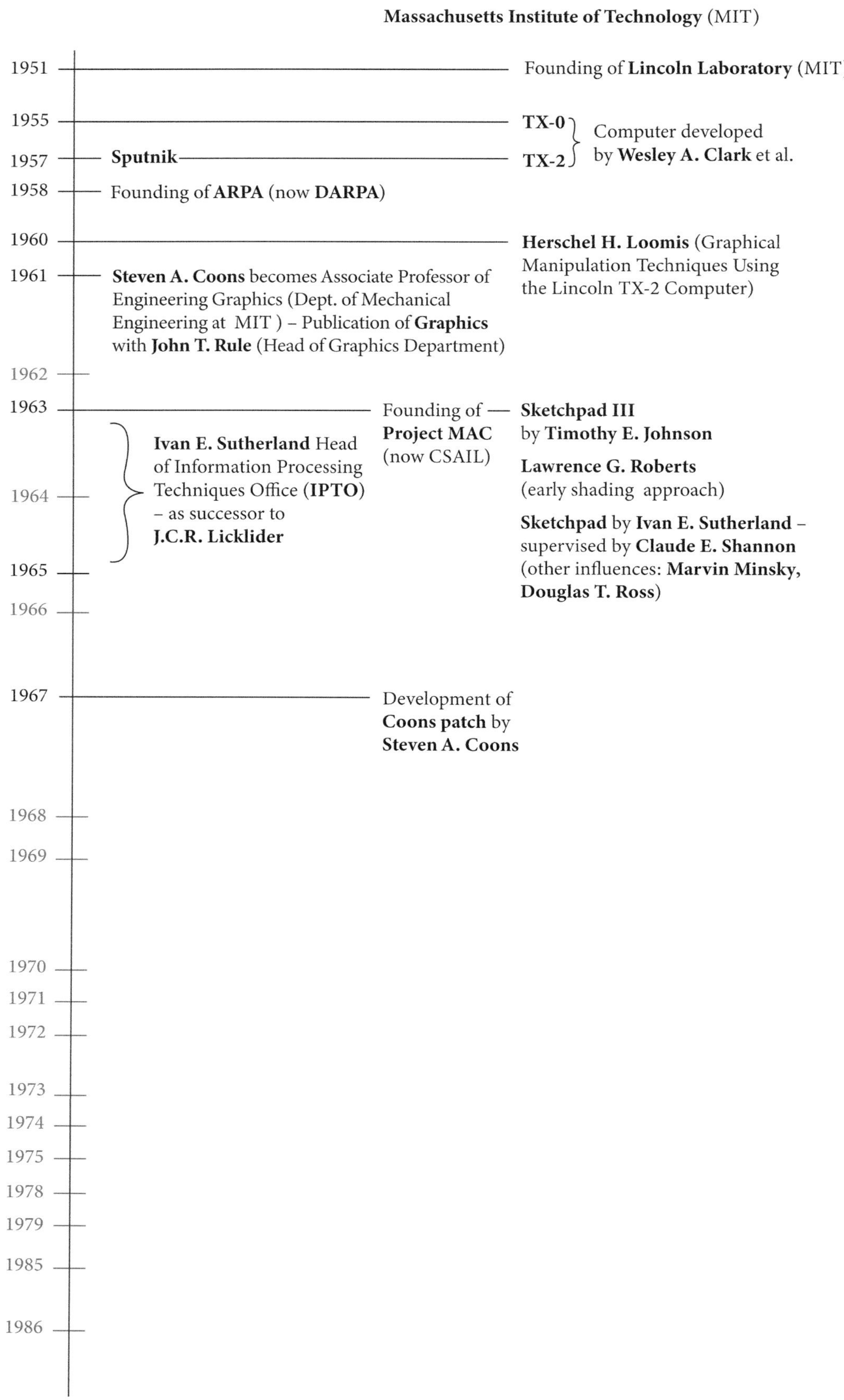
Massachusetts Institute of Technology (MIT)
1951
Founding of **Lincoln Laboratory** (MIT)
1955
TX-0
1957
Sputnik
TX-2
Computer developed by **Wesley A. Clark** et al.
1958
Founding of **ARPA** (now **DARPA**)
1960
Herschel H. Loomis (Graphical Manipulation Techniques Using the Lincoln TX-2 Computer)
1961
Steven A. Coons becomes Associate Professor of Engineering Graphics (Dept. of Mechanical Engineering at MIT) – Publication of **Graphics** with **John T. Rule** (Head of Graphics Department)
1962
1963
Founding of **Project MAC** (now CSAIL)
Sketchpad III by **Timothy E. Johnson**
Ivan E. Sutherland Head of Information Processing Techniques Office (**IPTO**) – as successor to **J.C.R. Licklider**
Lawrence G. Roberts (early shading approach)
1964
Sketchpad by **Ivan E. Sutherland** – supervised by **Claude E. Shannon** (other influences: **Marvin Minsky, Douglas T. Ross**)
1965
1966
1967
Development of **Coons patch** by **Steven A. Coons**
1968
1969
1970
1971
1972
1973
1974
1975
1978
1979
1985
1986

University of Utah Computer Science Department (now Kahlert School of Computing)	**Parallel Developments**	
		1951
		1955
		1957
		1958
		1960
		1961
	Douglas C. Engelbart (Publication of **Augmenting Human Intellect** at Stanford Research Institute)	1962
		1963
	Frieder Nake (6/7/64 Nr. 20, Zufälliger Polygonzug – in Germany)	1964
		1965
Project start **Graphical Man/Machine Communications** under the direction of **David C. Evans**	**William A. Fetter** (First Boeing Man) Founding of **MAGI**	1966
Chris Wylie, Gordon W. Romney, David C. Evans, Alan Erdahl (Half-tone perspective drawings by computer)	**Charles A. Csuri** (Sine Curve Man) **NASA/General Electric** (color and real-time computer graphics)	1967
	Founding of **Evans & Sutherland**	1968
Gordon W. Romney (Romney-Shading – first time in color) **John E. Warnock** (Warnock-Shading – first time in color)		1969
Gary S. Watkins (real-time display)		1970
Henri Gouraud (Gouraud shading)		1971
Project end **Graphical Man/Machine Communications**	**Alan Kay** (Smalltalk)	1972
Bui Tuong Phong (Phong shading)		1973
Edwin Catmull (textures)	**Edwin Catmull** at **NYIT**	1974
Martin E. Newell (teapot)		1975
James F. Blinn (bump maps)		1978
	Edwin Catmull at **Lucasfilm**	1979
	Anyflo (graphics software by **Michel Bret** from France)	1985
	ACCAD founded by Charles A. Csuri at Ohio State University **PIXAR** founded by **Edwin Catmull** and **Alvy Ray Smith**	1986